VISUAL QUICKSTART GUIDE

DIRECTOR 8

FOR MACINTOSH AND WINDOWS

Andre Persidsky

Peachpit Press

Visual QuickStart Guide
Director 8 for Macintosh and Windows
Andre Persidsky

Peachpit Press
1249 Eighth Street
Berkeley, CA 94710
(510) 524-2178
(510) 524-2221 (fax)

Find us on the World Wide Web at: http://www.peachpit.com

Peachpit Press is a division of Addison Wesley Longman

Editor: Marty Cortinas
Production Coordinator: Amy Changar
Compositor: Owen Wolfson
Copy Editor: Kathy Simpson
Indexer: Rebecca Plunkett

ISBN: 0-201-70258-4

0 9 8 7 6 5 4 3 2 1

Printed and bound in the United States of America

♻ Printed on recycled paper

Thank You

Marty Cortinas for a very thoughtful and thorough effort in editing this book.

Amy Changar of Peachpit Press for keeping production moving forward smoothly.

Nancy Ruenzel, publisher, Peachpit Press.

Leila Saadai, my muse and fountain of inspiration.

Pat and Zac at Director-Online.com for steering me towards some great sources for content featured in this book.

Simeon Rice (aka Noisecrime) for supplying some out-of-this-world Shockwave titles shown in this book.

Helmut Kobler for generous use of your office and being a supportive friend.

Special Thanks to the following organizations for making artwork available from the CD-ROM title *People in the Past, The Ancient Puebloan Farmers of Southwest Colorado*

Public Land Interpretive Association
6501 4th Street NW, Suite 1
Albuquerque, NM 87107

Produced for:
Anasazi Heritage Center
Bureau of Land Management
27501 Highway 184
Dolores, CO 81323
970-882-4811 (to order program call)

Produced by:
Paradox Productions
PO Box 331
Bluff, Utah 84512
435-672-2205

and
Living Earth Studios, Inc.
PO Box 317
Bluff, UT 84512
435-672-2277

For great technical articles, industry news, and developer features, visit Director Online at http://www.director-online.com

To view Noisecrime's cutting-edge Shockwave titles shown in several chapters in this book, go to http://www.simtek.dircon.co.uk/

Table of Contents

Introduction ix

Chapter 1: Director Basics 1

How Does Director Fit in the Mix? ... 2
About the Stage and Toolbar ... 4
About Cast, Score, and Stage Interaction ... 5
About Sprites and Cast Members ... 6
About Director Windows ... 7
About Director Inspectors ... 8
Getting Started ... 10
Creating a Movie ... 13
Director's Help System ... 24
Working Faster ... 26
General Preferences ... 27
Movie Properties ... 28
Updating Movies ... 29

Chapter 2: Assembling Casts 31

Creating Casts ... 33
Importing Cast Members ... 39
Working in List View ... 48
Working in Thumbnail View ... 53
Managing Cast and Cast Member Properties ... 57

Chapter 3: Building a Score 63

Using Frames and Channels ... 64
Working with Sprites ... 67
Changing Sprite Properties ... 78
Locking Sprites ... 91
Changing the Score View ... 92
Setting Markers ... 97

Chapter 4: Animating Sprites 99

Tweening ... 100
Adjusting Motion ... 105
Step Recording ... 109
Real-Time Recording ... 111
Building Animated Sequences ... 113
Making Film Loops ... 118
Animating Color Cursors ... 121
Incorporating Flash Movies ... 123

Chapter 5: Playing & Refining Movies **129**
Using the Control Panel 130
Setting Movie Tempo 134
Comparing Target Tempo with Actual Tempo . . 136
Locking Playback Speed 138
Setting Pauses in a Movie 139
Using Scene Transitions 140

Chapter 6: Using Paint Tools **143**
Getting Started 145
Selecting and Moving Images 148
Painting 153
Using Ink Effects 159
Ink Effect Choices. 160
Using Color and Pattern 161
Painting with Gradient Inks 168
Adding Text 173
Applying Effects 175
Using Ink Masks 180
Onion Skinning 182
Applying Image Filters 184

Chapter 7: Drawing Vector Shapes **185**
Creating Vector Shapes 186
Editing Vector Shapes 194

Chapter 8: Working on the Stage **201**
Setting Stage Properties 202
Zooming and Scrolling the Stage 204
Using Grids and Guides 206
Creating Shapes on the Stage 208
Creating Buttons on the Stage 211
Creating Text on the Stage 212

Chapter 9: Managing Color **213**
Color Depth 214
Color Mode 219
Color Choices 221
Color Palettes 224
Custom Color Palettes 226
Tactics for Limited Color Displays 233

Chapter 10: Adding Digital Video **249**
Importing Digital Video 250
Previewing a Digital Video 252
Incorporating Video 254
Setting Digital Video Properties 256

Editing Video 260
Importing Animated GIFs 262

Chapter 11: Adding Text **263**
Creating and Editing Regular Text 266
Importing Text 278
Embedding Fonts 280
Creating Field Text 282
Setting Text for Users to Change 284
Setting Text for Hyperlinks 286

Chapter 12: Adding Sound **287**
Importing Sounds 288
Placing Sounds in the Score 290
Synchronizing Sound to Actions 293
Compressing Sounds 297
Streaming Linked Shockwave Audio or
MPEG 3 Sound Files 300
Recording Sounds in Director (Mac) 302

Chapter 13: Creating a Projector **303**
Setting Projector Options 304
Making a Projector 308
Protecting Movie Files 312

Chapter 14: Making Movies for the Web **315**
Working with Shockwave 316
Creating a Shockwave Movie 317
Playing a Shockwave Movie 320
Making Stretchable Shockwave Movies 323
Working with Publish Settings 326
Making Streaming Shockwave Movies 335
Converting Multiple Movies 338

Chapter 15: Using Xtras **341**
Understanding Xtra Types 342
Installing Xtras 343
Using Xtras 344
Including Xtras in Distributed Movies 348
Including Xtras with Projectors 351
Using Xtras for Shockwave Movies 353
ActiveX Controls (Windows) 355

Chapter 16: Adding Behaviors **357**
Assigning Behaviors 358
Using the Behavior Inspector 361
Creating Behaviors 362
Modifying Behaviors 365

Chapter 17: Scripting Lingo 371
Understanding Scripts . . . 373
Writing Scripts . . . 377
Understanding Handlers, Messages, and Events . . . 384
Understanding Lingo Elements . . . 387
Scripting Navigation . . . 389
Using the Message Window . . . 396
Using Variables . . . 398
Making Sprites Interactive . . . 400
Using Lingo for Animated Cursors . . . 404
Setting Up Primary Event Handlers . . . 405

Chapter 18: Shockmachine 407
Understanding Shockmachine Basics . . . 408
Preparing Shockwave Movies for Playback in Shockmachine . . . 412

Glossary 415

Index 419

Introduction

This book teaches the fundamentals of using Macromedia Director, an exciting and challenging program for creating animation and multimedia productions for the Web, CD-ROM, or your local network.

With this *Director 8 Visual QuickStart Guide* you learn how to perform all the steps involved in creating Director projects, or *movies*, as most people call them. The book covers how to:

- Create and assemble cast members in Cast windows.
- Animate cast members on the stage.
- Build a movie frame-by-frame in the score.
- Create and edit cast members in the Paint window or Vector Shape window.
- Control movie playback, set scene transitions, alter color palettes, and add interactive controls to your movies using drag-and-drop behaviors.
- Produce a Shockwave-format file for distributing a movie on the Internet.
- Use Xtras, add-on modules that provide extra features.
- Introduce yourself to Lingo, Director's scripting language.

And much more!

About This Book

In the Visual QuickStart Guide format, this book provides clear instructions, supported by many illustrations. Where necessary, you'll find concise explanations—without any distracting fluff. The idea is to get you up and running as quickly as possible through practical examples.

How to Use This Book

If you have used other Visual QuickStart guides, you will find this book familiar. Each chapter offers a series of step-by-step instructions for completing essential tasks. As you work through the tasks, you gain an understanding of the program features and how to exploit them. Occasional tips provide hints for working efficiently, and illustrations demonstrate the techniques clearly.

The chapters unfold sequentially. The early chapters assume that you don't know anything that I introduce in a later chapter. You can use this book with the index to find out how to do something, but it's set up to make it easy to learn from scratch as you go through the book from chapter to chapter. You could skim some of the later chapters in the book because they detail how to do perform tasks that not all Director users need, but I recommend that you follow chapters one through five in order. Those first five chapters build on each other to help you quickly learn how to make and play a simple Director movie.

New in This Edition

This new edition of the book covers the latest version 8 features. Like the program itself, this edition of the book is completely updated to make it even easier to use than previous versions. Both the Macintosh and Windows versions of the program are covered in this one book, although you still have to buy two versions of the program to make movies for both platforms.

About Conventions in This Book

Different computer books use terms differently, so it's important to know how this book uses common terms.

Click means pressing down and releasing the Macintosh mouse button, or pressing down and releasing the left mouse button on Windows.

Drag means to hold the mouse button down and then move the mouse. You release the mouse button when you finish dragging.

Menu Commands

This book writes menu and command choices in the form of Menu name > Command > Subcommand. For example, if I need to tell you to choose Media Element from the Insert menu and then to select Bitmap from the submenu that pops out to the side, I can save us all a lot of trouble if I say instead, "Choose Insert > Media Element > Bitmap."

Keyboard Shortcuts

This book scatters keyboard shortcuts for commands sparingly throughout the chapters. There are two reasons for being stingy with the keyboard shortcuts in the step-by-step instructions:

- It's distracting to have a choice of how to do something when you're trying to learn new techniques.
- We all have so many PINs and passwords to remember that it's smart to be selective about what new things we commit to memory. Once you have worked with the program, you will know which commands you use so repeatedly that it's worth the trouble to learn the shortcut. Then refer to the handy tear-out reference card to the menus and their keyboard shortcuts.

About Cross-Platform Issues

Director 8 for Windows and Director 8 for Macintosh differ very little. That's why it makes sense to produce a single book that covers both versions of the program.

Illustrations

Figures that illustrate the tasks in this book come from both Mac and Windows versions of Director 8. Only a few elements of the program actually offer different choices in the two versions, and the other differences in the figures are merely cosmetic.

Modifier Keys

Modifier keys for keyboard shortcut commands differ on the Mac and on Windows. On Windows, the keys used are Shift, Ctrl, and Alt. These correspond to the Shift, Command, and Option keys on Mac. For example, I may say "Hold the Alt key (Windows) or Option key (Mac) while dragging the Lasso."

The Shift key generally works the same way on both types of computers.

The Command key on the Mac is the one that has the apple and cloverleaf symbols on it.

Features That Differ on Mac and Windows

Some techniques are performed differently on Windows and the Mac. Thus, in a few places a step has one method for Mac and one for Windows. Those steps are clearly labeled (and there aren't very many of them).

Even rarer are tasks that differ completely on the two types of computers. In those cases I've written totally different instructions, and I tell you about it in the heading for the task. For example, only the Macintosh can record sounds into Director, and so there is a task called "To record a sound in Director (Mac)."

1

Director Basics

Macromedia's Director is an extensive multimedia development tool. Use it to create animation, interactive movies, entertainment titles such as video games, e-merchandizing applications, corporate presentations, and much more. You can easily deliver Director content to your users via the Web, CD-ROM, or DVD.

Director's powerful tools take some getting used to because they work differently from most other programs you may have used. (If you've done sound sequencing or digital video editing, you might be in more familiar territory.)

This chapter begins by offering examples of the common types of projects you can create in Director and explaining how Director fits in with other Macromedia products. Then the chapter presents a visual overview of the program so that you can see how its main parts work together. If you're new to Director, you'll find it worthwhile to go through this chapter even if you're itching to get started. You'll be rolling up your sleeves and plunging into the program, creating a complete Director movie from start to finish, before the end of the chapter!

How Does Director Fit in the Mix?

Director is a core part of Macromedia's growing suite of software applications related to Web publishing and multimedia (**Figure 1.1**). Director is the tool you use to integrate and control a broad range of multimedia components that you create with applications such as Fireworks, Flash, Sonic Foundry SoundForgeXP, and FreeHand.

The end product of what you create in Director is called a *movie*. On the simple side, a movie can be what the name implies—an animation that your users sit back and watch without any participation. But the scope goes way beyond this when you start using Lingo, Director's powerful scripting language. The following is a partial list of the types of projects you can create in Director for delivery on the Web via Shockwave or through local storage means:

Entertainment/Education

Create cartoons, interactive animations, instructional titles such as language or math tutors, video games ranging from puzzles to fast-paced action (**Figures 1.2–1.3**), interactive music mixers, custom greeting-card generators, and much more.

Director
Create rich, immersive multimedia.

Dreamweaver
Make short work of Web site and HTML page production.

Drumbeat 2000
Easily create e-commerce and Web applications.

Fireworks
Design and optimize Web graphics for easy integration into your HTML pages.

Flash
Create animated vector-based Web sites.

Flash Player
View high-impact, vector-based Web sites.

FreeHand
Design and concept your sites.

Generator
Automate your Web site and production processes.

Shockwave Player
View entertaining rich-media content and animation.

Figure 1.1 Director is a core part of Macromedia's growing suite of Web publishing and development tools.

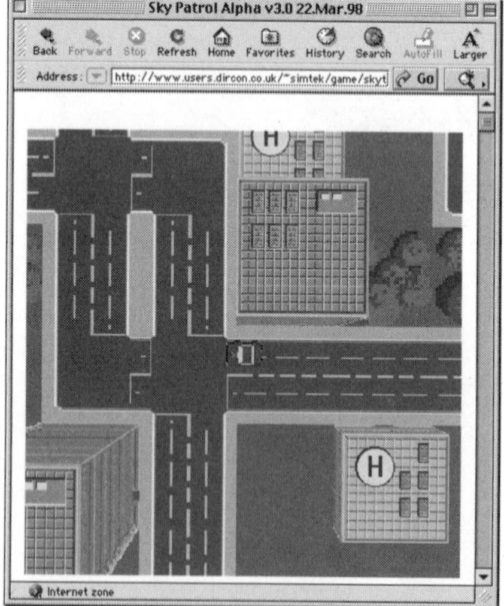

Figure 1.2 You can create fast-paced video games in Director that play back from the Web via Shockwave. This figure shows Noisecrime's GTA.

Figure 1.3 Sonic Rush Racing, created by Noisecrime.

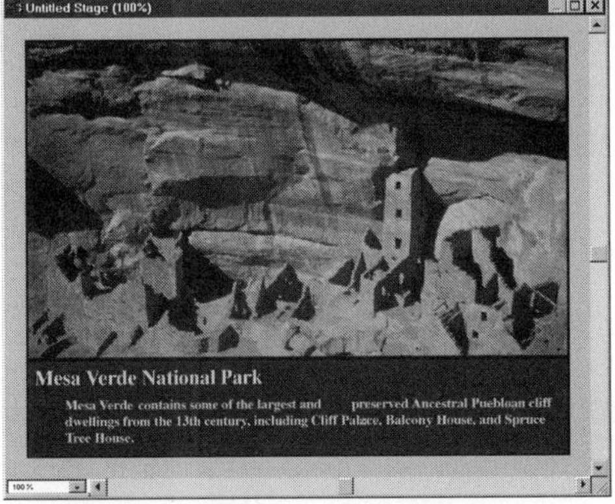

Figure 1.4 You can use Director to create the applications that run on kiosks, which often appear at museums or malls.

Business

Create interactive product simulations, corporate presentations, training applications, business applications with searchable databases, e-commerce interfaces, productivity applications, information kiosks (**Figure 1.4**), and much more.

Multiple-user applications

Director's Multiuser Server 2 allows you to create online applications such as interactive communities, avatar-type chat rooms, multiple-player online games, virtual meetings using a shared white board, and more.

Although Director excels at intelligently orchestrating multimedia elements to create just about any type of interface imaginable, it is not particularly geared to generating actual media, such as bitmaps, sounds, and QuickTime movies. Use applications such as Fireworks, Flash, and Premiere to generate media that you'll later import into Director. Also, though Director easily generates content for playback on the Web, it is not a Web-site development tool like Macromedia's Dreamweaver.

Now, on to the program!

About the Stage and Toolbar

The Director stage (**Figure 1.5**) serves as the window to the visual elements of a Director movie. Naturally, the stage is empty when you first open the program; it's your blank slate, awaiting your decisions about what to include in the movie.

The toolbar (**Figure 1.6**), which is nearly always visible while you work with Director, provides quick access to the most important Director commands.

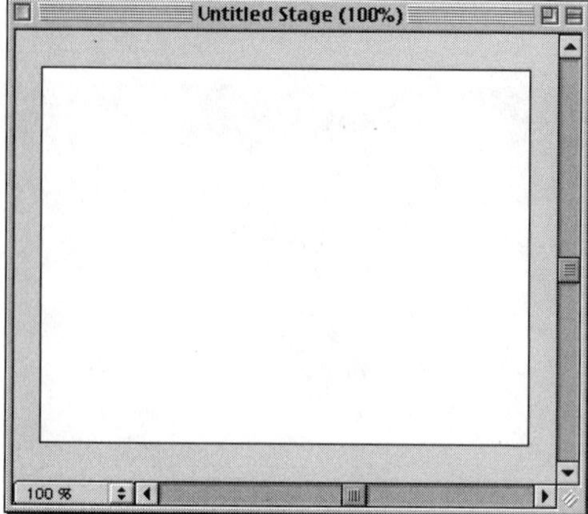

Figure 1.5 The stage opens empty when you first launch Director. The stage is where you arrange visual elements of your movie while authoring. It also defines the area that your users will see during playback.

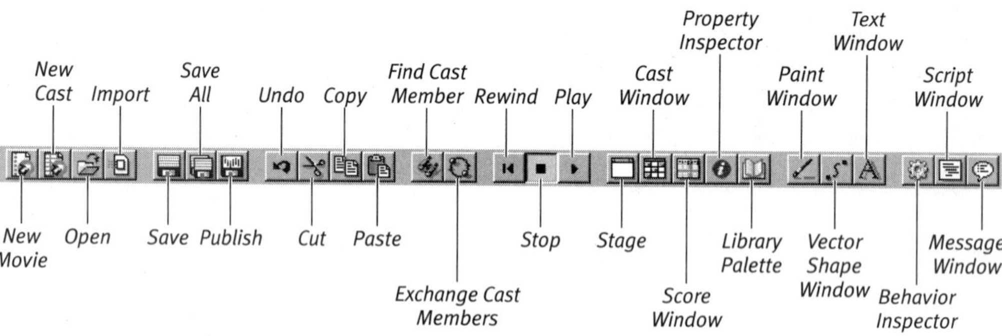

Figure 1.6 The toolbar provides buttons that serve as handy shortcuts to Director commands.

About Cast, Score, and Stage Interaction

You build a Director movie by placing cast members (**Figure 1.7**) in the score (**Figure 1.8**) over a range of frames. Visual cast members, such as bitmaps, appear on the stage in those frames (**Figure 1.9**), where you can position them as you want them to appear in your movie.

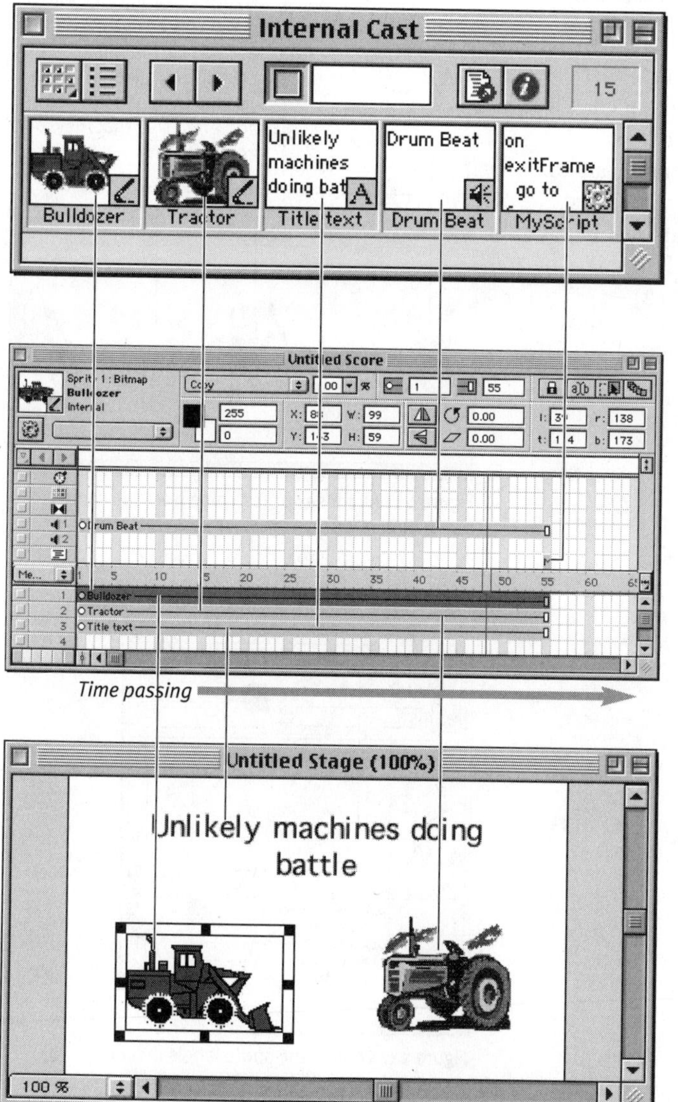

Figure 1.7 Cast members, stored in Cast windows, are the multimedia elements that comprise a movie. Cast members can be images, animation sequences, text, sounds, GIF animations, transitions, behaviors, and more.

Figure 1.8 The score shows a detailed grid that represents all the details of a movie over time. The score is organized into channels (rows), which hold specific cast-member types, and columns, which are the individual frames of your movie. The position of the playback head (which you can drag) dictates which frame is currently displayed on the stage.

Figure 1.9 You adjust the positions and other attributes of visual cast members on Director's stage to set the scene for one frame of the movie, which is much like a single frame of a Hollywood film. You create animation by rearranging the cast members on a frame-by-frame basis over a sequence of frames, which you can do so manually or with a Director animation technique such as tweening.

About Sprites and Cast Members

When you add a cast member (**Figure 1.10**) to a frame, you don't add a bulky copy of the cast member; you add an object called a *sprite* (**Figure 1.11**). The sprite points to the cast member but takes up very little space on disk and in computer memory, so you can make a movie of many frames populated with many sprites without overflowing your hard disk.

You can base many sprites on a single cast member. Each sprite of a cast member can have unique properties that define how, where, and when the cast member appears in a movie. You can think of a cast member as being a template and a sprite as an instance of the cast member. You can build a scene with only a few sprites (**Figure 1.12**).

Figure 1.10 You can create many sprites in a movie from a single cast member. They can all look alike, or you can change their appearance and add effects so that they look very different.

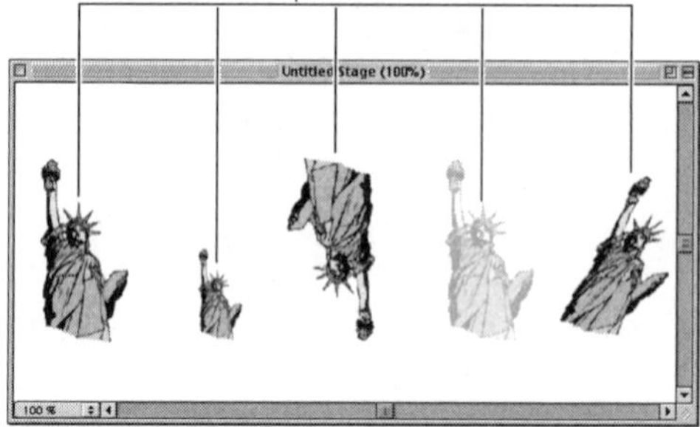

Figure 1.11 All these sprites come from the same cast member.

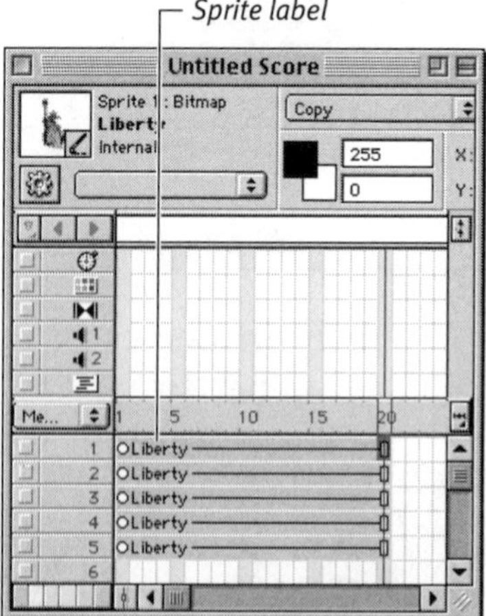

Figure 1.12 Look at the sprite labels in the score to see that all five of the sprites come from the same cast member.

About Director Windows

In addition to the stage, score, and Cast windows, Director provides work windows for specific tasks that you perform while making a movie. The Window menu (**Figure 1.13**) lets you access the work windows and tools of Director. Later chapters explain how to use these tools.

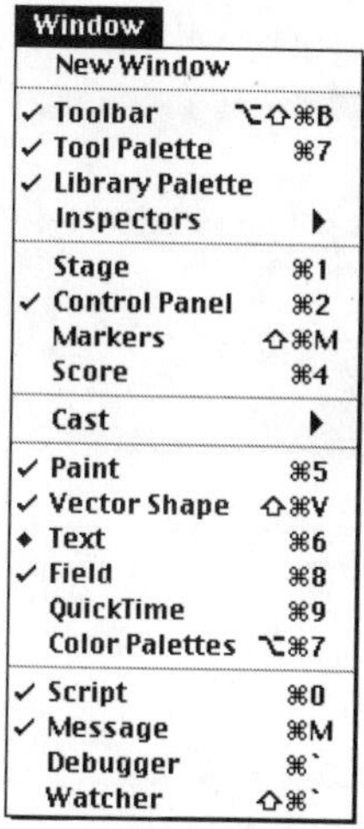

Figure 1.13 A check next to a command in the Window menu means that its window is open. A diamond or bullet indicates the active window.

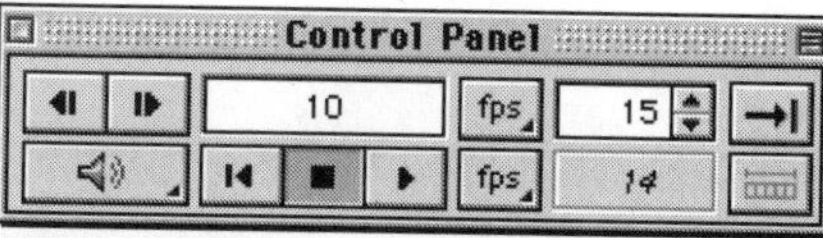

Control Panel

Message window

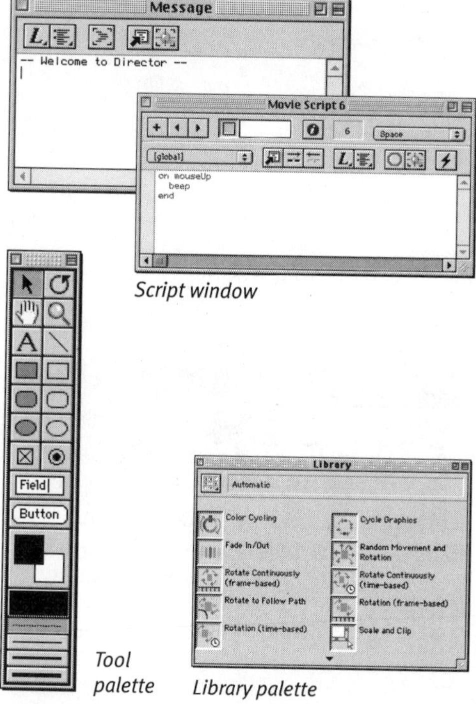

Script window

Tool palette

Library palette

Paint window

Vector Shape window

Field Text window

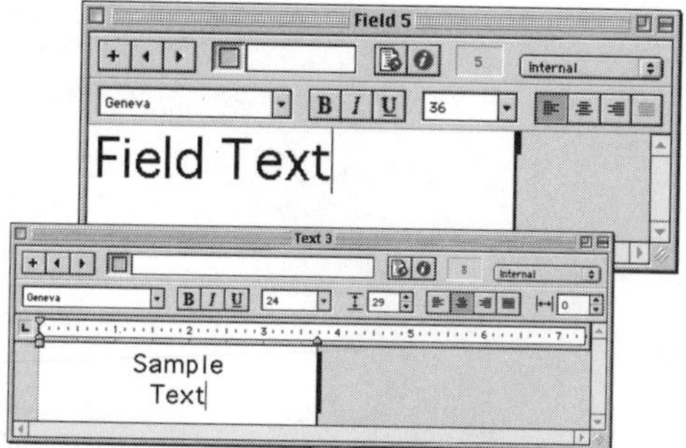

Text window

About Director Inspectors

In addition to the menus, dialog boxes, and toolbars that probably seem familiar if you've worked with other Mac or Windows programs, Director has *inspectors*. Inspectors (**Figures 1.14–1.18**) give you a glimpse of various properties and details of elements in a Director movie.

New to Director 8 is the Property Inspector, which you can use to view and set properties for various objects, including sprites, cast members, entire casts, and properties for your movie as a whole. Tabs in the Property Inspector vary depending on the object you select.

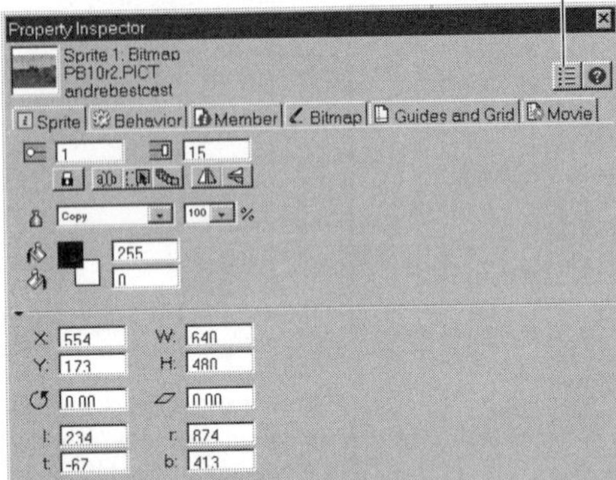

Figure 1.14 The Property Inspector is shown in Graphical view.

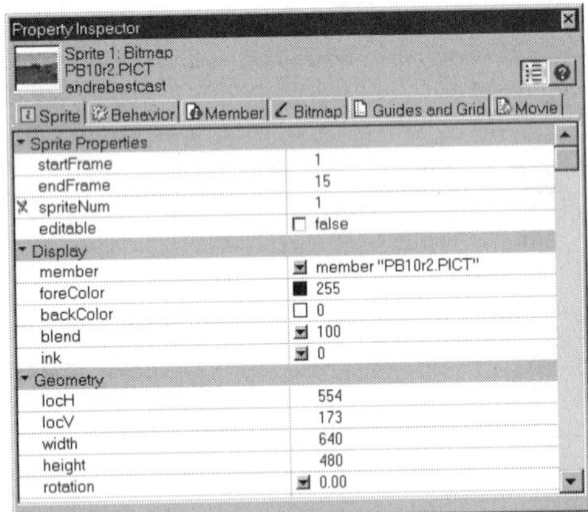

Figure 1.15 The Property Inspector is shown in List view.

Figure 1.16 Use the Text Inspector to adjust some of the text-formatting properties for a selected text sprite or cast member. This also is where you set text to act as a hyperlink (see Chapter 11, "Adding Text").

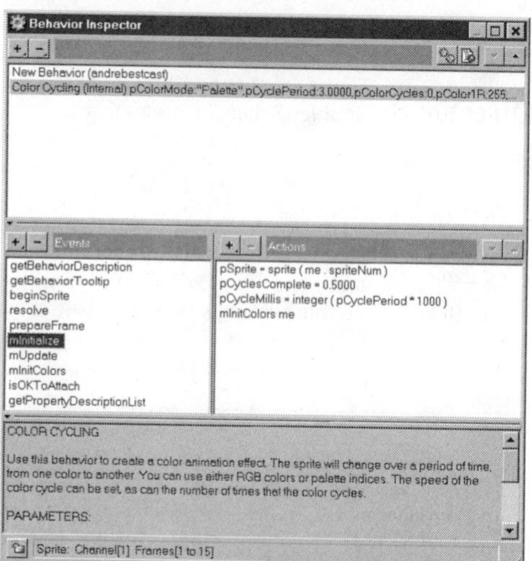

Figure 1.17 The Behavior Inspector contains controls for creating and customizing behaviors. Behaviors give you a way to quickly add scripting controls to a movie without having to use Lingo code (see Chapter 16, "Adding Interactive Behaviors," and Chapter 17, "Scripting Lingo").

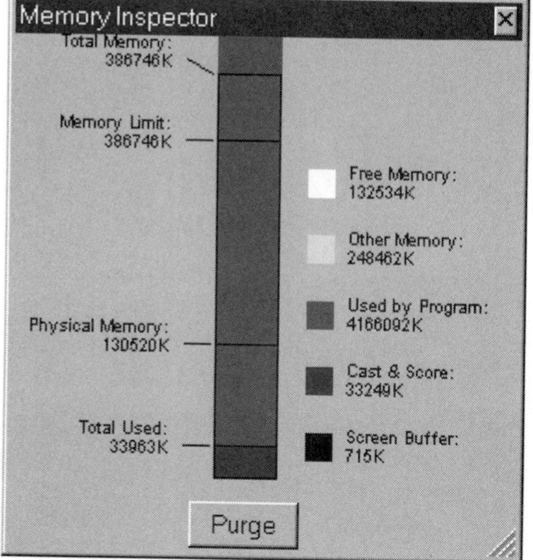

Figure 1.18 The Memory Inspector helps Director developers monitor memory use of a movie in progress. Knowing how much memory your cast and score take up helps you track whether the movie meets the target size for your finished project.

The Property Inspector offers two views: Graphical view and List view (**Figures 1.14–1.15**). Click the List View Mode button to toggle views. Note that in most cases, List view shows a more complete set of properties than Graphical view.

You access inspectors through the Window menu (**Figure 1.19**).

To open an inspector:

- Choose Window > Inspectors > *Inspector name.*

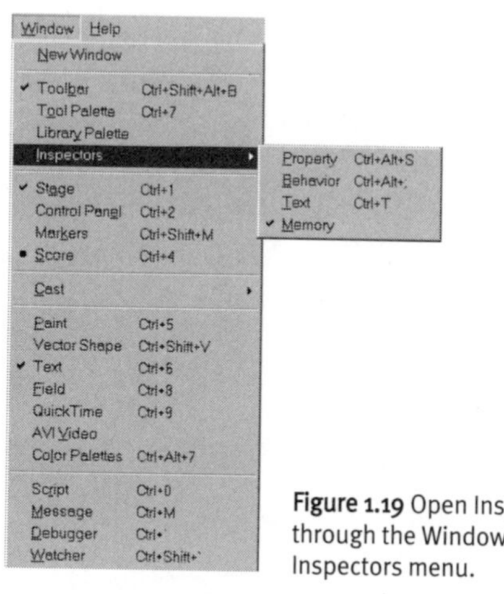

Figure 1.19 Open Inspectors through the Window > Inspectors menu.

Getting Started

If Director is not yet installed on your computer, you must install it according to the instructions that come with the program. (Make sure that you have enough room on your disk before installation.) The program installer leads you through the process.

To start Director:

1. Find the Director folder that was installed on your hard drive.
2. Open the folder by double-clicking it.
3. Double-click the Director application icon (**Figure 1.20**).

   or

   Double-click a Director movie icon (**Figure 1.21**).

To open an existing movie or external cast:

1. Choose File > Open to display the Open dialog box.
2. Select either a movie or external cast.
3. Click Open (**Figure 1.22**).

Figure 1.20 Launch Director by double-clicking its program icon.

Figure 1.21 You can open the program and a specific movie in one move by double-clicking a Director movie icon.

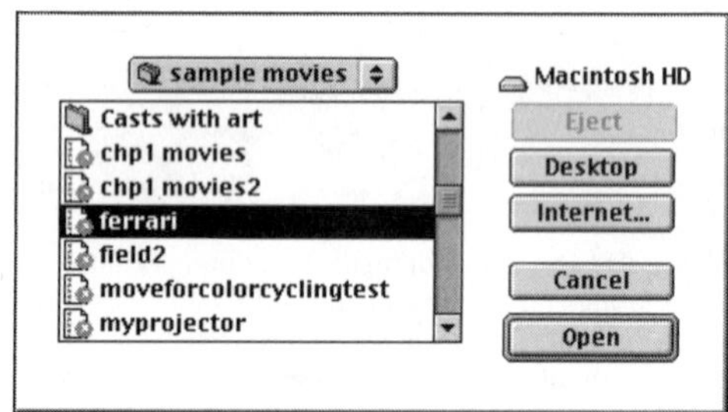

Figure 1.22 The Open dialog box.

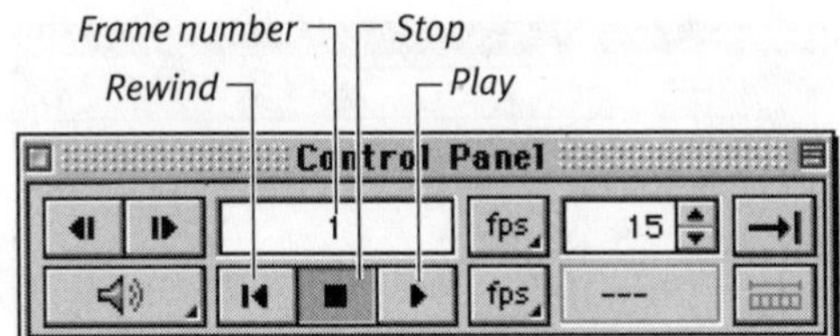

Figure 1.23 The Control Panel.

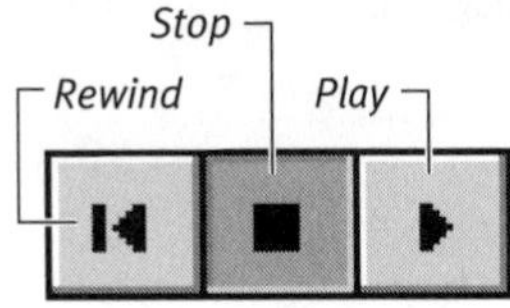

Figure 1.24 A portion of Director's toolbar.

You start a new project by opening a new movie. (A new movie opens automatically if you launch Director by double-clicking the program icon.)

To open a new movie:

- Choose File > New > Movie.

  If a movie is already open, Director prompts you to save it before proceeding.

  Whenever you work on a movie, you play it back repeatedly to check the results.

To play a movie:

1. Choose Window > Control Panel to display the Control Panel.
2. Click Rewind to move the playback head to frame 1 (**Figure 1.23**).

   or

   Click the frame box and type a frame number from which the movie should begin playing.
3. Click Play.

✔ Tip

- Director's main toolbar also offers Rewind, Stop, and Play buttons (**Figure 1.24**).

As you work, save the movie periodically to preserve your efforts.

To save a movie:

- Choose File > Save to save the current version of your movie to disk, writing over the movie's previous saved version.

  When you save a movie for the first time, Director opens the Save As dialog box (**Figure 1.25**), where you can name your movie and choose the area of your hard disk to which the movie should be saved.

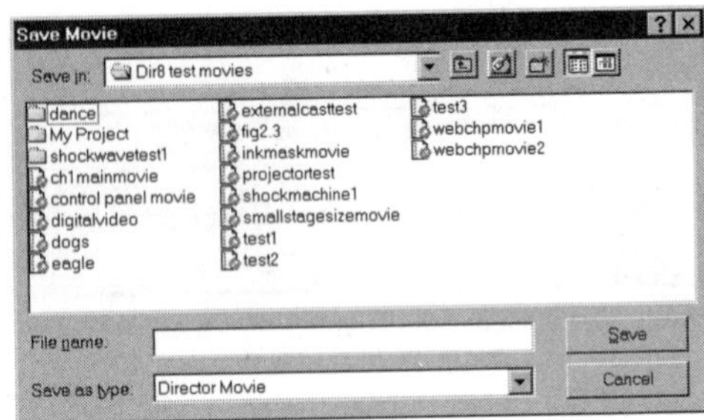

Figure 1.25 The Save As dialog box.

✔ Tip

- When you're ready to test your movie's performance, choose File > Save and Compact to save an optimized version of your movie under its original file name. Director reorders the cast, reduces the movie to its minimum size, and eliminates any unused space that might have accumulated in the original file.

If you want to try to undo something you've changed that can't be corrected with an Undo command, try the Revert command. This command works best when you want to go back to the previous saved version quickly.

To revert to the last saved version of your movie:

- Choose File > Revert to open the last saved version of your current movie.

Stage Size

Figure 1.26 Choose a stage size of at least 640X480 from the Stage Size pop-up menu.

Creating a Movie

Creating most kinds of Director movies usually involves the same general procedure. This section provides a seven-part outline of the entire process while building a simple but complete Director movie from start to finish. Each part of the outline includes a series of steps that collectively build a complete Director movie. Please follow the outline parts sequentially, and complete all steps within each part to build this example. Keep in mind that while the steps involved exemplify the movie-making process, they pertain specifically to this example, and would obviously differ for any other movie.

After working through this example, you'll have a good top-down grasp of a large part of Director. The only requirements before proceeding are having a bitmap and sound file available to complete the movie example.

Part I: Customize the authoring environment and movie properties

Before getting to the heart of creating a movie, take a moment to set the various preferences, view options, and properties that affect the movie as a whole, such as stage size.

To start making a Director movie:

1. Launch Director.

   This also opens a new movie.

2. Choose Modify > Movie > Properties to open the Property Inspector.

3. From the Stage Size pop-up menu, choose a size of at least 640x480 for this example (**Figure 1.26**).

4. Choose View > Guides and Grid, and turn off Show Grid and Show Guides in the submenu if they aren't already disabled.

continues on next page

5. Choose View > Sprite Overlay, and turn off Show Info and Show Paths in the submenu if they aren't already disabled.
6. Choose Control > Loop Playback to deselect Loop Playback.

   This step sets your movie to play through only once.
7. Choose Window > Score to open the score window.
8. Double-click the first frame in the Tempo channel to set the movie's rate (**Figure 1.27**).

   The Frame Properties: Tempo dialog box appears.
9. Use the slider to set a tempo of 30 frames per second (**Figure 1.28**).
10. Click OK.

Part II: Assemble the cast

The second step in creating a Director movie is to assemble the required cast members: the movie's multimedia participants, such as bitmaps, sounds, QuickTime movies, Lingo scripts, etc. You'll probably import most of these elements; others, you may create or edit in Director. You can keep them all in one cast, or you can organize them in different casts to manage them more conveniently (*see Chapter 2, "Assembling Casts"*).

To import cast members

1. Choose File > Import.
2. Choose Bitmap Image (**Figure 1.29**) from the Files of Type pop-up menu (Show pop-up menu on the Mac).
3. Select a bitmap file and click Add.

   Any image will do for this example.
4. Choose Sound from the Files of Type pop-up menu (Show pop-up menu on the Mac).

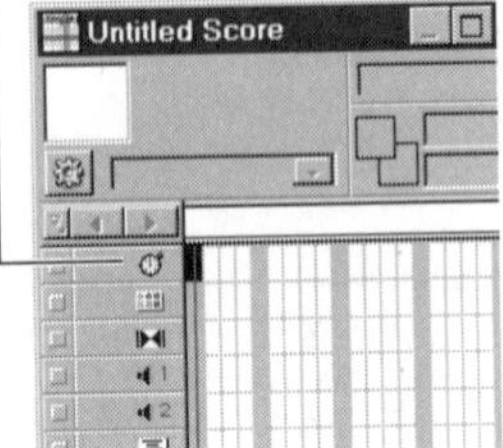

Figure 1.27 Double-click the first frame in the Tempo channel.

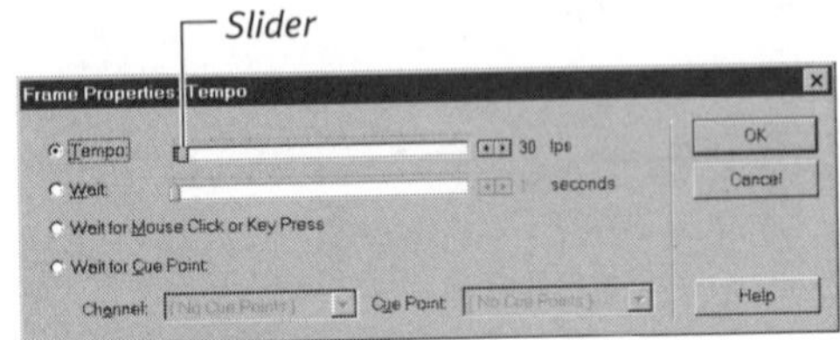

Figure 1.28 Set the tempo of your movie to 30 fps by using the slider.

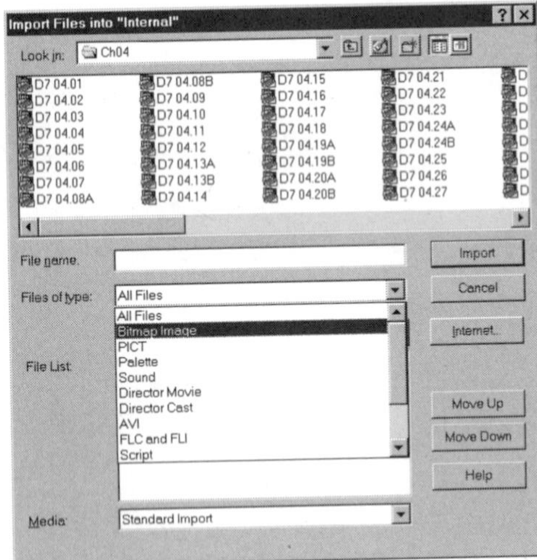

Figure 1.29 Choose Bitmap Image for the file type to import.

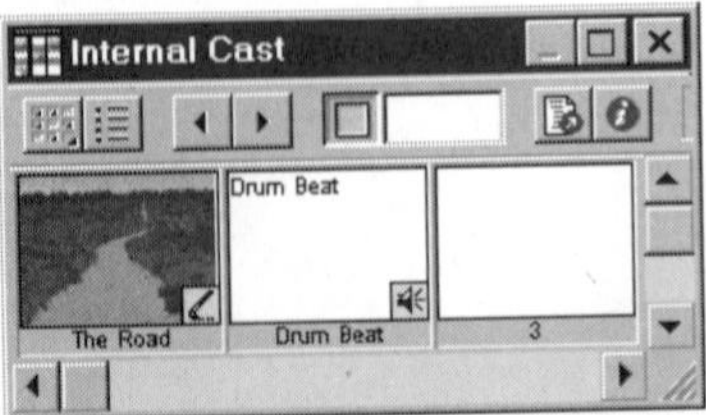

Figure 1.30 The imported cast members in a cast window.

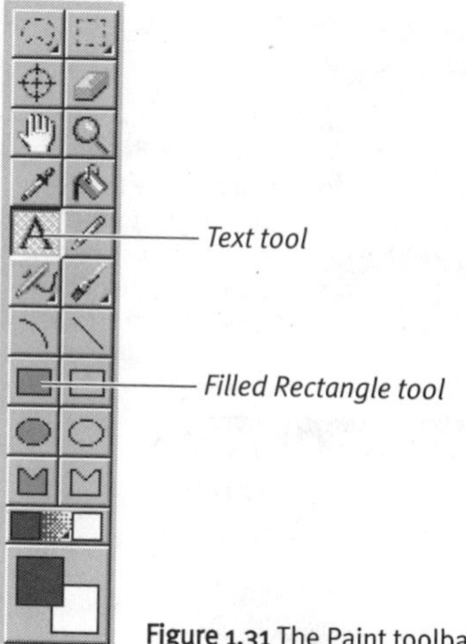

Figure 1.31 The Paint toolbar.

Figure 1.32 Using the Filled Rectangle tool, draw a rectangle in the paint window.

Figure 1.33 With the Text tool selected, click the top-left corner of the rectangle.

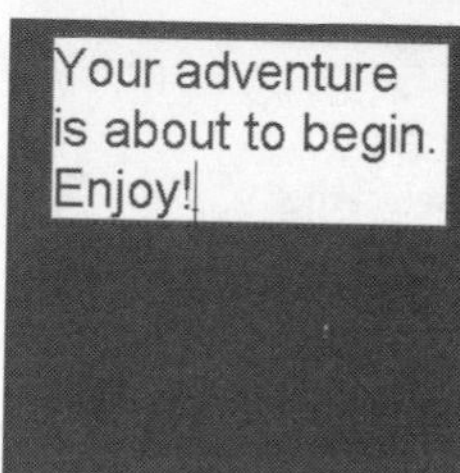

Figure 1.34 Type the text as shown.

5. Select a sound file and click Add.

   Any sound will work for this example. The sound file should be in one of the following formats: AIFF, WAV, MP3, AU, or Shockwave Audio.
6. Click Import.
7. If the Image Options dialog box appears, click OK.

   Your cast members are imported into the first available positions in the internal cast (**Figure 1.30**).

To create cast members internally

1. Choose Window > Cast to open the Cast window.
2. Select an empty cast-member position.
3. Choose Window > Paint to open the Paint window.
4. Click the Filled Rectangle tool (**Figure 1.31**).
5. Click the Foreground color chip and hold down the mouse button to display a color menu, and select any color you want to use.

   Leave the background color white.
6. Draw a rectangle in the Paint window approximately the size shown in **Figure 1.32**.
7. Click the Text tool.
8. Click the top-left corner of the rectangle to display a blinking text box (**Figure 1.33**).
9. Choose Modify > Font and choose 36 from the Size pop-up menu.
10. Click OK.
11. Type the text shown in **Figure 1.34** (or something else, if you prefer), pressing Enter or Return after the first line.

continues on next page

12. Before finalizing the bitmap text, drag the text box by one of its borders to position it roughly at the center of the rectangle (**Figure 1.35**).
13. Click outside the text box to finalize it.
14. Close the Paint window.

    A bitmap cast member is created in the selected cast-member slot when you close the window (**Figure 1.36**).

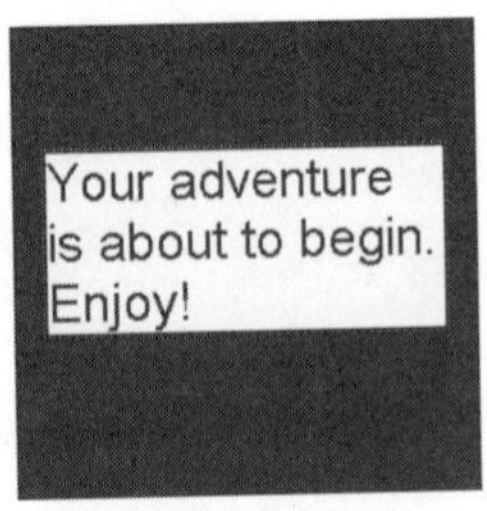

Figure 1.35 Before finalizing the text, drag the text box to the center of the rectangle (drag it by one of its borders).

Figure 1.36 The bitmap image you created in the paint window becomes a cast member.

To create cast members on the stage

1. Choose Window > Score to open the score window.
2. Click to select the first frame in the first sprite channel (**Figure 1.37**).
3. If the stage window is not visible, choose Window > Stage.
4. Choose Window > Tool Palette to display the Tool palette.
5. Click to select the Push Button tool in the Tool palette (**Figure 1.38**).
6. Click the bottom center of the stage to create a button cast member.

   A blinking insertion point appears in the push button.
7. Type **Start Movie** in the button and click outside it to finalize the button (**Figure 1.39**).

   The button becomes a cast member and is placed in the score automatically, because you created it on the stage.

Figure 1.37 Select the first frame in the first sprite channel.

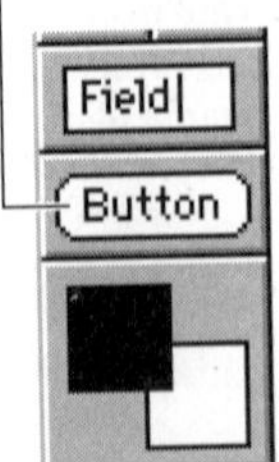

Figure 1.38 Select the Push Button tool.

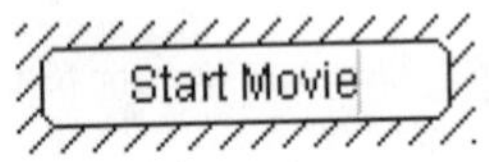

Figure 1.39 Type **Start Movie** in the button on the stage.

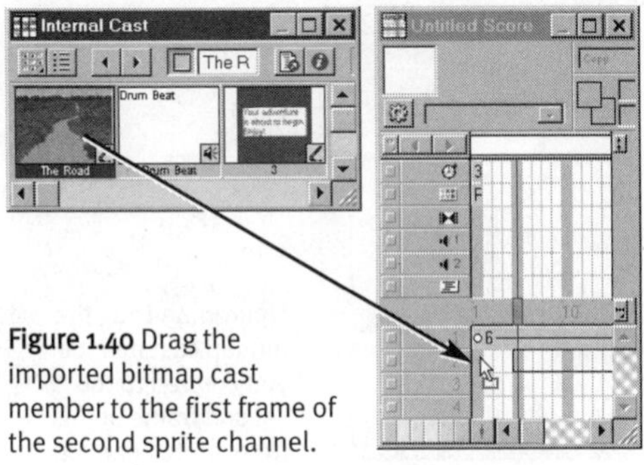

Figure 1.40 Drag the imported bitmap cast member to the first frame of the second sprite channel.

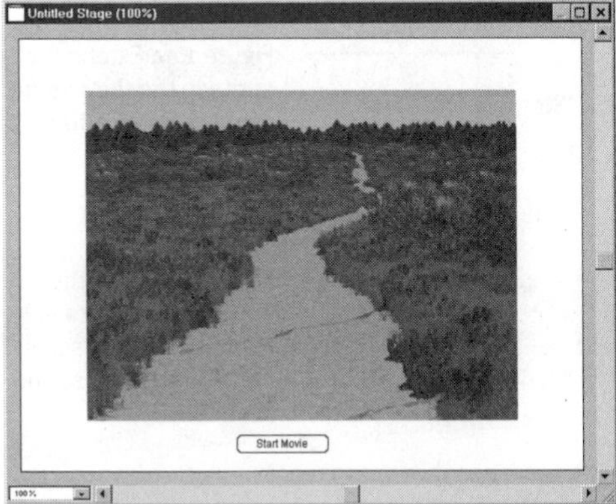

Figure 1.41 The cast member is positioned at the center of the stage.

Sprite occupies first frame only

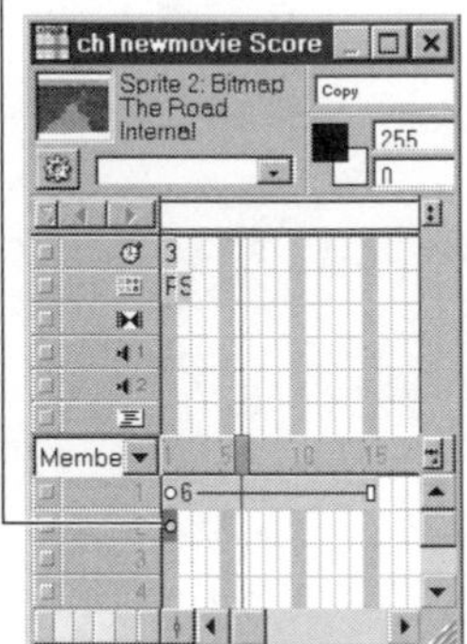

Figure 1.42 Shorten the sprite in the second sprite channel so that it occupies only the first frame.

Part III: Incorporate cast members into your movie

You start building an actual movie by placing cast members in the score to create sprites. You place the cast members over a range of frames in which you want them to be active. In the case of visual cast members, you place them in the frames where you want them to be visible on the stage (*see Chapter 3, "Building a Score"*).

To place cast members in the score

1. Choose Window > Score to open the score window, if it's not already open.
2. Open the cast window.
3. From the cast window, drag the bitmap cast member you imported to the first frame of the second sprite channel (**Figure 1.40**).

   Director positions the cast member in the center of the stage (**Figure 1.41**).
4. In the score, drag the end frame of this sprite (represented by a square) to the left to shorten the sprite so that it occupies only the first frame (**Figure 1.42**).

continues on next page

5. Drag the bitmap cast member of the rectangle with text you created earlier from the cast window into the second frame of the third sprite channel (**Figure 1.43**).

6. Drag the end frame of this sprite to the right to extend it to about the 100th frame (**Figure 1.44**).

7. Drag the sound cast member you imported into the second frame of the first sound channel (**Figure 1.45**) in the score (*see Chapter 12, "Adding Sound"*).

8. Extend this sound sprite in the same manner to about the 100th frame.

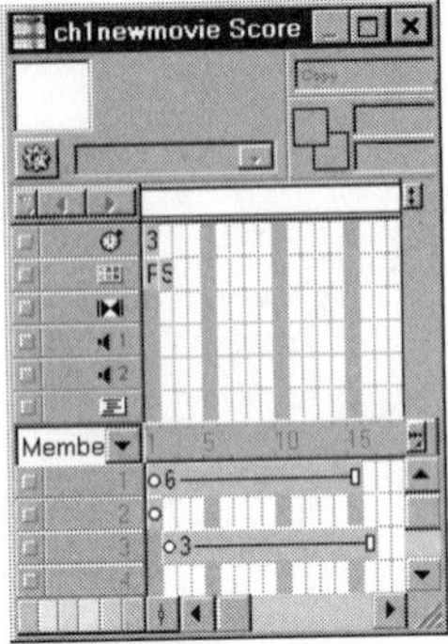

Figure 1.43 Drag the bitmap cast member you created to the second frame of the third sprite channel.

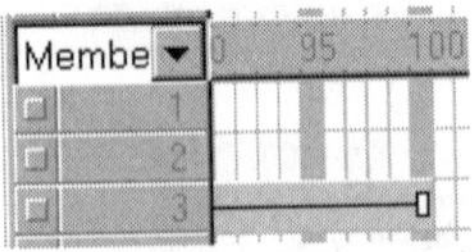

Figure 1.44 Extend the sprite in the third sprite channel to the 100th frame.

Figure 1.45 Drag the imported sound cast member into the second frame of the first sound channel.

Part IV: Customize and animate sprites

Change your sprites' properties to fit the requirements of your scene. You can change many properties, such as size, position, and rotation angle. You animate a sprite by changing its properties over a range of frames (*see Chapter 4, "Animating Sprites"*).

To change sprite properties

1. Open the Stage window, if it's not already visible.

2. In the score, click to select the end frame of the sprite (the rectangle-with-text sprite) in the third sprite channel.

   Just click the square symbol at the end of the sprite. You may need to use the score scrollbars to access it.

3. Choose Modify > Sprite > Tweening.

   The Sprite Tweening dialog box appears.

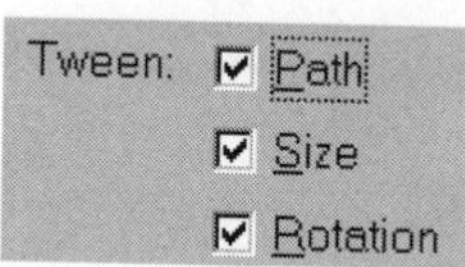

Figure 1.46 Choose the Path and Rotation options in the Sprite Tweening dialog box.

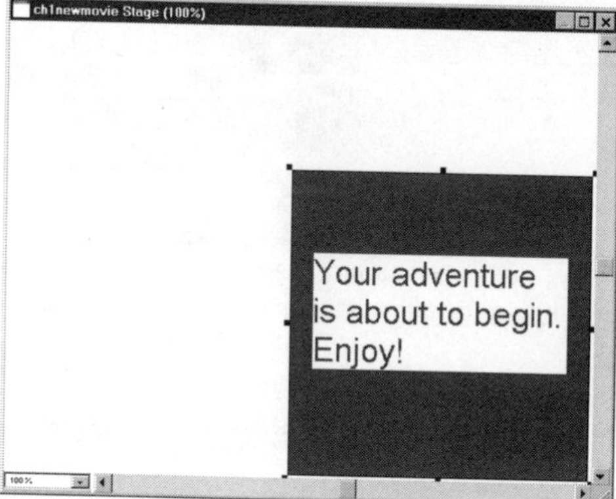

Figure 1.47 Drag the sprite to the bottom-right corner of the stage.

Figure 1.48 Type **720** in the Rotation Angle field of the Property Inspector.

Figure 1.49 Shrink the sprite to about one-fifth its original size by dragging its bottom-right handle upward and to the left.

4. Make sure that the Path and Rotation options are selected (**Figure 1.46**).

   These options are the sprite properties in this example that Director will *tween*, or automatically change for you gradually over a range of frames to create an animation.

5. Click OK to close the Sprite Tweening dialog box.

6. With the end frame of the sprite still selected in the score, drag the sprite to the bottom-right corner on the stage (**Figure 1.47**).

7. With the end frame of the sprite still selected in the score, choose Modify > Sprite > Properties to open the Property Inspector.

8. Type **720** in the Rotation Angle field (**Figure 1.48**).

9. Close the Property Inspector.

10. Click to select only the first frame of the sprite in the third channel.

    Just click the small circle at its start.

11. On the stage, drag the highlighted sprite to the top-left corner of the stage.

12. With the sprite still selected on the stage, drag the bottom-right handle upward and to the left to shrink the sprite to about one-fifth of its original size (**Figure 1.49**).

Part V: Add interactive controls

Director includes a powerful scripting language called Lingo, which allows you to add interactivity, and go beyond the linear approach of putting together a movie in the score *(see Chapter 17, "Scripting Lingo")*. Director also offers behaviors—prefabricated Lingo scripts—that you can drag and drop to add interactivity and other effects instantly *(see Chapter 16, "Adding Interactive Behaviors")*.

To add interactivity

1. Choose Window > Library Palette to open the Library palette.
2. Click the Library List button to display a pop-up menu of behavior categories.
3. Choose Navigation to display the Navigation-related behaviors.
4. Open the score window.
5. Drag the Go Loop behavior from the Library palette to the first frame of the script channel in the score (**Figure 1.50**).

   This behavior causes your movie to remain paused in the first frame during playback until some other action occurs.
6. Drag the Go to Frame X Button behavior from the Library palette to any part of the sprite in the first sprite channel in the score (the push-button sprite).

   The Parameters dialog box appears.
7. Type **2**, and click OK (**Figure 1.51**).

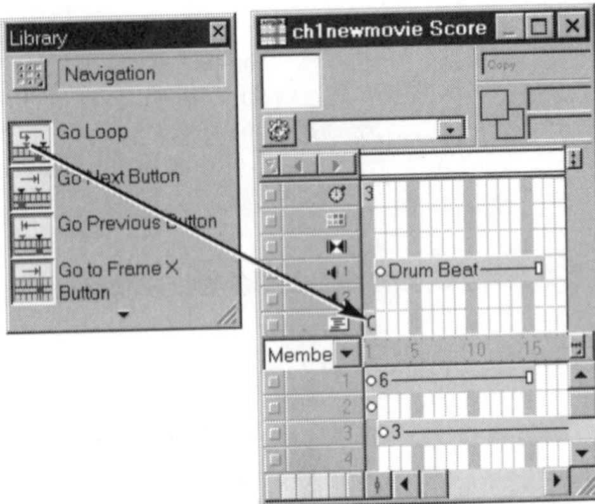

Figure 1.50 Drag the Go Loop behavior from the Library palette to the first frame in the script channel.

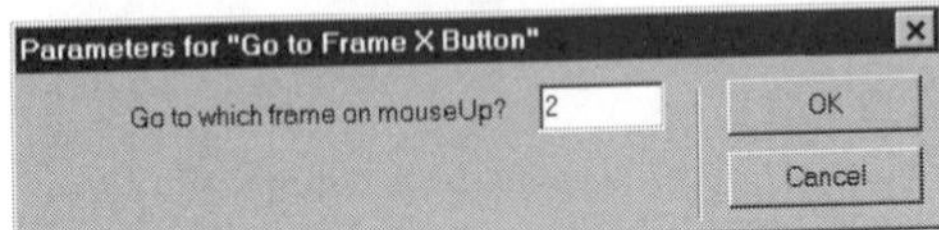

Figure 1.51 Type **2** in the Parameters dialog box.

CREATING A MOVIE

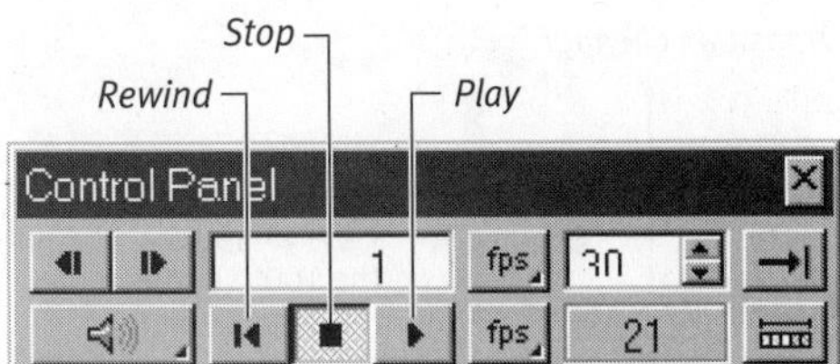

Figure 1.52 The Control Panel functions much like the buttons on a VCR for rewinding and playing your movie. You can also use it to set several other playback features, such as movie tempo.

Figure 1.53 The opening frame of the movie (your image will be different).

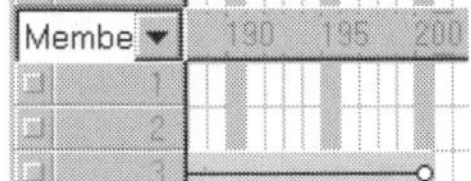

Figure 1.54 Extend the sprite in the third sprite channel to about the 200th frame.

Part VI: Test and refine the movie

Play back your movie-in-progress and make notes of any needed refinements. Then make adjustments in the score as necessary.

To fine-tune your movie

1. Choose Window > Control Panel to display the Control Panel (**Figure 1.52**).
2. Click Rewind to rewind your movie to frame 1.
3. Click the Play button.

   Your movie begins. On the stage, you should see the bitmap image that you imported and a push button below it (**Figure 1.53**).
4. Hide the Director interface by pressing Ctrl+Alt+1 (Command+Option+1 on the Mac).
5. Click the push button that you created at the bottom of the stage to start the animation.

   You should see the rectangle with text moving from the top-left corner to the bottom-right corner while rotating and growing in size. You also should hear the imported sound start to play.
6. When the movie finishes playing, press Ctrl+Alt+1 (Command+Option+1 on the Mac) again to display the Director interface.
7. Open the Score window.
8. In the score, click and drag the end frame of the sprite in the third sprite channel to the right to extend it to about the 200th frame (**Figure 1.54**).
9. Drag the end frame of the sprite in the sound channel to extend it to about the 200th frame as well.

continues on next page

10. Click Rewind in the Control Panel.

11. Click Play in the Control Panel and click the button on the stage.

    Your animation plays back slower but smoother, because now it occupies twice as many frames.

12. In the score, double-click the 100th frame in the transition channel (**Figure 1.55**) to add a scene transition.

    See Chapter 5, "Playing and Refining Movies," for more details on transitions.

    The Frame Properties: Transition dialog box appears.

13. Select the Dissolve category, and then select the Dissolve, Bits Fast transition (**Figure 1.56**).

14. Click OK.

15. Rewind and play back your movie.

    Notice the scene transition approximately halfway through the animation.

16. Double-click the first frame in the Tempo channel to change your movie's tempo or rate.

    The Frame Properties: Tempo dialog box opens.

17. Use the slider to set a faster tempo for your movie, such as 120 fps (**Figure 1.57**).

18. Click OK.

19. Rewind and play back your movie.

    Notice how much faster the animation is.

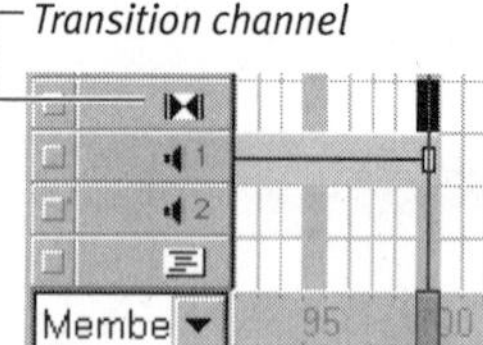

Figure 1.55 Double-click the 100th frame in the transition channel.

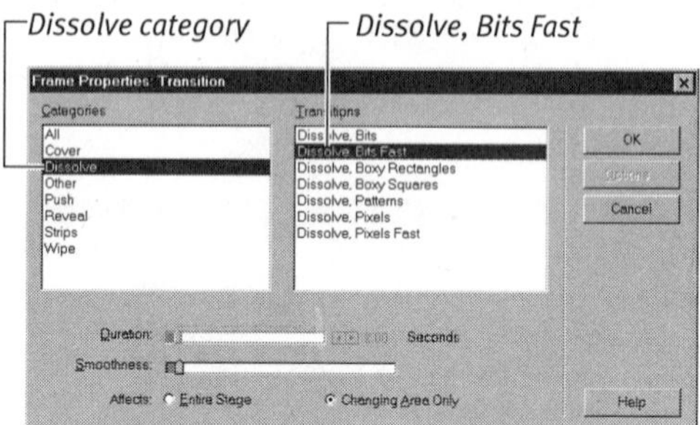

Figure 1.56 Select the transition shown here.

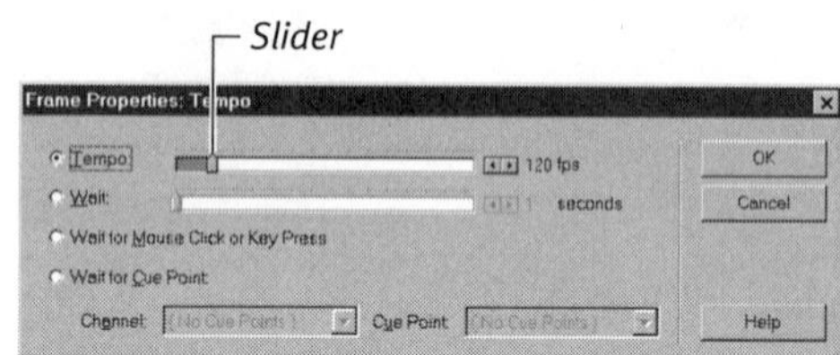

Figure 1.57 Set a much faster tempo for your movie, such as 120 fps.

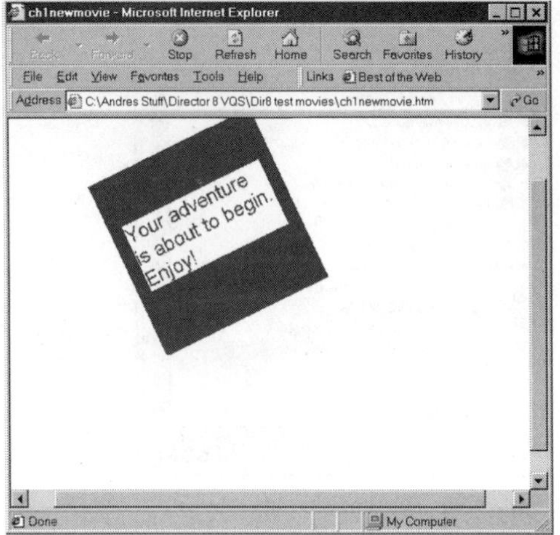

Figure 1.58 When you use the Publish command, Director creates a Shockwave version of your movie and plays it back in your default Web browser.

Part VII: Prepare the movie for distribution

When your movie works the way you want, convert it to a distribution format such as Shockwave or a projector. Shockwave movies play back in Web browsers, and projectors can run like stand-alone applications on the desktop. Before converting your movie, optimize it by compressing any elements that can be made smaller for faster downloads.

To publish your movie

1. Save your Director movie.
2. Choose File > Publish.

   Director creates a Shockwave version of your movie and embeds it in an HTML document. Director then launches your default Web browser (**Figure 1.58**) and plays back your Shockwave movie (*see Chapter 14, "Making Director Movies for the Web"*).

Director's Help System

You may have to resort to Director's built-in help system to find out how to handle a task. There are three ways to access the help information. If you want to browse around in the help system, here's how to hunt among the topics.

To browse Director help:

1. Choose Help > Director Help to display the Help Topics: Director 8 Help window.
2. Click the Contents tab to access help information by topics (**Figure 1.59**).

   The tiny book icons represent help topics.
3. Double-click to open the topic you want (**Figure 1.60**).

   or

   On the Mac only: Click the triangular arrows to the left of the books to open or collapse subtopics.
4. When you find the subtopic you want, double-click its page icon to open it.

To browse or search the Help index:

1. Choose Help > Director Help.
2. Click the Index tab to bring into view the alphabetical index of help contents (**Figure 1.61**).
3. Scroll to find a topic and click use the triangular arrows (on the Mac only) at the left edge to open or collapse subtopics.

   or

   Type a help topic to find.

✔ Tip

■ As soon as Director recognizes the word you're typing (or thinks it does), it jumps to the topic, so you can type just the first few letters of the topic.

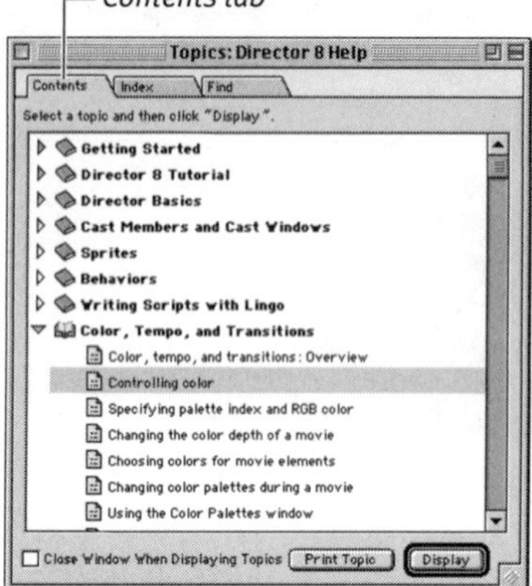

Figure 1.59 Click the Contents tab.

Figure 1.60 Double-click to open a topic page.

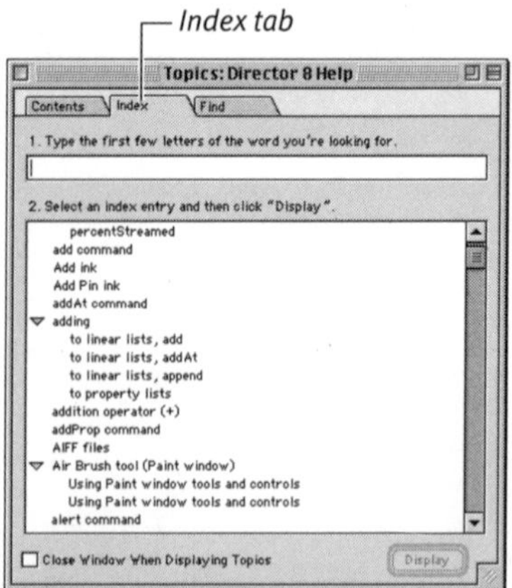

Figure 1.61 Click the Index tab.

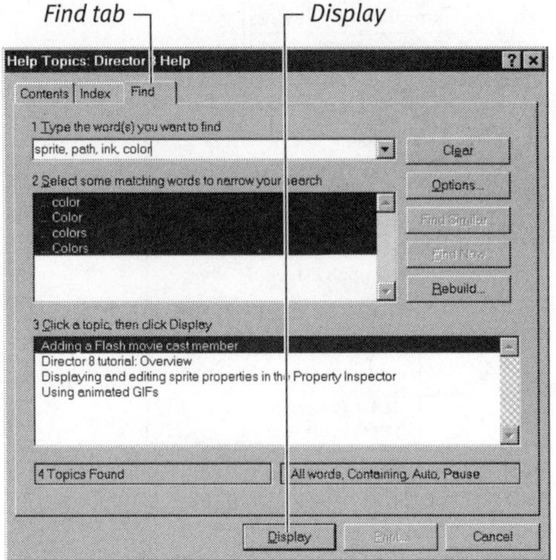

Windows version

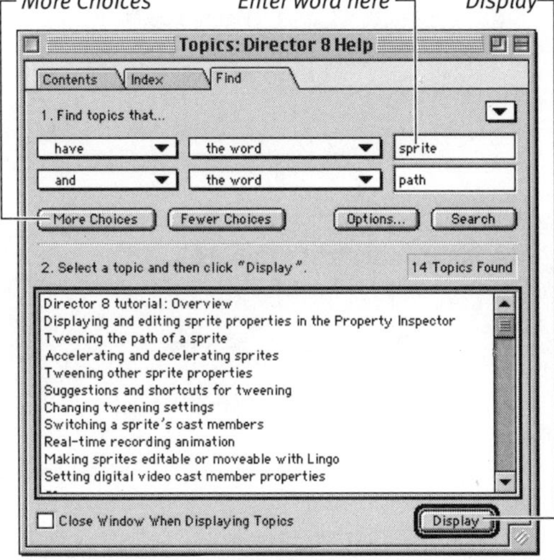

Mac version

Figure 1.62 Click the Find tab (Windows and Mac versions shown separately).

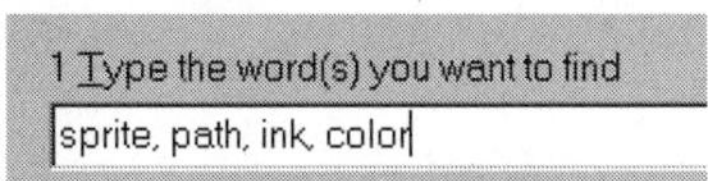

Figure 1.63 (Windows) Separate multiple search words with commas or spaces.

Director's help system allows you to retrieve help documents based on keyword use.

To find a help document that contains specific keywords:

1. Choose Help > Director Help.
2. Click the Find tab (**Figure 1.62**).
3. Type the words you want to find in Director help documents.

   (Windows) If you enter two or more words, separate them with commas or spaces (**Figure 1.63**).

   or

   (Mac) Click the More Choices button for each additional word you want to use as part of the search, and enter each word in the corresponding text box on the right side of the dialog box.
4. Click Options to change how the keywords are searched for.

   The Find Options dialog box opens.
5. Specify search criteria.
6. Click OK.

   Any help topics that meet your keyword search requirements are displayed at the bottom of the Help Topics dialog box.
7. Select a topic.
8. Click Display (**Figure 1.64**).

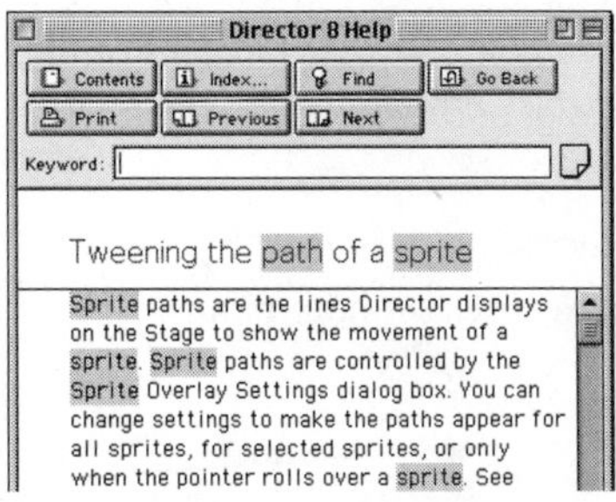

Figure 1.64 Your keywords are highlighted in the retrieved help document.

Working Faster

You can quickly access the relevant set of commands for many elements in Director by using a context menu.

To display a context menu:

- Right-click (Windows) or Control-click (Mac) an object, such as a sprite, or an interface element, such as a Director window (**Figure 1.65**), to display a context menu containing the most relevant commands.

  Many Director commands have a keyboard equivalent called a *keyboard shortcut*. To the right of most commands under the main menus, you find the keyboard-shortcut equivalents (**Figure 1.66**). *See the tear-out reference card for a list of keyboard shortcuts.*

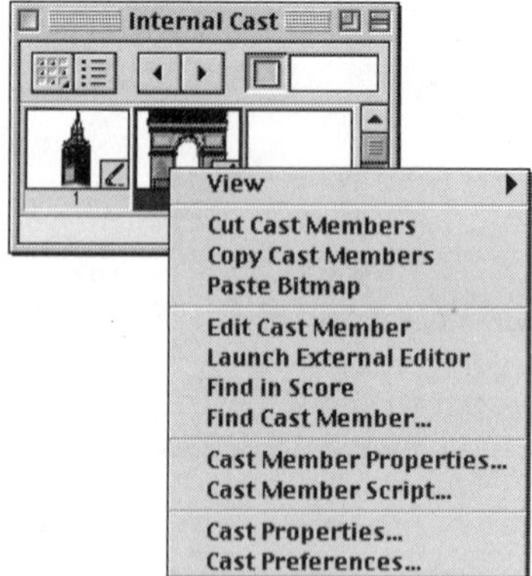

Figure 1.65 Right-click (Windows) or Control-click (Mac) to open a context menu for the given interface element or object.

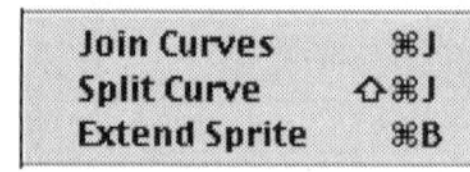

Figure 1.66 Menus display keyboard shortcuts alongside commands.

To perform a keyboard shortcut:

1. Hold down the specified modifier key or keys.

   The usual modifier keys are Shift, Control, and Alt in Windows. On the Mac, they're Shift, Command, and Option (**Table 1.1**). Ignore the little plus signs that are part of the keyboard shortcuts in Windows menus; they're punctuation, not keys that you need to hold down.

2. Press and release the activator key or keys.

   Press and hold Control/Command and then press and release O to open a new file, for example. To save a file, press and hold Control/Command and then press and release S.

3. Release the modifier key.

   Director executes the command.

Table 1.1

Mac menu shortcut symbols

Mac menu symbols	Key
⇧	Shift
⌘	Command
⌥	Option

General Preferences

General Preferences contain settings that relate to stage appearance and the user interface; you make choices according to how you like to work. If some of these choices seem confusing while you're new to the program, just leave the Director defaults until you learn more about the program by working through the tasks in this book.

To set General Preferences:

1. Choose File > Preferences > General to open the General Preferences dialog box (**Figure 1.67**).
2. Change settings as necessary in the dialog box.
3. Click OK to close the dialog box.

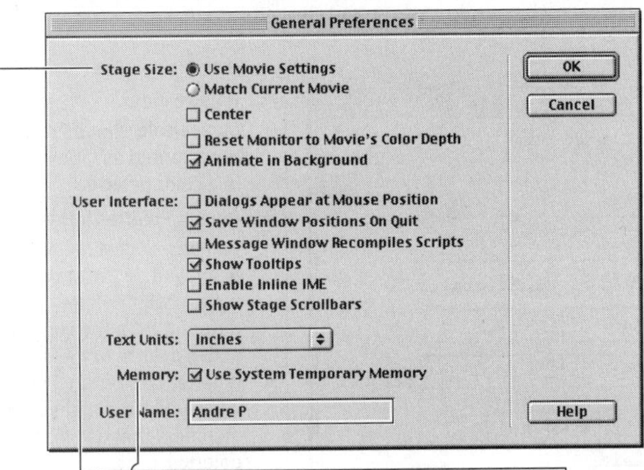

Figure 1.67 Use the General Preferences dialog box to control aspects of Director's stage and user interface.

Memory (Mac only) When this option is checked, Director uses available system memory when its own memory partition becomes full. If virtual memory is turned on, this option is disabled.

STAGE SIZE

Use Movie Settings makes the stage resize to the dimensions of any new movie that opens.

Match Current Movie makes the stage dimensions of any movie that is opened match the current movie.

Center centers the stage on the screen automatically. If this option is not checked, the movie's settings determine where on the stage it opens.

Reset Monitor to Movie's Color Depth (Mac only) makes your monitor's color depth change to match the color depth of any movie.

Animate in Background makes your movie capable of running in the background. You can work in other applications while a movie plays on the stage behind other program windows.

USER INTERFACE

Dialogs Appear at Mouse Position makes dialog boxes pop open at the position of the mouse pointer. If this option is not selected, the dialog boxes appear in the center of the screen.

Save Window Positions on Quit makes the program remembers where your Director windows are when you quit and reopens them in the same position the next time.

Message Window Recompiles Scripts is checked by default. If this option is not checked, you need to recompile Lingo scripts manually before entering any Lingo in the Message window.

Show Tooltips makes definitions appear when the mouse pointer is positioned over tools. This option is checked by default.

Show Stage Scrollbars displays scrollbars in the stage window.

Text Units Select the unit of measure for the Text and Field windows' rulers.

User Name assigns a user name to the movie.

Movie Properties

Movie properties are settings that affect an entire movie. You set the movie properties at the beginning of a project to make basic decisions about how your movie looks and operates. Some of the options may seem confusing before you know more about the program; don't worry, because the choices will make more sense later.

For your first efforts as you experiment with the program, you can skip this process and just accept Director's default settings.

To set movie properties:

1. Open an existing movie or create a new movie.
2. Choose Modify > Movie > Properties to display the Movie tab of the Property Inspector (**Figure 1.68**).
3. Adjust settings as necessary.

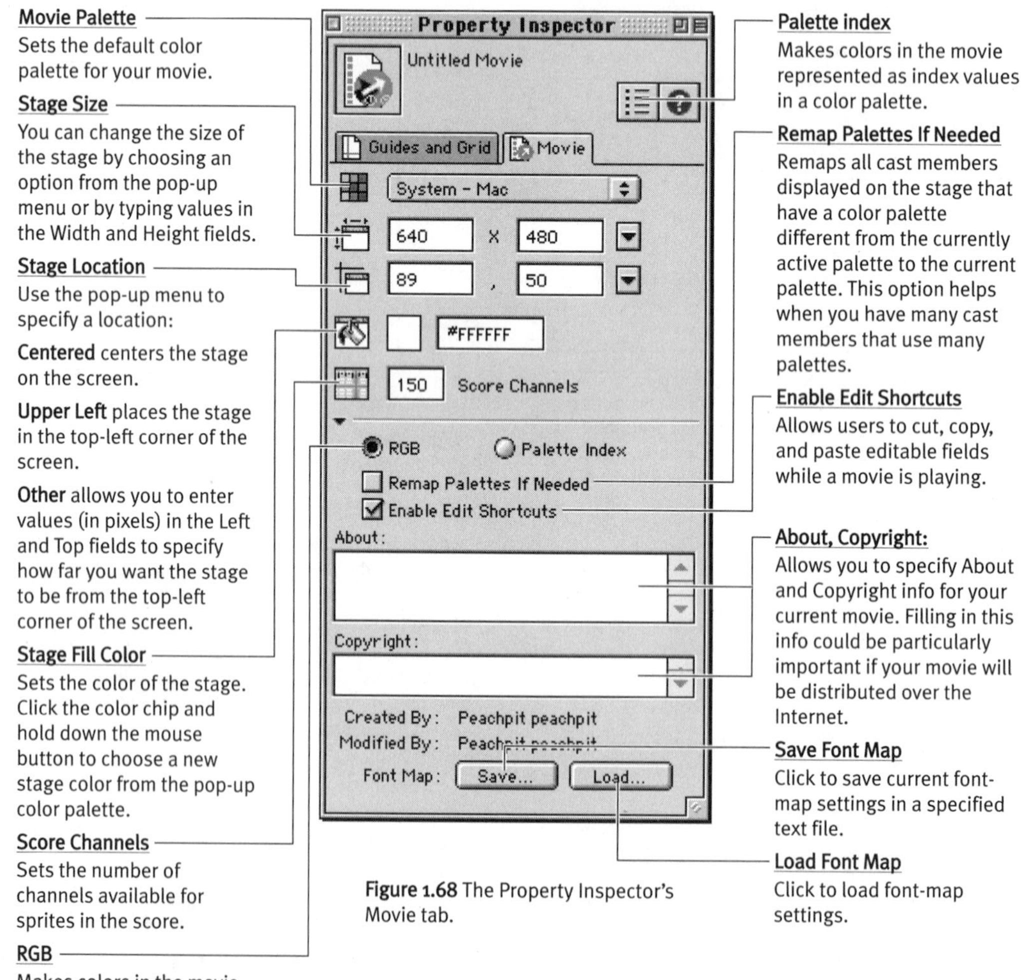

Movie Palette
Sets the default color palette for your movie.
Stage Size
You can change the size of the stage by choosing an option from the pop-up menu or by typing values in the Width and Height fields.
Stage Location
Use the pop-up menu to specify a location:
Centered centers the stage on the screen.
Upper Left places the stage in the top-left corner of the screen.
Other allows you to enter values (in pixels) in the Left and Top fields to specify how far you want the stage to be from the top-left corner of the screen.
Stage Fill Color
Sets the color of the stage. Click the color chip and hold down the mouse button to choose a new stage color from the pop-up color palette.
Score Channels
Sets the number of channels available for sprites in the score.
RGB
Makes colors in the movie represented as RGB values.
Palette index
Makes colors in the movie represented as index values in a color palette.
Remap Palettes If Needed
Remaps all cast members displayed on the stage that have a color palette different from the currently active palette to the current palette. This option helps when you have many cast members that use many palettes.
Enable Edit Shortcuts
Allows users to cut, copy, and paste editable fields while a movie is playing.
About, Copyright:
Allows you to specify About and Copyright info for your current movie. Filling in this info could be particularly important if your movie will be distributed over the Internet.
Save Font Map
Click to save current font-map settings in a specified text file.
Load Font Map
Click to load font-map settings.
Property Inspector
Untitled Movie
Guides and Grid
Movie
System - Mac
640
480
89
50
#FFFFFF
150
Score Channels
RGB
Palette Index
Remap Palettes If Needed
Enable Edit Shortcuts
About:
Copyright:
Created By:
Peachpit peachpit
Modified By:
Font Map:
Save...
Load...

Figure 1.68 The Property Inspector's Movie tab.

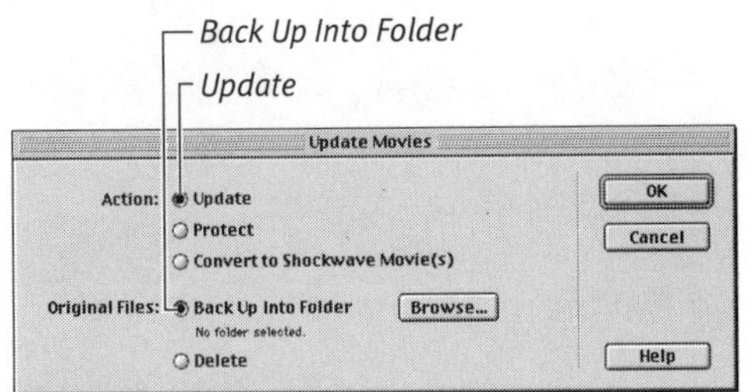

Figure 1.69 Choose Update in the Update Movies dialog box.

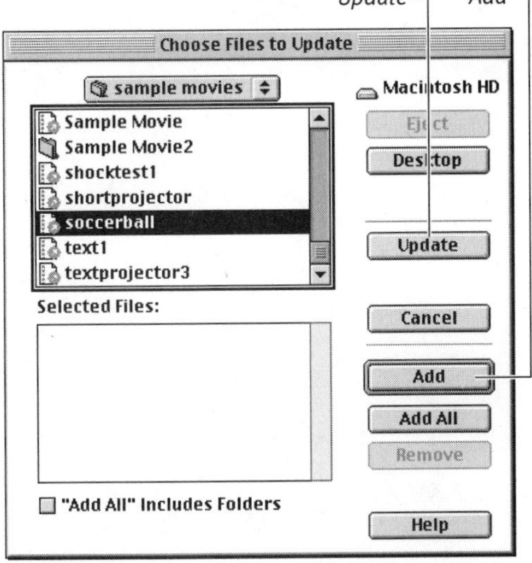

Figure 1.70 In the Choose Files to Update dialog box, select a Director 5 or later movie or cast file to update to version 8

✔ Tip

- If you're sure that you no longer need the original outdated Director files, or if you have secure backups on another disk, you can choose Delete in step 3. You can't undo and recover the deleted originals, though, so make sure that you don't need the files before you click OK.

Updating Movies

The Update Movies command in the Xtras menu is used for three purposes:

1. Converting older versions of Director movies and casts to the latest version
2. Protecting movies and casts from being opened or edited (*see Chapter 13, "Creating a Projector"*)
3. Converting movies and casts to the Shockwave format (*see Chapter 14, "Making Movies for the Web"*)

Use the following procedures to update Director 5 or later movies and casts to the Director 8 format.

To update Director movies and casts:

1. Choose Xtras> Update Movies to display the Update Movies Options dialog box.
2. Choose the Update option (**Figure 1.69**).
3. Choose the Back Up into Folder option.
4. Click Browse to select a storage folder for the original files.
5. Click Open.
6. Click OK.
   The Choose Files to Update dialog box opens.
7. Select a Director 5 or later movie file or cast that you want to update (**Figure 1.70**).
8. Click Add.
9. Repeat steps 7–8 to add all the files to update to the list at the bottom of the dialog box, or click Add All to add all the files in the current folder.
10. Click Update.

2

ASSEMBLING CASTS

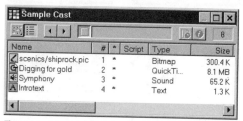

Sample Cast

Name	#	*	Script	Type	Size
scenics/shiprock.pic	1	*		Bitmap	300.4 K
Digging for gold	2	*		QuickTi...	8.1 MB
Symphony	3	*		Sound	65.2 K
Introtext	4	*		Text	1.3 K

Figure 2.1 A Cast window in List view.

Figure 2.2 A Cast window in Thumbnail view.

Director's Cast windows act as the storage bins for the multimedia elements—cast members—used in your movie. Cast members include elements such as pictures, sounds, text, color palettes, digital videos, film loops, and Lingo scripts. You can import cast members into Director from a wide variety of sources, or you can create them within Director by using the numerous built-in editing tools such as the paint and text windows.

You can choose to view a Cast window in either List view or Thumbnail view (**Figures 2.1–2.2**). In List view, cast members are represented by rows and columns of text, much like the List and Details view of a folder on your desktop. In Thumbnail view, each cast member is represented by a thumbnail image. A small icon in the bottom-right corner of each thumbnail identifies the cast member's type (**Figure 2.3**).

Director allows you to create and work with multiple independent casts within a single movie, organizing cast members by type or whatever is appropriate for your production. Each cast appears in its own window and can contain up to 32,000 cast members. You can include casts internally or make them external resources that you can share between Director movies.

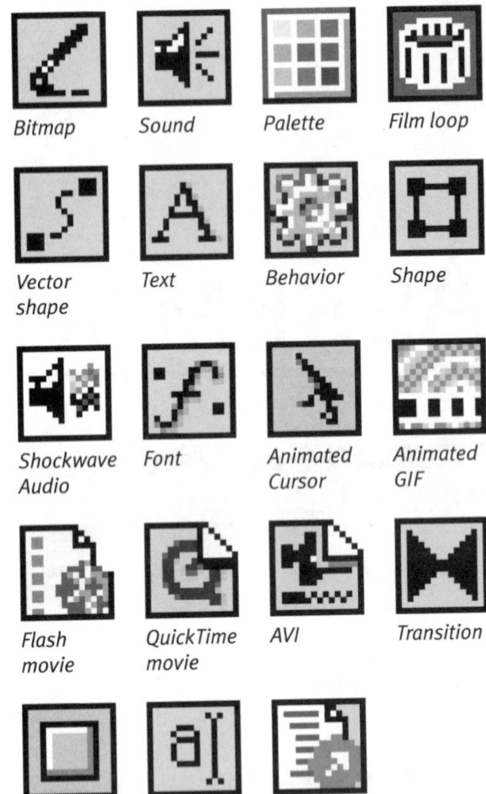

Figure 2.3 Symbols indicate the type of each cast member.

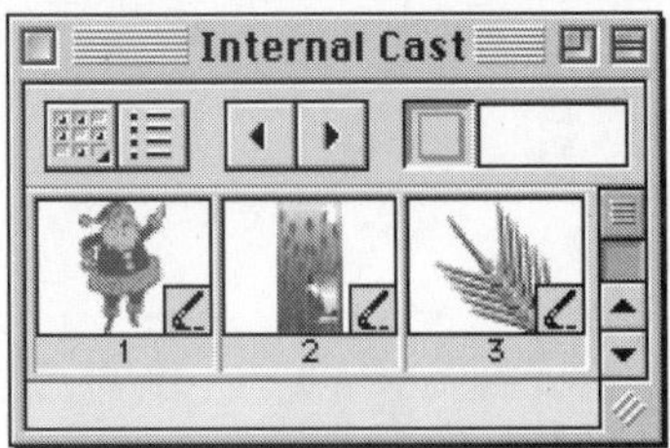

Figure 2.4 Each internal cast is stored inside the Director movie file.

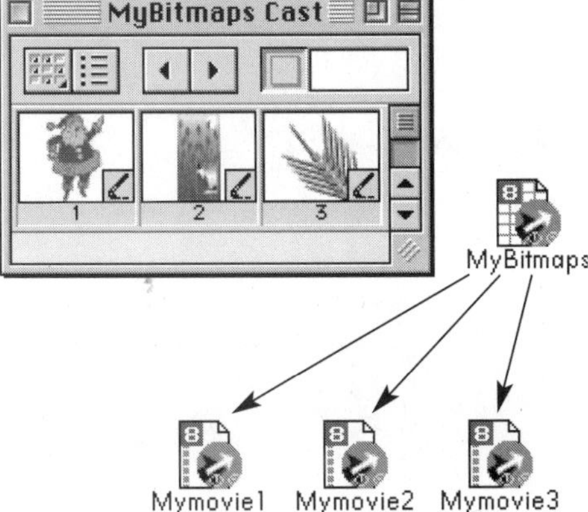

Figure 2.5 External casts are stored outside the Director movie file and can be shared by multiple Director movies.

Creating Casts

Whenever you create a cast in Director, you first must decide whether to make it internal or external. Director always saves all internal casts as part of the movie file itself. The program automatically creates one empty internal cast when you open a new movie (**Figure 2.4**). External casts (**Figure 2.5**), on the other hand, are separate files stored outside your movie and can be shared between Director movies. You must link an external cast to your movie before you can use any of its cast members *(see "To link an external cast to the current movie" later in this chapter).*

Director handles the packaging of internal and external casts somewhat differently between the two main Director movie distribution formats: Projectors and Shockwave movies. When you create a Projector file, all internal casts are automatically stored within it, and you have the option of embedding external casts as well. A Shockwave movie file also stores all internal casts within itself, but any necessary external casts can't be embedded and must be supplied along with the Shockwave file or linked to an address on the internet.

To decide whether to create an internal or external cast:

1. Decide whether the cast members you plan to put in the new cast ought to belong only to one movie.

   Internal casts belong only to the Director movie that contains them. Use an external cast for cast members that ought to be available for more than one movie, such as sound effects or characters that you plan to use in multiple movies.

2. Consider whether your project is simple or complex.

   In a simple movie, internal casts often make more sense. Complex projects may actually be composed of a series of related movies, requiring shared external casts.

   If you plan to distribute your movie via Shockwave, and you prefer it to be contained within a single file, use internal casts, because any external casts must be supplied separately.

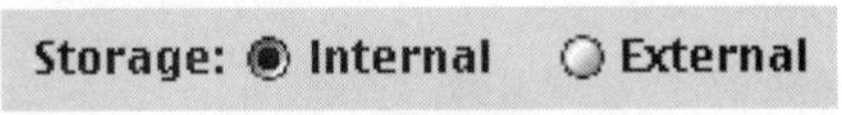

Storage: ◉ Internal ○ External

Figure 2.6 Choose Internal or External.

☑ Use in Current Movie

Figure 2.7 For external casts, check Use in Current Movie.

Figure 2.8 Type a name for the cast.

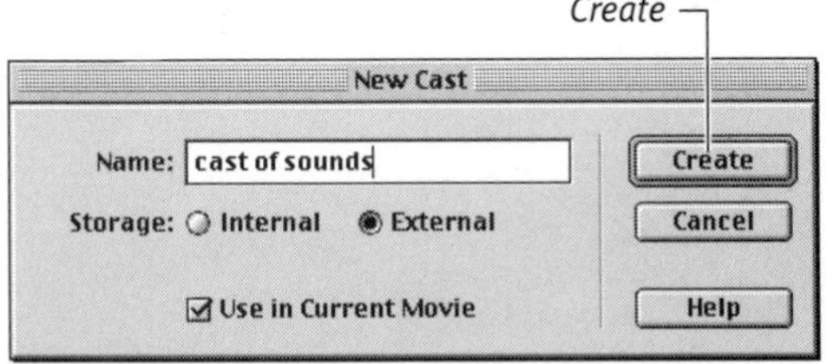

Figure 2.9 Click Create.

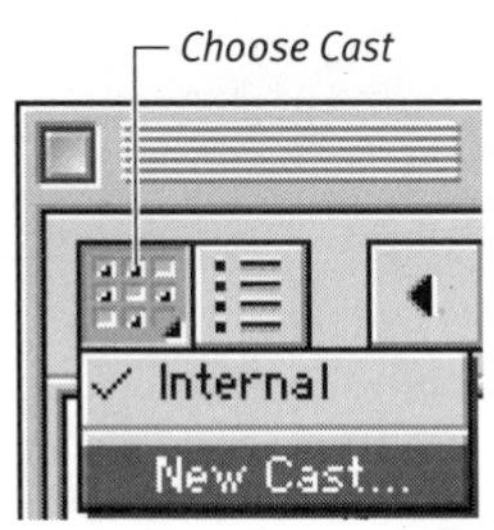

Figure 2.10 Create a new cast by clicking the Choose Cast button and choosing New Cast from the pop-up menu.

You can add as many internal or external casts to your movie as you want. If your movie involves a large number of cast members, it may help you work efficiently to group related cast members into separate casts. You may choose to create two casts: one for storing bitmaps and the other for sounds. If you're preparing a movie that will have versions in different languages, you can create different casts for the text in each language. Each cast is viewed in its own separate Cast window.

To create a new cast:

1. Choose File > New > Cast.
   The New Cast dialog box opens.
2. Choose internal or external as the cast storage type (**Figure 2.6**).
3. If the cast is external, check the Use in Current Movie checkbox to link the cast to the current movie (**Figure 2.7**).
4. Type a name for the cast in the text box (**Figure 2.8**).
5. Click Create (**Figure 2.9**).

✔ Tip

- You can also create a new cast by clicking the Choose Cast button in a Cast window and choosing New Cast from the pop-up menu (**Figure 2.10**).

To open a Cast window:

- Choose Window > Cast.

  or

  If multiple casts exist, choose Window > Cast > *name of cast.*

You can specify which actual cast appears in any open Cast window by clicking the Choose Cast button.

To choose a different cast for an open Cast window:

1. In an open Cast window, click the Choose Cast button to display a pop-up menu of available casts (**Figure 2.11**).

   The pop-up menu lists all internal casts, as well as external casts that have been linked to the current movie.

2. Choose a cast.

Internal and any linked external casts automatically open with the movie that contains them. If you want to access cast members from an external cast that is not currently linked to your movie, you must open that cast manually.

To open an external cast not linked to the current movie:

1. Choose File > Open.
2. Select an external cast file.
3. Click Open.

   The external cast opens in its own Cast window.

Figure 2.11 Click the Choose Cast button and choose a cast from the pop-up menu.

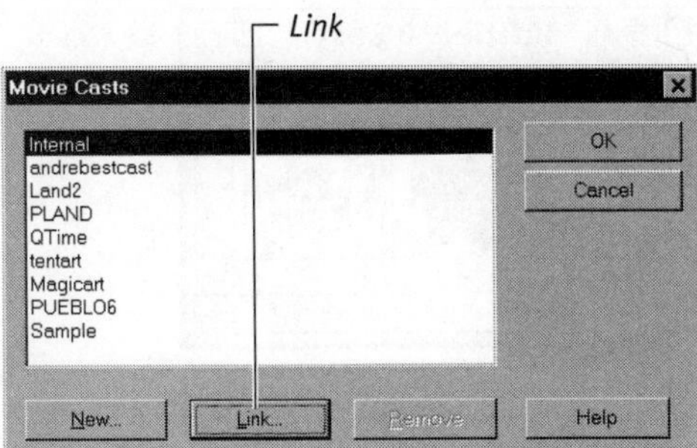

Figure 2.12 Click Link in the Movie Casts dialog box.

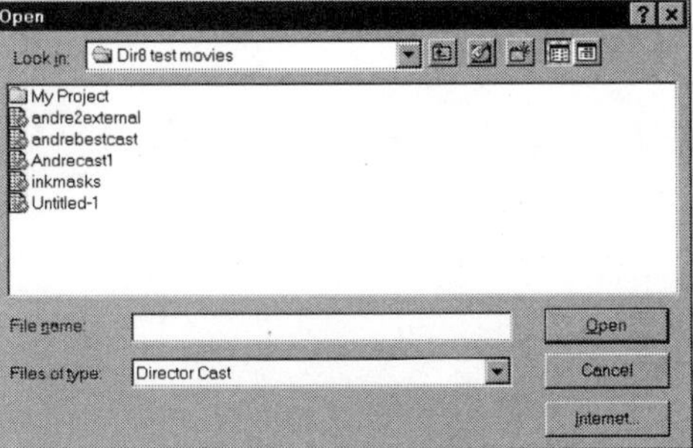

Figure 2.13 Select an external cast file.

Before you can use cast members from an external cast in a movie, you must link the external cast to the movie.

To link an external cast to the current movie:

1. Choose Modify > Movie > Casts.
   The Movie Casts dialog box opens (**Figure 2.12**).
2. Click Link.
   The Open dialog box appears.
3. Select the external cast file (**Figure 2.13**).
4. Click Open.
   After you link an external cast to the current movie, Director automatically opens that cast whenever you open the movie. Director also automatically saves any changes made in the external cast when you save the movie.

✔ Tips

- If you want to use a cast member in an external cast without linking to the cast, you can copy that cast member to either an internal cast or a linked external cast.
- Don't confuse linked external casts with linked cast members. A linked cast member can reside in any type of cast (internal, linked external, or unlinked external), but its actual media information is stored in a file outside Director. For details, see "To decide whether to use the Standard Import or Link to External file media option when importing a file" later in this chapter.

To unlink an external cast from the current movie:

1. Choose Modify > Movie > Casts to open the Movie Casts dialog box.
2. Select the external cast you want to unlink.
3. Click Remove.
4. Click OK.

When you make changes in an external cast that is not linked to your movie, you must explicitly save those changes, because they are not saved when you save the Director movie. On the other hand, if you link an external cast to your current movie, any changes you make in the cast are saved automatically when you save the Director movie.

To save changes in an external cast (linked or unlinked):

1. Make the external cast that you want to save the active window by clicking it (**Figure 2.14**).
2. Choose File > Save As.
3. Type a file name for the external cast.
4. Click Save.

✔ Tip

- To save your movie along with all casts—internal, external linked, and external unlinked—choose File > Save All.

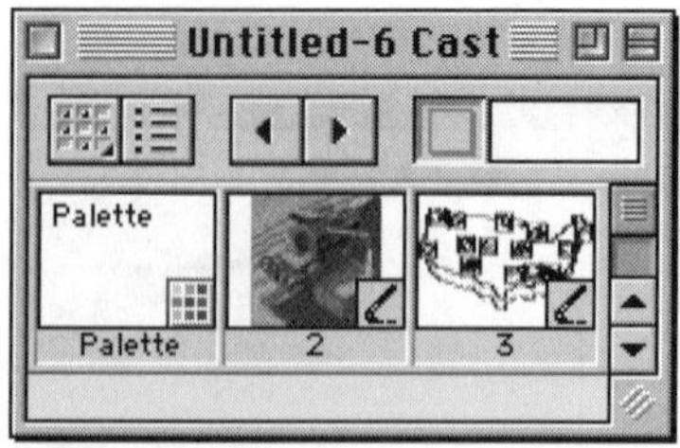

Figure 2.14 Click the external cast that you want to save to make it the active window.

Table 2.1

File Formats Imported by Director

File Type	File Formats
Animation and multimedia	Animated GIFs, Flash movies, Director movies, PowerPoint presentations
Still image	TIFF, PICT, Targa, BMP, GIF, JPEG, LRG (xRes), Photoshop 3.0 or later, MacPaint, PNG
Still image *Windows only*	PCX, Photo CD, WMF, PostScript
Multiple image file formats *Windows only*	FLI, FLC
Multiple image file formats *Mac only*	Scrapbook, PICS
Sound	AIFF, WAV (compressed and uncompressed), MP3, Shockwave Audio, AU
Sound *Mac only*	System 7 sounds
Video	QuickTime 2, 3, and 4; AVI
Text	ASCII, RTF, HTML
Palette	Photoshop, PAL, CLUT

Importing Cast Members

If you want your Director movie to incorporate graphics or sounds created in some other application (such as a background created in Photoshop or a set of sound effects compiled in SoundEdit Pro), you first have to import those elements into a Cast window.

Table 2.1 summarizes the objects and formats you can import into Director. Most people import at least some of the cast members for a Director movie.

To import a cast member:

1. Choose File > Import to display the Import Files dialog box (**Figure 2.15**).
2. From the Files of Type menu (Show menu on the Mac), choose the kind of cast member to import (**Figure 2.16**).

   Only files in the selected format are displayed in the dialog box.
3. At the top of the dialog box, find and open the folder that contains the file you want to import.

   or

   Click Internet (**Figure 2.17**) and specify a URL for the file in the Open URL dialog box.
4. Select the file and click Add (**Figure 2.18**).

   or

   Click Add All to add all the folder's displayed files to the list.

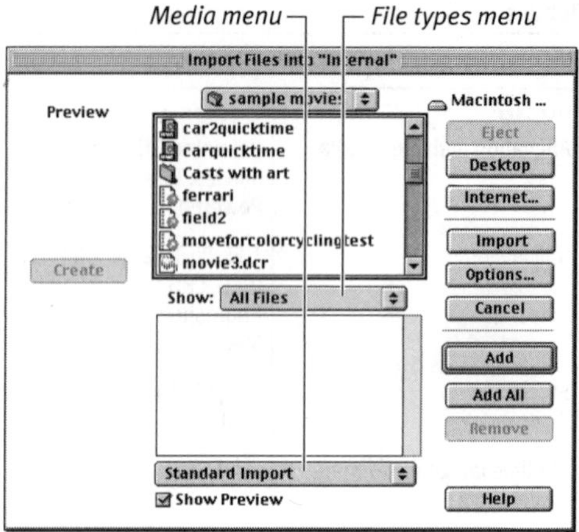

Figure 2.15 The Import Files dialog box.

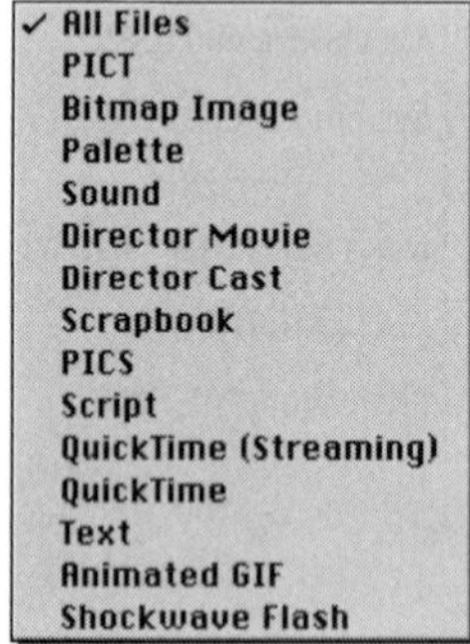

Figure 2.16 Select the type of cast member to import.

Figure 2.17 Select a file to import from a local drive, or click Internet to import a file via the Internet.

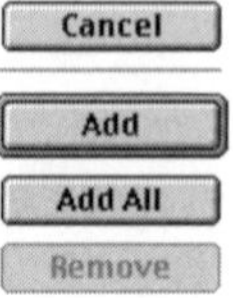

Figure 2.18 Click Add to choose one file or Add All to choose the entire folder.

✓ Standard Import
Link to External File
Include Original Data for Editing
Import PICT File as PICT

Figure 2.19 Choose one of four importing options from the Media pop-up menu.

5. Choose an option from the Media pop-up menu (**Figure 2.19**).

   Standard Import copies the contents of the file into your Director movie, so you won't need to provide the file when distributing your movie. (AVI and QuickTime movies are always linked to, even if you choose Standard Import.)

   Link to External File creates a link to an external file, allowing you to store cast member data outside your Director movie. Director imports this file from its source each time you run the movie. Text and RTF files are always stored inside your movie, regardless of whether you choose this option. *(See the following section for details.)*

   Include Original Data for Editing causes Director to keep a copy of the original cast member data inside the movie. Use this option when you have defined an external editor (via the File > Preferences > Editors command) for a particular media type, and you want Director to pass this original data along to the editor when you edit the cast member.

   Import PICT File as PICT keeps PICT files from being converted to bitmaps.

6. Click Import to bring the added cast member(s) into the active Cast window.

When you import a file into Director's cast, there are times when linking to the external file (as opposed to bringing in the data into your movie through Standard Import) is advantageous (**Figure 2.20**).

Choosing Standard Import or Link to External file when importing a file:

1. Consider whether downloading time or movie file size is an issue.

   Importing cast members with the Standard Import option increases your movie's file size.

   When you import a file by using the linking option, Director creates a cast member that stores only the name and location of the file. This information appears in the Member tab of the Property Inspector (**Figure 2.21**). Actual linked cast-member data is downloaded only if and when your movie requires it.

2. Consider whether cast-member data changes frequently in your movie.

   If it does, linking to a cast-member file—particularly at an Internet address—provides you the greatest flexibility in being able to update components of your movie without requiring your users to download the movie again and again.

3. Consider whether keeping the distribution process simple and reliable is more important than controlling file size.

   Linking external cast members adds some complexity and risk in distributing your movies, because you must include all linked cast members. The movie can come to a halt if a file is not found.

4. Decide whether your target audience can tolerate hiccups in movie playback.

   Linked external cast members sometimes cause playback delays as they load. In the worst case, if Director cannot find a linked file, it asks the viewer to locate the missing file before continuing.

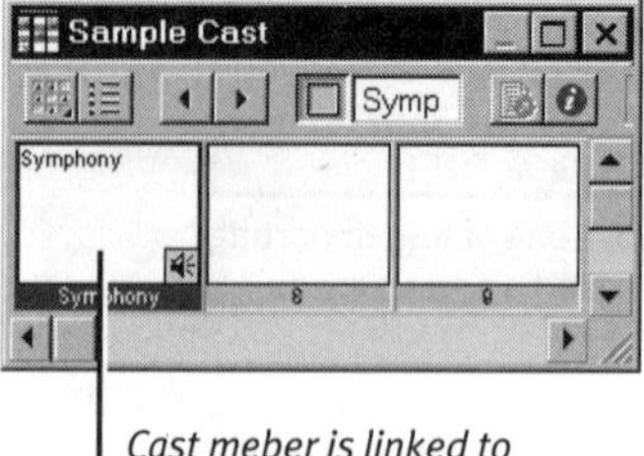

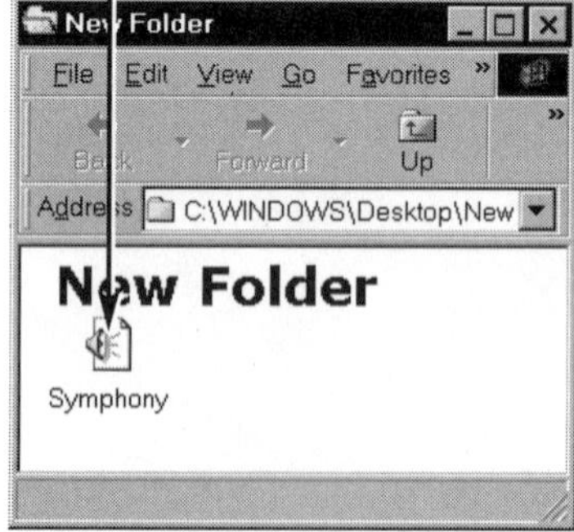

Figure 2.20 Linking to an external cast file has advantages, which include keeping your movie file smaller and being able to update cast-member media without requiring the user to download the entire movie from scratch.

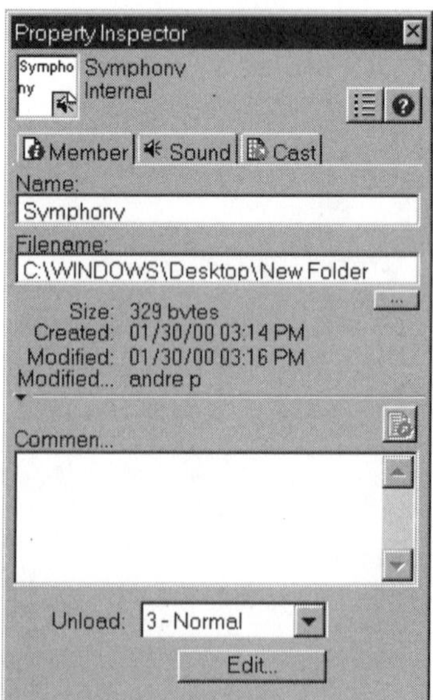

Figure 2.21 The Property Inspector for a linked sound cast member.

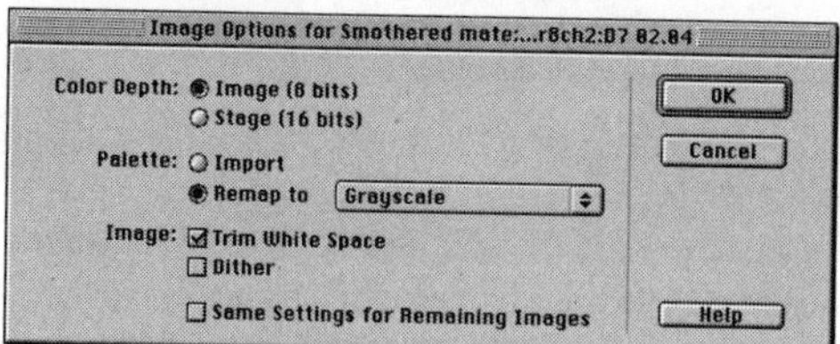

Figure 2.22 Options for importing images.

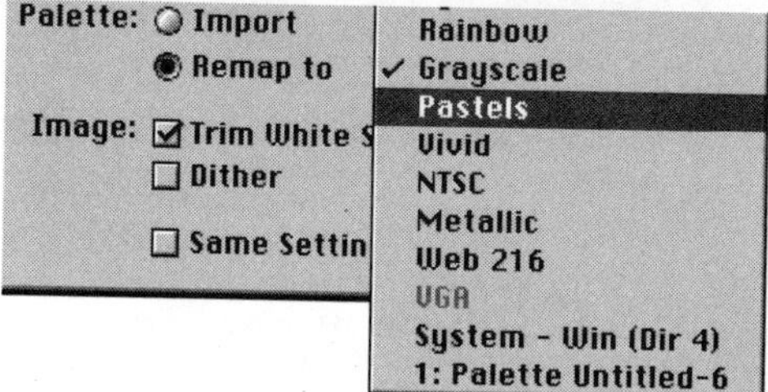

Figure 2.23 Choose a substitute palette.

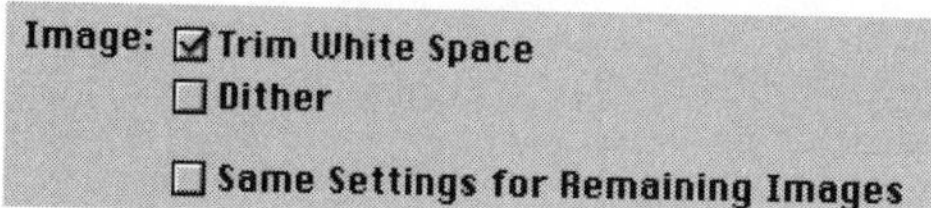

Figure 2.24 Choose the Trim White Space option to remove white pixels from the borders of an image.

✔ Tip

- If you're importing a batch of files, you can apply the options you choose to all the files at the same time. In the Image Options dialog box, check the Same Settings for Remaining Images checkbox; then click OK to bring in all the files.

When you import a bitmap cast member that uses a different palette or more colors than the current movie, the Image Options dialog box appears. In this dialog box, you specify color depth and palette attributes for the imported file (**Figure 2.22**).

To set image options for bitmap cast members:

1. In the Image Options dialog box, set the color depth option:

   Choose the Image option to import the image at its original color depth.

   or

   Choose the Stage option to import the image at the movie's color depth. *(For details on movie color depth, see Chapter 9, "Managing Color.")*

2. Set the Palette option:

   Click Import to keep the image's original color palette (the color palette becomes a cast member).

   or

   Click Remap To and choose a palette from the pop-up menu for the imported image to adopt (**Figure 2.23**). Choosing Remap To causes Director to replace the image's colors with the most similar colors from the palette you choose from the pop-up menu.

3. Set the Image option:

   Choose Trim White Space (**Figure 2.24**) to remove all white pixels from the borders of an image.

   or

   Choose Dither to blend colors in a new palette selection to better approximate the original colors in your image.

4. Click OK.

Sometimes, after you import a bitmapped cast member, you need to change its size.

To change a bitmapped cast member's size:

1. In a Cast window, select a bitmapped cast member.
2. Choose Modify > Transform Bitmap.
   The Transform Bitmap dialog box opens.
3. Type new values in the Width and Height boxes (**Figure 2.25**).
   Check the Maintain Proportions check-box to maintain the cast member's original proportions.
   or
   Type a value in the Scale box to size the cast member proportionately.

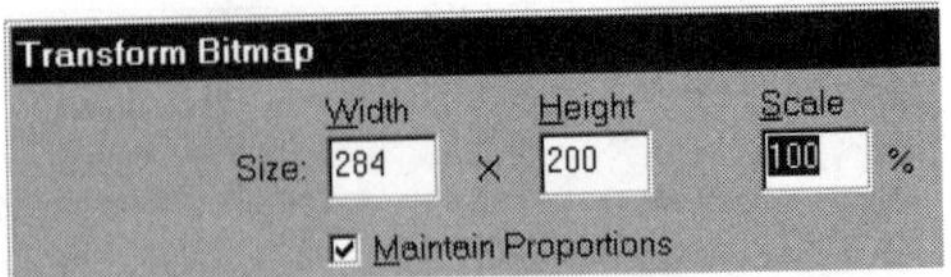

Figure 2.25 Resize a bitmap cast member by typing new values in the Width and Height boxes in the Transform Bitmap dialog box.

✔ Tip

- You cannot undo any changes made to a cast member via the Transform Bitmap command. Make sure that you have a duplicate of the original cast member before making any changes.

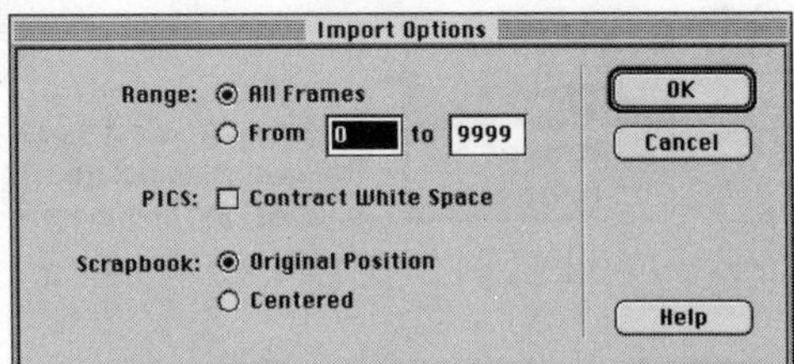

Figure 2.26 Importing options for Mac Scrapbook or PICS files.

Figure 2.27 Specify a range of frames to import.

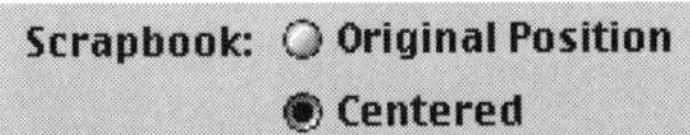

Figure 2.28 Position options for importing Mac Scrapbook images.

For Macintosh movies, when you import Scrapbook or PICS files, Director allows you to set several options in the Import Options dialog box (**Figure 2.26**).

To set import options for Scrapbook or PICS files (Mac):

1. Click Options in the Import Files dialog box.

   The Importing Options dialog box appears.

2. Click All Frames to import every frame in the file (each frame becomes a separate cast member).

   or

   Specify a range of frames to import by choosing the From option and typing the beginning and ending frame numbers in the text boxes (**Figure 2.27**).

3. Choose Contract White Space to import images without surrounding white space.

4. Choose Original Position for the Scrapbook option to import images in their original position.

   or

   Choose Centered (**Figure 2.28**) to import images centered in relation to other artwork in the sequence.

You may find that you've imported cast members that you haven't used in the movie. Director can find and delete them for you. Deleting unused cast members makes your movie more compact, quicker to load, and more efficient in using computer memory.

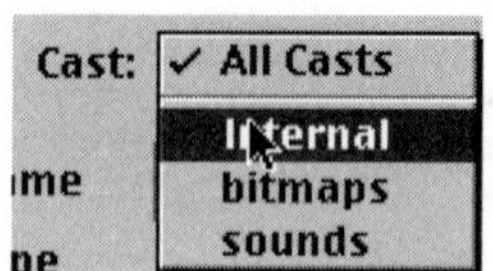

Figure 2.29 Select a cast from which to delete unused cast members.

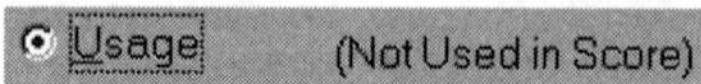

Figure 2.30 Click the Usage option.

To delete unused cast members:

1. Choose Edit > Find > Cast Member.
   The Find Cast Member dialog box opens.
2. From the Cast menu, choose a cast that has extraneous cast members (**Figure 2.29**).
3. Choose the Usage option (**Figure 2.30**).
4. Click Select All.
   Director finds and selects all unused cast members in the selected cast.
   You may first need to click the list to make the Select All button selectable.
   Cast members may be incorporated into your movie by way of Lingo scripts, in which case certain cast members would not necessarily appear in the score. So before deleting the cast members that Director finds, make sure that they are not used in any scripts.
5. Choose Edit > Clear Cast Members.

✔ Tip

- After you delete a series of cast members, save your movie by choosing File > Save and Compact. This operation reorders the cast, produces a more compact movie file, and optimizes movie playback.

Figure 2.31 Set the minimum PowerPoint slide duration.

Figure 2.32 Set the number of frames for PowerPoint effects.

Figure 2.33 Set a number of frames between keyframes for fly transitions in imported PowerPoint presentations.

Director includes an Xtras tool for importing presentations created in Microsoft PowerPoint, version 4. When you import a PowerPoint file, Director brings in the presentation in a form as true to the original as possible. Director imports the artwork, transitions, and text as cast members and converts each slide to a section in the score. PowerPoint build effects and any tempo changes also go into the score. You can play the presentation as imported or enhance it by adding interactivity, animations, and other Director effects.

To import a PowerPoint presentation:

1. Choose File > New > Movie.

   You must create a new movie to import a presentation.

2. Choose Xtras > Import PowerPoint File.

   Director brings in a copy of the PowerPoint file; the original presentation is not affected by the importing process.

3. Choose a presentation file and click Open.

   The PowerPoint Import Options dialog box appears.

4. Enter a value for Slide Spacing to specify the number of blank frames to allow between each pair of slides in the score.

5. Specify the Minimum Slide Duration, which is the minimum number of frames a slide occupies in the score (**Figure 2.31**).

6. If the presentation has build effects other than fly effects, enter a value for Item Spacing to specify the number of frames allocated for each item (**Figure 2.32**).

7. Specify Fly Transition Item Spacing, which is the number of frames between keyframes (**Figure 2.33**).

8. Click Import.

9. Play the movie.

10. If necessary, import the movie again with different settings.

Working in List View

When a Cast window is displayed in List view, cast members are represented by rows and columns of text attributes. List view is especially advantageous when you need to sort cast members by various attributes, such as name, size, or last time modified.

To toggle the view style for an open Cast window:

1. Select a Cast window to make it the active window.
2. Click the Cast View Style button (**Figure 2.34**) to toggle between List view and Thumbnail view.

   or

   Choose View > Cast >*view style.*

To set which column attributes are displayed for an open Cast window in List view:

1. Select a Cast window to make it the active window.
2. Choose File > Preferences > Cast.

   The Cast Window Preferences dialog box opens.
3. Select which list columns you want to display by checking the appropriate checkboxes (**Figure 2.35**).
4. Leave the Apply to All Casts checkbox unchecked if you want your column preferences to apply only to the Cast window you selected in step 1.

   or

   Check the Apply to All Casts checkbox to apply your column preferences to all Cast windows.

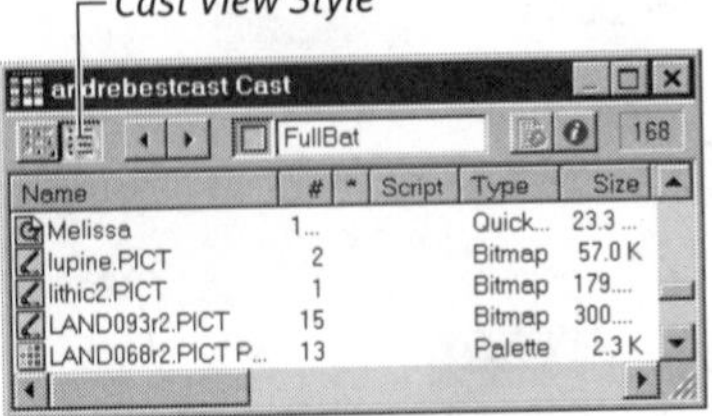

Figure 2.34 Use the Cast View Style button to toggle between List view and Thumbnail view.

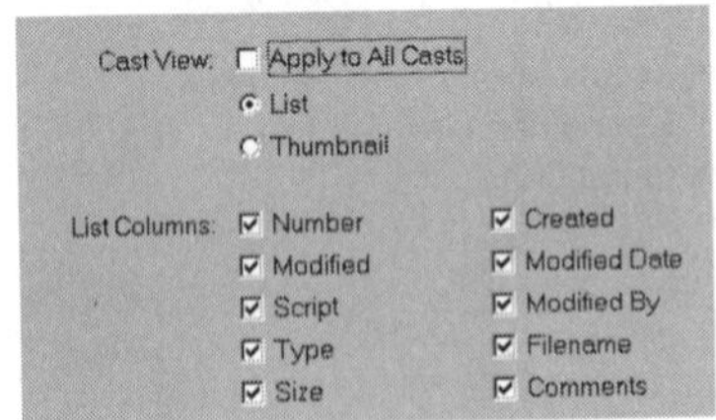

Figure 2.35 In the Cast Window Preferences dialog box, select which list columns you want to display.

✔ Tip

- Most of the column attributes are self-explanatory, but two need clarification: The Modified attribute corresponds to the column with the asterisk (*) header. An asterisk means that the cast member has been modified and not saved. The Script column indicates which cast members have a script attached.

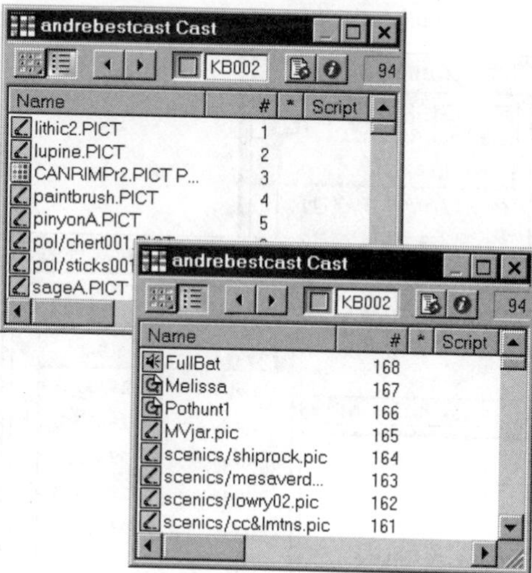
Figure 2.36 In Windows, click a column header to reverse the sort order.

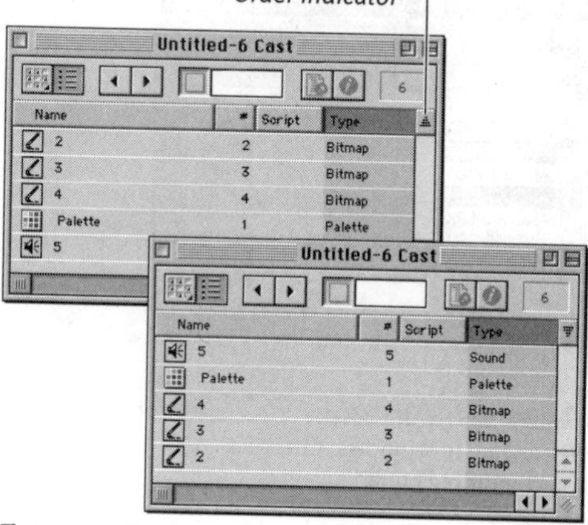

Figure 2.37 On the Mac, click the order indicator to reverse sort order.

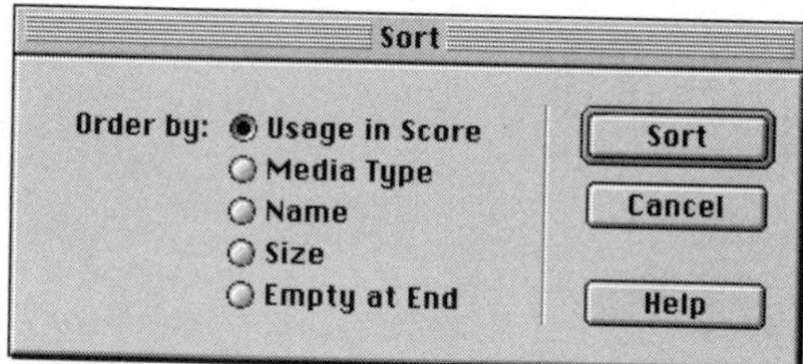

Figure 2.38 You can sort cast members by using the Sort dialog box.

To sort columns in a Cast window:

1. Open a Cast window and select List view:
2. Click any column header to sort the cast members by that column.
3. In Windows, click the column header again to reverse the sort order (**Figure 2.36**).

   or

   On the Mac, click the order indicator located above the vertical scroll bar to reverse sort order for the selected column (**Figure 2.37**).

✔ Tips

- When you sort by any column other than name, secondary sorting is performed by name.
- You can sort cast members by using the Modify > Sort command, which offers several sorting options that are unavailable through column sorting. To do so, first activate a Cast window and choose Edit > Select All. Then choose Modify > Sort and select a sort option in the Sort dialog box (**Figure 2.38**). The Sort command works in either cast view style.

To resize columns in a Cast window:

1. Open a Cast window and select List view.
2. Drag the separator between any column headers to resize the column to the left (**Figure 2.39**).

   Column widths can be customized for each Cast window.

To rename a cast member in List view:

1. Click the cast member that you want to rename.
2. In Windows, click the cast member a second time (not a double-click) to activate editing, or press F2.

   or

   On the Mac, wait one second or move the mouse outside the name to activate editing.

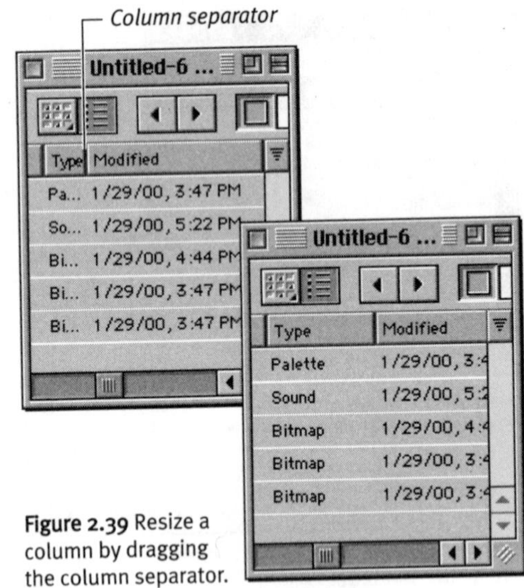

Figure 2.39 Resize a column by dragging the column separator.

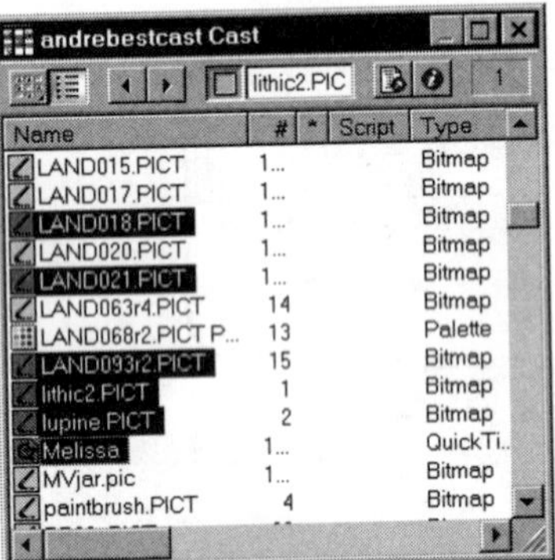

Figure 2.40 In Windows, Ctrl+click to select multiple nonadjacent cast members.

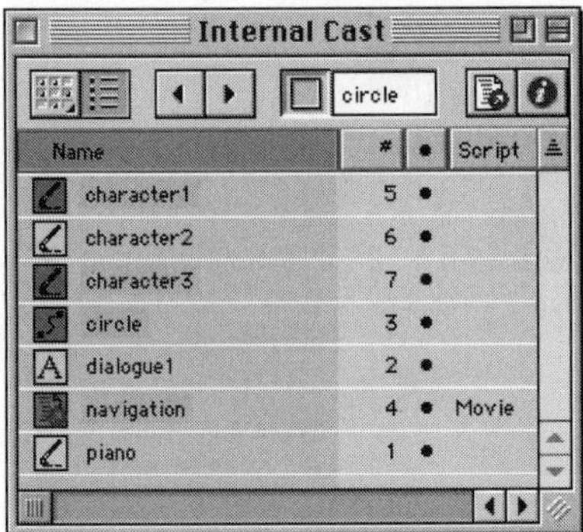

Figure 2.41 On the Mac, Shift+click to select multiple nonadjacent cast members.

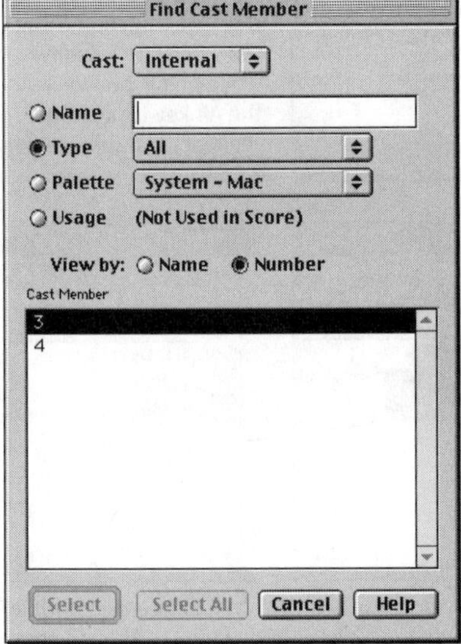

Figure 2.42 Use the Edit > Find > Cast Member command to find cast members by type, palette, or use.

To select cast members in List view (Windows):

1. Click the name or icon of a cast member to select it.

   Clicking any other column will not select the cast member.

2. Select a continuous range of cast members by Shift+clicking another cast member.

   or

   Ctrl+click to add or remove nonadjacent cast members (**Figure 2.40**).

To select cast members in List view (Mac):

1. Click any column of a cast member to select it.

2. Select a continuous range of cast members by using marquee selection (you don't need to select one cast member first).

   or

   Shift+click to add or remove nonadjacent cast members (**Figure 2.41**).

✔ Tips

- When a Cast window is active and a cast member's name is not being edited, you can select a cast member by typing its name. The cast member with the closest name match is selected.
- The Edit > Find > Cast Member command allows you to find and select cast members in any cast by type, palette, or use, which means that cast members not used in the score are selecte) (**Figure 2.42**). This command works in either cast view style.

To copy, move, or delete a cast-member selection in List view:

1. Select one or more cast members that you want to copy, move to a different cast, or delete (**Figure 2.43**).
2. Duplicate the cast-member selection within a Cast window by dragging and dropping the selection within the same window while holding down the Alt key (Option on the Mac) (**Figure 2.44**).

   or

   Copy the cast-member selection to a different cast window by dragging it there while holding down the Alt key (Option on the Mac) (**Figure 2.45**).

   or

   Move the selection by dragging it to a different Cast window (**Figure 2.46**).

   or

   Delete the selection by pressing Delete.

✔ Tips

- You cannot reorder cast members within a Cast window by dragging and dropping in List view. You can do so in Thumbnail view.
- You can duplicate a cast-member selection in a Cast window by choosing Edit > Duplicate.

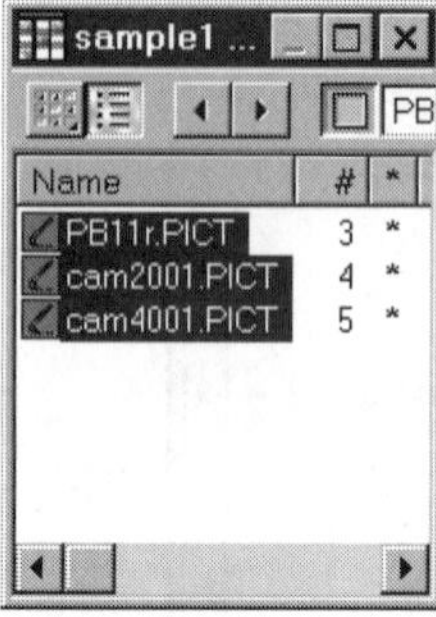

Figure 2.43 Make a cast-member selection.

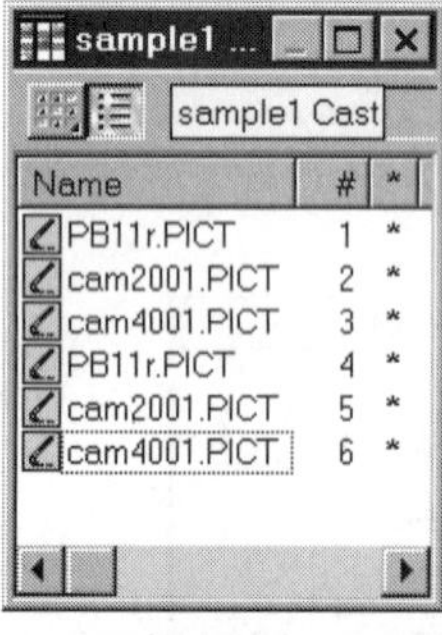

Figure 2.44 Drag and drop the selection within the same Cast window while holding down the Alt key (Option, on the Mac) to duplicate the selection.

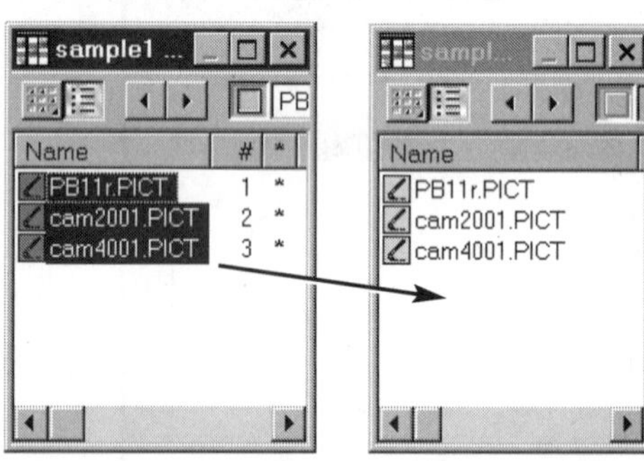

Figure 2.45 Drag the selection to a different cast while holding down the Alt key (Option, on the Mac) to copy it there.

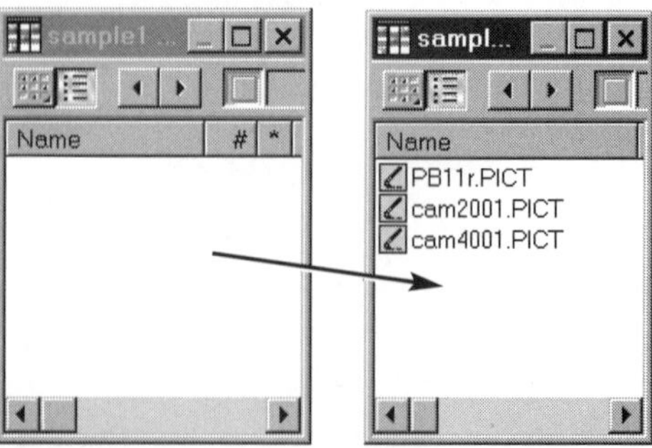

Figure 2.46 Drag to move the selection to a different cast.

Figure 2.47 Type a name in the Cast Member Name field.

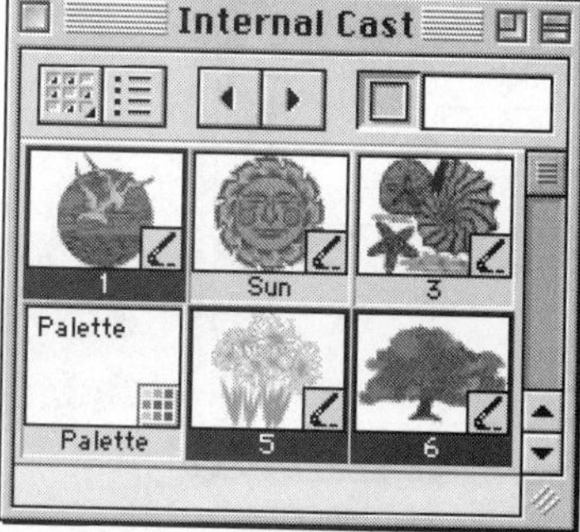

Figure 2.48 Ctrl+click (Command+click, on the Mac) to select multiple nonadjacent cast members.

Working in Thumbnail View

When a Cast window is displayed in Thumbnail view, cast members are represented by small images. When you have a large number of graphical cast members, Thumbnail view can be a more convenient way to view your cast than List view, because you can select cast members by sight. If you want to reorder cast members within a cast by dragging and dropping, you must use Thumbnail view. *(For details on displaying a Cast window in Thumbnail view, see "To toggle the view style for an open Cast window" earlier in this chapter.)*

By default, cast members are labeled with a number in the Cast window. You can give cast members descriptive names so that they're easier to recognize, find, and manage in the Cast window and throughout your entire movie.

To name a cast member in Thumbnail view:

1. Click to select a cast member in a Cast window.
2. Click the Cast Member Name field at the top of the Cast window.
3. Type a name for the cast member (**Figure 2.47**).

To select cast members in Thumbnail view:

- Click to select a single cast member.

  or

  Shift+click to select a range of cast members.

  or

  Ctrl+click (Command+click on the Mac) to select multiple nonadjacent cast members (**Figure 2.48**).

To reposition, copy, or move cast members in a Cast window in Thumbnail view:

1. In a Cast window, select a cast member or cast members (**Figure 2.49**).
2. Drag the selected cast member (or one cast member, in a multiple selection) to a new position in the Cast window (**Figure 2.50**).

   Alt+drag (or Option+drag, on the Mac) to copy the cast member instead of repositioning it.

   or

   Drag the selected cast member to another Cast window to move the cast members to a different cast. Alt+drag (or Option+drag, on the Mac) to copy the cast member instead.

   Multiple cast members are positioned sequentially from the point to which you drag them.

Figure 2.49 Make a cast-member selection.

Figure 2.50 Reposition a cast member by dragging it to a new position in the Cast window.

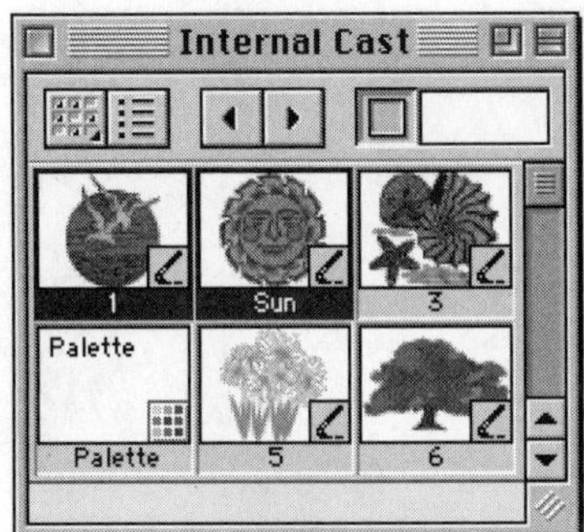

Figure 2.51 Select the cast member or cast members you want to move.

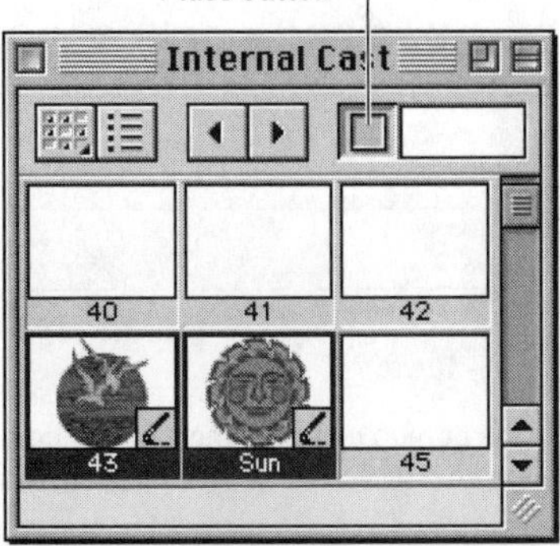

Figure 2.52 Drag the Place button to the new position in the Cast window or to a different Cast window.

The Place button comes in handy when you want to move some cast members to a new position in a Cast window, but it's not convenient to drag them-for example, when you can't see the destination at the time you're making the move.

To move cast members with the Place button:

1. In a Cast window, select the cast member or cast members you want to move (**Figure 2.51**).
2. Scroll through the Cast window to the position where you want to move the selected cast member(s).
3. Drag the Place button to the new position in the Cast window (**Figure 2.52**) or to a different Cast window.

   When you release the mouse button, the cast members move to the destination.

✔ Tip

- Hold down the Alt key (Option key, on the Mac) while dragging the Place button to copy selected cast members to their new position.

Director offers several display options for Cast windows in Thumbnail view, including thumbnail size, row width, and when media type icons should be displayed.

To change Cast-window preferences for Thumbnail view:

1. Activate a Cast window by clicking it.
2. Choose File > Preferences > Cast.

   The Cast Window Preferences dialog box opens (**Figure 2.53**).
3. Make choices from the pop-up menus in the Cast Window Preferences dialog box (**Figure 2.54**) to affect thumbnail size, quantity displayed, and the way labels and icons are displayed.

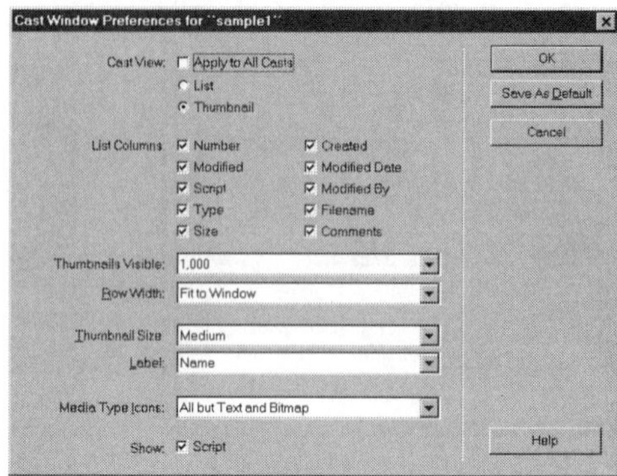

Figure 2.53 Change Thumbnail view preferences in the Cast Window Preferences dialog box.

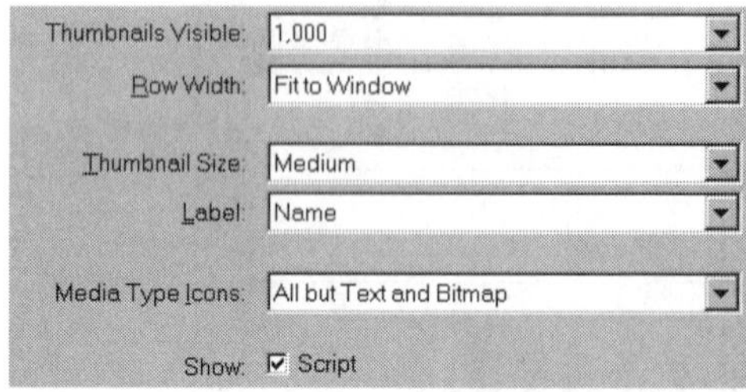

Figure 2.54 Use the pop-up menus in the Cast Window Preferences dialog box to change the way thumbnails are displayed.

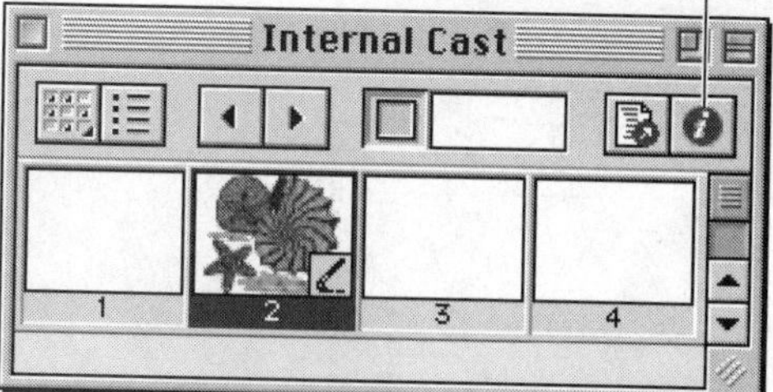

Figure 2.55 Click the Cast Member Properties button to open the Property Inspector.

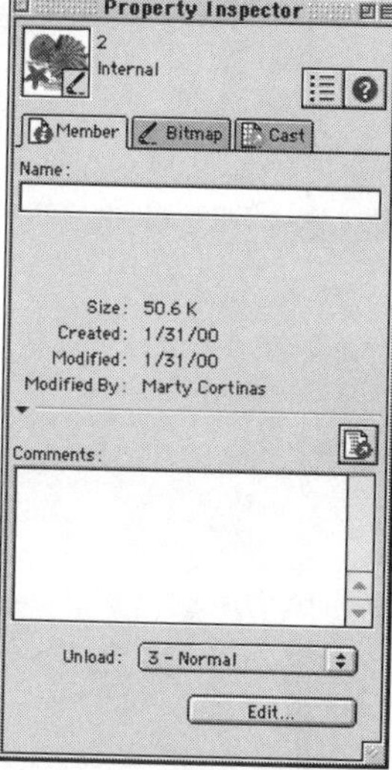

Figure 2.56 The Member tab for the Property Inspector.

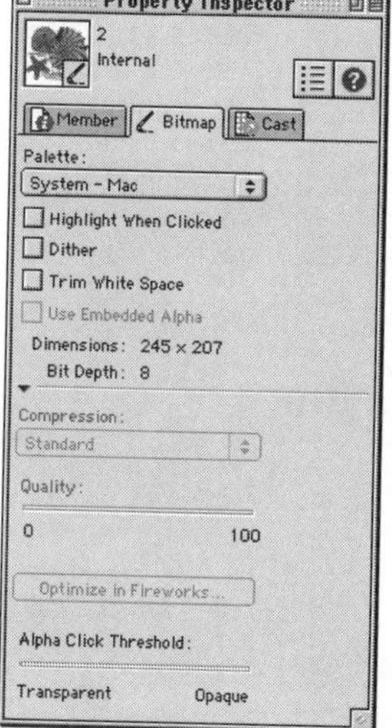

Figure 2.57 The Bitmap tab in the Property Inspector.

Managing Cast and Cast Member Properties

The new Property Inspector in Director 8 offers a much more integrated way of viewing cast and cast-member properties than in previous versions of Director.

To view or change cast and cast-member properties:

1. Select a cast member.
2. Choose Modify > Cast Member > Properties or click the Cast Member Properties button in the Cast window (**Figure 2.55**).

   The Property Inspector appears, displaying three tabs at the top.

   The first tab is the Member tab, which contains the same set of generic properties for all cast members (**Figure 2.56**).

   The second tab varies, depending on the type of cast member selected, and contains a specific set of properties for that type. If you select a bitmap cast member, for example, this tab contains properties such as palette and bit depth (**Figure 2.57**).

continues on next page

The third tab is the Cast tab, listing properties of the cast that contains the selected cast member (**Figure 2.58**).

3. Select the tab for which you want to set or view properties.
4. Click the List View Mode button to select either table or graphical view.

   Table view (**Figure 2.59**) generally shows a more complete set of properties than graphical view, which shows only the most commonly used properties.
5. Make any necessary changes in editable properties.
6. Close the Property Inspector.

   The many cast-member-specific properties are discussed throughout the book in sections relating to the specific media type.

✔ Tips

- When the Property Inspector is in table view, you can view a description of any property by holding the mouse pointer over the property name.
- When the Property Inspector is in table view, all properties that cannot be edited have a checkmark displayed next to their names.

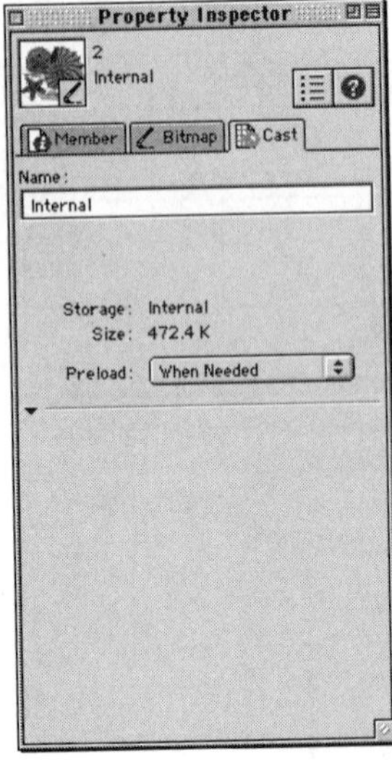

Figure 2.58
The Cast tab in the Property Inspector.

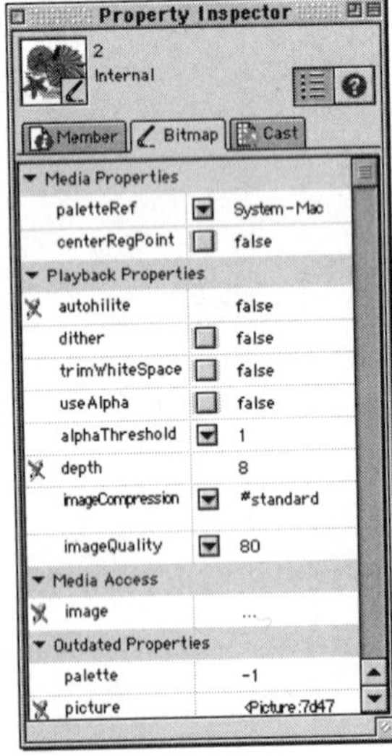

Figure 2.59
Table view in the Property Inspector shows a more complete set of properties than graphical view.

Table 2.2

Cast-Member Memory Priority

Unload Value	Priority in Memory
0 (Never)	Cast member is never purged from memory
1 (Last)	Cast member is among the last group to be purged from memory
2 (Next)	Cast member is among the next group to be purged from memory
3 (Normal)	Cast member is purged from memory as necessary

Unload: ✓ 3 - Normal
2 - Next
1 - Last
0 - Never

Figure 2.60 The Unload value determines the cast member's priority in memory.

When a user plays back your movie, Director sometimes must load and unload cast members from memory, juggling them to fit within the computer's memory constraints. You can control which cast members Director considers to be the most important to keep in memory—and which it considers to be the least important—by setting the cast members' Unload values in the Property Inspector (**Table 2.2**).

To set a cast member's priority in memory:

1. Select a cast member in a Cast window.
2. Choose Modify > Cast Member > Properties to display the Property Inspector.
3. Select the Member tab.
4. Click the List View Mode button to select graphical view.
5. Choose a setting from the Unload pop-up menu (**Figure 2.60**) (note that when the Property Inspector is in table view instead of graphical view, you set the Unload value by setting the purgePriority property). Unload settings range from 0 to 3. The 0 setting tells Director to never remove the cast member from memory; 3 means to unload this cast member from memory before anything with a 2 or 1 setting. Give the least important (or least frequently appearing) cast members a 2 or 3 setting. Give heavily used cast members a 0 setting.
6. Close the Property Inspector.

New to Director 8 are a set of asset-management fields (properties) that help project teams keep track of changes made in cast members. These fields are Created, Modified Date, Modified By, and Comments.

To view and set asset-management fields for a cast member:

1. Select a cast member in a Cast window.
2. Choose Modify > Cast Member > Properties to display the Property Inspector.
3. Select the Member tab (**Figure 2.61**).
4. Select graphical view by clicking the List View Mode button (if necessary).
5. View the Created, Modified Date, and Modified By fields in the top portion of the Property Inspector (**Figure 2.62**).

   These fields cannot be edited.
6. Enter comments for the cast member by typing them in the Comments box (**Figure 2.63**).

   Make sure that the bottom pane of the Property Inspector is open to display the Comments box.

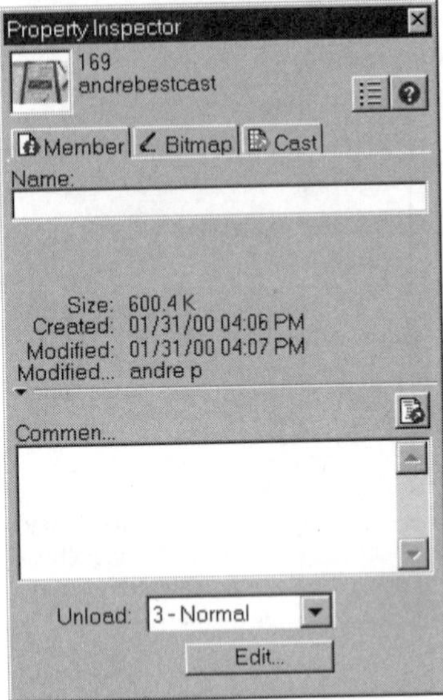

Figure 2.61 The asset-management fields for a cast member are located in the Member tab of the Property Inspector.

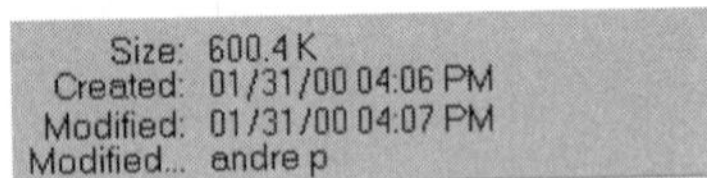

Figure 2.62 The asset-management fields.

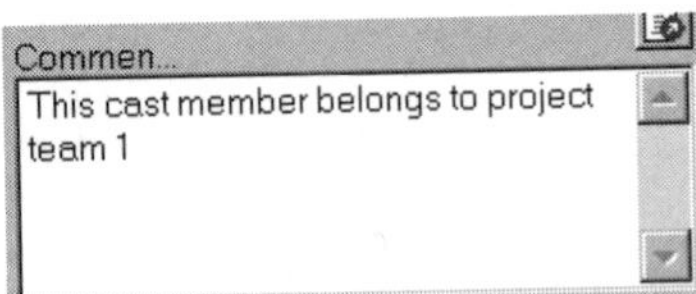

Figure 2.63 Enter comments for a cast member in the Comments box.

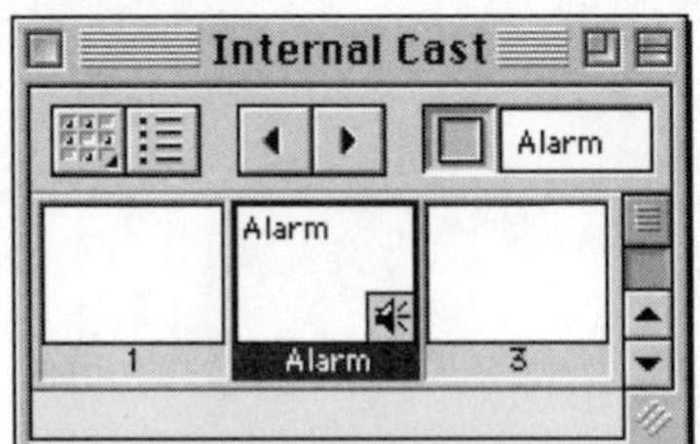

Figure 2.64 Select a cast member that needs a thumbnail.

Figure 2.65 Right-click (Ctrl+click, on the Mac) the thumbnail image in the top-left corner of the Property Inspector to display a pop-up menu.

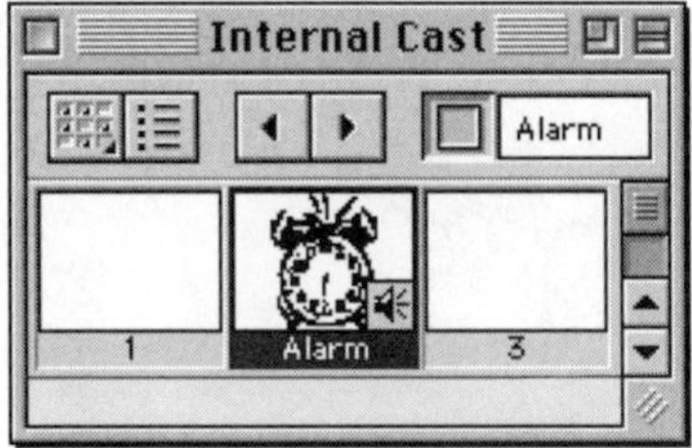

Figure 2.66 The new thumbnail.

You can replace a cast member's thumbnail image to make it more meaningful to you and your project team. Replacing a thumbnail does not affect the actual cast member in any way. Creating custom thumbnails can be especially useful for cast members for which Director does not automatically create a thumbnail image, such as sounds and behaviors.

To set a cast-member thumbnail:

1. Copy a bitmapped image that you want to use as the new thumbnail.

   You can copy this image from the paint window or another source.

2. Select a cast member (**Figure 2.64**).
3. Choose Modify > Cast Member > Properties to display the Property Inspector.
4. Right-click (Ctrl+click on the Mac) the thumbnail image in the top-left corner of the Property Inspector to display a pop-up menu (**Figure 2.65**).
5. Choose Paste Thumbnail.

   The Cast window shows the new thumbnail (**Figure 2.66**).

✔ Tips

- Choose Clear Thumbnail from the Thumbnail pop-up menu in the Property Inspector to return the cast member's original thumbnail image.
- You can copy and paste thumbnails by choosing the appropriate commands from the Thumbnail pop-up menu.

Building a Score

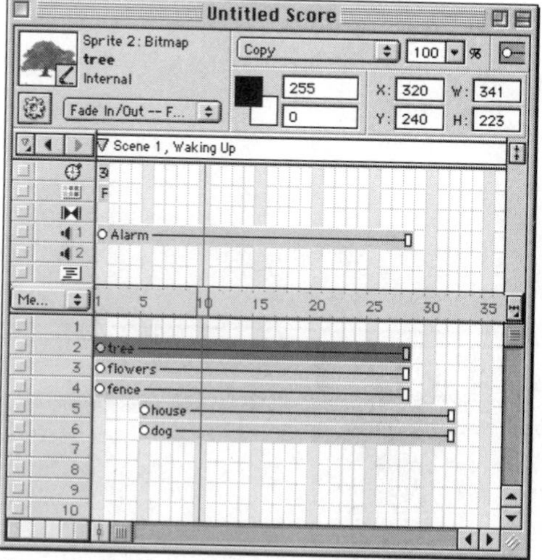

Figure 3.1 The score provides a frame-by-frame record of all the components that form your Director movie.

Director's score (**Figure 3.1**) works a bit like the script of a Hollywood movie. The score tells what your cast members should do and when they should do it. To a limited extent, the score even tells the cast members where on the stage they play their roles.

You assemble a Director movie by placing cast members (such as graphics and sounds) and events (such as visual transitions and playback tempo changes) in the score's frames, which represent brief segments of time in a movie.

Cast members placed in the score or on the stage are called *sprites*. A sprite consists of a cast member and a set of properties and behaviors that direct how, when, and where the cast member appears in your movie.

This chapter explains the basics of working with sprites in the score—basic training for building a Director movie. You learn how to create sprites from cast members and how to edit their properties and manipulate them in the score and on the stage. You also learn different ways to view the score.

Using Frames and Channels

As you learned in Chapter 1, the score abstractly represents everything in your movie within time (**Figure 3.2**). The vertical columns, or *frames*, represent small slices of time, like the frames in a movie. The horizontal rows, called *channels*, represent places where you can put movie contents, such as graphics, animation scenes, text, buttons, sounds, and programming scripts.

The intersections of the frames and channels make a grid of little boxes called *cells*, like those in a spreadsheet worksheet. Each cell represents the smallest unit of a movie: one frame's worth of a sprite. The whole thing works together like a control panel for your movie-a project-management grid that's interactive, so that what you do in the score actually manipulates what takes place on the movie stage.

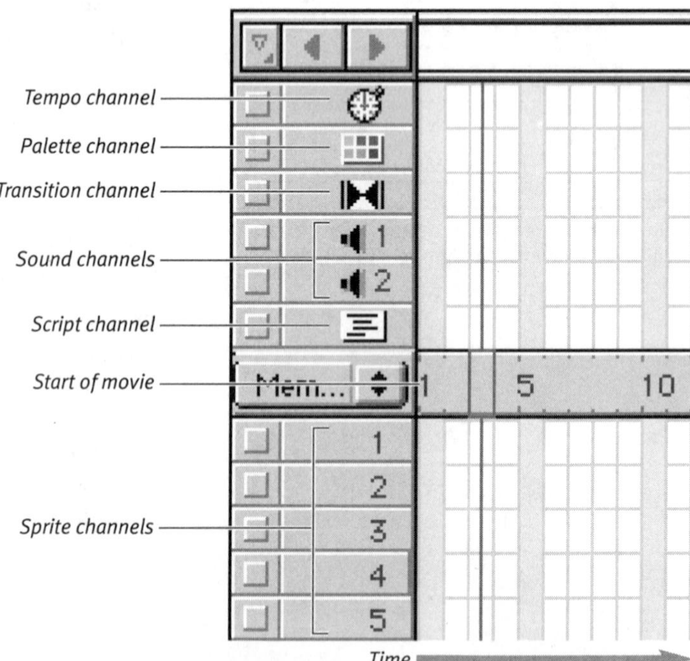

Figure 3.2 The score represents everything in your movie *within time*.

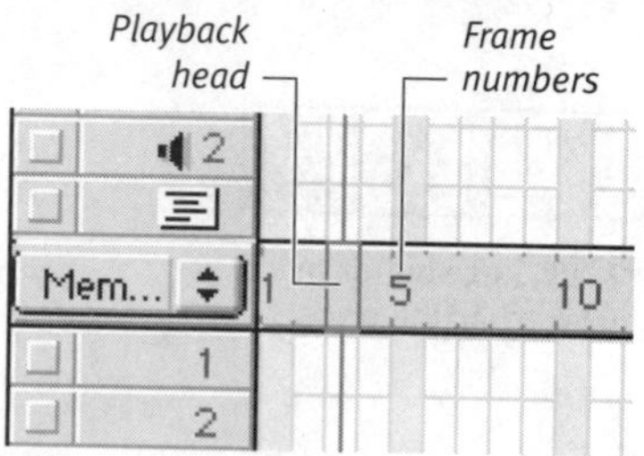

Figure 3.3 Each frame forms a column of cells, and the frames are arranged horizontally across the score window in sequential order.

Duration of sprite: 15 frames

Figure 3.4 Even sprites that appear only briefly in a movie take up a series of frames in the score.

Figure 3.5 Drag the playback head to a frame.

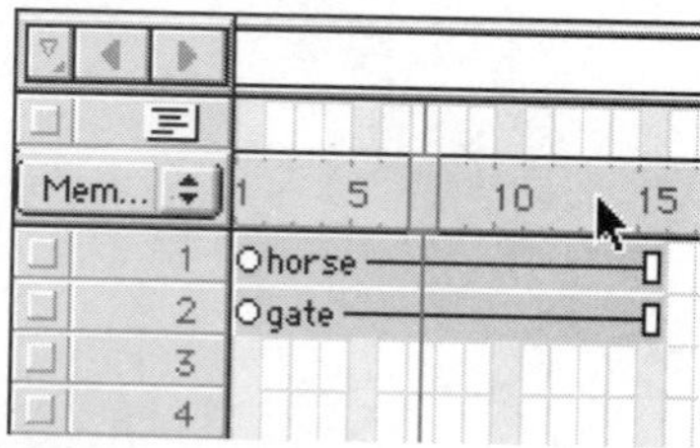

Figure 3.6 Click the frame you want to make active.

To open the score:

- Choose Window > Score.

  or

  Press Control+4 (Command+4, on the Mac).

One frame in the score, from top to bottom, is like a snapshot of the movie in time. The frames have numbers, visible between the effects and sprite channels, forming a horizontal band (**Figure 3.3**). The position of the *playback head* (the vertical line in the score that advances as the movie plays) indicates which frame is currently displayed on the stage.

There's no limit to the number of frames you can have in a movie, which means there's no technical limit to how long a Director movie can be (although there may be practical limits, such as how much room you have on a hard drive and Internet download times).

Because Director movies play at the speed of several (or many) frames per second, even sprites that appear only briefly in a movie take up a series of frames in the score (**Figure 3.4**).

Often, you need to select a frame of the score.

To select a frame:

- Drag the playback head left or right and release it in the desired frame (**Figure 3.5**).

  or

  Click the frame that you want to make active (**Figure 3.6**).

When you start exploring the score, you may want the stage to be open, too, so that you can watch how the two work together.

To open the stage:

Click the Stage button in the main toolbar (**Figure 3.7**).

Figure 3.7 Click the Stage button in the main toolbar to switch to the stage.

Using score channels

You manage and direct your cast elements and movie events by placing each of them in a channel of the score. Director reserves the first six channels at the top of the score for effects, including one channel for programming scripts. The channels below the frame-number row hold everything else-mostly, graphic sprites (**Figure 3.8**).

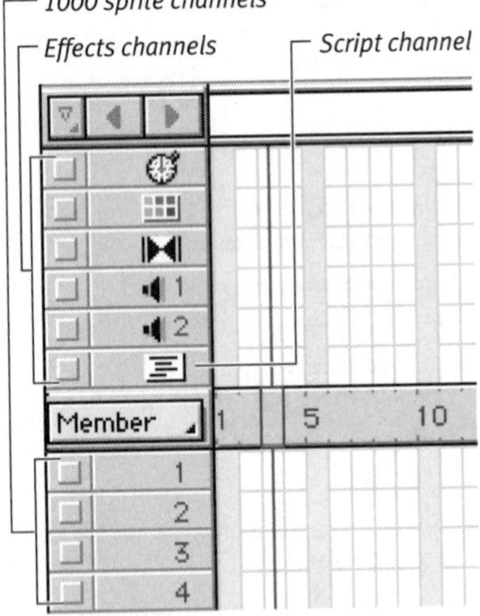

Figure 3.8 Each score channel forms a row of cells, labeled along the left side of the score.

Following is a brief summary of the function of each channel:

- **Tempo channel:** set the playback speed
- **Palette channel:** specify color palettes (mainly for low-memory, slow-processor situations)
- **Transition channel:** set transition effects between scenes, such as dissolves and wipes
- **Sound channels (two):** add sound effects, music, and voice tracks
- **Script channel:** incorporate Lingo programming scripts
- **Sprite channels:** animate cast-member graphics or (with some exceptions) include other types of cast members

Figure 3.9 A sprite's span, or duration.

Figure 3.10 The first frame of a sprite is a *keyframe*, which is an important landmark for animation. The end of a sprite is indicated by a square.

Working with Sprites

You can think of a sprite as one instance of a cast member used in your movie. Technically, a *sprite* is an object that consists of a cast member plus a set of properties and behaviors. The properties and behaviors determine how, where, and when a cast member appears in your movie. Changing a sprite's properties does not alter the original cast member (except in the case of text). You can create many sprites in your movie based on the same cast member. You work with sprites in two main environments: the score and the stage. In the score, each sprite is represented by a *sprite span* (**Figure 3.9**) that you place over a range of frames to indicate when the sprite appears during your movie.

On the stage, a sprite is represented by the image of its cast-member graphic (if it's a graphic cast member). You can resize or reposition it—or do both as part of an animation sequence.

Some cast members that you place in the score don't have a graphic representation on the stage. Such cast members, such as behaviors that you apply to frames in the script channel, have a place in the score—but just to show you where they are active. This book tries to keep the terminology clear by using *graphic sprites* for graphic elements and other terms that identify nonvisual sprites by the types of sprites they are, such as *sound sprite, transition sprite,* and *behavior sprite.*

The first frame of a sprite is a *keyframe* (**Figure 3.10**), which is a landmark for animation. The end frame of a sprite is indicated by a square.

You create a sprite as soon as you place a cast member in the score or on the stage, as described in the following two sections. This is a key step in creating a Director movie. (If you need to review how to work with cast members, see Chapter 2, "Assembling Casts.")

To create a sprite in the score:

1. Select one or more cast members.
2. Drag the cast-member selection to a cell in the score (**Figure 3.11**).

   As you drag, Director outlines the range of cells where sprites will be created. Director outlines only cells that can accommodate your cast members (sounds can be dragged only to cells in the sound channels, for example).

   When you release the mouse button, images of any graphical cast members you dragged to the score appear in the center of the stage as sprites (**Figure 3.12**).

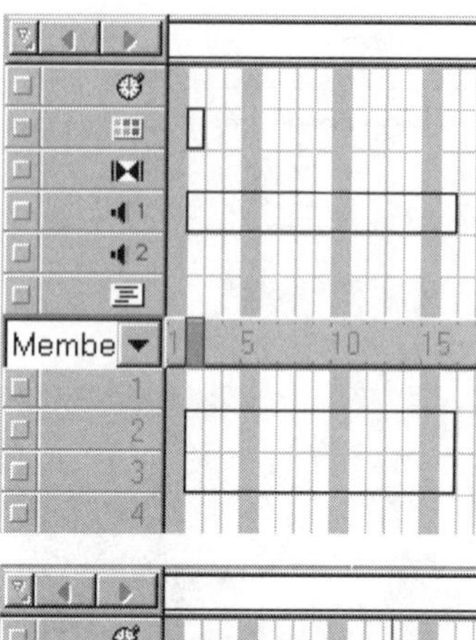

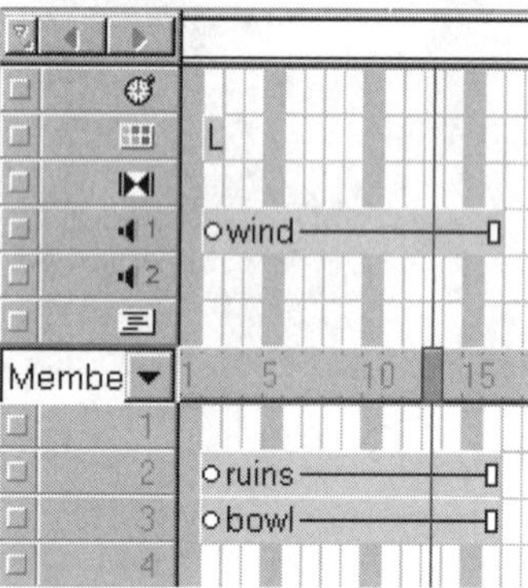

Figure 3.11 As you drag a cast-member selection into the score, Director outlines the range of cells where sprites will be created.

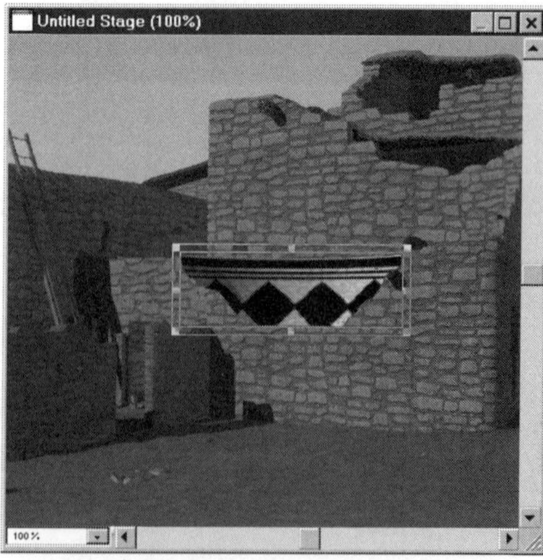

Figure 3.12 Graphical cast members dragged into the score appear at the center of the stage.

Figure 3.13 Open a Cast window.

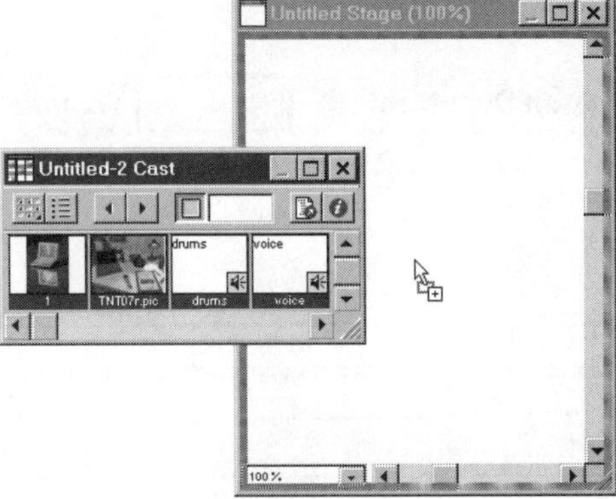

Figure 3.14 Drag cast members to the stage.

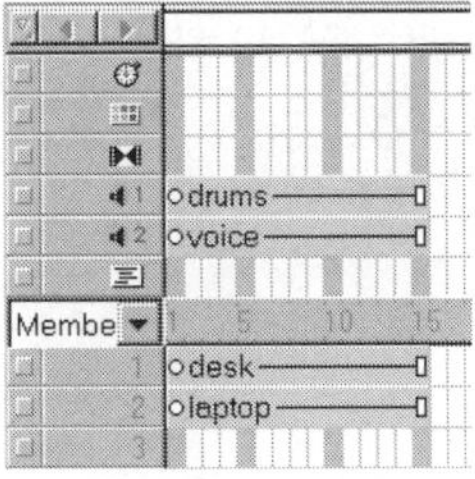

Figure 3.15 The new sprites appear in the score.

Figure 3.16 Graphical cast members appear on the stage as sprites overlapping at the location to which they were dragged.

To create a sprite by dragging cast members to the stage:

1. Choose Window > Score to open the score.
2. Open a Cast window (**Figure 3.13**).
3. If necessary, open the stage by clicking the Stage button in the main toolbar.
4. In the score, click where you want to place a sprite or group of sprites.
5. Drag a cast-member selection from the Cast window to the stage (**Figure 3.14**).

   Your new sprites appear in the score (**Figure 3.15**). Graphical cast members that are part of your selection also appear on the stage as sprites that overlap at the position where you dragged them (**Figure 3.16**).

Each new sprite that you create has a default duration of 28 frames, called the *span duration*. You can change Director's default sprite-span duration.

To change the default sprite-span duration:

1. Choose File > Preferences > Sprite.

   The Sprite Preferences dialog box opens (**Figure 3.17**).

2. Enter a value for the Span Duration option (**Figure 3.18**).

   or

   Choose Width of Score Window to have new sprites span the width of the score.

3. Check the Terminate at Markers checkbox to have new sprites end one frame before the next marker. (*See "Setting Markers" for details on using markers)*

You can select a sprite in the score in several ways. Following are a few ways to select sprites.

To select an entire sprite:

- Click the horizontal line within a sprite's span (**Figure 3.19**).

  or

  Click the sprite on the stage.

  When an entire sprite is selected, any changes you make in its properties affect all its frames.

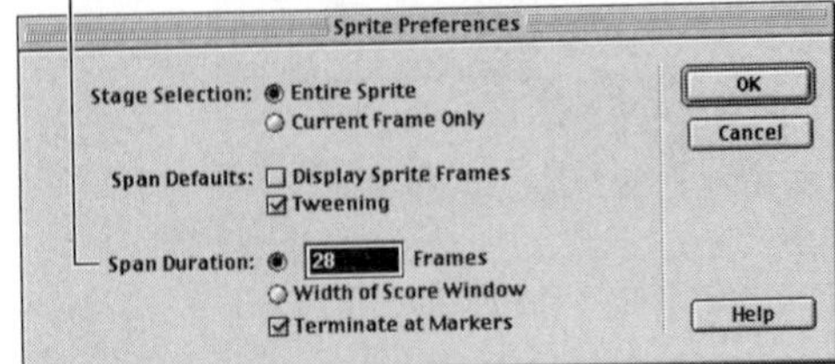

Figure 3.17 The Sprite Preferences dialog box.

Figure 3.18 Type a number of frames for the span duration.

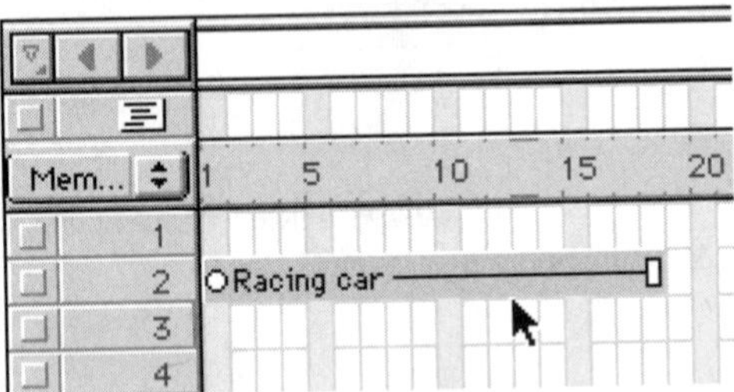

Figure 3.19 Click within a sprite's span to select it.

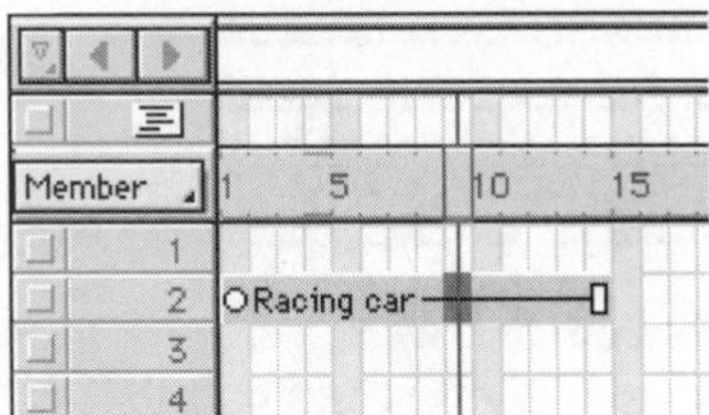

Figure 3.20 Select an individual frame in a sprite by Alt+clicking it (Windows) or Option+clicking it (Mac).

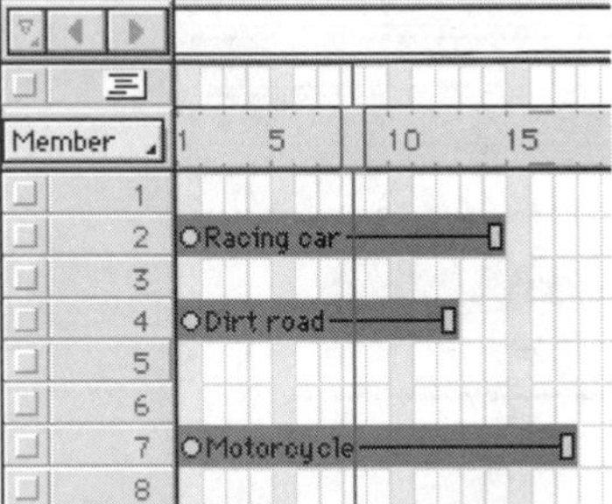

Figure 3.21 Select a range of sprites in the score by clicking the first sprite and then Shift+clicking the last sprite.

Sometimes, you need to manipulate only one frame of a sprite.

To select one frame in a sprite:

- Alt+click the frame (Option+click, on the Mac) (**Figure 3.20**).

  or

  Alt+click (Option+click, on the Mac) the sprite on the stage while the frame you want is active.

✔ Tip

- If the single frame you want to select is a keyframe or end frame, simply click that frame in the score. You don't need to hold down the Alt or Option key while you click.

To select multiple frames within a sprite:

- Select multiple nonadjacent frames in a sprite by Control+Alt+clicking (Command+Option+clicking, on the Mac).

  or

  Shift+Alt+click (Shift+Option+click, on the Mac) to select a continuous range of frames.

Often, you need to perform the same action on a group of sprites.

To select multiple sprites:

- In the score, drag to select multiple sprites. You need not enclose a sprite completely within the selection rectangle to select all of it.

  or

  Drag to select multiple sprites on the stage.

✔ Tip

- You can select a continuous range of sprites in the score by clicking the first sprite and then Shift+clicking the last sprite (**Figure 3.21**). Control+click (Command+click, on the Mac) to select multiple sprites that are not adjacent.

You move a sprite in the score to specify when it appears in a movie, or whether it appears in the foreground or background of a scene (see "To change the order of overlapping sprites" later in this chapter).

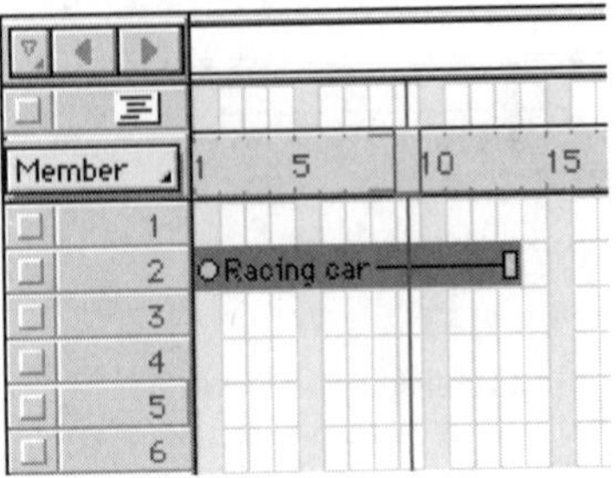

Figure 3.22 Click a sprite.

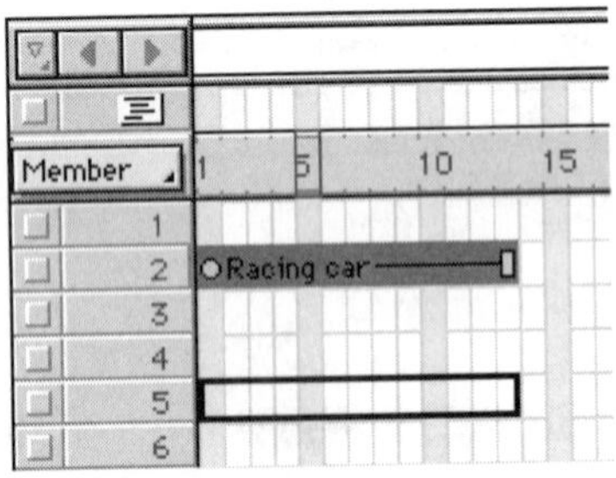

To move a sprite to a new location in the score:

1. In the score, click a sprite (**Figure 3.22**).
2. Drag the sprite to a new frame and/or channel in the score.
   Director outlines the new range of frames for the sprite (**Figure 3.23**).
3. Release the mouse button to place the sprite in the outlined frames.

Figure 3.23 Drag the sprite to a new frame and/or channel.

You can also move sprites in the score by cutting and pasting.

To cut and paste sprites in the score:

1. In the score, select the sprite or range of sprites.
2. Choose Edit > Cut Sprites or Edit > Copy Sprites.
3. Click the cell in the score where you want to paste the sprite selection.
4. Choose Edit > Paste Sprites.
   If the placement of the sprite selection threatens to overwrite any existing sprites, the Paste Options dialog box appears.
5. If the Paste Options dialog box appears, make one of the three choices and then click OK (**Figure 3.24**).

Overwrite Existing Sprites
Truncate Sprites Being Pasted
Insert Blank Frames to Make Room

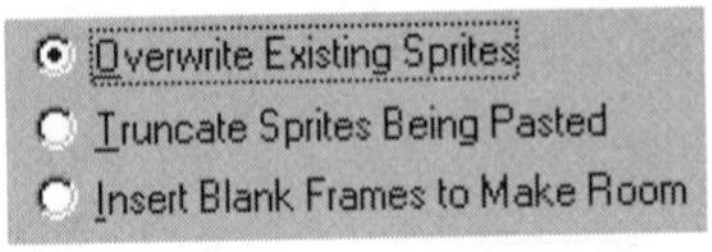

Figure 3.24 Specify in the Paste Options dialog box how sprites should be pasted.

✓ Tips

- You can paste a sprite selection in a way that inserts it into the score rather than overwrites any data. To do so, choose Edit > Paste Special > Insert.
- To delete a sprite selection instead of moving it, choose Edit > Clear Sprites in step 2 above.

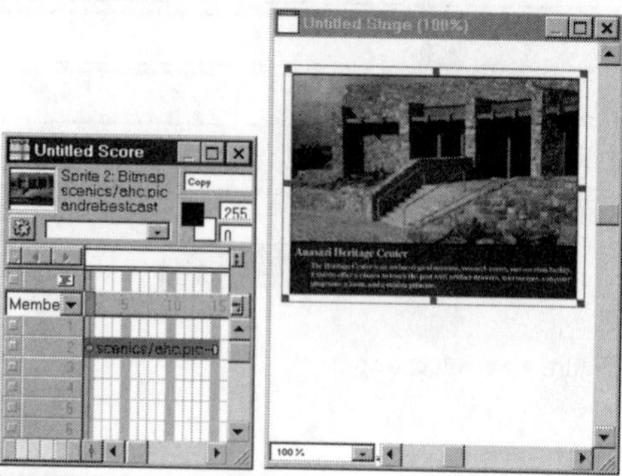

Figure 3.25 Selecting a sprite in the score also highlights it on the stage.

Figure 3.26 Drag the sprite to its new location on the stage.

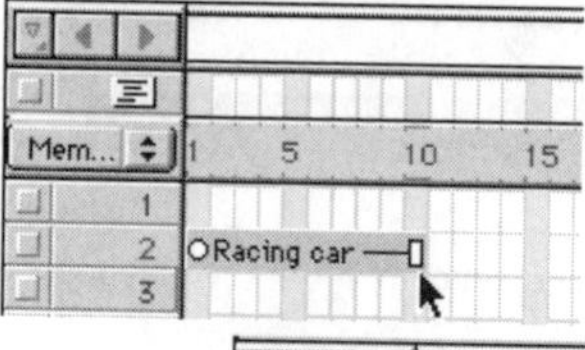

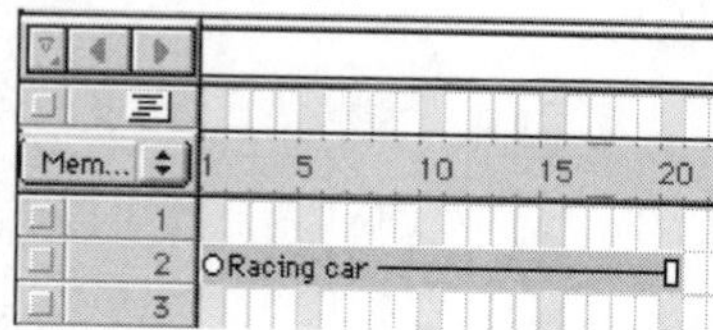

Figure 3.27 Change a sprite's span by dragging the frame at either end.

Figure 3.28 Change a sprite's span by entering new values in the Sprite toolbar or the Property Inspector.

To reposition a sprite on the stage:

1. Open the score.
2. Click a sprite.

   The sprite is highlighted in the score and on the stage (**Figure 3.25**).
3. Drag the sprite to its new position on the stage (**Figure 3.26**).

   This step repositions the sprite throughout all of the frames in its span.

✔ Tip

- You can reposition selected frames of a sprite. First, select sprite frames (as described in "To select one frame in a sprite" earlier in this chapter); then reposition the sprite.

You can shorten or lengthen the span of a sprite so that it occupies any number of frames in the score.

To change the length of a sprite's span:

1. Open the score.
2. Drag the keyframe at the beginning of a sprite span to a new start or drag the end frame to a new end point (**Figure 3.27**).

✔ Tip

- You can also change a sprite's span by entering the values in the Start and End fields of the Sprite toolbar in the score (**Figure 3.28**). If the Sprite toolbar is not visible, choose View > Sprite Toolbar.

To extend a sprite:

1. Select a sprite in the score (**Figure 3.29**).
2. Click the place in the frame channel to which you want to extend the sprite (**Figure 3.30**).

   Director repositions the playback head in the selected frame.
3. Choose Modify > Extend Sprite.

   Director extends the sprite to meet the playback head (**Figure 3.31**).

✔ Tip

- You can use the same process to shorten a sprite. Click a frame within the sprite to reposition the playback head where you want the sprite to end. When you choose Modify > Extend Sprite, the sprite shortens.

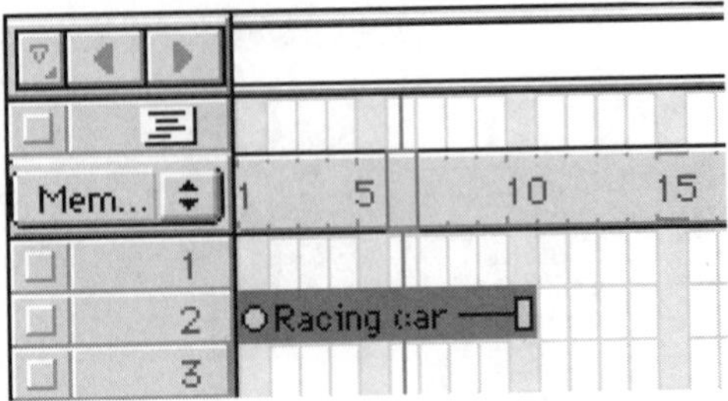

Figure 3.29 Select a sprite.

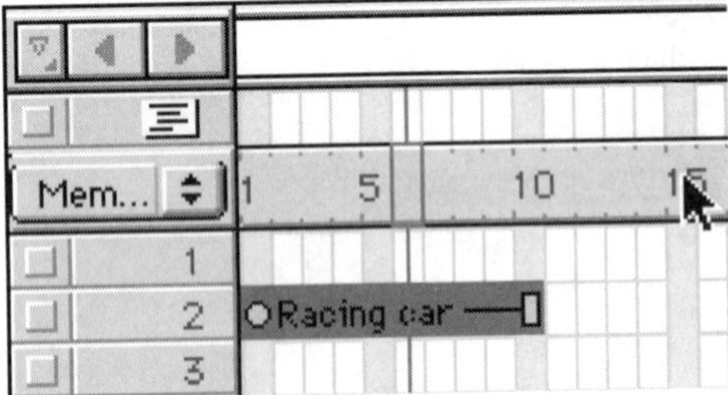

Figure 3.30 Click the Frame channel where you want the extended sprite to end.

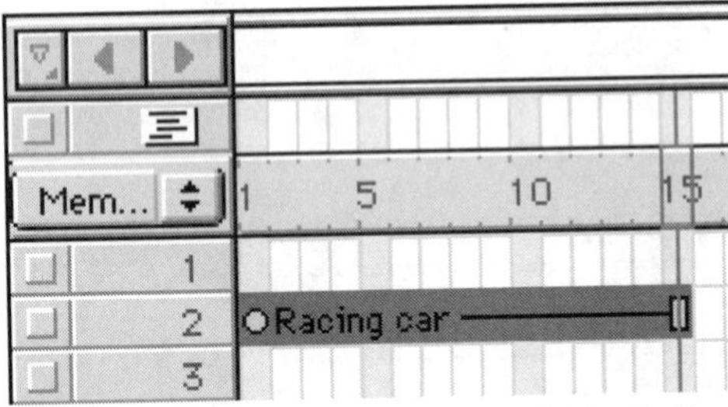

Figure 3.31 The sprite extends to meet the playback head.

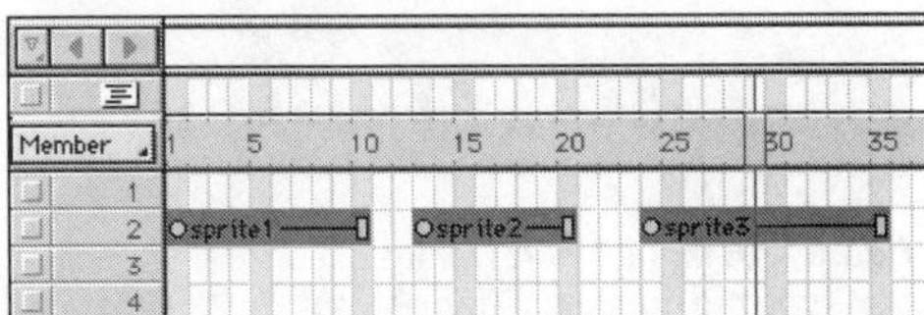

Figure 3.32 In a single channel of the score, select the sprites that you want to join.

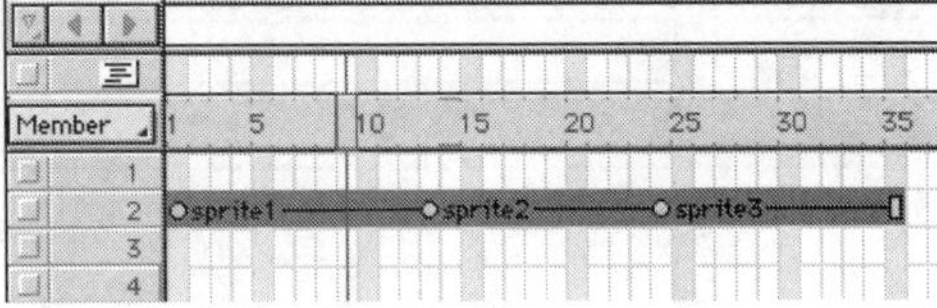

Figure 3.33 The sprites merge into a single sprite.

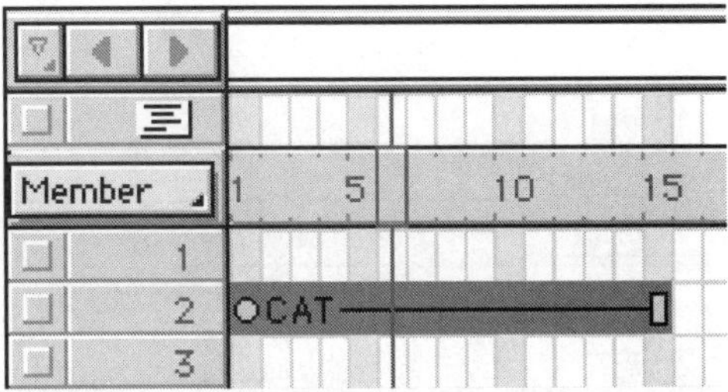

Figure 3.34 In a sprite, click the frame where you want to divide it.

Figure 3.35 The sprite divides in two.

Sometimes, you need to combine two or more sprites into one. Joining sprites is useful when, for example, you have created a series of animation sequences as separate sprites and need to consolidate them into a single sprite.

To join sprites:

1. Select sprites in the score.

   The sprites can have gaps between them, but they must all occupy the same channel (**Figure 3.32**).

2. Choose Modify > Join Sprites.

   The sprites join up (**Figure 3.33**).

A scene may work better if you divide a sprite into two or more sequences.

To split a sprite:

1. In the score, click the frame within a sprite where you want to divide it (**Figure 3.34**).

2. Choose Modify > Split Sprite.

   The sprite divides into two new sprites at the location of the playback head (**Figure 3.35**).

Normally, clicking a sprite in the score or on the stage selects the entire sprite. If, during the animation process, you frequently adjust a sprite's properties one frame at a time, save yourself some trouble by setting the sprite for frame-by-frame editing.

To edit individual sprite frames:

1. In the score, click a sprite.
2. Choose Edit > Edit Sprite Frames.

   Now when you click a frame within the sprite, only that single frame is selected.

✔ Tip

- Turn off frame selection by selecting any frame in the sprite and then choosing Edit > Edit Entire Sprite.

To insert frames into the score:

1. Click the frame in the score where you want to insert one or more frames.
2. Choose Insert > Frames.

   The Insert Frames dialog box opens.
3. Enter the number of frames to insert (**Figure 3.36**).

   If the frame you select contains sprites, Director inserts frames into each sprite, moving their end frames farther to the right. If the frame you select coincides with a keyframe in any sprite, new keyframes are inserted for those sprites.

To remove a frame from the score:

1. Click the single frame that you want to remove (**Figure 3.37**).
2. Choose Insert > Remove Frame (**Figure 3.38**).

   If any sprites are in this frame, they are effectively shortened by one frame.

Figure 3.36 In the Insert Frames dialog box, type the number of frames you want to insert into the score.

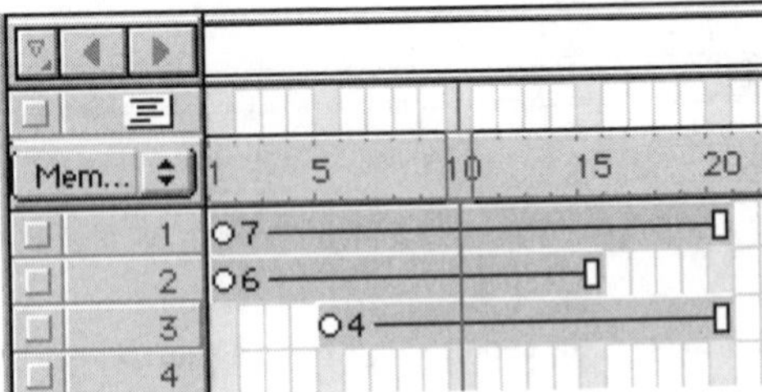

Figure 3.37 Click the single frame you want to remove.

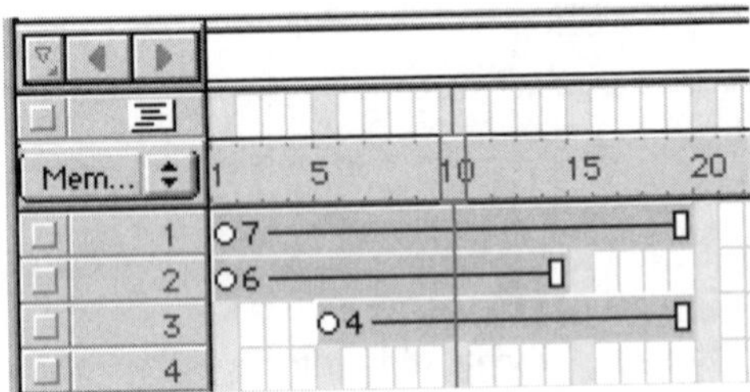

Figure 3.38 The frame is deleted.

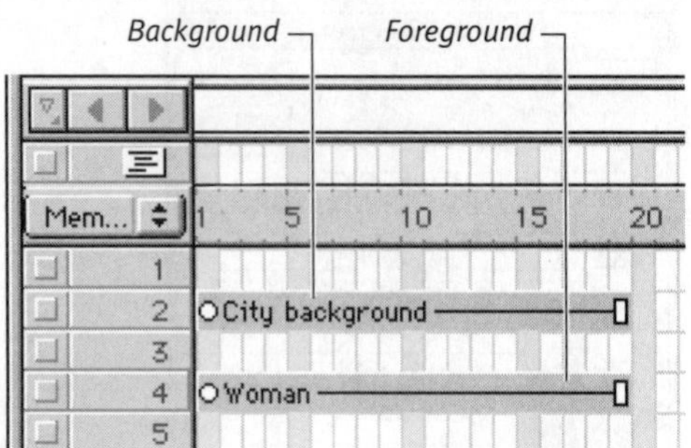

Figure 3.39 When sprites overlap on the stage, the sprite in the higher-numbered channel appears in the foreground.

Figure 3.40 Here, the sprite of a woman walks in the foreground; the city sprite is in the background.

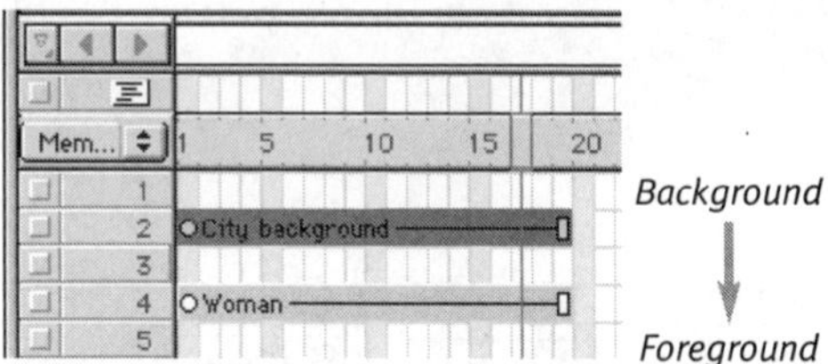

Figure 3.41 Select a sprite to move forward or backward.

Bring to Front	⇧⌘↑
Move Forward	⌘↑
Move Backward	⌘↓
Send to Back	⇧⌘↓

Figure 3.42 Use the Modify > Arrange menu to change the overlapping order.

When sprites overlap on the stage, the sprite in the higher-numbered channel appears in the foreground (**Figure 3.39**).

If you are animating a character walking down a street, for example, the character may appear to walk in front of buildings (**Figure 3.40**) but behind parked cars, street lamps, and signposts.

To change the order of overlapping sprites:

1. In the score, select a sprite to move forward or backward on the stage (**Figure 3.41**).
2. Choose Modify > Arrange, and choose the appropriate command from the pop-up menu (**Figure 3.42**).

   Bring to Front places the selected sprite in the foreground of all other sprites. Move Forward places the sprite one step closer to the foreground. The other two commands accomplish the opposite tasks.

Changing Sprite Properties

Each sprite includes a set of properties that describes how the sprite looks in your Director movie. These properties include a sprite's stage-location coordinates, size, blend percentage, ink effect, start frame and end frame, rotation, and skew angles, as well as animation options. You can vary these properties frame by frame as part of the animation process (see Chapter 4, "Animating Sprites").

You can change some sprite properties—such as size and stage coordinates—by moving or resizing a sprite on the stage. You can also change these properties and many others by using the Property Inspector's Sprite tab or the Sprite Toolbar in the score (**Figures 3.43** and **3.44**).

To open the Property Inspector for a sprite:

1. Select a sprite.
2. Choose Modify > Sprite > Properties.
   The Property Inspector opens, with the Sprite tab displayed.

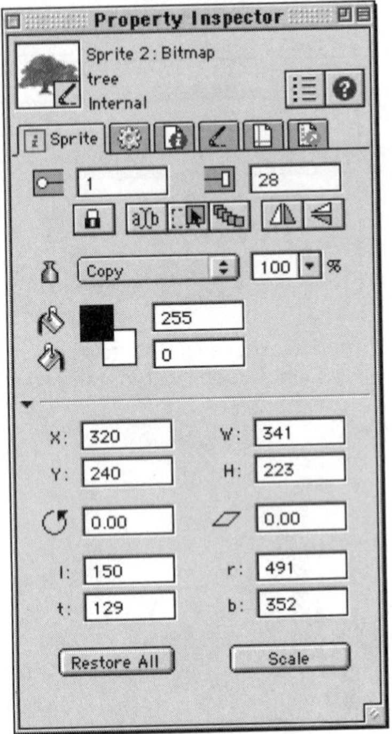

Figure 3.43 The Property Inspector's Sprite tab.

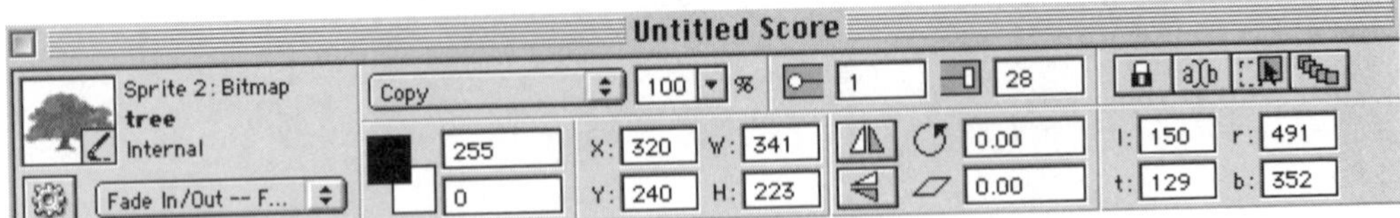

Figure 3.44 Set sprite properties in the score's Sprite toolbar.

Figure 3.45 Turn on the Show Info option to view sprite details in a small panel below a sprite.

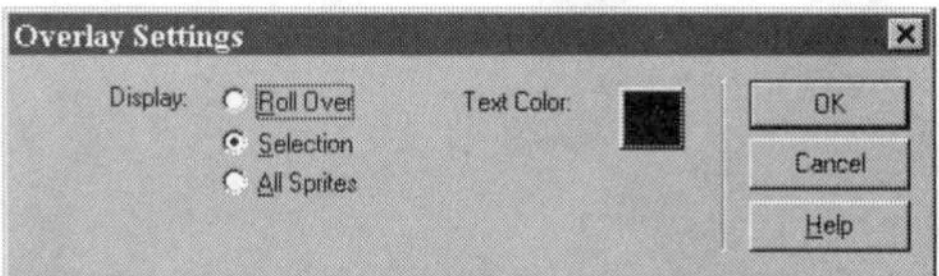

Figure 3.46 In the Overlay Settings dialog box, specify how Director displays the sprite information panel.

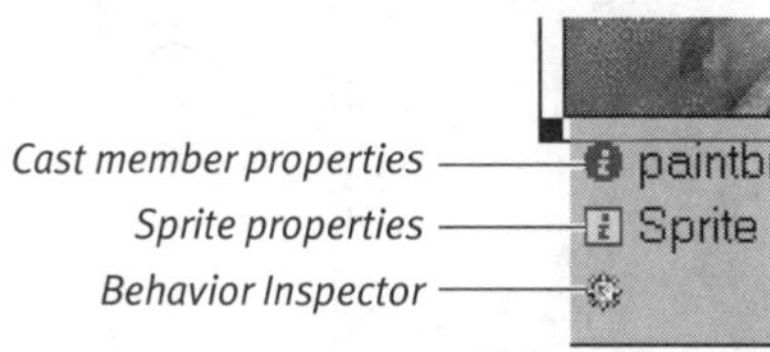

Figure 3.47 Click the small center icon in the panel below the sprite to edit the sprite's properties.

✔ Tip

- Click the small center icon (**Figure 3.47**) on the left side of a Sprite Overlay panel to edit the sprite properties in the Property Inspector. Click the top icon to edit the Cast Member Properties. Click the bottom icon to edit the behavior of the given sprite.

You can also change sprite properties in the Sprite toolbar, which contains the same set of properties as the Property Inspector. Which you use is a matter of preference.

To toggle the display of the Sprite toolbar:

1. Open the score.
2. Choose View > Sprite Toolbar or use the shortcut Ctrl-Shift-H (Command-Shift-H on Mac)
3. Select a sprite to view its properties in the Sprite toolbar.

While working on the stage, you can view a set of commonly used sprite properties (sprite coordinates, ink effect, and blend percentage) right on the stage in a small information panel called the *sprite overlay* without having to go back and forth between the stage and Property Inspector.

To view sprite properties on the stage:

1. Choose View > Sprite Overlay > Show Info.

   Sprite properties are displayed in a small rectangular panel below a sprite (**Figure 3.45**).
2. Choose View > Sprite Overlay > Settings to open the Overlay Settings dialog box.
3. Choose an overlay setting to define how sprites display the information panel (**Figure 3.46**).

   Click Roll Over if you want sprite properties to be displayed when you roll the mouse pointer over a sprite on the stage.

   Click Selection if you want properties to be displayed only for selected sprites.

   Click All Sprites if you want properties to be displayed for all sprites on the stage.

You can change the size and appearance of a sprite by stretching or squeezing it horizontally or vertically. The change affects only the selected sprite; the original cast member remains unchanged. For ways to use resizing in animation, see Chapter 4, "Animating Sprites."

To resize a sprite:

1. In the score, select a sprite.

   A rectangular outline with little square resizing handles surrounds the sprite on the stage (**Figure 3.48**).
2. Drag one of the sprite's handles to stretch or squeeze the sprite (**Figure 3.49**).

   Hold the Shift key while dragging a corner handle of the sprite to resize it proportionately.

✔ Tips

- You can resize multiple sprites at the same time by selecting them together in the score and then resizing one of the selected sprites on the stage. All the selected sprites resize in the same way.
- You can also resize a sprite by entering width and height dimensions in the Scale Sprite dialog box (**Figure 3.50**). Open it by first selecting a sprite, opening the Property Inspector dialog box, and then clicking the Scale button. Check the Maintain Proportions option to maintain the sprite's original proportions while changing width and height values, or type a value in the Scale box to resize your sprite proportionately.

Figure 3.48 A selected sprite on the stage has eight small resize handles.

Figure 3.49 Drag resize handles to stretch or squeeze a sprite.

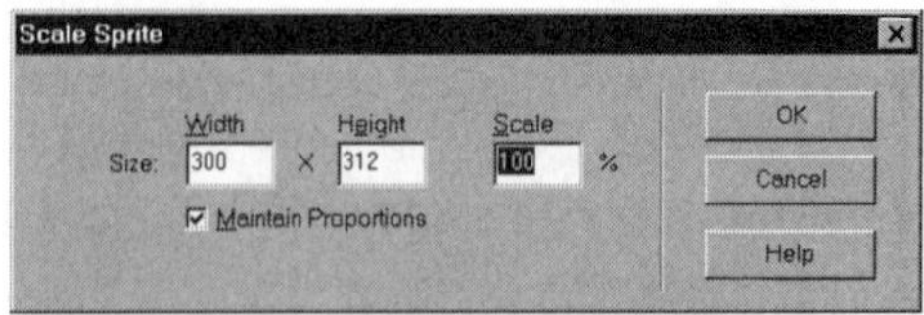

Figure 3.50 Resize a sprite by entering width and height dimensions in the Scale Sprite dialog box.

Figure 3.51 Select a sprite to rotate.

Figure 3.52 In the Property Inspector, type how many degrees to rotate.

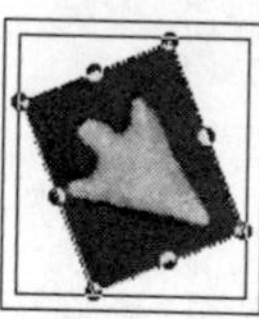

Figure 3.53 The sprite, rotated 45 degrees clockwise.

Figure 3.54 You can also rotate sprites with the Rotation and Skew tool in the Tool palette.

To rotate a sprite:

1. Select a sprite.

   A rectangular outline surrounds the selected sprite on the stage (**Figure 3.51**).

2. Choose Modify > Sprite > Properties to display the Property Inspector .

3. Type a number of degrees in the Rotation Angle field (**Figure 3.52**).

   A positive number rotates the sprite clockwise (**Figure 3.53**); a negative number rotates it counterclockwise.

✔ Tips

- You can also rotate sprites with the Rotation and Skew tool in the Tool palette. First, choose Window > Tool Palette, and click the Rotation and Skew tool (**Figure 3.54**). Next, click a sprite to rotate on the stage. Move the Rotation and Skew tool into the selected sprite to select the Rotation tool. Click and drag to rotate the sprite; release the mouse button when the result looks right to you.

- To rotate a sprite in 90-degree increments, select a sprite and then choose Modify > Transform > Rotate Left or Modify > Transform > Rotate Right.

You can also change sprites by flipping them, creating mirror images of the sprites.

To flip a sprite:

1. Select a sprite.
2. Choose Modify > Sprite > Properties.
3. Click Flip Horizontal or Flip Vertical (**Figure 3.55**) to flip the sprite either horizontally or vertically (**Figure 3.56**).

Figure 3.55 The Flip Horizontal and Flip Vertical buttons of the Property Inspector's Sprite tab.

Figure 3.56 Flip sprites horizontally or vertically.

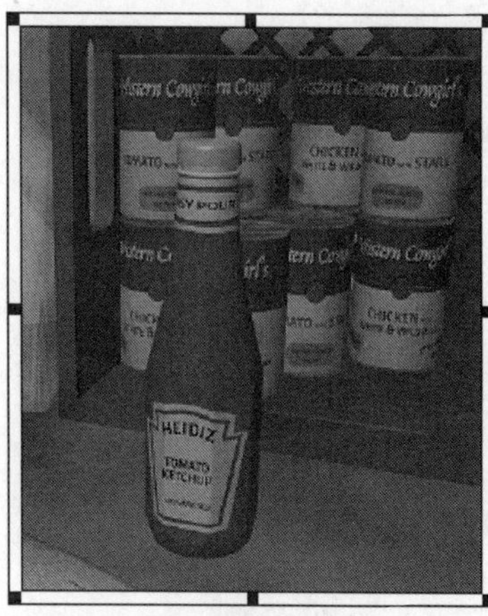

Figure 3.57 Select a sprite to skew.

Figure 3.58 Type a value in the skew-angle field.

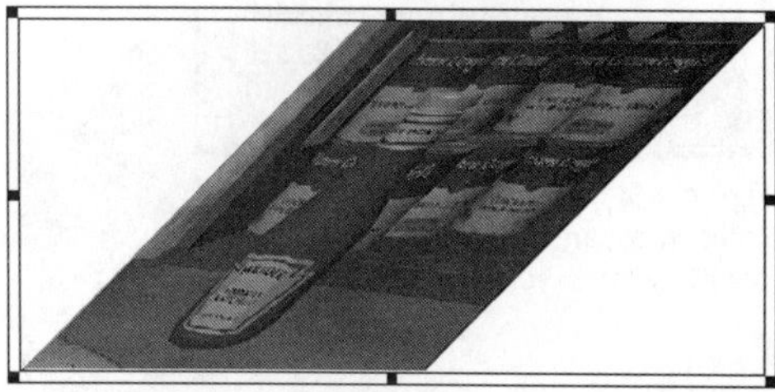

Figure 3.59 The sprite, skewed 45 degrees to the right.

Figure 3.60 The Rotation and Skew tool.

To skew a sprite:

1. Select a sprite (**Figure 3.57**).
2. Choose Modify > Sprite > Properties.
3. Type a value in the skew-angle box (**Figure 3.58**).

   A positive value skews the sprite to the right (**Figure 3.59**); a negative value skews it to the left. Entering 90 (degrees) flattens the sprite.

✔ Tips

- You can also skew sprites with the Rotation and Skew tool in the Tool palette. First, choose Window > Tool Palette, and click the Rotation and Skew tool (**Figure 3.60**). Next, click a sprite on the stage. Move the Rotation and Skew tool to the border of the selected sprite to select the Skew tool. Click and drag to skew the sprite.
- After resizing, rotating, and skewing a sprite, you may want to restore its original shape and orientation. To do so, select the sprite and then choose Modify > Transform > Reset All.

You can change a sprite's foreground and background colors, but doing so requires attention to detail. *(For details on color palettes, see Chapter 9, "Managing Color.")* The simplest color changes are from all black to a single color.

If a cast member is painted in multiple colors, changing the color of its sprite changes any parts of it that were black to the new color you select. The nonblack colors change in an unintuitive fashion. Basically, these colors are offset by the same distance in the current color palette as the distance the new color you select is from black in the palette.

To change a sprite's color:

1. Select a sprite.
2. If necessary, first switch a single-color cast member's color to black by using the Switch Colors command, as explained in Chapter 6, "Using Paint Tools."

   Changing the color of a sprite whose cast member is not black probably will result in an unexpected color.
3. Choose Modify > Sprite > Properties.
4. Click the foreground or background color chip and hold down the mouse button to open a pop-up color palette (**Figure 3.61**).
5. Choose a color.
6. If necessary, choose Color Picker or Edit Favorite Colors in the pop-up palette to select a more specific color.

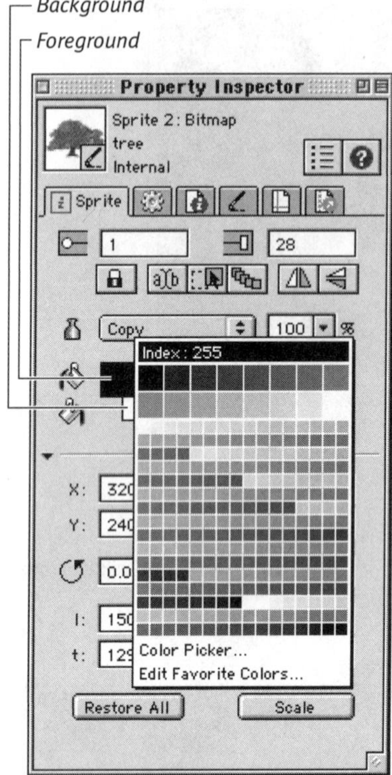

Figure 3.61 Foreground and background color chips, and the pop-up color palette, in the Property Inspector.

Figure 3.62 Set a new blend percentage in the Property Inspector.

The blend percentage of a sprite controls its transparency level. A 100 percent blend is completely opaque, and a 0 percent blend makes a sprite totally transparent. Like other sprite properties, this one can be used with the animation tools described in Chapter 4, "Animating Sprites."

To set the blend percentage of a sprite:

1. Select a sprite or range of sprites.
2. Choose Modify > Sprite > Properties.
3. Type a new value in the Blend box (**Figure 3.62**).

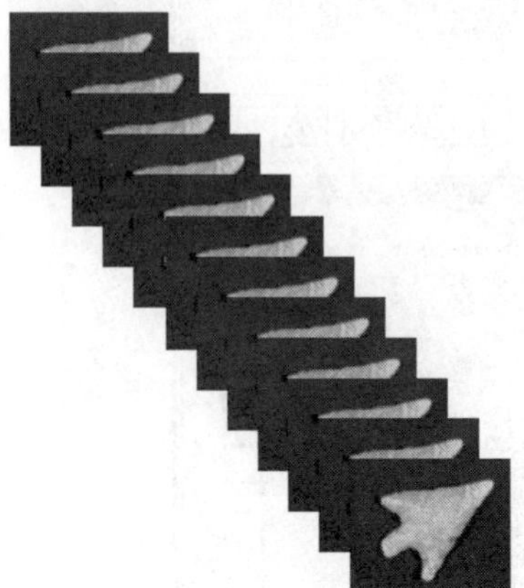

Figure 3.63 You can set a sprite to leave a trail of images as it moves.

Using a sprite's Trails property makes a moving sprite leave a trail of images on the stage (**Figure 3.63**). This feature creates a convincing animated handwriting effect (wherever the sprite moves it leaves a mark, as though someone were writing with a pencil), as explained in the next chapter.

To set a sprite's Trails property:

1. Select a sprite or range of sprites.
2. Choose Modify > Sprite > Properties.
3. Click the Trails button (**Figure 3.64**).

Figure 3.64 The Trails button in the Property Inspector.

Setting the Moveable property of a sprite allows users to drag the sprite on the stage while your movie is playing. This feature could be useful in an educational game in which children rearrange items on the screen.

To set sprites to be movable during movie playback:

1. In the score, select a sprite or range of sprites.

   Users can move the sprites only during the frames that contain the selected sprites.
2. Choose Modify > Sprite > Properties.
3. Click the Moveable button in the Property Inspector (**Figure 3.65**).

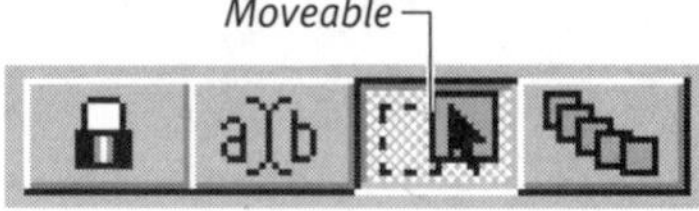

Figure 3.65 The Moveable button in the Property Inspector.

Director features many ink effects that change the way sprites look. This feature is especially effective when sprites overlap. You can use sprite ink effects to make sprites transparent or to darken or lighten them.

Note that sprite ink effects are different from those that you can apply to bitmaps in the Paint window. Ink effects in the Paint window change the actual cast member; sprite ink effects affect only sprites, not the cast member on which they are based. The names and functions of the ink effects in the two sets have differences as well.

To set an ink effect for a sprite:

1. Select a sprite or range of sprites on the stage or in the score.
2. Choose Modify > Sprite > Properties.
3. From the Ink pop-up menu, choose an ink effect (**Figure 3.66**).

   The "Score Ink Effects" list describes the effects of the inks on sprites.

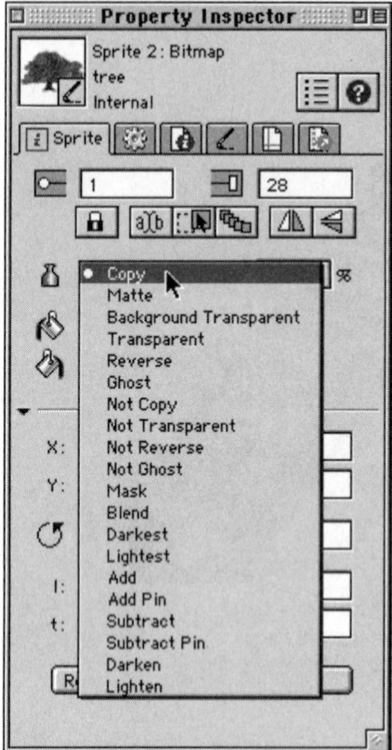

Figure 3.66 Use the Ink pop-up menu in the Property Inspector to choose an ink effect for a selected sprite.

✔ Tip

- Using ink effects other than the default Copy effect can slow your movie's animation. Try to use ink effects in strategic places, rather than across the board, if speedy animation is important in your project.

Score Ink Effects

Although these explanations help you imagine the differences from one effect to another, the best way to understand them is to try them out.

Copy

Sprites painted with this default ink effect are surrounded by a bounding box. This box is invisible on a white stage. When the sprite rests on a colored stage or passes in front of another sprite, the bounding box is visible. Director animates sprites painted in the Copy ink more quickly than those that use any other ink.

Matte

Sprites appear without the white bounding box associated with the Copy ink effect, but they use more memory and animate less quickly than those that use the Copy ink.

Background Transparent

Pixels in the sprite that were painted in the background colors are transparent, so you can see the background through them.

Transparent

All colors are transparent, so you can see any artwork behind them.

Reverse

White pixels in the sprite become transparent, so the background shows through.

Ghost

When two sprites overlap, any black pixels in the foreground sprite turn the pixels beneath the sprite white. Any white pixels in the foreground sprite become transparent.

Not Copy, Not Transparent, Not Reverse, Not Ghost

These inks act like the standard Copy, Matte, Transparent, and Ghost effects, except that they first reverse the foreground colors of a sprite.

Mask

This effect allows you to specify which parts of a sprite should be transparent and which should be opaque. For Mask ink to work, you must design a special 1-bit mask cast member, which you place in the Cast window in the position immediately after the cast member you want to mask. (See "Using Ink Masks" in Chapter 6 for more information on creating masks.)

Blend

The colors of a sprite painted in this ink blend with the colors of the background sprite that it passes over. Because this blend is created on the fly, this option can significantly impair the speed of animation. Director creates the blend based on the percentage specified in the Sprite Properties dialog box.

Darkest

With this ink effect, Director compares the pixel colors of foreground and background sprites and uses whichever pixels of the two are darker to color the foreground sprite. In other words, the darker colors of two overlapping sprites are made visible.

Lightest

This effect works like the Darkest ink effect, except that the lighter pixels of two overlapping sprites are visible.

Add

When two sprites overlap, Director repaints that area in a new color that is created by adding the colors of the overlapping pixels. If the value of the new color is greater than the maximum color value, Director wraps the new color value around to the beginning of the color palette *(see Chapter 9, "Managing Color")*.

Add Pin

This effect works the same way as the Add ink effect, except that the new color value can't exceed the maximum color value.

Subtract

This effects works the same way as the Add ink effect, except that the new color for overlapping sprites is created by subtracting the foreground sprite's color value from the background sprite's color value. If the value of the new color is less than the minimum color value, Director wraps the new color value around to the top of the color palette.

Subtract Pin

This effects works the same way as the Subtract ink effect, except that the new color value can't be less than the current palette's minimum color value, and no wrap occurs.

Sometimes, you need to align sprites on the stage so that they match up in all frames of an animation.

You can align sprites on the stage by using the Align command. You can align sprites with respect to their centers, registration points (see "To view and set a cast member's registration point" later in this chapter), or any of the eight points around the bounding box that encompasses each sprite. Aligning sprites does not change their cast members' registration points.

Figure 3.67 Select the sprites you want to align.

To align sprites:

1. In the score or on the stage, select all the sprites that you want to align (**Figure 3.67**).
   The last sprite you select is the sprite with which the others will be aligned.
2. Choose Modify > Align to display the Align dialog box (**Figure 3.68**).
3. Click an area within the preview window to specify how the sprites should aligned.
   or
   Use the horizontal and vertical pop-up menus to choose horizontal and vertical alignment options (**Figure 3.69**).
4. Click Align.
   The sprites line up in relation to the last sprite you selected (**Figure 3.70**).
5. Close the Align dialog box.

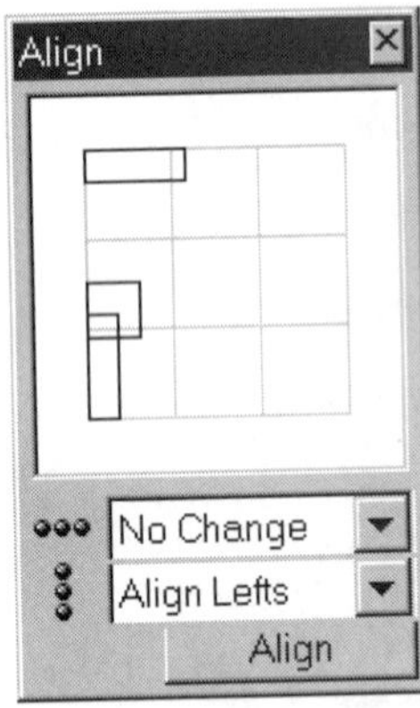

Figure 3.68 The Align Sprites dialog box.

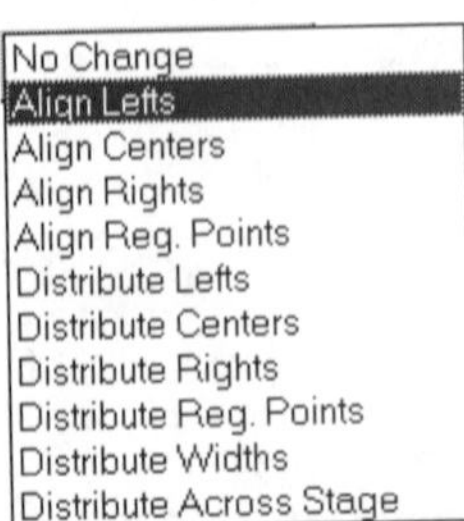

Figure 3.69 Use the pop-up menus in the Align Sprites dialog box to choose alignment options.

Figure 3.70 Sprites align with respect to the last sprite selected.

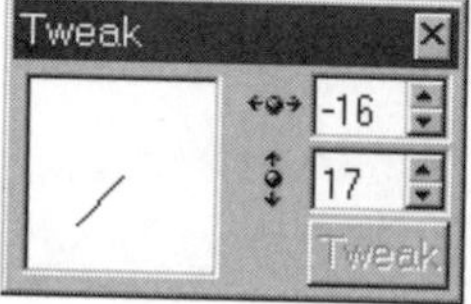

Figure 3.71 The Tweak window.

Use the Tweak window when you need to move sprites a precise number of pixels on the stage.

To tweak sprites:

1. Select one or more sprites.
2. Choose Modify > Tweak.
   The Tweak dialog box opens (**Figure 3.71**).
3. Drag the image in the left side of the Tweak dialog box to specify visually how far to move the selected sprites.
   or
   Click the up and down arrows to specify how far (in pixels) to move the selected sprites in horizontal and vertical directions.
4. Click Tweak to move the sprites.

A *registration point* is a fixed point of reference in a bitmapped image. Every bitmapped cast member in your movie has a default registration point directly at its center (**Figure 3.72**).

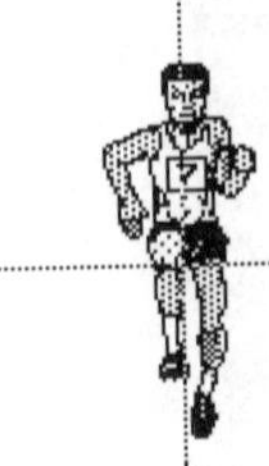

Figure 3.72 Resetting cast-member registration points can improve animation smoothness.

When you play back cast members for an animation sequence, they may appear to jump or shift from one frame to the next. To eliminate the jerky motion, you can adjust the registration points. If you are animating several frames of an athlete running, for example, you could reset the registration point for all the runners to the point where the character's feet touch the ground, to ensure that the runner's feet never hit above or below ground level.

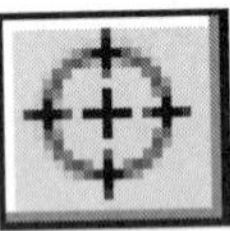

Figure 3.73 The Registration Point tool.

To view and set a cast member's registration point:

1. Open a cast member in the Paint window.
2. Select the Registration Point tool (**Figure 3.73**).
   The current registration point appears at the intersection of the dotted lines.
3. Move the crosshair pointer where you want to place the new registration point, and click (**Figure 3.74**).

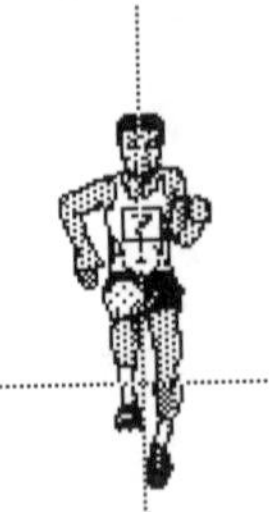

Figure 3.74 Click to set a new registration point.

✔ Tip

- To restore a registration point to its default position (the center of the cast member), open the cast member in the Paint window; then double-click the Registration Point tool in the Paint Tool palette.

Figure 3.75 Click the Lock button to lock selected sprites.

Figure 3.76 Locked sprites are displayed with a lock symbol in the score.

Figure 3.77 A locked sprite on the stage.

Locking Sprites

You can lock a sprite in Director 8, preventing any of its properties from being changed inadvertently. This feature can be particularly useful when you don't want to accidentally move or delete a carefully positioned sprite on the stage. Locked sprites remain visible on the stage but can't be selected from the stage.

To lock a sprite or group of sprites:

1. In the score or on the stage, select a sprite or range of sprites that you want to lock.

   You can select multiple nonadjacent sprites. Note that you cannot lock part of a sprite.

2. Choose Modify > Lock.

   or

   Click the Lock button in the Property Inspector (**Figure 3.75**) or Sprite toolbar.

The locked sprites are displayed with a lock symbol in the score (**Figure 3.76**). When selected in the score, a locked sprite is surrounded by a red border on the stage, which includes a lock symbol in the top-right corner (**Figure 3.77**). Property fields are dimmed for locked sprites in both the Property Inspector and the Sprite toolbar.

To unlock a sprite or group of sprites:

1. In the score, select a sprite or ranged of locked sprites that you want to unlock.
2. Choose Modify > Unlock.

✔ Tip

- You can change a property (such as blend percentage) of a multiple sprite selection consisting of both locked and unlocked sprites, but only the unlocked sprites change.

Changing the Score View

In addition to standard viewing controls, such as the scroll bars, you have several viewing options in the score.

To center the playback head in the window:

- Click the Center Current Frame button to reorient the score so that the frame that contains the playback head is displayed at the center of the score (**Figure 3.78**).

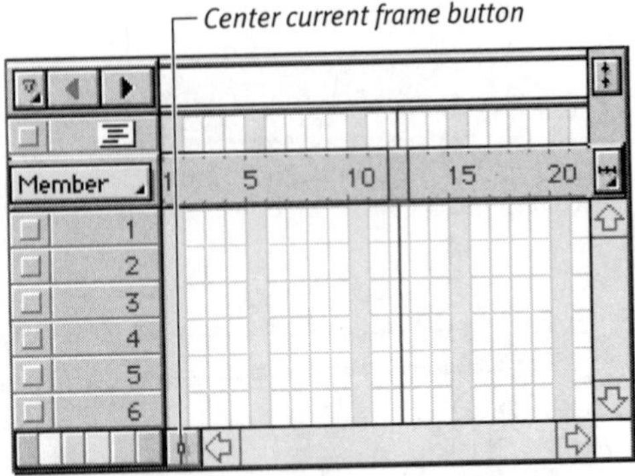

Figure 3.78 Click the Center Current Frame button to center the frame that contains the playback head.

Sometimes, you don't need the effects channels. You can hide them to use more of your screen for the sprite channels.

To hide or show the effects channels:

- Click the Hide/Show Effects Channel button to toggle the display of the effects channels (**Figure 3.79**).

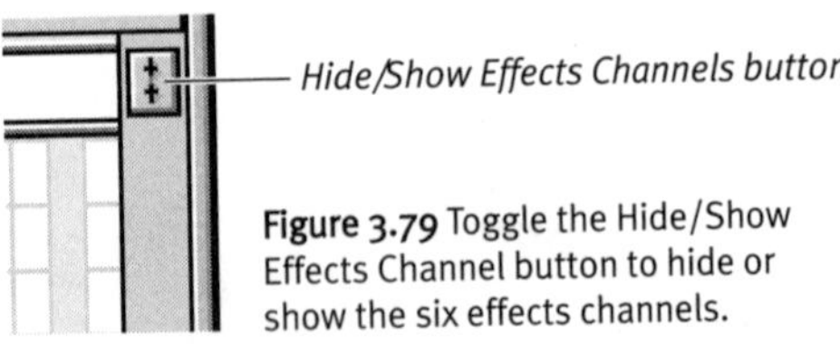

Figure 3.79 Toggle the Hide/Show Effects Channel button to hide or show the six effects channels.

You may find it helpful to be able to zero in on a close-up view of the score.

To zoom in or out:

- Click the Zoom Menu button, and choose a magnification percentage from the pop-up menu (**Figure 3.80**).

Choose a percentage greater than 100 to zoom in and see more detail in each frame. Choose a percentage smaller than 100 to zoom out and see large portions of the score.

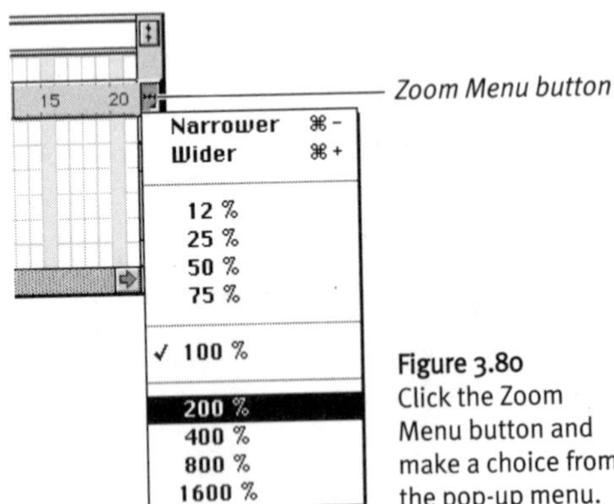

Figure 3.80 Click the Zoom Menu button and make a choice from the pop-up menu.

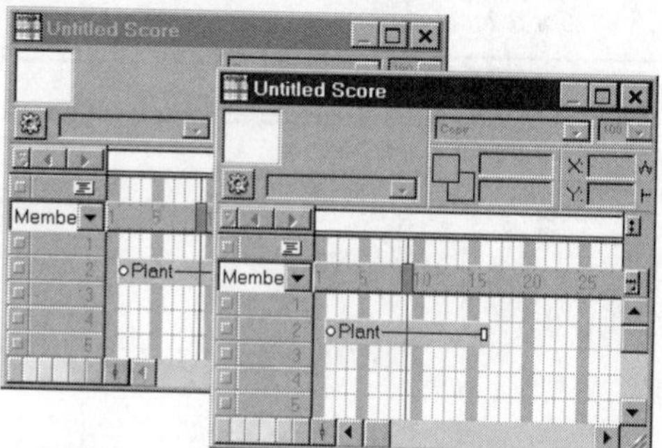

Figure 3.81 Open extra score windows to view and edit different parts of the score at the same time.

You can view and edit different parts of the score at the same time by opening additional score windows. With extra windows open, you can easily drag sprites between different parts of the score without excess scrolling.

To view multiple score windows:

1. Select the score window.
2. Choose Window > New Window to display an additional score window (**Figure 3.81**).
3. Use the scroll bars to navigate in the new window.

   You can open as many additional score windows as you need.

Some people find the little circular keyframe indicators in the sprite spans to be distracting. You can clean up the the score by hiding those indicators; later, you can restore them just as easily.

To show or hide keyframes in the score:

- Choose View > Keyframes to toggle the display of keyframe indicators in the score.

The text that identifies the sprite span is called a *sprite label*. Sprite labels make it much easier to work with sprites and edit your movie by providing key information, such as the name or number of the cast member on which a sprite is based (**Figure 3.82**).

To view sprite labels in the score:

1. Open the score.
2. Choose View > Sprite Labels and then choose an option from the pop-up menu.

   The option determines where in a sprite span the sprite label appears (**Figure 3.83**). The actual information displayed by a sprite label is determined by the score display option *(see "To change the display option for sprite labels" later in this chapter).*

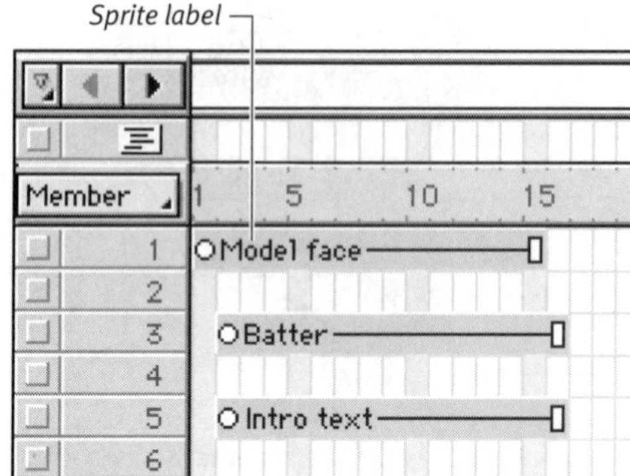

Figure 3.82 Sprite labels make it much easier to work with sprites in the score.

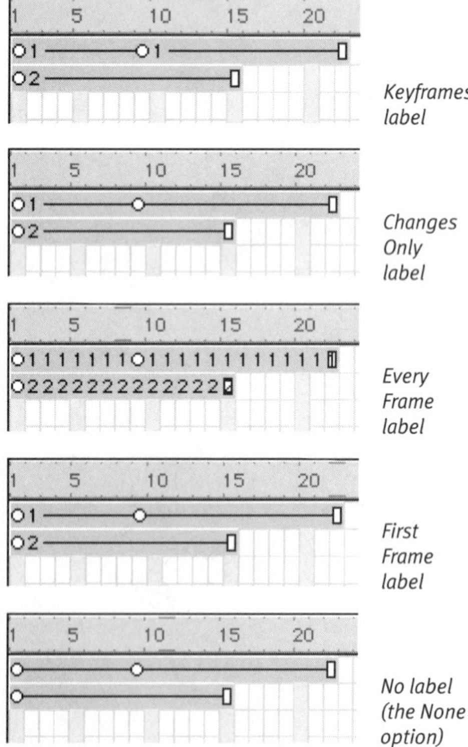

Figure 3.83 Sprite-label options.

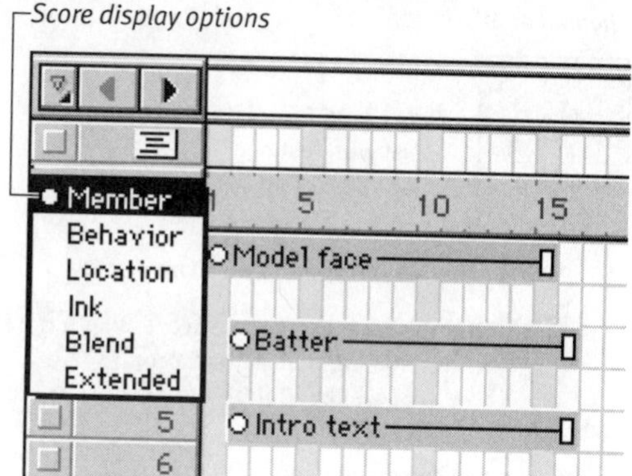

Figure 3.84 Select sprite-label options in the score.

Score Window Preferences

Extended Display: ☒ Cast Member
☒ Behaviors
☒ Ink Mode
☒ Blend
☒ Location
☐ Change in Location

Figure 3.85 When you choose the Extended sprite-label option, you can specify which combination of display options appear by using the Score Window Preferences dialog box.

You can change the type of information that appears in sprite labels by setting the display option for the score.

To change the display option for sprite labels:

- Open the display options menu in the score and make a choice (**Figure 3.84**).

  or

  Choose View > Display and then choose an option from the pop-up menu.

  Following are the display options:

  - Choose Member to display the name and number of each sprite's cast member.
  - Choose Behavior to display the behavior assigned to each sprite.
  - Choose Location to display the coordinates of each sprite's registration point, which Director uses to match up images in animation sequences.
  - Choose Ink to display the ink effect applied to sprites.
  - Choose Blend to show each sprite's blend percentage.
  - Choose Extended to view any combination of display options specified in the Score Window Preferences dialog box (**Figure 3.85**), which you open by choosing File > Preferences > Score.

By default, all channels in the score are turned on, but you can turn some off to make it easier to test or work on a portion of the score.

Channel on/off button

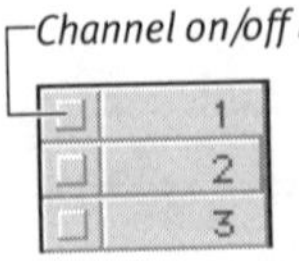

Figure 3.86 Turn a channel off or on to assist with testing.

To turn a channel on or off:

1. Click the button at the left side of a channel to turn the channel off during movie playback (**Figure 3.86**).

   Director ignores all information in the disabled channel, including any sprites; this technique may speed playback.

   Turning the Script channel off causes Director to ignore all scripts during playback.

2. To turn a channel back on, click the button again.

The score in Director 8 features many improvements over its counterpart way back in Director 5, most notably in the way that sprites are displayed. In some cases, you may still prefer to view the score using the old format-when you are editing a Director 5 movie, for example.

To use the Director 5-style score display:

1. Open the score.
2. Choose File > Preferences > Score.

   The Score Window Preferences dialog box appears.

3. Check the Director 5 Style Score Display checkbox (**Figure 3.87**).

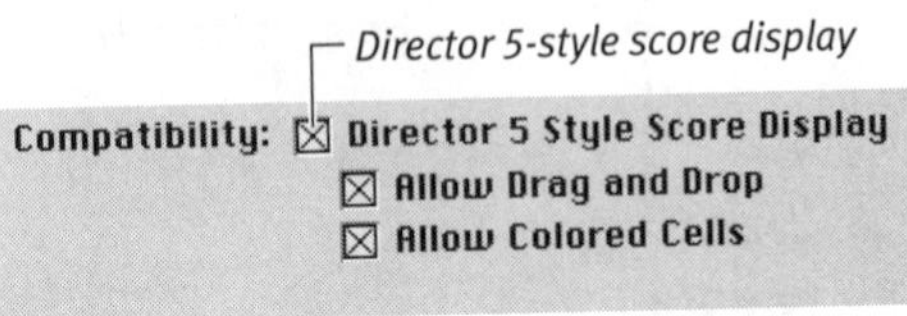

Figure 3.87 You can display the score to look like a Director 5 score, if you prefer.

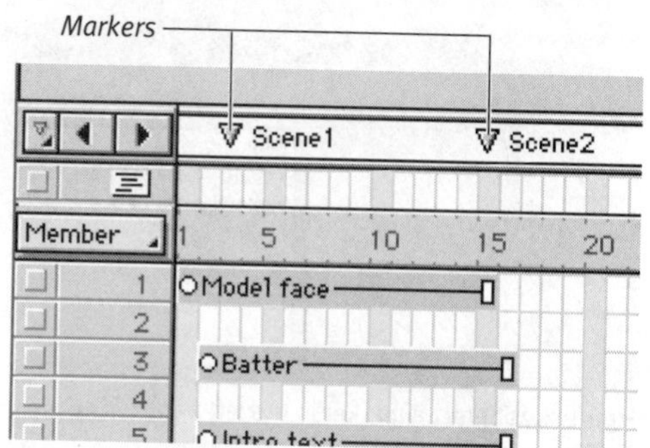

Figure 3.88 Place markers in the score to label movie sections.

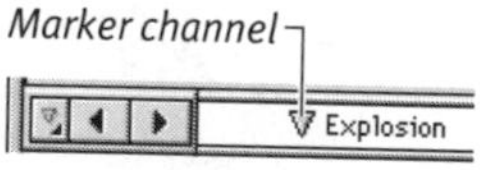

Figure 3.89 Click the marker channel to position a new marker.

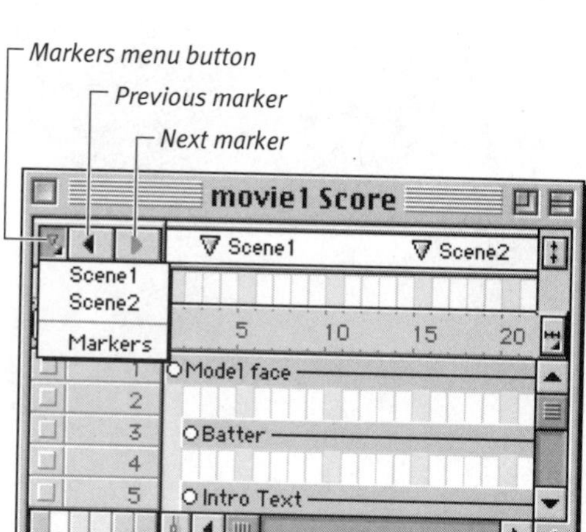

Figure 3.90 In the score, use the Previous/Next Marker buttons or the Markers pop-up menu to move to a new marker position in the score.

Setting Markers

One way to manage a movie composed of many frames is to use markers to label important sections (**Figure 3.88**).

Lingo scripts that navigate through your movie almost always refer to marker names rather than to changeable frame numbers. *(For more information on scripts, see Chapter 17, "Scripting Lingo.")*

To create a marker:

1. In the score, click a frame in the marker channel where you want to insert a new marker (**Figure 3.89**).
2. Type a name for the marker.
3. Press Enter or Return.

To reposition a marker:

- Drag a marker left or right to a new frame.

To delete a marker:

- Drag the marker out of the marker channel.

To navigate through a score by markers:

1. Click the Previous Marker button to jump back to the marker before the current frame (**Figure 3.90**).
2. Click the Next Marker button to jump forward to the marker after the current frame.
3. Jump directly to a specific marker by opening a pop-up menu called Markers menu and selecting the name of the marker.

Director includes a Markers window that allows you to add descriptive comments to markers—scene descriptions or any other notes that might help someone understand what purpose the marked frames serve in your movie.

To annotate markers in the Markers window:

1. With the score open, choose Window > Markers to display the Markers window.
2. In the left pane of the window, click the name of the marker that you want to annotate (**Figure 3.91**).

   Director immediately moves the playback head to the frame that contains the selected marker. It also copies the name of the marker in the right pane of the window.
3. Click the right pane of the Markers window to deselect the marker name that's repeated there.
4. Press Enter or Return after the marker name to start the comments on a new line.
5. Type the comments (**Figure 3.92**).
6. Close the Markers window.

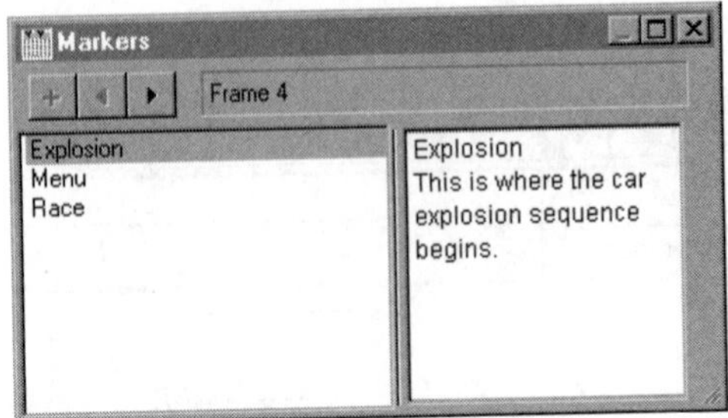

Figure 3.91 Select a marker in the left pane of the Markers window.

Explosion
This is where the car
explosion sequence
begins.

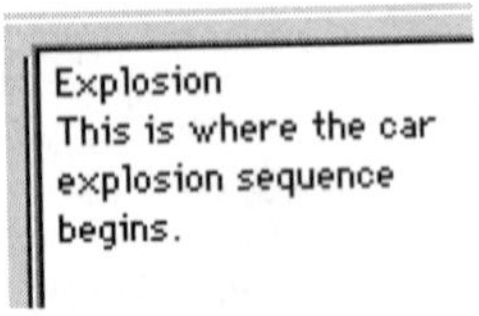

Figure 3.92 Type a note.

4

Animating Sprites

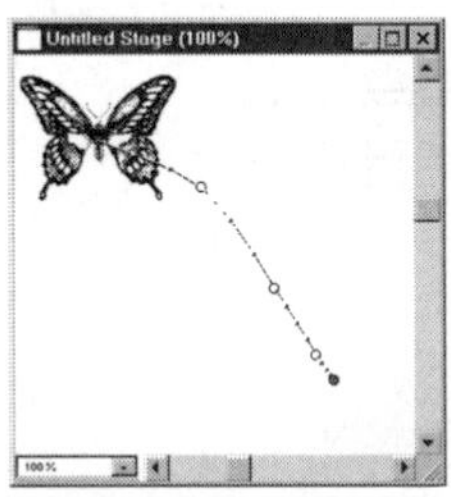

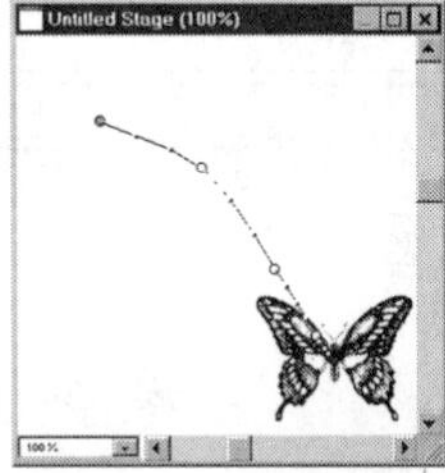

Figure 4.1 You can animate a sprite by changing its position on the stage.

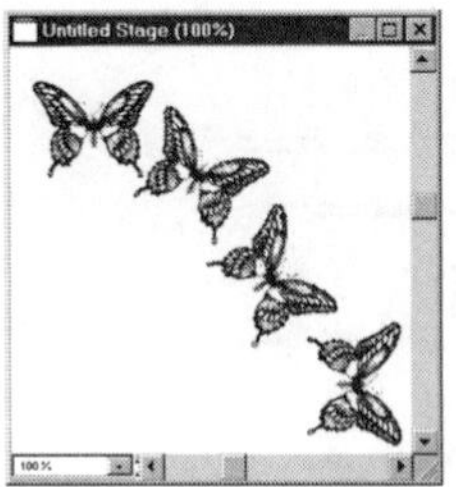

Figure 4.2 You also can animate a sprite by gradually changing a property of its image, such as Rotation Angle.

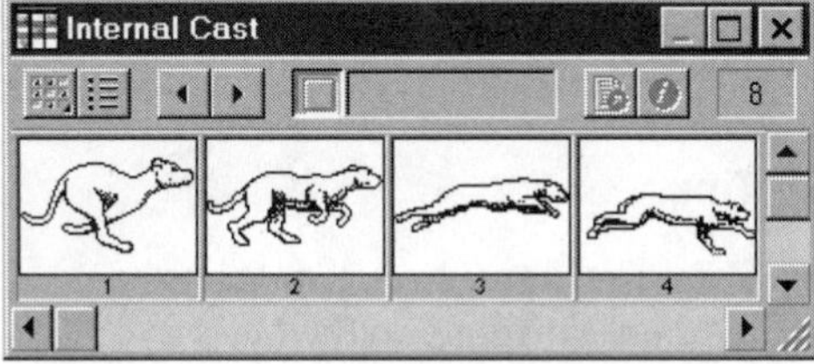

Figure 4.3 An animated sequence consists of a series of related cast members that alternate on the stage.

You can animate sprites in Director in two ways. The first way is to change a sprite's position on the stage over a series of frames to create the appearance of motion (**Figure 4.1**). The second way is to alter a sprite's image little by little over a series of frames. Often, animators combine both methods in a single animation, moving the image and changing it at the same time.

You can change a sprite's image in several ways:

- Gradually change one or more of its properties, such as Rotation Angle (**Figure 4.2**), size, or color over a series of frames.
- Exchange a sprite's image with another cast-member graphic. This technique allows you to create an *animated sequence*, which is a series of related cast members (**Figure 4.3**) alternating on the stage.

This chapter covers all the basic techniques of moving and changing sprites to create animation.

✔ Tip

- To make the best use of this chapter, you must first understand the material in chapters 1 through 3.

Tweening

Tweening offers a quick way to animate a sprite. All you need to do is set up keyframes within a sprite; Director automatically generates all the in-between frames.

You can tween these sprite properties:

- Path
- Size
- Rotation angle
- Skew angle
- Foreground and/or background color
- Blend percentage

A *keyframe*—represented by a circle within a sprite span in the score—is a frame in which any tweenable property of a sprite can change. Tweening occurs between two keyframes that contain the before and after states of a sprite property. When you tween the path of a sprite, for example, the first keyframe holds the sprite's starting location on the stage, and the second keyframe shows the destination (**Figure 4.4**). Director generates all the frames between the keyframes to create an animation of the sprite gradually moving from one place to another (**Figure 4.5**). You can create as many keyframes within a sprite as it has frames in its span, with tweening occurring between each pair. You could create 10 or more keyframes within a sprite to define a complex path for it to follow.

To create a keyframe:

1. Select a sprite in the score.
2. Select a frame (**Figure 4.6**).
3. Choose Insert > Keyframe (**Figure 4.7**).

Figure 4.4 The boats represent two keyframes with the sprite at opposite sides of the stage.

Figure 4.5 By tweening, Director creates the images between the keyframes to create animation. Here, the boat sails from right to left. (This figure shows 10 frames.)

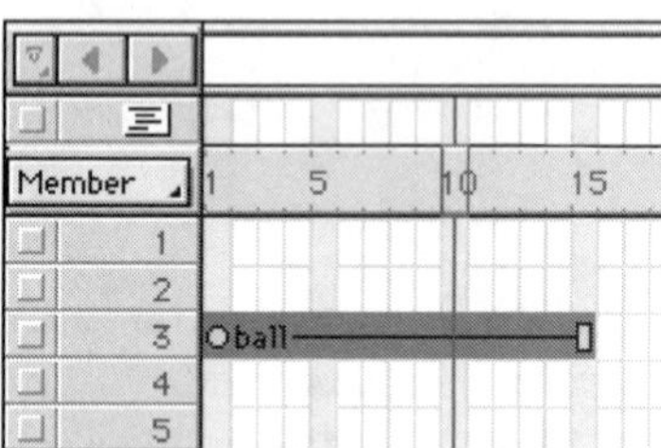

Figure 4.6 Click a frame to position a keyframe.

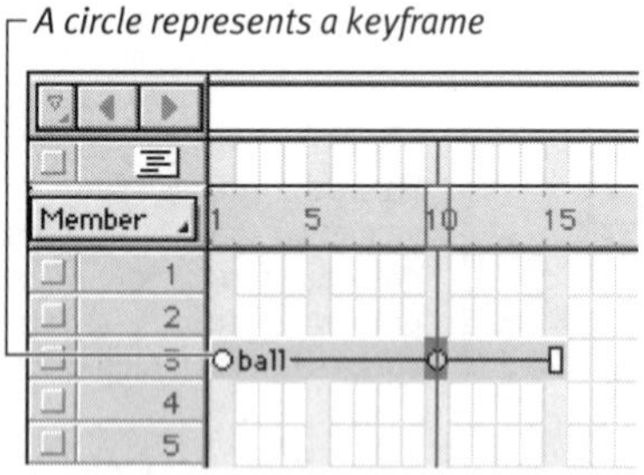

A circle represents a keyframe

Member 1 5 10 15

1 2 3 ball 4 5

Figure 4.7 The selected frame becomes a keyframe.

✔ Tips

- Copy a keyframe by Alt+dragging (Option+dragging, on the Mac) it to a new frame.
- The end frame of a sprite is not a keyframe, but you can place one there.

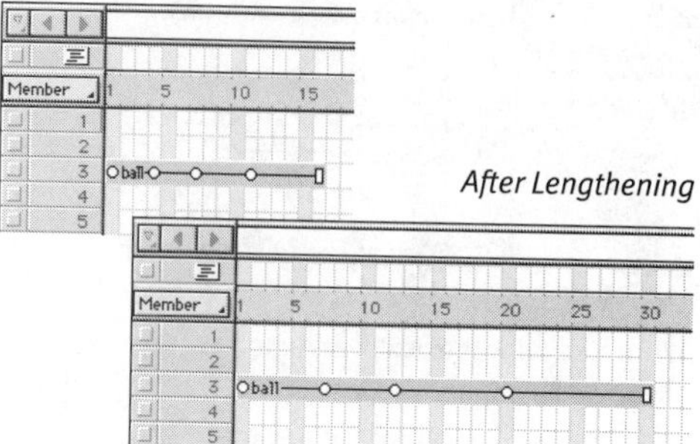

Figure 4.8 When you extend a sprite, its keyframes move proportionately farther apart.

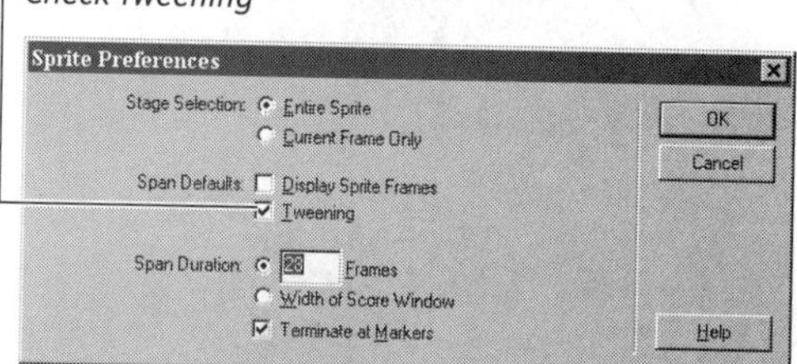

Figure 4.9 Choose Tweening in the Sprite Preferences dialog box.

Figure 4.10 Click the first keyframe in the sprite.

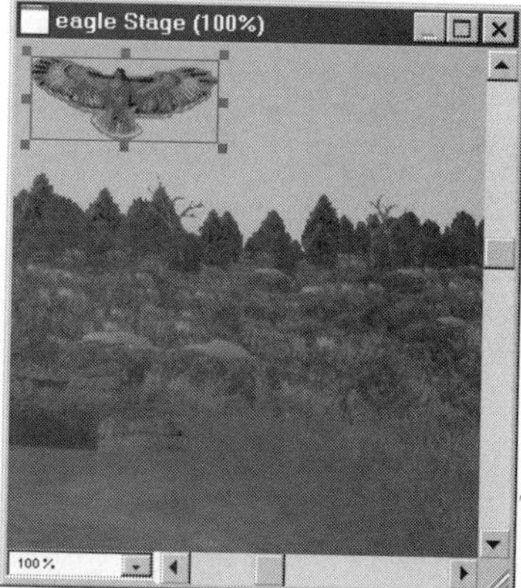

Figure 4.11 Set the sprite's initial properties in the first keyframe.

By changing the number of frames between keyframes, you can control how smooth tweening looks during playback.

To reposition keyframes in the score:

- Drag the keyframe to another frame in the same channel to create more or fewer frames between the keyframes.

✔ Tips

- When you drag the start or end keyframe of a sprite to shorten or lengthen its span, all keyframes within the sprite move proportionately closer or farther apart (**Figure 4.8**).
- Hold down the Control key (Command, on the Mac) while dragging the start or end frame of a sprite to extend it without moving other keyframes.

No matter which sprite properties you tween, the process is basically the same.

To tween a sprite:

1. Turn on tweening by choosing File > Preferences > Sprite, and check the Tweening option in the dialog box that opens (**Figure 4.9**).
2. In the score, create and position all the keyframes that you will need within a sprite.
3. Adjust the sprite's initial properties for the tween by clicking the first keyframe in the sprite (**Figure 4.10**) and editing any tweenable property, such as position, color, blend, and rotation.
   Change tweenable sprite properties by using the Property Inspector, by using the Sprite toolbar in the score, or by changing a property (such as size or position) directly on the stage (**Figure 4.11**).

continues on next page

TWEENING

4. Click to select the next keyframe within the sprite (**Figure 4.12**), and edit its properties to define the end state for the tween relative to the last keyframe (**Figure 4.13**).

   Director automatically generates all frames between this keyframe and the preceding one.

5. Repeat step 4 for each additional keyframe.

6. Click to select the entire sprite within the score.

7. Choose Modify > Sprite > Tweening to display the Sprite Tweening dialog box (**Figure 4.14**).

8. Check to enable the sprite properties you want tweened between keyframes (**Figure 4.15**).

   You can tween multiple sprite properties (such as size and path) at the same time by selecting multiple tweening options in this dialog box.

9. Click OK.

10. Rewind and play back the movie to see how the animation looks.

11. Refine the tweening, if necessary.

✔ Tips

- You can create the illusion of a sprite rotating in 3D by tweening its skew angle through 90 degrees or more.
- Tween the blend property of a sprite from a high value to a low value to make a sprite appear to fade out, or vice versa to make it appear to fade in.
- If you want to tween the size of a cast member, you will achieve the best results by using Flash or vector-shape cast members. Tweening the size of a bitmap cast member may result in noticeable distortion.

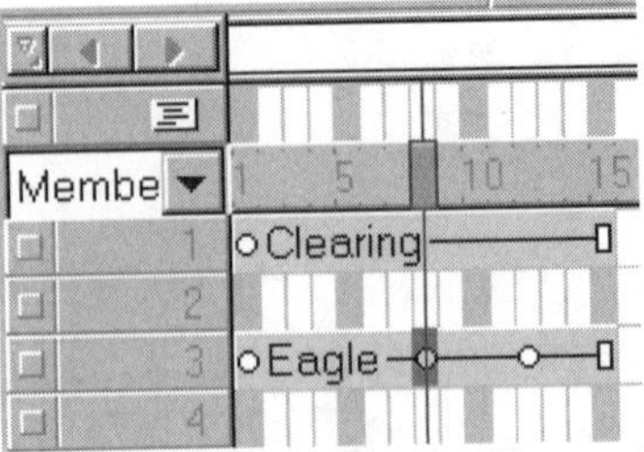

Figure 4.12 Click the next keyframe within the sprite.

Figure 4.13 Change the sprite's properties to define the end state for the tween.

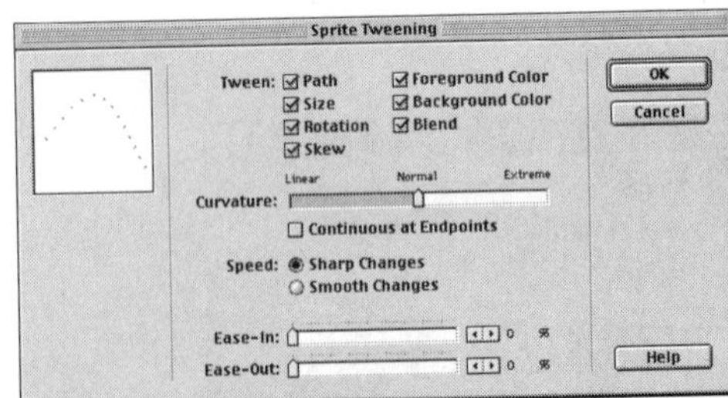

Figure 4.14 The Sprite Tweening dialog box.

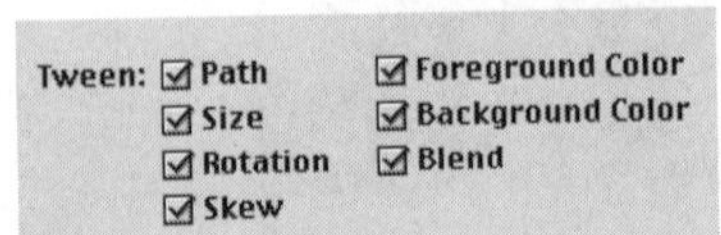

Figure 4.15 Enable the sprite properties you want tweened.

After you play back a tweened animation, you may find that you need to make some adjustments.

To refine tweening:

1. Select the sprite.
2. To improve animation or create a smoother path of animated movement, create additional keyframes, make more states of the sprite, and tween them again.

   To re-tween, you don't need to do anything special. As long as the sprite property you are changing is enabled in the Sprite Tweening dialog box, just change the property in any keyframe, and Director handles re-tweening automatically.
3. For more gradual transitions, add frames between keyframes.

   The more frames that separate your keyframes, the more gradual the transition in the tweened property is. If you're tweening motion across the stage, for example, using two keyframes separated by 100 frames produces fairly smooth motion. If only five frames separate the keyframes, the sprite appears to move suddenly and in a very jerky fashion.

There's a shortcut for changing a sprite property and creating a new keyframe in one step. This method comes in handy if you're setting up many keyframes and tweens within a sprite.

To create a keyframe and change a sprite property at the same time:

1. Enable single-frame selection (see Chapter 3, "Building a Score").
2. Make sure that the sprite property you are changing is set for tweening in the Sprite Tweening dialog box.

   You open the Sprite Tweening dialog box by choosing Modify > Sprite Tweening.
3. Click a frame in the sprite (**Figure 4.16**).
4. Change one or more of the sprite's tweenable properties, such as position or size (**Figure 4.17**).

   Director creates a keyframe in the selected frame (**Figure 4.18**) and changes the sprite according to your specifications.

✔ Tip

- Alt+click (Option+click, on the Mac) to select a single frame in the sprite if single-frame selection is not enabled (**Figure 4.19**).

Figure 4.16 Click a frame in the sprite.

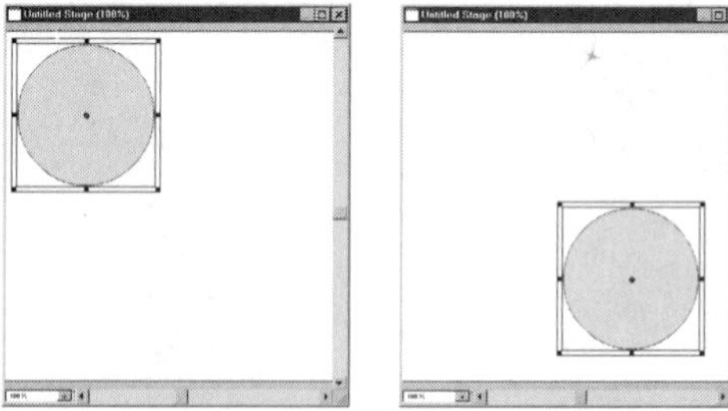

Figure 4.17 Change one or more sprite properties, such as position.

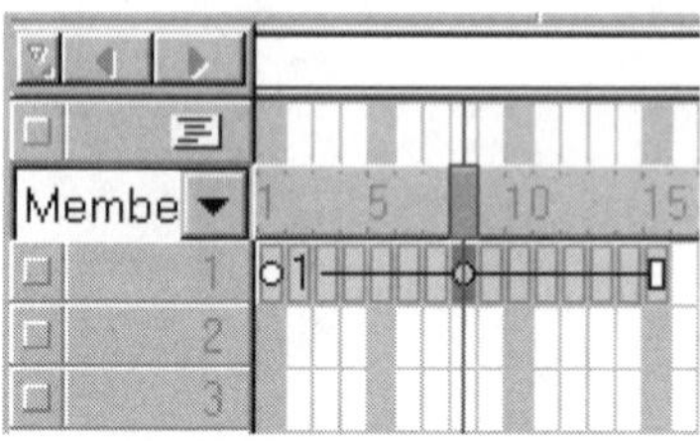

Figure 4.18 Director creates a keyframe.

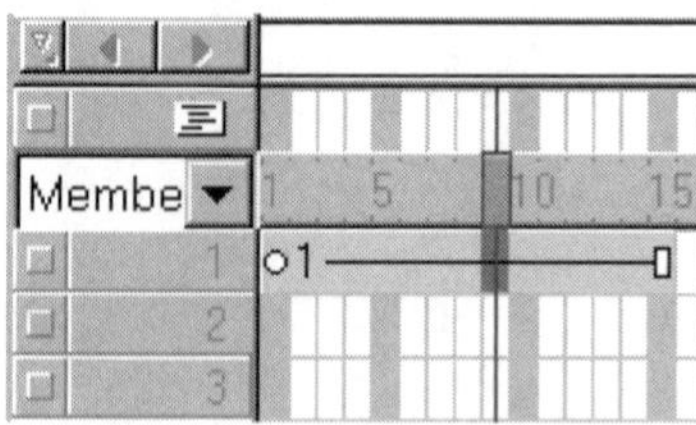

Figure 4.19 Alt+click or Option+click (Mac) to select a single frame in a sprite.

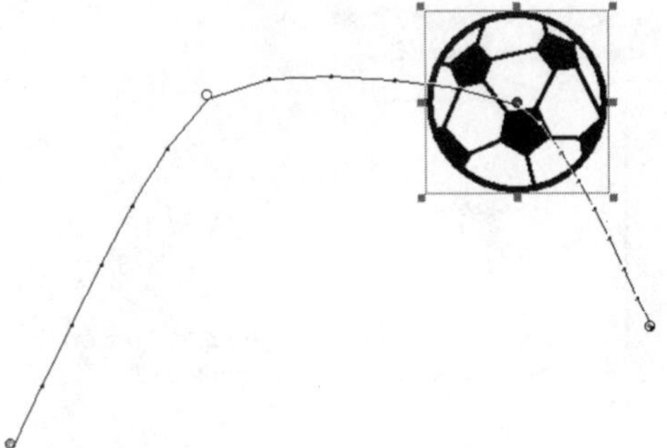

Figure 4.20 The path of the sprite is shown on the stage.

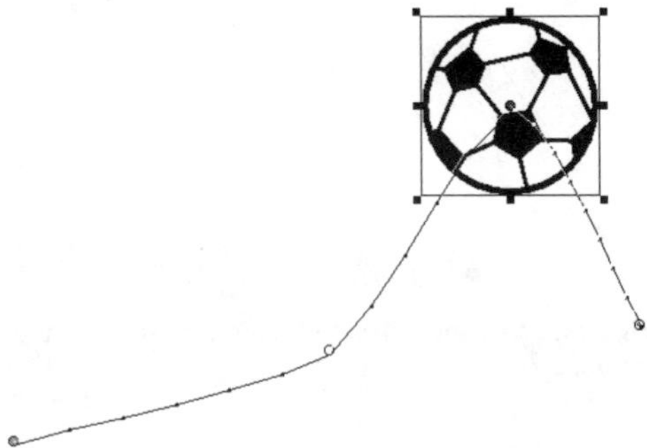

Figure 4.21 You can adjust the path by dragging any keyframe.

Adjusting Motion

After you tween a path for a sprite to follow, you can make numerous adjustments in the motion of the sprite (such as adding acceleration) to create a more realistic animation.

The quickest and most convenient way to adjust the path of a sprite is to use Sprite Overlay view, which allows you to see the complete path of the sprite—and its keyframes—on the stage.

To view and adjust the path of a sprite on the stage:

1. In the score, select the sprite whose path you want to view or adjust.
2. Choose View > Sprite Overlay > Show Paths.

   The complete path of the sprite appears on the stage (**Figure 4.20**). Keyframes within the path are symbolized by small circles; regular frames, by small dots.
3. Drag any keyframe symbol in the overlay to a new position (**Figure 4.21**).

   The sprite's path adjusts immediately.

✔ Tip

- When you select an entire sprite in the score and then change its position on the stage, you move the entire sprite throughout all its frames relative to the new position (as opposed to adjusting the position in a single keyframe).

When a sprite uses three or more keyframes, you can make the path between them follow a curve rather than a straight line.

To add curvature to a sprite's tweened path:

1. In the score, select a sprite whose path needs adjustment.
2. Choose Modify > Sprite > Tweening.
3. In the Sprite Tweening dialog box, drag the Curvature slider to adjust how much curvature is in the sprite's path.

   You can preview the adjusted path on the left side of the Sprite Tweening dialog box (**Figure 4.22**).

   Drag the slider to the Linear end to move the sprite between keyframes in straight lines (**Figure 4.23**).

   Drag to the Normal end to give the sprite's path moderate curvature.

   Drag to the Extreme end for maximum curvature in the path between keyframes (**Figure 4.24**).

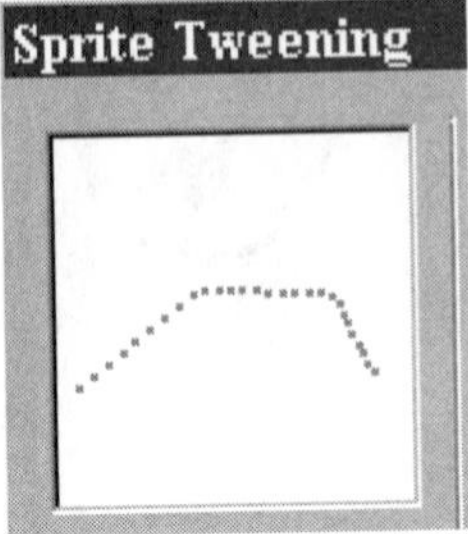

Figure 4.22 Preview the tweening path.

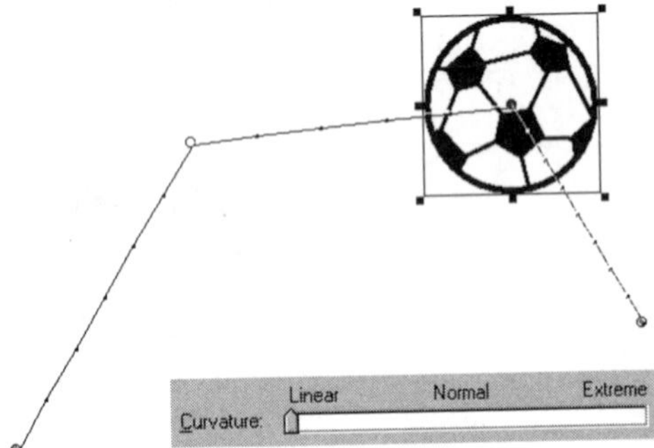

Figure 4.23 Linear path settings produce straight-line motion.

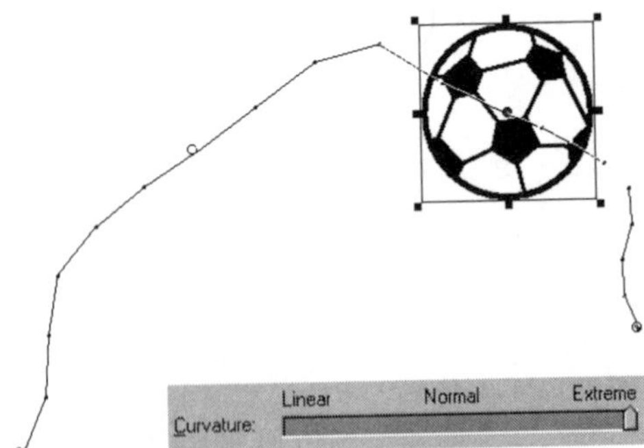

Figure 4.24 Extreme curvature produces a curved path for the sprite.

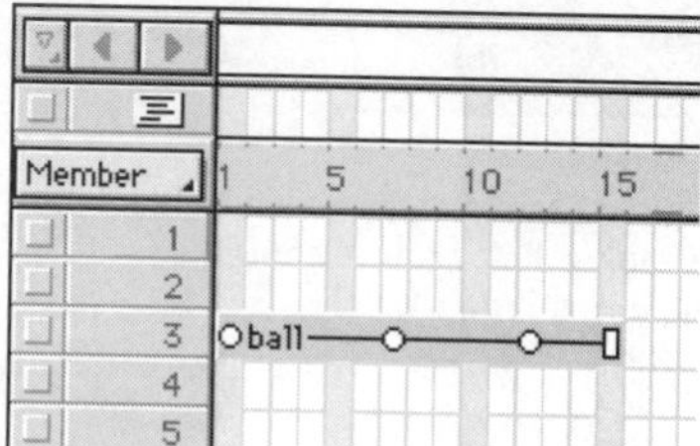

Figure 4.25 Create three keyframes.

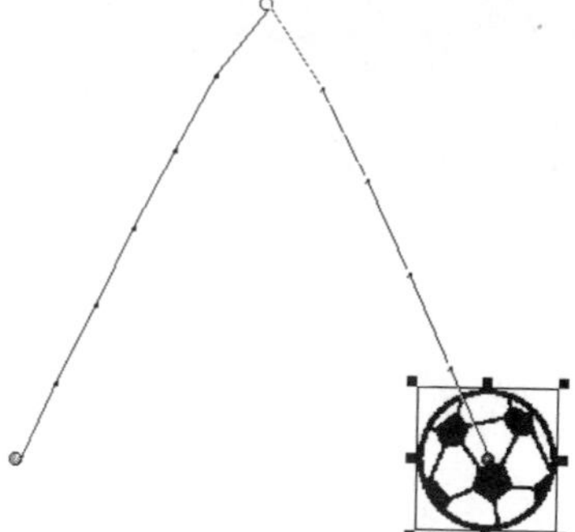

Figure 4.26 Position the sprite's keyframes in a triangle.

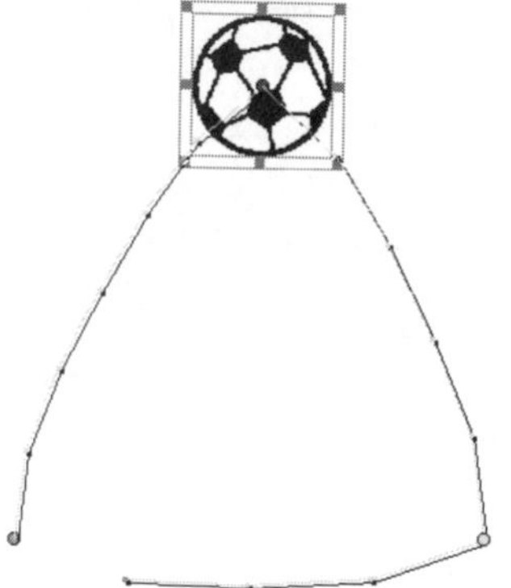

Figure 4.27 The closed path still looks triangular.

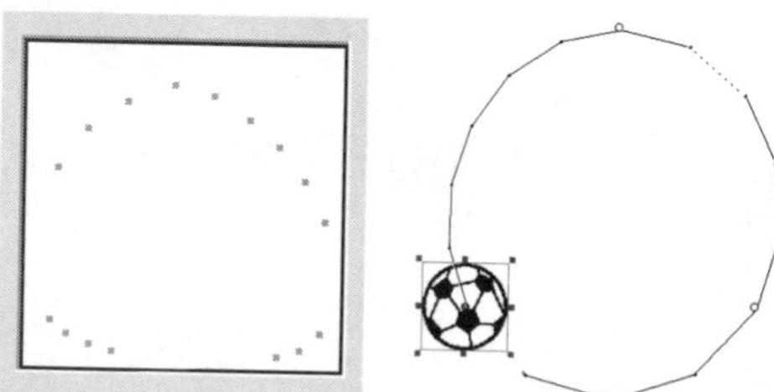

Figure 4.28 The path preview and the circular path after adjustment.

When you want a sprite to move in a circular path, use this method.

To create a circular path for a sprite:

1. Place a cast member in the score to create a sprite.
2. Create a total of three keyframes within the sprite (**Figure 4.25**).

   You can use the start frame, but don't create a keyframe at the end frame.
3. Choose View > Sprite Overlay > Show Paths to turn on the display of sprite paths.
4. On the stage, position the sprite's keyframes as corners of an equilateral triangle (**Figure 4.26**).
5. Select the sprite in the score and choose Modify > Sprite > Tweening.

   The Sprite Tweening dialog box opens.
6. Check the Continuous at Endpoints checkbox.

   That option makes the path a closed triangular path (**Figure 4.27**).
7. Drag the Curvature slider to the right to make the sprite's path resemble a circle.

   Use the path preview on the left side of the Sprite Tweening box as a guide (**Figure 4.28**).
8. Click OK.
9. Fine-tune the circular path, if necessary, by dragging the keyframes (represented by circles) within the Sprite Overlay on the stage.

When you tween a sprite along any path, you can make it change speed at the beginning or end to add a touch of realism.

To accelerate or decelerate a sprite along its path:

1. Set up keyframes and tween your sprite along a path.
2. Select the sprite in the score.
3. Choose Modify > Sprite > Tweening.
4. In the Sprite Tweening dialog box, drag the Ease-In and Ease-Out slider bars to control the sprite's acceleration along its path.

   Ease-In controls the beginning speed. High percentages make the sprite take a longer time to reach top speed along the path. Ease-Out controls the ending speed. High percentages for Ease-Out make the sprite take a long time to slow down (**Figure 4.29**).

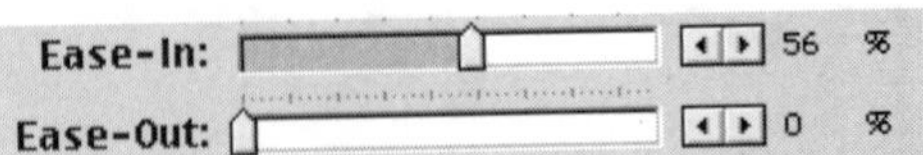

Figure 4.29 Drag the Ease-In and Ease-Out slider bars in the Sprite Tweening dialog box to control a sprite's acceleration and deceleration.

When a sprite follows a tweened path, it may move smoothly and slowly between certain keyframes but then suddenly speed up and move abruptly between other keyframes. These abrupt speed changes occur when too few frames lie between keyframes. Use the following to smooth abrupt speed changes.

To smooth the speed changes of a moving sprite:

1. Select the sprite whose speed changes you want to smooth.
2. Choose Modify > Sprite > Tweening.
3. In the Sprite Tweening dialog box, check the Smooth Changes speed option (**Figure 4.30**).

   Sharp Changes is the default selection.
4. Click OK.

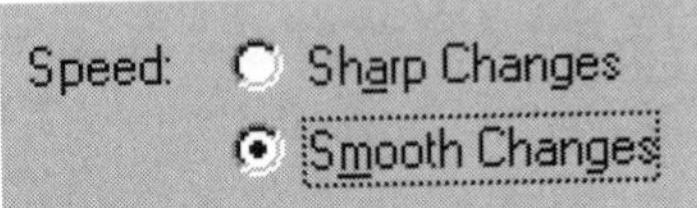

Figure 4.30 Click Smooth Changes in the Sprite Tweening dialog box to make speed changes more gradual.

Figure 4.31 Select sprites for step recording and click the frame where you want to start. An indicator appears in each channel that contains a selected sprite.

Figure 4.32 The sprite in frame 1.

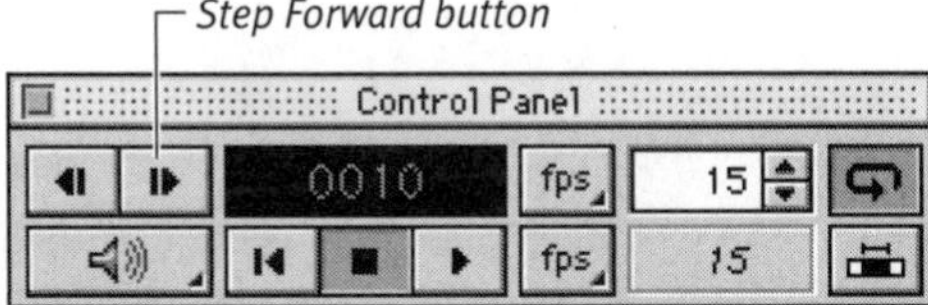

Figure 4.33 Click the Step Forward button to record a frame.

Step Recording

Unlike tweening, in which Director creates animation frames for you, step recording is a technique in which you animate a sprite one frame at a time. You manually adjust the properties of a sprite, such as position, to create an animation. You can use step recording to refine a tweened sprite. You also can step-record a complex scene in which sprites need to move in coordination. Use step recording when you need precise, frame-by-frame control of your sprite animation.

To step-record:

1. In the score, select one or more sprites.
2. Click the first frame for step recording.
3. Choose Control > Step Recording.

   An indicator appears next to selected sprites in the score (**Figure 4.31**).
4. Choose Window > Control Panel.
5. Arrange the sprite on the stage for the first frame (**Figure 4.32**).

   If you selected more than one sprite for step recording, the sprites move in unison.
6. Click the Step Forward button in the Control Panel (**Figure 4.33**) to record the frame to the score and advance to the next frame.

   If you step past a sprite's last frame, Director automatically extends the sprite into the next frame.

continues on next page

7. Arrange the selected sprites for the next frame of the step recording.

   You can cancel step recording for a particular sprite by selecting the sprite and deselecting Step Recording in the Control menu.

8. Repeat steps 6 and 7 to step-record as many frames as you need.

9. When you finish, select the sprites that you step-recorded and choose Control > Step Recording.

   A step-recorded sprite path and the resulting score might look something like **Figure 4.34**.

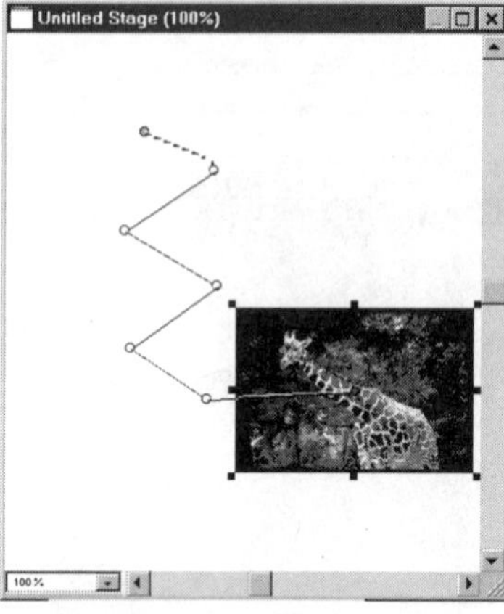

Figure 4.34 An example of a step-recorded path.

Figure 4.35 Click the start frame for your real-time-recording animation.

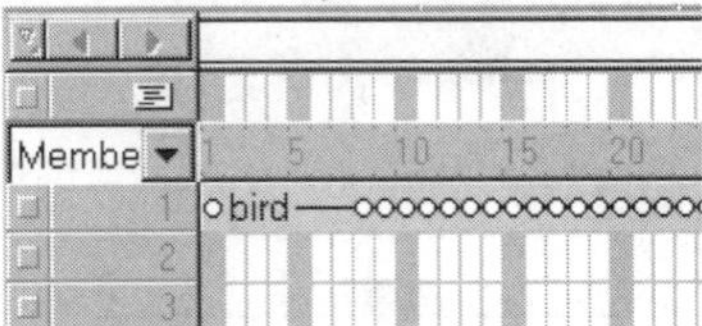

Figure 4.36 The score after a real-time recording.

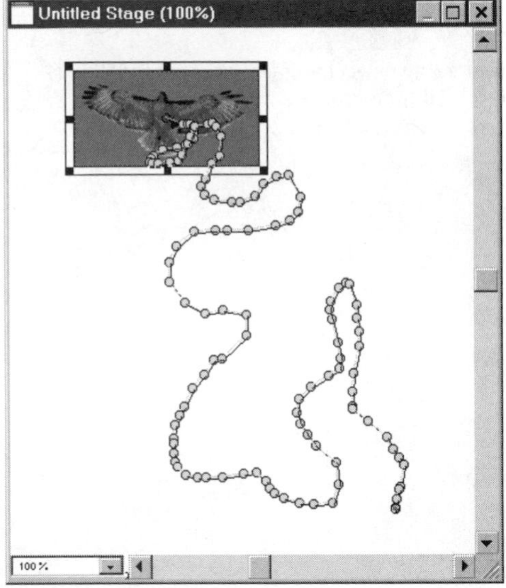

Figure 4.37 An example of a real-time-recorded path

Real-Time Recording

One of the most direct ways to animate sprites in Director is to use real-time recording. For real-time recording, you drag a sprite around the stage while Director automatically records its movement to the score. Real-time recording works well when you want to animate a sprite along a natural, free-flowing path with many changes in direction. The drawback of real-time recording is that the motion generated by your hand often looks considerably less smooth than you might like, although you can correct it later.

To real-time-record:

1. Select a sprite.

   You can real-time-record multiple sprites by selecting them as a group.

2. Click to select the starting frame for your real-time recording (**Figure 4.35**).

   Choose a frame within the sprite's span.

3. Arrange the sprite on the stage as it should appear in the first frame of the animation.

4. Choose Control > Real-Time Recording.

   A real-time recording indicator appears in any channel that contains a selected sprite (**Figure 4.35**).

5. Drag selected sprites around the stage to start real-time recording.

6. Release the mouse button to stop recording (**Figures 4.36–4.37**).

   If you record beyond the last frame of a sprite, Director automatically extends the sprite through the score until you stop recording or until the start of another sprite is reached in the same channel. (In the latter case, recording stops automatically, because real-time recording does not overwrite other sprites.)

continues on next page

7. Play back and review the animation.
8. Adjust individual frames, if necessary, to refine the motion.

✔ Tips

- If real-time recording seems to be too sensitive to your mouse movements, try slowing the recording tempo. In the Control Panel, set a new tempo by entering a new value (in frames per second) in the Tempo display (**Figure 4.38**). You can reset the tempo to a higher rate to play back the animation.
- You can create a handwriting effect by selecting a real-time recorded sprite and clicking the Trails box in the score's Sprite toolbar (**Figure 4.39**). As the sprite moves across the stage, it leaves behind a trail.

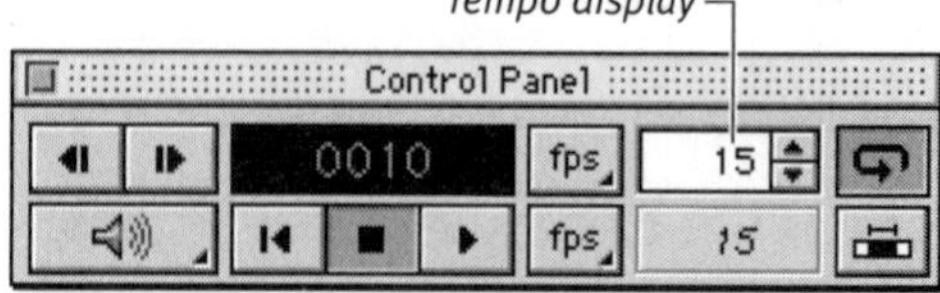

Figure 4.38 Slow the recording tempo in the Control Panel for more control.

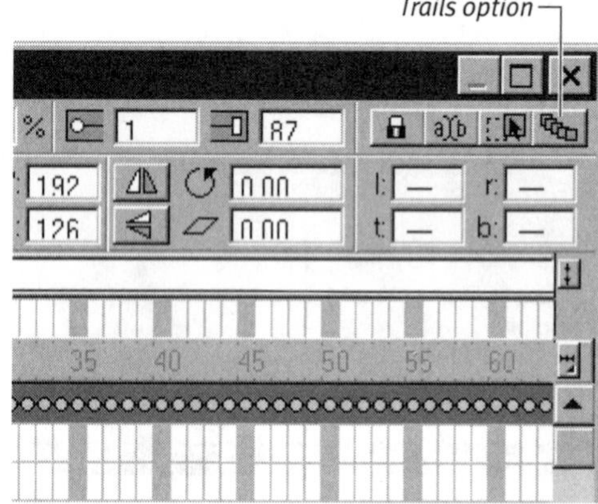

Figure 4.39 Select the Trails option for a real-time-recorded sprite to create a handwriting effect.

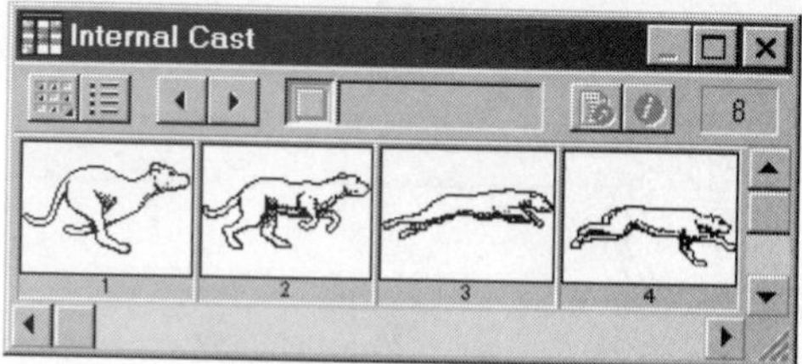

Figure 4.40 An animated sequence is a series of related cast members that alternate on the stage.

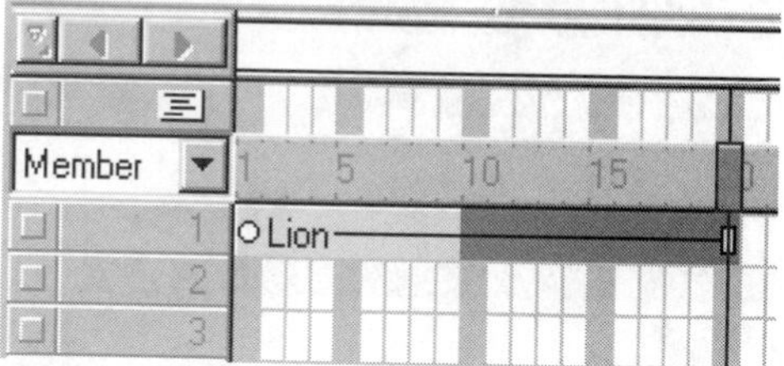

Figure 4.41 Select the frames in which you want to substitute a different cast member.

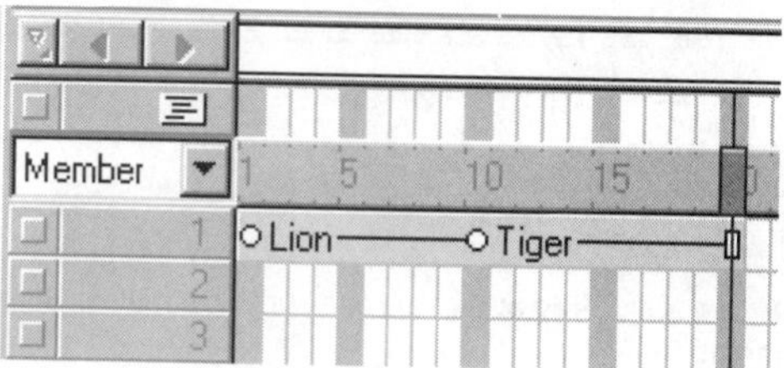

Figure 4.42 The revised sprite.

Building Animated Sequences

An *animated sequence* in Director consists of a series of related cast members (**Figure 4.40**) that alternate on the stage to create a more realistic animation than change of position or sprite properties can.

Up to now, you have worked with sprites that display only one cast-member graphic. You can create a sprite that displays multiple cast-member images throughout its span, which simplifies the process of creating animated sequences. A sprite can display one cast member for the first 10 frames and another cast member in the next 10 frames, for example.

You can change the cast member on which a sprite is based for either the entire sprite or for a range of frames. The path of a sprite (if any) remains the same when you change the cast members.

To exchange a cast member within a sprite:

1. In the score, select the range of frames within a sprite where you want to exchange the cast member on which the sprite is based (**Figure 4.41**).

   or

   Select the entire sprite if you want to exchange the cast member throughout all its frames.

2. In the Cast window, select a cast member to exchange for the sprite you selected in step 1.

3. Choose Edit > Exchange Cast Members.

   The cast member is exchanged, and sprite labels within the sprite span are updated (**Figure 4.42**).

The Cast to Time command offers a convenient way to create an animated sequence by moving a series of cast members from a Cast window to sequential frames in the score, forming a single sprite.

To place a series of cast members in frames as one sprite:

1. In the Cast window, organize some cast members into a sequence.
2. In the score, click a cell as the starting point where your cast members should be placed (**Figure 4.43**).
3. In the Cast window, select the sequence of cast members that you want to move into the score (**Figure 4.44**).

   You can choose adjacent cast members or make noncontiguous selections.
4. With the Cast window still active, choose Modify > Cast to Time.

   Director creates a sprite that consists of as many frames as there are cast members in your selection, with each frame containing one of the cast members (**Figure 4.45**).
5. Play back the movie to check the animated sequence.

✔ Tips

- As a shortcut for the Modify > Cast to Time command, you can hold down the Alt key (Option, on the Mac) while dragging the cast members from the Cast window into the score.
- Sometimes, a sequence of cast members placed in the score may appear to jump or shift as your movie plays. In this case, their registration points may need to be aligned (*see "To set a new registration point" in Chapter 3*).

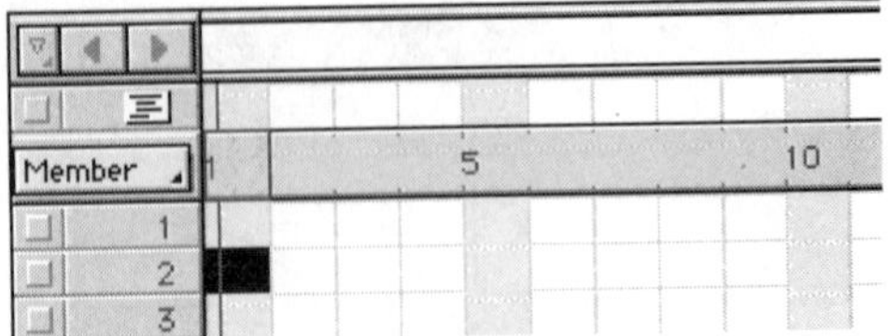

Figure 4.43 Select a cell as a destination for the cast members.

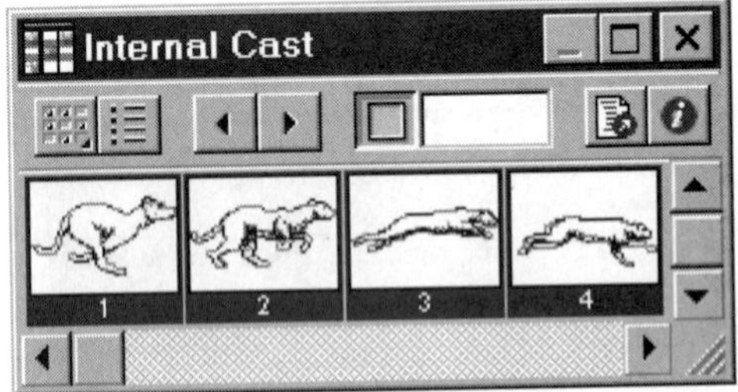

Figure 4.44 Select a series of cast members.

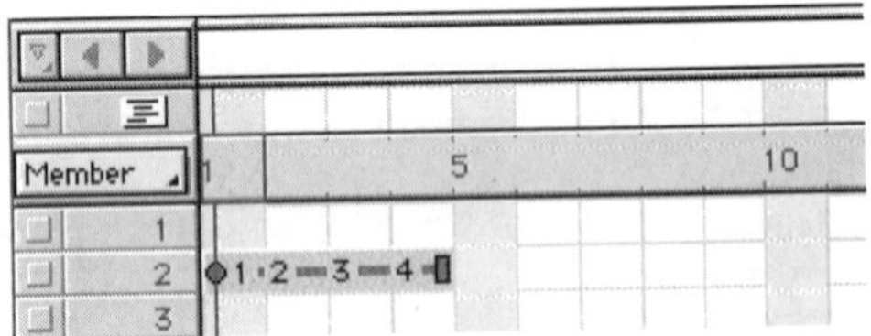

Figure 4.45 Director creates one sprite from the cast members.

Figure 4.46 Drag cast members for the sequence to the stage—in order.

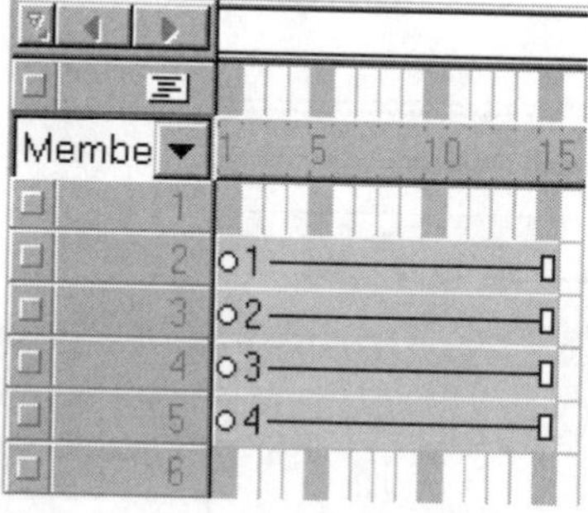

Figure 4.47 The cast members are placed in sequential channels in the score.

Figure 4.48 Carefully position the sprites on the stage as they should appear in the animated sequence.

Figure 4.49 Limit the sprites' span duration to one frame.

In the process of creating an animated sequence, animators often find it helpful to temporarily place all the cast members in a single frame in the score, so as to view them all at the same time on the stage and check positioning. When you finish checking the positioning, you can use Director's Space to Time command to convert all the sprites in that one frame to a single sprite to form an animated sequence.

To convert sprites in one frame to an animated sequence:

1. Select a cell in the score as the destination for your animated sequence.
2. One by one, drag the cast members for the animated sequence from the Cast window to the stage (**Figure 4.46**).

   Be sure to drag the cast members to the stage in the correct order. Director automatically places the cast members in sequential channels in the score, creating separate sprites (**Figure 4.47**).
3. Arrange the sprites on the stage as they should appear in the animated sequence (**Figure 4.48**).
4. Select all the sprites that you just created in the score.
5. Limit the sprites' span duration to one frame (**Figure 4.49**) by entering the same frame number for the start frame and end frame in the Property Inspector or the score's Sprite toolbar.

continues on next page

6. Choose Modify > Space to Time.
7. In the Space to Time dialog box, enter a Separation value to indicate how many frames should separate the sprites within the new combined sprit.
8. Click OK.

   All the selected sprites condense into a single sprite in a single channel (**Figure 4.50**).

Figure 4.50 The multiple sprites are converted to a single sprite.

The Paste Relative command aligns the start position of one sprite on the stage with the end position of the preceding sprite (**Figure 4.51**). This method comes in handy when you want to create an animated sequence moving across the stage, with each iteration of the sequence starting where the preceding one left off.

Figure 4.51 Align the sprites end to end with the Paste Relative command.

To link an animated sequence with Paste Relative:

1. In the score, select a sprite that contains an animated sequence (**Figure 4.52**).
2. Choose Edit > Copy Sprites.
3. In the score, choose the cell immediately after the last cell of the selected sprite (**Figure 4.53**).
4. Choose Edit > Paste Special > Relative (**Figure 4.54**).

   Director copies your animated sequence onto the stage, beginning exactly where the previous sequence ends (**Figure 4.51**).

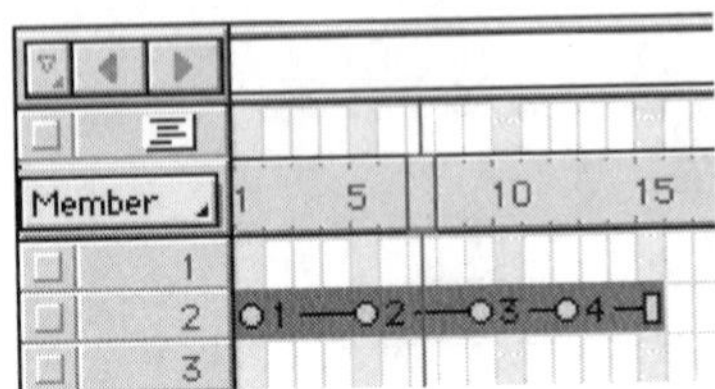

Figure 4.52 Select a sprite.

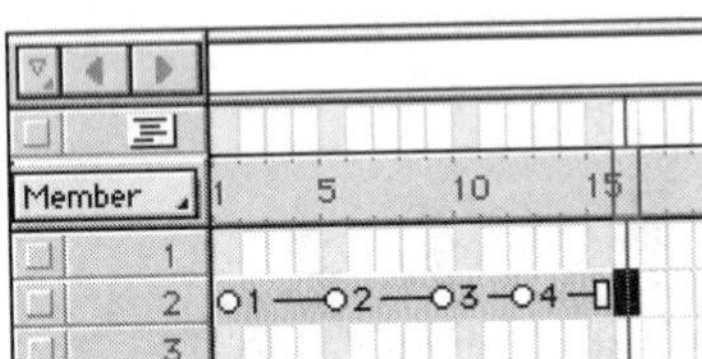

Figure 4.53 Select the next cell after the sprite.

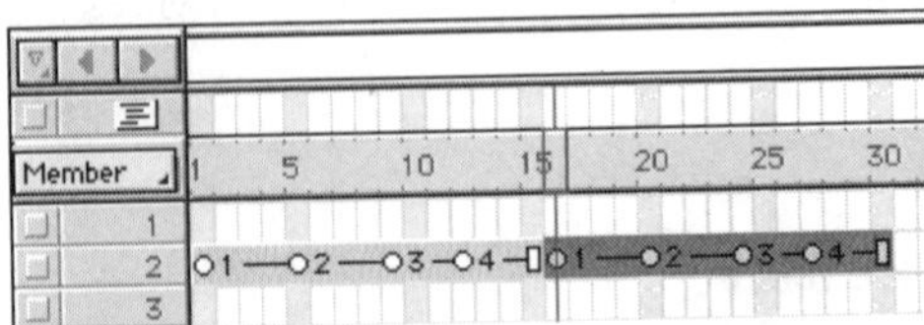

Figure 4.54 Using Paste Relative, copy the sprite into place.

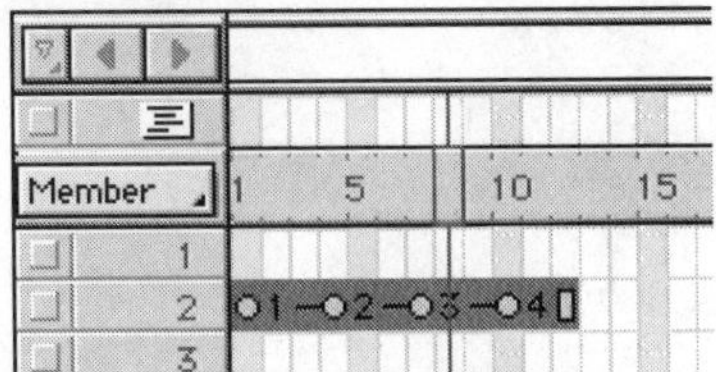

Figure 4.55 Select a sprite to reverse.

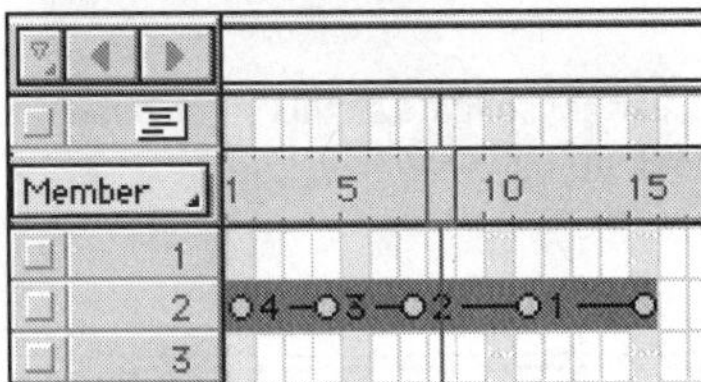

Figure 4.56 The reversed sprite.

You can reverse the order of a sprite in the score, so that the end of its span becomes the starting frame, and vice versa. If the sprite comprises an animated sequence, the order of all cast members in the sprite reverses as well.

To reverse a sequence:

1. In the score, select a sprite that you want to reverse (**Figure 4.55**).
2. Choose Modify > Reverse Sequence (**Figure 4.56**).

Making Film Loops

Film loops consolidate many sprites and effects over a range of frames into a single cast member (**Figure 4.57**). When you place a film-loop cast member in the score, you create a single sprite that consists of all the consolidated sprite data in the film loop (**Figure 4.58**).

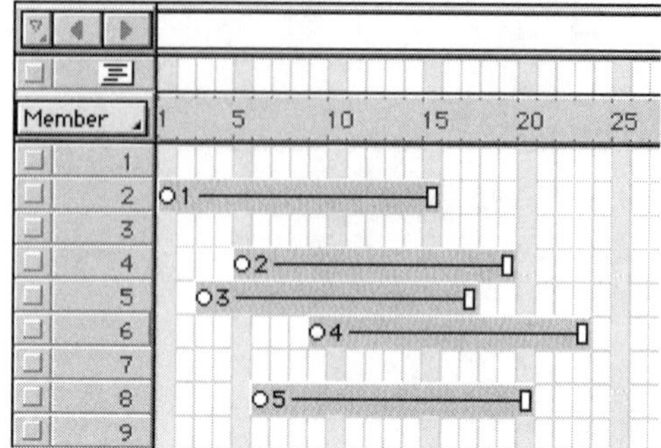

Figure 4.57 You can consolidate all this sprite data into a single film-loop cast member.

Film loops make it much easier to develop large and complex animations. They also make it easier to work with animated sequences. Suppose that you have a sprite that consists of the four cast members shown in **Figure 4.59**, forming an animated sequence. If you create a film-loop cast member from that sprite, you can simply place that single film-loop cast member in the score whenever you need it, instead of hassling with four separate cast members.

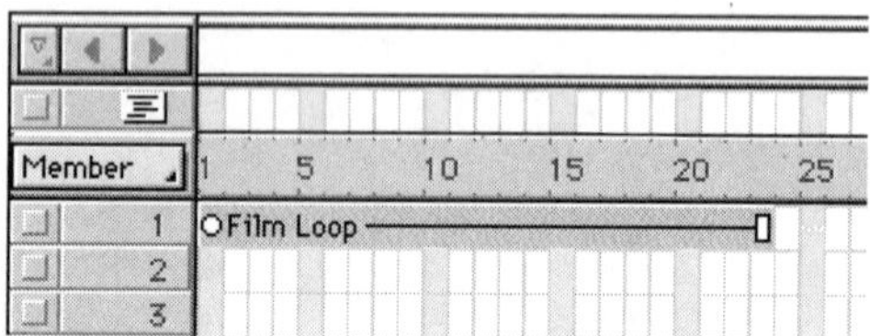

Figure 4.58 A single film loop replaces all the score data.

You can tween film loops just as you would any other cast member or apply real-time recording with them to create complex animations. The film loop of a bird flapping its wings, for example, can be tweened to fly across the screen.

Figure 4.59 A sprite that consists of four cast members.

A film loop itself can be composed of other film loops. Suppose that you have two film loops in the score: one of a walking man and the other of a running dog. You can create a single film loop to include both loops.

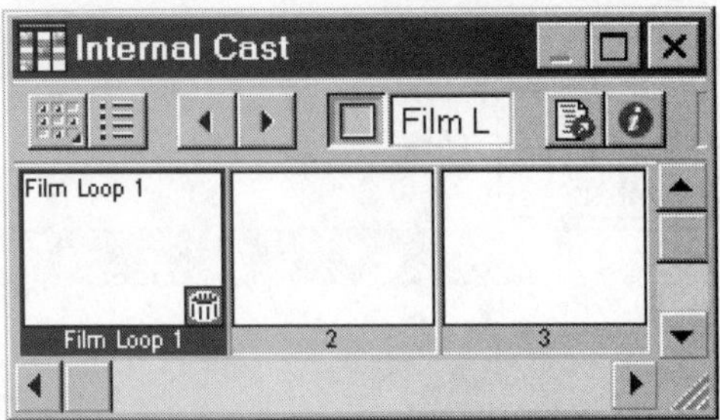

Figure 4.60 A film-loop cast member in a Cast window.

Figure 4.61 Name the film loop.

Director stores film loops, like other cast members, in a Cast window, identified by the film-loop icon (**Figure 4.60**).

To create a film loop:

1. In the score, select all the sprites for the film loop.

   You can include effects sprites from the effects channels.

2. Choose Insert > Film Loop.

   The Create Film Loop dialog box opens.

3. Type a name for the film loop (**Figure 4.61**).

4. Click OK.

   Director puts the film loop in the next available position in the Cast window.

5. Place the film loop in the score or stage as often as you need it.

6. Add frames in the score, if necessary, to provide enough room for the loop to play at least once all the way through.

   Film loops animate only when you play your movie; you won't see the animation if you step through the frames or drag the playback head across the frames.

✔ Tips

- You cannot apply score ink effects to film loops. You must apply ink effects to the individual sprites before you include them in a film loop.
- As a shortcut, create a film loop by dragging a selection of frames from the score to a Cast window.

You can use real-time recording to record a path for a film-loop cast member to follow across the stage. The process is very similar to real-time recording with other cast members, as described earlier in this chapter.

To real-time-record with a film loop:

1. In the score, select a film-loop sprite (**Figure 4.62**).
2. With the sprite still selected, click a frame (within the sprite's range of frames) to indicate the start frame for real-time recording (**Figure 4.63**).
3. Arrange the sprite on the stage for the initial frame of the animation, if necessary.
4. Choose Control > Real-Time Recording.
5. Drag the selected sprite on the stage to start real-time recording.
6. Release the mouse button to end your real-time recording session.

Figure 4.62 Select a film-loop sprite.

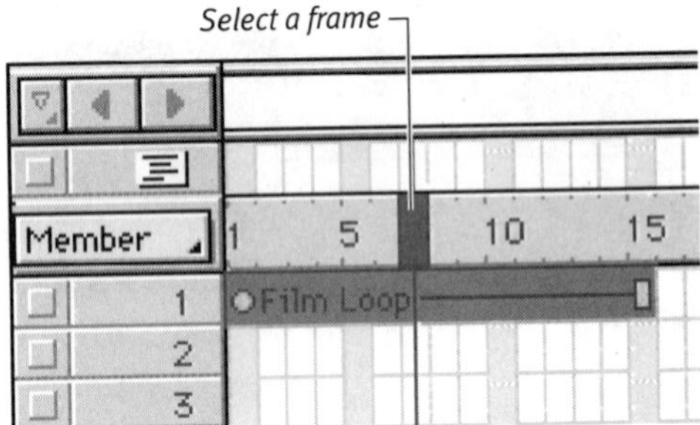

Figure 4.63 Select a frame for the start of real-time recording.

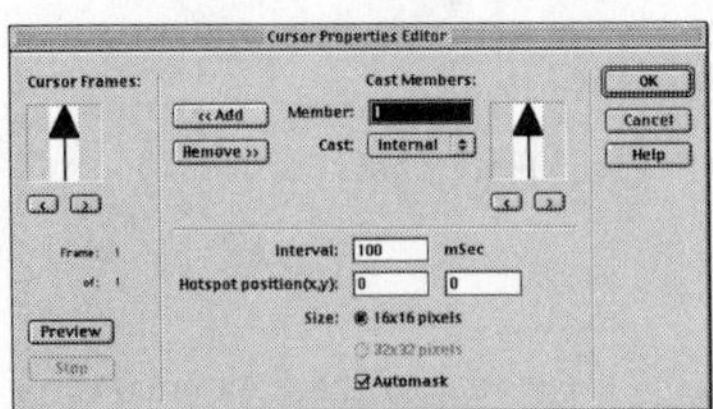

Figure 4.64 Use the Cursor Properties Editor to create an animated cursor.

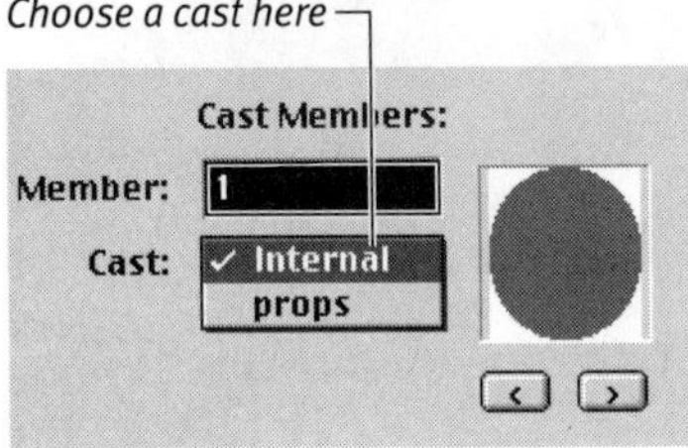

Figure 4.65 Choose a cast.

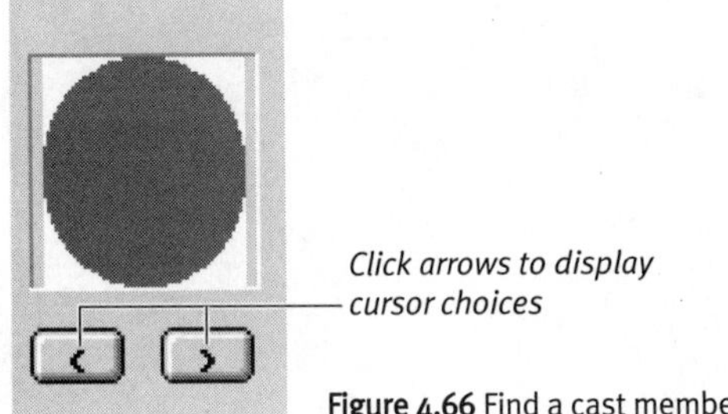

Figure 4.66 Find a cast member.

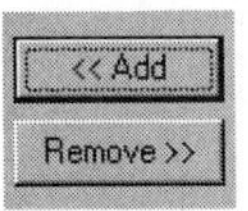

Figure 4.67 Click Add to select a cast member. Click Remove to delete one.

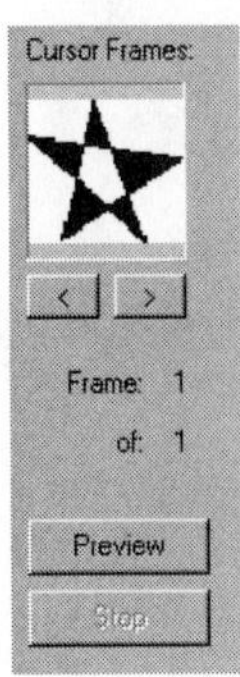

Figure 4.68 Check the cursor frames you've added.

Animating Color Cursors

By creating an animated cursor, you can bring life to the boring static cursor, transforming it into a miniature animation. You can activate an animated cursor during a rollover, for example, as a way to communicate to your users that some action is possible when the mouse pointer is on a certain icon.

An *animated cursor* essentially is an animated sequence of a series of bitmapped cast members. You activate an animated cursor by writing a Lingo script (*see "Lingo for Animated Cursors" in Chapter 17*).

To create an animated color cursor:

1. Make sure that all the cast members you want to use for the animated cursor are in casts that are currently linked to your movie.
2. Choose Insert > Media Element > Cursor.

   The Cursor Properties Editor dialog box opens (**Figure 4.64**).
3. From the Cast pop-up menu, choose the cast that contains the cast members for the animated cursor (**Figure 4.65**).

   You can use members from more than one cast.
4. Click the arrows below the Cast Members section (right side of the dialog box) to browse choices and select a cast member (**Figure 4.66**).

   Only suitable cast members (8-bit color bitmapped images) show up as choices.
5. Click Add (**Figure 4.67**).
6. Repeat steps 4 and 5 to add all the cast members you need.
7. Use the arrows in the Cursor Frames section of the dialog box to review the frames you have added (**Figure 4.68**).

continues on next page

8. Click Remove to delete a previewed frame, if necessary.
9. Enter a value (in milliseconds) in the Interval field to set the time delay between frames of the cursor.

   This interval governs the entire cursor, regardless of the movie's playback tempo.
10. Enter x and y values in the Hotspot Position field to define your cursor's hot spot—the place that activates whatever you click (**Figure 4.69**).

    (0,0) marks the top-left corner.
11. Click a size option to select the maximum size of your cursor.

    Depending on your system, only one option may be available.
12. Check Automask to make white pixels in the cursor transparent (**Figure 4.70**).
13. Click Preview to see the cursor animation.
14. When you are satisfied with the cursor animation, click OK.

    The cursor goes into the cast. You need to use Lingo to add it to a movie *(see Chapter 17, Scripting Lingo).*

✔ Tips

- You can create an animated cursor that appears to have a variable frame rate by creating identical consecutive cursor frames. If your Interval is 100 milliseconds, for example, you can create a cursor frame that appears to last 500 milliseconds (half a second) by creating five identical cursor frames that you place back to back.
- If you select Automask to make white pixels transparent, you still can have opaque "white" pixels in your cursor by selecting the lightest shade of gray from the color palette for those pixels.

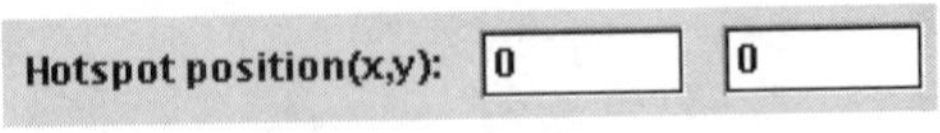

Hotspot position(x,y): 0 0

Figure 4.69 Define the cursor's hot spot.

☑ Automask

Figure 4.70 Check Automask to make white pixels transparent.

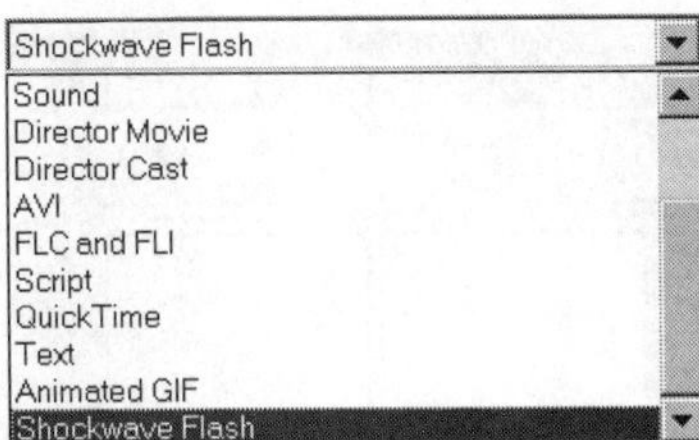

Figure 4.71 Choose Shockwave Flash as the file type to import.

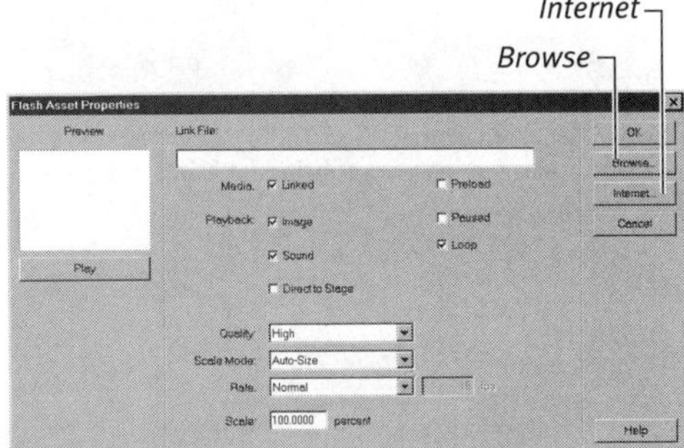

Figure 4.72 The Flash Asset Properties dialog box.

Incorporating Flash Movies

Director 8 allows you to import Flash movies and incorporate them into your movie as you would any other cast member. Flash is a vector-based animation development tool that produces compact animations ideally suited for use in Shockwave movies. Because Flash movies are vector-based, you can manipulate them on Director's stage with scaling, rotation, and other tools without reducing sharpness.

You animate Flash sprites the same way you animate any graphic cast member in Director. You can tween the properties of a Flash sprite to create complex compound animations, such as a Flash movie rotating and moving across the stage while shrinking.

Director 8 can import Flash 2, 3, and 4 movies, and it supports all the latest features in Flash 4.

To import a Flash movie:

1. Choose File > Import.
2. In the dialog box, choose Shockwave Flash from the Files of Type pop-up menu (Show pop-up menu, on the Mac) (**Figure 4.71**).
3. Select a Flash movie file.
4. Click Import.

✔ Tip

- If you want to set options for your Flash cast member before it's imported, add the Flash cast member by choosing Insert > Media Element > Flash Movie. In the Flash Asset Properties dialog box (**Figure 4.72**), set options and then click Browse or Internet to select the Flash movie you want to import.

You can set media options for a Flash movie to control whether the movie data is linked to or brought into actual memory. You can set these options before a Flash movie is imported or reset the options after the Flash movie has been imported.

To set media options for a Flash cast member:

1. If the Flash cast member has already been imported, double-click it in the Cast window (**Figure 4.73**).

   or

   Choose Insert > Media Element > Flash Movie to set media options for a new Flash movie before it's imported.

   The Flash Asset Properties dialog box opens.

2. Check the Linked checkbox (**Figure 4.74**) if you want to link to an external Flash movie file so that Director loads it into memory only when the Flash sprite appears on the stage.

   or

   Leave the Linked checkbox unchecked if you want Director to load the entire Flash movie into the cast and memory.

   If the Flash cast member has already been imported as an internal cast member when you choose the Linked option, specify the new file in the Link File box (**Figure 4.75**). The internal Flash cast member is erased.

3. Choose the Preload option if you have linked to an external Flash movie and want Director to load the entire Flash movie into memory before playing the first frame of your Director movie.

   or

   Deselect the Preload option if you want your Director movie to start playing immediately while the Flash movie streams into the cast and memory.

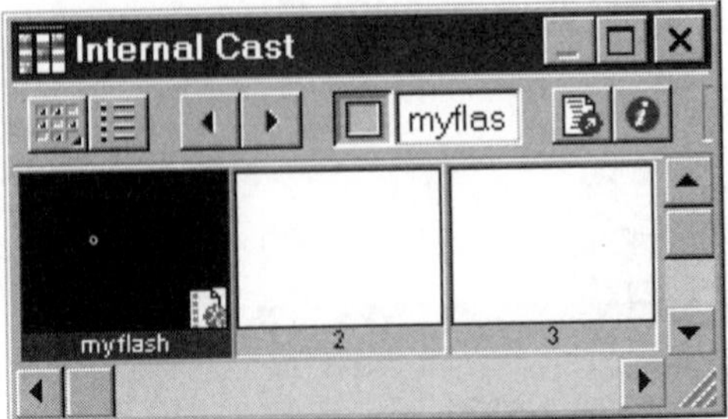

Figure 4.73 Double-click a Flash cast member.

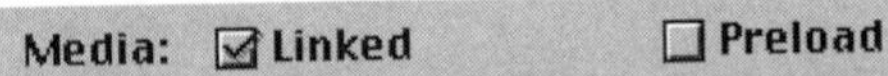

Figure 4.74 Select the Linked option to link to an external Flash file instead of bringing it into the cast and memory.

Figure 4.75 Specify the file name for the linked Flash movie.

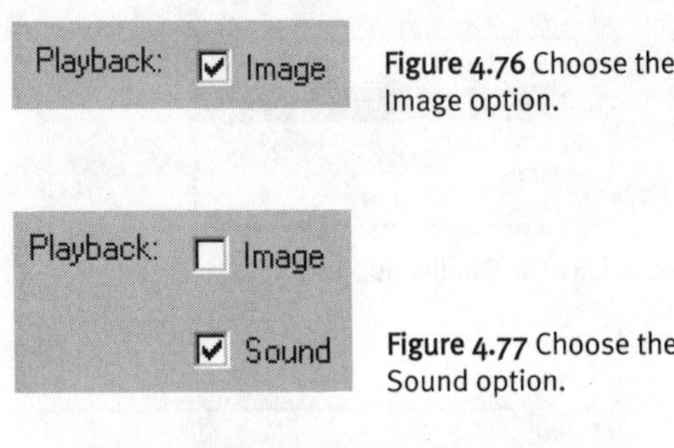

Figure 4.76 Choose the Image option.

Figure 4.77 Choose the Sound option.

Figure 4.78 Choose the Paused option.

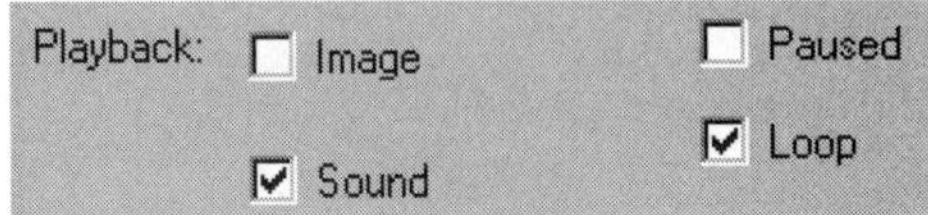

Figure 4.79 Choose the Loop option.

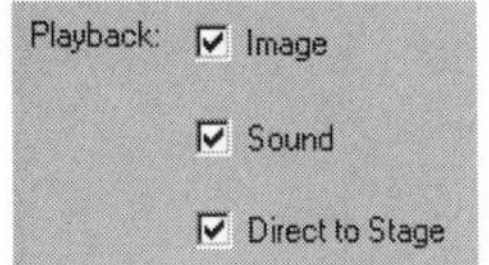

Figure 4.80 Choose the Direct to Stage option.

The playback options in the Flash Asset Properties dialog box control how Director plays your Flash movie in a projector or Shockwave movie, as well as in the authoring environment.

To set playback options for a Flash cast member:

1. If the Flash cast member has already been imported, double-click it in the Cast window.

   or

   Choose Insert > Media Element > Flash Movie to set playback options for a new Flash movie before it's imported.

   The Flash Asset Properties dialog box opens.

2. Choose the Image option (**Figure 4.76**) to display images in the Flash movie sprite.
   Deselect Image to keep the images invisible.

3. Choose the Sound option to play any sounds in the Flash movie sprite (**Figure 4.77**).

   Deselect Sound for a silent Flash movie.

4. Choose the Paused option (**Figure 4.78**) to display only the first frame of the Flash movie when the Director movie plays.

   Deselect Paused to play the Flash sprite immediately after it appears on the stage.

5. Choose the Loop option (**Figure 4.79**) to repeat the Flash movie after it finishes.

   Deselect Loop to play the Flash movie only once.

6. Choose the Direct to Stage option (**Figure 4.80**) if you want Director to display the Flash movie as soon as it appears on the stage, ignoring any applied ink effects, and placing it on top of all other sprites regardless of channel placement.

continues on next page

This option can improve playback performance.If you deselect this option, Director first loads the Flash movie sprite into memory along with all the other sprites, applies ink effects, and takes channel order into account before displaying it.

7. Choose a Quality setting (**Figure 4.81**).

   Choose High to play the Flash movie with anti-aliasing turned on, which slows playback.

   Choose Low to turn off anti-aliasing during playback.

   Choose Auto-High to start playing with anti-aliasing on but then to turn it off if Director can't meet the required tempo.

   Choose Auto-Low to start playing with anti-aliasing off but then to turn it on if Director can maintain the tempo.

8. Choose a scaling option (**Figure 4.82**).

   - Choose Show All to maintain the Flash movie's aspect ratio and fill in any gaps, if necessary, using your movie's background color.
   - Choose No Border to preserve the aspect ratio by cropping borders.
   - Choose Exact Fit to stretch the Flash movie to fit the sprite dimensions.
   - Choose Auto-Size to make the Flash sprite's bounding box fit a rotated, flipped, or skewed movie.
   - Choose No Scale to place the sprite on the stage without scaling.

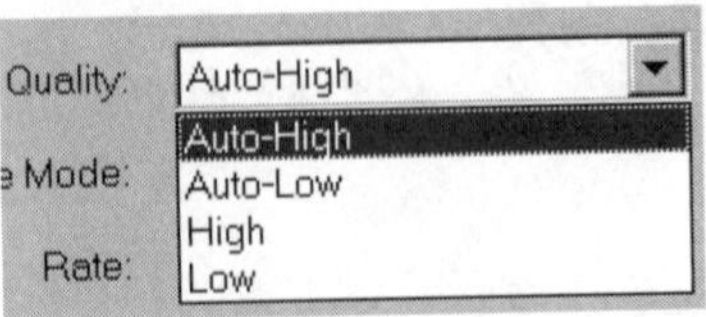

Figure 4.81 The Quality pop-up menu.

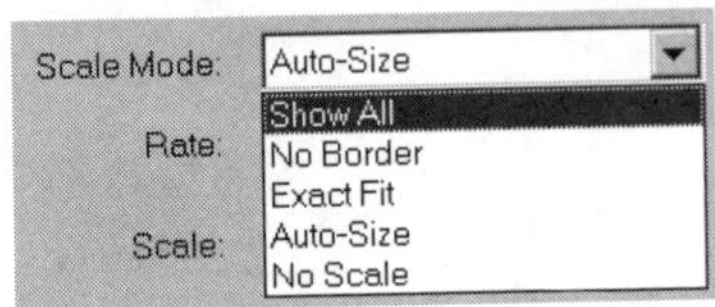

Figure 4.82 The Scale Mode pop-up menu.

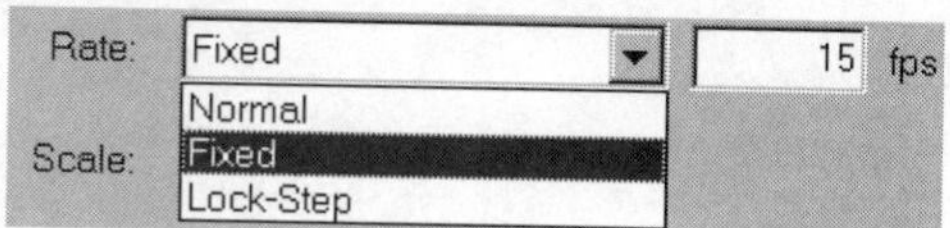

Figure 4.83 The Rate pop-up menu.

Figure 4.84 Enter a scaling value. The default value is 100 percent

9. Choose a playback rate for the Flash movie from the Rate pop-up menu (**Figure 4.83**).
   - Choose Normal to play the Flash movie at its original tempo.
   - Choose Fixed to play it at a rate that you enter. (Director tries to keep up but may not if the rate is too fast.)
   - Choose Lock-Step to play at a rate of one frame for every Director frame.
10. Enter a scaling value (**Figure 4.84**).
11. Click OK

✔ Tips

- If you need more precise control of how a Flash movie plays back, such as changing the frame rate on the fly or displaying a specific frame in the movie, use Lingo to control the many Flash movie properties. (choose Help > Director Help and type "flash movies" in the index for more details.)
- A Flash movie plays only when its sprite is in the score. To loop a Flash sprite, extend it through all the frames.
- Only the Copy, Transparent, Background Transparent, and Blend ink effects work with a Flash sprite.

5 Playing & Refining Movies

While producing a Director movie, you repeatedly play back the movie to check results and make improvements. In this chapter you learn how to use the Control Panel to play back a movie in different ways.

This chapter also covers *tempo*—how fast the frames play back. You'll learn how to set tempo in the tempo channel and how to test playback speed on different computers to compare performance with the assigned tempo.

When you play a movie, you'll inevitably notice places where the scenes jump too abruptly from one to another. That's a place to choose a scene transition effect, also explained in this chapter. *Transitions* range from simple wipes (a new frame slides in from one side to replace the original frame) and dissolves (one frame melts into another) to more elaborate effects.

Using the Control Panel

Director includes a set of buttons called the Control Panel that behaves much like the controls for a videotape or audiotape player (**Figure 5.1**). With the Control Panel, you can play and rewind, or step forward and step backward through the frames of your movie. The Control Panel also allows you to adjust volume and set loop playback.

Because you play and rewind a movie repeatedly, the tasks in this section include keyboard shortcuts. You may want to learn these keyboard shortcuts right away.

Figure 5.1 Play back movies, set tempo and volume, and specify looping with the Control Panel.

Figure 5.2 Click the Rewind button to return to the start of a movie.

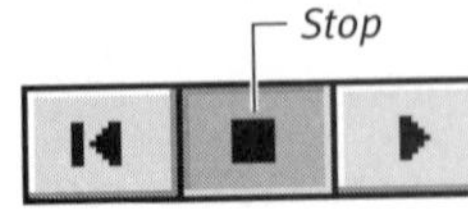

Figure 5.3 The Stop button halts the playback of a movie.

To open the Control Panel:

- Choose Window > Control Panel.

  or

  Press Control+2 (Command+2 for Mac).

To rewind the movie to frame 1:

1. Open the Control Panel.
2. Click the Rewind button (**Figure 5.2**).

   or

   Press Control+Alt+R (Command+Option+R for Mac).

   This resets the movie to frame 1. Clicking Rewind during playback stops the movie and rewinds to frame 1.

To stop playback:

1. Open the Control Panel, if necessary.
2. Click the Stop button (**Figure 5.3**).

   or

   Press Control+period (Command+period for Mac).

Figure 5.4 Click the Play button to start playback.

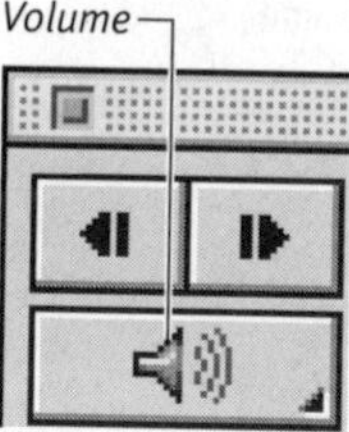

Figure 5.5 Set the sound level for a movie with the Volume button.

Figure 5.6 Click to move ahead one frame at a time, or hold down to step forward continuously.

To start playback:

1. Open the Control Panel, if necessary.
2. Click the Play button (**Figure 5.4**).

   or

   Press Control+Alt+P (Command+Option+P for Mac).

To set the volume of your movie:

1. In the Control Panel, click the Volume button (**Figure 5.5**).
2. Select a volume level from the pop-up menu.

   Setting the volume in the Control Panel determines the sound level for an entire movie.

Sometimes you need to walk through a scene one frame at a time.

To step through a movie:

1. Select a frame to start.
2. Open the Control Panel.
3. Click the Step Forward button to move forward one frame at a time (**Figure 5.6**). Hold down the mouse button to step forward continuously.

   or

   Press Control+Alt+Right Arrow (Command+Option+Right Arrow for Mac) to step the movie forward one frame.

✔ Tip

- When a score channel is in step-recording mode, click the Step Forward button to copy the contents of the current frame to the next frame.

To step backward:

1. Select a frame to start.
2. Open the Control Panel.
3. Click the Step Backward button to move back one frame at a time (**Figure 5.7**). Hold down the mouse button to go backward continuously.

   or

   Press Control+Alt+Left Arrow (Command+Option+Left Arrow for Mac) to go back one frame.

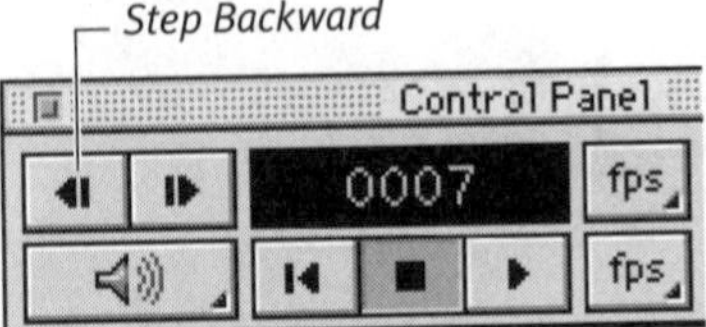

Figure 5.7 Click to move back one frame at a time, or hold down to step back continuously.

Looping playback sets a movie to play repeatedly. It automatically starts over from frame 1 each time it reaches the last frame. By default, movies are set to loop (**Figure 5.8**).

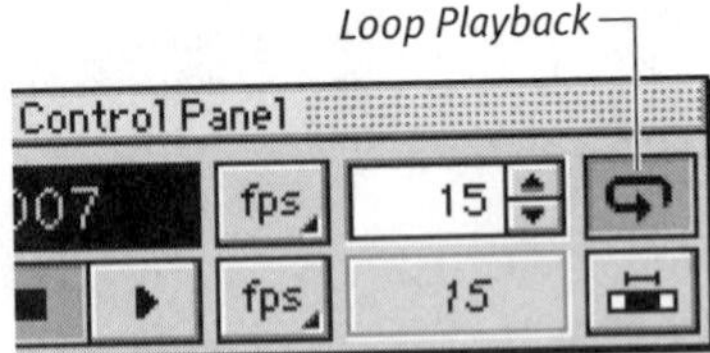

Figure 5.8 Until you turn off looping, all movies are set to repeat when they end.

To stop/start loop playback:

1. Open the Control Panel.
2. Click the Loop Playback button to toggle looping off or on (**Figure 5.9**).

   The current movie will loop or stop looping, depending on what state you started in.

Loop enabled (default) *Loop disabled*

Figure 5.9 The Loop Playback button changes to show whether looping is turned on or off.

✔ Tip

- Toggle looping with this keyboard shortcut: Control+Alt+L (Command+Option+L for Mac).

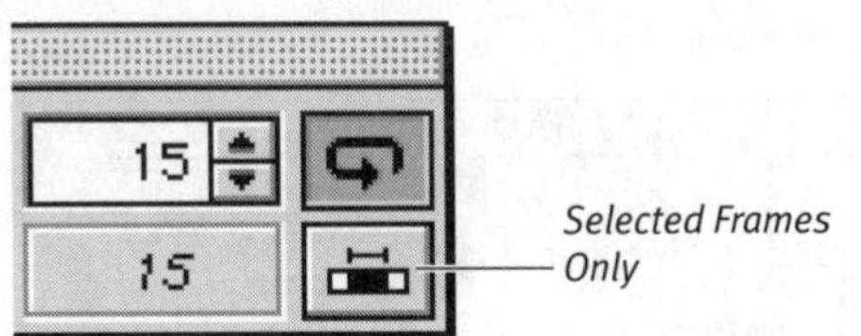

Figure 5.10 Set playback for only part of the movie.

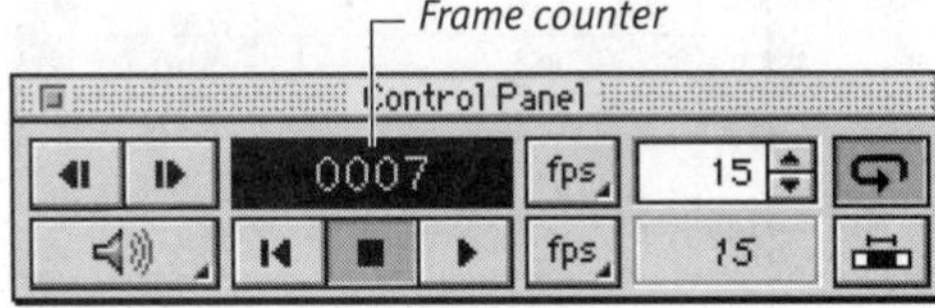

Figure 5.11 The frame counter shows the current frame number.

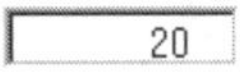

20

Figure 5.12 Type the number of the frame you want to view.

When you're troubleshooting a movie, you often need to play back just a portion of the movie.

To play only part of a movie:

1. Open the score.
2. Select the frames you want to play.
3. Open the Control Panel.
4. Click the Selected Frames Only button (**Figure 5.10**).

   A green bar appears in the score above the selected frames.
5. Click the Play button.

   Only the marked frames play.
6. When you finish viewing the movie segment, click the Selected Frames Only button again to remove the green bar and turn off the selection.

Sometimes the quickest way to reach a place in a movie is to go to its frame address.

To jump to a specific frame:

1. Open the Control Panel.
2. Double-click the number displayed in the frame counter (**Figure 5.11**).

   The frame counter tells you which frame of a movie is currently displayed on the stage and where the playback head rests in the score.
3. Type the number for the frame you want to view (**Figure 5.12**).

Setting Movie Tempo

Director plays your movie at a particular tempo, or speed, which you can easily adjust. The movie's tempo is measured in *frames per second* (fps). The higher the tempo rate (15 fps, 24 fps, 30 fps, and so on), the faster Director plays back animation. With a high tempo (say, 60 fps), you can make sprites zoom across the stage; you can use a low tempo to create a slow-motion effect.

The fastest theoretical tempo Director 8 supports is 999 frames per second, though it's unlikely any movie could actually play at this rate.

You can apply one tempo to an entire movie, or you can vary the tempo frame by frame. You set a movie's tempo in the tempo channel of Director's score (**Figure 5.13**).

The tempo you set affects the speed at which cast-member sprites are animated on stage; it does not affect the playback rate of sounds or digital videos.

You may set a high tempo in a movie, but the computer running it must be powerful enough to keep up with the specified pace. A complex scene —for example, one with many animated sprites, special ink effects, 24-bit or 32-bit color cast members, complex transitions, or color-palette manipulation—may slow playback. In this case, you must settle for this slow playback speed, buy a faster computer, or redesign the movie's scene so that it is less demanding.

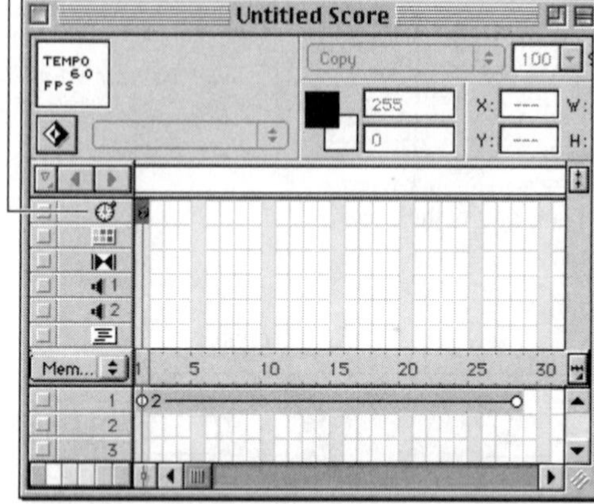

Figure 5.13 The tempo channel is marked with a stopwatch symbol.

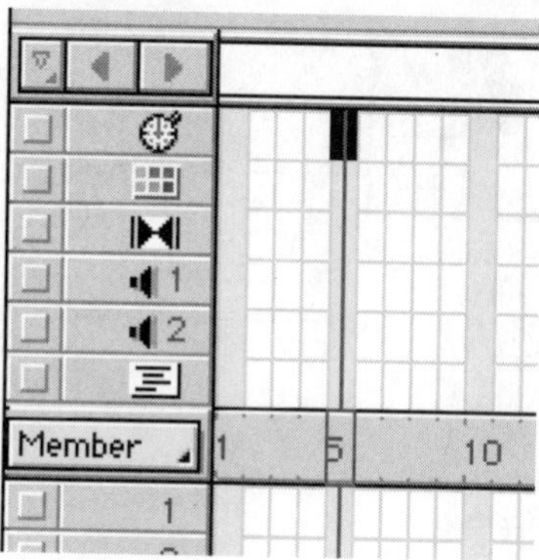

Figure 5.14 Select a cell for a new tempo.

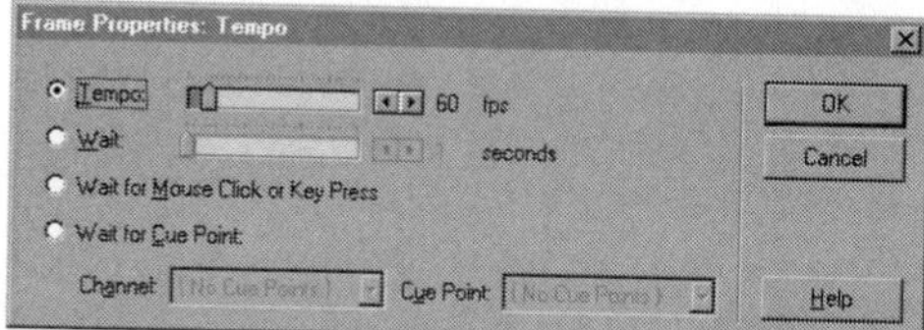

Figure 5.15 The Frame Properties: Tempo dialog box.

Figure 5.16 Drag the Tempo slider or click the arrows to set a new tempo.

When you set a new tempo in the tempo channel, that tempo applies to all the following frames of your movie (until you set another tempo change).

To set a new movie tempo:

1. Open the score.
2. In the tempo channel, select a cell for the new tempo (**Figure 5.14**).
3. Choose Modify > Frame > Tempo.
   The Frame Properties: Tempo dialog box opens (**Figure 5.15**).
4. In the dialog box, click the Tempo button and slide the Tempo scroll bar to set the movie's tempo in frames per second (**Figure 5.16**).
5. Click OK.
   Director uses the new tempo from the selected frame until it reaches a different tempo setting in the tempo channel.

✔ Tips

- You can select a cell and open the dialog box in one move by double-clicking the cell in the tempo channel.
- If you expect your movie to play on a variety of computer models, try to set a tempo that even low-end systems will be able to keep up with. Otherwise, owners of low-end computers may be disappointed by your movie's performance. The best way to test how well a particular computer will play your movie is to play it on that machine and compare the movie's target tempo with its actual playback tempo.

Comparing Target Tempo with Actual Tempo

Director tries to play a movie at the tempo you've set in the tempo channel, which functions as the *target tempo*, or the maximum tempo. The actual playback speed may fall short when the movie includes complex animation. If you plan to run your movie on a wide range of systems, comparing the set tempo with the actual tempo (**Figure 5.17**) on a slower computer allows you to set appropriate tempo values for the frames, so that the actual tempo never falls below the set tempo.

To compare the set tempo with the actual tempo:

1. Open the Control Panel.
2. Rewind the movie to the first frame.
3. Click the Step Forward button (**Figure 5.18**).
4. Compare the tempo and actual-tempo displays (**Figure 5.19**).

   The actual-tempo value is how fast the computer managed to play back the given frame. The tempo setting shows the target frame rate you set in the tempo channel for the given frame. If no tempo setting has been made for a frame, Director displays a default tempo.
5. Use the arrows to adjust the tempo for any frames, if necessary.

   The effect is the same as setting a tempo for a frame in the tempo channel.

✔ Tip

- A tempo you set in the tempo channel overrides any value you set in the control panel's tempo display.

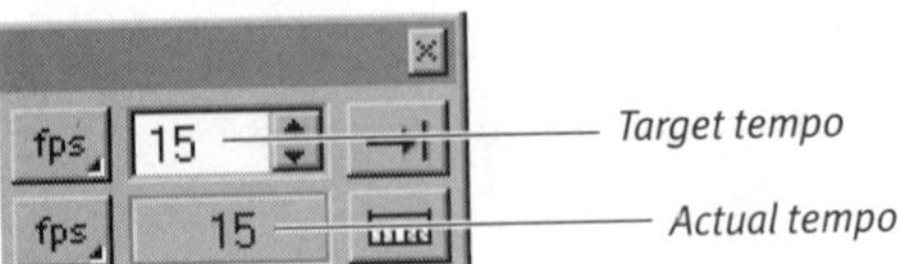

Figure 5.17 The Control Panel shows both the target tempo and the actual tempo.

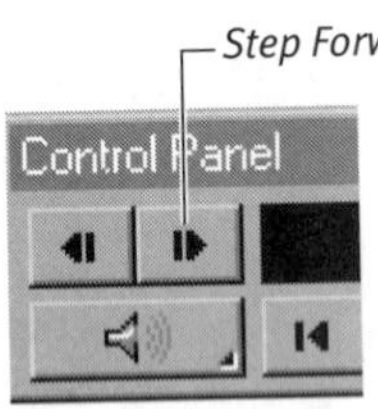

Figure 5.18 Rewind and then click the Step Forward button.

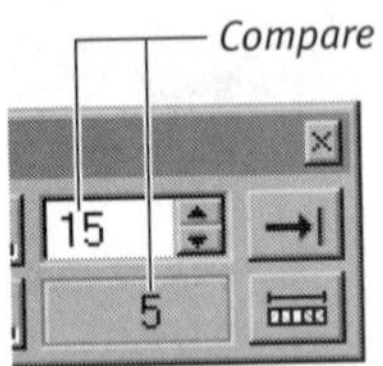

Figure 5.19 Actual and target tempo displays may show discrepancies when you step through a movie.

Figure 5.20 Open the pop-up menu to reset the units for the tempo display.

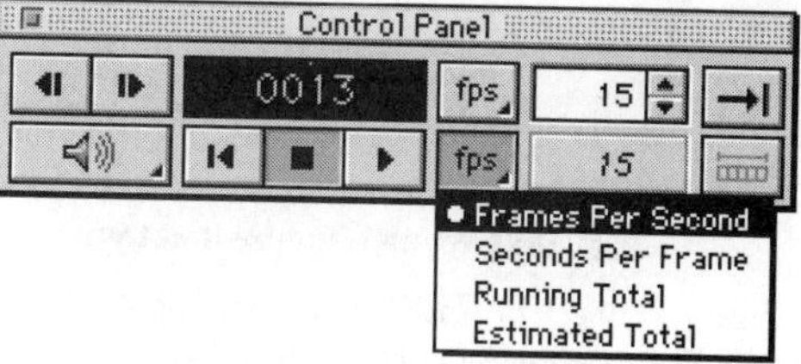

Figure 5.21 Open the pop-up menu to reset the mode for the actual-tempo display.

You can choose to view the tempo in frames per second (fps) or seconds per frame (spf).

To change the target-tempo units:

1. Open the Control Panel.
2. Use the tempo mode pop-up menu (**Figure 5.20**) to choose frames per second or seconds per frame.

You can also choose one of four options for the actual-tempo display. In addition to frames per second and seconds per frame, you have two other choices.

To change actual-tempo display:

1. Open the Control Panel.
2. Use the actual-tempo pop-up menu (**Figure 5.21**) to choose an option.

   Your choices are Frames Per Second, Seconds Per Frame, Running Total, and Estimated Total.

   - Running Total indicates the total elapsed time, in seconds, from the start of your movie to the current frame.
   - Estimated Total is similar to Running Total but is more accurate because it includes palette changes and transitions in its calculation of the frames' length.

✔ Tip

- Don't leave your actual-tempo display in Estimated Total mode; this mode may reduce the playback speed due to its more-intensive calculations.

Locking Playback Speed

When you've determined the proper tempo for your movie, you can lock that speed so that it's used by whatever computer your movie happens to play on. Doing so guards against a movie being played too fast on an advanced system but does not prevent the movie from playing back slower on a less-powerful computer. If you're trying to set the movie's tempo to play successfully on even low-end computers, first establish a tempo that those computers can keep up with; then lock that tempo.

To lock playback speed:

1. Set the tempo for the frames of your movie.
2. Open the Control Panel.
3. Rewind and then play back your movie from beginning to end (**Figure 5.22**).

   Director records the actual speed at which it plays each frame and stores these values in the Actual Tempo display in the Control Panel. If the movie branches off into multiple segments (in an interactive presentation, for example), make sure you play through all these segments.
4. Choose Modify > Movie > Playback.

   The Movie Playback Properties dialog box appears.
5. In the dialog box, check the Lock Frame Durations option and click OK (**Figure 5.23**).

   Each frame is now locked to play at the actual speed recorded when the movie was played back.
6. To unlock the movie's playback speed, reopen the dialog box, uncheck the Lock Frames Duration checkbox, and click OK.

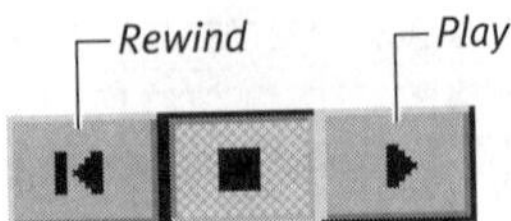

Figure 5.22 Rewind and play a movie to record the playback speeds it contains.

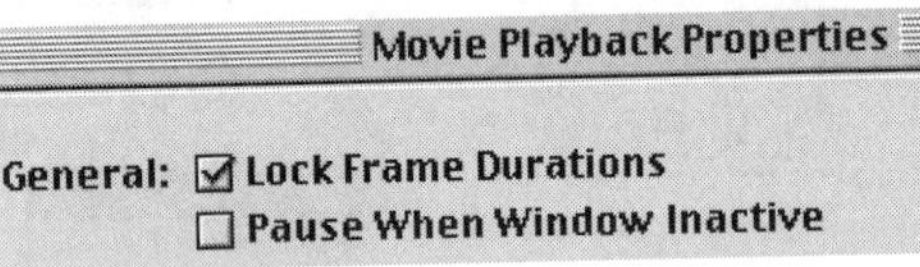

Figure 5.23 Check the Lock Frame Durations checkbox in the Movie Playback Properties dialog box.

Figure 5.24 Wait options for pauses in a movie.

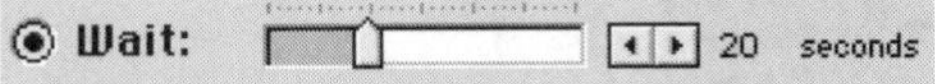

Figure 5.25 Set the length for the pause by dragging the slider or clicking the arrows.

Figure 5.26 Select the second Wait option to pause until the user either clicks the mouse or presses a key.

Figure 5.27 The Wait for Cue Point option pauses your movie until a specified cue point is reached.

Setting Pauses in a Movie

You can use the tempo channel to create a pause in the playback of a movie. You can pause a movie for a specified number of seconds, create a pause until a mouse click or key press occurs, or set a pause that waits for a cue point to be reached in a specified channel.

To set a pause in a movie:

1. In the tempo channel, select a frame for the pause.
2. Choose Modify > Frame > Tempo.
   The Frame Properties: Tempo dialog box appears.
3. In the dialog box, select a wait option (**Figure 5.24**).
   - Select the first Wait option if you are creating a timed pause. Then use the adjacent slider to specify the duration in seconds (**Figure 5.25**).
   - Select the Wait for Mouse Click or Key Press option for your movie to remain paused until the mouse or a key is pressed (**Figure 5.26**).
   - To pause a movie until a specific cue point is reached in a sound or a digital video, select the Wait for Cue Point option (**Figure 5.27**). Use the channel pop-up menu to select the channel of the cue sound or digital video. Then use the Cue Point pop-up menu to select a cue point in the chosen channel.
4. Click OK.

✔ Tip

- If you create a pause that waits for a cue point in a sound or digital video, make sure that the sound or video clip begins playing before the frame where the pause takes place.

Using Scene Transitions

Director offers more than 50 special effects transitions—such as dissolves, wipes, and fades—that you can use to move smoothly from one scene in a Director movie to another. Without transitions, scenes cut abruptly from one to another, often creating a jarring effect for the viewer.

Director features too many transition types to attempt to describe here, and in any case, you'll best understand the differences among them by trying them out. Experiment with the different transition types before selecting one for your scene. You can even create a sample movie that includes the transitions you want to test.

You place transitions in the transition channel of Director's score, at the frame where you want the transition to occur.

To set a transition:

1. Open the score.
2. In the transition channel, select a cell for the transition (**Figure 5.28**).

   The transition begins between the frame that you select and the frame that precedes it. To transition between two scenes, you set the transition at the first frame of the second scene, not the last frame of the first scene.
3. Choose Modify > Frame > Transition, or double-click the cell selected in the transition channel.

   The Frame Properties: Transition dialog box opens (**Figure 5.29**).
4. In the dialog box, scroll through the transitions to find a suitable transition.

   Each transition has a descriptive name.
5. Click a transition to apply (**Figure 5.30**).

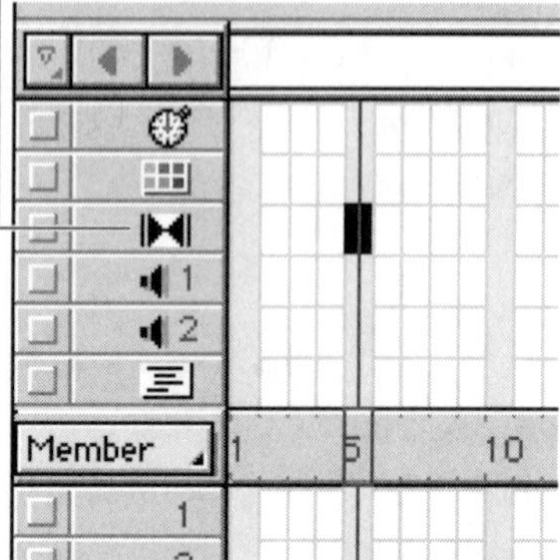

Figure 5.28 Select a cell in the transition channel.

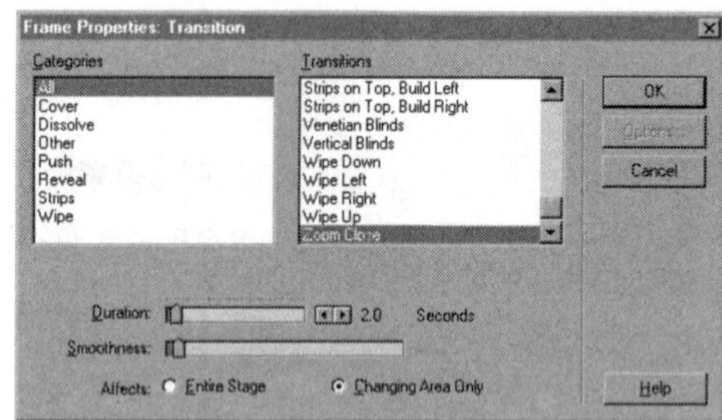

Figure 5.29 The Frame Transitions dialog box lists categories of transitions on the left. When you select a category, the transitions in the category appear in the list on the right.

Figure 5.30 Select a transition.

Figure 5.31 Choose an area for the transition.

Figure 5.32 Drag the slider or click the arrows to set a length for the transition.

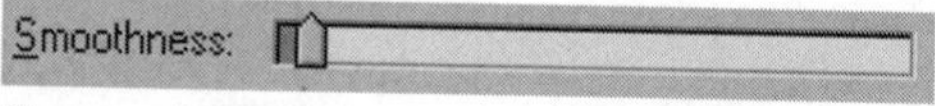

Figure 5.33 Drag to set the transition smoothness.

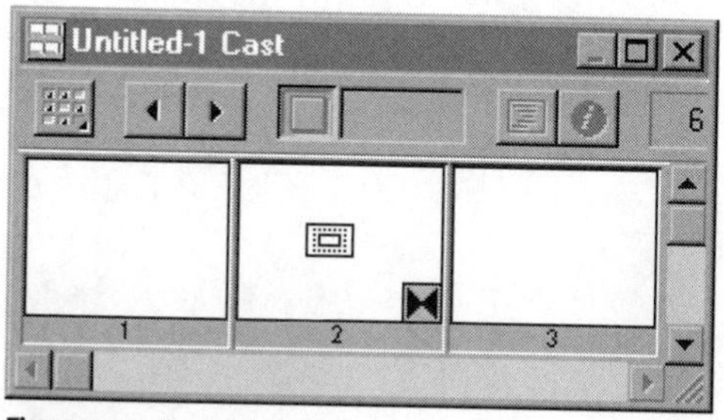

Figure 5.34 Transition cast members have an icon that looks like a bow tie.

6. Specify where on the stage to apply the transition (**Figure 5.31**).

   Choose the Entire Stage option to apply the transition to all of Director's stage.

   Choose the Changing Area Only option to apply the transition only to areas of the stage that change in the switch between scenes (in other words, where sprites are present but then are not, or vice versa).

7. Set the transition duration with the slider (**Figure 5.32**).

8. Drag the Smoothness slider to set how gradual or abrupt the transition is (**Figure 5.33**).

   Director measures smoothness by how big a chunk of the stage (size in pixels) changes during the transition.

9. Click OK.

   The transition goes into the active Cast window as a transition cast member (**Figure 5.34**).

If you don't find exactly the transition you want within Director, you can add new transitions by installing them as Xtras.

To add Xtra transitions to Director:

1. Install a transition by copying the Xtra transition file to the Xtras folder inside the Director program folder. (Also see Chapter 15, "Using Xtras")

2. In the score, double-click a cell in the transition channel where you want to apply the transition.

3. In the dialog box that opens, find and select the Xtra transition.

   Xtras transitions show up in the dialog box with a special icon.

4. Click OK.

6

USING PAINT TOOLS

Figure 6.1 The Paint window with the tool palette and without rulers.

Director includes a simple paint program that make it easy for you to create and edit bitmapped cast members without having to open another program, such as Adobe Photoshop. All the painting and editing takes place in the Paint window (**Figure 6.1**). Every new image you create in the Paint window becomes a cast member.

In addition to tools that probably will seem familiar to anyone who has used any other paint program (**Figure 6.2**), Director includes an important animation tool: onionskinning. This unique painting feature speeds the creation of a sequence of images for animation (see "Onion Skinning" later in this chapter).

In addition to its own tools, Director can use image filters from Photoshop or Premiere to modify bitmapped cast members in the Paint window (see "Applying Image Filters" later in this chapter).

✔ Tips

- Everything in this chapter takes place in the Paint window.
- When using the Rectangle or Ellipse tool, hold down the Shift key to constrain the shape to either a square or circle. Also, when using the Arc and Line tools, you can hold down the Shift key to constrain a line to 45-degree increments.

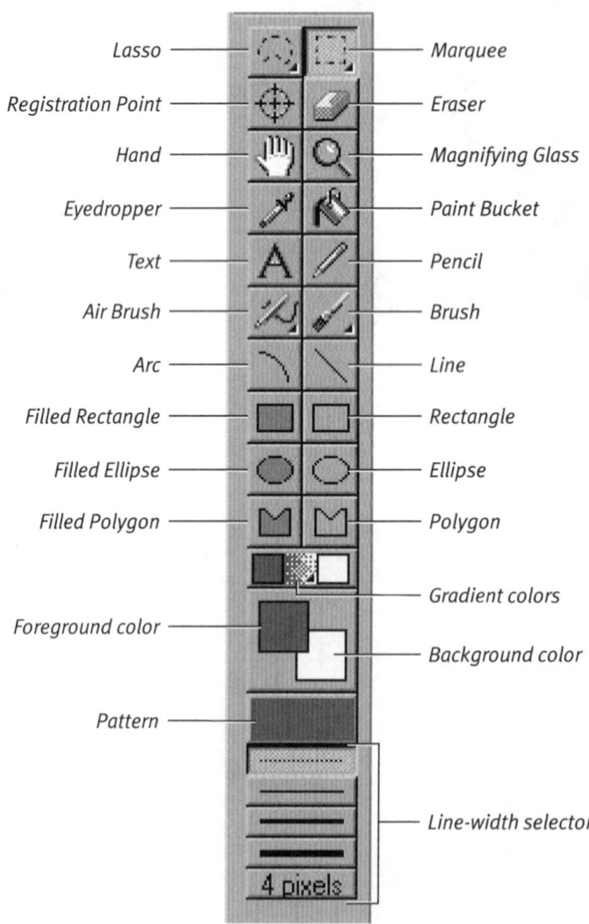

Figure 6.2 The Paint window tool palette.

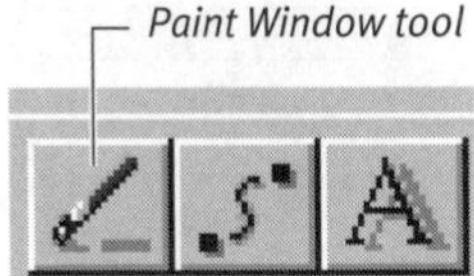

Figure 6.3 Open the Paint window by clicking its tool in the main toolbar.

Figure 6.4 An image in the Paint window becomes a cast member.

Figure 6.5 Drag the Place button from the Paint window to the stage to place the current image there.

Getting Started

Before you start creating images in the Paint window, you have a few things to set up and a few basics to learn.

To start, you need to open the Paint window, where all the work in this chapter takes place. When you have the Paint window open, you can find out how to create cast members there and how to add them to the score.

To open the Paint window:

1. Choose Window > Paint.

   or

2. Click the Paint Window tool in the main toolbar (**Figure 6.3**).

To add a cast member from the Paint window:

1. Click the New Cast Member button to create a new cast member (**Figure 6.4**).
2. Create an image.
3. Close the Paint window.
   Director puts the image you draw in the first available position in the Cast window.

To place a graphic on the stage from the Paint window:

1. Open the Paint window.
2. Create or open an image.
3. Drag the Place button (**Figure 6.5**) onto the stage.
   Director places the image from the Paint window on the stage and in the score.

You can display a set of horizontal and vertical rulers in the Paint window (**Figure 6.6**) to help you align and measure your artwork. The rulers can display measurement values in inches, centimeters, or pixels.

To show or hide rulers:

1. Open the Paint window.
2. Choose View > Ruler.

   To hide the ruler, choose the command again.

✔ Tips

- You can also press Ctrl+Shift+Alt+R to toggle the Ruler (Press Command+Shift+Option+R on Mac).
- You can set a ruler's zero points by dragging anywhere within the horizontal or vertical ruler space to the point where you want the new zero point to be.
- To display the ruler's measurements in a new unit (inches, centimeters, and so on), click the top-left corner where the horizontal and vertical rulers meet (**Figure 6.7**).

If you need more work space in the Paint window, you can hide the tool palette, as shown in **Figure 6.6**.

To show or hide the paint tool palette:

1. Select the paint tool you want to use.
2. Choose View > Paint Tools to hide the paint tool palette or press Ctrl+Shift+H (Command+Shift+H on Mac).

   Choose the command again to restore the tool palette to view.

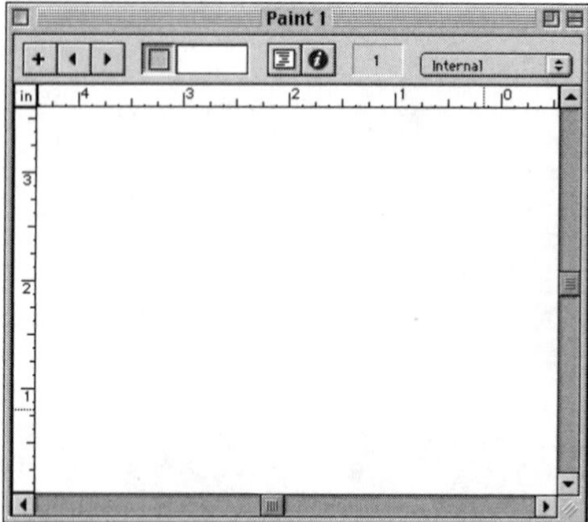

Figure 6.6 Horizontal and vertical rulers can border the Paint window, if you prefer. This window has no tool palette visible.

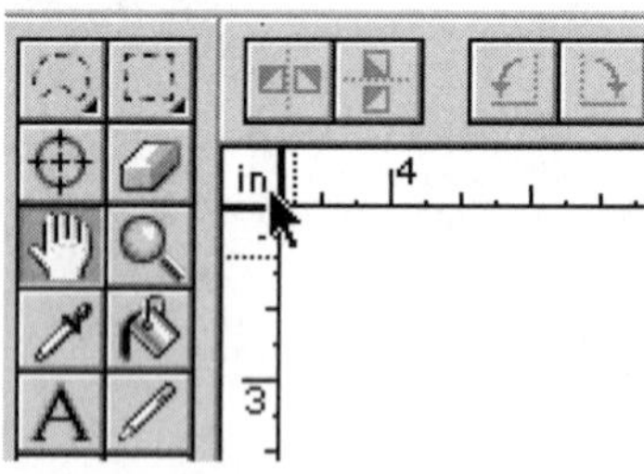

Figure 6.7 Click the box where the rulers intersect to change the unit of measurement.

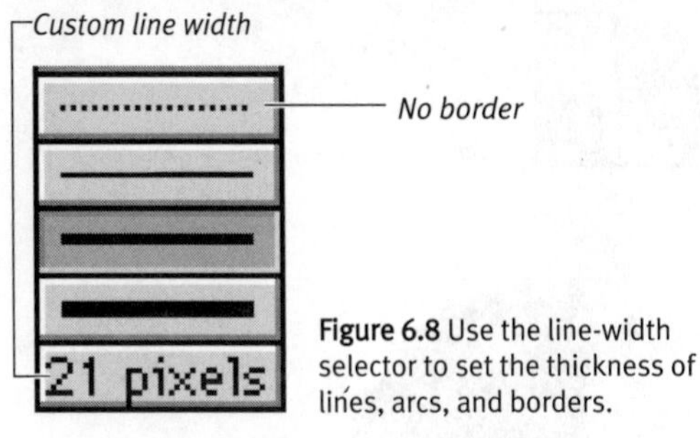

Figure 6.8 Use the line-width selector to set the thickness of lines, arcs, and borders.

Figure 6.9 Create a custom line thickness by dragging the slider in the Paint Preferences dialog box.

You can change the width of a line or border drawn by the Paint window's Line, Rectangle, Arc, Ellipse, and Polygon tools.

To set the width of a line or shape's outline:

1. In the paint tool palette, click a line style in the line-width selector (**Figure 6.8**).
2. Choose the dotted-line item in the selector to draw filled shapes with no border.
3. In the paint tool palette, select one of the following tools: Line, Rectangle, Arc, Ellipse, or Polygon.

   When you draw with the tool, it will use the line thickness you just selected.

To create a custom line width:

1. Choose File > Preferences > Paint to display the Paint Window Preferences dialog box.
2. Use the "Other" Line Width slider or the increase/decrease arrows at the center of the dialog box to set the line thickness (**Figure 6.9**).
3. Choose the custom selection in the Line Width Selector.

✔ Tip

- Double-click the custom selection in the Line Width Selector to open the Paint Preferences dialog box.

Selecting and Moving Images

Like most paint programs, Director's Paint window features selection tools that allow you to select all or just parts of cast-member artwork. Selection is almost always the first step of any operation. First, you select the image or a portion of it and then you do something to it—move it to another region of the Paint window, cut or copy it, rotate it, change its colors, warp it, and so on.

Lasso and Marquee Tools

A selection rectangle called the Marquee selects everything within its bounds. The Lasso, on the other hand, allows you to make a selection of any shape. Some of Director's paint features work only with artwork selected by one of the two selection tools; make sure that you follow the selection instructions in the tasks later in this chapter.

To select with the Marquee:

1. Click the Marquee tool in the tool palette (**Figure 6.10**).

   The pointer becomes a crosshair pointer.

2. Position the crosshair pointer at one corner of your selection.

3. Hold down the mouse button and move the pointer diagonally to the opposite corner to create a selection box around the artwork (**Figure 6.11**).

   A dotted rectangle called a *marquee* appears as you drag.

4. Release the mouse button when the marquee encloses what you want to select.

✔ Tip

- Double-click the Marquee tool to select the entire visible portion of the Paint window.

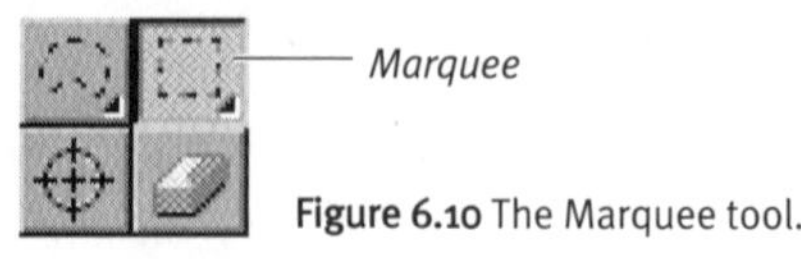

Figure 6.10 The Marquee tool.

Figure 6.11 Drag diagonally to make a rectangular selection.

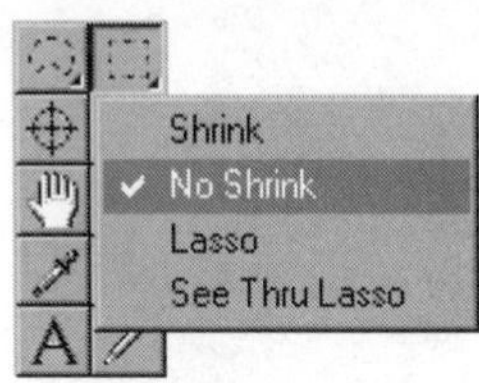

Figure 6.12 Open the Marquee tool's Options pop-up menu.

Shrink

No Shrink

Lasso

Figure 6.13 The first three Marquee tool options.

You can control how the Marquee behaves as you use it to select artwork.

To choose Marquee tool options:

1. Click the Marquee tool and hold down the mouse button until the Options pop-up menu appears (**Figure 6.12**).
2. Drag to select one of the four options.
3. Your choices are Shrink, No Shrink, Lasso, and See Thru Lasso (**Figure 6.13**).
   - **Shrink** makes the rectangular selection marquee tighten around whatever object you've selected.
   - **No Shrink** leaves the selection exactly as you draw it.
   - **Lasso** makes the selection marquee tighten around whatever object you've selected, as though you had used the Lasso tool.
   - **See Thru Lasso** is similar to the Lasso option, but it makes all white pixels in the selection transparent.

To select with the Lasso tool:

1. Click the Lasso tool (**Figure 6.14**).
2. Position the Lasso wherever you want to begin your selection.
3. Hold down the mouse button and move the Lasso to draw a line around the art you want to select (**Figure 6.15**).
4. Try to end the selection at the point where you started it.
5. Release the mouse button.

   Director highlights the selected area.

   If you did not entirely enclose your selection, Director automatically connects its starting and ending points.

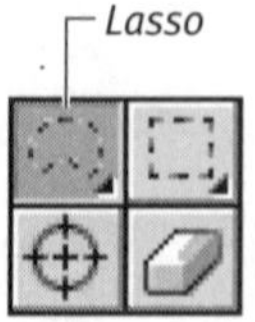

Figure 6.14 Use the Lasso tool to select irregular shapes.

Figure 6.15 Drag the Lasso around your selection.

✔ Tip

- You can use the Lasso tool to select a polygon. Hold down the Alt key (Windows) or Option key (Mac) while dragging the Lasso to create an anchor point and draw a straight selection line. Add line segments to encase the artwork. Double-click to end your selection.

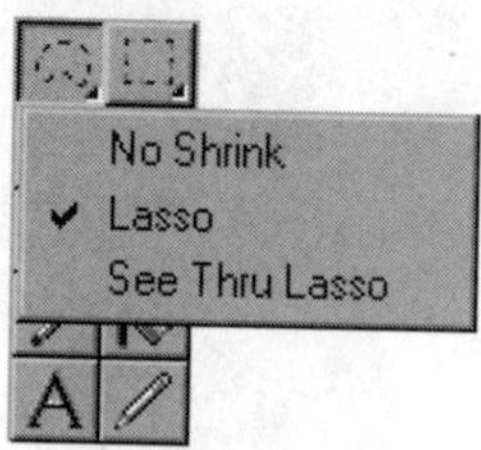

Figure 6.16 Open the Lasso tool's Options pop-up menu.

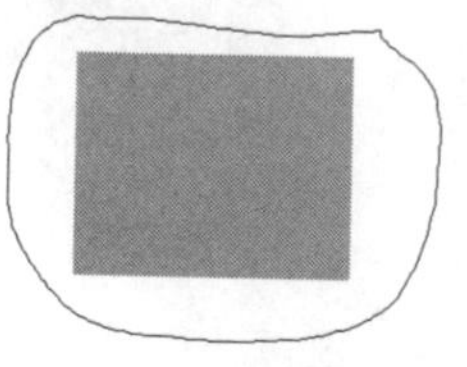

No Shrink *Shrink*

Figure 6.17 The No Shrink Lasso tool selection option.

Figure 6.18 Drag a selection to move it.

You can control how the Lasso behaves when selecting artwork.

To choose Lasso options:

1. Click the Lasso tool and hold down the mouse button until the Options pop-up menu appears (**Figure 6.16**).
2. Select an option.
3. Your choices are No Shrink (**Figure 6.17**), Lasso, and See Thru Lasso.
   - **No Shrink** selects all the artwork that you enclose with the Lasso and does not alter the selection marquee.
   - **Lasso** makes the selection marquee tighten around whatever object you've selected. Director tries to identify an object's border by looking for color differences among pixels.
   - **See Thru Lasso** makes all the white pixels in your selection transparent.

To reposition a selection:

1. Make a selection with the Marquee or Lasso tool.
2. Drag the selection to a new location (**Figure 6.18**).

To copy a selection:

1. Select the image with the Marquee tool.
2. Hold down the Alt key (Option key for the Mac) and drag the selection to a new place.

   The original image is left in place.

Figure 6.19 Drag while holding down the Control or Command key to stretch a selection.

To stretch/compress a selection:

1. Make a selection with the Marquee tool.
2. Hold down the Control key (Windows) or Command key (Mac), click anywhere in the selection, and drag (**Figure 6.19**).

   Drag away from the center to stretch the image; drag toward the center to compress.

✔ Tip

- To stretch or compress along either the x- or y-axis, press Control+Shift (Windows) or Command+Shift (Mac) while dragging.

To erase a selection:

1. Make a selection.
2. Press the Backspace or Delete key.

Scrolling the Paint window with the Hand tool often is more convenient than using the scroll bars:

To scroll the paint window:

1. Click the Hand tool (**Figure 6.20**).
2. Drag the image in any direction.

✔ Tip

- You can press and hold down the spacebar on the keyboard to select the Hand tool momentarily. Then drag the image and release the spacebar to return to the preceding tool.

Hand tool

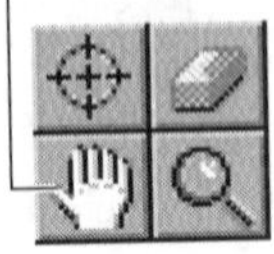

Figure 6.20 Move selections with the Hand tool.

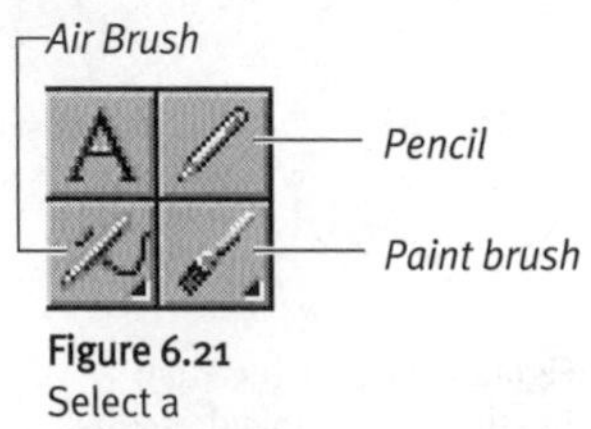

Figure 6.21 Select a painting tool.

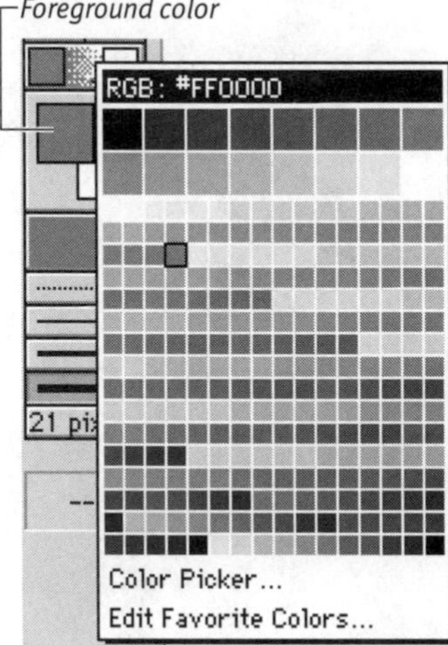

Figure 6.22 Click the Foreground color chip and make selection from the Color menu.

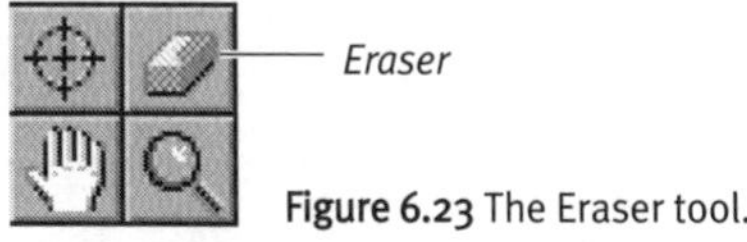

Figure 6.23 The Eraser tool.

Painting

This section shows you how to use the free-form painting tools of Director's Paint window.

To paint:

1. Select the Pencil, Paint Brush, or Air Brush tool in the paint tool palette (**Figure 6.21**).
2. Click the Foreground color chip, hold down the mouse button, and select a foreground color from the Color menu (**Figure 6.22**).
3. Drag to paint.

   The Air Brush lays down a thicker layer of its spatter pattern as you drag over the same area.

✔ Tips

- Double-click the Pencil tool to zoom in on an image at the maximum zoom level.
- You can change the Air Brush and Paint Brush shapes, but the Pencil always puts down a thin line of the selected color.

To erase:

1. Select the Eraser tool in the paint tool palette (**Figure 6.23**).
2. Drag to erase.

✔ Tip

- Double-click the Eraser tool to erase the entire contents of the Paint window.

Director's Paint Brush offers five shapes—labeled Brush 1 through Brush 5—that you can choose each time you select the Brush. You can change and customize these brush shapes in Director's Brush Settings dialog box.

To choose a Paint Brush shape:

1. Click the Paint Brush tool in the paint tool palette and hold down the mouse button.

   A pop-up menu appears, listing the brush shapes that you can choose (**Figure 6.24**).
2. Select a brush shape.

You can assign different shapes (even shapes that you have customized) to the pop-up menu, replacing the default styles.

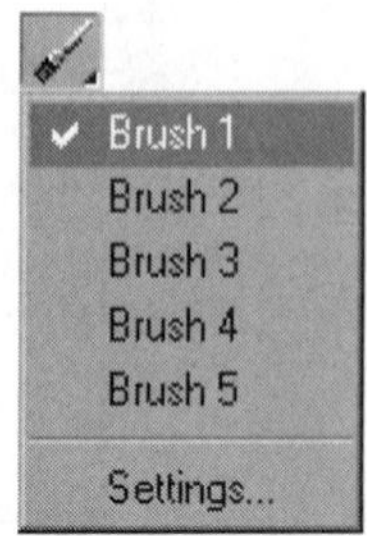

Figure 6.24 Click the Paint Brush tool and hold down the mouse button to open a pop-up menu of brush selections.

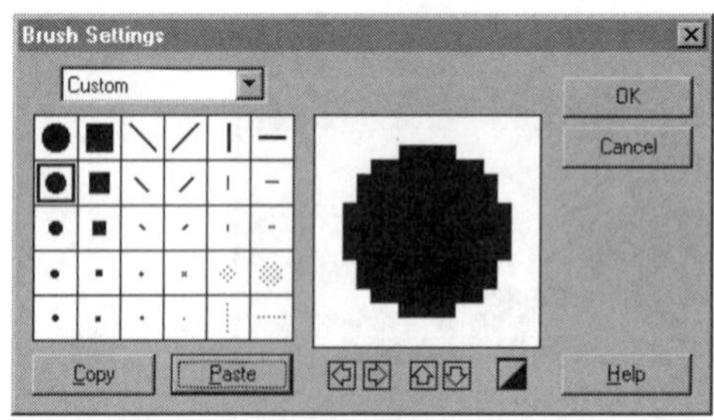

Figure 6.25 Select a new brush shape in the Brush Settings dialog box.

To change a brush shape:

1. Click the Paint Brush tool in the paint tool palette and hold down the mouse button.
2. Select the brush shape that you want to change.

   Because you can have only five choices in the menu, you must eliminate one whenever you add a choice to the menu.
3. Open the Paint Brush pop-up menu again and choose Settings.

   The Brush Settings dialog box opens.
4. Select a brush shape to add to the menu (**Figure 6.25**).
5. Click OK.

   The new brush shape takes its place in the pop-up menu.

✔ Tip

- Double-click the Paint Brush tool to open the Brush Settings dialog box.

Brush Tools: ☑ Remember Color

Figure 6.26 Choose the Remember Color option in the Paint Preferences dialog box to make Director remember which color is associated with each brush shape.

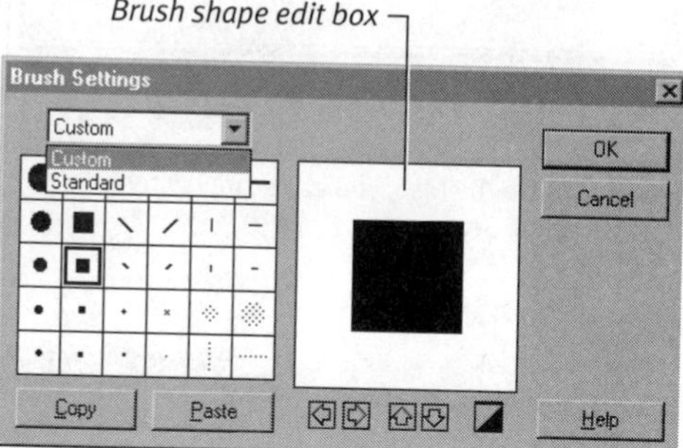

Figure 6.27 Choose Custom to begin creating a new brush shape.

You can tell Director to automatically select a particular color when you paint with a particular brush—red for Brush 1, green for Brush 2, and so on.

To assign a color to a brush:

1. Choose File > Preferences > Paint to open the Paint Preferences dialog box.
2. Check the Remember Color checkbox (**Figure 6.26**).

Although Director features a variety of Paint Brush shapes, you can design your own brush styles. You simply rearrange the pixels that make up a brush's shape.

To edit a Paint Brush shape:

1. With Director's Paint window open, double-click the Paint Brush tool to open the Brush Settings dialog box.
2. Choose Custom from the pop-up menu (**Figure 6.27**).

   Standard shapes cannot be changed.
3. Select a custom brush shape to edit.

   An enlarged version of the selected brush appears in the Brush Shape edit box.
4. In the Brush Shape edit box, click empty spaces to add pixels to the brush or click pixels to erase them.
5. Click the arrows below the edit box to move the brush within the space.
6. When you're happy with your new brush design, click OK.
7. Try out the brush and then make adjustments, if necessary.

✔ Tip

- Director lets you copy any pattern in the Paint window and use it as a brush shape. To do so, open the Brush Settings dialog box and click any pattern outside the dialog box to pick it up.

To store a set of custom brush shapes:

1. Double-click the Paint Brush tool.
2. In the Brush Settings dialog box, click Copy.
3. On the Mac: Choose Apple > Scrapbook, and then choose Edit > Paste to store the brushes in the Scrapbook (**Figure 6.28**).

   or

   In Windows: Open the Windows Clipboard Viewer and choose File > Save As to save the brush shapes (**Figure 6.29**).

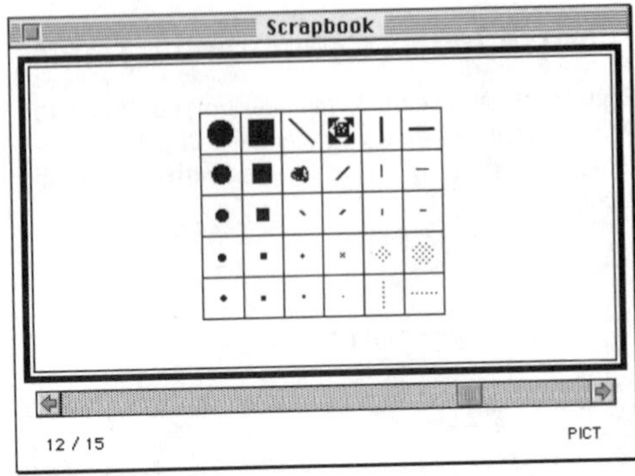

Figure 6.28 On the Mac, you can store custom brushes in the Scrapbook.

To retrieve stored custom brush shapes:

1. On the Macintosh: Open the Scrapbook, find the entry with the brush shapes, and choose Edit > Copy.

   or

   In Windows: Open the Clipboard Viewer and open the file that contains the desired brush set.
2. Return to Director's Paint window.
3. Double-click the Paint Brush tool (**Figure 6.30**) to open the Brush Settings dialog box.
4. Click Paste to install the stored brush set.

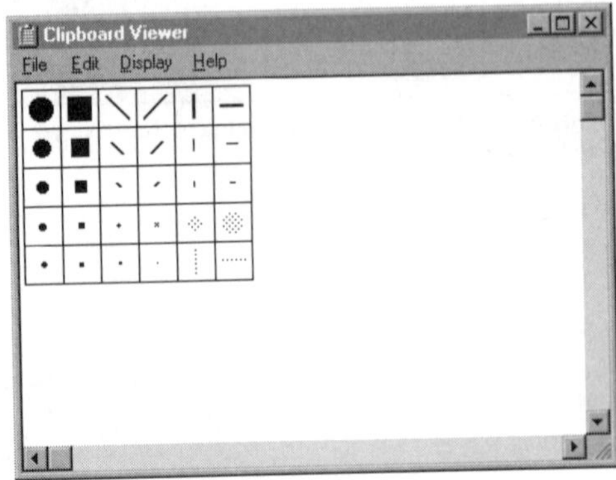

Figure 6.29 In Windows, you can store custom brushes in the Clipboard Viewer.

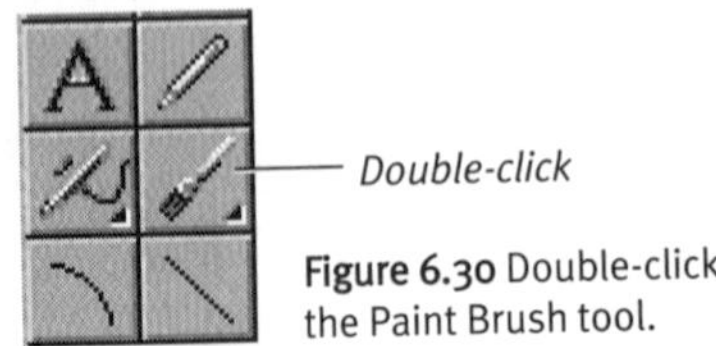

Figure 6.30 Double-click the Paint Brush tool.

PAINTING

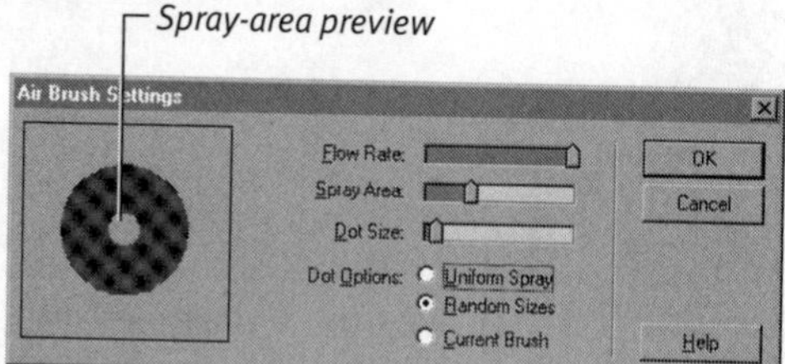

Figure 6.31 Use the Air Brush Settings dialog box to adjust the spray pattern of Air Brush, and to preview the spray area of the brush

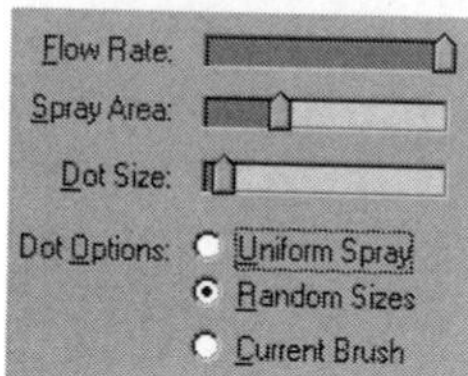

Figure 6.32 Air Brush setting controls.

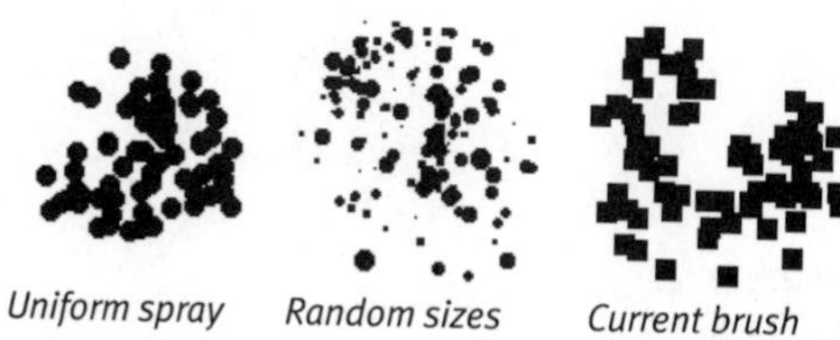

Figure 6.33 The Air Brush can spray three different types of dots.

You can adjust the size of the Air Brush's spray area, the size of the ink dots it sprays, and the speed at which it sprays them.

To adjust the Air Brush spray pattern:

1. With the Paint window open, click the Air Brush tool, hold down the mouse button, and choose Settings from the pop-up menu that appears.

   The Air Brush Settings dialog box opens (**Figure 6.31**).

2. Drag the Flow Rate slider to adjust the speed at which the Air Brush sprays the dots (**Figure 6.32**).

3. Drag the Spray Area slider to change the diameter of the Air Brush stream.

4. Drag the Dot Size slider to adjust the size of the dots the Air Brush sprays.

   As you adjust the scroll-bar values, Director displays a preview of how the new settings affect the Air Brush tool. The gray circle in the preview shows the size of the Air Brush's spray area; the light circle inside represents the size of the dots themselves.

5. Choose a dot option (**Figure 6.33**).

   The Uniform Spray setting makes dots of identical size; Random Sizes randomly varies the size of dots sprayed. The Current Brush settings cause the Air Brush to spray in the shape that's currently selected for the Paint Brush tool.

6. Click OK.

   The new Air Brush settings take effect.

Director remembers five Air Brush settings—labeled Air Brush 1 through Air Brush 5—for you to choose when you select the Air Brush tool. You can change these settings, just as you change those of the Paint Brush.

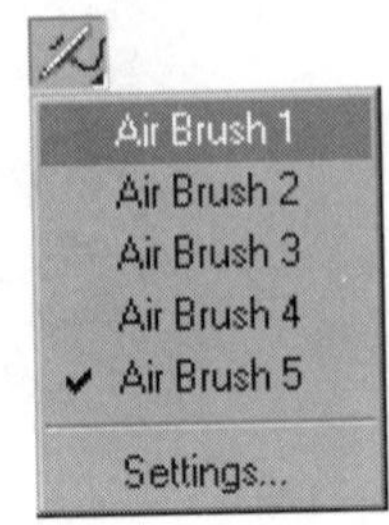

Figure 6.34 Click the Air Brush tool and hold down the mouse button to display brush choices.

To choose an Air Brush shape:

1. Click the Air Brush tool in the paint tool palette and hold down the mouse button.

   A pop-up menu appears (**Figure 6.34**), listing the five brush presets.

2. Choose a brush shape.

You can replace each of the five Air Brush settings with your own settings.

To assign a shape to a brush:

1. Open the Air Brush pop-up menu and choose a brush to change.
2. Double-click the Air Brush tool to open the Brush Settings dialog box.
3. Change the Air Brush's Flow Rate, Spray Area, and Dot Size settings as necessary.
4. Click OK.
5. Try out the new Air Brush and make adjustments, if necessary.

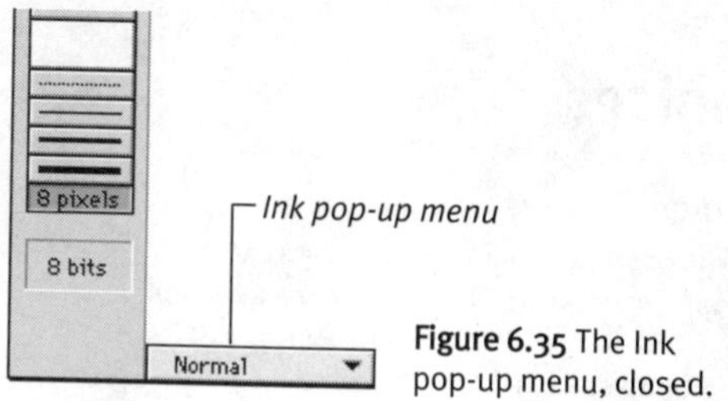

Figure 6.35 The Ink pop-up menu, closed.

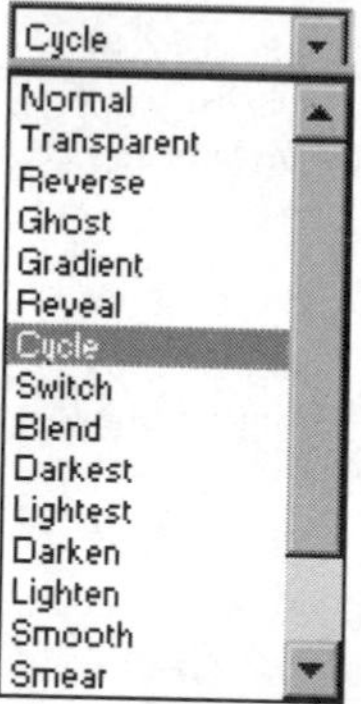

Figure 6.36 The Ink pop-up menu, open.

Using Ink Effects

Director features many ink effects that you can apply to the artwork you create in the Paint window. You can smear the edges of a cast member destined for the background of a scene, for example, or darken a foreground cast member. Applying ink effects to the cast members in the Paint window makes the effect part of any sprite based on the cast member.

You also can apply ink effects to sprites in the score, but in that case you modify only the sprite, not the original cast member, and the result may look very different. (See Chapter 3, "Building a Score," for details on how to use ink effects in the score.)

In the Paint window, you apply each effect with a specific paint tool, such as the Paint Bucket or Paint Brush.

See the sidebar "Ink Effect Choices" in this section for a description of the ink effects.

To choose an ink effect:

1. In the Paint window, select a tool in the paint tool palette for applying the ink effect.

   Director remembers which ink effect you select for a specific tool.

2. Click the Ink selector in the bottom-left corner of the Paint window (**Figure 6.35**).

   The Ink pop-up menu appears (**Figure 6.36**).

3. Choose an ink effect.

Ink Effect Choices

Normal

Normal is the default ink setting. This ink is simply the current foreground color and any selected pattern.

Transparent

Transparent ink makes the background color used in patterns transparent. When you paint with Transparent ink, you can see any artwork behind the pattern.

Reverse

Any color that you paint over using Reverse ink changes to its "mirror" color at the opposite end of the color palette. For example, a color ten spaces from the top of the palette changes to the color ten spaces from the bottom of the palette.

Ghost

Ghost ink paints with the current background color.

Gradient

Gradient allows you to paint with a blend of colors, ranging from the current foreground color to the current gradient destination color. The gradient options are set in the Gradient Settings dialog box.

Reveal

Reveal ink makes use of the previous cast member. As you paint with reveal ink, you uncover the previous cast member in its original foreground color.

Cycle

As you paint with Cycle ink, the color cycles through all the colors in the color palette between the current foreground color and destination color. Choose black and white for the foreground and gradient destination colors to cycle through the entire color palette.

Switch

As you paint with Switch ink, any pixels in the current foreground color that you paint over are changed into the gradient destination color.

Blend

Blend is a transparent ink. As you paint over your artwork, it remains visible, but its colors blend with the current foreground color. You can set the percentage of blend in the Paint Window Preferences dialog box.

Darkest

As you paint over an image with Darkest ink, Director compares the level of darkness of the foreground color to the pixels that you are painting over. If the foreground color is darker, the pixels of the image are replaced with its color.

Lightest

As you paint over an image with Lightest ink, Director replaces the pixels with the foreground color anywhere the foreground color is lighter than the pixels of the image.

Darken

Darken ink reduces the brightness of artwork as you paint over it. You can set the rate of this Ink effect in the Paint Window Preferences dialog box.

Lighten

Lighten ink increases the brightness of artwork as you paint over it.

Smooth

Smooth ink blurs artwork as you paint over it. It is useful for smoothing out jagged edges. It only has an effect on existing artwork.

Smear

Smear ink causes the paint of your artwork to spread or smear as you drag the Paint Brush across it. The smear occurs in the direction you drag the Paint Brush.

Smudge

Similar to Smear ink, except the colors fade faster as they are smudged.

Spread

Spread ink works with the Paint Brush. As you drag the brush across the artwork, the image under the brush is picked up and becomes the new shape for the Paint Brush.

Clipboard

Uses the contents of the clipboard as the pattern for your brush.

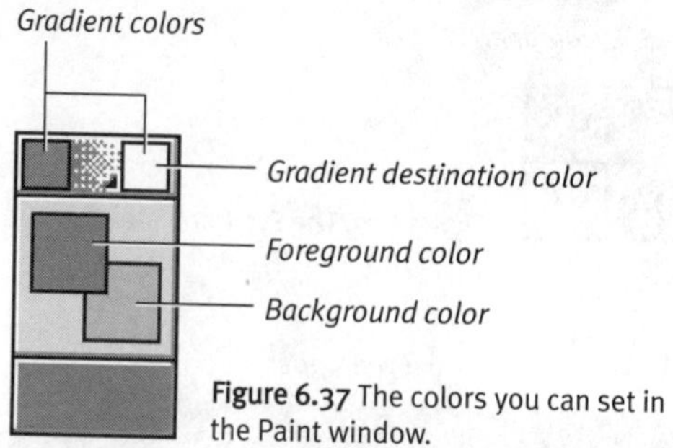

Figure 6.37 The colors you can set in the Paint window.

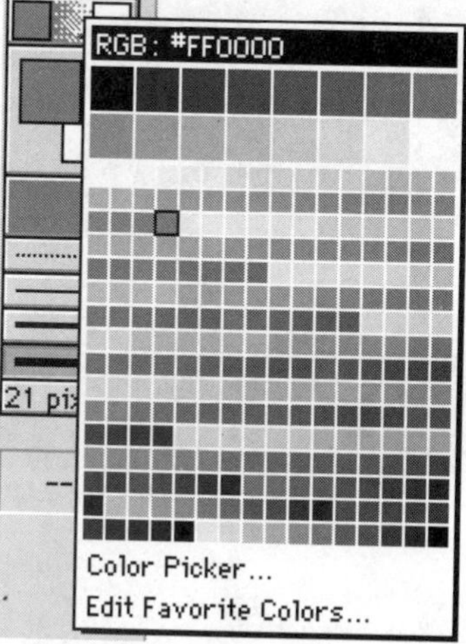

Figure 6.38 Click the Foreground, Background, or Gradient Destination color chip to open the Color menu.

Using Color and Pattern

Because color and pattern are so important in creating images for animation, Director's Paint window includes tools for controlling the color and pattern of cast members.

Color Paint Techniques

Three color specifications in the Paint window help you color your cast member artwork:

- **Foreground color**. Foreground color is Director's main color. The current foreground color serves as the default color for everything you create with Director's paint tools, such as the Paint Brush, Air Brush, and Pencil. The foreground color also is the fill color for solid patterns, and it serves as the primary color in multicolor patterns.
- **Background color**. Director's background color serves as the secondary color in multicolor patterns.
- **Gradient destination color**. This color serves as the ending color of gradient blends that start with the foreground color.

The paint tool palette displays the current foreground color, background, and gradient destination colors (**Figure 6.37**).

The colors available to you in the Paint window depend on the color-depth settings of your movie and the current color palette (see Chapter 9, "Managing Color").

To choose a color:

1. Click the Foreground, Background, or Gradient Destination color chip and hold down the mouse button.

   A pop-up color palette appears (**Figure 6.38**).
2. Drag to the desired color.
3. Release the mouse button.

Director makes it easy to isolate a particular color in a cast member and then switch that color with any other color.

To switch colors in a cast member:

1. Make sure that your cast member is displayed in Director's Paint window.
2. Click the Eyedropper tool in the tool palette (**Figure 6.39**).
3. Move the Eyedropper to a color in your cast member that you want to replace and click the mouse (**Figure 6.40**).
   The color that the Eyedropper clicks becomes the new foreground color.
4. In the paint tool palette, click the Gradient Destination color chip and hold down the mouse button.
   A pop-up color palette appears.
5. By dragging, select the color that will be the new color in your cast member.
6. Use the Marquee or Lasso tool to select the portion of the image where the color switch should take place.
7. Click the Switch Colors button in the Effects toolbar (**Figure 6.41**).

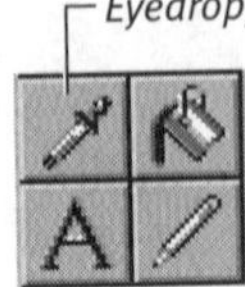

Figure 6.39 The Eyedropper tool.

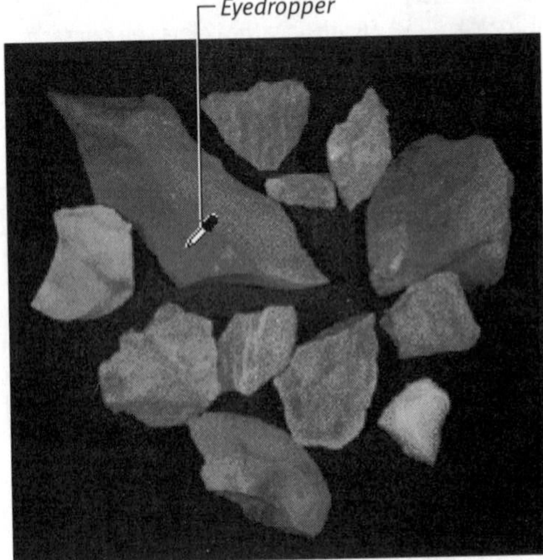

Figure 6.40 Use the Eyedropper tool to sample a color.

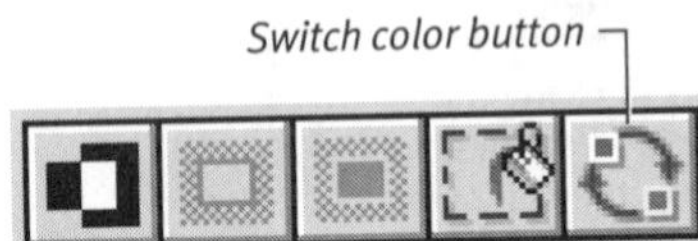

Figure 6.41 Click the Switch Colors button in the Effects toolbar.

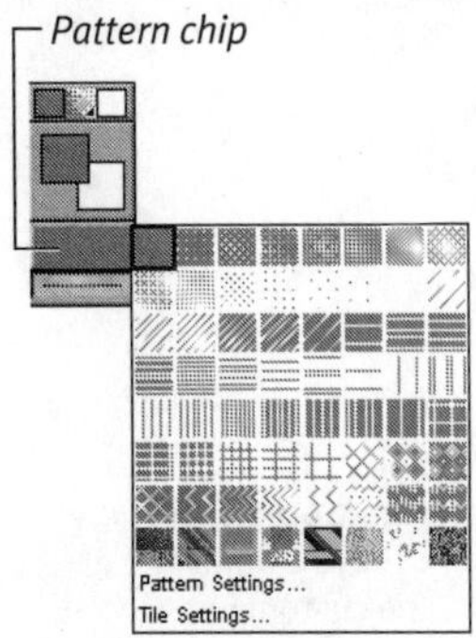

Figure 6.42
Click the pattern chip and hold down the mouse button to open the pattern palette.

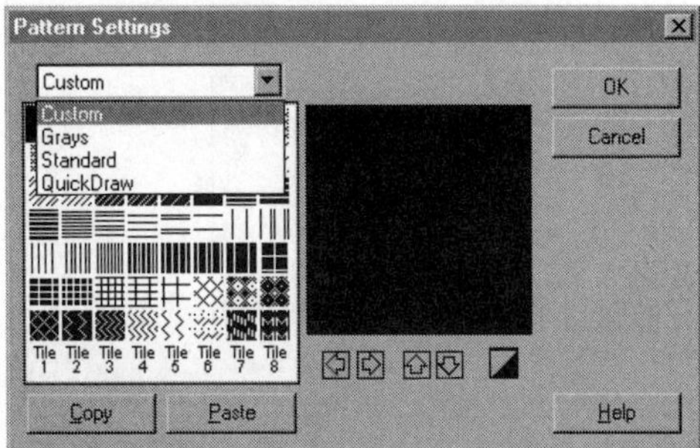

Figure 6.43 Choose the Custom pattern set and find a pattern to edit.

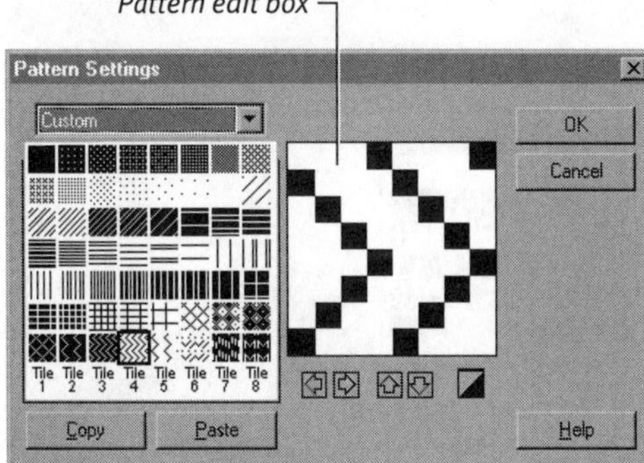

Figure 6.44 The Pattern Edit box displays an enlarged version of any pattern you select.

Pattern Techniques

You can use some painting tools—the Paint Bucket, Paint Brush, and Air Brush—to paint with a pattern instead of a solid color.

The paint tool palette includes a pattern chip that shows the currently selected pattern. The pattern chip also serves as a pattern selector. Director includes preset patterns, but you can add your own patterns.

To choose a pattern:

1. Click the pattern chip in the paint tool palette (**Figure 6.42**) and hold down the mouse button.
2. Drag to a pattern in the pop-up menu and release the mouse button.

Director features four sets of patterns. The custom set can be edited. The other three sets—Grays, Standard, and QuickDraw—cannot be changed.

To edit or create a pattern:

1. With Director's Paint window open, click the Pattern chip, hold down the mouse button, and select Pattern Settings at the bottom of the pop-up palette.
   The Pattern Settings dialog box opens.
2. Choose Custom from the pop-up menu (**Figure 6.43**).
3. Select a pattern to edit.
   An enlarged version of the pattern appears in the Pattern Edit box (**Figure 6.44**).
4. In the Pattern Edit box, click open spaces to place a black pixel in the pattern. Click existing pixels to make them white.
5. Click the directional arrows to move the pattern shape up, down, and sideways.
6. When you're happy with the pattern, click OK.
   Director adds the pattern to the custom pattern library.

You can store sets of custom patterns by copying them to and from the Mac's Scrapbook or the Windows Clipboard Viewer.

To store custom pattern sets:

1. Click the Pattern chip and hold down the mouse button to open the pop-up menu.
2. Choose Pattern Settings to open the Pattern Settings dialog box.
3. Click Copy (**Figure 6.45**).
4. Click Cancel.
5. On the Mac: Open the Scrapbook, paste the custom patterns there, save, and close the Scrapbook (**Figure 6.46**).

   or

   In Windows: Open the Clipboard Viewer, paste the custom patterns, and then choose File > Save As to save the pattern set (**Figure 6.47**).

✔ Tip

- Director lets you pick up a pattern displayed in its Paint window and edit it in the Pattern Settings dialog box. To do so, open the Pattern Settings dialog box and then click the pattern in the artwork inside the Paint window.

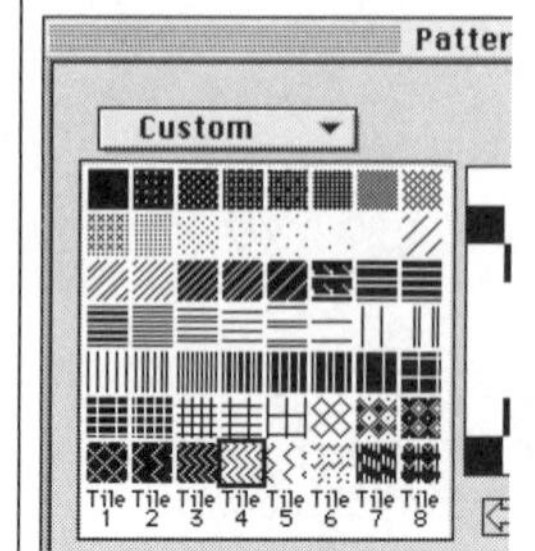

Figure 6.45 Click Copy to save a duplicate of the custom pattern set.

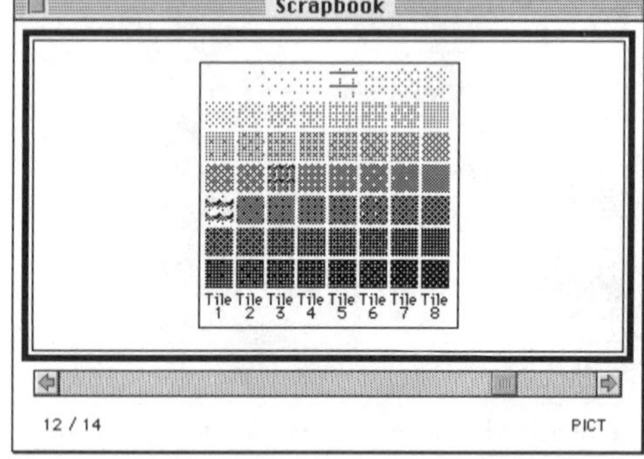

Figure 6.46 On the Mac, you can store custom patterns in the Scrapbook.

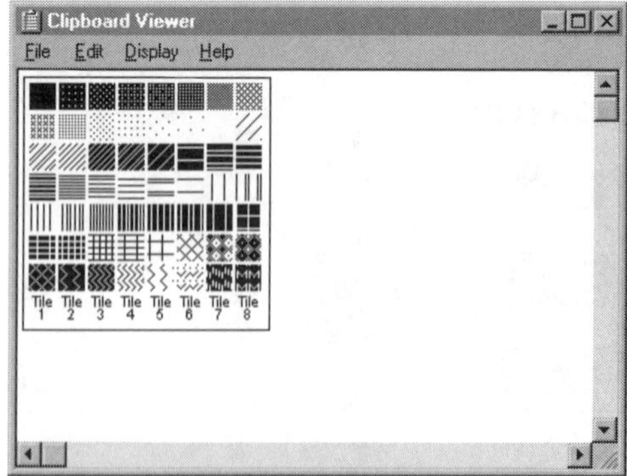

Figure 6.47 In Windows, you can store custom patterns in the Clipboard Viewer.

To reinstall stored patterns (Mac):

1. Open the Scrapbook.
2. Open the entry that contains the patterns you want to use.
3. Choose Edit > Copy.
4. Return to Director's Paint window.
5. Open the Pattern Settings dialog box.
6. Click Paste to install the copied pattern set.
7. Click OK to close the dialog box.

To reinstall stored patterns (Windows):

1. Open the Clipboard Viewer.
2. Open the entry that contains the patterns you want to use.
3. Return to Director's Paint window.
4. Open the Pattern Settings dialog box.
5. Click Paste to install the copied pattern set.
6. Click OK to close the dialog box.

Even though you can't directly edit the patterns contained in Director's Grays, Standard, and QuickDraw patterns, you can copy those predefined patterns into Director's Custom set and edit them from there.

To edit Director's preset patterns:

1. Open the pattern palette that contains the patterns you want to edit.
2. Select the pattern you want to edit.
3. Click Copy.
4. Open the Custom pattern palette.
5. Paste the copied pattern into the Custom palette.
6. Edit the pattern as necessary.
7. Click OK.

Tile Pattern Techniques

Tiles are pattern building blocks that you can repeat in an image to create textures or fillers. You create tiles from an existing cast member. If you have a cast member of a brick, for example, you can turn it into a tile to paint a brick wall. Because tiles are based on existing cast members, they can feature more than the simple foreground/background color combination that limits traditional patterns.

To create a tile from a cast member:

1. Make sure that the cast member on which you want to base your tile is already in a Cast window.

   Creating the tile has no effect on the cast member.

2. In the Paint window, click the pattern chip, hold down the mouse button, and choose Tile Settings from the pop-up menu (**Figure 6.48**).

   The Tile Settings dialog box appears (**Figure 6.49**).

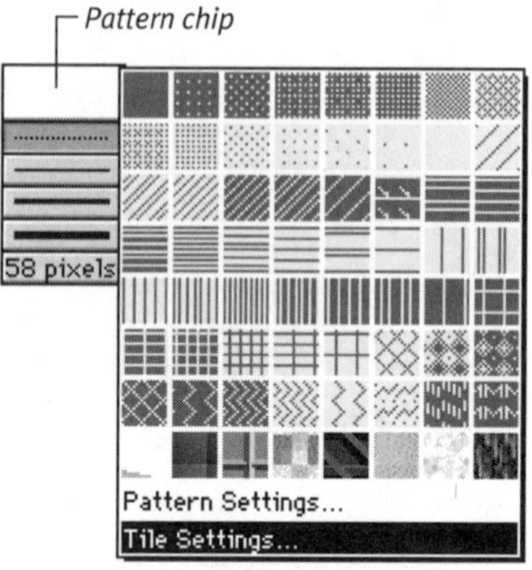

Figure 6.48 Click the Pattern chip and choose Tile Settings from the pop-up menu.

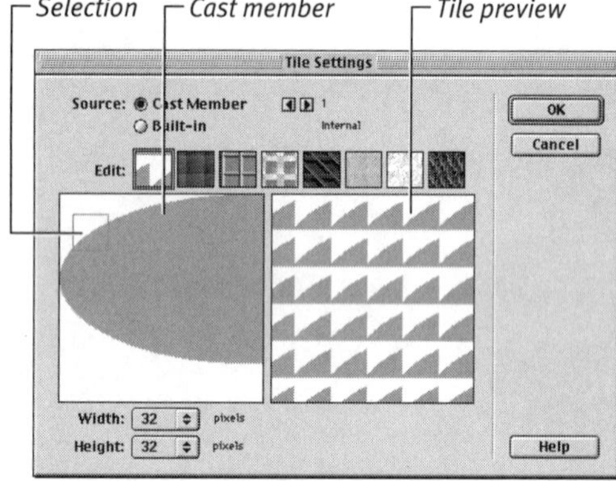

Figure 6.49 The Tile Settings dialog box.

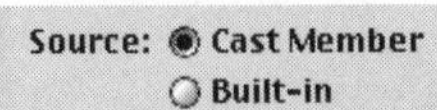

Figure 6.50 Select the Cast Member option in the Tile Settings dialog box.

Figure 6.51 Use the arrows in the Tile Settings dialog box to locate a cast member to use for a tile.

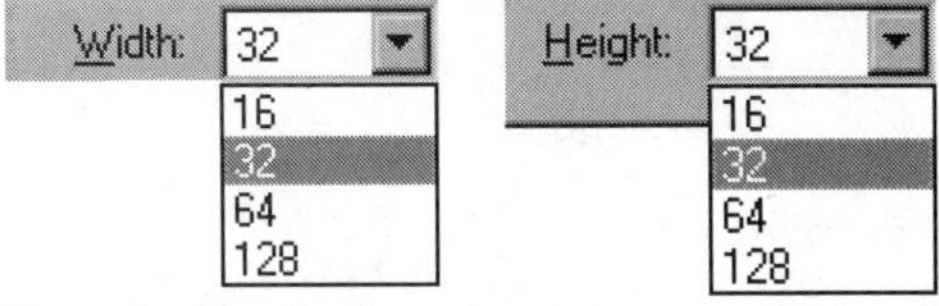

Figure 6.52 Set tile dimensions.

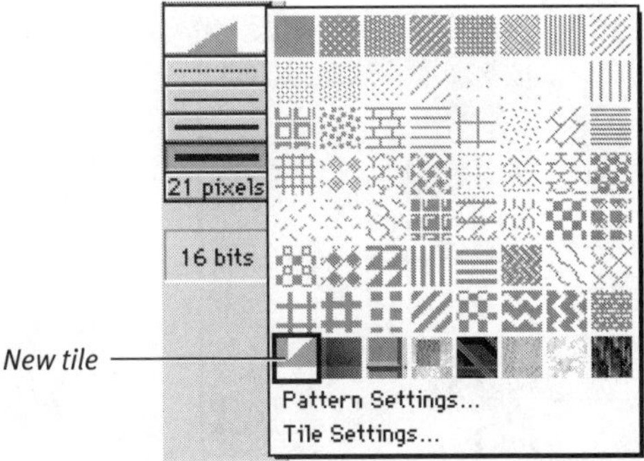

Figure 6.53 The Pattern palette displays the new tile.

3. Select the Cast Member option (**Figure 6.50**).

   This option is dimmed if the movie has no color cast members. Cast members for tiles must be saved in at least two-bit color depth (four colors total).

4. Click the left or right arrow (**Figure 6.51**) next to the Cast Member option to find the cast member you want to turn into a tile.

   All the cast members appear on the left side of the Tiles dialog box. The right side of the box displays the tile preview.

5. Use the Width and Height menus to set the dimensions (in pixels) of the tile (**Figure 6.52**).

   The range of dimensions goes from 16-by-16 to 128-by-128 pixels.

6. Drag the dotted marquee on the left side of the dialog box to select the part of the cast member you want to turn into a tile.

7. View the preview of the pattern based on the tile on the right side of the dialog box.

8. When you're satisfied with the tile, click OK to create a new tile based on the selection.

   Your new tile appears at the bottom of the Paint window's Pattern palette (**Figure 6.53**).

Painting with Gradient Inks

You can paint bitmapped artwork with a *gradient*, which is a blend of two colors that you select. Setting up a gradient is simple: You set the foreground color, which also is the beginning color for the blend, and then choose the gradient destination color, which is the ending color for the blend. Director automatically blends the two colors to display a range of colors in between (**Figure 6.54**) when you paint with a tool that can use the blend. You might want to use gradient ink to create a sunset with colors blending from red to yellow, for example.

Gradient inks work with several of Director's paint tools, including the Paint Brush, Paint Bucket, Ellipse, Rectangle, and Polygon.

Figure 6.54 When you use a gradient ink, you can paint or fill with a blend of colors.

To create a gradient:

1. In the paint tool palette, select a paint tool that works with gradients (the Paint Brush or Paint Bucket, for example).
2. Click the first gradient color chip, hold down the mouse button, and select a color from the pop-up color palette (**Figure 6.55**).

   This step sets both the foreground color and the beginning gradient color.
3. Click the second gradient color chip, hold down the mouse button, and choose an ending color for the gradient.
4. Click to open the Ink pop-up menu at the bottom of the paint window, and choose the Gradient .

   The paint tool that you selected in step 1 now paints with the gradient rather than a solid color.

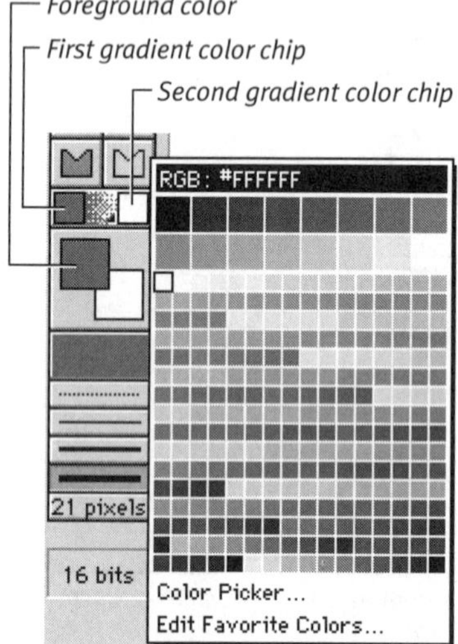

Figure 6.55 Click the first gradient color chip to select a beginning color for the gradient. The foreground color and the starting gradient color always match.

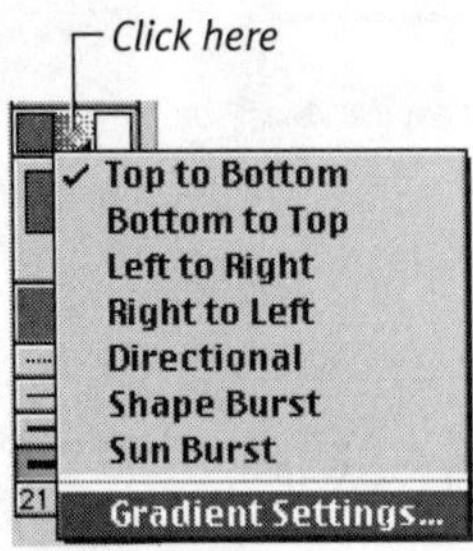

Figure 6.56 Click between the gradient color chips and choose Gradient Settings from the pop-up menu.

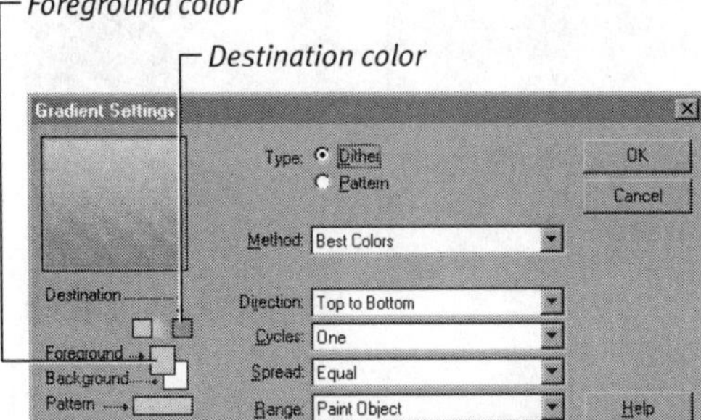

Figure 6.57 Use the Gradient Settings dialog box to set specific characteristics of the gradient.

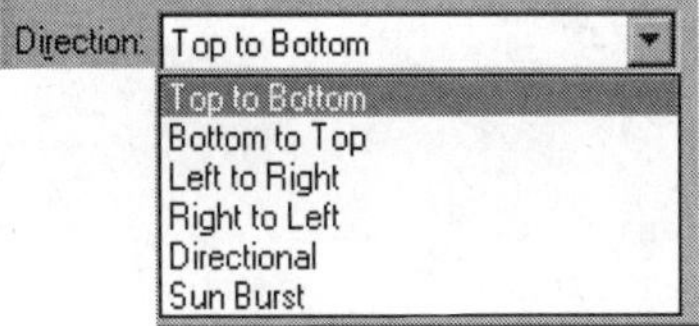

Figure 6.58 The Direction pop-up menu.

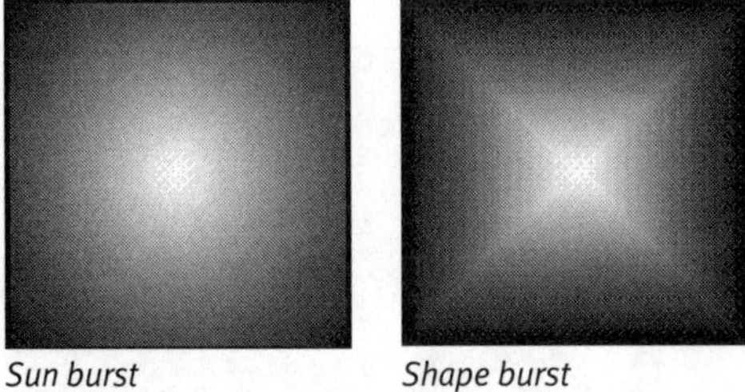

Figure 6.59 Two kinds of gradient directions.

Director allows you to customize a color gradient. You can control the slant of the gradient, how often the gradient repeats, and other specifics that change its appearance.

To use the Gradient Settings dialog box:

1. Make the Paint window active, if necessary.
2. In the paint tool palette, click between the gradient color chips and choose Gradient Settings from the pop-up menu (**Figure 6.56**).

   The Gradient Settings dialog box opens (**Figure 6.57**).
3. Use the dialog box's pop-up menus to fine-tune the characteristics of your gradient.

   For specific guidelines for setting characteristics, see the tasks that follow.
4. Click OK.

Gradient direction is the orientation of the blend within the line or shape you paint.

To set the gradient direction:

1. Open the Gradient Settings dialog box.
2. Make a choice from the Direction pop-up menu to specify how the gradient fills a particular area (**Figure 6.58**).

   The first four choices have self-explanatory names.

   The **Directional** option allows you to set a custom direction whenever you use the paint tool with the gradient.

   Sun Burst begins a gradient at the outer edges of an area and moves toward the center in concentric circles (**Figure 6.59**).

   Shape Burst creates a gradient that starts at the outer edges of an area and then fills inward while following the contours of the area (**Figure 6.59**).
3. Click OK or select other settings.

To set the gradient repeat settings:

1. Open the Gradient Settings dialog box.
2. Make a choice from the Cycles pop-up menu which specifies how many times a gradient repeats within an area (**Figure 6.60**), and whether the edge of the gradient repeat looks sharp or smooth

   You can set the gradient to cycle through its color spectrum up to four times in a given area. Sharp cycles repeat from start to finish with a crisp edge between. Smooth gradient cycles repeat with the colors reversed, with a gradual transition between repeats (**Figure 6.61**).
3. Click OK or select other settings.

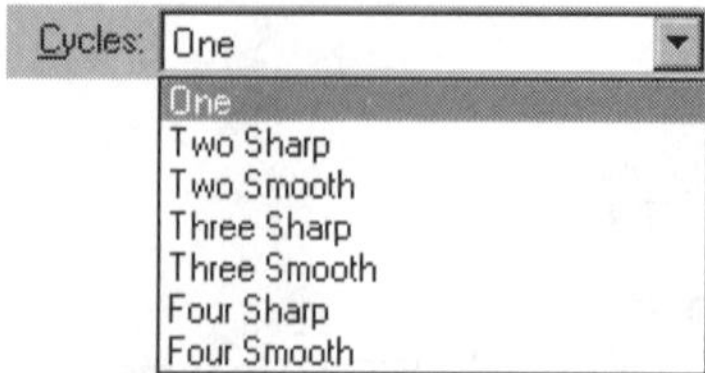

Figure 6.60 The Cycles pop-up menu controls how the gradient repeats within a shape.

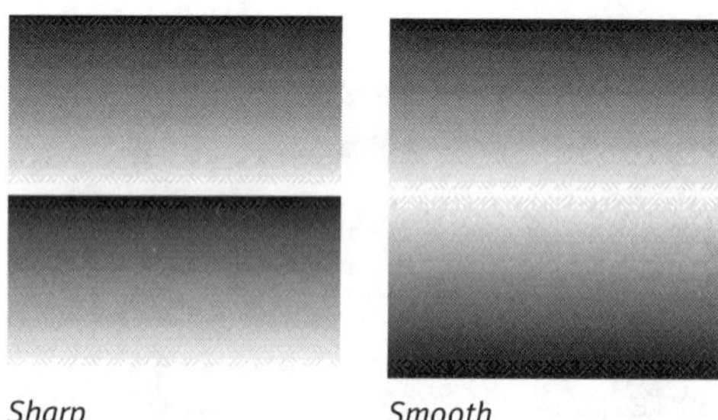

Sharp *Smooth*

Figure 6.61 Sharp and smooth gradient repeat cycles.

To set the gradient color-blending method:

1. Open the Gradient Setting dialog box.
2. Click Dither or Pattern (**Figure 6.62**).

   Choose Pattern when you want to use the currently selected pattern with the gradient color blend. Choose Dither when you want the color blend to use a subtle alternating-pixel pattern that Director chooses. Dither gives you more choices for the color-blending method.
3. Use the Method pop-up menu to select a type of blending.

   All the color-blending methods for the Dither type gradient use a subtle dithered pattern:

   - **Best Colors** uses only colors that create a continuous blend between your foreground and destination colors.
   - **Adjacent Colors** creates the gradient blend by using all the colors in the current color palette that happen to occur between the foreground and destination colors, even if those in-between colors do not create a smooth blend.

Figure 6.62 Use the gradient Type and Method settings to define how the colors blend.

- **Two Colors** blends only the foreground and destination colors.
- **One Color** fades the foreground color.
- **Standard Colors** blends the foreground and destination colors, adding several blended colors.
- **Multi Colors** blends similarly to Standard Colors, but the dithered pattern is randomized.

  All the color-blending methods for the Pattern-type gradients use the currently selected pattern as the underlying pattern for the blend.
- **Best Colors** uses only colors that create a continuous blend between your foreground and destination colors. The Transparent version of this option makes any white pixels in the blend transparent.
- **Adjacent Colors** creates the gradient blend by using all the colors in the current palette that happen to occur between the gradient's foreground and destination colors, even if those in-between colors do not create a smooth blend. The Transparent version of this option makes any white pixels in the blend transparent.

4. Click OK or select other settings.

To set the gradient spread:

1. Open the Gradient Settings dialog box.
2. Make a choice from the Spread pop-up menu to control how Director distributes the colors of your gradient within an area (**Figure 6.63**).

   The Equal option spaces the gradient's colors evenly throughout an area. More Foreground (**Figure 6.64**) and More Destination increase the amount of foreground or destination color in a gradient, respectively. More Middle devotes more space to the gradient's middle colors.
3. Click OK or select other settings.

To set the gradient color range:

1. Open the Gradient Settings dialog box.
2. Make a choice from the Range pop-up menu to apply the entire color range of gradients to objects, cast members, or the Paint window (**Figure 6.65**).

   Choose Paint Object if you want to see the full range of the gradient's colors in any size brush stroke or fill area (**Figure 6.66**). If you choose Cast Member or Window, you may not see a full range of colors in any one object.
3. Click OK or select other settings.

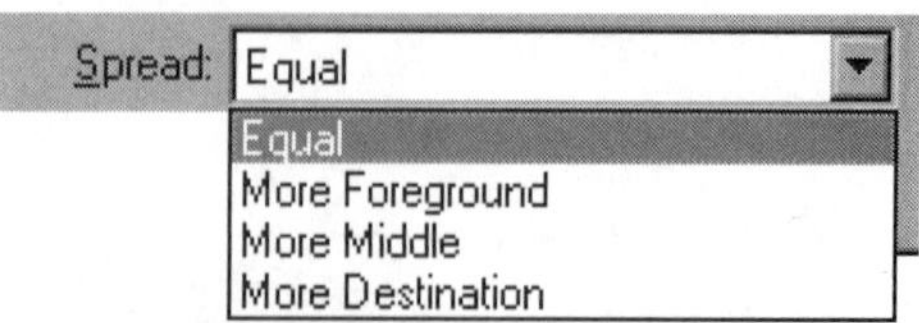

Figure 6.63 The Spread pop-up menu provides options for spacing the colors of a gradient within a region.

More Foreground *More Destination*

Figure 6.64 Two kinds of gradient spreads.

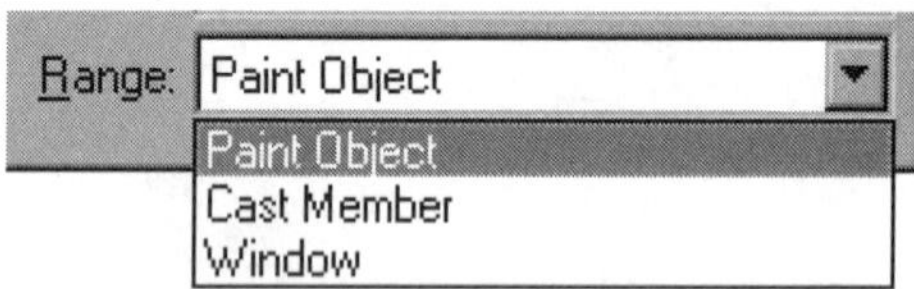

Figure 6.65 The Range pop-up menu.

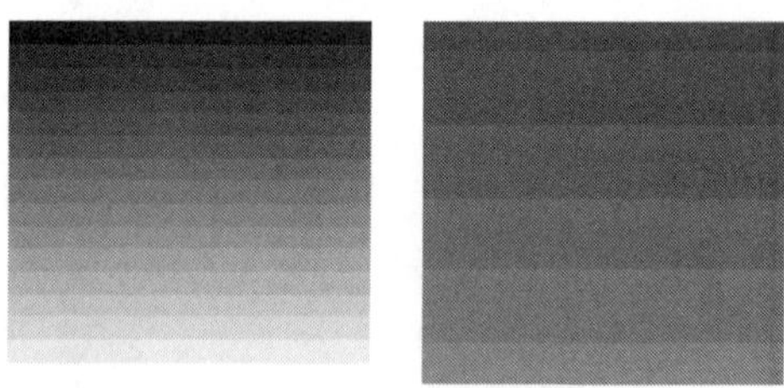

Paint Object *Window*

Figure 6.66 Examples of gradient range choices.

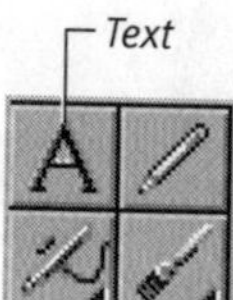

Figure 6.67 The Text tool.

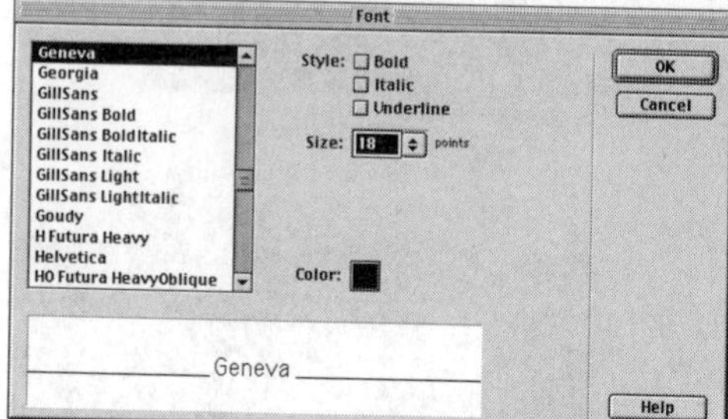

Figure 6.68 Set the font, size, and style of text in the Font dialog box.

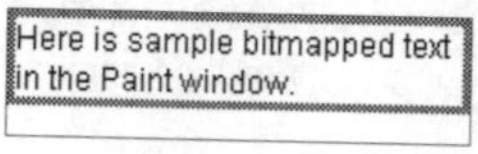

Here is sample bitmapped text in the Paint window.

Figure 6.69 Type directly in the text box.

Adding Text

The most notable feature of bitmapped text, created only in the Paint window, is that it's hard to edit. If you decide to change a word, the typeface, the text's spacing, and so on, you must erase the original text and start again. On the other hand, you can transform and manipulate bitmapped text just as you would any other bitmapped image with the Paint-window effects. You can rotate, warp, and flip bitmapped text. You also can easily incorporate bitmapped text into other painted artwork you might have. The print quality of bitmapped text is anemic compared with that of other text types, though.

Your movie viewers don't need to have the same fonts installed on their systems to view bitmapped text in your movie.

For a complete discussion of using other types of text in Director, see Chapter 11, "Adding Text".

To create bitmapped text:

1. Choose Window > Paint to open the Paint window.
2. Click the Text tool (**Figure 6.67**).
3. Click where you want the text to appear.
   A text box appears, with a blinking insertion point.
4. Set the font, size, and style by choosing Modify > Font and making choices in the Font dialog box (**Figure 6.68**).
5. Type the text (**Figure 6.69**).
   If you want multiple lines of text, press Return to start each new line.

continues on next page

6. If necessary, adjust the placement of the text within the rest of the image by dragging any edge of the text box (**Figure 6.70**).

7. Proofread the text carefully.

   Remember that you cannot easily edit the style, font, spelling, wording, or placement of the text in the image after you finish.

8. When the text is finished, click outside the text box.

   The bitmapped text becomes a bitmap cast member in the current Cast window.

Figure 6.70 You can reposition a text box by dragging any of its edges.

Applying Effects

Director's Effects toolbar (**Figure 6.71**) offers a variety of effects and functions that you can apply to existing artwork. These features include flips and rotations of cast members, edge traces, color switches, and image distortions such as warp and perspective. You generally can apply an effect to a portion of an image or the whole thing.

For most of these effects, you must use the Marquee tool, not the Lasso, to make the selection.

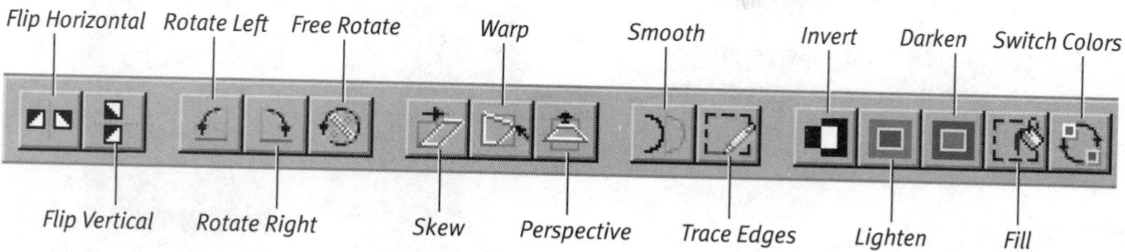

Figure 6.71 The Effects toolbar.

To rotate artwork 90 degrees:

1. Use the Marquee tool to select some artwork to rotate (**Figure 6.72**).
2. Click Rotate Right or Rotate Left in the Effects toolbar (**Figure 6.73**) to rotate the selected artwork 90 degrees.

   The selected image rotates (**Figure 6.74**).

To freely rotate artwork in 1-degree increments:

1. Use the Marquee tool to select artwork to rotate.
2. Click Free Rotate in the Effects toolbar.

   Notice that Director places little handles at each corner of your selection.
3. Drag one of the handles to rotate your art selection in 1-degree increments (**Figure 6.75**).

Figure 6.72 Select the artwork to rotate.

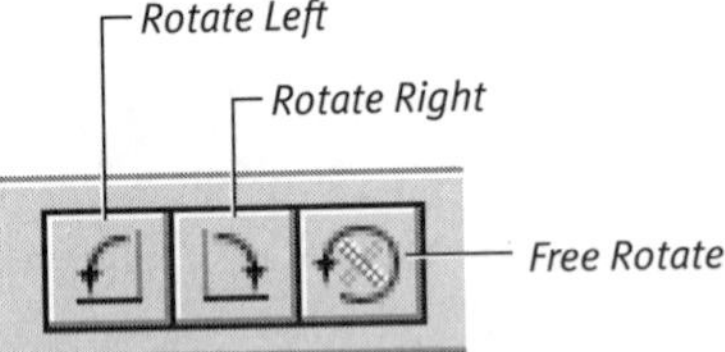

Figure 6.73 Click one of the Rotation tools.

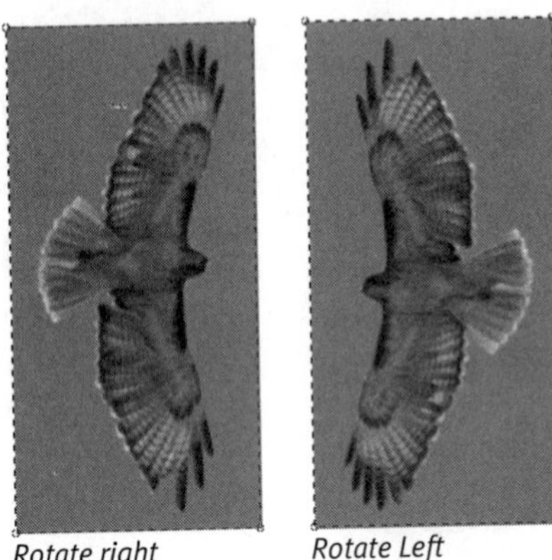

Figure 6.74 The result of rotating the image.

Figure 6.75 Drag a handle to rotate a selection in 1-degree increments with the Free Rotate tool.

Original

Flip Horizontal

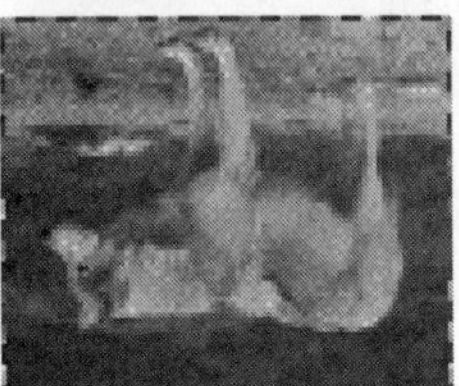
Flip Vertical

Figure 6.76 The results of flipping an image.

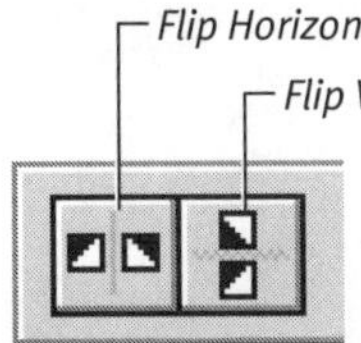

Figure 6.77 Click Flip Horizontal or Flip Vertical to vary the image.

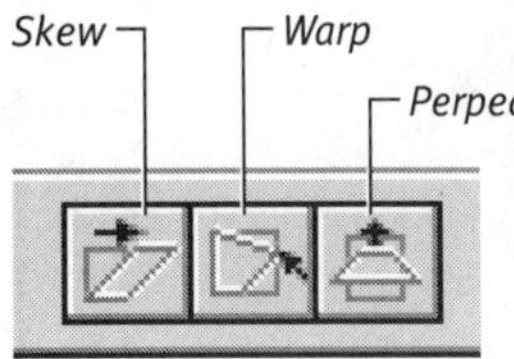

Figure 6.78 Use the Skew, Warp, or Perspective tool to alter the shape and dimensions of an image.

Figure 6.79 The results of distorting an image.

Director lets you flip an artwork selection to create variations (**Figure 6.76**).

To flip artwork:

1. Use the Marquee tool to select the artwork to flip.
2. Click the Flip Horizontal or Flip Vertical tool in Director's Effects toolbar (**Figure 6.77**).

You can alter the shape and dimensional appearance of artwork by using the Skew, Warp, and Perspective tools. Skew slants the artwork while maintaining a parallelogram shape. Warp allows you to bend and stretch artwork; Perspective makes the artwork seem as though it is being viewed from a particular vantage point, with one part of the image appearing to be closer than another.

To distort artwork:

1. Use the Marquee tool to select the artwork to alter.
2. Choose the Skew, Warp, or Perspective tool in Director's Effects toolbar (**Figure 6.78**).

   Notice that Director places handles at each corner of the selection.
3. Drag one of the handles to apply the desired effect to the artwork (**Figure 6.79**).

✔ Tip

- You may want to make a copy of your artwork before distorting it, in case you don't like the results.

To apply other toolbar special effects:

1. Use the Marquee or Lasso tool to select the artwork to change.

   The Lasso works for all effects except Trace Edges.

2. Choose the Smooth, Trace Edges, Invert Colors, Lighten, Darken, Fill, or Switch Colors tool in Director's Effects toolbar (**Figure 6.80**).

   - **Smooth** softens the edges of your artwork by adding pixels that blend the colors at the edges (**Figure 6.81**).
   - **Trace Edges** creates an outline around the edges of the artwork you've selected. Select Trace Edges repeatedly to increase the number of outlines in the trace.
   - **Invert Color** affects all colors. In black-and-white images, white pixels turn to black and vice versa, creating a negative image. In an image with more than two colors, Director flips the color palette so that all the colors are reassigned. (See Chapter 9, "Managing Color," for more information on palettes.)
   - **Lighten** increases and **Darken** decreases the brightness.
   - **Fill** fills the selected area of the Paint window with the foreground color and pattern.
   - **Switch Colors** is explained earlier in this chapter in "To switch colors in a cast member."

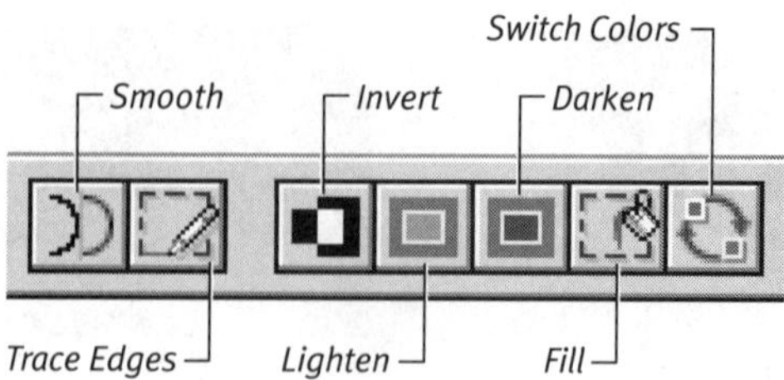

Figure 6.80 More effects tools in the Effects toolbar.

Figure 6.81 The results of applying some paint effects.

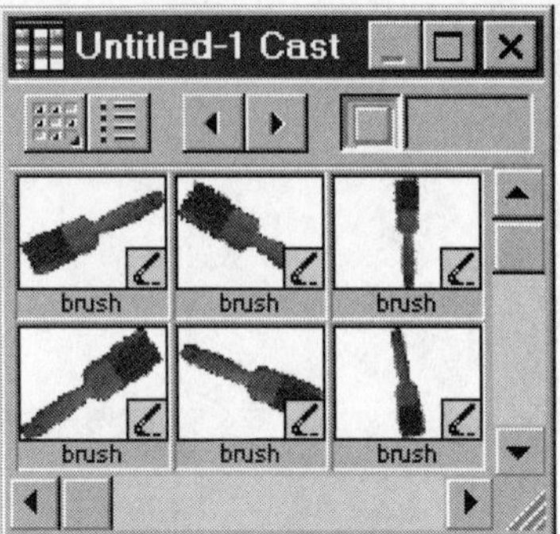

Figure 6.82 The results of using Auto Distort with the Free Rotate command to create a series of in-between rotated images.

Figure 6.83 In the Auto Distort dialog box, enter the number of in-between cast members to create.

Director's Auto Distort command creates in-between images for artwork that you skew, warp, perspective, or rotate. Suppose that you use the Free Rotate command to rotate a picture by 350 degrees—almost a full circle. You can then use Auto Distort to create versions of the artwork in several rotated positions between 0 and 350 degrees—at 60 degrees, 120 degrees, 180 degrees, 240 degrees, and so on (**Figure 6.82**). Director places each of these in-between images into the current Cast window, where they can be incorporated into a movie as an animation sequence.

To create a sequence of in-between images:

1. Use the Marquee tool to select the artwork to Auto Distort.
2. Click the Skew, Warp, Perspective, or Rotate tool in the Effects toolbar.

   Director places handles at each corner of the selection.
3. Drag one of the handles to rotate or distort the selected art.
4. While the Marquee is still active, choose Xtras > Auto Distort.

   The Auto Distort dialog box opens.
5. Type the number of in-between cast members that you want to create (**Figure 6.83**).
6. Click Begin.

   Director creates the new in-between cast members and adds them in the next available positions in the active Cast window.

Using Ink Masks

An *ink mask* allows you to make certain parts of a bitmap cast member transparent so that you can see through it to other cast members in the background while other parts of the cast member remain opaque. This feature can be extremely useful. Imagine a scene in which a room with a brick wall has a window in it, and you want to be able to see the moon outside. (**Figures 6.84** and **85**). In such a scene, the wall would be opaque but the window transparent, so that a cast member of a moon would be visible through it.

Figure 6.84 The window in the brick wall is made transparent via an ink mask.

Figure 6.85 The cast member of the moon, which is underneath the brick wall, is visible through the transparent window.

Color Depth: 1 Bit

Figure 6.86 Select 1 Bit from the Color Depth pop-up menu in the Transform Bitmap dialog box.

To create a mask:

1. Open the cast member that you want to mask in the Paint window—in other words, the cast member that you want to make transparent in certain places.
2. Choose Edit > Duplicate.
3. While the cloned cast member is active in the Paint window, choose Modify > Transform Bitmap.
   The Transform Bitmap dialog box opens.
4. Choose 1 Bit from the Color Depth pop-up menu (**Figure 6.86**).
   This option changes the duplicate cast member to black and white (1-bit color depth), which is required to make a mask.
5. Click Transform.
6. In the paint tool palette, click the Paint Bucket, Paint Brush, or other drawing tool.
7. Fill the parts of the cloned cast member that should be opaque (that is, that should not be transparent).
   Be sure not to paint outside the borders of the cloned cast member.

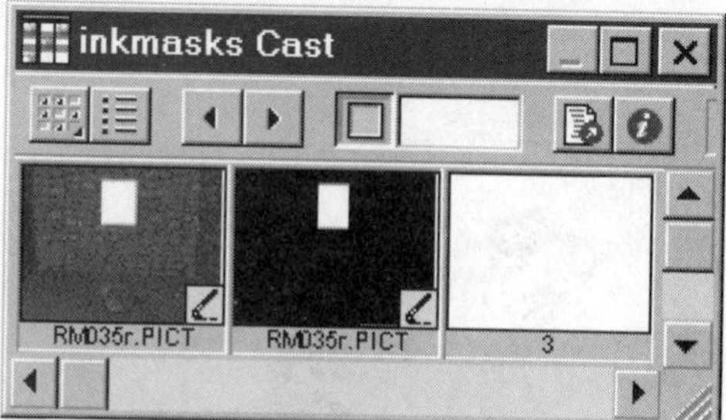

Figure 6.87 In the cast window, make sure that the cloned cast member is positioned immediately after the original cast member.

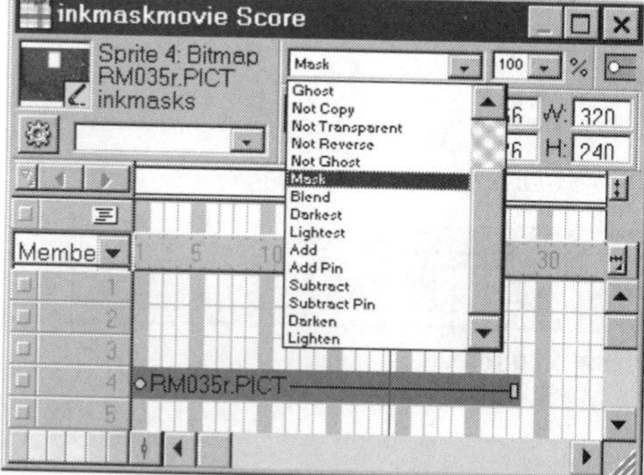

Figure 6.88 In the score, choose Mask from the pop-up menu.

8. In the Cast window, make sure that the duplicate cast member immediately follows the original version of the cast member (**Figure 6.87**).

   If it is not already there, drag the filled-in duplicate to the appropriate location.

9. Choose Window > Score.
10. Place in the score the original cast member that you want to mask.
11. Select the frames in the score that contain the cast member you want to mask.
12. In the score, choose Mask from the pop-up menu (**Figure 6.88**).

    Director displays your cast member masked in the selected frames.

13. Make sure that other cast members that you want to be visible through the transparent portion of your masked cast member are placed in earlier channels in the score; otherwise, they will appear on top of your masked cast member.

Onion Skinning

Onionskinning allows you to create a new cast member in the Paint window while viewing one or more existing cast members as reference images. The reference images appear dimmed in the background, as though you had tracing paper over them (hence the name of the technique, after a form of lightweight tracing paper once used by animators). You draw on top of the reference images, tracing the parts of their features that you need for the new cast member. The cast members used as references are not altered in the process.

Onion skinning comes in very handy when you create sequences of closely related cast members, which would be hard to generate precisely without the reference images.

The following procedures allow you to create a new cast member while viewing a previously rendered cast member as a background reference image.

To use onion skinning:

1. In the Paint window, open the cast member you need to use as the background reference image (**Figure 6.89**).
2. Choose View > Onion Skin.
3. Click Toggle Onion Skinning in the Onion Skin toolbar (**Figure 6.90**).
4. Click Set Background.
5. Click the New Cast Member button in the Paint window (**Figure 6.91**).
6. Click Show Background in the Onion Skin toolbar.

   The reference cast member appears dimmed in the Paint window (**Figure 6.91**).
7. Draw the new cast member on top of the image.

Figure 6.89 Open the reference cast member in the Paint window.

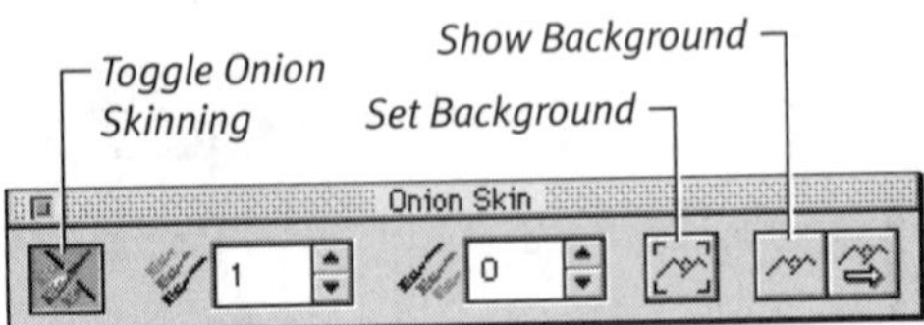

Figure 6.90 The Onion Skin toolbar.

Figure 6.91 The reference cast member appears dimmed in the Paint window. Draw the new cast member on top of this image.

ONIONSKINNING

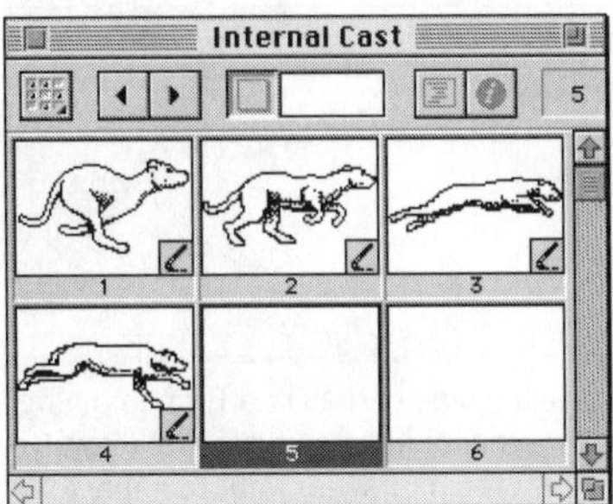

Figure 6.92 Create an empty position in the Cast window.

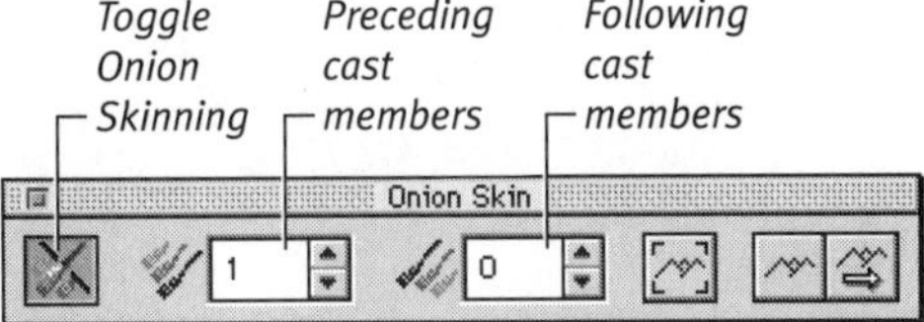

Figure 6.93 Display your reference cast members by clicking the Preceding or Following cast member arrows in the Onion Skin toolbar.

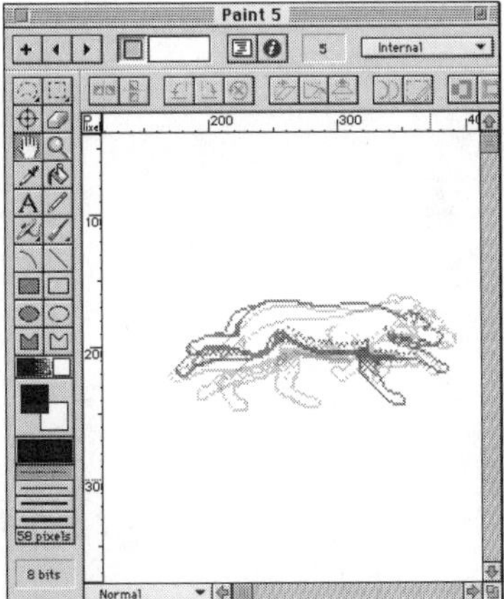

Figure 6.94 Your reference cast members appear on top of each other in the Paint window.

As you create a cast member that is part of an animation sequence, it helps to view several preceding frames of the sequence at the same time, so that the new cast member fits in appropriately. With this technique, your reference cast members appear on top of one another in the Paint window, with decreasing levels of brightness. This allows you to create your new cast member in precise relation to the entire sequence.

To create a cast member with a reference sequence:

1. Open the Cast window that contains the reference cast members.

   Make sure that the reference cast members are grouped together.

2. Create an empty position immediately following or preceding the reference cast members.

3. Select the empty cast position (**Figure 6.92**).

4. Choose Insert > Media Element > Bitmap.

   The Paint window opens.

5. Choose View > Onion Skin.

6. Click Toggle Onion Skinning in the Onion Skin toolbar to turn it on.

7. Click the Preceding or Following cast member arrows in the Onion Skin toolbar to display the reference cast members (**Figure 6.93**).

   Display as many reference images as you need by setting the appropriate value. The reference images are displayed on top of one other in the Paint window (**Figure 6.94**). The farther away the reference cast members are from the new cast member in the cast window, the dimmer they appear.

8. Draw the new cast member on top of the reference images.

Applying Image Filters

Director allows you to apply Photoshop or Premiere image filters to your bitmapped cast members.

For Director to have access to the filters, you must first place them in the Xtras folder in the Director program folder. Then you can apply a filter to modify a portion of a bitmapped cast member or to modify multiple cast members. You can apply image filters either in the Paint window or in the Cast window.

To apply a filter to a bitmapped cast member:

1. Open the cast member in the Paint window.
2. Use the Marquee or Lasso tool to select part of the cast member to modify.
3. Choose Xtras > Filter Bitmap to open the Filter Bitmap dialog box.
4. On the left side of the Filter Bitmap dialog box, select a category of filters (**Figure 6.95**).

   Choose All to view every available filter.
5. On the right side of the Filter Bitmap dialog box, select the filter to apply to your cast member.
6. Click Filter.

   At this point, the filter probably displays its own dialog box, in which you enter filter settings. If the filter doesn't have a custom dialog box, it will be applied immediately after you click Filter.
7. Make selections and apply the filter.

✔ Tip

- You can apply a filter to a selection of multiple cast members in a Cast window. Select the cast members in a cast window and then choose Xtras > Filter Bitmap.

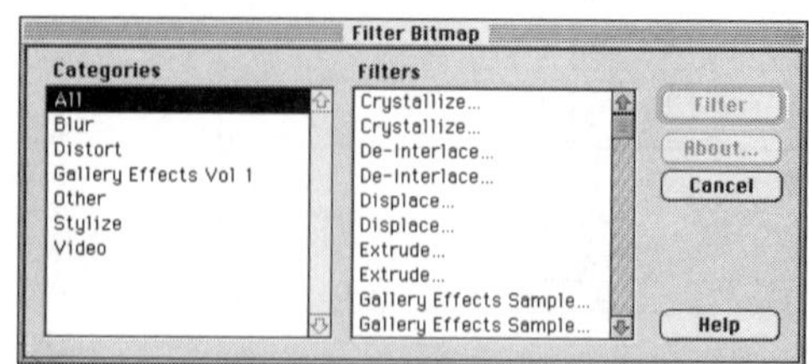

Figure 6.95 On the left side of the Filter Bitmap dialog box, select the category of filters you want to view. On the right side, select the filters you want to apply to your cast member and click Filter.

7

Drawing Vector Shapes

Vector-shape cast members offer a distinct advantage over bitmaps in that they use much less storage space and consequently require less download time from the Internet or other network. In addition, you can resize vector shapes without distortion, unlike bitmaps, which often look coarse when enlarged.

Also unlike bitmaps, vector shapes are limited by having to be defined in terms of lines and vertices, which makes them more suitable for simple designs than complex scenes. On the upside, Director 8 allows a single vector-shape cast member to consist of multiple distinct shapes, paving the way for possibilities such as creating text phrases from a single vector cast member.

If you need complex, realistic objects that require pixel-level editing, bitmaps are still the best choice. Use vector shapes when your movie calls for simple shapes with minimal detail and when it requires quick animation or downloading.

Creating Vector Shapes

Instead of being composed of an array of pixels of various colors, like a bitmap, a vector shape is defined by a geometrical description: line thickness, fill color, line slope, and so on. You create a vector shape by plotting points to define a path and by controlling the curvature of the line between the points (**Figure 7.1**). In Director 8, a single vector-shape cast member can consist of multiple distinct shapes (**Figure 7.2**). If you have used any vector drawing programs, such as Freehand or Illustrator, these techniques will be familiar.

If you're not familiar with vector drawing, start with the shape tools. The basic shape tools allow you to quickly create geometric shapes that you can later modify. You can also draw straight and curved lines and then combine them in a single path or closed shape.

To create a basic vector shape:

1. Choose Window > Vector Shape.
   The Vector Shape window opens (**Figure 7.3**).
2. Select a shape tool (**Figure 7.3**).
3. Use the Stroke Width pop-up menu to choose a line thickness.
4. Drag diagonally in the Vector Shape window to draw the shape (**Figure 7.4**).

✔ Tips

- Hold down the Shift key while dragging to constrain the shape to perfect proportions. A constrained rectangle makes a square; a constrained ellipse makes a circle.
- You can add multiple basic shapes to a single vector-shape cast member. Do so by simply selecting a shape tool again and drawing the next shape in the Vector Shape window.

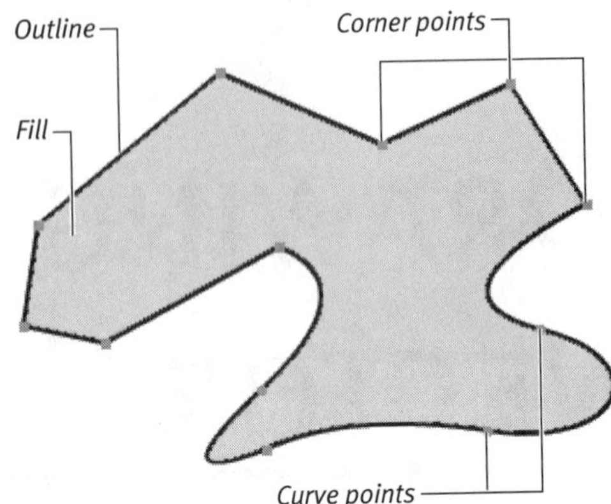

Figure 7.1 You create a vector shape by specifying a set of points through which a line passes and controlling the curvature of the line between the points.

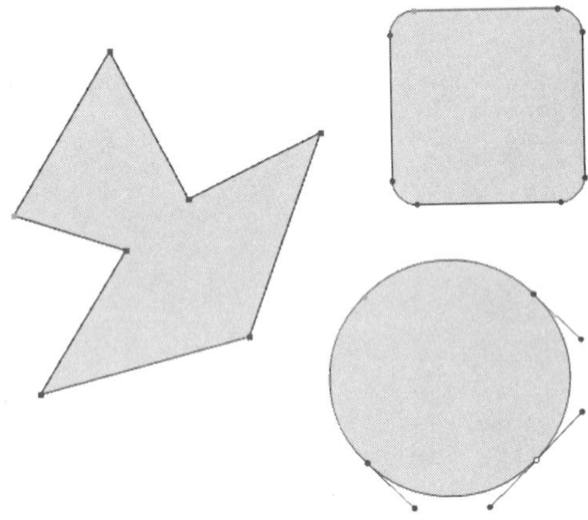

Figure 7.2 A single vector-shape cast member can consist of multiple distinct shapes.

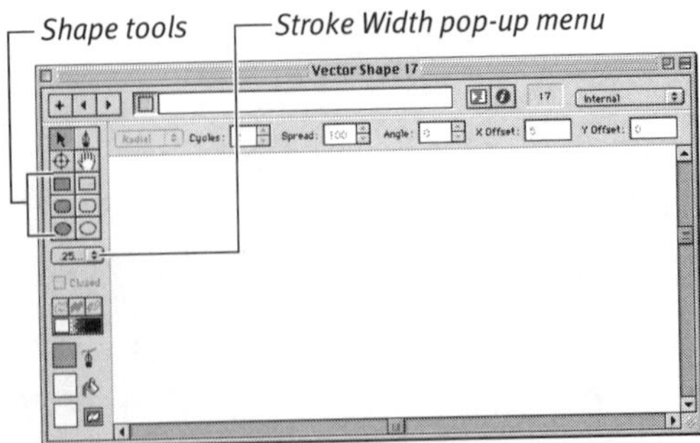

Figure 7.3 Create vector shapes in the Vector Shape window.

Figure 7.4 With a basic vector shape tool selected, drag diagonally to size and create the shape.

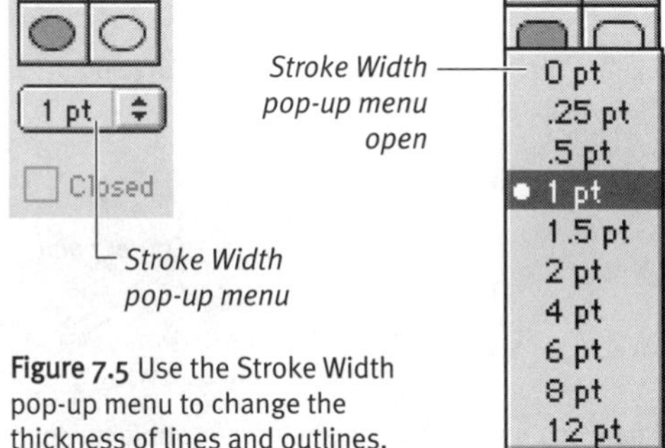

Figure 7.5 Use the Stroke Width pop-up menu to change the thickness of lines and outlines.

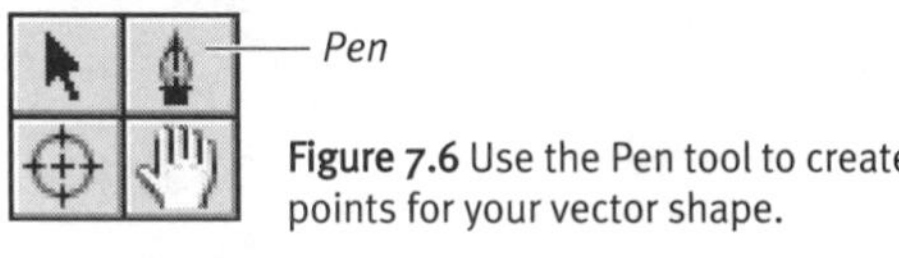

Figure 7.6 Use the Pen tool to create points for your vector shape.

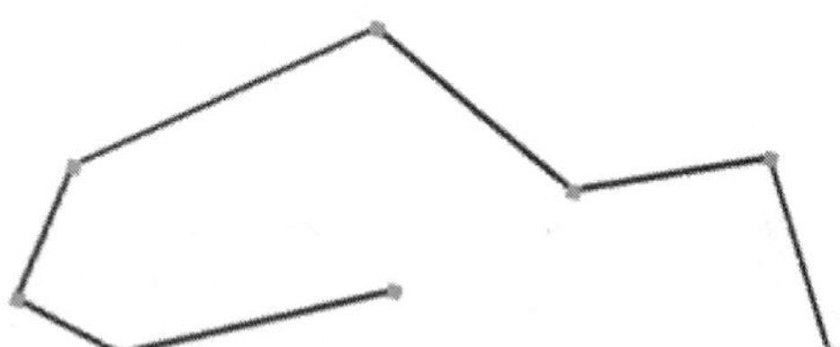

Figure 7.7 Using the Pen tool, click to create a corner point or drag to create a curve point.

To draw a vector shape composed of straight lines:

1. Open the Vector Shape window.
2. If the Vector Shape window opens with an existing cast member displayed, you may want to click the New Cast Member button to start creating a new vector-shape cast member.
3. Choose a line thickness from the Stroke Width pop-up menu (**Figure 7.5**).

   You can use only one line thickness in any single vector-shape cast member.
4. Select the Pen tool (**Figure 7.6**).

   The pointer turns into a crosshair pointer when it's within the drawing portion of the Vector Shape window.
5. Click in the Vector Shape window to start the first line segment.

   Clicking (as opposed to dragging) creates a corner point, which means that the next end point will be connected to this point by a straight line. The first point is green, indicating the starting point of the shape.
6. Click again to define the end of the line segment.
7. Position the crosshair pointer where you want the next segment to end; then click.
8. Continue to click to add segments until you have the path you want (**Figure 7.7**).

   Notice that the last point added is always red, indicating the end point of the shape. Points between the starting and ending points are blue.
9. If you want to close the path to create a shape that you can fill, either check the Closed checkbox to the left of the drawing area or click the green starting point.

   Director automatically connects the end points. Uncheck the Closed checkbox to keep the shape open.

To create a vector shape composed of curved lines:

1. Open the Vector Shape window.
2. Choose a line thickness from the Stroke Width pop-up menu.

   You can use only one line thickness in any single vector shape.
3. Select the Pen tool.

   The pointer turns into a crosshair pointer when it's within the drawing portion of the Vector Shape window.
4. Drag to start the curved line.

   Dragging creates a curve point with control handles. These curves are also called *Bézier curves.*
5. Create additional points by dragging.
6. If you want to close the path to create a shape that you can fill, either check the Closed checkbox to the left of the drawing area (**Figure 7.8**) or click the green starting point.

   Director automatically connects the end points. Uncheck the Closed checkbox to keep the shape open.

✔ Tip

- You can combine straight and curved segments by clicking to create a corner point and then resuming dragging to create curve points (**Figure 7.9**).

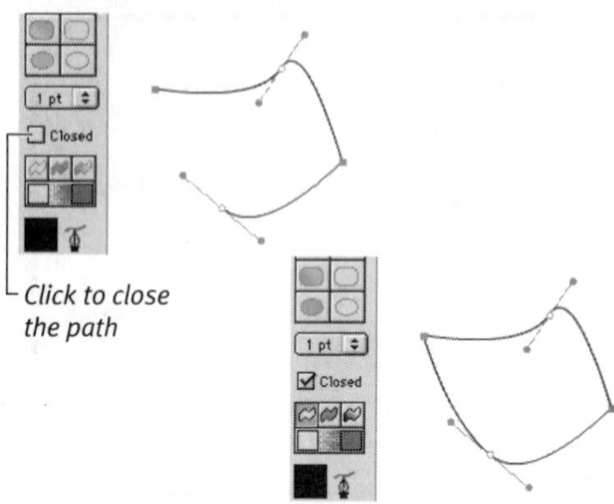

Figure 7.8 Choose the Closed option to join the ending points of a path automatically.

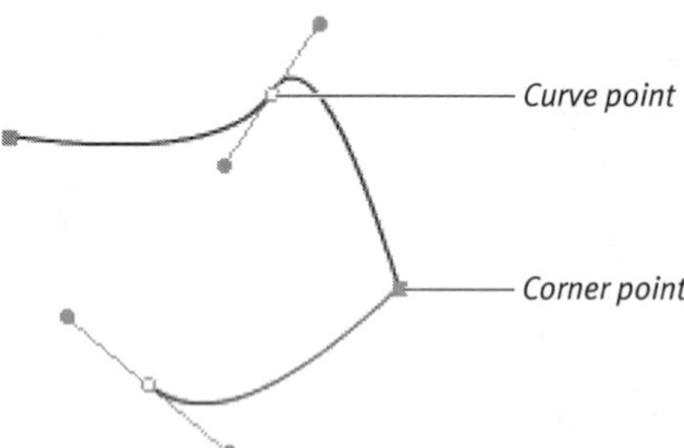

Figure 7.9 Combine curves, angles, and straight lines in a single path by clicking wherever you need an angle or straight-line segment.

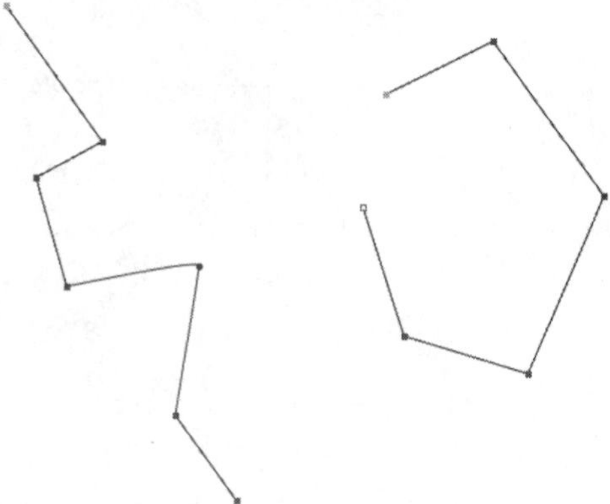

Figure 7.10 Double-click with the Pen tool to end a distinct vector shape.

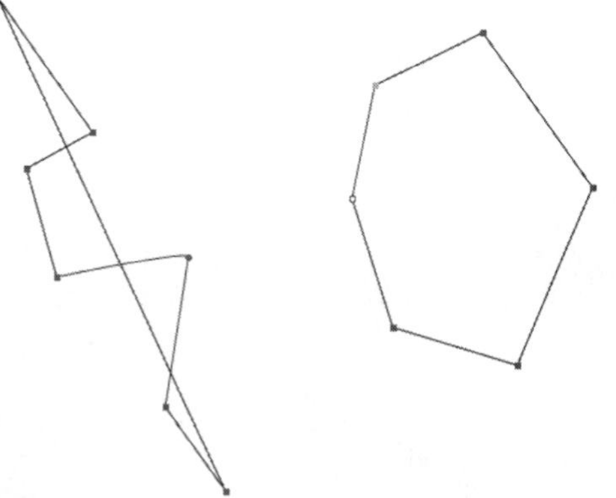

Figure 7.11 Choose the Closed option to close all the vector shapes.

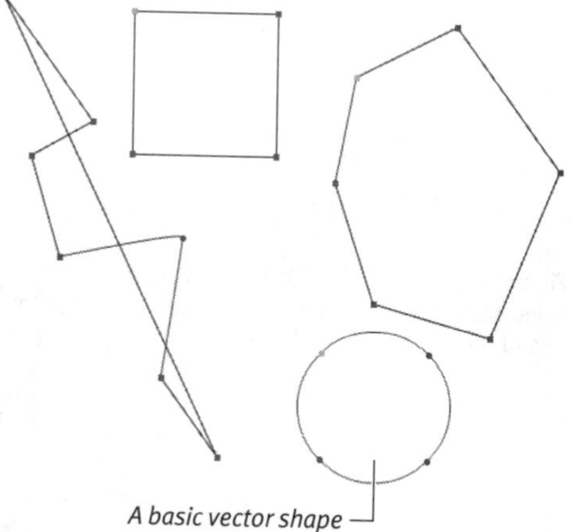

Figure 7.12 You can add multiple basic vector shapes to your vector-shape cast member.

When you know how to create a single vector shape with straight or curved lines, you can easily create multiple shapes in a single vector cast member.

To create a single vector-shape cast member composed of multiple distinct shapes:

1. Create a vector shape as described in the preceding sections, but don't close it or create the endpoint.
2. With the Pen tool still selected, double-click to create the last point in the first shape.

   This action tells Director to end the first shape.
3. Click in the Vector Shape window to create the starting point for your next vector shape.
4. Continue clicking or dragging to create additional points and segments of the new vector shape.
5. Double-click to end the shape (**Figure 7.10**).
6. Repeat steps 3-5 to add as many distinct shapes to your cast member as you want.
7. If you want to close all the vector shapes, check the Closed checkbox in the Vector Shape window (**Figure 7.11**).

   Keep in mind that all vector attributes—such as line thickness, the Closed setting, and color—affect all the shapes within a single vector-shape cast member.

✔ Tip

- You can add basic vector shapes (ellipse, rectangle, and so on) to a vector cast member with multiple shapes (**Figure 7.12**). For these tools to be selectable, though, the Closed checkbox must be checked, because you can't mix open and closed shapes in a single vector cast member.

In Director 8, you can split a vector shape into two distinct shapes.

To split a vector shape:

1. Select the Arrow tool in the Vector Shape window.
2. While holding down the Shift key, select any two adjacent points in a vector shape.
3. Choose Modify > Split Curve.

   The selected points become new start and end points, which connect to the previous start and end points to form two separate shapes (**Figure 7.13**).

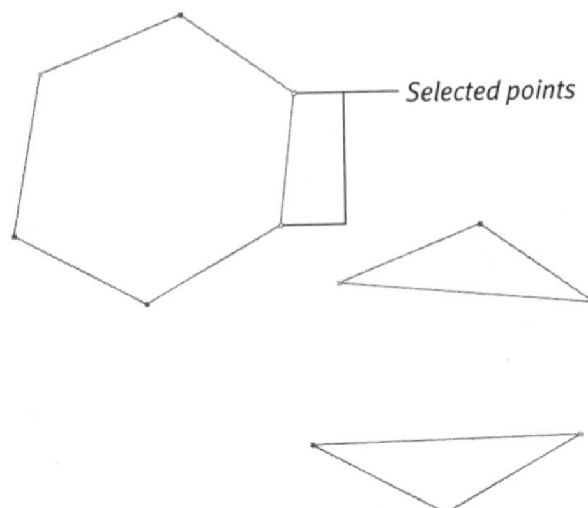

Figure 7.13 Split a vector shape to create two new shapes.

Director 8 allows you to join two vector shapes or curves at their end points. You cannot join points in the midsections of vector shapes.

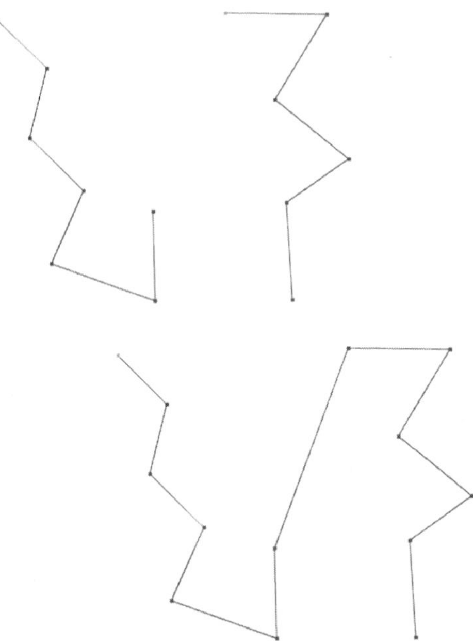

Figure 7.14 When midpoints in both curves are selected, the start of the second curve is joined to the end of the first curve.

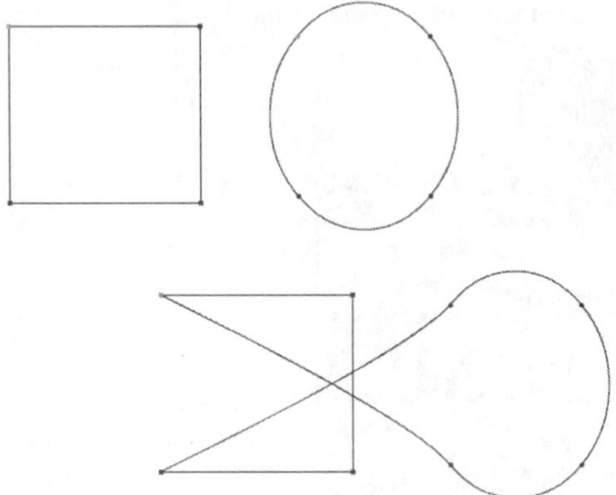

Figure 7.15 Joining two closed shapes forms a new closed single shape.

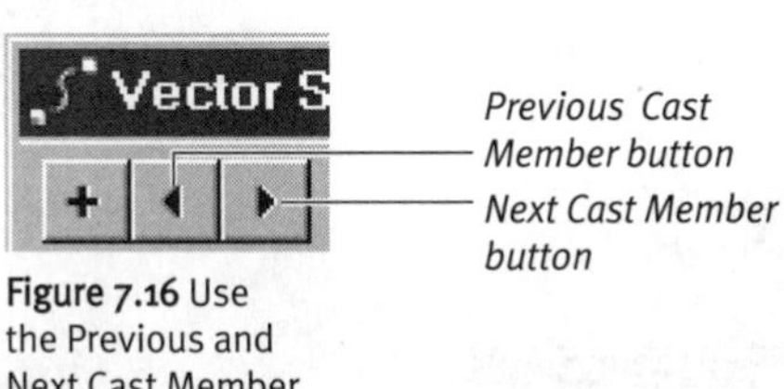

Figure 7.16 Use the Previous and Next Cast Member buttons to select the appropriate vector shape.

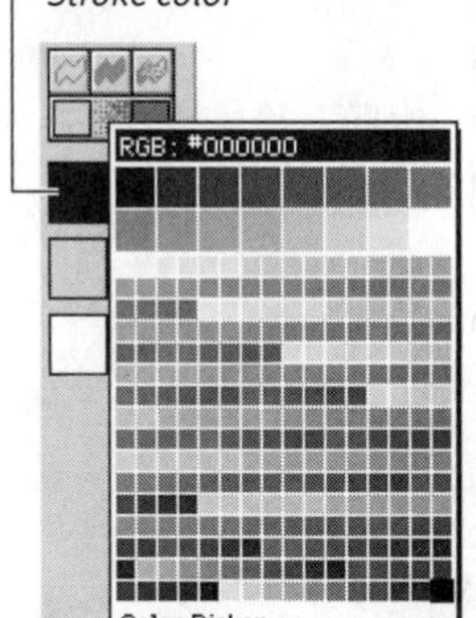

Figure 7.17 The stroke color defines the color of the outline of your vector shape.

To join two vector shapes or curves:

1. While holding down the Shift key, select one point in each of the vector shapes or curves that you want to join.

   If you select points in the middle of each curve, the start of the second curve (*second curve* means the second curve drawn) will be joined to the end of the first curve (**Figure 7.14**). If the shapes are closed, the start of the first shape will also be joined to the end of the second shape to form a new closed shape (**Figure 7.15**).

   If you select end points, those end points will be joined.

2. Choose Modify > Join Curves.

To set a vector shape's outline color:

1. Click the Previous and Next Cast Member buttons in the Vector Shape window to display the vector shape for which you want to change the color outline (**Figure 7.16**).

2. Click the stroke color in the Vector Shape window and select a new stroke color (**Figure 7.17**).

To set background color:

1. Click the Previous and Next Cast Member buttons in the Vector Shape window to display the vector shape for which you want to change the background color.
2. Click the background color in the Vector Shape window and select a new background color (**Figure 7.18**).

To fill a vector shape with a solid color:

1. Click the Previous and Next Cast Member buttons in the Vector Shape window to display the vector shape for which you want to change the fill color.
2. Click the fill color in the Vector Shape window (**Figure 7.19**) and select a new fill color.

To undo a fill:

Click the No Fill button in the Vector Shape window (**Figure 7.20**).

✔ Tips

- If a vector shape is closed and filled, and you want its border to be visible, make sure that the stroke color (which is the border color) is different from the fill color.
- Remember that if a vector-shape cast member consists of multiple shapes, all of them are affected by any color changes.

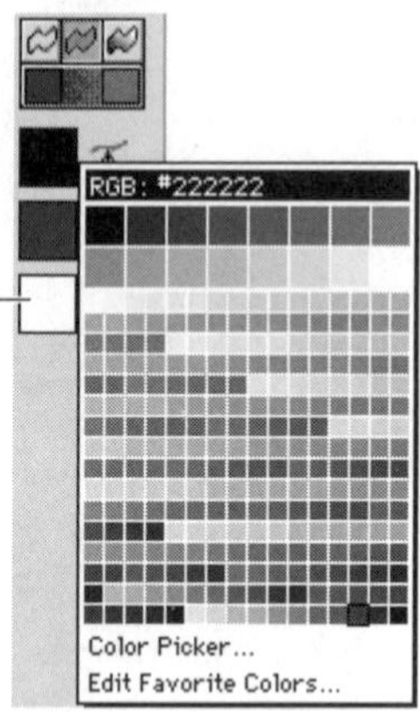

Figure 7.18 The background color defines the color outside the edges but within the bounding box of your vector shape.

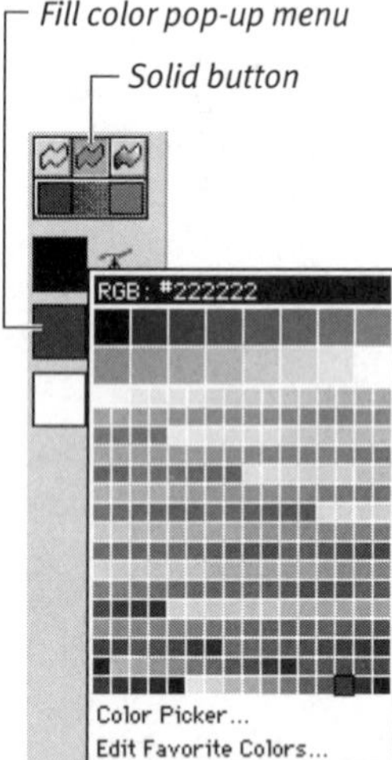

Figure 7.19 The fill color defines the interior color of a vector shape.

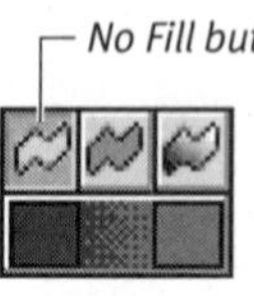

Figure 7.20 Click the No Fill button to leave your vector shape hollow.

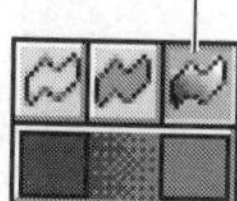

Figure 7.21 Click the Gradient button to fill the inside of your vector shape with a gradient.

Figure 7.22 Select the starting color for your gradient.

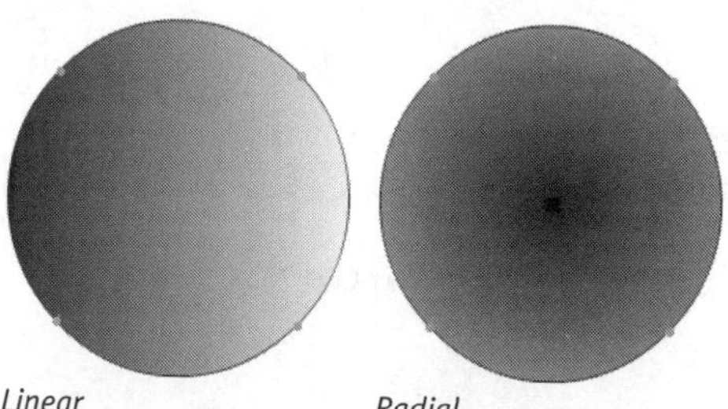

Figure 7.23 Compare linear and radial gradients.

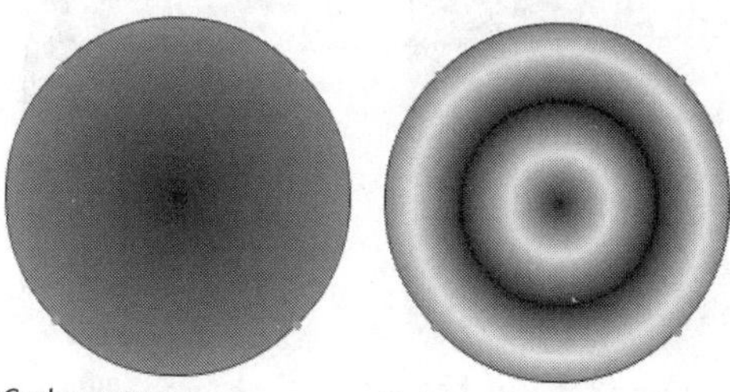

Figure 7.24 Gradient cycles control how many times the gradient repeats in a shape.

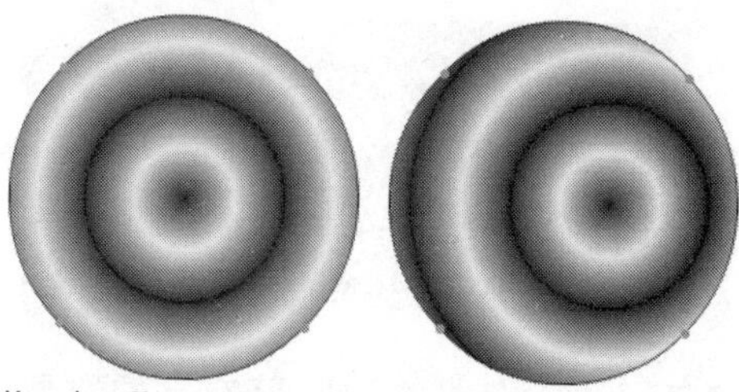

Figure 7.25 You can create gradients with different offsets.

To set a gradient fill:

1. Open or create a closed vector shape in the Vector Shape window.
2. Click the Gradient button (**Figure 7.21**).
3. Click the left color chip below the Gradient button and select the starting color for the gradient from the color menu that opens (**Figure 7.22**).

   This color is the same as the fill color.
4. Click the right color chip below the Gradient button and select the ending color for the gradient from the color menu that opens.
5. Choose Linear or Radial from the Gradient Type pop-up menu.

   Linear distributes a gradient across a shape. Radial creates a gradient which emanates from a central point (**Figure 7.23**)
6. Enter a value for Cycles.

   The Cycles setting defines how many times the gradient repeats from start color to end color within the given vector shape (**Figure 7.24**).
7. Enter a Spread value.

   The Spread value controls whether the gradient is weighted more toward the start color or the end color. A value of 100 makes the gradient evenly distributed between start and end colors. Values less than 100 weigh toward the end color; values greater than 100 weigh the gradient toward the start color.
8. Rotate a linear gradient by entering a value in the Angle field.
9. To offset a gradient within a vector shape, enter values in the X Offset and Y Offset fields (**Figure 7.25**).

Editing Vector Shapes

After you create a vector shape, you can modify it by moving and changing the corner points and curve points. Adding points also provides an opportunity to change the shape. Removing points changes the shape instantly. These editing techniques apply equally to a vector-shape cast member that consists of multiple shapes.

To move a point in a vector shape:

1. In a Cast window, double-click a vector shape (**Figure 7.26**).
2. Click the Selection tool in the Vector Shape window (**Figure 7.27**).
3. Drag a point to a new location (**Figure 7.28**).
4. Release the mouse button.

   The lines connecting to the point adjust dynamically when you release the point.

To move multiple points:

1. In a Cast window, double-click a vector shape.
2. Click the Selection tool in the Vector Shape window.
3. Select multiple points by Shift+clicking or by dragging a selection rectangle around them.

   Points turn hollow when selected. Multiple points can span distinct shapes within a vector cast member.
4. Drag any point to a new location to move all the points together (**Figure 7.29**).

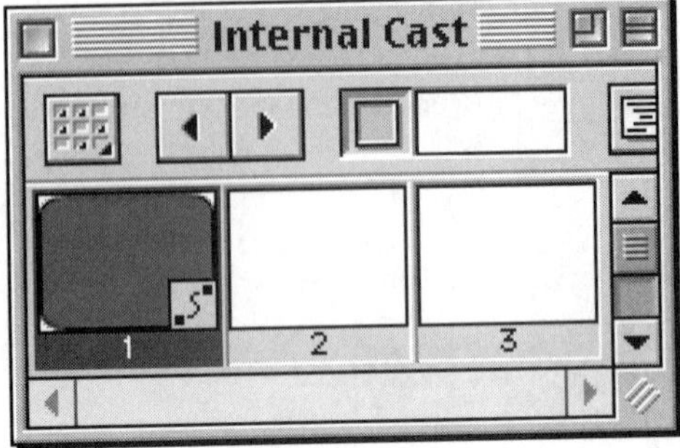

Figure 7.26 Double-click a vector-shape cast member to open it in the Vector Shape window.

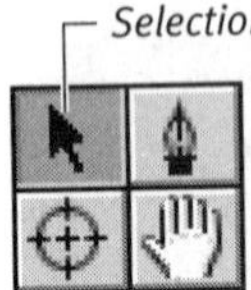

Figure 7.27 Click the Selection tool.

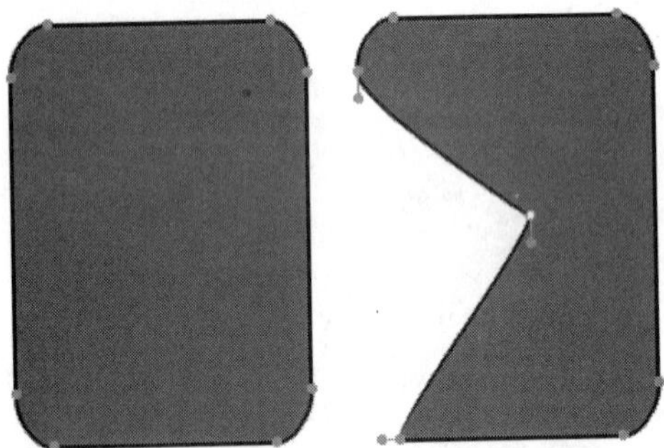

Figure 7.28 Moving a point can have a drastic effect on a shape.

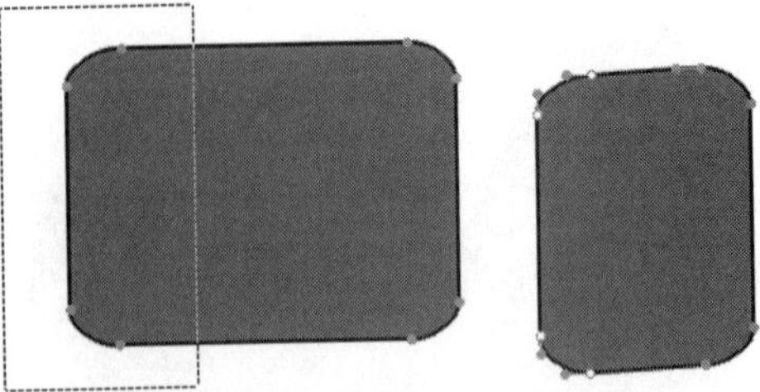

Figure 7.29 Move multiple points in a vector shape at the same time by first selecting them together.

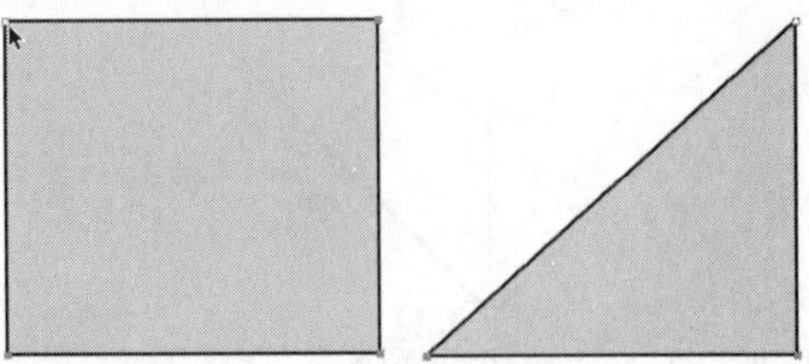

Figure 7.30 Deleting a point also changes a shape.

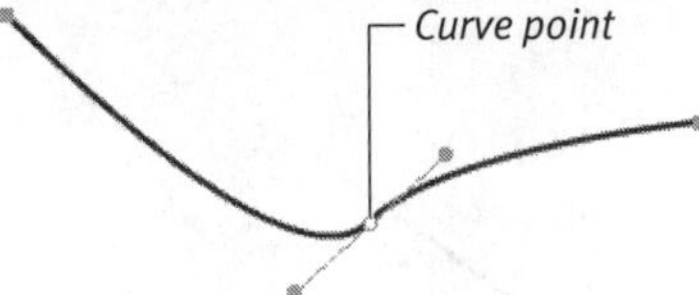

Figure 7.31 When you select a curve point, its handles appear.

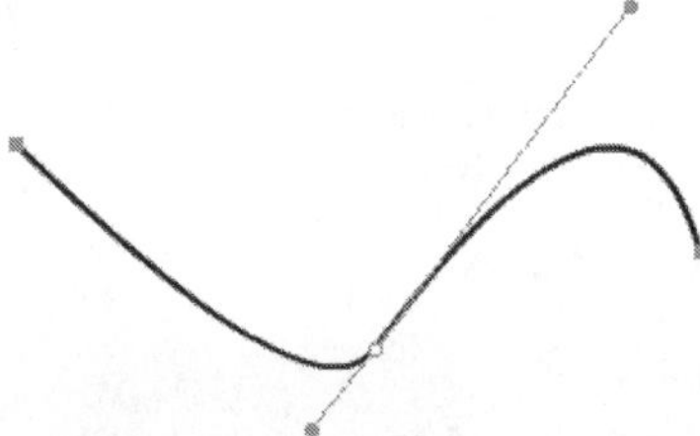

Figure 7.32 Drag a handle to shorten or lengthen the adjacent curve.

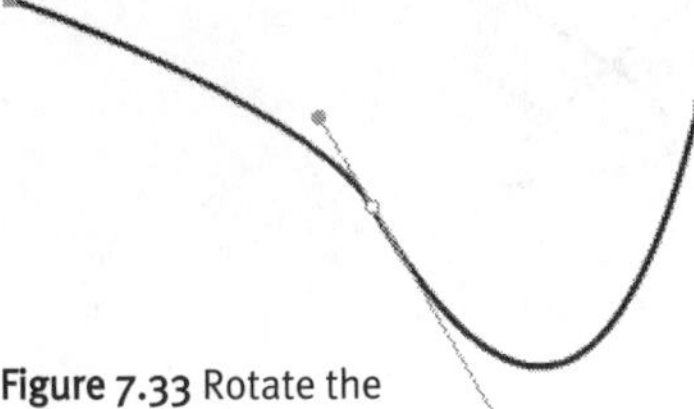

Figure 7.33 Rotate the curve around the point by dragging and rotating a control handle.

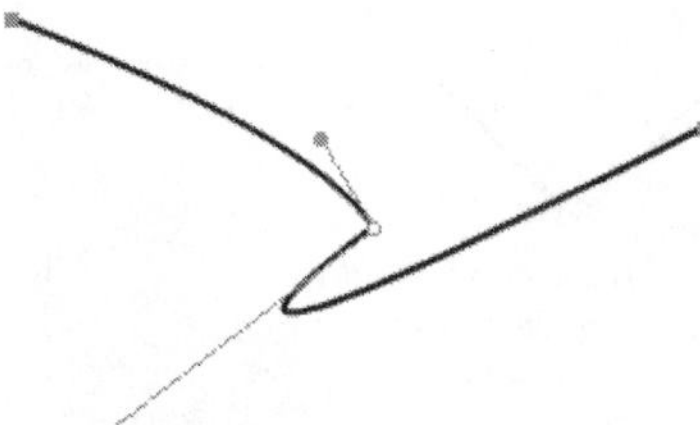

Figure 7.34 You can independently rotate either control handle by holding down the Control key (Windows) or Command key (Mac) and dragging either control handle.

To delete points:

1. In a Cast window, double-click a vector shape.
2. Click the Selection tool in the Vector Shape window.
3. Select a point or points.
4. Press Delete (**Figure 7.30**).

   The lines connecting to the point or points you delete are also removed.

To adjust a curve point:

1. In a Cast window, double-click a vector shape.
2. Click the Selection tool in the Vector Shape window.
3. Click to select the curve point to adjust.

   Two handles appear (**Figure 7.31**). These handles normally are 180 degrees apart.
4. Shorten or lengthen the curve on either side of the point by dragging the corresponding handle (**Figure 7.32**).
5. Rotate the curve around the point by dragging and rotating either control handle (**Figure 7.33**).

✔ Tips

- Hold down the Control key (Windows) or Command key (Mac) to independently drag and rotate one of the handles, which rotates only one side of the curve around the point (**Figure 7.34**).
- Hold down the Shift key while dragging a control handle to constrain it to movements of 45-degree increments.

To convert a corner point to a curve point:

1. Select a corner point (**Figure 7.35**).

   Corner points are represented by small squares.
2. Alt+click (Windows) or Option+click (Mac) and drag the point in the direction of the first control handle you want to place (**Figure 7.36**).

   The corner point converts to a curve point, which is represented by a small circle with a control handle.
3. Alt+click/Option+click and drag the point again to extend the second control handle and shape the curve.

To convert a curve point to a corner point:

1. Select a curve point (**Figure 7.37**).
2. Drag one control handle into the point to make it disappear.
3. Drag the second control handle into the point.

   The curve becomes a corner (**Figure 7.38**).

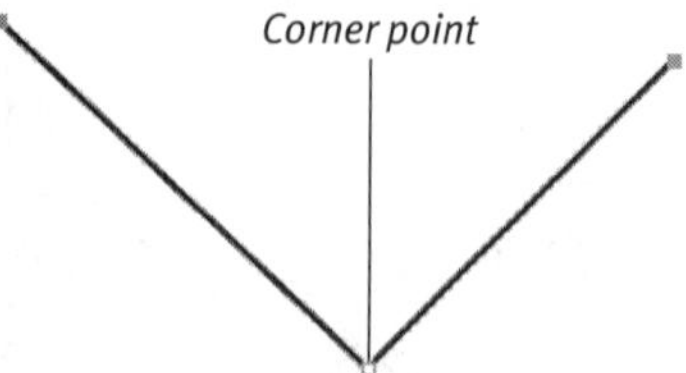

Figure 7.35 Select a corner point.

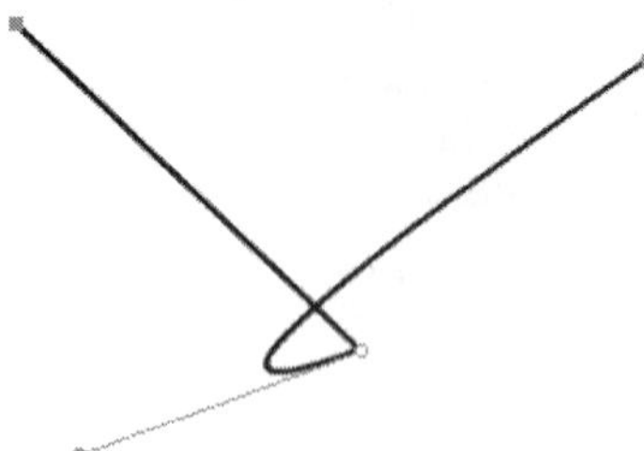

Figure 7.36 Convert a corner point to a curve point by Alt+clicking (Windows) or Option+clicking (Mac) and dragging to extend a control handle.

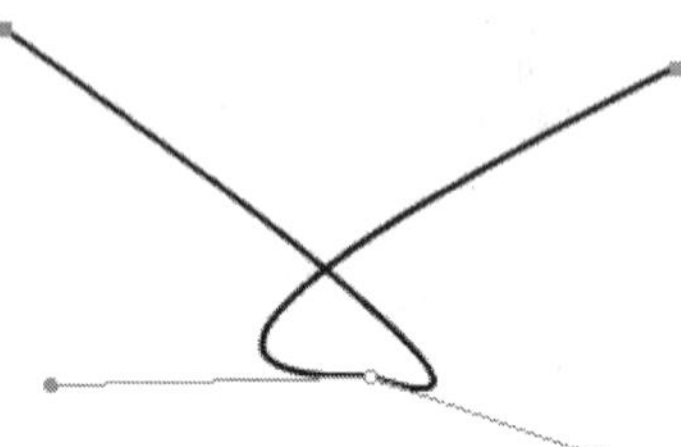

Figure 7.37 Select a curve point.

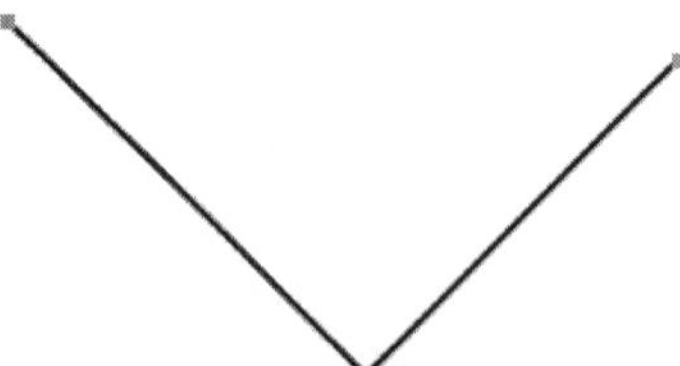

Figure 7.38 Convert the curve point to a corner point by dragging the handles into the point.

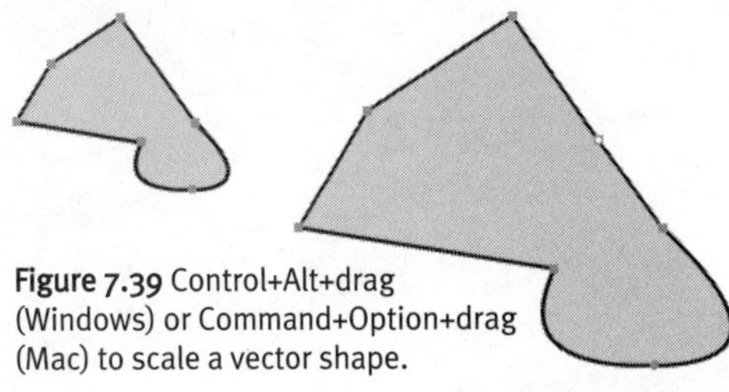

Figure 7.39 Control+Alt+drag (Windows) or Command+Option+drag (Mac) to scale a vector shape.

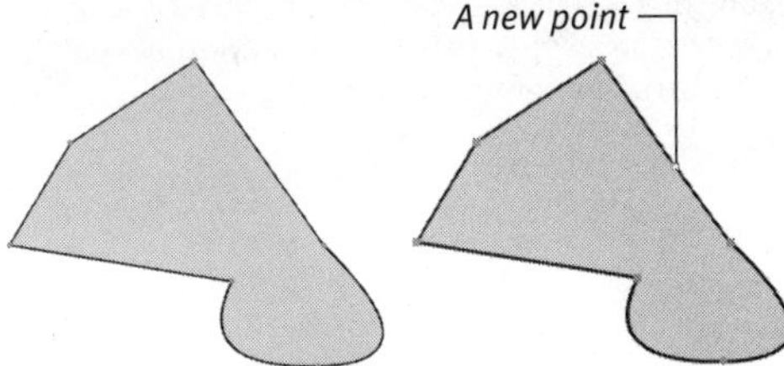

Figure 7.40 Click or drag to add a new point to a path or shape.

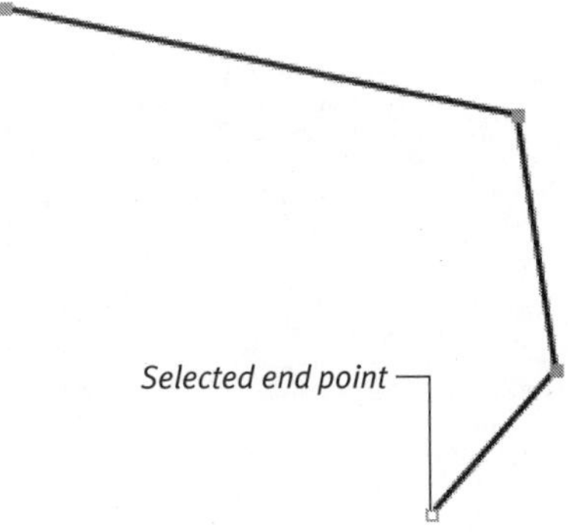

Figure 7.41 Select an end point on the path.

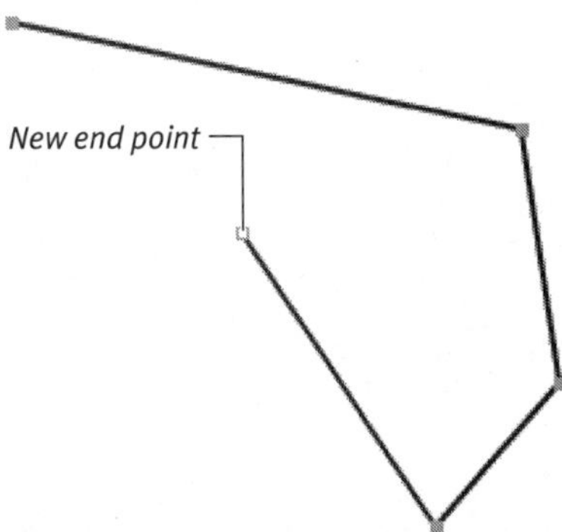

Figure 7.42 With the Pen tool, click to create a new corner end point, or drag to create a new curve end point.

To resize a vector shape:

1. In a Cast window, double-click a vector shape.
2. Click the Selection tool in the Vector Shape window.
3. Control+Alt+drag (Windows) or Command+Option+drag (Mac) to scale the vector shape proportionally (**Figure 7.39**).

To add a point to a closed vector shape:

1. In a Cast window, double-click a closed vector shape.
2. Select the Pen tool.
3. Click anywhere on a path to create a new corner point (**Figure 7.40**).

   or

   Drag anywhere on a path to create a new curve point.

To add a new end point to an open vector shape:

1. In a Cast window, double-click an open vector shape.
2. Click the Selection tool.
3. Click to select either end point of the path (**Figure 7.41**).

   A selected point becomes hollow.
4. Select the Pen tool.
5. Click anywhere to create a new corner end point (**Figure 7.42**).

   or

   Drag anywhere to create a new curve end point.

To add a new point to an open vector shape:

1. In a Cast window, double-click an open vector shape.
2. Select the Pen tool.
3. Alt+click (Windows) or Option+click (Mac) anywhere on the path to add a new corner point (**Figure 7.43**).

   or

   Alt+drag or Option+drag to add a new curve point.

   If your vector cast member consists of multiple shapes, you can easily change the relative positions of these shapes.

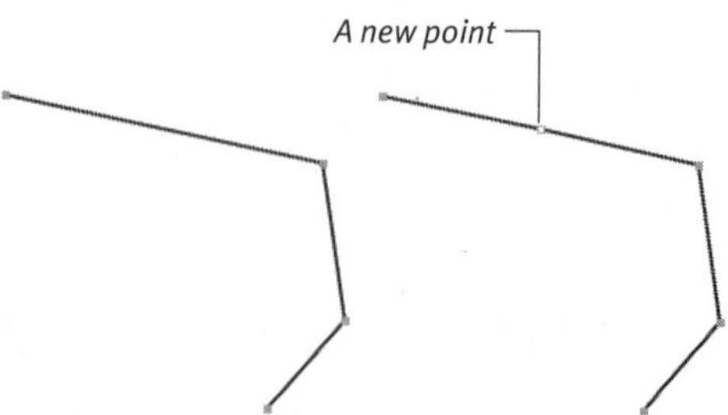

Figure 7.43 Alt+click (Windows) or Option+click (Mac) anywhere on an open path to add a new corner point, or drag to add a new curve point.

To move a shape within a multiple-shape vector cast member:

1. In a Cast window, double-click a vector shape.
2. Move the mouse pointer over any edge of a shape that you want to reposition.

   Notice that the pointer color inverts.
3. Drag the shape to its new location (**Figure 7.44**).

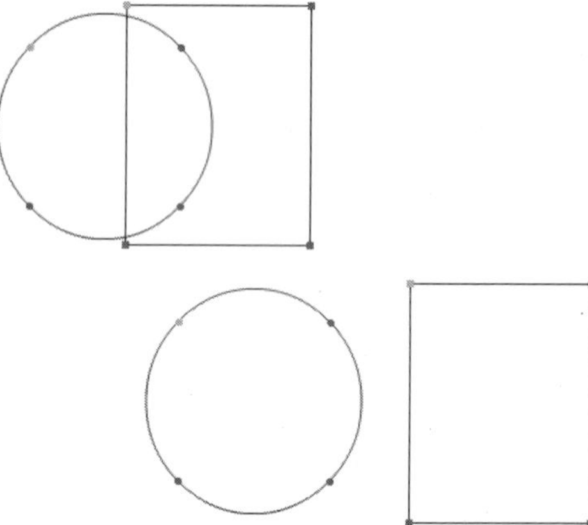

Figure 7.44 Drag a shape by its edge to move it.

✔ Tips

- You can move multiple shapes at the same time by first selecting all their points with the Selection tool and then dragging a selected point to a new location.
- If the shape that you want to move is filled, you can move it simply by dragging its interior.

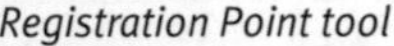

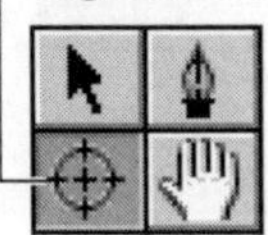

Figure 7.45 Select the Registration Point tool.

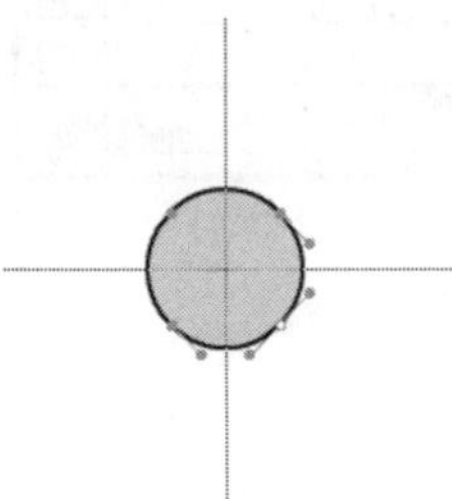

Figure 7.46 The registration point initially falls at the center of any vector shape.

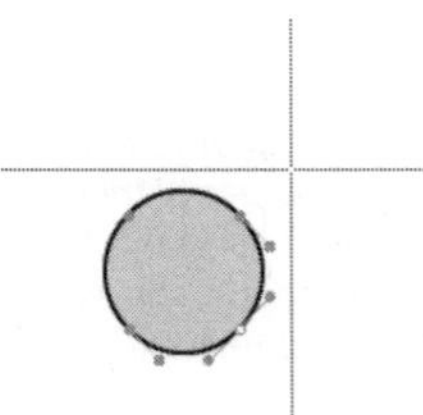

Figure 7.47 With the Registration Point tool selected, click to set a new registration point.

When you place a vector shape on the stage, the shape is placed relative to its registration point. You can change the registration point, just as you can for bitmapped cast members.

To adjust the registration point for a vector shape:

1. In a Cast window, double-click a vector shape.
2. Select the Registration Point tool in the Vector Shape window (**Figure 7.45**).

   The default registration point appears as a crosshair at the center of the vector shape (**Figure 7.46**).
3. Click anywhere in the window to set a new registration point (**Figure 7.47**).

✔ Tip

- Double-click the Registration Point tool to reset the registration point to the center of the vector shape.

To anti-alias a vector shape:

1. Select a vector-shape cast member in a Cast window (**Figure 7.48**).
2. Select a cast member with edges that appear too jagged in the movie (**Figure 7.49**).
3. Choose Modify > Cast Member > Properties.

   The Property Inspector opens.
4. Select the Vector tab.
5. Choose the Anti-Alias option (**Figure 7.50**).

   The anti-aliased vector shape has blurred edges, which improves the appearance of vector shapes that use thick lines (**Figure 7.51**).

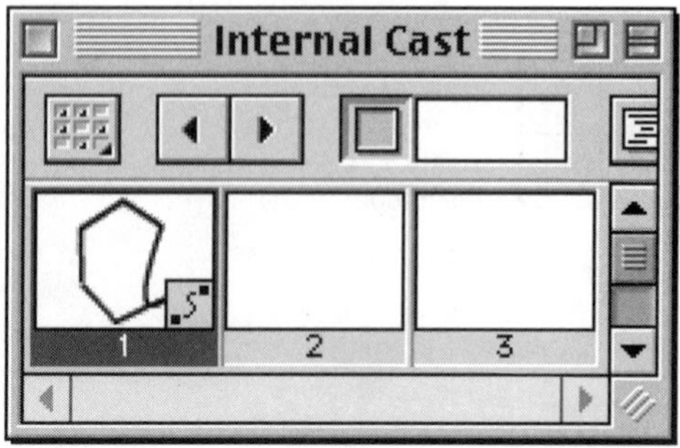

Figure 7.48 Select a vector-shape cast member.

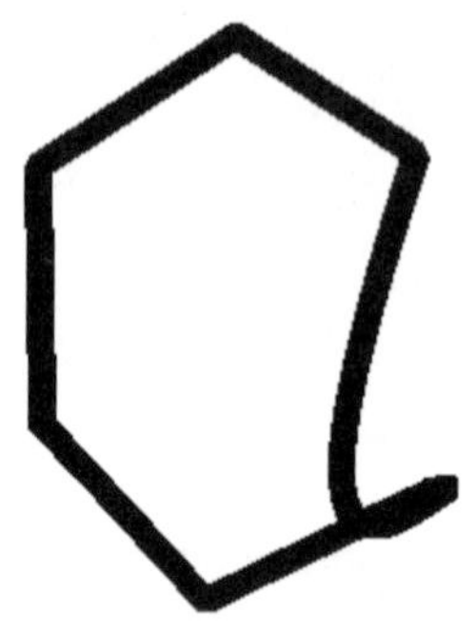

Figure 7.49 Notice the jagged edges of the curved lines of this vector shape, shown before anti-aliasing.

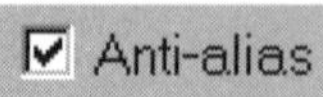

Figure 7.50 Check the Anti-Alias option.

Figure 7.51 A vector shape has smoother, blurry edges after anti-aliasing.

WORKING ON THE STAGE

Figure 8.1 Director's stage is where your movies play.

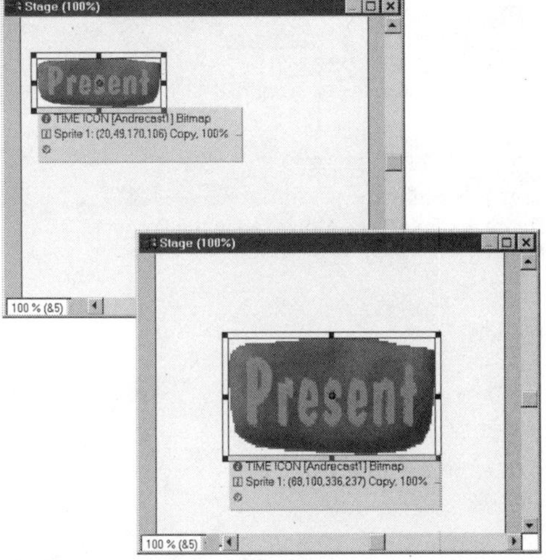

Figure 8.2 You can edit components of your movie directly on the stage.

As you well know by now, Director's stage is where your movies play (**Figure 8.1**). You also frequently use the stage to help build your movies, such as by dragging and positioning cast members and resizing sprites (**Figure 8.2**). Understanding how to manipulate the stage and its various properties while authoring will help you maximize creative possibilities.

This chapter covers how to change various stage attributes, such as size and color; how to zoom the stage; and how to use grids and guides for aligning sprites. The chapter also covers the drawing, button, and text tools in the Tool Palette, which allow you to create cast members directly on the stage instead of using a media editor, such as the Paint or Vector window.

Setting Stage Properties

The size and location of the stage form an important part of your users' viewing experience. If you plan to distribute your movie in Shockwave on the Web, for example, you may want the movie to play in a relatively small window at the center of a Web browser so that other information around it is visible (**Figure 8.3**). Other movies, such as projector-based entertainment titles, may demand that the stage occupy the full screen.

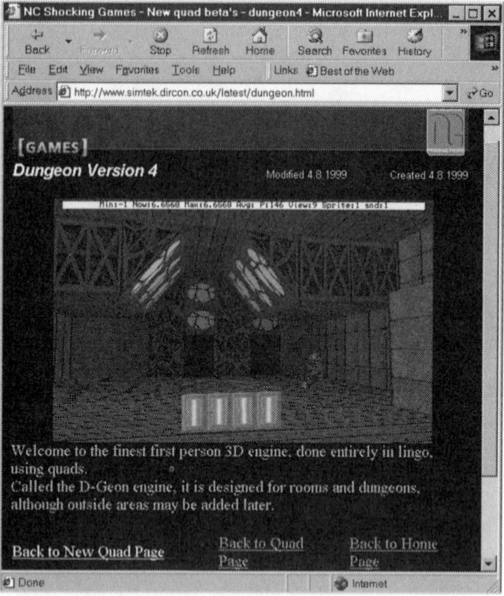

Figure 8.3 You can make the stage any size you want. (Screen shot of Dungeon created by NoiseCrime.)

To change the size and location of the stage for your movie:

1. Choose Modify > Movie > Properties.
2. Select the Movie tab in the Property Inspector (**Figure 8.4**).
3. Click the List View Mode button, if necessary, to place the Property Inspector in Graphical Layout mode.
4. Choose a new stage size from the Stage Size pop-up menu.
5. Choose a new stage location from the Stage Location pop-up menu.

   Your choices are Centered, Upper Left, and Other. If you choose Other, specify coordinates by entering them in the adjoining boxes.

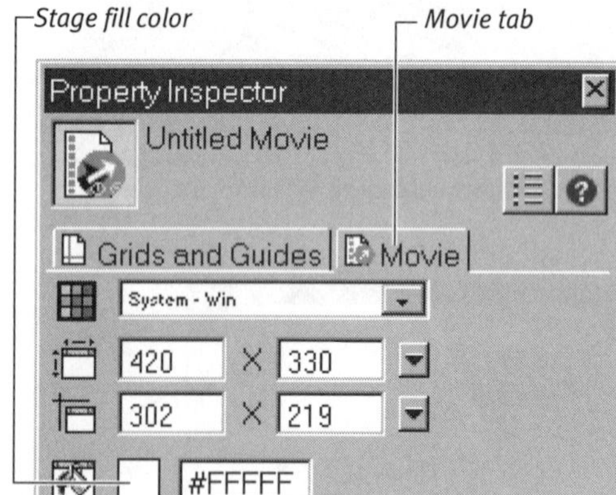

Figure 8.4 Select the Movie tab in the Property Inspector.

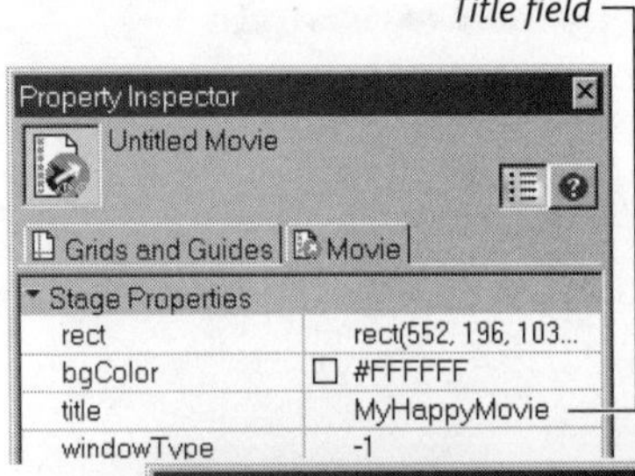

Figure 8.5 Title your stage by entering a name in the Title field.

You can view your movie in Full Screen mode during authoring or playback, which hides all of Director's user-interface features. The actual stage size remains the same.

To view the stage in Full Screen mode:

Choose View > Full Screen to toggle Full Screen mode, or press Ctrl+Alt+1 (Command+Option+1 on the Mac).

To change the background color of the stage:

1. Repeat steps 1-3 from the section titled "To change the size and location of the stage for your movie".
2. Click the Stage Fill Color chip to select a color (**Figure 8.4**).

To set the title of the stage:

1. Choose Modify > Movie > Properties.
2. Select the Movie tab in the Property Inspector.
3. Click the List View Mode button, if necessary, to place the Property Inspector in Table mode.
4. In the Title field, type a name for the title bar of the stage (**Figure 8.5**).

Zooming and Scrolling the Stage

While editing your movie, you may often find it helpful to change the zoom factor of the stage (**Figure 8.6**). All normal editing operations, such as moving and aligning sprites, work as usual in a zoomed state.

To zoom the stage window:

◆ Choose View > Zoom, and select a magnification level from the pop-up menu .

or

Press Ctrl+[+] or Ctrl+[-] to zoom in or out one level (Command+[+] or Command+[-] on Mac).

✔ Tips

- You also can zoom the stage by using the Magnifying Glass tool in the Tool Palette (**Figure 8.7**). Choose Window > Tool Palette, and select the Magnifying Glass in the palette. Click the stage to zoom in or Alt+click (Option+click on the Mac) to zoom out. The advantage of using this tool is that wherever you click the stage determines the new center of the zoom.
- When your stage is zoomed in or out, you can choose View > Standard View to set the stage zoom level back to 100 percent. You can return to your original zoom level by choosing View > Restore View.

Figure 8.6 You can zoom in and out when working on the stage. Here is the same scene at 50 percent, 100 percent, and 200 percent.

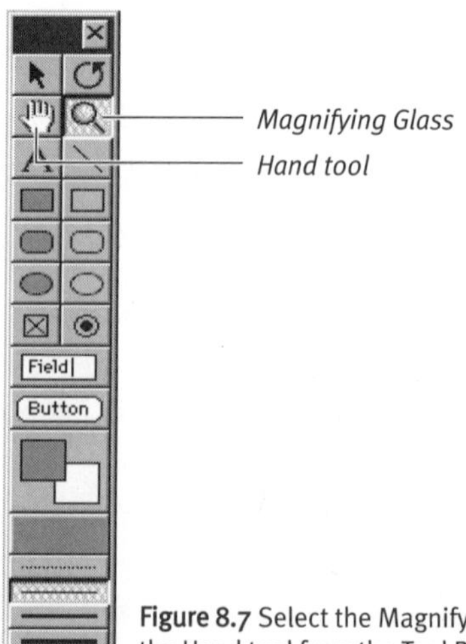

Figure 8.7 Select the Magnifying Glass or the Hand tool from the Tool Palette.

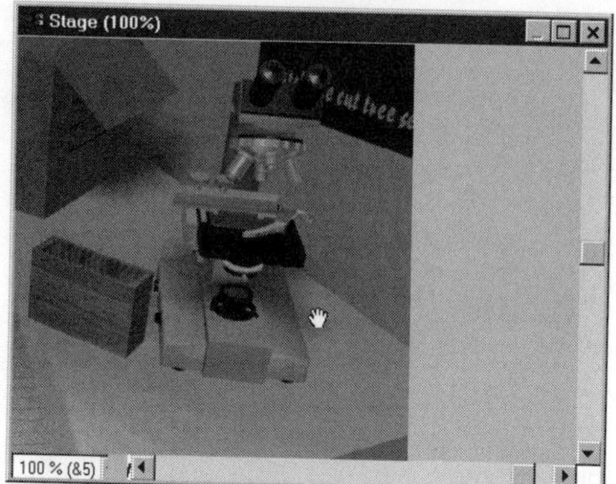

Figure 8.8 Drag the stage with the Hand tool to scroll it in any direction.

Depending on the stage zoom level, it often is necessary to scroll the stage to make certain sprites visible. You can use the stage scroll bars, but it may be more convenient to use the Hand tool in the Tool Palette (**Figure 8.7**).

To scroll the stage with the Hand tool:

1. Choose Window > Tool Palette.
2. Select the Hand tool in the Tool Palette.
3. Drag the stage to scroll it in any direction (**Figure 8.8**).

Using Grids and Guides

Director has a grid that you can use to align sprites on the stage (**Figure 8.9**).

To display and configure the stage grid:

1. Choose View > Grids and Guides > Show Grid.

   The grid appears.

2. Choose View > Grids and Guides > Settings to adjust grid settings.

   Make sure that the bottom pane of the Property Inspector is open. This pane is where you can set the color and line spacing of the grid (**Figure 8.10**).

3. Choose View > Grids and Guides > Snap To to toggle this feature.

   When Snap To is on, any time you drag a sprite and release it close to the grid, the edge of the sprite automatically scoots over to cling to the nearest part of the grid.

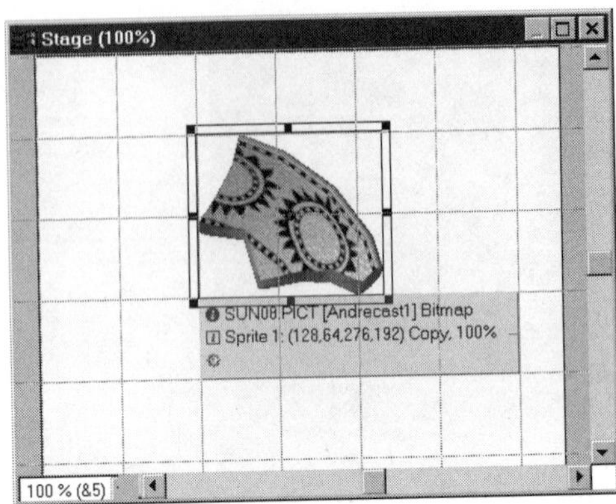

Figure 8.9 Sprites can align to Director's stage grid.

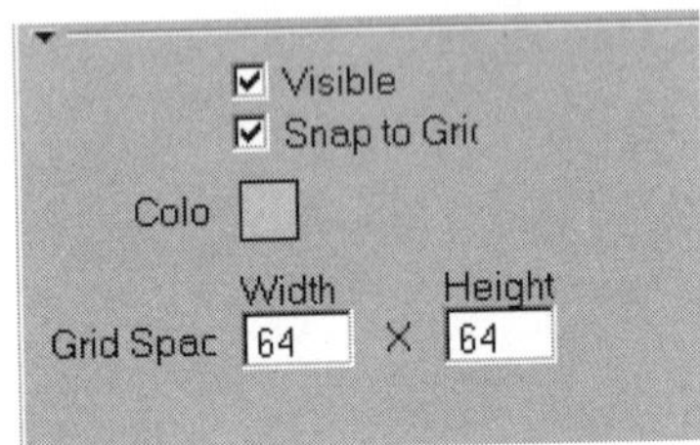

Figure 8.10 Set grid attributes in the Grid and Guides tab of the Property Inspector.

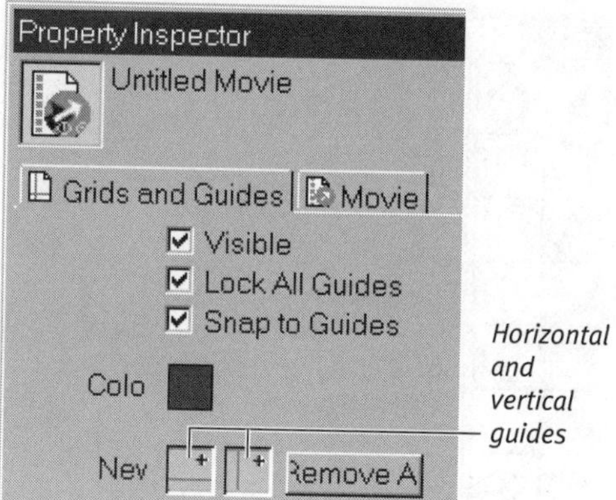

Figure 8.11 Place a horizontal or vertical guide line on the stage by dragging it from the corresponding symbol in the Property Inspector.

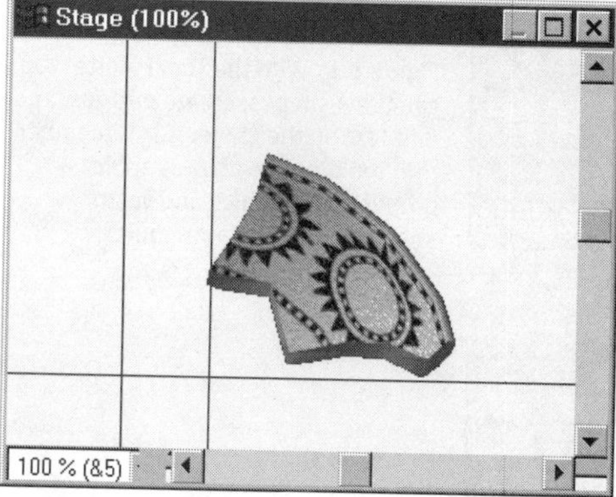

Figure 8.12 Guides on the stage.

Sometimes, you need to align sprites to a specific position on the stage that does not coincide with a grid line. In this case, you can add custom guide lines, much like those in a page-layout program, and align sprites to them.

To add guides to the stage:

1. Choose View > Grids and Guides > Settings.
2. In the Property Inspector, drag a guide from the horizontal or vertical guide symbol to the desired place on the stage (**Figures 8.11** and **8.12**).

   You can add as many guides as you need.
3. Select the Visible option in the Property Inspector to make guides visible on the stage.
4. If you want sprites to snap to your guides, select the Snap to Guides option.
5. Select Lock All Guides to prevent them from being moved on the stage.
6. Choose an alternative color for the guides by clicking the Color chip and choosing the color from the Color menu.

✔ Tip

- Click the Remove button in the Property Inspector below the Grid and Guides tab to remove all guides from the stage.

Creating Shapes on the Stage

You can create shape, text, and button cast members directly on the stage by using the Tool Palette (**Figure 8.13**).

Shapes created with the Tool Palette are QuickDraw graphics, which have a couple of advantages over bitmaps and vectors—and some real drawbacks. QuickDraw shapes (including lines) can be resized and edited on the stage. They consume much less memory than bitmap images and print much better on laser printers (if printing is something that you expect people to do with your project).

On the downside, QuickDraw graphics created with the Tool Palette animate more slowly than bitmaps or vector shapes. Also, you cannot edit QuickDraw graphics in the Paint window or Vector Shape window.

Figure 8.13 With the Tool Palette, you can draw shapes, create buttons, and edit text on the stage. Just remember that the other Director graphics—bitmapped graphics and vector shapes—animate more quickly.

To draw a line:

1. Click the Line tool (**Figure 8.14**).
2. Choose a line width from the bottom of the Tool Palette (**Figure 8.15**).
3. With the Line tool, drag on the stage to draw a line.
4. Release the mouse button when the line is the right length and direction.

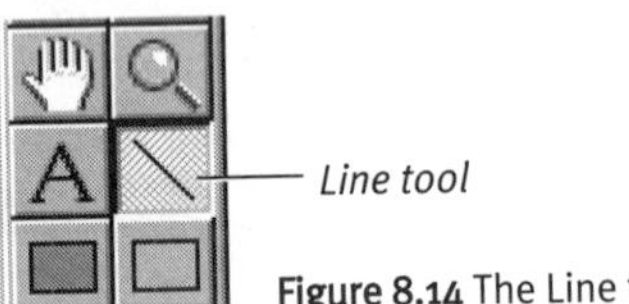

Figure 8.14 The Line tool.

✔ Tip

- Hold down the Shift key while dragging the Line tool to make 45-degree lines.

Figure 8.15 Click a line option to choose a line thickness.

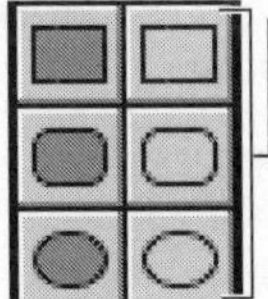

Figure 8.16 Choose a hollow shape tool to draw an unfilled geometric figure.

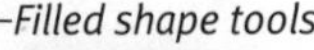

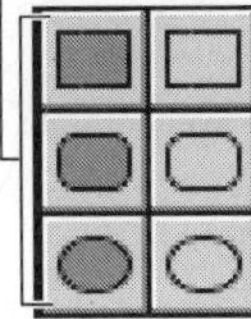

Figure 8.17 Choose a filled shape tool to draw geometric figures filled with the current color and pattern.

Figure 8.18 Click a line selection to choose a line thickness. Choose the dotted line if you want no border on a filled shape.

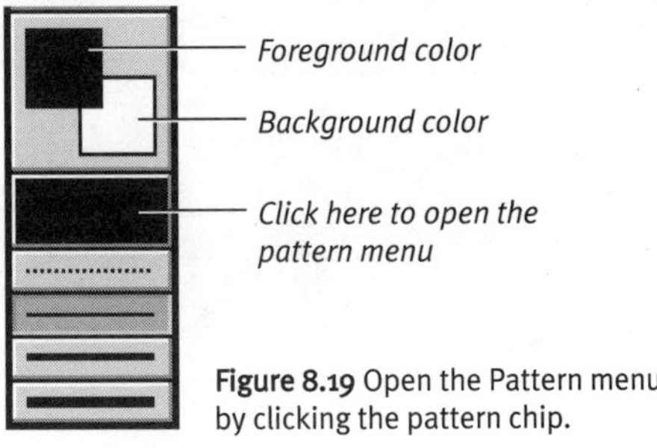

Figure 8.19 Open the Pattern menu by clicking the pattern chip.

To draw a hollow shape:

1. Click a hollow shape tool (**Figure 8.16**).

   Your choices are Rectangle, Rounded-Corner rectangle, and Ellipse.

2. Choose a line width from the bottom of the Tool Palette.

3. On the stage, drag diagonally to make a shape.

4. Release the mouse button when the shape is the right size and proportion.

✔ Tip

- Hold down the Shift key while dragging a rectangle to produce a square. Do the same with the Ellipse tool to make a circle.

To draw a filled shape:

1. Click a filled shape tool (**Figure 8.17**).

2. Choose a line width for the shape's border from the bottom of the Tool Palette (**Figure 8.18**).

   Select the dotted line if you want no border to show.

3. Click and hold the foreground color chip to select a color for the shape from the pop-up Color menu.

   or

   Click and hold the Pattern chip to choose a pattern from the Pattern pop-up menu (**Figure 8.19**).

4. Drag diagonally on the stage to make a shape.

5. Release the mouse button when the shape is the right size and proportion.

To set the color and pattern of QuickDraw graphics on the stage:

1. Select a QuickDraw line or shape on the stage.
2. Click the foreground or background color chip in the Tool Palette to select a color from the Color menu (**Figures 8.20** and **8.21**).

   The foreground color applies to the color of a shape or line, to the fill color of a filled shape, and to the foreground color of any pattern.

   The background color affects only the background color of any applied patterns.
3. Click the Pattern chip to select a pattern, which is visible in filled shapes only.

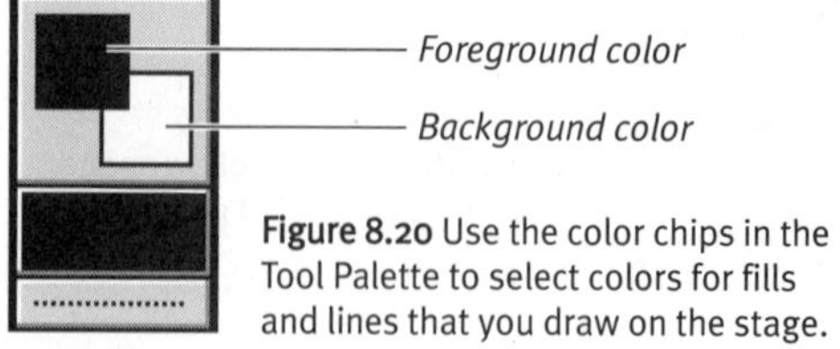

Figure 8.20 Use the color chips in the Tool Palette to select colors for fills and lines that you draw on the stage.

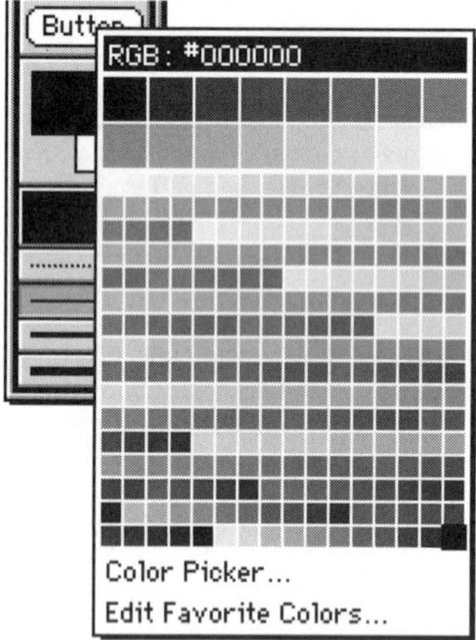

Figure 8.21 Choose a new foreground color from the Color pop-up menu.

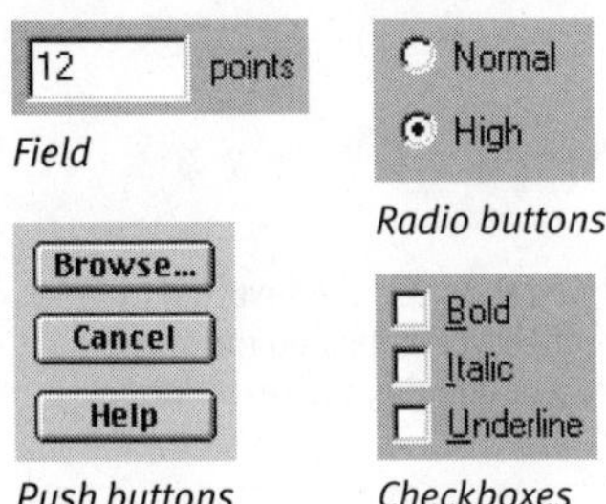

Figure 8.22 You can draw fields, buttons, checkboxes, or radio buttons with the Tool Palette.

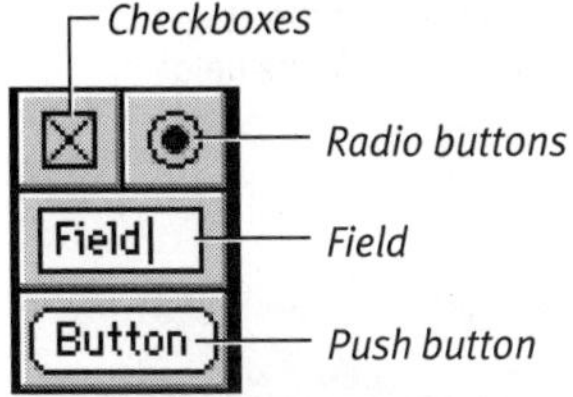

Figure 8.23 When you click a button tool in the Tool Palette, you also choose what kind of button or field to draw.

Creating Buttons on the Stage

With the tools in the Tool Palette, you can draw and set text for fields, push buttons, and sets of checkboxes or radio buttons (**Figure 8.22**).

Radio buttons and checkboxes always come in sets. Use *radio buttons* for "choose one" situations, in which a user can click only one radio button in the set at a time. Use *checkboxes* when users can check all that apply. Push buttons trigger just one action.

Fields are places where the user can enter text.

During movie playback, buttons that you draw on the stage appear to respond when clicked but trigger no other action unless you attach a Lingo script (see Chapter 17, "Scripting Lingo").

To draw buttons and checkboxes:

1. Open the Tool Palette.
2. Choose a frame and make the stage visible.
3. Click one of the button tools in the Tool Palette (**Figure 8.23**).
   You can choose radio buttons, a push button, a field, or checkboxes.
4. Drag the mouse to create a rectangle on the stage where the button will go.
5. Choose the font, size, and style for any text that goes with the buttons or checkboxes.
   Reach the text-formatting tools by choosing Modify > Font or by using the Text Inspector (see Chapter 11, "Adding Text").
6. Type the text that belongs with the button, field, or checkboxes.
   When you place the artwork on the stage, Director creates a button or field cast member.

✔ Tip

- You can also edit button or field text on the stage.

Creating Text on the Stage

On the stage, you can use the Text tool (**Figure 8.24**) and Field tool (**Figure 8.25**) as alternatives to opening the Text and Field windows (**Figure 8.26**). When you create text on the stage with the Text or Field tool, you create a text cast member, just as you would if you used the Text or Field window instead.

See Chapter 11, "Adding Text," for a complete discussion of the advantages of one type of text over another in Director. That chapter also provides complete instructions for creating and editing text and field text on the stage.

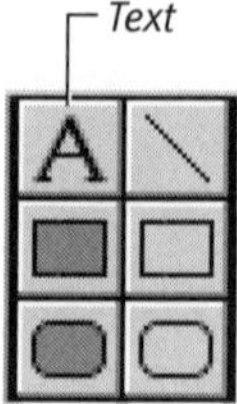

Figure 8.24 Use the Text tool to create and edit text on the stage without opening the Text window.

Figure 8.25 Use the Field tool to create Field text on the stage, in addition to creating the fields themselves.

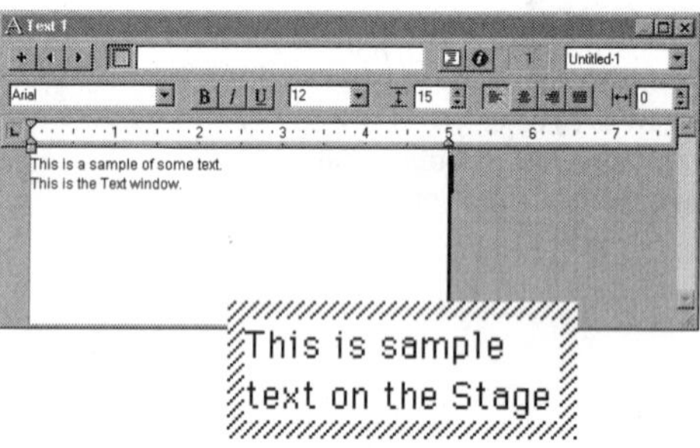

Figure 8.26 Text in the Text window and Text on the stage in a simple text box.

9

MANAGING COLOR

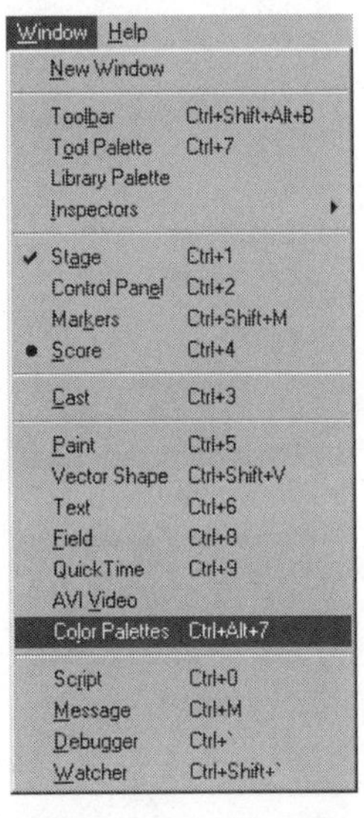

Figure 9.1 Throughout this chapter, you open the palettes window by choosing Window > Color Palettes.

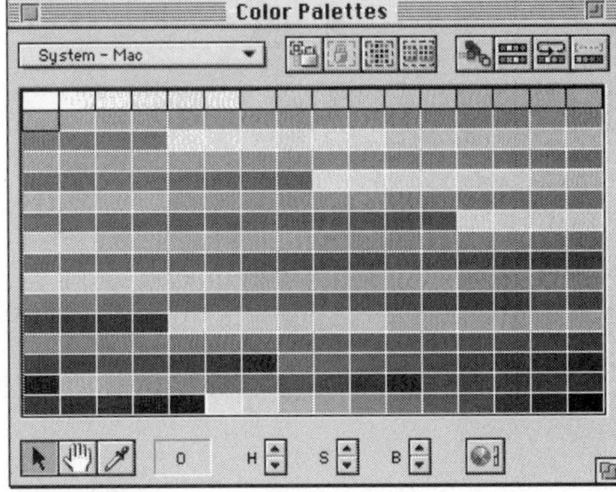

Figure 9.2 Edit cast member colors in the Color Palettes window.

Imagine animation without color. Hard to picture, right? Color makes a big impact in animation. But lots of rich color graphics also can make a file fat and slow.

Managing color in Director amounts to balancing the best color effects against the size they take up in memory and on disk, and against the time they take to download.

Even if you don't need to worry about download time or wedging your movies into a fixed number of megabytes, in this chapter you can learn the basics that are the foundation of animating color changes in sprites.

This chapter covers all color basics, such as how to use the color menu and how to customize palettes to keep favorite colors at hand. You'll learn about movie and cast-member color depth and how these settings relate to color palettes. You'll create and edit palettes (**Figures 9.1-9.2**) and learn how to take the most commonly used colors from a variety of cast members and arrange them in a palette that all cast members share.

This chapter also explains how to create impressive visual effects through palette transitions and a special technique called color cycling, which makes cast members appear to animate and pulse.

Color Depth

The first thing to understand about color in Director is color depth. *Color depth*, sometimes called *bit depth*, relates to the number of colors that a computer can display at the same time. The maximum number of colors is governed by how much room (in bits) a computer has to store information about each dot, or *pixel*, on the screen (**Table 9.1**). The more bits of color data the computer stores for each pixel, the more colors the computer can display (**Figure 9.3**).

Today, most new computers can display at least 16-bit color. Sometimes, however, you need to limit the color depth of a movie or some of its elements to make it download faster over the Web or other network or to make a scene display quickly.

Movie Color Depth

When you specify the color depth for an entire movie, you set the maximum number of colors for all the images it contains. A movie set to 8-bit color depth displays any 16-bit or 32-bit cast members in 8-bit color, substituting the closest colors available out of 256 colors. The results may not be pretty, so it's best to decide the maximum bit color depth at the start of a project and then assemble the cast accordingly.

✔ Tip

- If you need to strike a balance between a few rich graphics and the need for a compact movie file, set the movie depth to match the cast elements or background with the most colors. Then set all other cast elements individually to the lowest bit depth that looks acceptable, so that they take up the least amount of space and load and animate as quickly as possible.

32 bits per pixel

16 bits per pixel

8 bits per pixel

4 bits per pixel

2 bits per pixel

1 bit per pixel

Figure 9.3 This series of images suggests how the color depth affects the appearance of a cast member. Try it yourself and see the results in color.

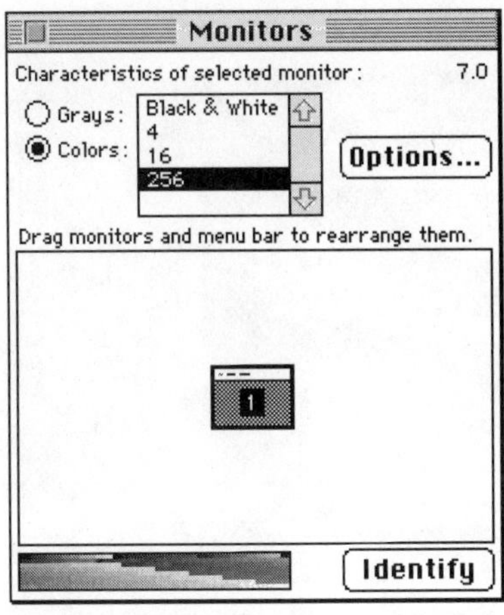

Figure 9.4 The Mac Monitors control panel.

Figure 9.5 Choose the color depth.

Table 9.1

Color depth compared with colors displayed and file size for a cast member

BITS PER PIXEL	NUMBER OF COLORS DISPLAYED	SIZE OF EXAMPLE (IN KB)
1 bit	black & white only	12
2 bits	4	24
4 bits	16	48
8 bits	256	96
16 bits	32,768	192
32 bits	16.7 million	384

You change the color depth for an entire movie by resetting the color depth for the computer you're using to develop the project. That means that the process is different for Mac and Windows users. It also means that the maximum bit depth for a movie is the bit depth of the computer on which you prepare your movie as a Projector or Shockwave movie.

To change movie color depth (Mac):

1. Choose Apple > Control Panels > Monitors.

   The Monitors control panel appears (**Figure 9.4**).

2. Set the number of colors to display in the current Director movie (**Figure 9.5**).

3. Save the movie.

✔ Tip

- On the Macintosh, you can make Director change the monitor's color depth setting automatically to match the current movie. Choose File > Preferences > General. In the General Preferences dialog box, select Reset Monitor to Movie's Color Depth.

You change color depth in Windows through the Display Properties dialog box.

To change movie color depth (Windows):

1. Open the Control Panel and double-click the Display icon.

   The Display Properties dialog box appears.
2. Click the Settings tab (**Figure 9.6**).
3. Set the number of colors to display in the current Director movie (**Figure 9.7**).
4. Save the movie.

Here's a way to find the color-depth setting of a movie.

To check the movie color depth:

1. Open the Paint window.
2. Click the plus sign in the top-left corner of the window, as if to create a new cast member.
3. Look in the bottom-left corner of the window for the movie's current color depth (**Figure 9.8**).

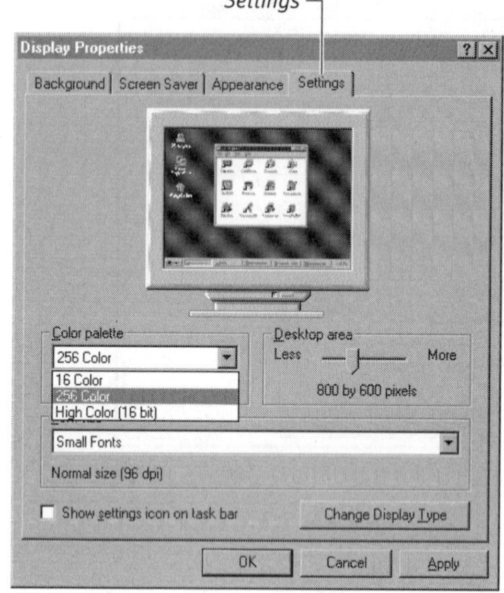

Figure 9.6 Display Properties settings.

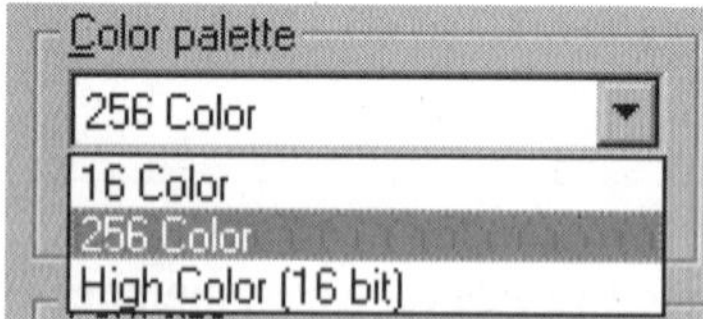

Figure 9.7 Color-depth choices.

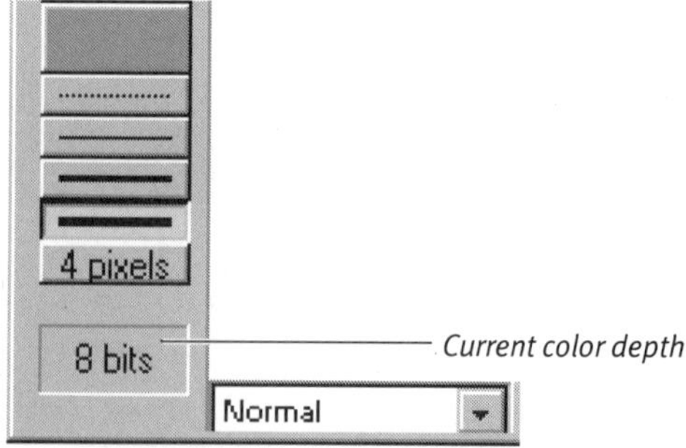

Figure 9.8 Find the current movie's color depth in the corner of the Paint window.

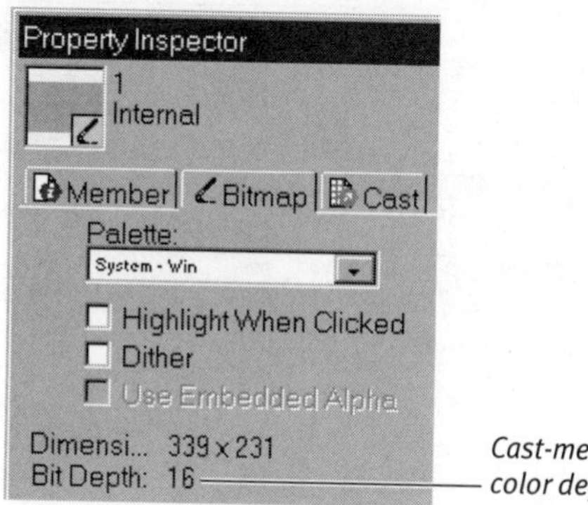

Figure 9.9 View a cast member's color depth.

Cast-Member Color Depth

Each bitmapped cast member in Director has its own color-depth setting, which can differ from the movie color depth. The greater a cast member's color depth, the more memory it requires and the more time it takes to animate. Most new computer systems today can handle 16-bit color depth.

For a cast member to display its entire range of colors in a movie, the movie color-depth setting must be at least as high as the cast-member color depth. If you want to accurately display a 16-bit cast member (32,768 colors), for example, the movie color-depth setting must be at least 16 bits.

You may sometimes want to check a cast member's color depth.

To view cast-member color depth:

1. Open a Cast window.
2. Select a bitmap cast member.
3. Choose Modify >Cast Member > Properties.
4. Select the Bitmap tab.

   The cast member's bit depth appears next to either Bit Depth or Depth, depending on the view mode selected in the Property Inspector (**Figure 9.9**).

To change a cast member's color depth:

1. If you want to preserve an original of the cast member at its original color depth, make a backup copy of the cast member. You can't reverse a color-depth change.
2. In the Cast window, select a cast member.
3. Choose Modify > Transform Bitmap. The Transform Bitmap dialog box appears (**Figure 9.10**).
4. Select the new depth for the cast member (**Figure 9.11**).
5. Click Transform (**Figure 9.12**).

✔ Tip

- If cast members have higher color depth settings than the movie that contains them, the extra colors do not display, but the sprites based on the cast members animate more slowly, as though the computer were processing all the original colors. In most cases, you should transform cast members to the color depth setting of the movie—or lower.

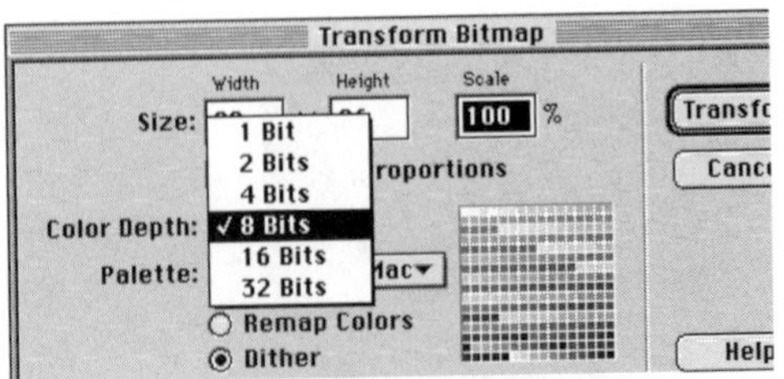

Figure 9.10 The Transform Bitmap dialog box.

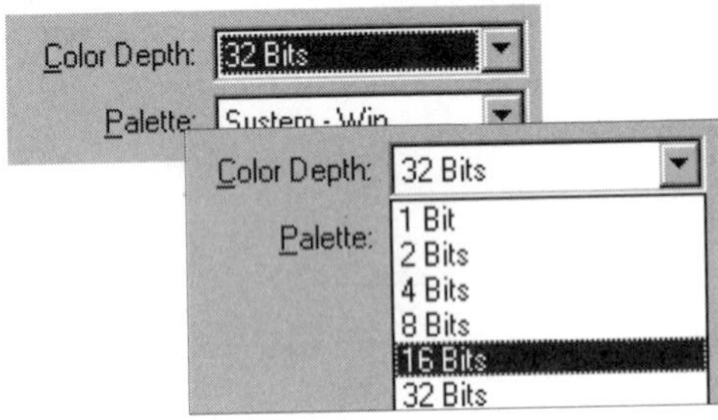

Figure 9.11 Choose a new color depth.

Figure 9.12 Click Transform.

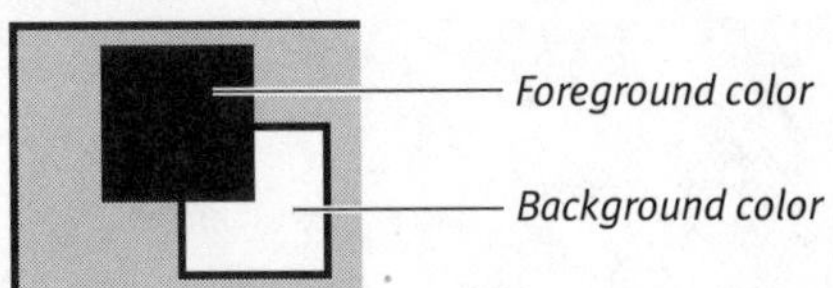

Figure 9.13 Click foreground or background color chips to open the color menu.

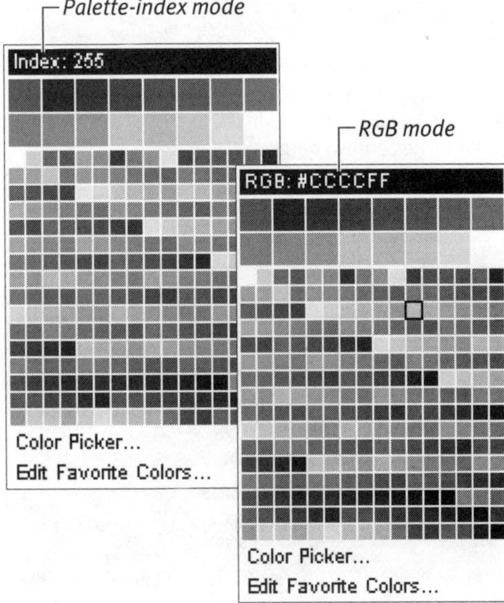

Figure 9.14 The color menu indicates color mode.

Color Mode

Director offers a choice of two basic color modes for your movies and authoring process: *RGB* for thousands of colors and *palette index* for 8-bit color or other constrained situations.

Opening a color menu is the first step in performing many tasks with Director's color features.

To open a color menu:

1. Choose a sprite or a cast member.
2. Open a window or tool with access to a color menu.

   Any tools with foreground and background color chips (**Figure 9.13**) can access the color menu. You can find a color menu in the Property Inspector when a sprite is selected; in the Tool Palette; and in the Score, Vector Shape, or Paint window.
3. Click the foreground or background color chip.

   The color menu opens.

The current color mode appears at the top of the color menu.

To check the current color mode:

1. Open a color menu.
2. Look at the top of the color menu for the color mode indicator (**Figure 9.14**).
3. Close the color menu.

RGB Mode for Nearly Anyone

People who don't need to worry about their movies playing in 8-bit color generally work in RGB mode because it's much simpler. RGB mode offers the most accurate way of specifying colors in Director because you can choose them from a continuous spectrum (**Figure 9.15**). In this mode, Director represents colors in *RGB values*: percentages of red, green, and blue mixed to form a color. You can use RGB mode for all movies, but keep in mind that even though 8-bit movies in RGB mode can represent colors as RGB colors, you are still limited to the 256 colors of the current palette for any one scene.

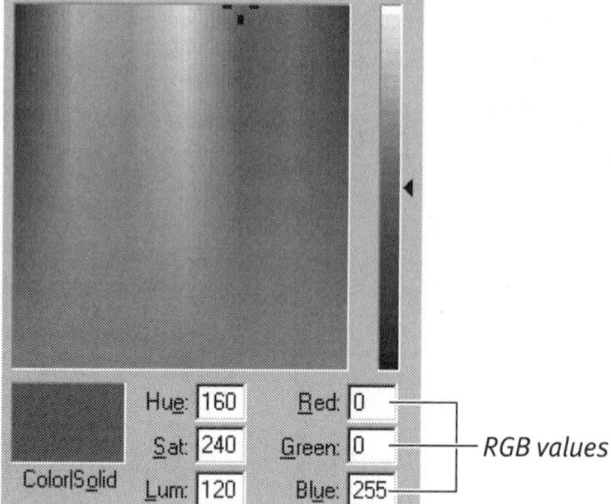

Figure 9.15 In RGB mode, colors are defined by values of red, green, and blue, which you can enter in the Color Picker, shown here.

In movies with 16-bit color depth or greater, palettes are strictly a means of selecting colors. Changing the current palette has no effect on cast-member colors. Color palette transitions and color cycling also have no effect.

Palette-Index Mode for 8-Bit and Less

In palette-index mode, colors are numbered 0 through 255, which refer to positions in the current color palette (**Figure 9.16**). This color mode makes the most sense for movies with limited color depth—8 bits or lower.

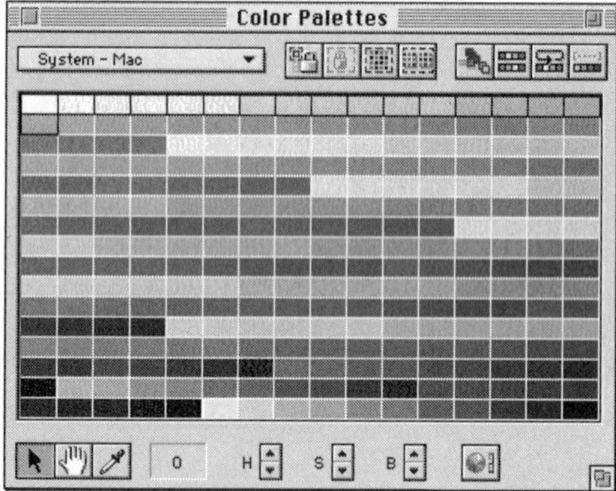

Figure 9.16 In palette-index mode, colors are defined by a number between 0 and 255, representing the position in the current palette.

Even though there's no obvious advantage in doing so, you can choose to use palette-index mode with 16-bit color (or greater) movies. Even in palette-index mode, 16-bit (or greater) movies can display more than 256 colors, but the colors are represented by index values rather than RGB values.

Figure 9.17 Choose RGB or Palette Index color mode.

To set the color mode:

1. Choose Modify > Movie > Properties.

   Make sure that the bottom page of the Property Inspector is expanded.

2. Click the Color Selection option you want: RGB or Palette Index (**Figure 9.17**).

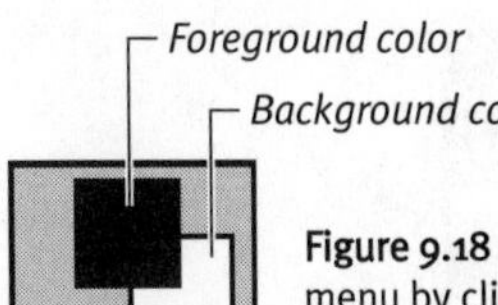

Figure 9.18 Open the color menu by clicking a foreground or background color chip.

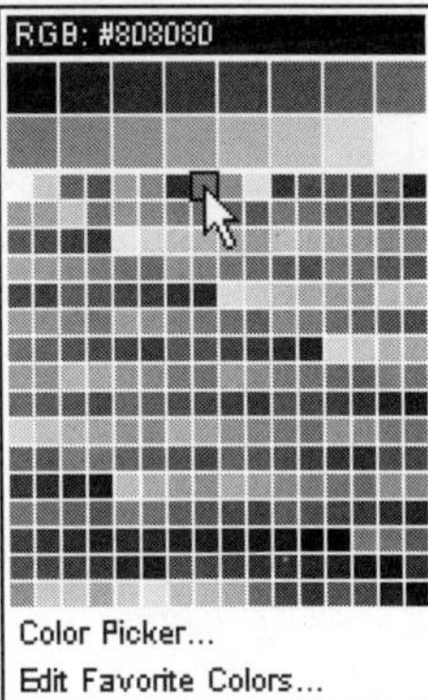

Figure 9.19 Choose a new color.

Color Choices

Whenever you need to specify a color in Director—to paint a new cast member in the Paint or Vector Shape window, for example—you make the selection from the color menu.

To choose a color to work with:

1. Select a cast member or sprite.
2. Open a window or tool with access to a color menu.

   Any tools with foreground and background color chips (**Figure 9.18**) can access the color menu. You can find a color menu in the Property Inspector when a sprite is selected; in the Tool Palette; and in the Score, Vector Shape, or Paint window.
3. Click the foreground or background color chip.

   The color menu opens.
4. Click a new color in the color menu (**Figure 9.19**).

✔ Tip

- Remember that if you are trying to change the color of a sprite, sprites colored black are the easiest to change (see Chapter 3, "Building a Score").

The color menu and current color palette share a direct relationship. Colors in the current palette determine those in the color menu.

To change or set the current color palette:

1. Choose Window > Color Palettes.
   The Color Palettes window appears.
2. Select a palette from the pop-up menu (**Figure 9.20**).

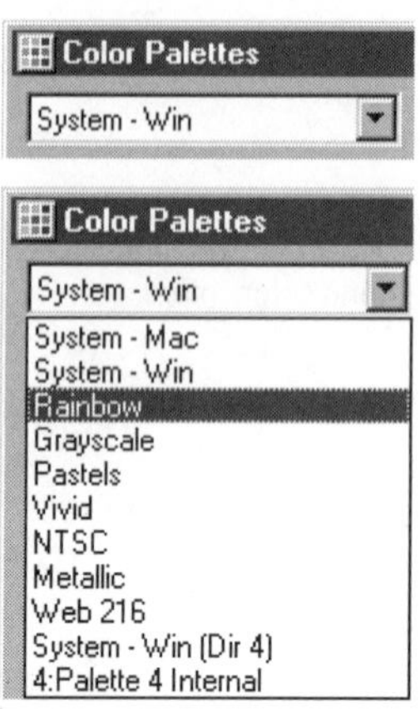

Figure 9.20 Choose a color palette.

✔ Tip

- You can also set the current palette with the color palette channel in the score. When you play a movie, settings in the score (**Figure 9.21**) override any other current palette settings if they differ.

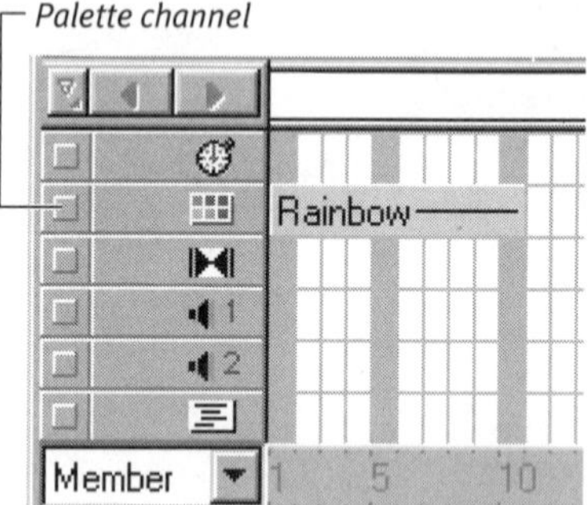

Figure 9.21 Current palette settings that you make in the score override choices that you make in the Color Palettes window.

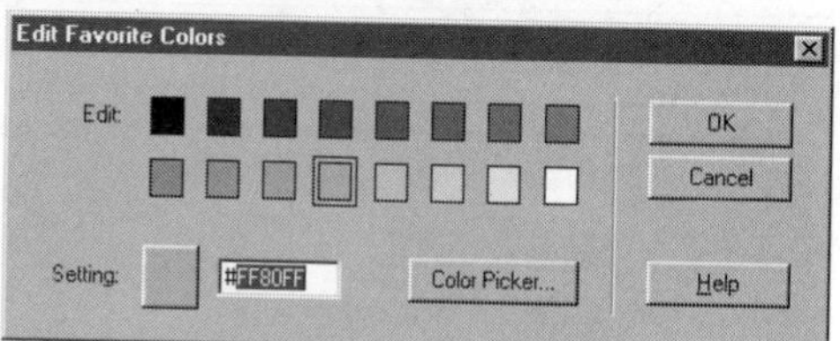

Figure 9.22 The Edit Favorite Colors dialog box.

Figure 9.23
Click Color Picker.

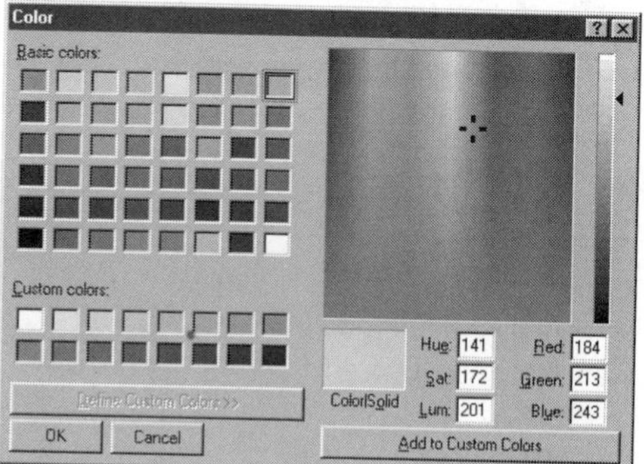

Figure 9.24 In Windows, choose a color by clicking or by entering values.

The top of the color menu holds a bank of 16 colors that remain constant no matter how often you change palettes in a movie. In those 16 spots, you can put your favorite colors, the colors common to the interface you're designing, the colors of a corporate logo and contrasting accents, the shared colors for a set of cast members that appear throughout a movie, and so on. Even when you change palettes, the 16 favorites remain until you decide to edit them.

To specify a favorite color, you edit one of the default favorite colors.

To edit favorite colors:

1. Open a color menu.
2. Choose Edit Favorite Colors.

   The Edit Favorite Colors dialog box appears (**Figure 9.22**), displaying 16 colors.
3. Select a color you want to change.
4. Click Color Picker (**Figure 9.23**) to display the Color Picker.
5. Choose a color.

   In Windows, enter Hue, Saturation, and Luminosity values or RGB values to specify the color. Alternatively, click a color in the color spectrum box (**Figure 9.24**).

   On the Mac, first select one of the color models and then select a new color, using its controls.
6. Click OK to close the Color Picker.
7. Change all the other favorite colors you want to change by repeating steps 4–6.
8. In the Edit Favorite Colors dialog box, click OK.

Color Palettes

A *color palette* is essentially a set of colors to choose among when you are working with graphics in Director (**Figure 9.25**).

In 16-bit (or greater) movie color, you use color palettes simply to choose and organize colors.

In palette-index mode (8-bit movie color depth or lower), the colors of your cast member graphics are tied directly to positions in a color palette. If position 15 in a palette is red and your cast member is filled with that red color, changing the color at position 15 to green would make your cast member green. In 8-bit (or less) movie color depth, Director can display only the colors of the current palette.

Director comes with some built-in 8-bit color palettes for you to use, or you can create your own color palettes. You can also import color palettes into Director. Palettes that you create or import become cast members.

You can import a color palette file into Director directly, or you can bring in a palette on the coattails of an image you import, as described in the task on the next page.

To import a color palette:

1. Choose File > Import.
   The Import dialog box appears.
2. Choose Palettes from the Files of type pop-up menu (**Figure 9.26**).
3. Select the palette file to import.
4. Click Import.

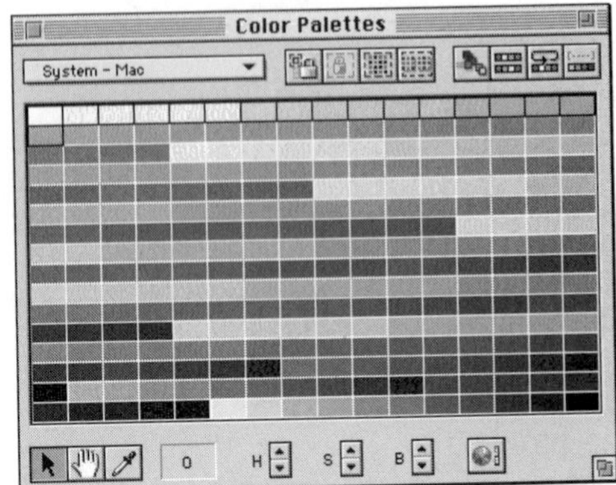

Figure 9.25 Pick a color from the color palette.

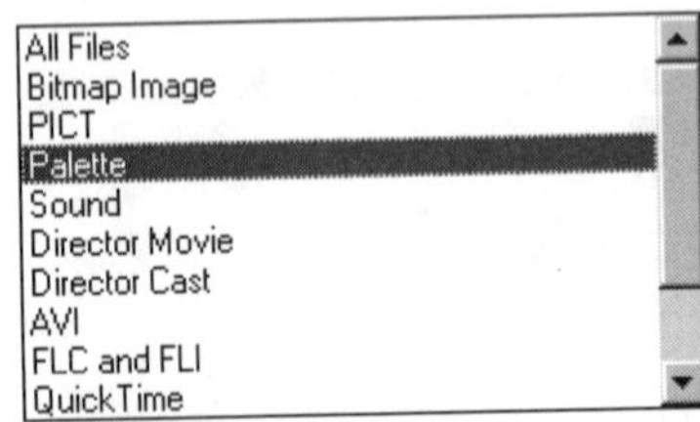

Figure 9.26 Choose Palettes as the type of file to import.

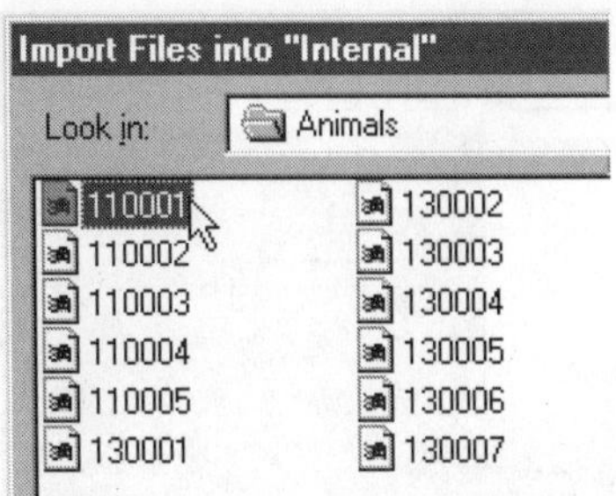

Figure 9.27 Select an image.

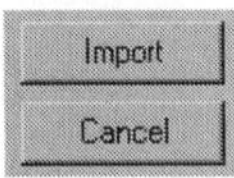

Figure 9.28 Click Import.

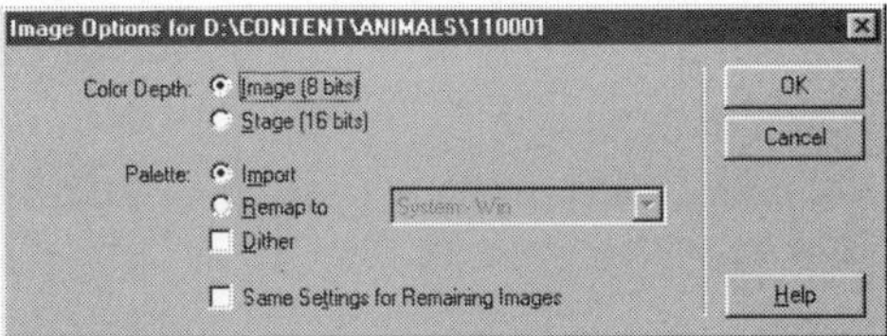

Figure 9.29 The Image Options dialog box.

There's a shortcut for bringing in a color palette: importing an image that uses the palette you want to import.

To import a color palette with an image:

1. Choose File > Import.
   The Import dialog box appears.
2. Select an image file that uses the color palette you want to import (**Figure 9.27**).
3. Click Import (**Figure 9.28**).
   If the image's color palette is different from the currently active color palette, the Image Options dialog box appears (**Figure 9.29**). In the dialog box, choose the Import option for the palette.
4. Click OK.
   The color palette goes into the active Cast window. (See "Importing Cast Members" in Chapter 2, "Assembling Casts," for more details on the Image Options dialog box.)

Custom Color Palettes

If you want to create a custom color palette, you start by creating a duplicate of one of Director's standard palettes (which cannot be modified). Then you can change any color in the duplicate palette or even replace all the colors.

To duplicate a color palette:

1. Choose Window > Color Palettes.
2. In the window that opens, choose a color palette from the Palette pop-up menu (**Figure 9.30**).
3. Choose Edit > Duplicate.
4. In the dialog box that opens (**Figure 9.31**), type a name for the duplicate palette.
5. Click OK.

   Director stores the palette in the active Cast window (**Figure 9.32**).

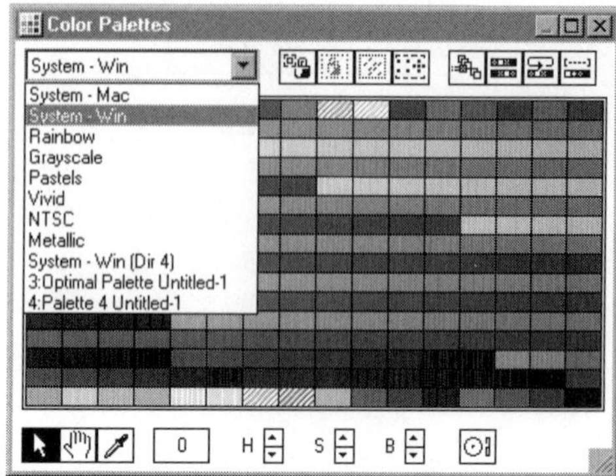

Figure 9.30 Select a palette to duplicate.

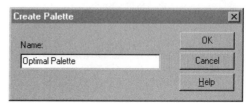

Figure 9.31 Name the new palette.

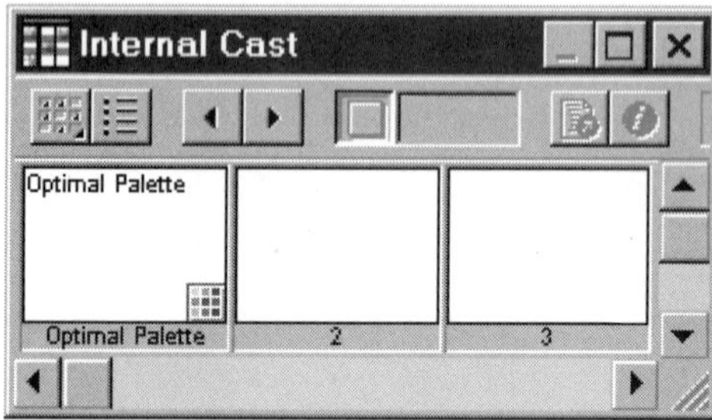

Figure 9.32 Director puts the new palette in the active Cast window.

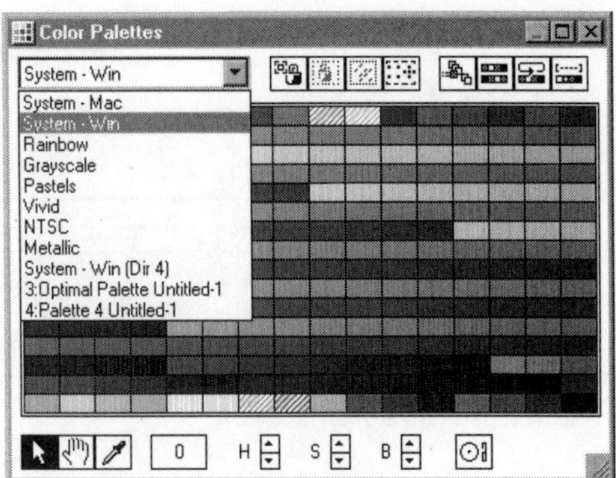

Figure 9.33 Select a palette to edit.

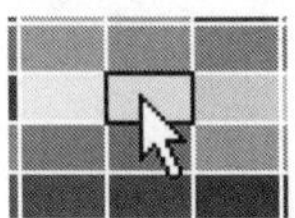

Figure 9.34 A selected color swatch.

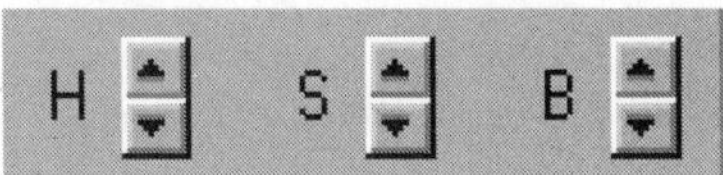

Figure 9.35 Hue, saturation, and brightness controls.

Figure 9.36 Click the arrows to increase or decrease the color values.

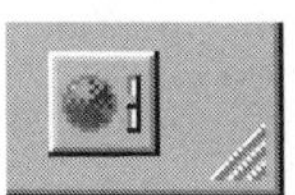

Figure 9.37 Click the Color Picker button to define a new color.

Sometimes you need to tailor a color palette to a project by adding new colors.

To edit colors in the Color Palettes window:

1. Choose Window > Color Palettes.
2. In the window that opens, choose a color palette from the Palette pop-up menu (**Figure 9.33**).

   Because you cannot modify the standard preset Director palettes, the Create Palette dialog box prompts you to duplicate the palette if you try to edit a standard palette.
3. With the Selection tool, click a color swatch.

   The selected color is highlighted and has a black border (**Figure 9.34**).
4. Adjust the hue, saturation, and brightness by clicking the arrow controls (labeled H, S, and B) (**Figure 9.35**) at the bottom of the window (**Figure 9.36**).

   or

   Click the Color Picker button (**Figure 9.37**) and then define a new color by entering numeric values or by using the color wheel or box.

   Director places the new color in the palette.

✔ Tip

- When you edit a color swatch, you may want to copy it and paste it into an empty spot in the palette. This way, you can easily return to the original color.

You can use Director's Copy and Paste commands to move colors from one palette to another or to rearrange colors within a single palette.

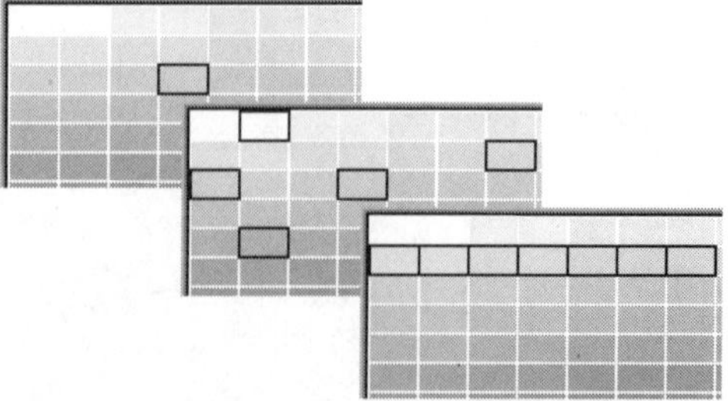

Figure 9.38 Select a single color swatch, several swatches, or a range of swatches.

To copy and paste colors within a palette:

1. Open a color palette.
2. In the Color Palettes window, use the Selection tool or hand pointer to select one or more color swatches.

   Hold down the Control key (Command key for Mac) to make multiple, discontinuous selections, or Shift+click to select a range between two color chips (**Figure 9.38**).
3. Choose Edit > Copy Colors.
4. If necessary, choose a different destination palette from the Palette pop-up menu.
5. Click a swatch in the palette as a destination for pasting the color (**Figure 9.39**).

   The moved color replaces the destination swatch.
6. Choose Edit > Paste into Palette.

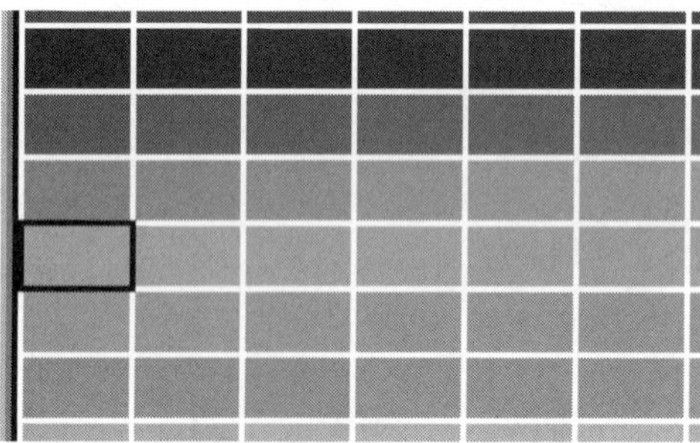

Figure 9.39 Click a destination for the swatch or swatches.

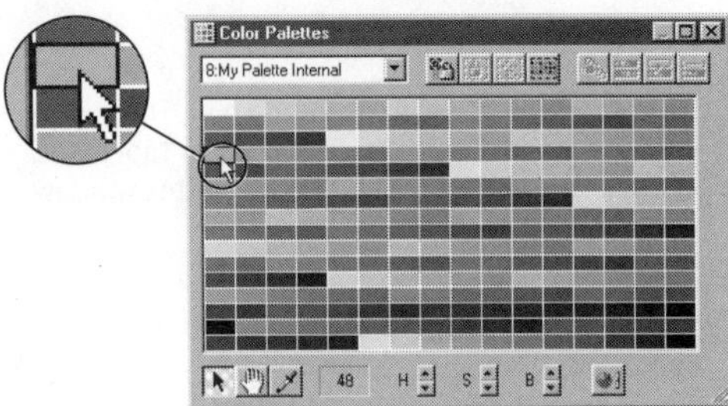

Figure 9.40 Click the starting color of the blend.

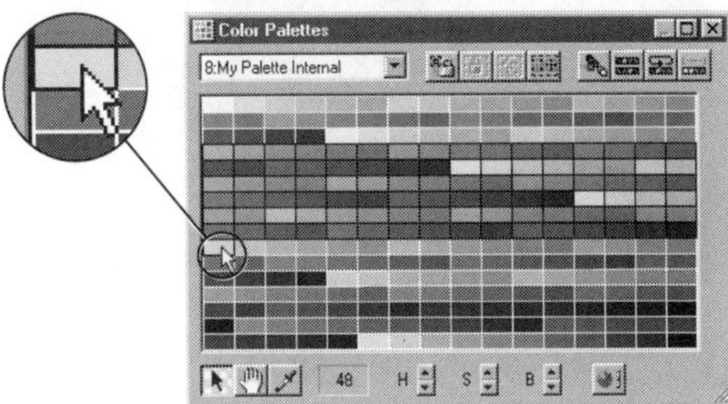

Figure 9.41 Shift+click the blend's ending color.

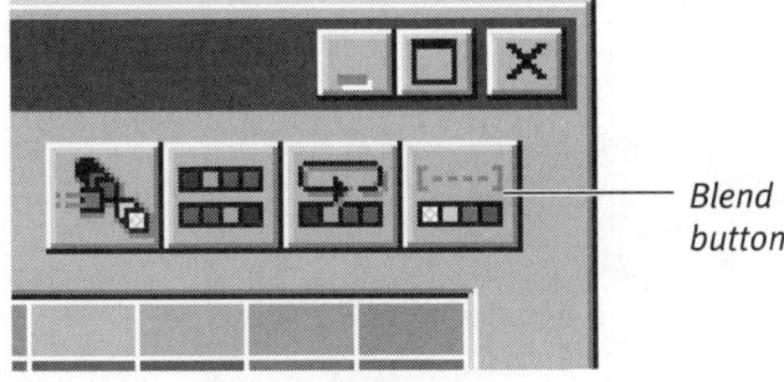

Figure 9.42 Click the Blend button.

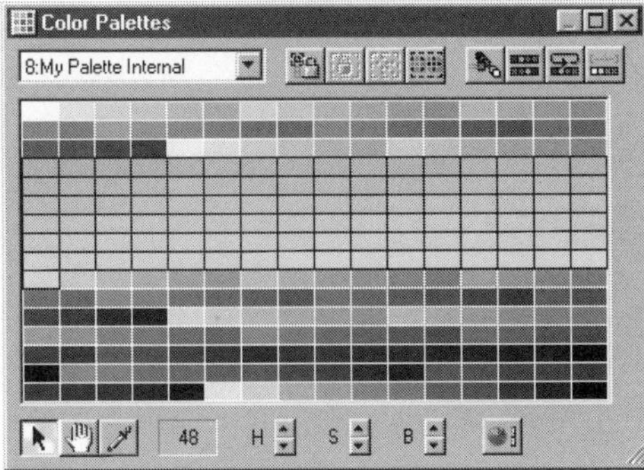

Figure 9.43 The swatches for the blend.

You can create a range of colors that blends gradually from one color to another and then save the series in a palette. If you are creating a sunset backdrop, for example, you might need a blend of colors from red to yellow. A graduated set of colors in a palette comes in handy for creating subtle gradient fills, smooth color cycling, and tasteful animation of foreground or background colors.

To blend colors within a palette:

1. Choose Window > Color Palettes.
2. In the window that opens, choose a palette from the Palette pop-up menu.
3. With the Selection tool, select the starting color for the blend (**Figure 9.40**).

   Pick the red swatch to blend from red to yellow, for example.
4. Hold down the Shift key and click the blend's destination color (**Figure 9.41**). If you're blending from red to yellow, select the yellow color swatch.
5. Click the Blend button (**Figure 9.42**).

   The palette blends from the first selected color to the destination color (**Figure 9.43**).

✔ Tips

- To control the number of color swatches for a blend, move the start and end colors closer together or farther apart in the palette and then click the Blend button. Move a color swatch with the hand pointer.
- You may want to work with a duplicate of your original palette; creating a blend can radically change it.

Director's Eyedropper tool makes it easy to find a color swatch to match any color in any cast member on the stage.

To match colors in sprites:

1. Make sure the color that you want to match is in one of the sprites on the stage.
2. Choose Window > Color Palettes.

   The Color Palettes window appears.
3. Select the Eyedropper tool (**Figure 9.44**).
4. Drag any palette swatch to the color on the stage that you want to pick up.
5. Release the mouse button when the tip of the Eyedropper tool touches the color you want (**Figure 9.45**).

   This color appears in the Color Palettes window in the selected swatch (**Figure 9.46**). If no exact match is in the current palette, Director highlights the color in the current palette that is closest to the one you sampled with the Eyedropper.

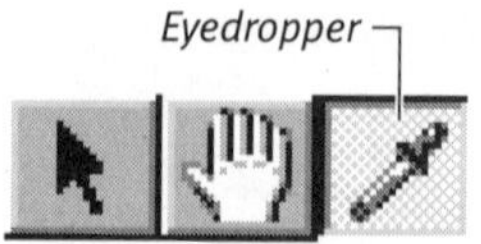

Figure 9.44 The Eyedropper tool in the Color Palettes window.

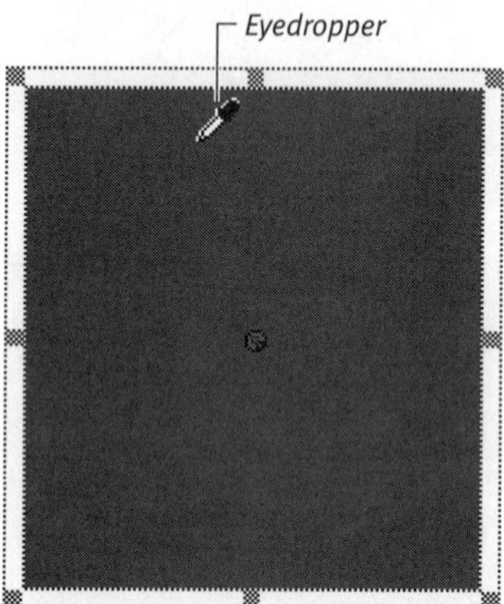

Figure 9.45 Release the mouse button to pick up the color.

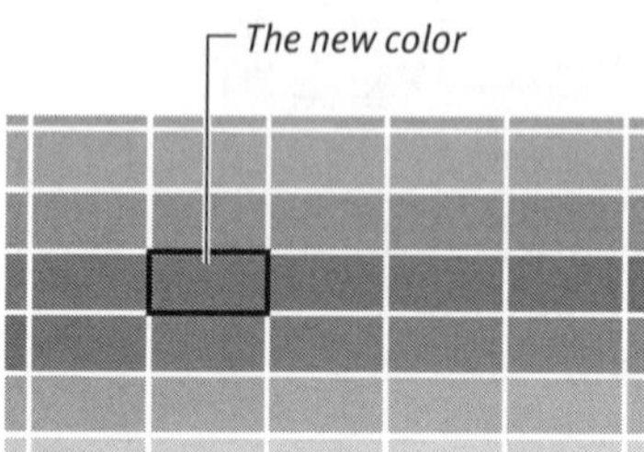

Figure 9.46 The new color in the palette.

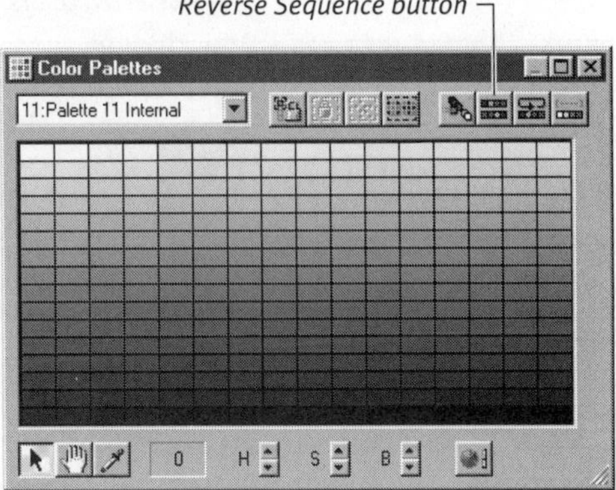

Figure 9.47 Select the colors.

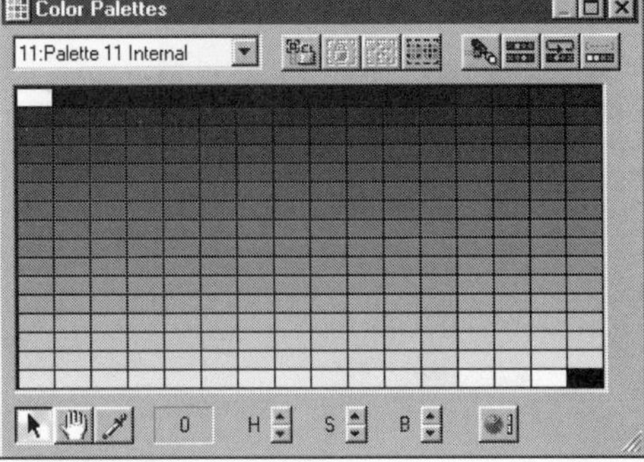

Figure 9.48 The reversed colors.

You can reverse the order of all the colors in a palette or just within a selected range.

Remember that changing the position of colors in an indexed palette (when you're working in movies of 8-bit or less color depth) may change the coloring of cast members that are based on that particular palette.

To reverse the order of a palette's colors:

1. Choose Window > Color Palettes.
2. In the Color Palettes window, select the first color swatch in the range (**Figure 9.47**).
3. Hold down the Shift key and select the last swatch in the range.
   All swatches between the two colors are highlighted.
4. Click the Reverse Sequence button.
   Director reverses the order of all the selected colors (**Figure 9.48**).

✔ Tip

- When you're working in 8-bit (or less) color depth, reversing the color order in a palette affects the coloring of cast members that use the palette. In that case, you may want to work with a duplicate of the palette and then apply the new palette to cast members selectively.

Director can sort the colors in a color palette by their hue, saturation, or brightness values. This feature helps you compare colors in a palette.

Remember that in movies of 8-bit (or less) color depth, changing the position of colors in an indexed palette may change the coloring of cast members that are based on that palette.

To sort colors in a palette:

1. Choose Window > Color Palettes to display the Color Palettes window.
2. Using the Selection tool, select the first color swatch in the range.
3. Hold down the Shift key and select the last swatch in the range.
   All color chips between the two selections are highlighted (**Figure 9.49**).
4. Click the Sort button (**Figure 9.50**).
5. In the Sort Colors dialog box, choose which color attribute to sort by (**Figure 9.51**).
   The three choices are hue, saturation, and brightness. Sorting by hue arranges similar colors together in the palette.
6. Click Sort.

✔ Tip

- Like most other changes in a color palette with 8-bit color depth (or less), sorting the color order affects the coloring of cast members using that palette. To prevent unexpected results that you can't undo, create a duplicate of the palette, sort the colors in the copied palette and then apply the new palette to cast members one at a time, making backups of the cast members as necessary.

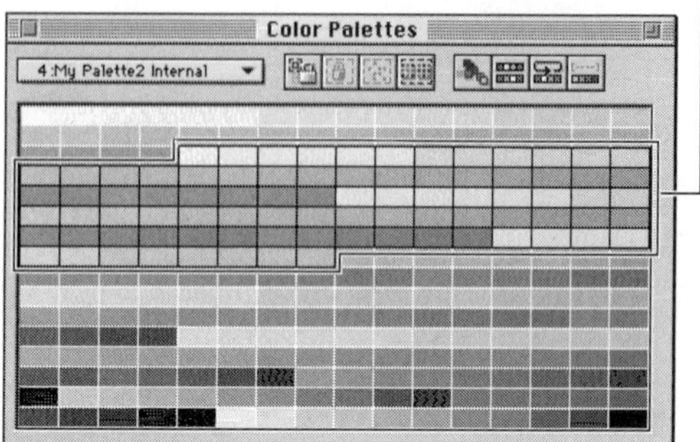

Figure 9.49 Select the colors.

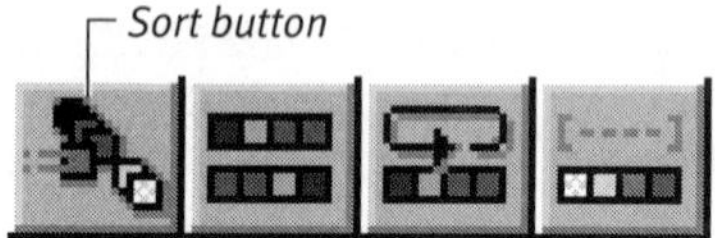

Figure 9.50 Click the Sort button.

Figure 9.51 Specify how to sort.

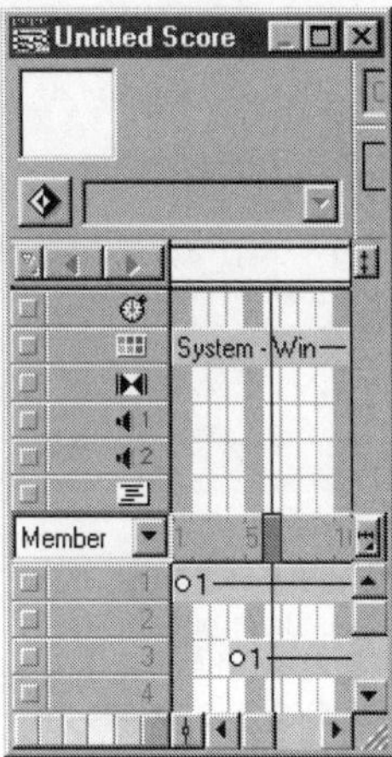

Figure 9.52 The current palette governs everything in the frame.

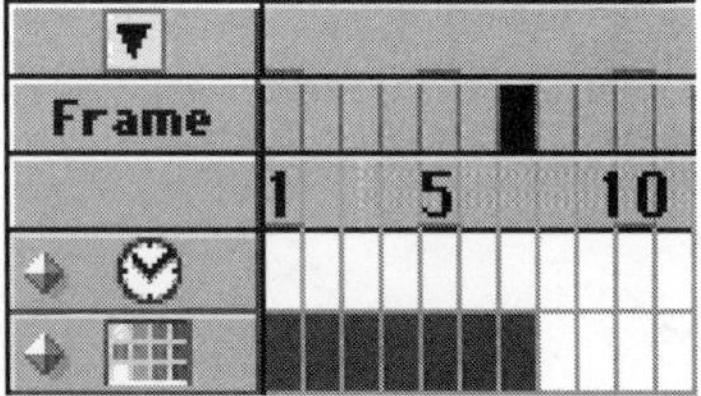

Figure 9.53 You set a palette in the palette channel.

Tactics for Limited Color Displays

People working with the tightest constraints—those creating movies for displays limited to 8-bit color or less—must learn how to juggle color palettes as described in this section. People using previous versions of Director had to learn the tricky art of managing color palettes. Now it's a more arcane art, though not quite so outdated as alchemy.

The tasks in this section apply only when you create movies with 8-bit or less color depth. When you develop a movie of 16-bit (or greater) color depth, your color choices are not constrained in the same way, and the color-management issues in this section do not apply.

The Current Color Palette

Only one color palette can be active in any single frame of a movie; this palette is called the *current color palette* (**Figure 9.52**). All cast members in the frame share the colors of the current palette. The colors that can appear in any single frame of your movie simultaneously must be in the current color palette set for that given frame.

An 8-bit Director movie can display more than 256 unique colors—just not in the same frame. You can use additional colors in other frames by switching the current palette. You can set a different current palette for each frame of a movie by using the score's palette channel (**Figure 9.53**).

To review how to set a palette, see "To change or set the current color palette," earlier in this chapter.

Cast Members and Color Palettes

Each 2-, 4-, and 8-bit bitmap cast member in Director is mapped to a particular color palette. In other words, the color of each pixel in the cast member corresponds to the color in a certain position in its palette. If you display a cast member using a current palette other than its mapped palette, the cast member probably will display the wrong colors. The cast member's pixels would be mapped to positions on a palette that probably contain the wrong colors.

Figure 9.54 shows an example of cast-member colors mapped to specific color positions.

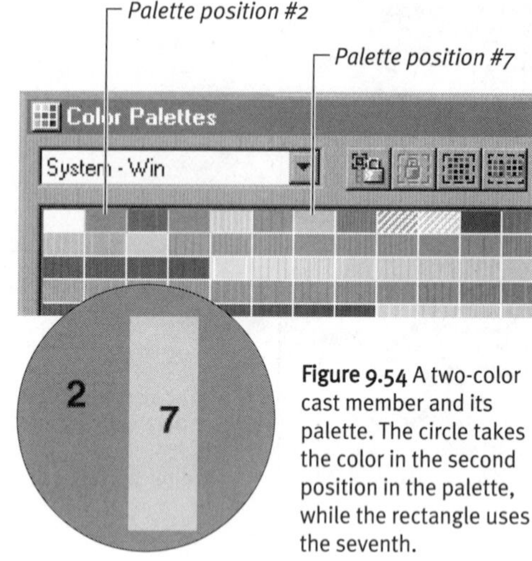

Figure 9.54 A two-color cast member and its palette. The circle takes the color in the second position in the palette, while the rectangle uses the seventh.

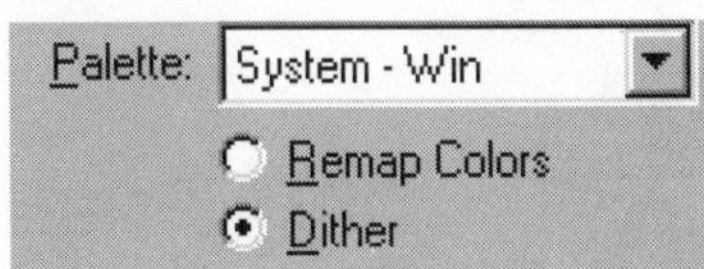

Figure 9.55 View the palette of a cast member.

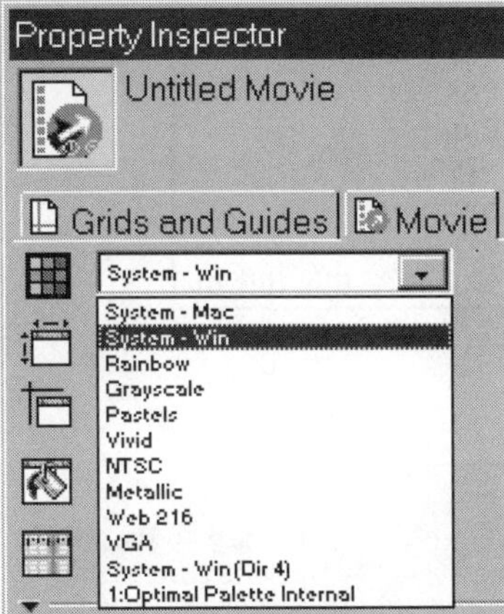

Figure 9.56 Select a default palette.

In the course of managing color in a movie, you may need to check which palette a cast member is assigned.

To check a cast member's palette:

1. Select a cast member.
2. Choose Modify > Transform Bitmap.
3. In the Transform Bitmap dialog box, note the name of the palette in the Palette menu (**Figure 9.55**).

When you create a new Director movie, you can set a palette that is automatically used as the movie's current palette. This default palette serves as the current color palette in all frames unless you set a different palette in the palette channel.

To set a default color palette:

1. Choose Modify > Movie > Properties.
2. Choose a palette from the Movie Palette pop-up menu (**Figure 9.56**).
3. Click OK.

When Director plays a movie, it displays its cast members using a color palette specified in the palette channel of the score. You can swap palettes repeatedly in the palette channel to display a sequence of distinct cast members in their original palettes. You can also create unique visual effects by changing between palettes over time.

When you place on the stage a cast member that uses a palette other than the currently active palette, Director automatically substitutes that cast member's palette as the current palette and uses it for all subsequent frames until you set a new palette. Setting a new palette is easy.

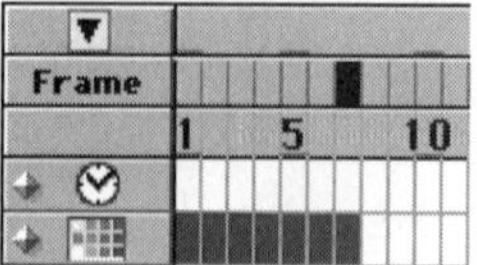

Figure 9.57 Select a range of frames.

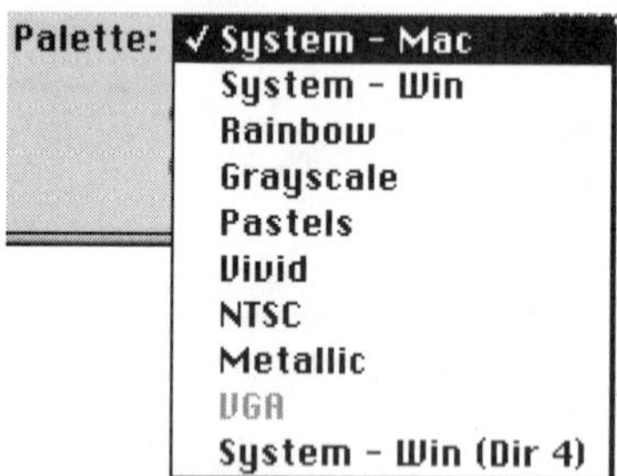

Figure 9.58 Select a palette.

To assign a color palette to certain frames:

1. In the palette channel, select a frame or frames (**Figure 9.57**).
2. Choose Modify > Frame > Palette.
3. In the Frame Properties dialog box, choose a palette from the Palette pop-up menu.

   Your choices include all of Director's built-in palettes (System, Rainbow, Pastels, and so on), plus any you've created (**Figure 9.58**).
4. Click OK.

   Director sets the new palette in the selected frames (**Figure 9.59**).

   Don't be surprised if the cast members in those frames suddenly change colors—they are now displayed in the colors of your new palette.

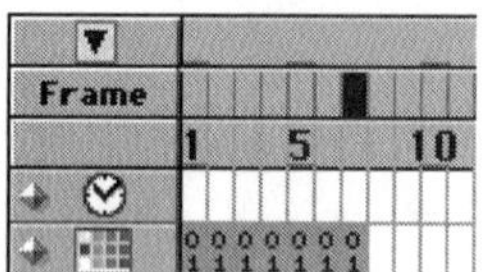

Figure 9.59 The new palette governs the colors in the selected frames.

✔ Tip

- You can double-click a frame in the palette channel to open the Frame Properties dialog box.

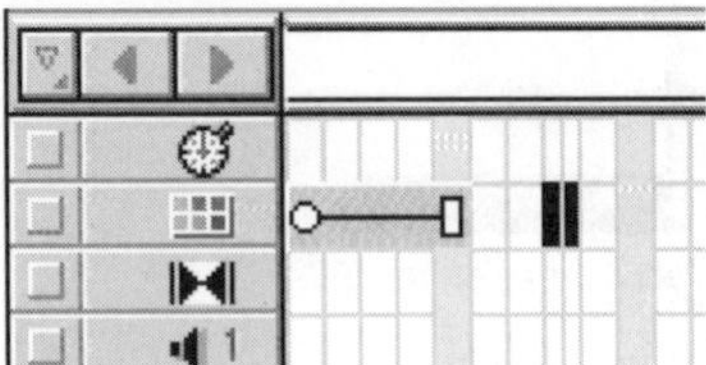

Figure 9.60 Select a frame for the transition.

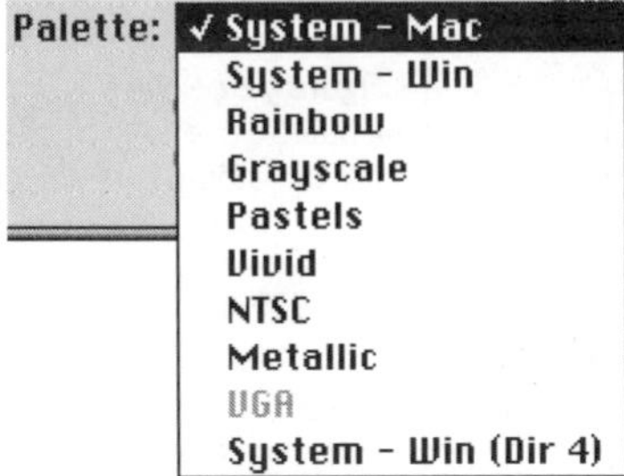

Figure 9.61 Choose a palette to end the transition.

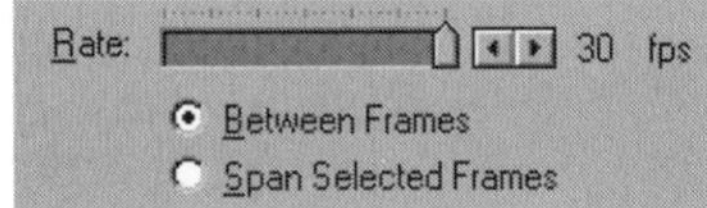

Figure 9.62 Set a speed.

Switching palettes during a scene can be a little jarring: You see one set of colors, and in the next frame the color set looks entirely different. Director provides a palette transition so that you can control the speed at which colors change, smoothing the switch from one palette to the next.

To set a color-palette transition over a single frame:

1. In the palette channel of the score, select a cell for the transition (**Figure 9.60**).
2. Choose Modify > Frame > Palette.
3. In the Frame Properties dialog box, choose the ending palette for the transition from the Palette pop-up menu (**Figure 9.61**).

   Remember that the palette you set in this frame should be different from the palette used in the channel's previous frames.
4. In the Frame Properties dialog box, specify the rate for the transition between the old and new palettes.

   The speed can be set anywhere between 1 and 30 frames per second (**Figure 9.62**). During playback, your movie will pause in this frame while the transition takes place.
5. Select Between Frames.
6. Click OK.

Just as you can set a smooth palette transition in one frame, you can make a gradual transition over a series of frames. That makes the transition between color palettes more subtle, and your animation continues without interruption.

To set a color-palette transition over a series of frames:

1. In the palette channel, select a series of frames (**Figure 9.63**).
2. Choose Modify > Frame > Palette.
3. In the Frame Properties dialog box, choose an ending palette from the Palette pop-up menu (**Figure 9.64**).
4. Select Span Selected Frames (**Figure 9.65**).
5. Click OK.

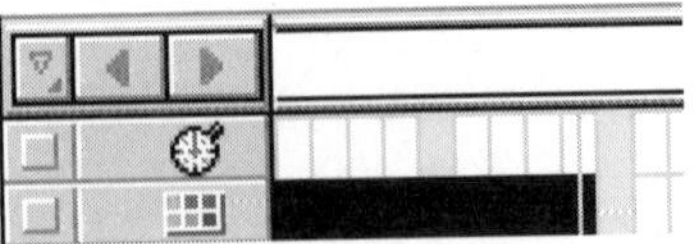

Figure 9.63 Select a range of frames.

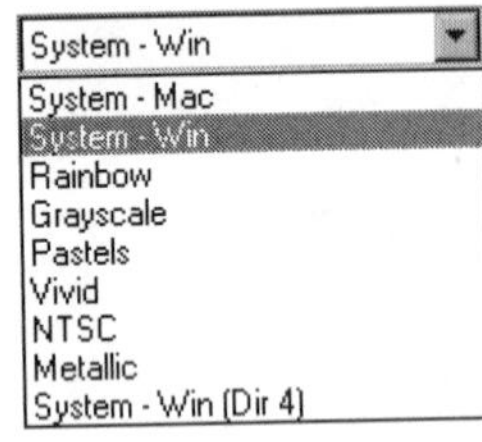

Figure 9.64 Select a palette to end the transition.

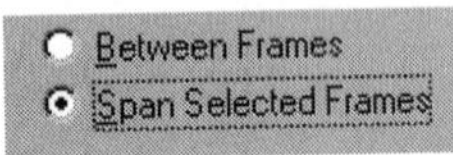

Figure 9.65 Select Span Selected Frames.

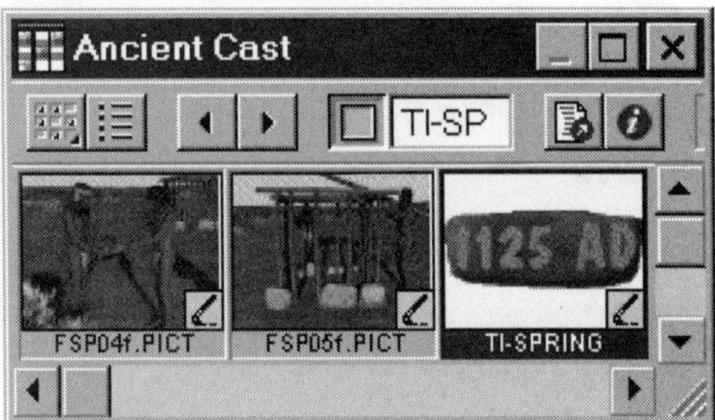

Figure 9.66 Select a cast member.

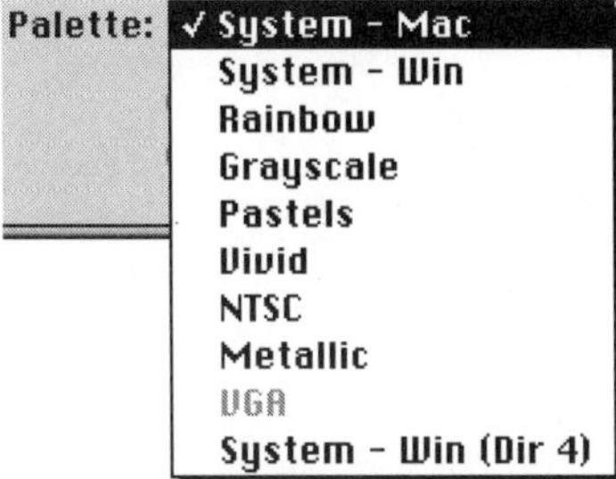

Figure 9.67 Choose a new palette.

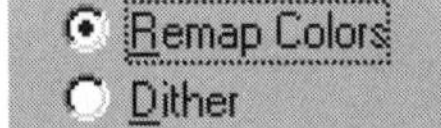

Figure 9.68 Select Remap Colors.

Director lets you remap a cast member to a different palette. Director first examines the cast member's original colors pixel by pixel; then it remaps the pixels to positions in the new palette that contain colors that best match the original colors. The process often leads to a close, but not identical, match of colors. For best results, choose a palette with colors similar to the cast member's original palette.

To remap a cast member to a different color palette:

1. Select a cast member (**Figure 9.66**).
2. Make a copy of the cast member.

   Because remapping a cast member can distort its colors, it's a good idea to perform the process on a copy of the cast member. If you don't like the result, you can revert to an earlier color scheme.
3. Choose Modify > Transform Bitmap.
4. In the Transform Bitmap dialog box, choose a new palette for the cast member from the Palette pop-up menu (**Figure 9.67**).
5. Select Remap Colors (**Figure 9.68**).
6. Click Transform.
7. Check the results by playing the movie or by examining the cast member closely in the Paint window.

✔ Tip

- If your movie will be played by a Web browser, it's a good idea to remap all 8-bit cast members to Director's Web216 palette. That palette contains the set of colors used by both Netscape Navigator and Internet Explorer.

When you have cast members on the stage that rely on color palettes different from the current palette, these cast members do not show their true colors. You can have Director remap all such cast members to the current color palette automatically—on the fly. Remapping on the fly affects the appearance only of cast members on the stage; it does not permanently remap the stored cast members.

To remap sprites on the stage to the current palette:

1. Choose Modify > Movie > Properties.
2. In the Movie Properties dialog box, check the Remap Palettes If Needed checkbox (**Figure 9.69**).
3. Click OK.

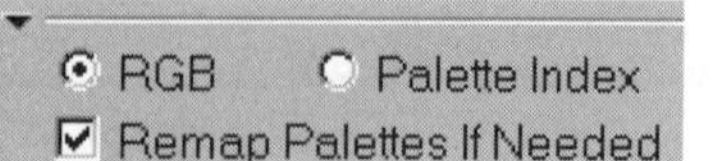

Figure 9.69 Check Remap Palettes If Needed.

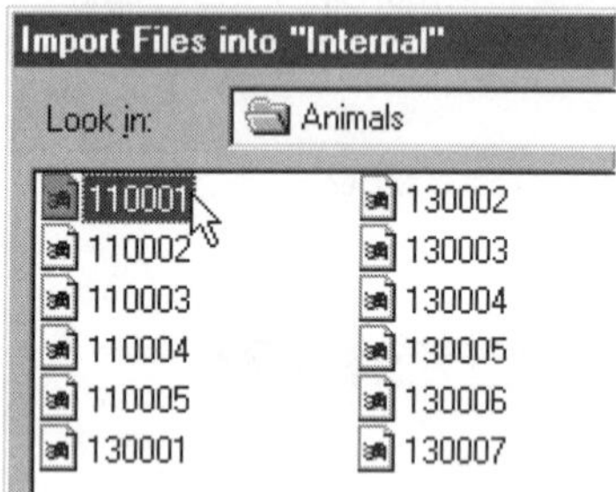

Figure 9.70 You can bring a cast member's palette in when you import it.

When you import a 2-, 4-, or 8-bit image from any graphics program, such as Photoshop, you can also import its original palette. You can use that as the current palette to preserve the cast member's original colors.

To display original colors in an imported cast member:

1. Import the cast member with its linked color palette, as explained on page 225 of this chapter (**Figure 9.70**).
2. Use the cast member's original color palette as the current palette in frames that include sprites based on that cast member.

✔ Tip

- You could instead adapt the cast member by remapping it to a palette that suits both it and the scene that contains it.

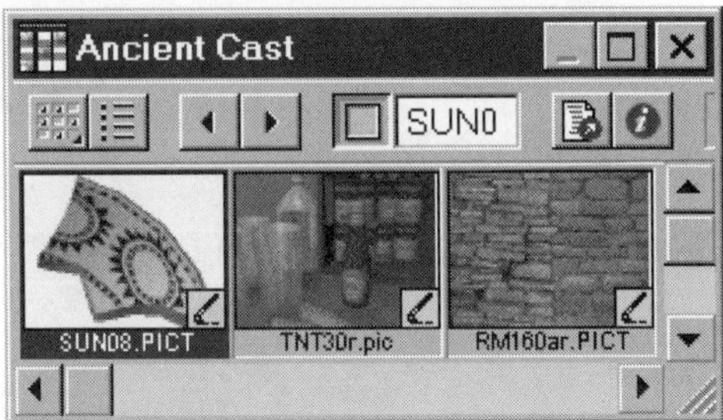

Figure 9.71 Select a cast member with only a few colors.

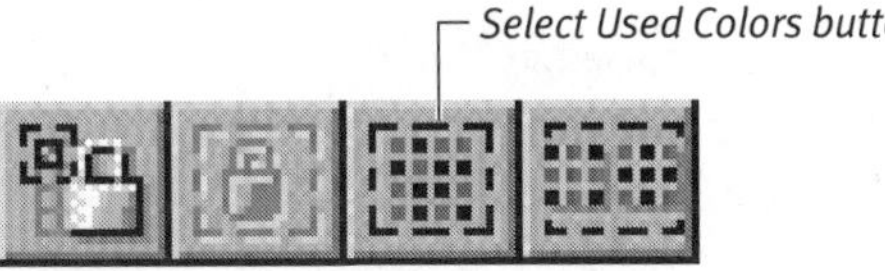

Figure 9.72 Click the Select Used Colors button.

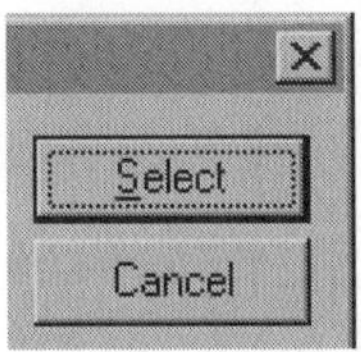

Figure 9.73 Click Select in the Select Used Colors dialog box.

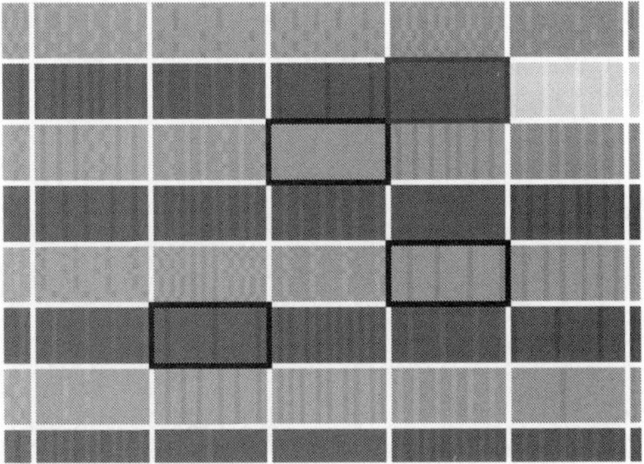

Figure 9.74 Colors used in the cast member are highlighted.

A Single Optimal Color Palette

It's possible to create a single, specialized palette that incorporates colors that all your cast members can share. After you create an optimal palette, you can remap all your cast members to it. This approach allows your movie to operate from a single common palette, keeping colors consistent throughout.

Remember, however, that if your optimal palette does not contain all the colors used in a cast member, Director substitutes the nearest match for any missing colors.

The process is a bit involved, but if you follow all the tasks in this section in order, you'll complete the job.

You start building an optimal palette by creating a palette based on the colors of a single cast member.

To begin building an optimal color palette for all cast members:

1. Select a cast member (**Figure 9.71**).
   Start with a cast member that uses only a small number of colors in its palette.
2. Make the cast member's assigned palette the current palette.
3. Choose Window > Color Palettes.
4. In the Color Palettes window, click the Select Used Colors button (**Figure 9.72**).
5. In the dialog box that opens, click Select (**Figure 9.73**).
   Director highlights all the colors used by the cast member. (**Figure 9.74**).
6. Choose Edit > Duplicate.
   Copy the palette that so you're free to work without disturbing the cast member's current coloring.
7. In the dialog box that opens, name the palette and click OK.

The next part of building an optimal color palette makes it easy for you to find places to put the other colors you will soon add.

To make used colors easy to find among unused colors:

1. Starting with the foundation palette you created in the preceding task, make sure that all the colors used in the cast member are still highlighted, as shown in **Figure 9.75**.
2. In the Color Palettes window, use the hand pointer to drag one of the highlighted colors to the second color position in the first row of colors—the position immediately to the right of white (**Figure 9.75**).

   Director rearranges the selected colors into a continuous range.
3. Click the Invert Selection button (**Figure 9.76**).

   This step selects all the unused colors in the palette.
4. Click the Blend button (**Figure 9.77**).

   Director changes all unused colors into a continuous blend of similar colors, so that you can easily tell them apart from the used colors that form the backbone of your optimal palette (**Figure 9.78**). In this area of blended colors, you can paste additional colors from other color palettes.

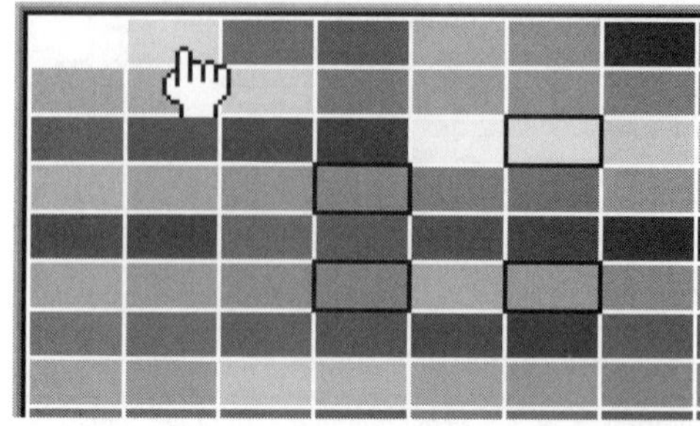

Figure 9.75 Drag a used color to the second position in the palette.

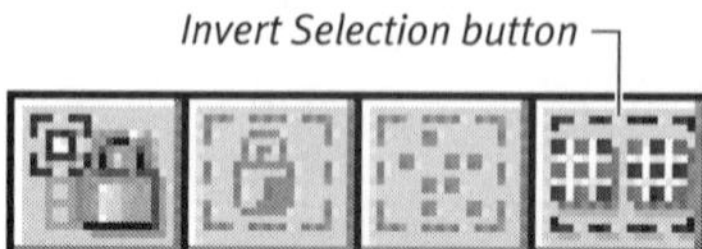

Figure 9.76 Click the Invert Selection button.

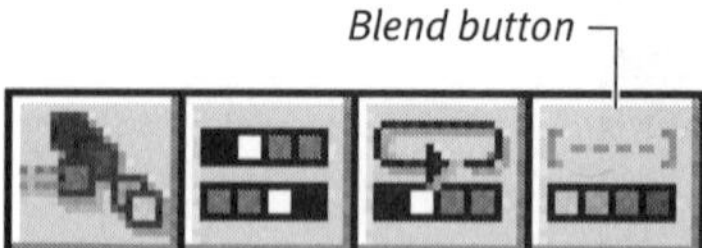

Figure 9.77 Click the Blend button.

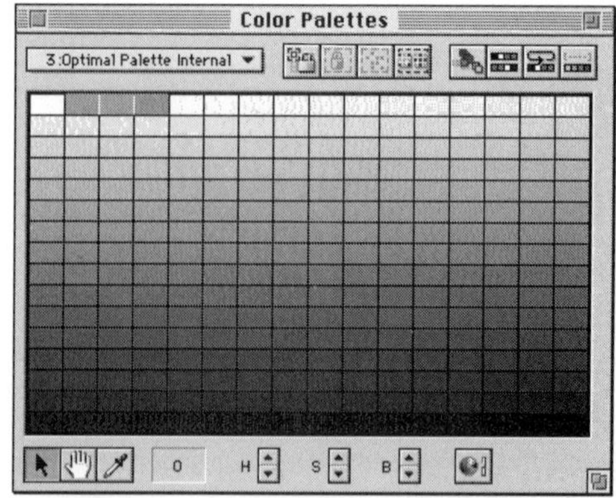

Figure 9.78 The unused colors form a blend.

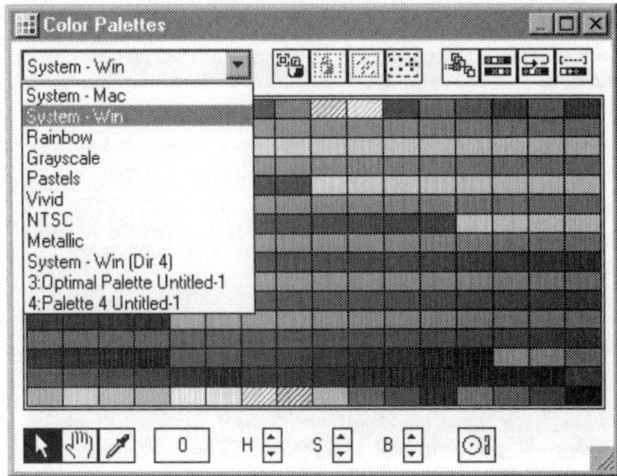

Figure 9.79 Select another palette.

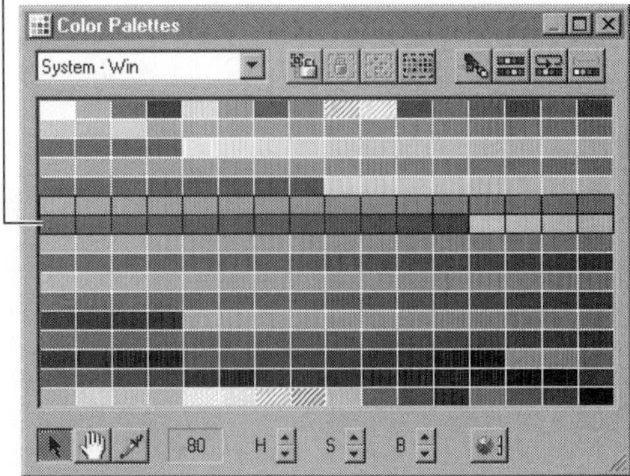

Figure 9.80 Select colors to add to the optimal palette.

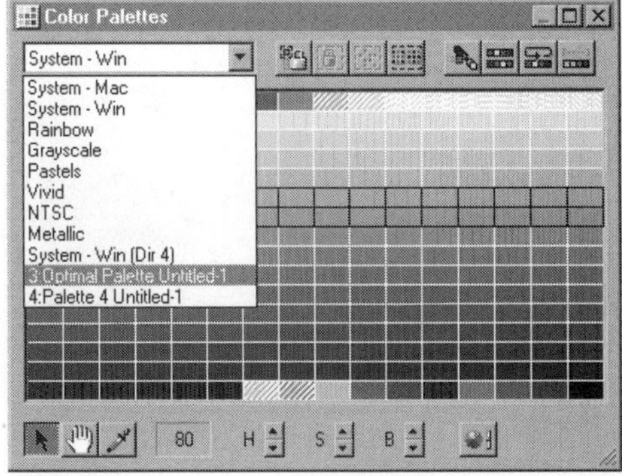

Figure 9.81 Open the optimal palette-in-progress.

For the next stage of creating an optimal palette, you add colors from other cast members to complete the palette.

To add colors to the optimal palette:

1. In the Color Palettes window, open the Palette pop-up menu and choose a palette used by other cast members in your movie (**Figure 9.79**).
2. In the Color Palettes window, select colors to add to your optimal palette (**Figure 9.80**).

   or

   Select a cast member that uses the palette and then click the Select Used Colors button in the Color Palettes window to highlight all the colors the cast member uses.
3. Choose Edit > Copy Colors.
4. In the Color Palettes window, choose the optimal palette you created earlier from the Palette menu (**Figure 9.81**).
5. In the optimal palette, select the first position that follows the last used color (**Figure 9.82**).

   Make sure that you have enough unused swatches to accommodate the new colors.
6. Choose Edit > Paste Into Palette (**Figure 9.83**).
7. Repeat steps 1-6 to continue adding colors from other color palettes.
8. Close the Color Palettes window when you've filled the optimal palette.

Now you're ready to remap your movie's cast members to the optimal palette you've just created. To do so, follow the steps outlined in "To remap a cast member to a different color palette"

✔ Tips

- If you don't have room for all the colors for every cast member, try to select a few colors that best represent the color range of each palette. Pick a couple of reds, a couple of blues, a few grays and greens, and so on.
- Creating an optimal palette may require a great deal of trial and error. After your first attempt, you may need to adjust the palette so that all the cast members look right.

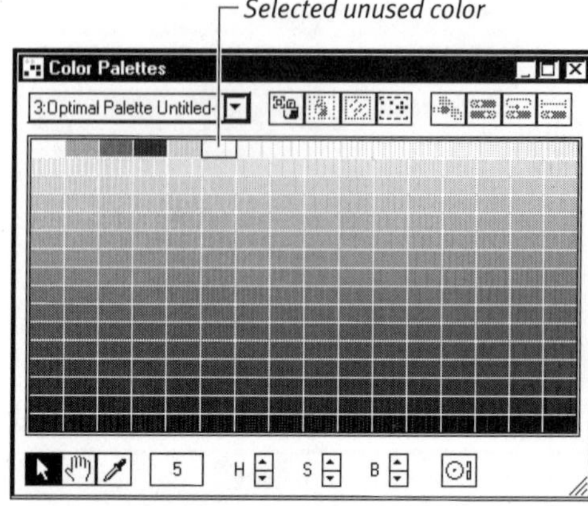

Figure 9.82 Select the first unused color.

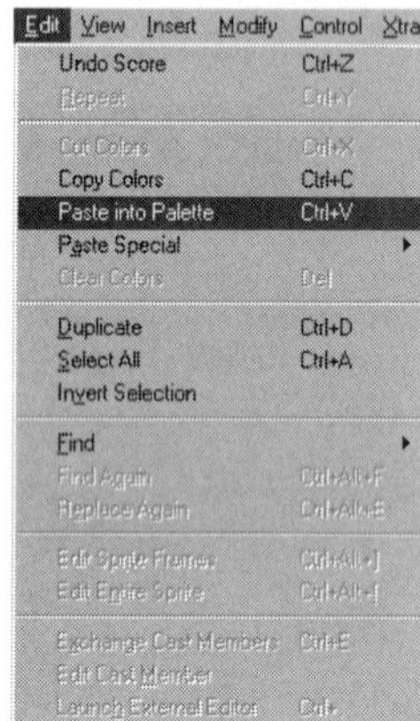

Figure 9.83 Paste the selected colors into the palette.

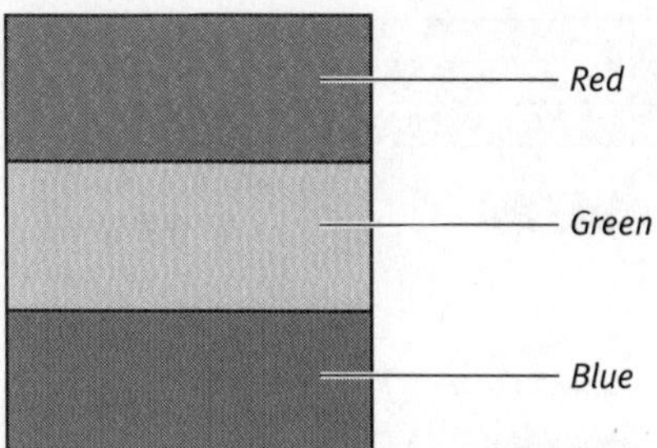

Figure 9.84 Colors before cycling.

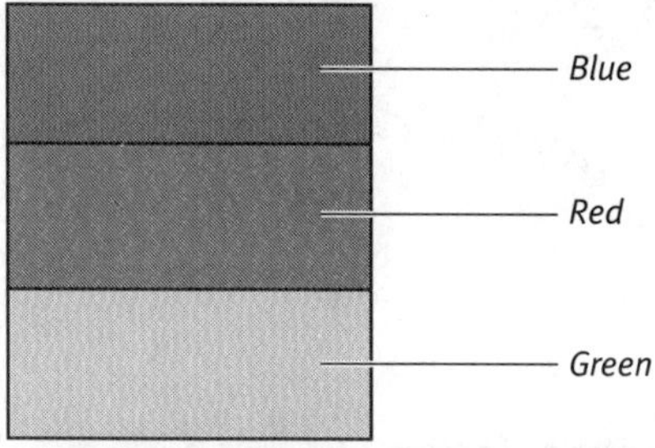

Figure 9.85 Color cycling, first step.

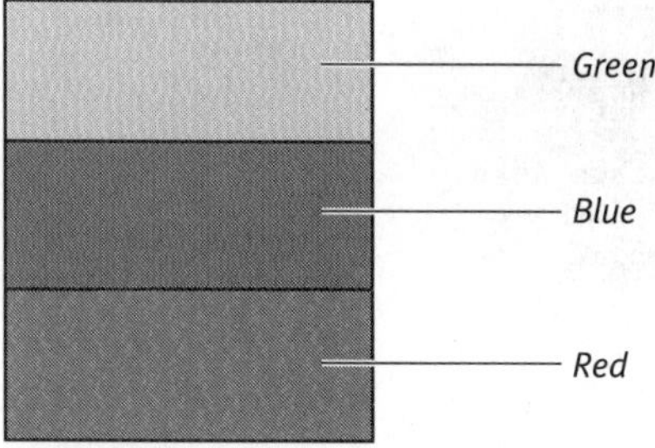

Figure 9.86 Colors cycling, last step.

Color Cycling

You've probably seen cycling colors used to animate TV weather maps; a storm front appears to pulsate through a range of dark and light shades of blue. It's also handy for effects such as fire and explosions, in which color pulses through a series of reds, yellows, and oranges.

Color cycling achieves the illusion of animation by rotating a selected range of colors in a palette over time. Take a cast member that is painted red on top, green in the middle, and blue at its base (**Figure 9.84**). Color cycling can rotate the colors so that in the first step of the cycle, the red color shifts to the cast member's middle, the green to its base, and the blue to its top. In the next step of the cycle, the red shifts to the cast member's base, the green to its top, and the blue to the middle (**Figures 9.85** and **9.86**).

You can set color cycling to repeat, to stop after going through all the colors once, or to cycle in reverse at the end of a cycle.

You apply color cycling to a selected range of colors over a series of frames. Within those frames, the selected colors cycle in any cast members that have those colors.

To cycle colors in a palette:

1. In the score's palette channel, select the series of frames that contain the sprites you want to color cycle (**Figure 9.87**).

   Select a single frame to color cycle a stationary sprite (one that doesn't move while being cycled). You can cycle color throughout an animation by selecting a range of frames in the palette channel.

2. Choose Modify > Frame > Palette.
3. If necessary, edit the palette so the colors you want to cycle appear in adjacent swatches (see "To copy and paste colors within a palette" earlier in this chapter).
4. In the Frame Properties dialog box, select Color Cycling (**Figure 9.88**).
5. Select a palette from the Palette pop-up menu.
6. In the palette of the Frame Properties dialog box, select a range of colors to cycle.

   Shift+click two color swatches to select the range of colors between them (**Figure 9.89**).

7. Select Between Frames (**Figure 9.90**) if you want a complete color cycle to occur in each frame.

   or

   Select Span Selected Frames (**Figure 9.91**) if you want the color cycle to take place over a range of selected frames.

8. If you select the Between Frames option, type the number of cycles in the Cycles box to indicate the number of complete color cycles per frame. Then drag the

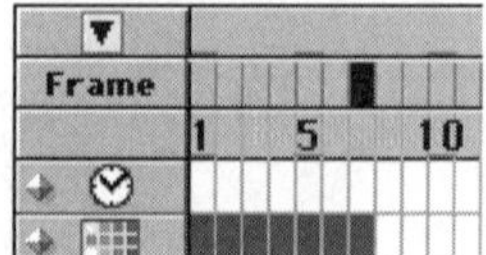

Figure 9.87 Select frames for color cycling in the palette channel.

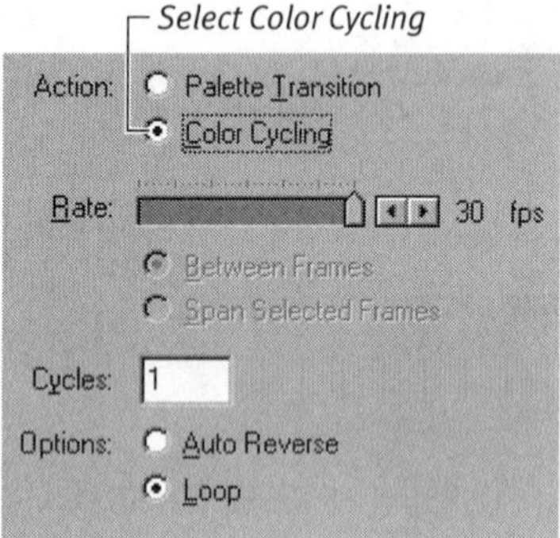

Figure 9.88 Select Color Cycling.

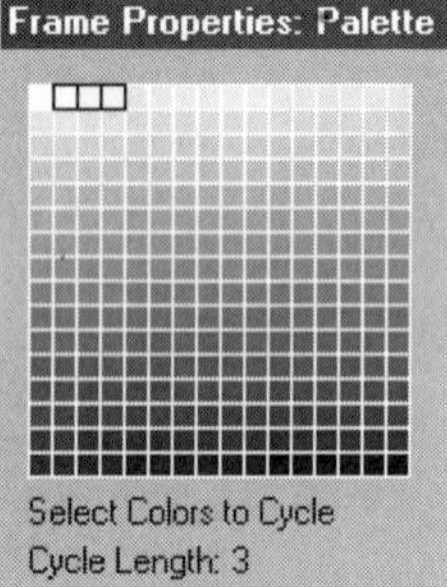

Figure 9.89 Select the range of colors.

TACTICS FOR LIMITED COLOR DISPLAYS

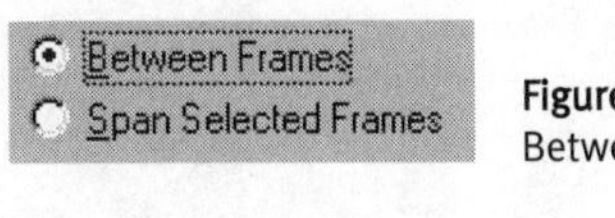

Figure 9.90 Select Between Frames...

Figure 9.91 ...or select Span Selected Frames.

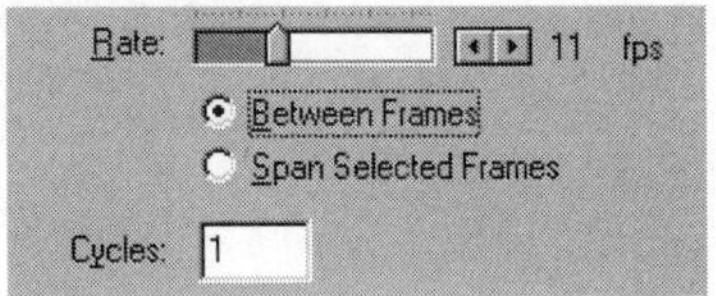

Figure 9.92 Choose the color-cycle rate.

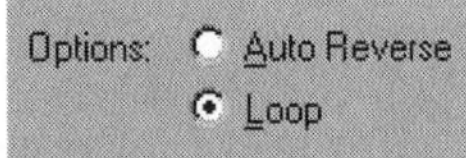

Figure 9.93 Choose color-cycle options.

Rate slider to set the speed of the color cycle, in frames per second (**Figure 9.92**).

Director defines one cycle as displaying all the selected colors one time.

9. Select Loop if you want the color cycle to repeat from the beginning (**Figure 9.93**).

   or

   Select Auto Reverse if you want the color cycling to reverse at the end of a cycle—to cycle colors from red to blue first and then from blue to red, for example.

10. Click OK to apply the color cycling to the selected frame or frames in the score.

10

Adding Digital Video

Director does more than serve as a computer animation stand. It also allows you to incorporate full-motion digital video into your productions—alongside your sprite animations—to create a rich multimedia experience.

Director 8 supports Apple's QuickTime 4 standard for Mac and Windows, which allows streaming off the Web. To play or create movies that use QuickTime cast members, you must have QuickTime installed on your system, which you can download for free from Apple's Web site.

Director also fully supports AVI movies in Windows and can convert them to QuickTime on the Macintosh.

Director provides very basic video-editing tools in its QuickTime window, where you can rearrange frames by cutting, copying, and pasting. More extensive editing requires a specialized program such as Adobe Premiere. Most people complete all editing before importing video clips into Director.

Importing Digital Video

Director allows you to import QuickTime and Windows AVI movies (**Figure 10.1**). Because a video file can be large, Director always imports it as a linked external file rather than embedding it internally; this helps limit movie size. Consequently, it's important to keep your video files in a constant location relative to your Director movie. Otherwise, if the location changes and the links aren't updated, the video won't play. When you distribute your movie, you must provide all video files—or current Web links from which they can be downloaded—along with it.

Because video files are linked, if you edit a video in Director, the external video changes to match. Conversely, if you modify the external video, the linked imported video also changes.

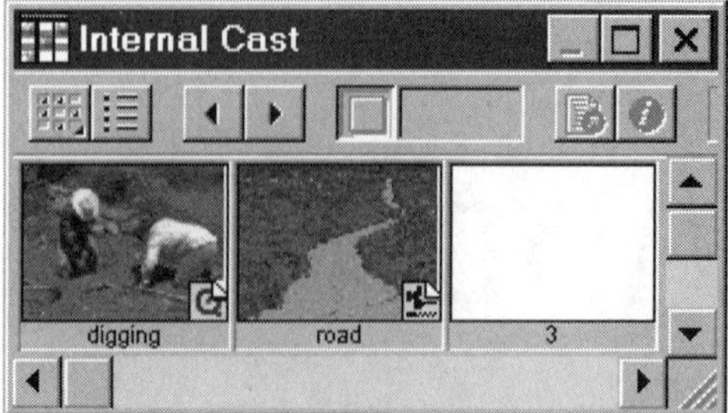

Figure 10.1 You can import both QuickTime and AVI digital movies into a cast.

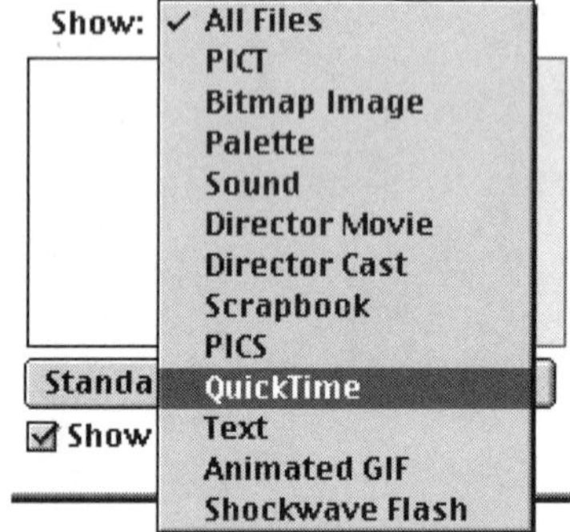

Figure 10.2 Choose the file type for the digital movie you're importing.

To import digital video files:

1. Choose File > Import to display the Import Files dialog box.
2. From the Files of Type pop-up menu (Show pop-up menu on the Mac), choose QuickTime or AVI (**Figure 10.2**).

   QuickTime is the only option available on the Mac.

   It is not necessary to set an option in the Media pop-up menu, because digital video files are always imported as linked cast members.
3. At the top of the Import dialog box, find and open the folder that contains the file you want to import.

   or

   Click Internet and specify a URL for the file.

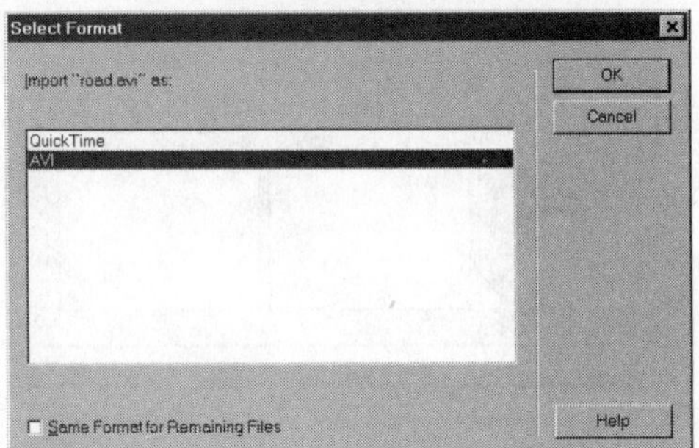

Figure 10.3 You can import an AVI movie as an AVI or QuickTime movie.

4. Select the file and click Add.

   or

   Click Add All to add all the folder's displayed files to the list.

5. Click Import.

   (Windows only) If the video is an AVI movie, you are given the choice of importing it as an AVI or a QuickTime movie (**Figure 10.3**). QuickTime generally offers more playback controls and flexibility than AVI movies.

✔ Tip

- If you plan to make any edits of a video within Director, the actual linked video file will change, so you may want to keep a backup of the original.

Previewing a Digital Video

You can use Director's QuickTime or AVI windows to playback a digital video. This can be useful before incorporating a video into your movie to double-check that it's the one you want.

To preview an imported QuickTime video:

1. Double-click a QuickTime cast member to open it in the QuickTime window (**Figures 10.4–10.5**).
2. Click the Play button at the bottom-left corner of the window to start the movie (**Figure 10.6).**
3. Click the Play button again to stop the movie.

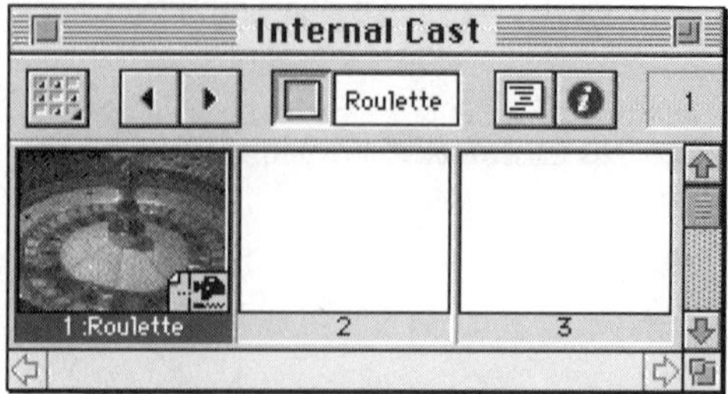

Figure 10.4 Double-click a QuickTime cast member.

Figure 10.5 The QuickTime movie opens in the QuickTime window.

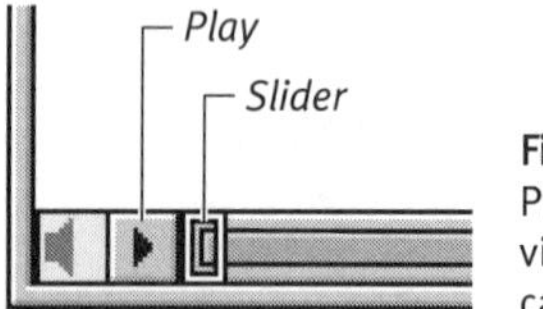

Figure 10.6 Click the Play button to start viewing a digital video cast member.

Figure 10.7 Double-click an AVI cast member to open it in the AVI Video window.

Figure 10.8 The AVI movie opens in the AVI Video window.

To preview an imported AVI movie (Windows only):

1. Double-click an AVI cast member to open it in the AVI Video window (**Figures 10.7–10.8**).
2. Double-click inside the AVI Video window to start playing the AVI movie.
3. Click inside the AVI Video window to stop the movie.

   Notice that unlike the QuickTime window, the AVI Video window offers no playback controls.

Incorporating Video

Unlike sounds, which you place in special sound channels, you incorporate video cast members into your movie by placing them in the sprite channels. You then adjust sprite duration and various playback options to tailor the video to your requirements.

To place digital video in a movie:

1. Choose Window > Score.
2. Drag a digital video cast member from its Cast window into a sprite channel at the frame where the video should begin playing (**Figure 10.9**).

   For the video to play to completion, it must occupy enough frames in the score to match its playing length; otherwise, it ends prematurely.
3. Position the video sprite on the stage by dragging it (**Figure 10.10**).
4. Play the movie to test the video.
5. Adjust the number of frames, if necessary.

✔ Tip

- You can synchronize your digital video to other events in your movie by creating cue points in the video file and then setting a wait option in the tempo channel to pause your movie until a specified cue point is reached. *(See "Setting Pauses in a Movie" in Chapter 5, "Playing & Refining Movies.")*

Figure 10.9 Place the digital video cast member in the score.

Figure 10.10 Place the video sprite where you want it on the stage.

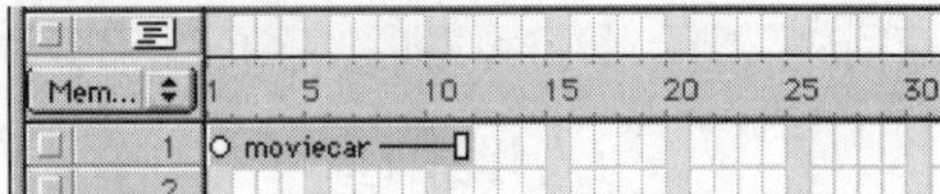

Figure 10.11 A sprite that needs more frames.

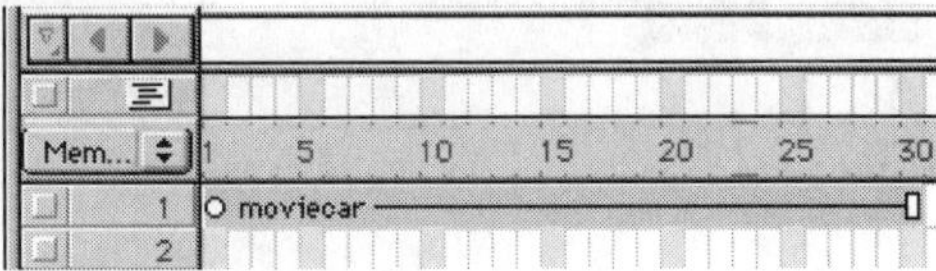

Figure 10.12 The extended sprite.

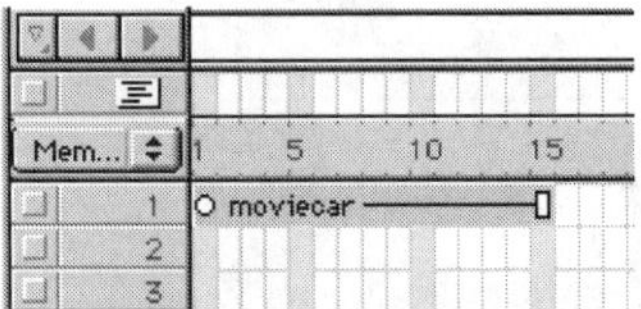

Figure 10.13 Adjust the sprite so that the video finishes playing in the last frame.

To extend a video sprite to cover enough frames:

1. Choose Window > Score.
2. Select a digital video sprite that needs more frames (**Figure 10.11**).
3. Extend the video sprite over more frames than necessary (**Figure 10.12**).

   Estimate the needed number of frames by multiplying the length of the video, in seconds, by the number of frames per second set as the movie tempo.

   If the duration of the video is 5 seconds, for example, and the movie frame rate is 30 frames per second, the digital video sprite requires approximately 150 frames.
4. Play the movie back and watch the playback head in the score.
5. Note the frame where the video finishes playing and adjust the sprite duration accordingly (**Figure 10.13**).

Setting Digital Video Properties

Digital video cast members have a wide range of properties you can set to affect various aspects of playback performance and appearance. Some of the most commonly used properties can be set in the Property Inspector window.

There are some differences between the properties available for QuickTime and AVI videos; generally, more properties and flexibility favor QuickTime. If you need to access and set the full range of video cast member properties, you'll need to write Lingo scripts instead of using the Property Inspector. (For a complete list of video properties, see the Lingo by Feature section for Digital Video in Director's Help system.)

To set digital video cast member properties with the Property Inspector:

1. Select a digital video cast member in a Cast window (**Figure 10.14**).
2. Choose Window > Inspectors > Property to display the Property Inspector.
3. If necessary, click the List View Mode button to select Graphical View mode.
4. Select the Member tab.
5. Click the Browse button if you need to link to a new video file on your local drive or on the Internet (**Figure 10.15**).

   This step is necessary only if your file has moved or you want to link to a different file.
6. Select the QuickTime or AVI tab (**Figure 10.16**).

Figure 10.14 Select a digital video cast member.

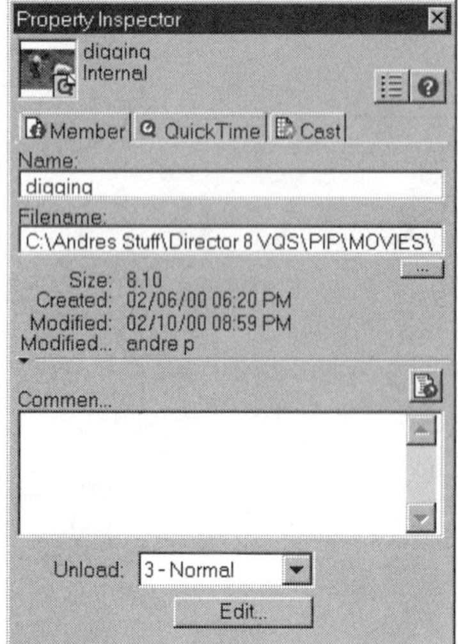

Figure 10.15 Click Browse to link to a new video file.

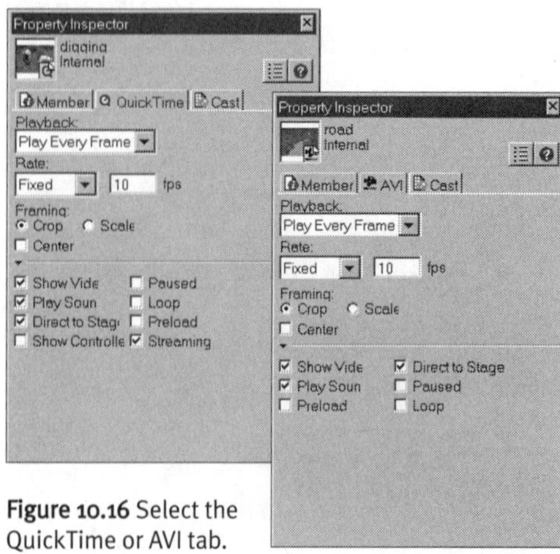

Figure 10.16 Select the QuickTime or AVI tab.

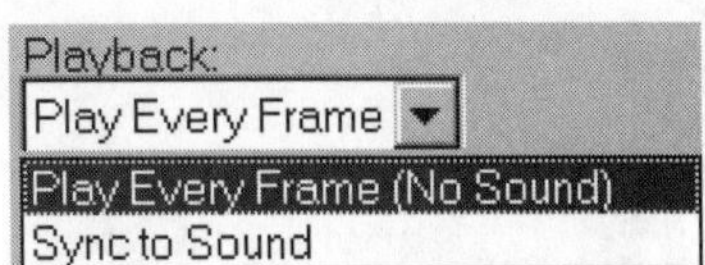

Figure 10.17 Choose a playback option from the Playback pop-up menu.

Here are the properties you can set that are common to both QuickTime and AVI movies:

- **Direct to Stage.** For best performance of QuickTime or AVI movie playback, turn on the Direct to Stage option. This option hands complete control of video playback to QuickTime or Windows AVI. There are tradeoffs for faster playback: Director doesn't compose the video with other sprites, so the video always appears in front of other sprites regardless of priority in the sprite channels, and ink effects don't affect the video.
- **Show Video.** Select this option to make sure that the video portion of your movie is displayed. The only time to disable this option is if your digital video uses only sound.
- **Play Sound.** Select this option for the soundtrack of your video to be heard. If your video doesn't use sound, deselect it to improve playback performance.
- **Paused.** When this option is selected, your video will be paused when it appears on the stage. You use Lingo to start the video at some later point.
- **Loop.** This option causes your video to loop (repeat from the beginning) when the video reaches its end and the playback head is still in a frame containing the video.
- **Preload.** When this option is selected, Director loads as much of the video as possible into RAM before playing. Preload improves playback performance, but at the expense of waiting while the video loads. When this option is unselected, Director plays from the linked file.
- **Playback pop-up menu.** Choose Sync to Soundtrack to make the video skip frames if necessary to keep up with its soundtrack, or choose Play Every Frame to play each frame of your video, sacrificing the sound instead (**Figure 10.17**).

- **Rate pop-up menu** (available only when Play Every Frame is selected in the Playback pop-up menu). Choose a speed from the Rate pop-up menu (**Figure 10.18**). Choose Normal to play each frame at the video clip's normal rate, without skipping any frames. Choose Maximum to play the video as quickly as possible without dropping frames. Choose Fixed to play the movie back using the frame rate you set.
- **Crop:** When this option is selected, whenever you resize the bounding box for the corresponding video sprite on the stage, the video is cropped rather than scaled (**Figure 10.19**).
- **Scale:** When this option is selected, whenever you resize the bounding box for the corresponding video sprite on the stage, the video is scaled rather than cropped (**Figure 10.20**).
- **Center** (available only when the Crop option is set). When this option is selected, the cropped video is centered within its bounding box.

Additional properties for QuickTime only:

- **Show Controller** (available only when the Direct to Stage option is set): When this option is selected, a controller bar is displayed at the bottom of your QuickTime movie, giving users control of video playback (**Figure 10.21**). When it appears on stage, the video is initially paused.
- **Streaming.** Set this option to allow your QuickTime movie to be streamed. The Direct to Stage option must also be set. QuickTime 4 must be installed on the user's system for streaming to occur. *Streaming* means that when a user starts to download your Director movie from the Web, the QuickTime video can start playing as soon as it appears in the movie while the rest of it loads in the background.

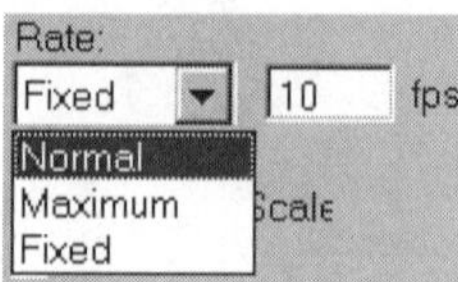

Figure 10.18 Choose a speed from the Rate pop-up menu.

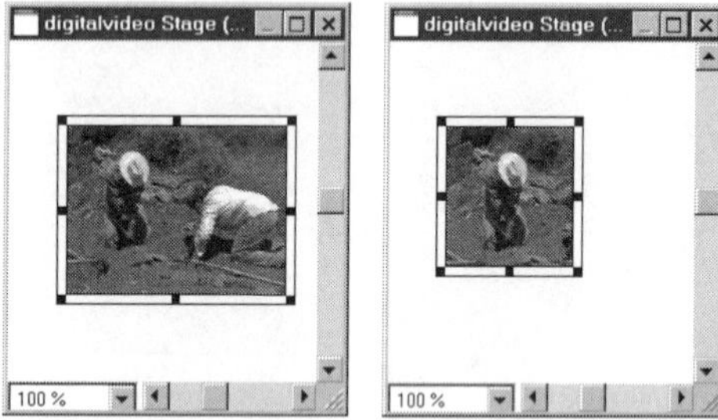

Figure 10.19 Drag the borders of the window to establish the new dimensions of the cropped video-playback window.

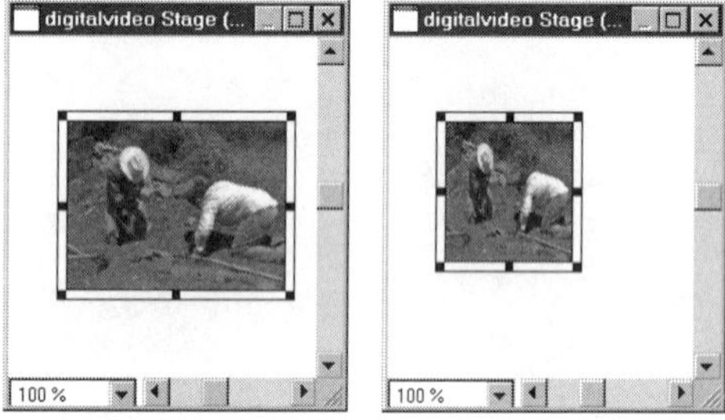

Figure 10.20 Drag the handles in the border to resize the playback area.

Figure 10.21 Check Show Controller to give users playback controls for the QuickTime video clip.

Figure 10.22 Select a digital video sprite.

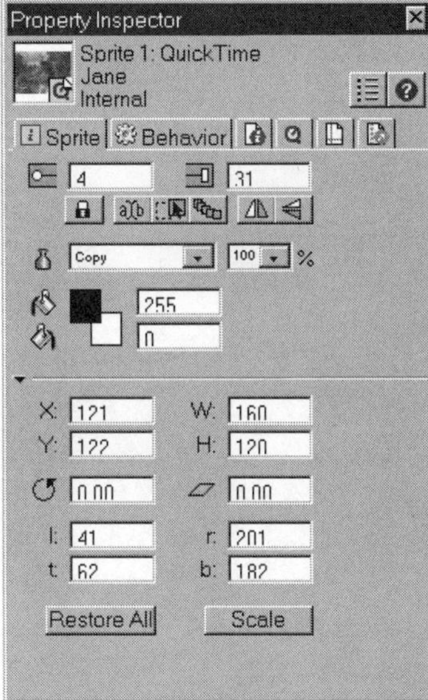

Figure 10.23 Select the Sprite tab.

Just like regular cast members, digital videos placed in the score have sprite properties independent of their parent cast members' properties. Using the Property Inspector window, you can set just about all the same types of properties for a digital video sprite that you can for a regular bitmap sprite. The exceptions are rotation and skew angles (You can use Lingo to set the rotation property for a video cast member to play all sprites based on it at an angle.)

You can tween most sprite properties for a digital video to create potentially impressive or undesirable effects. You can move a digital video across the screen while it plays; you can blend a digital video sprite to make it appear to fade in or out; you can gradually enlarge a digital video; you can change the foreground and background colors of a video and even apply ink effects to it. Keep in mind that these effects can slow video playback considerably.

To set digital video sprite properties:

1. Select a digital video sprite on the stage or in the score (**Figure 10.22**).
2. Choose Window > Inspectors > Property to display the Property Inspector.
3. Select the Sprite tab (**Figure 10.23**).
4. Set the desired sprite properties. *(See Chapter 3, "Building a Score," for details on sprite properties.)*

✔ Tip

- If the Direct to Stage cast-member property is not on, you can remove any white bounding box around a digital video sprite on the stage by applying the Background Transparent score ink.

Editing Video

Although complex video editing tasks require a specialized program, you can perform very simple tasks, such as reordering a sequence of frames, within Director. Such editing is restricted to the QuickTime window.

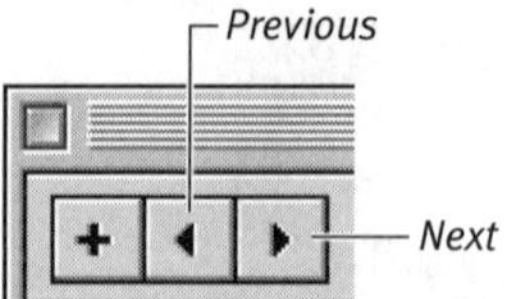

Figure 10.24 Use the Next and Previous buttons to find a cast member in the QuickTime window.

To copy and paste digital video frames:

1. Choose Window > QuickTime to open the QuickTime window
2. Use the Previous and Next cast member buttons to display a particular digital video cast member (**Figure 10.24**).
3. Drag the slider at the bottom of the window to move to the section you want to copy.

   If you want to select a range of frames, hold down the Shift key and drag the slider until you reach the last frame you want to select. The portion of the slider that corresponds to the multiple-frame selection turns black (**Figure 10.25**).

   or

   If you want to select only one frame, when you reach that video frame, you have effectively selected it.
4. Choose Edit > Copy or Edit > Cut.

   Keep in mind that cutting changes the linked video file.

Figure 10.25 The slider bar darkens to represent the selected portion.

Figure 10.26 Select a frame that appears right before the spot where you want to paste the video insert.

5. In the QuickTime window, use the Previous and Next cast member buttons to display the digital video cast member where you plan to paste.

   or

   Click the New Cast member button to make the video insert a new cast member.

6. Using the slider, display the frame in the video window that precedes the spot where you want to paste the video insert (assuming that you're not creating a new video cast member) (**Figure 10.26**).

7. Choose Edit > Paste.

   If you are pasting into a new digital video, Director prompts you to name the new linked cast-member file.

8. Play the video and make any necessary adjustments.

Importing Animated GIFs

Many Web sites include GIF (graphic inline format) animation sequences that you can add to a Director movie. You can import and incorporate an animated GIF into a Director movie just as you would a digital video clip.

Director supports the GIF89a and GIF87 formats. You can import only GIFs that have a global color table.

To set animated GIF options:

1. Select the animated GIF cast member.
2. Choose Modify > Cast Member > Properties to display the Property Inspector.
3. Click More Options to display the Animated GIF Asset Properties dialog box (**Figure 10.27**).
4. If necessary, change the animated GIF cast member's link status (**Figure 10.28**).

   If the GIF cast member is linked to an external file, you can switch the link to another file by entering a new path name in the Link File field. Or click Internet to specify a URL to link to a file on the Internet.
5. Select the Direct to Stage option if you want the fastest playback rate (**Figure 10.29**).

   If you turn on Direct to Stage, ink effects don't work on the GIF, and other sprites always appear underneath the animated GIF.
6. Choose an option from the Rate pop-up menu (**Figure 10.30**).

   Choose Normal to play the GIF at its original rate. Choose Fixed to play at the frame rate you specify in the text box to the right of the menu. Choose Lock-Step to play the GIF at the same rate as your Director movie.
7. Click Play in the left side of the dialog box to preview your Animated GIF.

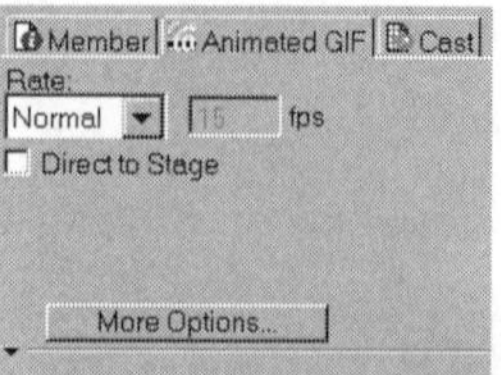

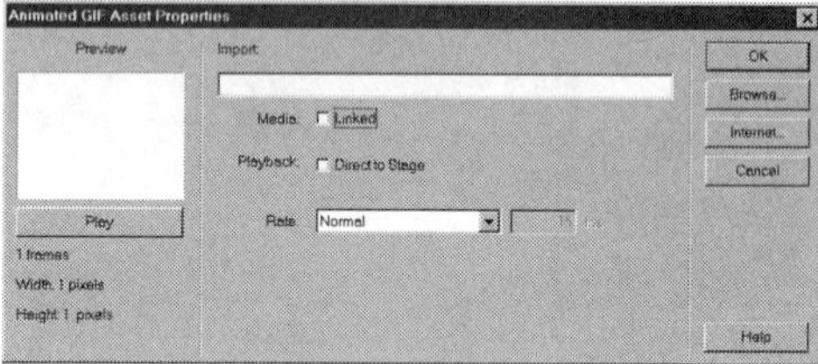

Figure 10.27 The Animated GIF Asset Properties dialog box.

Figure 10.28 Specify a link file, if necessary.

Figure 10.29 Check Direct to Stage for fast playback that puts the GIF animation in front of any sprites in the scene.

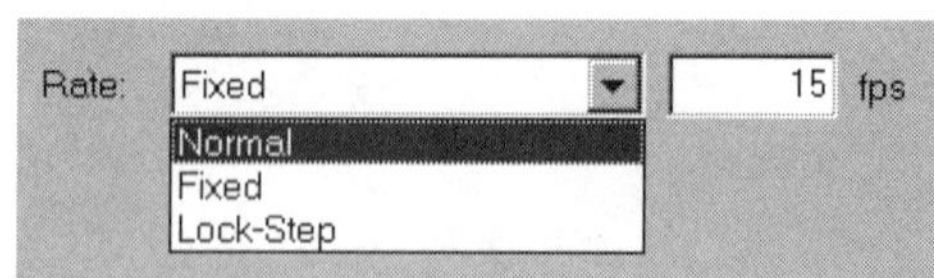

Figure 10.30 Choose a Rate option for the animated GIF.

11

Adding Text

Figure 11.1 Bitmapped text, created in the Paint window, becomes part of the image, where you can modify it with tools or effects.

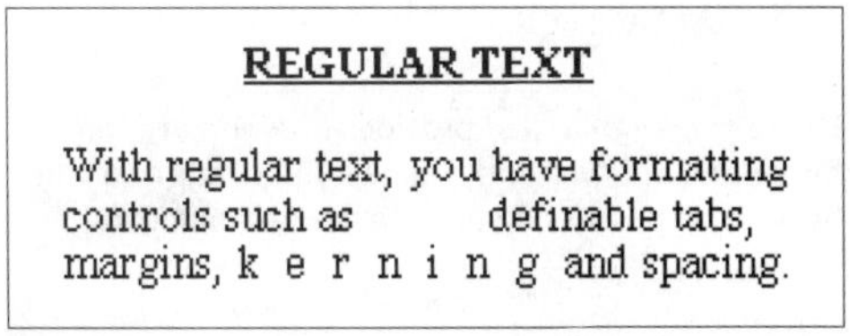

REGULAR TEXT

With regular text, you have formatting controls such as definable tabs, margins, k e r n i n g and spacing.

Figure 11.2 Regular text works more like word-processor text.

Regular Text has been anti-aliased.

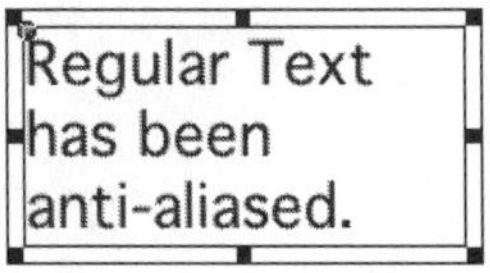

Figure 11.3 Regular text looks good at large sizes because you can anti-alias it.

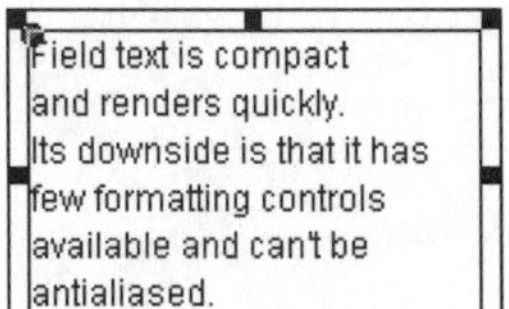

Field text is compact and renders quickly. Its downside is that it has few formatting controls available and can't be antialiased.

Figure 11.4 Field text works best for short passages in small sizes.

Director gives you four ways to incorporate text in your movies. You can import text, or you can create three sorts of text within Director. Each type of text has its advantages and limits:

- *Bitmapped text*, created in the Paint window (**Figure 11.1**), which is covered in detail in Chapter 6, "Using Paint Tools."
- Text that you can edit much like word-processor text, which is nicknamed *regular text* to distinguish it from Director's other kinds of text (**Figures 11.2–11.3**).
- *Field text*, which is compact and renders quickly but has few formatting options (**Figure 11.4**).

You can import into Director plain ASCII text; text in Rich Text Format, which preserves the styling from a word-processing document; and HTML text from Web pages.

You also can embed fonts in movies to avoid font substitutions on the viewer's desktop when you use field text or regular text.

Use **Table 11.1** to select the right text type for the job.

To choose the right text for the job:

1. Consider how important size is for the movie that includes the text.

   Field text takes up the least space; it downloads fastest.

2. Consider how important graphics effects are for the text.

   If you want to warp or rotate the text, or add a drop shadow, choose bitmapped text (**Figure 11.5**).

3. Decide whether you can afford the space to use embedded fonts for the text.

   Embedded fonts are necessary for regular text and fields, but not for bitmapped text.

4. Decide whether you need editing and formatting options.

   Regular text has the most style and formatting choices; it's also the easiest to revise (**Figure 11.6**). You cannot edit the wording or change the font of bitmapped text after you place the text in a Cast window; you'd have to start over or change the text with paint tools.

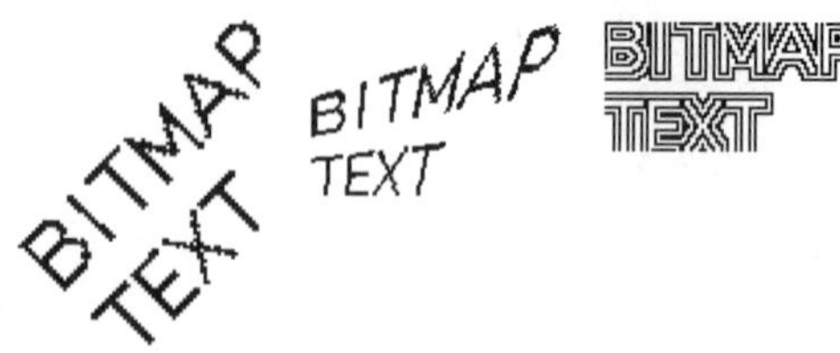

Figure 11.5 Bitmapped text is more image than text. You create it in the Paint window and can treat it just like any other image, rotating it or adding effects, such as warping or trace edges.

Bold
Italic
Choice of sizes
Choice of typefaces
Adjustable margins
and indents
Tabs that you can
set and edit

Figure 11.6 Regular text provides a wealth of formatting options, and it allows you to edit text with basic word-processing tools in the Text window.

TEST

Bitmapped text

TEST

Field text

TEST

Regular text

Figure 11.7 At large sizes, bitmapped text and field text show stairstep jaggies in diagonal and curved strokes of the letters. Regular text looks better than the other choices at large sizes.

5. Decide whether the text needs to be large.

   Use regular text for large sizes if you want the text to look smooth; the other two kinds of text look jaggy at large sizes (**Figure 11.7**).

6. Ask yourself whether the text passage will be long or short.

   Field text is best suited for short passages, because you can't control its appearance.

7. Decide whether you'll ever want to use the text as a hypertext link to a Web address.

   Regular text is the only option for hypertext links (see "Setting Text for Hyperlinks" later in this chapter).

Table 11.1

Comparing Director's varieties of text

	Regular Text	Field Text	Bitmapped Text
Cast member size	Large	Small	Medium
Animation speed	Medium	Fast	Fastest
Word processing tools	Yes	—	—
Author can revise easily	Yes	Yes	—
Can set for users to edit during playback	Yes	Yes	—
Created where	Text window, stage	Field window, stage	Paint window
Editable during play	Yes	Yes	—
Need embedded fonts	Yes	Yes	—
Supports hyperlinks	Yes	—	—
Can be anti-aliased	Yes	—	—
Movie viewers see the same font as author, even without embedding fonts	—	—	Yes
Can be incorprated into bitmapped images	—	—	Always
Modify with paint tools/effects	—	—	Yes

Creating and Editing Regular Text

Regular text (often just called *text* in Director) offers the most flexibility and versatility of any text in Director. It provides the most extensive formatting controls and can be anti-aliased to minimize jagged edges on large characters. You also can set regular text so that users can edit it during playback. Regular text is the only kind of text you can use in Director for automated hyperlinks.

Creating text directly on the stage is the quickest, most straightforward method of incorporating text into a movie.

To create text on the stage:

1. In Director's score, select a cell for the text cast member (**Figure 11.8**).
2. Choose Window > Tool Palette to display the tool palette.
3. Click the Text tool (**Figure 11.9**).
4. On the stage, click and drag to set the boundaries of the box for the text and then release the mouse button.

   The text box appears.
5. Type the text (**Figure 11.10**).

   The text wraps to a new line automatically as you type.
6. If necessary, press Return to start a new paragraph (**Figure 11.11**).
7. Click outside the text box.

   Director places the text on the stage and in the active Cast window.

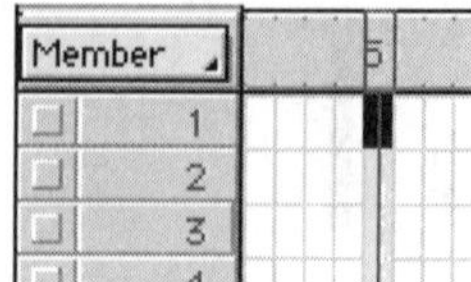

Figure 11.8 Select a place in the score for the text cast member.

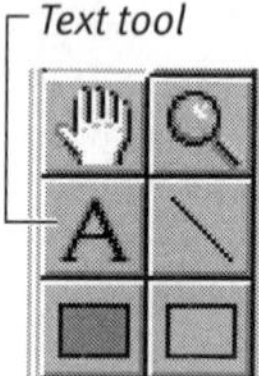

Figure 11.9 The Text tool.

Sample Text

Figure 11.10 Type text in the text box.

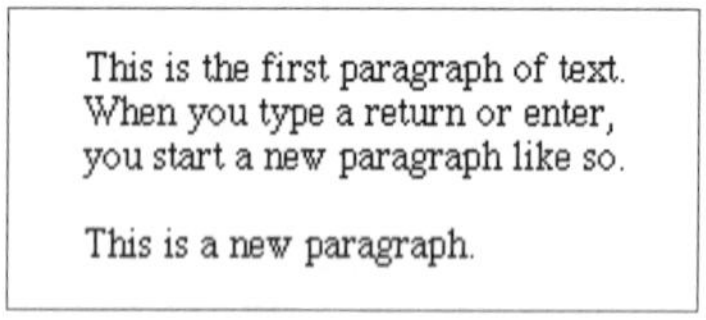

This is the first paragraph of text. When you type a return or enter, you start a new paragraph like so.

This is a new paragraph.

Figure 11.11 Press Return to start a new paragraph.

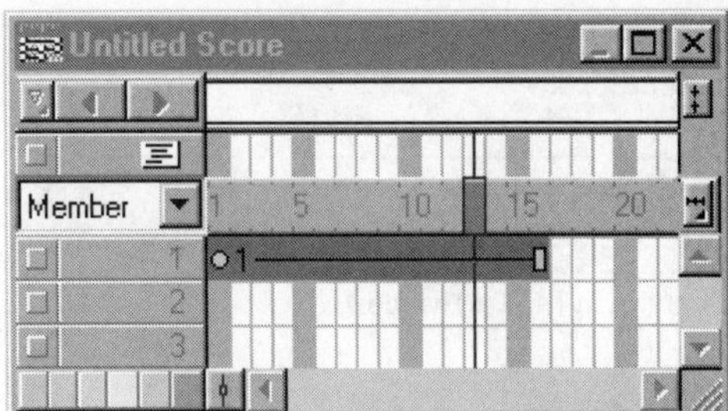

Figure 11.12 Select the text sprite that you want to edit.

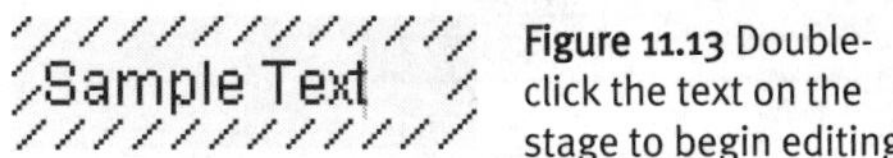

Figure 11.13 Double-click the text on the stage to begin editing.

8. If necessary, click the text box and drag its handles to accommodate the text.

   You can reshape the text box horizontally but not vertically.

9. If necessary, double-click the text box and revise the text.

After you create a text cast member and place it in the score, you can edit the text directly on the stage.

To edit text on the stage:

1. In the score, select a text sprite (**Figure 11.12**).
2. Double-click the text on the stage (**Figure 11.13**).

   An insertion point appears in the text.

3. Edit the text.
4. Click outside the text box.

✔ Tips

- Any changes you make in a text sprite affect the original text cast member and all other sprites based on the same text cast member.
- If the Paint window opens when you double-click text on the stage, you have selected bitmapped text, which is covered in Chapter 6, section "Adding Text."

You can add and edit text in the Text window. Work in the Text window if you expect to use extensive formatting or if you want to create several text cast members one after another and place them throughout your movie later.

The Text window provides the features of an elementary word processor, offering tab and margin controls, paragraph formatting, line spacing, type styles and sizes, and more.

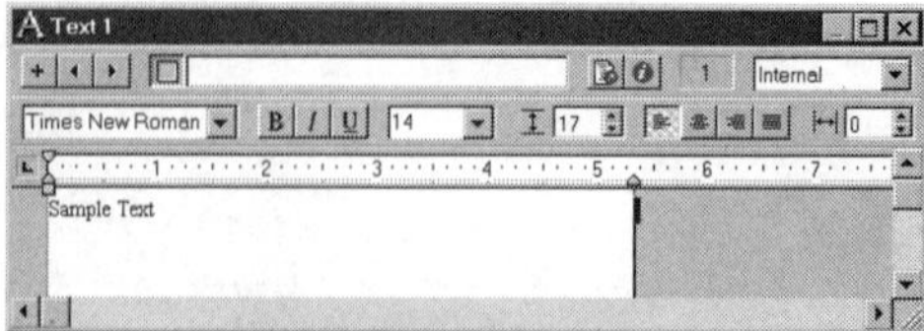

Figure 11.14 The Text window.

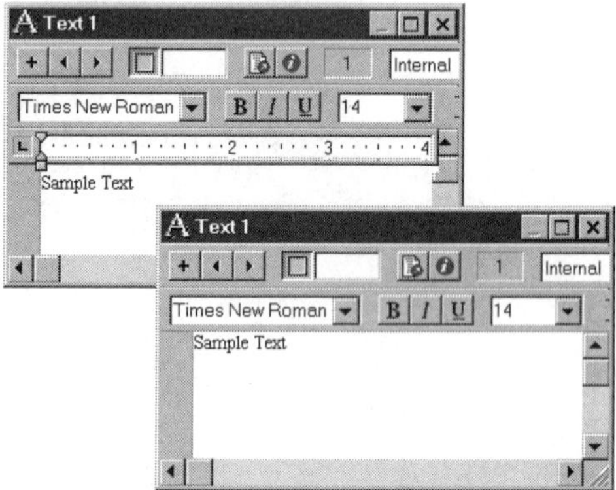

Figure 11.15 The Text window, with and without the ruler.

To create text in the Text window:

1. Select an empty cast-member position in a cast window.
2. Choose Window > Text.
   The Text window opens (**Figure 11.14**).
3. If necessary, display the ruler by choosing View > Ruler (**Figure 11.15**).
4. Type the text.
   Text wraps as you type. You also can press Return to begin a new line.
5. When you finish creating text, close the Text window.
   Director enters the text as a cast member in the current Cast window (**Figure 11.16**).

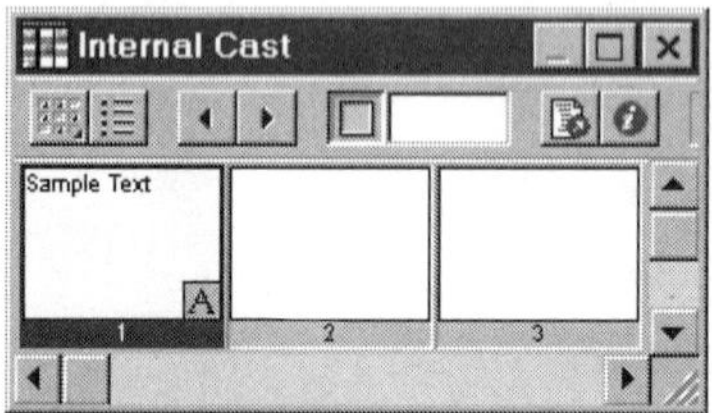

Figure 11.16 Director enters the text as a cast member.

✔ Tip

- You can create several text cast members one after another within the Text window. When you finish creating one block of text, click the New Cast Member button at the top of the Text window (**Figure 11.17**). Director clears the window and makes a place in the Cast window to accommodate the new text.

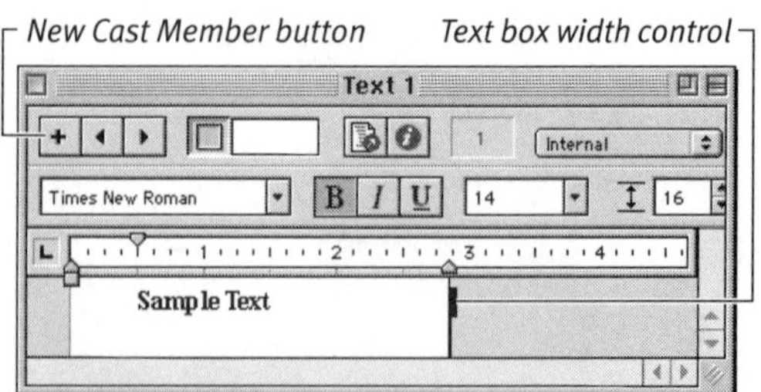

Figure 11.17 Click the New Cast Member button to create a new text cast member.

Creating and Editing Regular Text

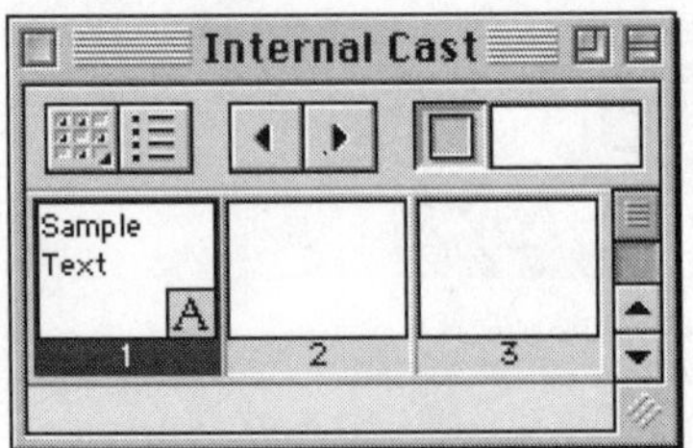

Figure 11.18 Text cast member in a Cast window.

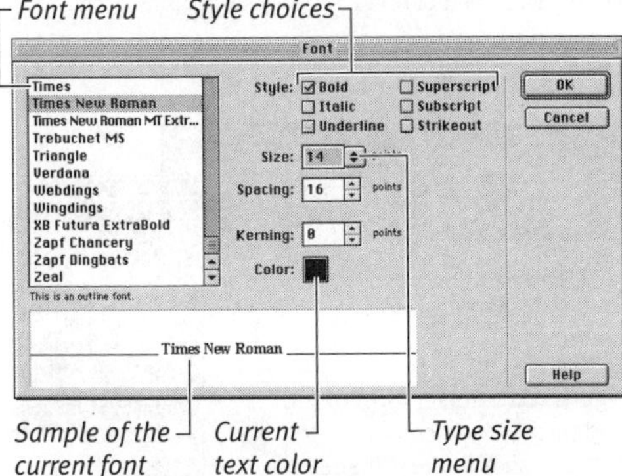

Figure 11.19 Set a text cast member's font, style, and size in the Font dialog box.

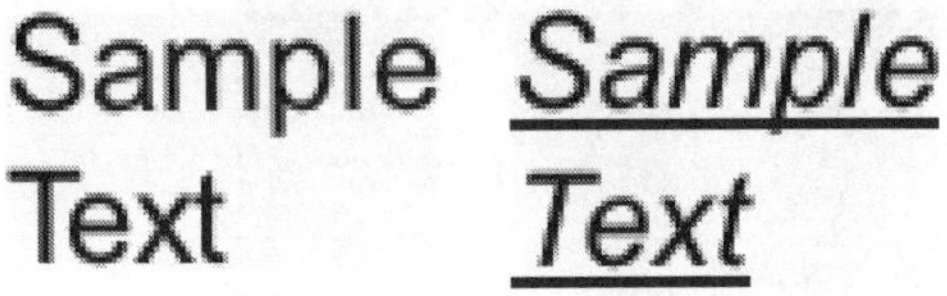

Sample Text   *Sample Text*

Figure 11.20 The font of the text has been modified (shown before and after on the stage).

To edit in the Text window:

1. In the Cast window, double-click a text cast member.
2. Make changes in wording, type styles, or other formatting.
3. Close the Text window.

✔ Tip

- You can change the width of the text box by dragging the width control—the heavy black tab in the top-right corner of the text area (**Figure 11.17**).

To change the font of a text cast member:

1. Select a text cast member in a Cast window (**Figure 11.18**).
2. Choose Modify > Font to display the Font dialog box.
3. Set the text's font, style, and size (**Figure 11.19**).
4. Click OK (**Figure 11.20**).

✔ Tip

- You can change a text cast member's font and other text properties from several other points in Director. Choose Window > Text to open the Text window, and enter font attributes at the top of the window. Or choose Window > Inspectors > Text to use the floating Text Inspector window.

To change a text cast member's color:

1. Double-click a text cast member in a cast window.
2. In the Text window, select the part of the text for which you want to change the foreground color (**Figure 11.21**).
3. Choose Window > Inspectors > Text to open the Text Inspector.
4. Click the Foreground Color chip in the Text Inspector, hold down the mouse button, and choose a new color from the Color menu (**Figure 11.22**).
5. Click the Background Color chip, hold down the mouse button, and choose a new background color for the entire text block.

To change a text sprite's color:

1. Select a text sprite on the stage or in the score.
2. Make sure that the text cast member that the sprite is based on is black in the foreground and white in the background. Otherwise, your sprites' colors will change in unpredictable ways.
3. Choose Modify > Sprite > Properties to display the Property Inspector .
4. Click the Foreground or Background Color chip and hold down the mouse button to display the Color menu.
5. Choose the appropriate color (**Figure 11.23**).

✔ Tip

- You can select a transparent ink for a text sprite, so that its text box seems to disappear when overlapping other sprites on the stage. You do this by using the Ink pop-up menu in the Property Inspector for the given text sprite (**Figure 11.23**).

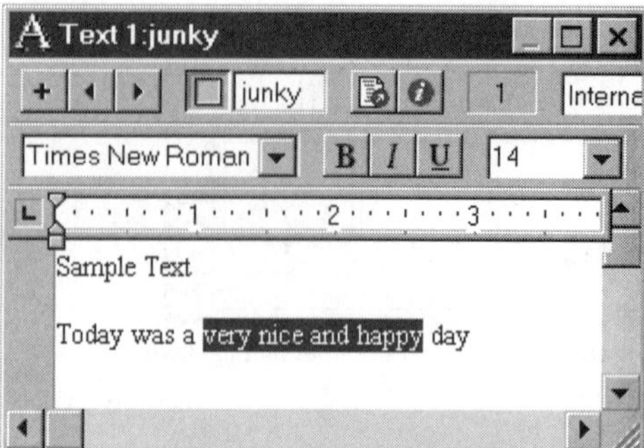

Figure 11.21 Select text to change its color.

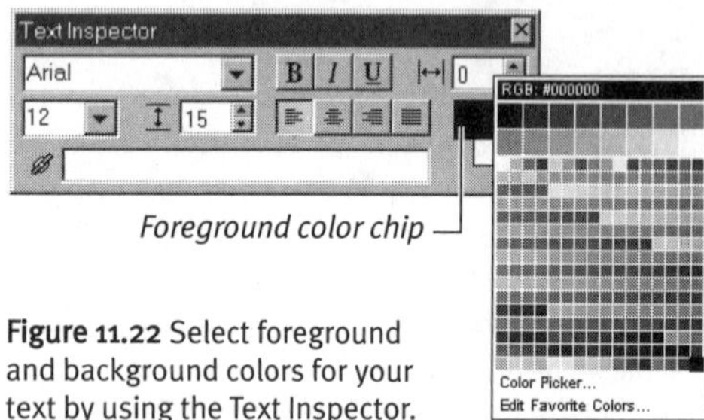

Figure 11.22 Select foreground and background colors for your text by using the Text Inspector.

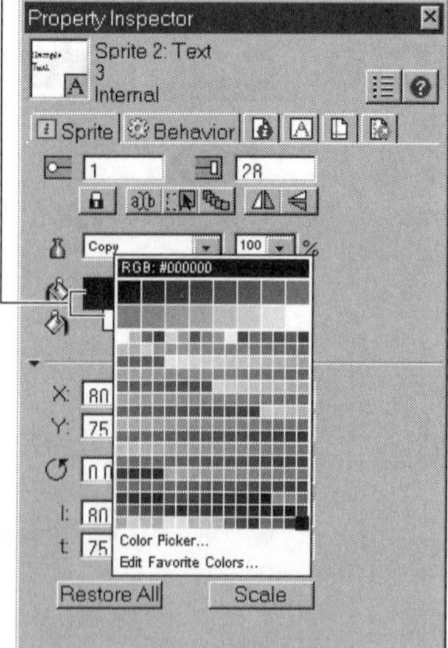

Figure 11.23 Use the Property Inspector to set colors and inks for your text sprites.

CREATING AND EDITING REGULAR TEXT

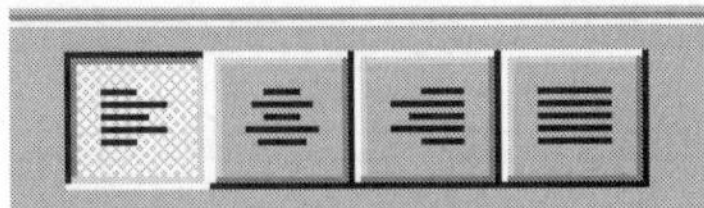

Figure 11.24 Text-alignment buttons in the Text window.

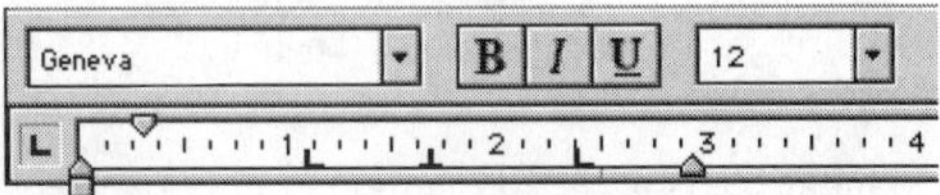

Figure 11.25 The ruler in the Text window contains controls for margin and tabs.

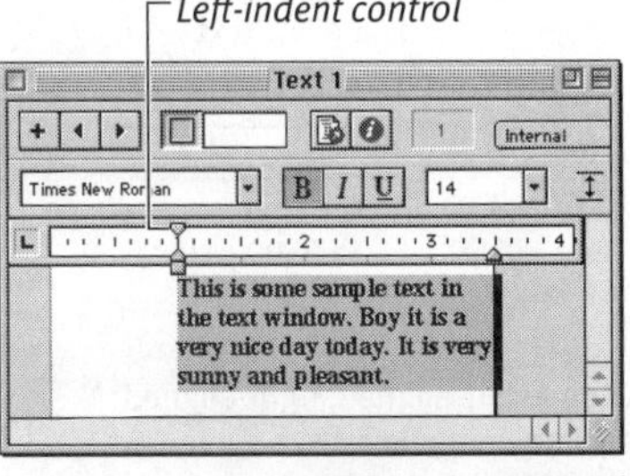

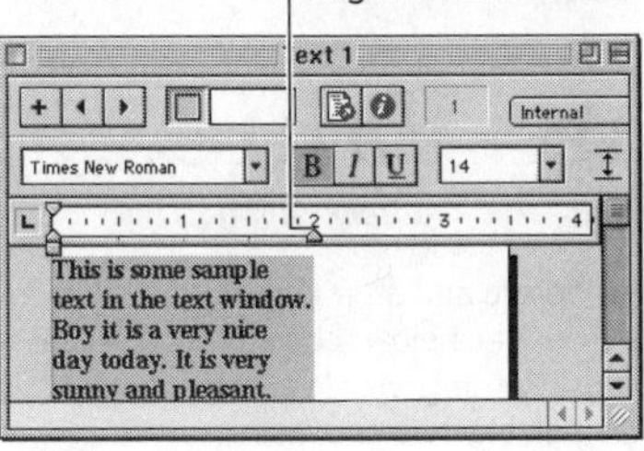

Figure 11.26 Set the margins by dragging the controls along the ruler.

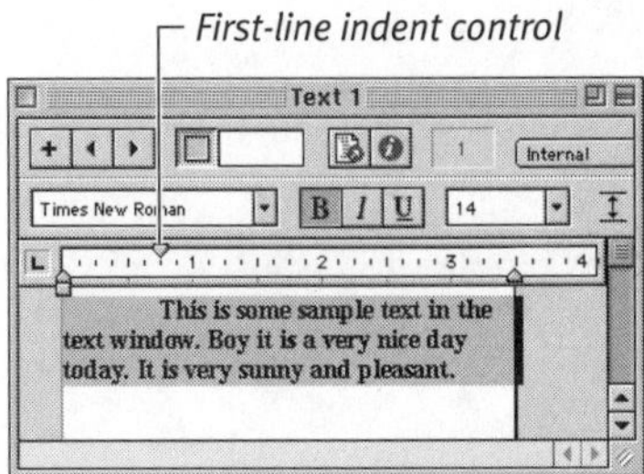

Figure 11.27 Adjust the indent of the first line of a paragraph by dragging the first-line indent in the ruler.

To align text margins:

1. In the Cast window, double-click a text cast member.

   The Text window opens.
2. If necessary, display the ruler by choosing View > Ruler.
3. Click within the paragraph of text or drag to select multiple paragraphs.
4. Click an alignment button to set the alignment of the text (**Figure 11.24**).

To change text margins:

1. In the Cast window, double-click a text cast member.

   The Text window opens.
2. If necessary, display the ruler by choosing View > Ruler (**Figure 11.25**).
3. Click within a paragraph or drag to select multiple paragraphs.
4. Adjust the right or left margin by dragging one of the indent controls in the ruler (**Figure 11.26**).

   The left-indent control is the little house-shaped control. It has two parts that work differently: the little box and the triangular roof.

   Drag the box to control the left margin for all the lines of your selection. Drag the triangular roof to change the left margin for the first line of your selection.
5. If necessary, set a different indent for the first line of the selected text by dragging the first-line indent along the ruler (**Figure 11.27**).

To set and change tabs in the Text window:

1. Open a text cast member.
   The Text window opens.
2. If necessary, display the ruler by choosing View > Ruler.
3. Click the tab well to select the type of tab you want (**Figure 11.28**).
   The type of tab changes each time you click; keep clicking until the type of tab you want appears in the tab well (**Figure 11.29**).
4. Click the ruler where you want to set a new tab.
5. If necessary, change a tab's location by dragging it on the ruler.
6. Remove a tab by dragging it off the ruler.

Kerning controls the spacing between certain pairs of characters (**Figure 11.30**). Kerning can greatly improve the appearance of text at large sizes but does very little to improve small text. Director includes kerning settings, called a *kerning table*, for pairs of letters that typically need kerning help at larger sizes. You can customize those kerning settings for a cast member.

✔ Tip

- If you want to use kerning, you must use standard text; it doesn't work on field text or bitmapped text.

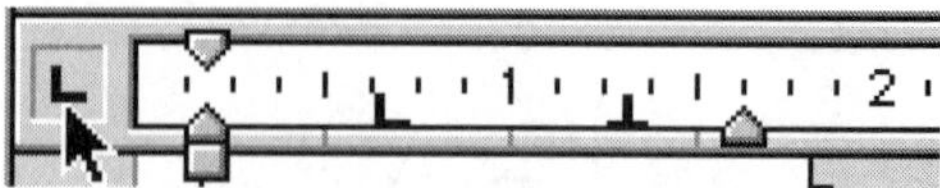

Figure 11.28 Click the tab well to select the type of tab.

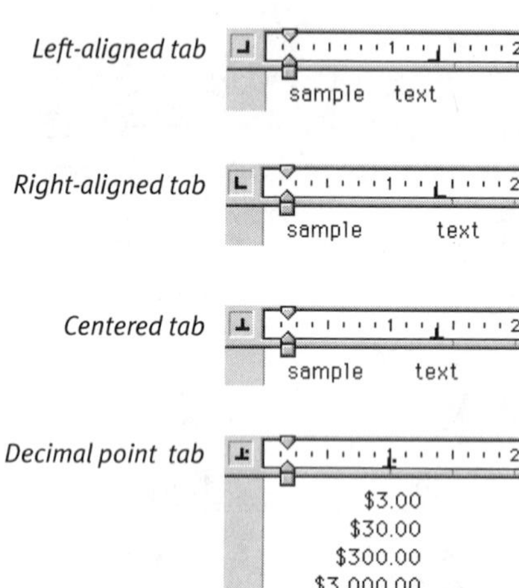

Figure 11.29 Choose left-aligned, right-aligned, centered, or decimal -aligned tabs.

Value Value

Before kerning *After kerning*

Figure 11.30 Text before and after kerning. Notice that the *a* nestles below the *V* in the kerned text. Before kerning, words in large type sometimes look like two chunks of letters rather than a single word.

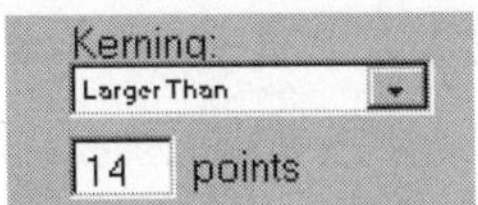

Figure 11.31 Kerning options for an entire cast member.

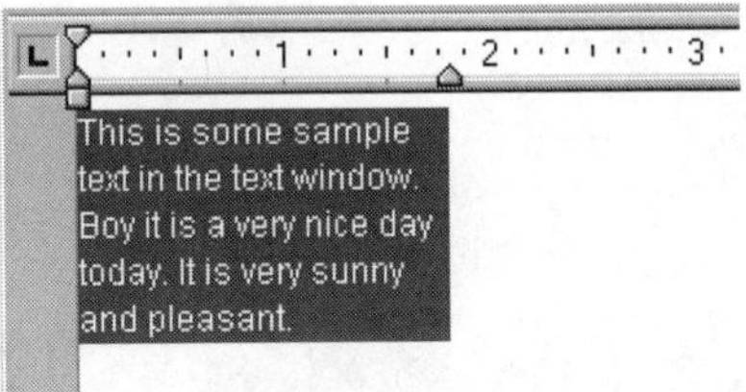

Figure 11.32 Select the text you want to kern.

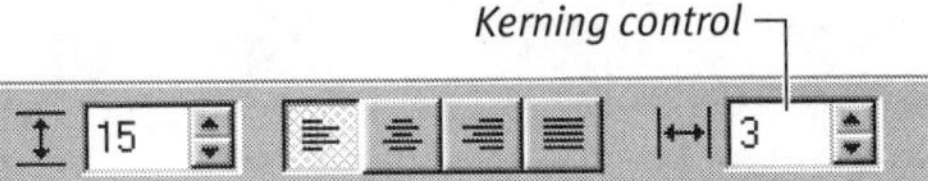

Figure 11.33 Type a value or click the up and down arrow controls to change kerning for selected text.

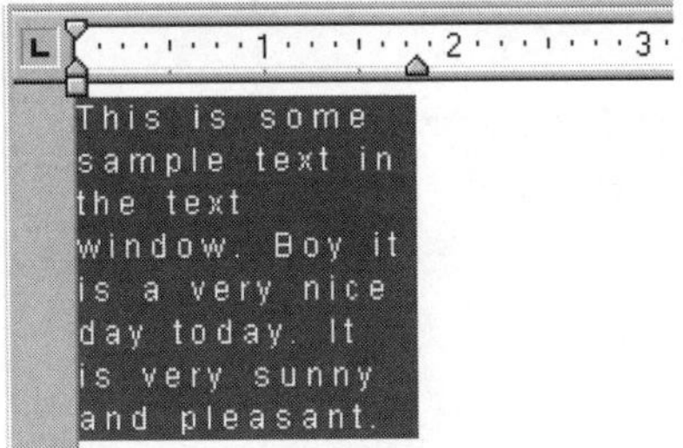

Figure 11.34 Director kerns the text, including the spaces. In this example, everything in the selection is farther apart after kerning.

To change kerning for an entire text cast member:

1. Select a text cast member.
2. Choose Modify > Cast Member > Properties to display the Property Inspector .
3. Click the List View button, if necessary, to select the graphical view in the Property Inspector.
4. Choose a kerning option from the Kerning pop-up menu (**Figure 11.31**).

   Choose All Text to kern all text in the cast member according to Director's kerning table.

   Choose Larger Than and enter a point size to change the size at which Director applies kerning in the cast member.

   Choose None to turn off kerning in the cast member.

You can kern selected text to refine letter spacing without affecting the kerning for an entire text cast member. You also can select all text in a cast member and open the spacing or close all the spaces more tightly.

To kern text selections individually:

1. Open a text cast member.
2. Drag to select the portion of text you want to kern (**Figure 11.32**).
3. Type a number in the kern box (**Figure 11.33**) or click the up and down arrows to change the kerning value.
   Director kerns the text (**Figure 11.34**).

✔ Tip

- Negative numbers in the kern box make characters scoot very close together or overlap.

Line spacing controls the vertical spacing between lines of text.

To change text line spacing:

1. Open a text cast member.
2. Drag to select a portion of the text (**Figure 11.35**).
3. Type a number of points in the line-spacing box or click the up and down arrows to add or subtract space between lines (**Figure 11.36**).

   Type `0` if you want Director to make automatic adjustments between lines.

   Director adjusts the line spacing (**Figure 11.37**).

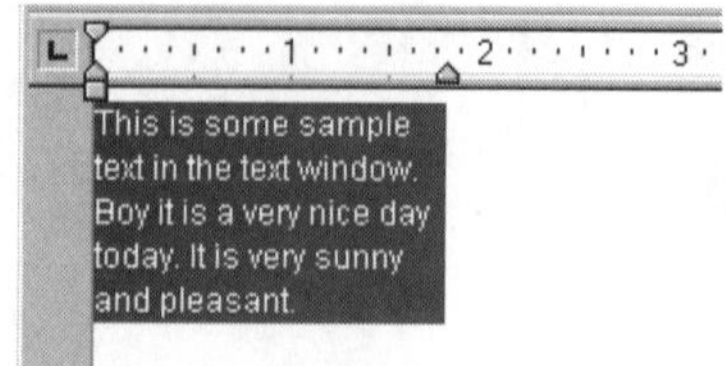

Figure 11.35 Select the text for which you want to change the line spacing.

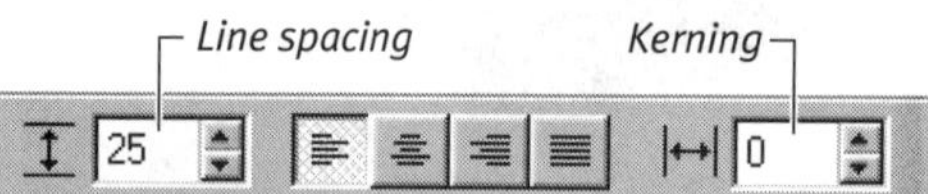

Figure 11.36 Type a value or click the up and down arrows to change the line spacing.

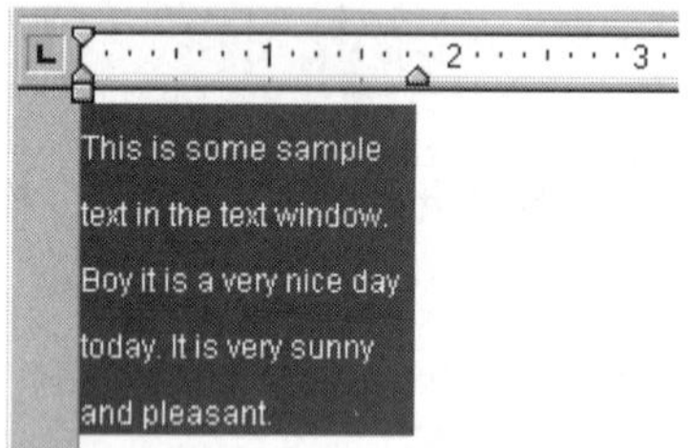

Figure 11.37 Director adjusts the line spacing.

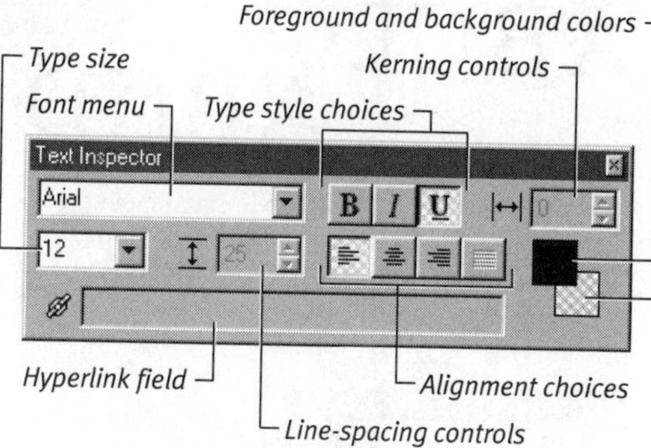

Figure 11.38 The Text Inspector contains some of the formatting controls that the Text window contains.

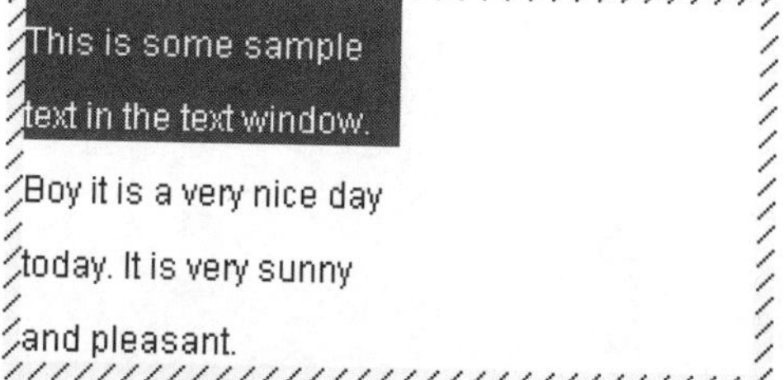

Figure 11.39 Select some text to reformat.

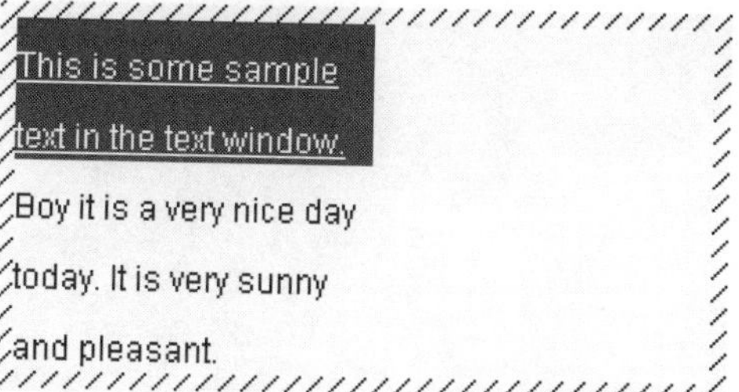

Figure 11.40 The modified text, now underlined.

The Text Inspector offers most of the text-formatting tools in yet another guise. You can use the Text Inspector to modify both regular text and field text. With the Text Inspector, you can change text formatting on the stage without having to go to the Cast window and open the text in the Text window.

To reformat text with the Text Inspector:

1. Choose Window > Inspectors > Text.

   The Text Inspector opens (**Figure 11.38**).

2. Double-click a text sprite on the stage and drag to select the portion of text that you want to reformat (**Figure 11.39**).

   or

   Click the sprite once to select all of it for reformatting.

3. Make the formatting adjustments in the Text Inspector.

   The text changes (**Figure 11.40**).

4. Close the Text Inspector.

Anti-aliasing smoothes the jagged edges and curves of text—but only Director's standard text. Anti-aliasing makes the biggest difference for text at large sizes (**Figure 11.41**). By default, anti-aliasing is turned on for regular text in Director.

To reset text anti-aliasing:

1. In the Cast window, select a text cast member.
2. Choose Modify > Cast Member > Properties to open the Property Inspector.
3. Choose an option from the Anti-Alias pop-up menu (**Figure 11.42**).

   Choose All Text to smooth all text in the cast member.

   Choose Larger Than and type a point size to change the size at which anti-aliasing is turned on in the cast member.

   Choose None to turn off anti-aliasing in the cast member.

✔ Tip

- When you work with small type sizes, turn off anti-aliasing because blurring the edges of characters usually makes small text harder to read.

ABCD ABCD

Figure 11.41 When you turn on anti-aliasing, Director blurs the edges of the characters to smooth out the jagged stairstep effect on curved and diagonal strokes. The edges look smoother on-screen.

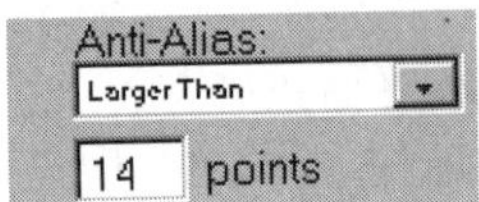

Figure 11.42 Choose one of the three anti-aliasing options.

Text in the Text window before conversion to bitmap

The converted text opens in the Paint window.

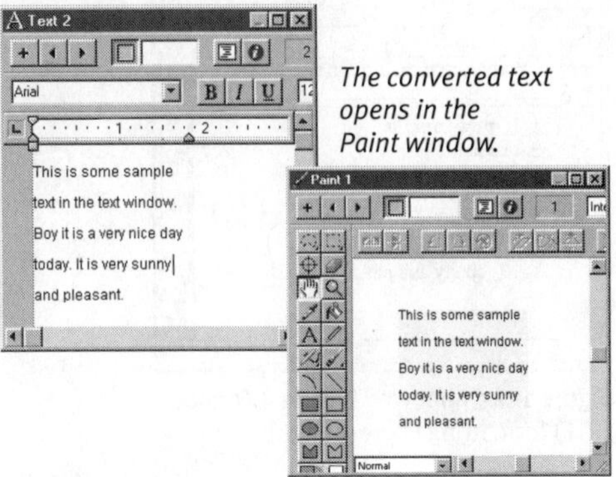

Figure 11.43 Text before and after being converted to a bitmap.

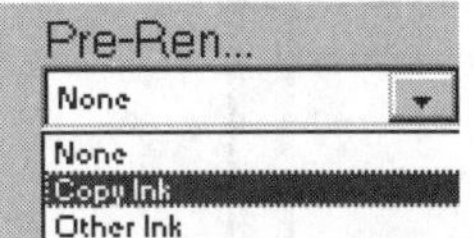

Figure 11.44 Choose an option from the Pre-Render pop-up menu to speed display of text.

You can convert regular text and field text cast members to bitmapped cast members (but not the other way around).

To convert regular text or field text to bitmapped text:

1. Select a text or field cast member in a Cast window.
2. Choose Modify > Convert to Bitmap.

   Once converted, the text behaves like a bitmapped image (**Figure 11.43**); you can no longer change it with any of the text tools.

You can control how fast text appears in your movie by using one of the pre-render options in the Property Inspector. When you do so, Director renders the text when it is first loaded into your movie, as opposed to when it first appears on stage.

To speed the display of text in your movie:

1. In a cast window, select a text cast member that you want to pre-render.
2. Choose Modify > Cast Member > Properties to open the Property Inspector.
3. Choose an option from the Pre-Render pop-up menu (**Figure 11.44**).

   Choose Copy Ink to optimize pre-rendering for the Copy ink.

   Choose Other Ink to optimize pre-rendering for all other inks.

Importing Text

Director allows you to import text files in three formats:

- Rich Text Format (RTF) (**Figure 11.45**)
- Plain text (ASCII) (**Figure 11.46**)
- HTML document (**Figure 11.47**)

To import text:

1. Choose File > Import.
2. In the dialog box that appears, choose text as the file type to import (**Figure 11.48**).
3. Select the text file by browsing through your files and then clicking the file name.
4. Click Import.

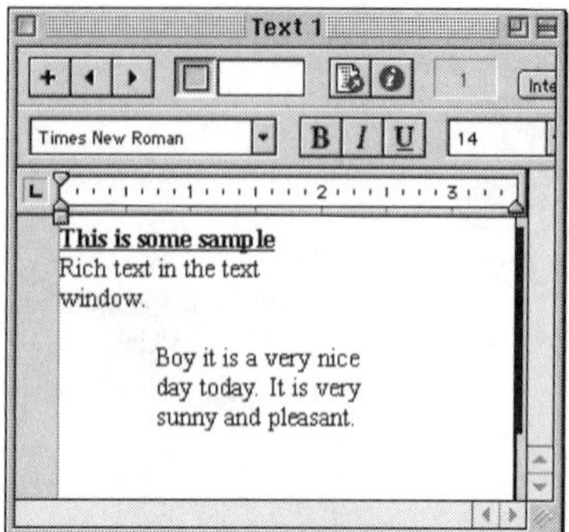

Figure 11.45 Imported Rich Text Format (RTF) formatting is preserved.

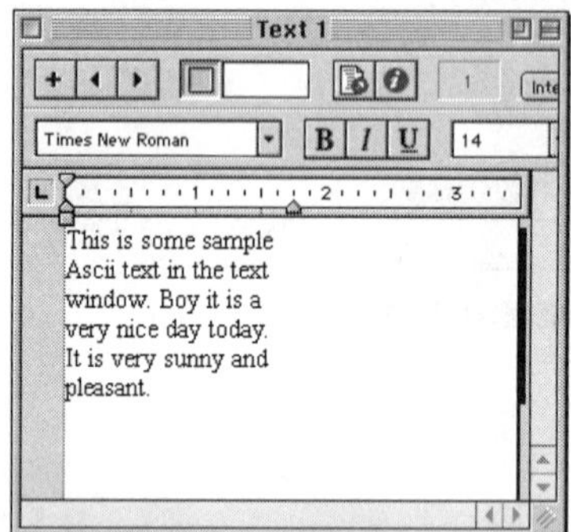

Figure 11.46 Imported plain ASCII text.

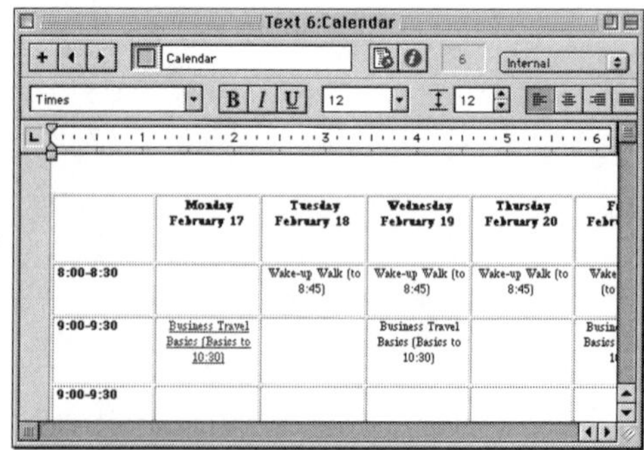

Figure 11.47 Imported HTML document.

Figure 11.48 Choose text as the file type in the Import dialog box.

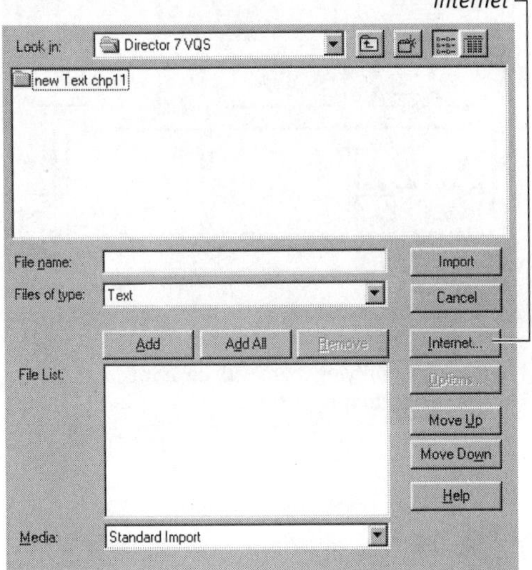

Figure 11.49 Click Internet.

Figure 11.50 Type the URL for the HTML document you want to import.

You can import an HTML document from the Web. When you do so, Director does its best to approximate formatting. It recognizes most standard HTML tags and parameters, but no embedded objects except tables. Director does not recognize `<FORM>`, `<APPLET>`, `<FRAME>`, `<INPUT>`, and `<IMAGE>` tags.

To Import an HTML document from the Web:

1. Choose File > Import to open the Import dialog box.
2. Choose text as the file type to import.
3. Click Internet to display the Open URL dialog box (**Figure 11.49**).
4. Type the URL for the HTML document that you want to import (**Figure 11.50**).
5. Click OK.
6. Click Import.

✔ Tip

- You can import an HTML document that's on your computer's hard disk or that's stored on another disk you can reach on a network without connecting to the Internet. In that case, you specify the location of the HTML file instead of clicking Internet in step 3.

Embedding Fonts

Director allows you to make sure that the text you create displays with the intended fonts when viewers play it on their own computers. You do so by embedding font information in the movie file—for any of the fonts already installed on the computer you're using to create the Director movie.

If you choose not to embed a font that a user doesn't have installed, the Director projector substitutes a font from the computer that's running the movie.

Director compresses and stores embedded fonts as cast members (**Figure 11.51**).

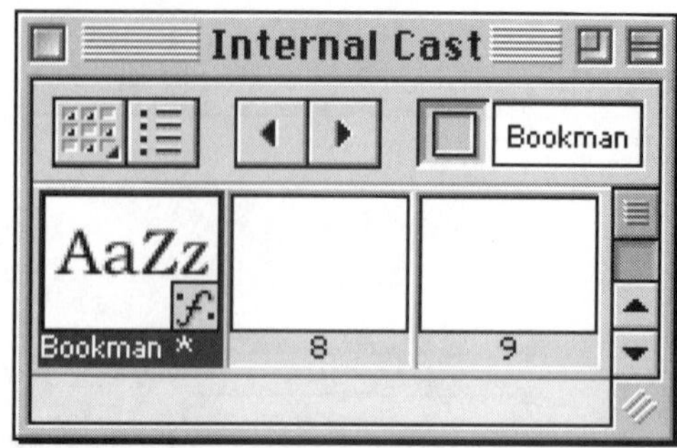

Figure 11.51 Director stores embedded fonts as cast members, identifying them with an embedded-font icon in the bottom-right corner.

To embed a font in your movie:

1. Choose Insert > Media Element > Font to display the Font Cast Member Properties dialog box .
2. From the Original Font menu, choose the font to embed (**Figure 11.52**).
3. If the font has custom faces, such as Bold, Italic, or BoldItalic, choose the specific font face from the pop-up menu below the Original Font menu.

   The default font face is plain.
4. Click OK.

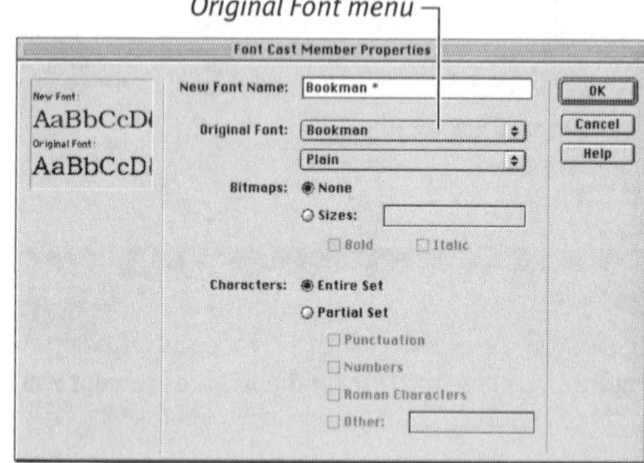

Figure 11.52 Choose the font to embed from the Original Font pop-up menu.

If you know that your movie uses a subset of characters with a particular font, you can embed only those characters—instead of the entire font—to help limit file size.

To keep file size down with embedded fonts:

1. In a Cast window, select the font cast member whose file size you want to keep minimum.
2. Choose Modify > Cast Member > Properties to open the Property Inspector.

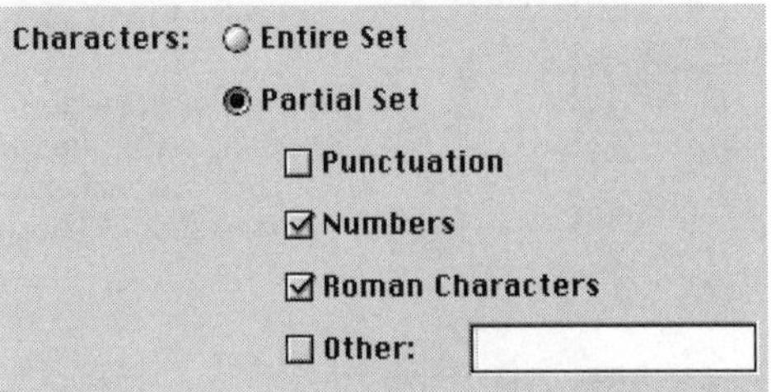

Figure 11.53 Select Partial Set and one or more checkboxes below to limit the font to a subset of characters.

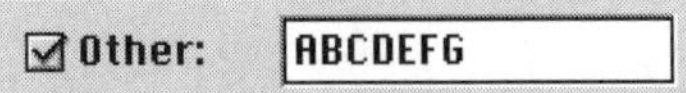

Figure 11.54 Click the Other button and type the characters of the font to include with your movie.

Figure 11.55 Click the Sizes button and type which point sizes to include with the font.

3. Click More Options.

   The Font Cast Member Properties dialog box opens.

4. Click the Partial Set button for Characters, and click one or more checkboxes below to indicate which subset of characters you want to limit the font to (**Figure 11.53**).

   You can specify your own custom group of characters by selecting the Other option and typing the characters to include—without any spaces. Type **ABCDEFG**, for example (**Figure 11.54**).

If your movie uses text at small point sizes, consider including bitmapped versions of those fonts. Small text generally looks better in bitmapped fonts rather than standard fonts. Unfortunately, including bitmapped versions increases file size; you have to make the decision whether legibility is more important than file size for your movie.

To embed fonts that look best at small sizes:

1. In a Cast window, select a font cast member.
2. Choose Modify > Cast Member > Properties to open the Property Inspector.
3. Click More Options to open the Font Cast Member Properties dialog box.
4. Click the Sizes button for Bitmaps and type the point sizes to include, separated by commas but no spaces.

   Type **7,8,9**, for example (**Figure 11.55**).
5. If necessary, click Bold and/or Italic to include bitmapped versions of bold and/or italic characters with the font.

Creating Field Text

Field text cast members consume the least amount of memory of all the text types available in Director—an important consideration for movies distributed via the Web. On the other hand, Director can't anti-alias field text and provides fewer formatting controls for it; you can't insert tabs or set special margin alignments in field text.

When your movie calls for a short passage of small-point text with simple formatting, field text generally works best. Also opt for field text when memory, media space, or network bandwidth for your movie is limited.

You can create field text on the stage or in the Field window.

To create field text on the stage:

1. In the score, select the cell where you want to place the field cast member (**Figure 11.56**).
2. Choose Window > Tool Palette to open the tool palette.
3. Click the Field tool (**Figure 11.57**).
4. Position the crosshair pointer on the stage, and drag to set the width of the field box.

   When you release the mouse button, a field text box appears (**Figure 11.58**).
5. Choose Modify > Font.

   The Font dialog box appears (**Figure 11.59**).
6. Set the field's font, style, color, and size.
7. Click OK.
8. Type the text.
9. When the text is finished, click outside the box.

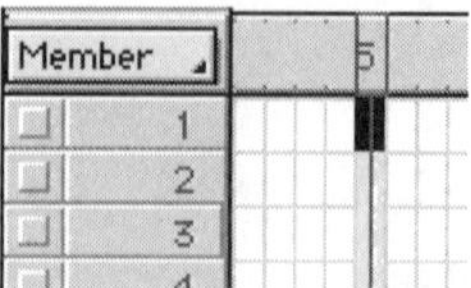

Figure 11.56 In the score, select the cell where you want to place the field cast member.

Figure 11.57 Click the Field tool in the tool palette.

Figure 11.58 A field text box on the stage.

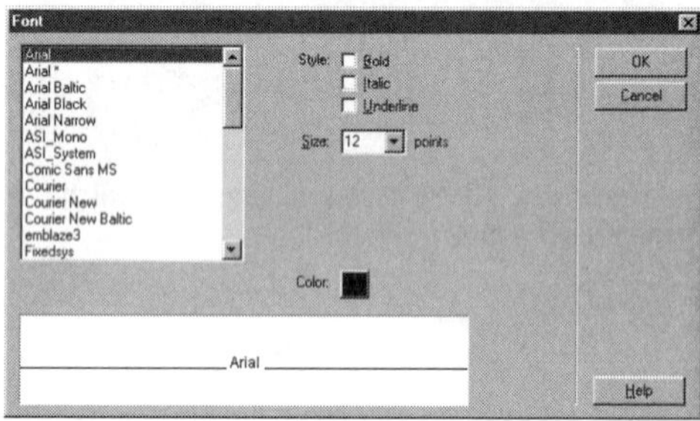

Figure 11.59 The Font dialog box.

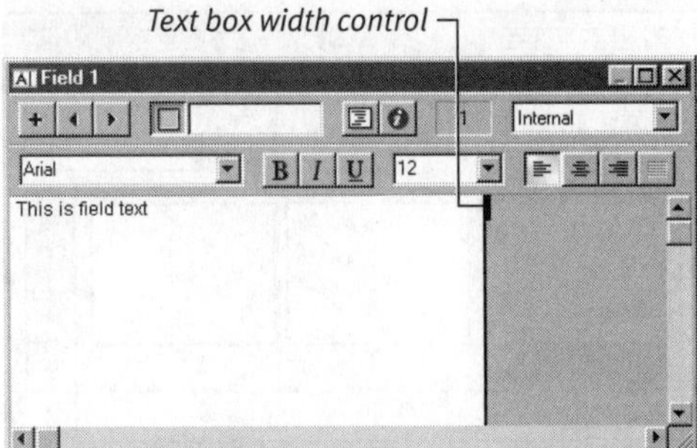

Figure 11.60 Enter text in the Field window.

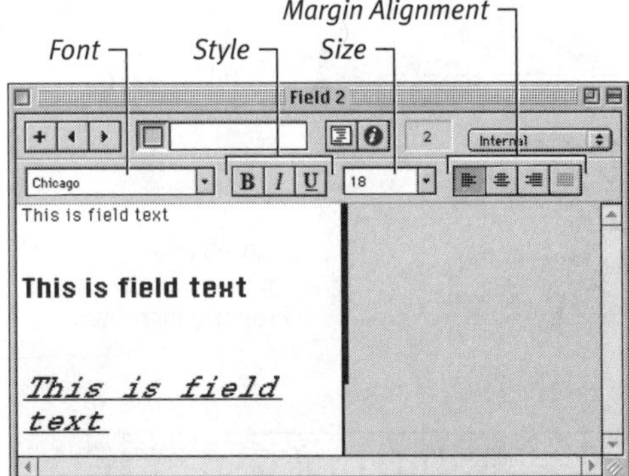

Figure 11.61 Style the text with the controls in the Field window.

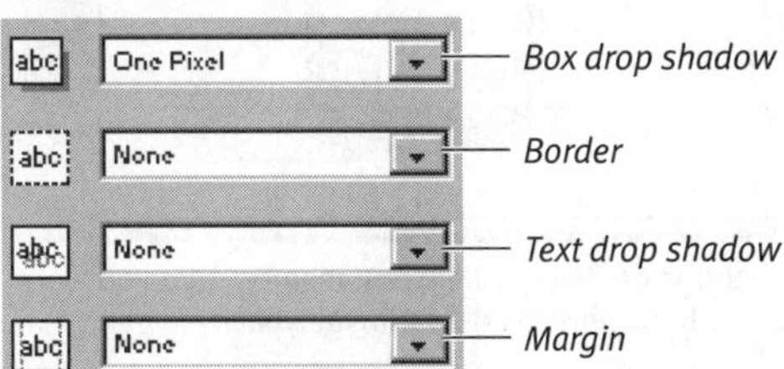

Figure 11.62 Add drop shadows and borders to field text for a selected field cast member by using the pop-up menus in the bottom pane of the Property Inspector.

The Field window works much as the Text window does, except that the ruler (with tab and indent controls), paragraph , and spacing and kerning controls are not available. If you need those controls, use regular text.

To create field text by using the Field window:

1. Select an empty cast-member position where you want to store the field text cast member.
2. Choose Window > Field.
   The Field window opens.
3. Type the text (**Figure 11.60**).
4. Style the text as necessary by using the font, style, and size controls (**Figure 11.61**).
   There is no ruler in the Field window, so you cannot adjust text margins within the text box, but you can choose flush-left, flush-right, or centered alignment of the text within the box.
5. When the text is finished, close the Field window.
   Director creates a field cast member in the current Cast window.

✔ Tips

- You can change the width of the text box by dragging the width control—the heavy black tab in the top-right corner of the text area (**Figure 11.60**).
- You can add drop shadows and borders to field text by selecting the field cast member, choosing Modify > Cast Member > Properties, and then using the pop-up menus in the bottom pane of the Property Inspector (**Figure 11.62**).

Setting Text for Users to Change

You can set regular text and field cast members so that users can edit the text as the movie plays. If your movie calls for users to enter their names, for example, include an editable text or field sprite that users can click to type.

Keep in mind that any edits made in a text or field sprite also change the original text or field cast member, as well as all sprites created from it throughout your movie.

To make a text cast member editable during movie playback:

1. Select the text cast member in the Cast window (**Figure 11.63**).
2. Choose Modify > Cast Member > Properties to open the Property Inspector.
3. Choose Editable.
4. Close the Property Inspector (**Figure 11.64**).

Just as you can set regular text for users to modify during playback, you can specify field text sprites to be editable during playback.

To make a field text cast member editable during movie playback:

1. Select the field text cast member in the Cast window (**Figure 11.65**).
2. Choose Modify > Cast Member > Properties to open the Property Inspector.
3. Choose Editable.
4. Close the Property Inspector (**Figure 11.66**).

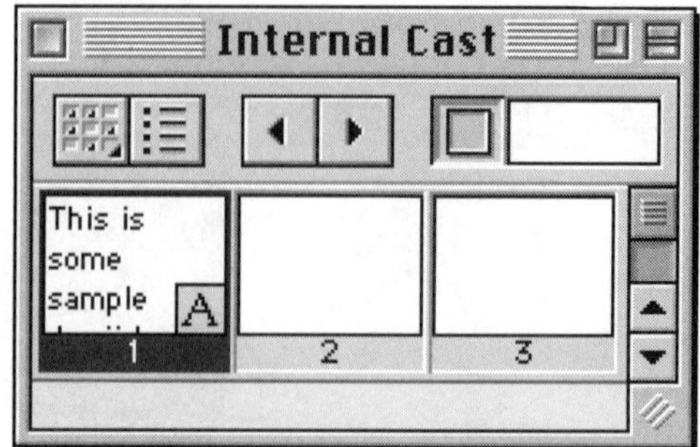

Figure 11.63 Select the text cast member that you want to allow users to modify while they play your movie.

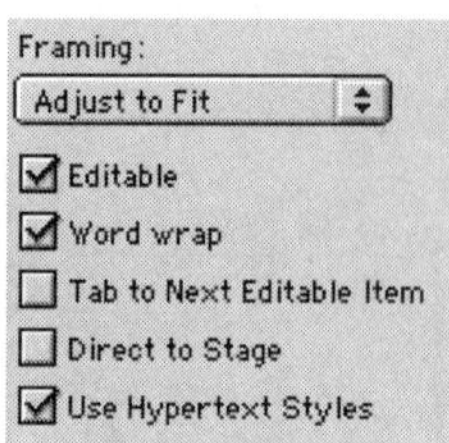

Figure 11.64 Choose Editable in the Property Inspector.

Figure 11.65 Select a field cast member that you want users to be able to edit during playback of your movie.

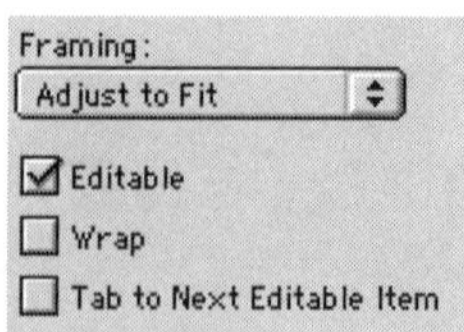

Figure 11.66 Choose Editable.

Figure 11.67 Select the range of frames in which you want the text or field sprite to be editable.

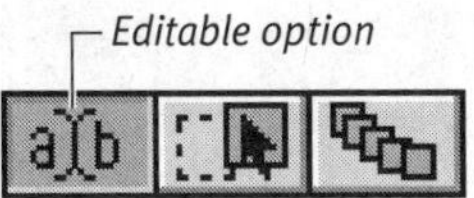

Figure 11.68 Click the Editable option in the score.

Sometimes you want users to be able to change text—but not until a particular point in your movie. You can specify when the users can edit a text or field sprite.

To make fields editable during a certain range of frames:

1. Make sure that the Editable option is turned off for your selected field cast member.
2. In the score, select the range of frames in a field sprite where you want the text to be editable (**Figure 11.67**).

   Ctrl+Alt and Shift+Alt+click to select a range of frames within a sprite (Command+Option and Shift+Option+click on the Mac).
3. If the sprite toolbar is not visible in the score, choose View > Sprite Toolbar.
4. Select the editable option in the score (**Figure 11.68**).

Setting Text for Hyperlinks

You can style any portion of a text cast member as a hypertext link, or *hyperlink* for short. Director applies the Web's standard link formatting to the text, so that it appears blue at first and turns purple after a viewer clicks the link.

For anything to happen when a user clicks the hypertext during a movie, you must write an `on hyperlinkClicked` event handler in Lingo (see Chapter 17, "Scripting Lingo"). With the handler script, you can make the hypertext link to a Web-site address (URL) or perform some other action.

Bitmapped text and field text do not work for hypertext links. You must use regular text for the links.

To style text for hyperlinks:

1. On the stage, double-click the text that you want to use as a hypertext link.
2. Drag to select the portion of text that you want to style as a hypertext link (**Figure 11.69**).
3. Choose Window > Inspectors > Text to display the Text Inspector .
4. In the hyperlink box at the bottom of the Sprite Inspector, type the URL or other message that you want to send to the `hyperlinkClicked` handler (**Figure 11.70**).
5. Press Enter (Return on the Mac).

   Director styles the text automatically (**Figure 11.71**).

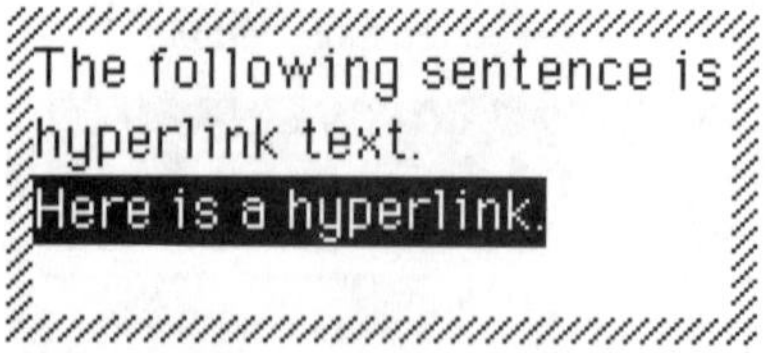

The following sentence is hyperlink text.
Here is a hyperlink.

Figure 11.69 Select the portion of text that you want to style as a hyperlink.

Hyperlink box

Figure 11.70 Type the URL or other message in the hyperlink box at the bottom of the Text Inspector.

The following sentence is hyperlink text.
Here is a hyperlink.

Figure 11.71 The text styled as a hyperlink. It shows up as blue on-screen until someone clicks it.

12

Adding Sound

Sounds—music, narration, sound effects—bring animation to life. Adding sounds to Director movies is easy: You simply import a sound cast member and place it in one of Director's two sound channels in the score.

Director offers very limited means of editing an imported sound. You should do so before importing by using a program such as SoundEdit 16 or Peak LE 2 on the Mac, and Sound Forge 4.0 or Cool Edit 96 in Windows. You also can use these programs to set cue points in sound files, which makes it much easier to synch sprite animations to narrations, for example.

Although Director's score offers only two sound channels, a total of eight channels are available. The other six can be accessed only through Lingo commands. Even though you could theoretically have eight sounds playing at the same time, the practical limitations of RAM, computer speed, and download times make this scenario unrealistic in most situations.

This chapter covers all the basics of incorporating sounds through the score. If you need more precise control of how and when your sounds play—in a fast-paced video game, for example, in which slight sound delays could be very noticeable—you should use Lingo's sound methods and properties, several of which are discussed in this chapter.

Importing Sounds

You have the choice of importing a sound into Director as an internal sound cast member or as a linked sound cast member. After you import the sound, it becomes a cast member that you can place in one of the score's sound channels (**Figure 12.1**).

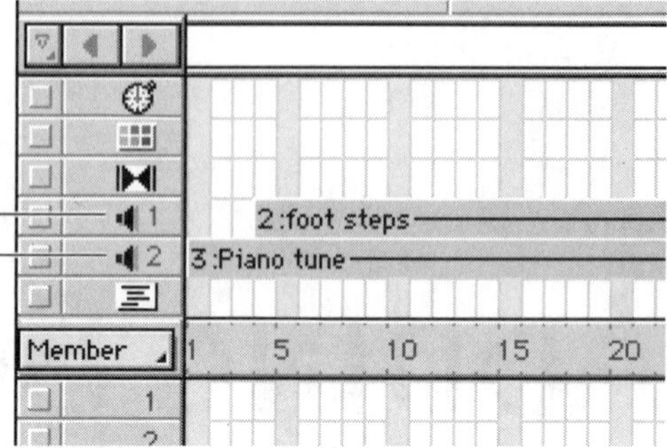

Figure 12.1 After you import a sound, you can place it in the score in one of the two sound channels.

Internal Sound Cast Members

All the data for an internal sound cast member is stored in either your movie or cast file. Director loads internal sounds into memory completely before playing them. Short sound effects such as beeps or footsteps that repeat often throughout your movie work best as internal sound cast members.

Linked External Sounds

Long-playing sounds, such as a voice narrative, are best imported as linked sound cast members. Data for a linked sound cast member is stored outside Director. Every time a linked sound begins to play, Director must load it into memory from its source. Director can *stream* linked Shockwave Audio and MP3 sounds, which means that you hear the sound start playing immediately while the rest of it loads. Linking sounds helps keep your movie file small.

Import Formats

You can import a wide range of sound file formats into Director 8, including AIFF, compressed and uncompressed WAV, Shockwave Audio, AU, MP3, and Macintosh sounds. Macromedia recommends using sounds with an 8- or 16-bit depth and with a sampling rate of 11.025, 22.050, or 44.1 kHz.

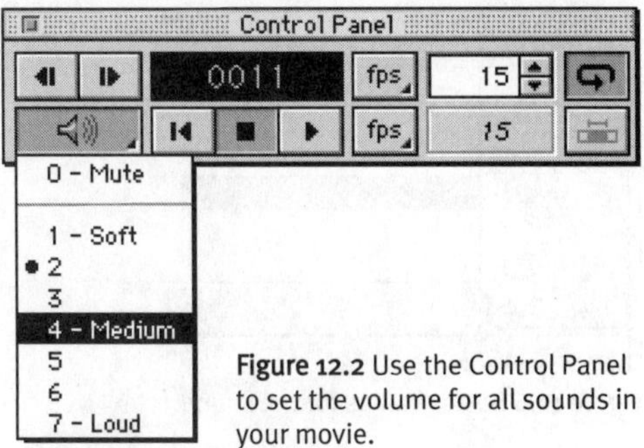

Figure 12.2 Use the Control Panel to set the volume for all sounds in your movie.

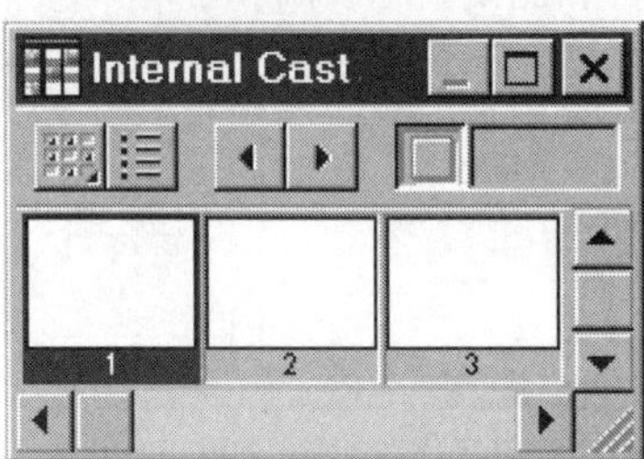

Figure 12.3 Select a home for the sound cast member you're about to import.

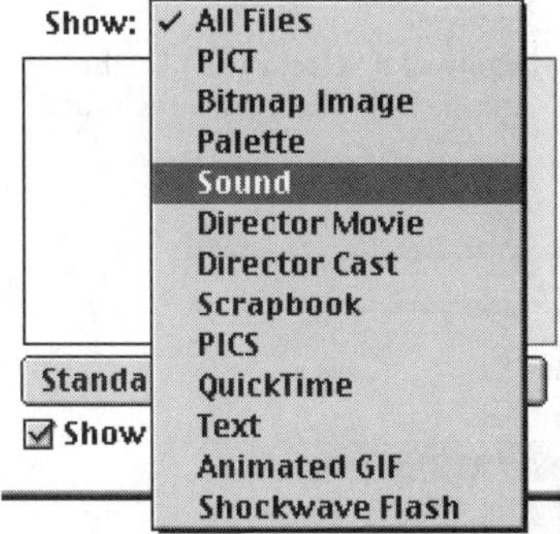

Figure 12.4 Choose Sound as the type of file to import.

✓ Standard Import
Link to External File
Include Original Data for Editing
Import PICT File as PICT

Figure 12.5 Choosing Standard Import brings the sound into Director as an internal cast member.

Volume

You can set the volume for your entire movie (all eight sound channels are affected) by using the Control Panel's Volume button (**Figure 12.2**). Alternatively, you can control the volume level for individual sound channels by setting the volume system property through a Lingo script (for details, see the Lingo Dictionary's volume system property).

To import a sound:

1. In a Cast window, select a place for the sound that you'll import (**Figure 12.3**).
2. Choose File > Import to display the Import dialog box.
3. Choose Sound from the Files of Type pop-up menu (**Figure 12.4**).
4. At the top of the dialog box, find and open the folder that contains the file you want to import.

   or

   Click Internet and specify a URL for the file.
5. To bring in the sound as an internal cast member, choose Standard Import from the Media pop-up menu at the bottom of the Import dialog box (**Figure 12.5**).

   or

   To import the sound as a linked cast member, choose Link to External File from the Media pop-up menu.
6. Select the sound file and click Add.

   or

   Click Add All to add all the folder's displayed files to the list.
7. Click Import.

Placing Sounds in the Score

After you import sounds into an internal or external cast, you place them in the score.

Most sounds need more than one frame in the score to play completely. A laser blast might require 20 frames, whereas a musical score could fill hundreds. If you assign a sound too few frames, the sound cuts off abruptly in the movie, but you can extend it to occupy additional frames in the score.

You can also set sounds to loop, or repeat, to make a compact sound fill in longer passages of time in the movie.

To place sounds in the score:

1. Make sure that the sound you want to use has already been imported into a Cast window.
2. In the score, select the frames in a sound channel where you want to place the sound (**Figure 12.6**).
3. Choose Modify > Frame > Sound.

   The Frame Properties: Sound dialog box opens (**Figure 12.7**).
4. From the list in the dialog box, select the sound to place in the score.
5. If necessary, click Play to preview the sound (**Figure 12.8**).
6. Click OK to place the selected sound in the score (**Figure 12.9**).

✔ Tip

- You can drag a sound directly into one of the score's sound channels from a Cast window. When you do so, the number of frames assigned to the sound sprite is determined by the Span Duration setting in the Sprite Preferences dialog box. View and alter this setting by choosing File > Preferences > Sprite.

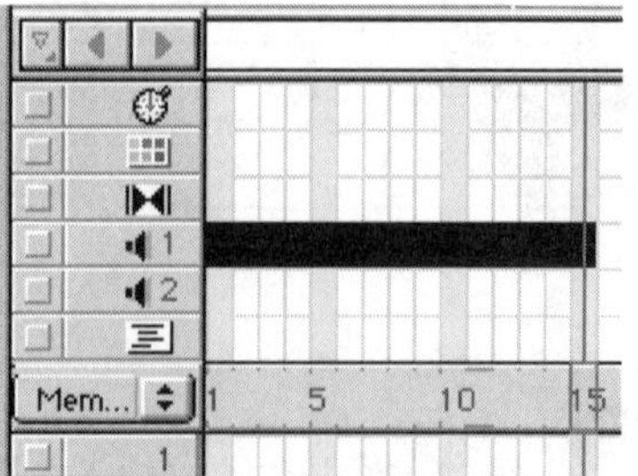

Figure 12.6 Select frames for the sound.

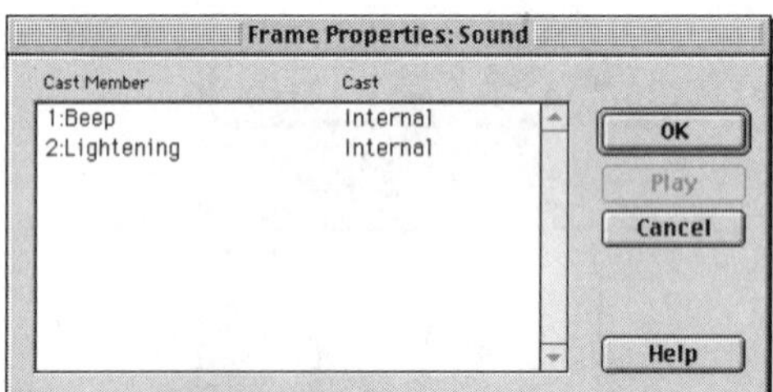

Figure 12.7 Use the Frame Properties: Sound dialog box to select which sound to place in the score.

Figure 12.8 Select a sound in the list and click Play to preview the sound.

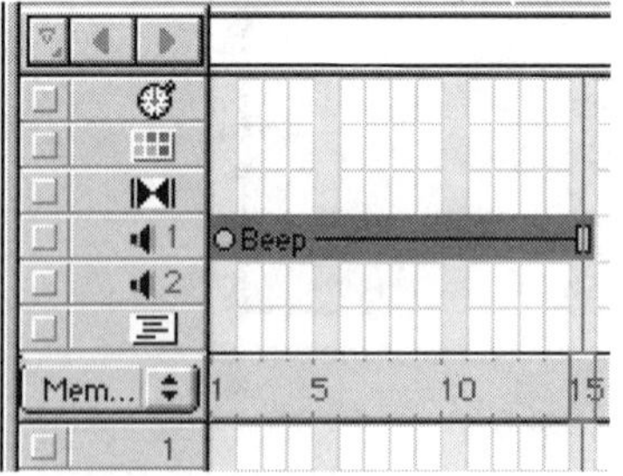

Figure 12.9 The sound goes into the score after you click OK.

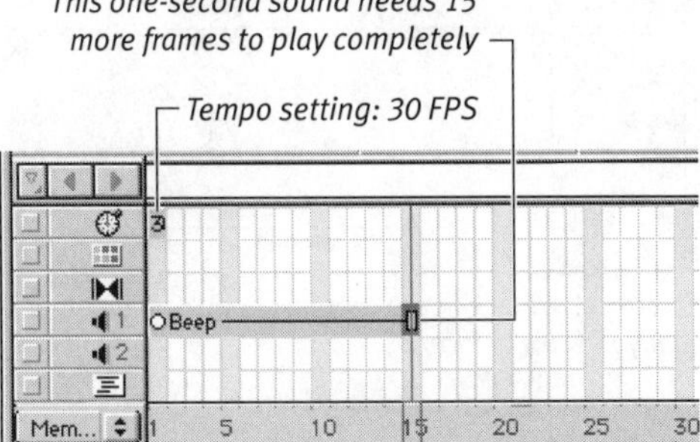

Figure 12.10 Calculate how many frames the sound needs.

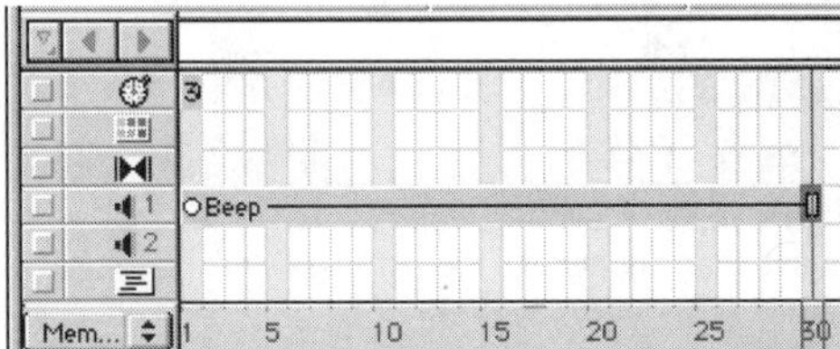

Figure 12.11 Extend the sound sprite to allow complete playback of the sound.

To extend sounds to play completely:

1. Figure out how many frames the sound needs to play completely (**Figure 12.10**).

   Multiply the length of the sound (in seconds) by the movie's tempo of frames per second. A sound designed to last 2 seconds in a movie with a tempo of 30 fps needs 60 frames (2 times 30 frames) to play completely. If you assign only 45 frames, the sound ends in the 45th frame without finishing.
2. Click the sound sprite you want to extend.
3. Click in the frame channel to mark the frame in the score's sound channel where the sound should finish.
4. Choose Modify > Extend Sprite (**Figure 12.11**)to extend the sprite to the marked frame.
5. Play back the movie to confirm that the sound now plays completely.
6. If necessary, extend the sound sprite into additional frames by repeating steps 2 through 4.

✔ Tips

- If you assign a sound to more frames than it requires, the sound does not repeat unless you set it to loop (see "To loop a sound").
- To quickly determine the number of frames a sound requires, extend it into more frames than it can possibly require; then play back the movie and watch the score. Listen for the sound and note the frame at which it finishes. (As the movie plays, Director highlights each frame it moves through.) Cut out any extra frames that the sound occupies.

To loop a sound:

1. Place in the score a sound cast member that you want to loop (**Figure 12.12**).
2. Determine how many frames the sound requires to play through once *(see "To extend sounds to play completely")*.
3. Extend the sound sprite through all the frames in the score in which you want it to repeat over and over.

   If the sound requires 10 frames to play once, for example, and you want it to repeat five times, extend it through 50 frames.
4. In the Cast window, select the sound cast member (**Figure 12.13**).
5. Choose Modify > Cast Member > Properties to display the Property Inspector.
6. Choose the Loop option (**Figure 12.14**).
7. Play back the movie to make sure that the sound repeats as often as needed.

✔ Tip

- You can also repeat a sound by placing multiple sound sprites next to one another in the score based on the same cast member (**Figure 12.15**). For this technique to work, you must separate the sprites by at least one frame. Separating the sprites tells Director to retrigger the sound at the start of each sprite.

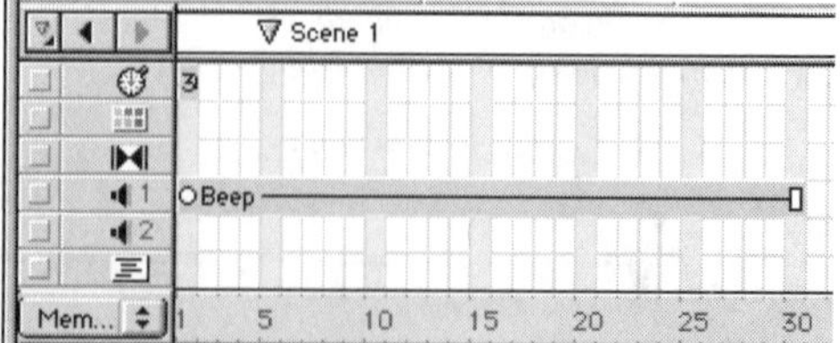

Figure 12.12 Place in the score a sound cast member that you want to loop.

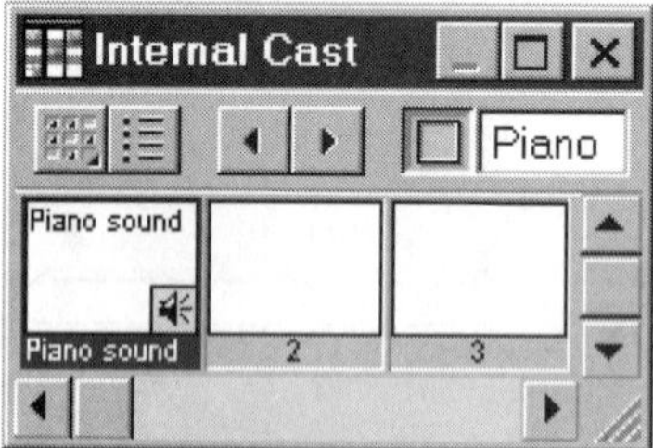

Figure 12.13 Select the sound cast member and open the Property Inspector.

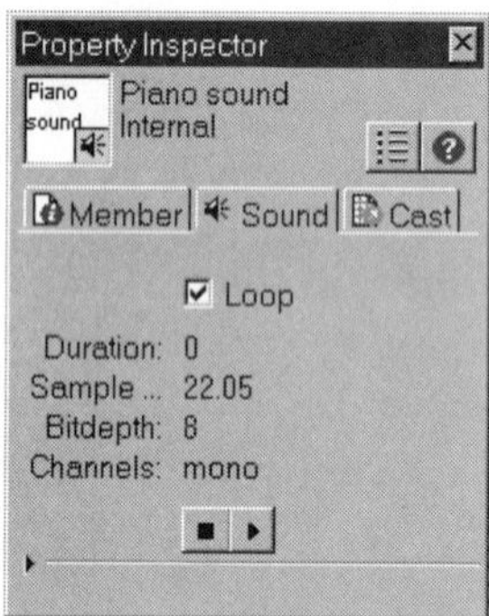

Figure 12.14 Check the Loop checkbox to turn on looping for your sound.

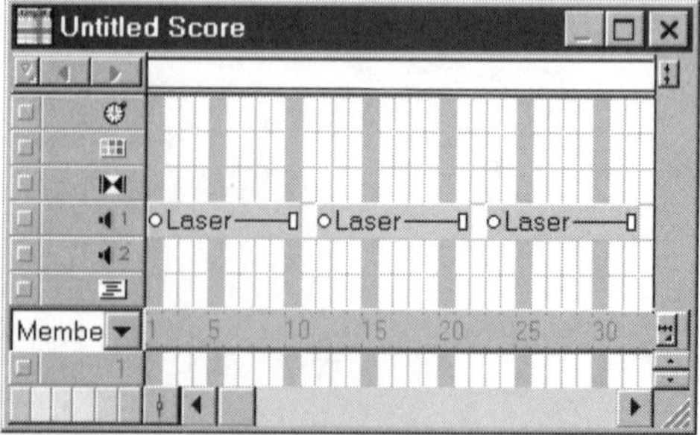

Figure 12.15 You can repeat a sound by placing it in the score multiple times. Make sure that you separate each instance by at least one frame for Director to replay the sound.

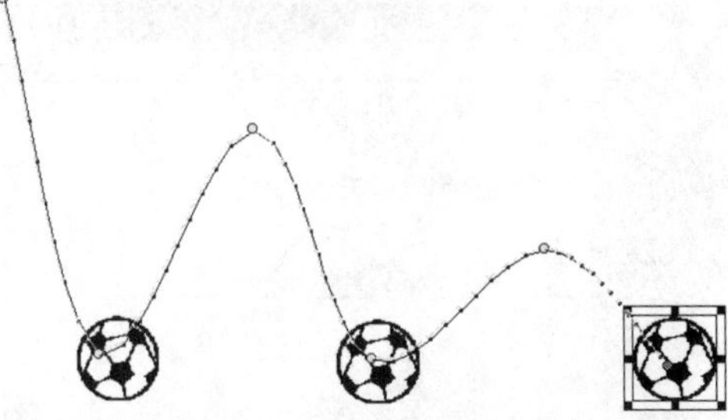

Figure 12.16 To roughly match sound with the ball's bounces, place keyframes where the ball meets the ground, and match the sounds with them. Add markers, if you prefer.

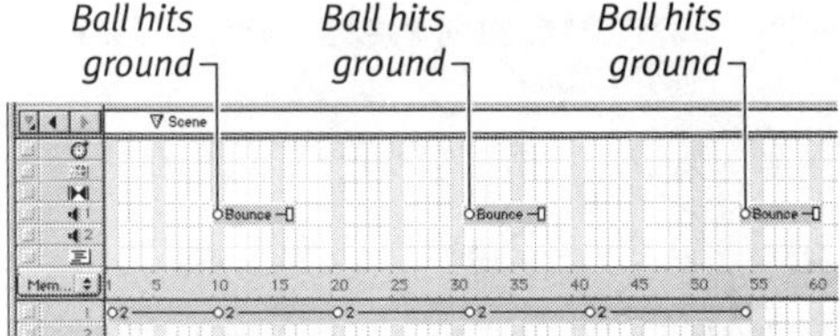

Figure 12.17 Place sounds in the score to match the frame with the action.

Synchronizing Sound to Actions

Some movies call for playing a musical piece throughout an entire animation. In such a case, you usually can place the music in a sound channel through a range of frames. At other times, though, you need to synchronize sound to specific events in a movie.

By using the sound channels only, you can roughly match sounds with scenes by placing sounds to coincide with the action (**Figures 12.16–12.17**). This approach works best for short internal sounds. If you want Director to play the sound of a ball bouncing as it reaches the ground, for example, you first animate the ball's motion, note the frames in which it touches the ground, and then place the sounds accordingly.

Unfortunately, this method does not guarantee precise synchronization of sound. The problems are worsened when you are using large linked sound cast members, which Director does not preload into memory. In such cases, the sound may lag the animation by as much as several seconds, causing confusion, especially in fast-paced games or animations.

There are two ways around this problem. One way is to place cue points in a sound file and then use the tempo channel to wait for them to be reached before starting the corresponding animation. Another way is to use Lingo to queue and control sound playback directly.

To synch animation to sound by using cue points:

1. Create all necessary cue points in your sound file at the locations where visual elements of your scene should be synchronized to the sound.

   To set the cue points, use a program such as Peak LE 2 or Sound Edit 16 on the Mac, or Sound Forge 4.0 or Cool Edit 96 in Windows.

   If you have a soundtrack of a car chase ending with a big crash, for example, and you want to animate an explosion at the moment of the crash, create a cue point at the very start of the crashing sound in the sound file.

2. Import the sound.

3. Place the sound cast member in one of the two sound channels.

4. In the tempo channel of the score, select the frame where you want the playback head to pause until the desired cue point is reached.

   This frame should be within the range of frames where the sound is placed in the score.

   For the example in step 1, you would select the starting frame of the explosion animation (**Figure 12.18**).

5. Choose Modify > Frame > Tempo.

   The Frame Properties: Tempo dialog box opens.

6. Choose the Wait for Cue Point option (**Figure 12.19**).

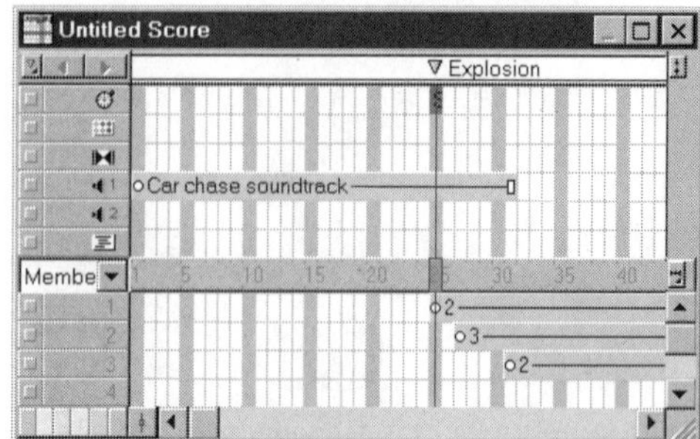

Figure 12.18 In the tempo channel, select the frame where you want to pause your movie until a specified cue point in your sound is reached.

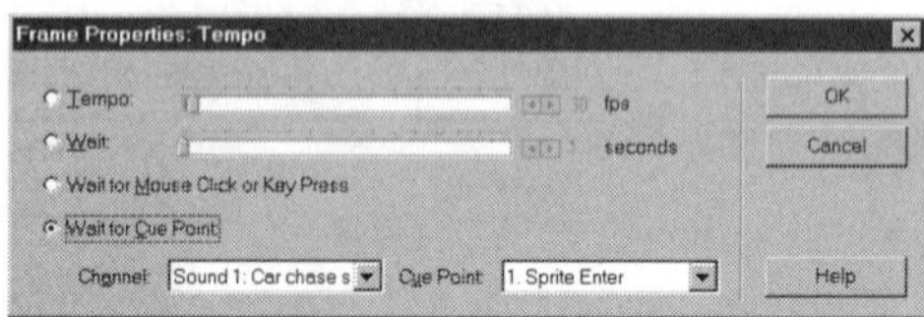

Figure 12.19 Choose the Wait for Cue Point option toward the bottom of the Frame Properties: Tempo dialog box.

Figure 12.20 Use the Channel and Cue Point pop-up menus to select the sound and the cue point within it to wait for.

7. From the Channel pop-up menu, choose the sound channel that contains your sound file (**Figure 12.20**).
8. From the Cue Point pop-up menu, choose the cue point to wait for (**Figure 12.20**).

✔ Tip

- If you want to synch an animation to start at the point when a sound finishes playing, you don't need to create a cue point. The end of the sound is already considered to be a cue point, and you can choose it from the Cue Point menu in the Frame Properties: Tempo dialog box.

  The most sure-fire way to ensure that a sound plays back exactly when it's supposed to is to use Lingo commands. This approach is especially appropriate for interactive movies such as video games, which have nonlinear events, such as gunfire, that must be precisely synched to sound.

To play a sound at a precise moment by using Lingo:

Include the following lines in your Lingo script:

```
sound(channel#).queue(member("member
→ name"))
sound(channel#).play()
```

The following example creates a cast member that plays a sound each time it's clicked:

1. Import a sound and name it in the Cast window.
2. Open the Script window.
3. Type the following (**Figure 12.21**), entering your sound's name for *member name*:

   ```
   on StartMovie
     sound(1).queue(member("member name"))
   end
   ```

   This script cues up the sound in channel 1 (Director loads it into its RAM buffer) at the start of the movie so that it's ready to play at a moment's notice.
4. In the Cast window, select a graphical cast member that appears in your movie, and click the Script button.
5. Type the following line (**Figure 12.22**) between the two provided lines in the script window, entering your sound's name for *member name*:

   ```
   sound(1).play()
   sound(1).queue(member("member name"))
   ```
6. Close the Script window, play your movie, and click the cast member to hear the sound.

✔ Tip

- Many additional sound properties and methods are available through Lingo, a topic that is beyond the scope of this book. See Director's Lingo Dictionary or Lingo by Feature section for more information.

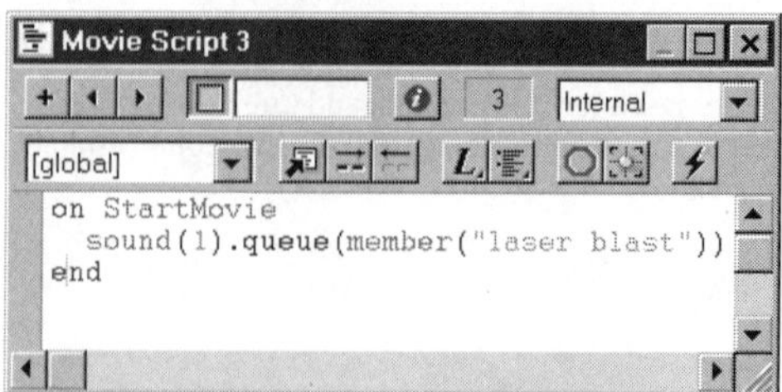

Figure 12.21 Type this text in the Script window.

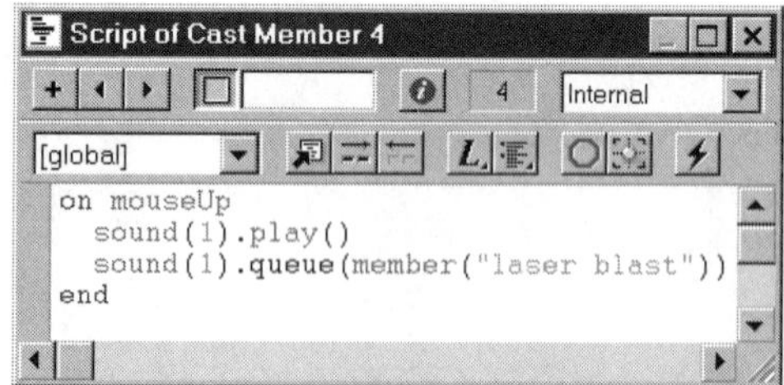

Figure 12.22 Type the two middle lines between the lines already provided in the Script window.

Compressing Sounds

You can use Shockwave Audio (SWA) to compress all internal sound cast members. You can also link to external compressed Shockwave Audio files.

SWA compression makes sound data much smaller in a movie file—by a ratio of as much as 12-to-1 without noticeable sound-quality loss—which in turn decreases download time and/or disk space. The tradeoffs are that after a movie is downloaded, it may take a little longer to start, because files have to be decompressed, and sound quality can suffer if compression levels are too high. Nevertheless, when your movie uses a great deal of sound, audio compression is a great way to go, especially when you're distributing on the Internet.

SWA compression actually occurs only when you compress your Director movie with the Create Projector, Update Movies, or Publish command. Also, you cannot choose to apply SWA compression to a partial set of internal sound cast members. It's all of them or none, and you can't vary the SWA settings among them.

✔ Tip

- If your movie uses Shockwave Audio compression, you must include the appropriate Xtras when you distribute your movie to allow Director to decompress and play the sounds.

To compress internal sounds:

1. Choose File > Publish Settings to display the Publish Settings dialog box.
2. Select the Compression tab (**Figure 12.23**).
3. Select Compression Enabled to turn on compression (**Figure 12.24**).
4. Choose a bit-rate setting from the kBits/second pop-up menu (**Figure 12.25**).

   Low values mean more compression, which produces lower sound quality.
5. Choose Convert Stereo to Mono to convert a stereo file to monaural (**Figure 12.26**).

   All stereo sounds are converted to monaural at a bit rate lower than 48.
6. Click OK.

   If you are distributing your movie as a projector, you must also select the Compress (Shockwave Format) option in the Projector Options dialog box for audio compression to occur (**Figure 12.27**). *(See "To set projector playback options" in the Creating a Projector chapter for more details.)*

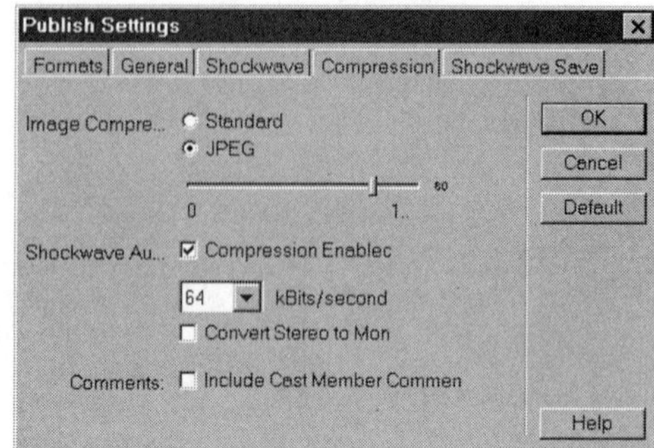

Figure 12.23 Select the Compression tab in the Publish Settings dialog box.

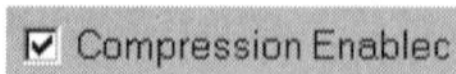

Figure 12.24 Turn on compression.

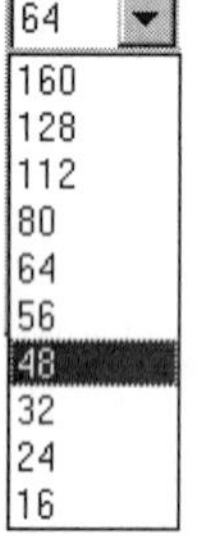

Figure 12.25 Specify a bit-rate setting to set the level of compression. Lower values mean more compression.

Convert Stereo to Mon

Figure 12.26 For stereo sounds, check the Convert Stereo to Mono checkbox if you want to convert to mono sound.

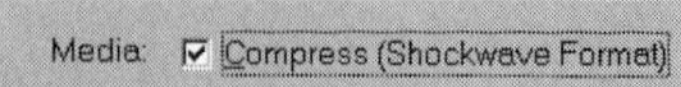

Figure 12.27 Choose Compress (Shockwave Format) in the Projector Options dialog box if you are compressing internal sounds and will be distributing your movie as a projector.

Compressing Sounds

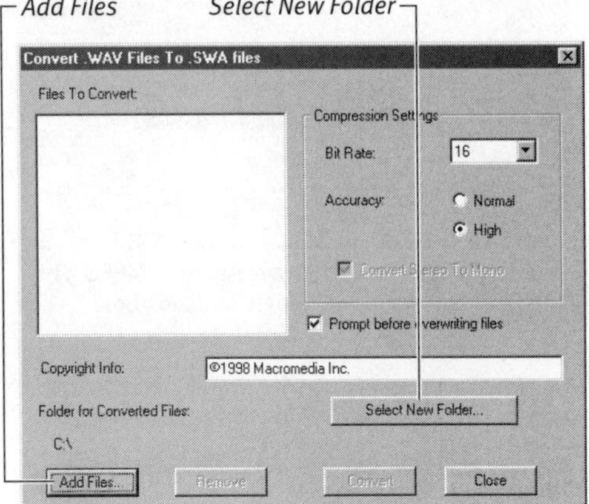

Figure 12.28 In Windows, you can create external Shockwave Audio files by using the Convert .WAV To .SWA files dialog box.

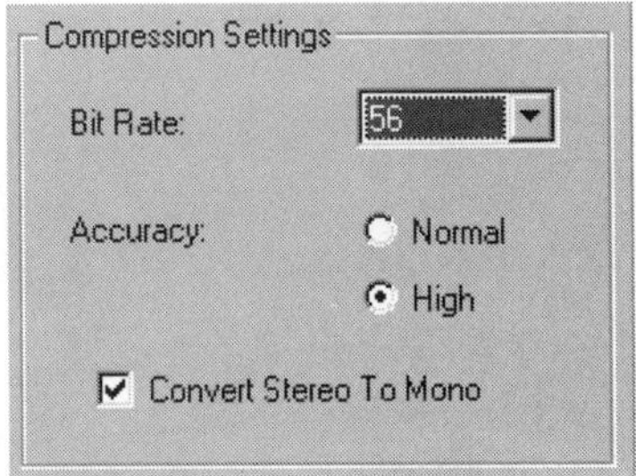

Figure 12.29 Choose compression options for WAV files that you're converting to Shockwave Audio.

Compression for External Sounds

Instead of storing and compressing a sound internally in Director, you may prefer to link to an external Shockwave Audio file. You can compress sound as low as 8 kbps, but most developers use at least 16 kbps for Internet delivery.

On the Mac, you need a separate application such as Peak LE 2 or SoundEdit 16 to create a Shockwave Audio file. In Windows, Director provides a way of doing so internally.

External Shockwave Audio has two benefits: it decreases movie file size, and it allows you to stream the sounds *(see "Streaming Linked Shockwave Audio or MP3 Sound Files").*

To create Mac external Shockwave Audio files:

1. Create or import a sound with SoundEdit 16, Peak LE 2, or another audio-editing program.
2. Export the sound in Shockwave Audio format.

To create Windows external Shockwave Audio files:

1. In Director, choose Xtras > Convert WAV to SWA.

   The conversion dialog box opens (**Figure 12.28**).
2. Click Add Files.
3. Select the WAV files to convert.
4. Choose compression settings (**Figure 12.29**).
5. Click Select New Folder and designate or create a folder for the converted files.
6. Check Prompt Before Overwriting Files to avoid deleting existing files by mistake.
7. Save the converted file.

Streaming Linked Shockwave Audio or MPEG 3 Sound Files

Director can stream linked Shockwave Audio or MPEG 3 sound files, which means that the sound starts to play right away when the scene or Web page first appears as the rest of the sound continues to load from its source. Internal sounds, compressed or not, can't be streamed.

To stream a linked Shockwave or MPEG 3 sound in a movie, you create a Shockwave Audio cast member that controls the streaming process.

To set a linked Shockwave Audio or MPEG 3 sound to stream:

1. Choose Insert > Media Element > Shockwave Audio.

   The SWA Cast Member Properties dialog box opens.

2. Click Browse and select a Shockwave Audio or MPEG 3 file on disk (**Figure 12.30**).

   or

   Type a URL in the Link Address field (**Figure 12.31**).

3. Set the volume level of the sound with the slider (**Figure 12.32**).

4. From the Sound Channel pop-up menu, choose Any as the channel for the Shockwave Audio (**Figure 12.33**).

   Choosing Any prevents conflicts with other sounds.

5. Use the Preload Time pop-up menu to specify how many seconds of streaming sound Director should download initially (**Figure 12.34**).

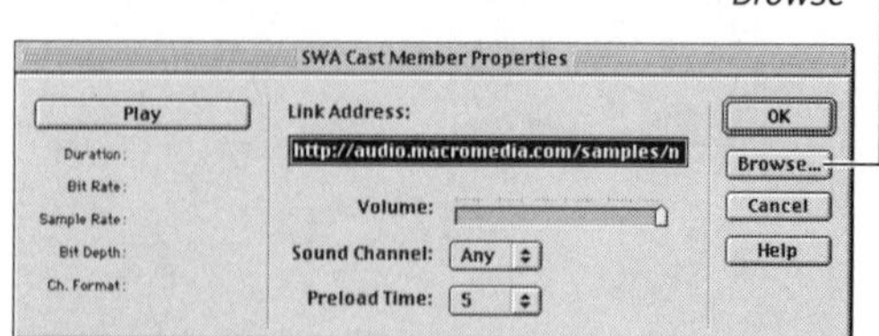

Figure 12.30 Select a Shockwave Audio or MPEG 3 file in the SWA Cast Member Properties dialog box.

Figure 12.31 You can link to a Shockwave Audio or MPEG 3 file on the Web.

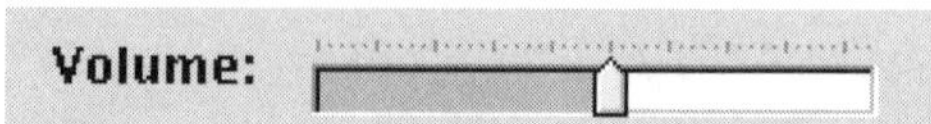

Figure 12.32 Drag the slider to set the sound's volume.

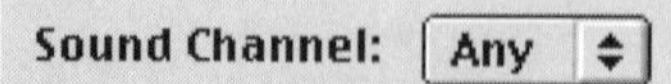

Figure 12.33 Select Any in the Sound Channel pop-up menu.

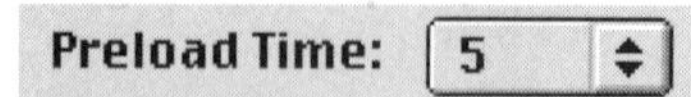

Figure 12.34 Choose a preload time.

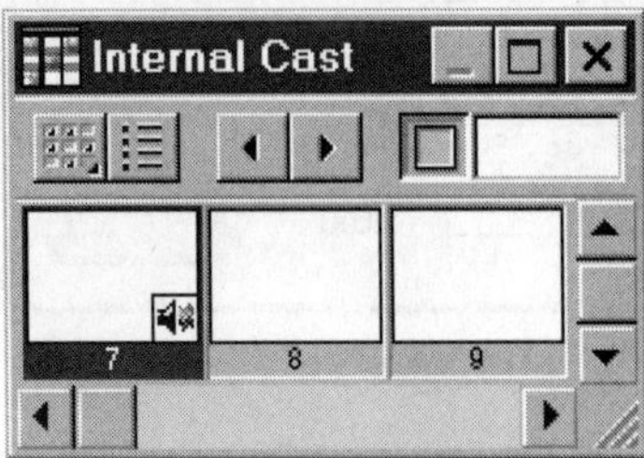

Figure 12.35 Select a linked Shockwave Audio or MPEG 3 cast member and drag it to the score.

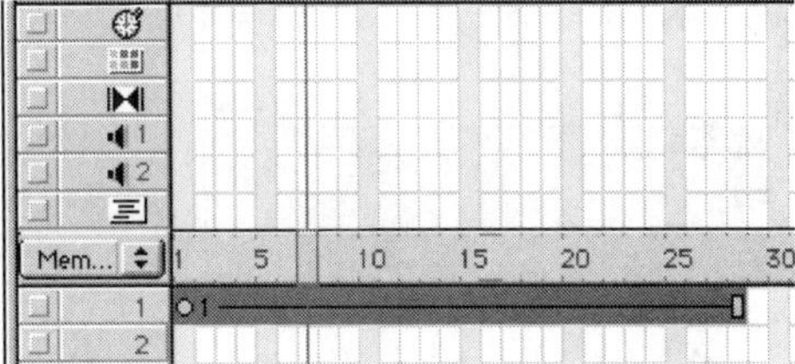

Figure 12.36 Extend the sprite as necessary to provide enough frames for the sound.

Director tries to load enough of the sound to play it without hiccups for the preload duration you set. The shorter the preload time, the less bulk you add to the initial download file. The longer the preload time, the longer the sound can play continuously while the rest of the movie loads.

6. Click OK.

To stream a linked Shockwave Audio or MPEG 3 sound:

1. From a Cast window, drag a linked Shockwave Audio or MPEG 3 cast member that you created in the preceding section to a sprite channel in the score (**Figure 12.35**).
2. Position the sprite in the range of frames where you want the sound to play (**Figure 12.36**).
3. Play the movie and listen to the results.
4. Extend the sprite, if necessary, to allow the entire sound to play.

✔ Tip

- You never place streaming Shockwave Audio cast members in sound channels.

Recording Sounds in Director (Mac)

On Macintosh computers only, you can record, or *digitize*, sounds within Director with the handheld microphone that ships with most Macintosh models. Although Director doesn't have sophisticated controls for top-notch sound production, it does offer a quick and easy way to engineer short sounds for your movies.

Figure 12.37 On the Mac only, you can record sounds within Director.

To record a sound in Director (Mac):

1. Make sure that you have a microphone attached to the Macintosh.
2. In Director, choose Insert > Media Element > Sound.

   The recording window opens (**Figure 12.37**).
3. Click Record and begin recording a sound with the attached microphone.
4. If necessary, click Pause to pause a recording session; click Record to resume.
5. When you finish recording, click Stop.
6. Click Play to listen to the recorded sound.
7. Click Save and name the sound.

   Director places the sound in the active Cast window (**Figure 12.38**).

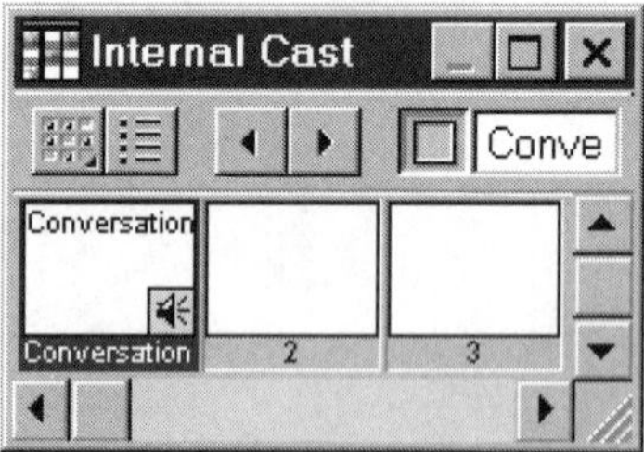

Figure 12.38 The newly recorded sound takes a place in the Cast window.

Creating a Projector

Figure 13.1. A projector encapsulates your Director movie so users can play it without having Director installed on their computers. Projectors have a distinctive icon so you can identify them at a glance.

When you want to distribute a Director movie that can be played without a Web browser, you need to create a projector. A *projector* is a file that works as a play-only version of your movie or sequence of movies (**Figure 13.1**), which the operating system recognizes as an application program. Users don't need to own a copy of Director to run the projector file; as long as their computers meet minimum hardware requirements, they can play it.

Users can't open or edit a projector file even if they have Director. In fact, even the author can't open or edit a projector. All editing must take place in the original movie files.

To create a projector for Windows, you must use Director for Windows. Likewise, to create a Macintosh version, you need Director for Macintosh. If you need a movie that can *stream* (play as it loads from an Internet connection), make a Shockwave movie, as described in the next chapter, rather than a projector. You can distribute a projector file via the Internet, but it must be fully downloaded before it can play, and it can't play within a Web browser.

This chapter covers setting projector options, creating projectors, packaging projectors and external files for distributions, and more. If you plan to include Xtras in a projector, see Chapter 15, "Using Xtras," for details.

Setting Projector Options

Before you create a projector, take a moment to specify general settings that affect all the movies combined in a single projector.

A few options are specific to the computer on which you create the projector. Set the Windows-only and Mac-only options as well as the options that apply to both platforms.

To set projector playback options:

1. Save any currently open Director movies.
2. Choose File > Create Projector.
   The Create Projector dialog box opens.
3. Click Options (**Figure 13.2**).
   The Projector Options dialog box opens.
4. If you plan to include several movies in one projector and want them all to play, check the Play Every Movie checkbox (**Figure 13.3**).
   If you leave this option unchecked, the projector plays only the first of any movies that you include.
   The Play Every Movie option plays the movies in the order of the play list. You also can control the order in which movies play through Lingo scripts, as described later in the section "To create a projector that's easy to modify."
5. If you want the projector to continue playing when users switch to another application, choose Animate in Background (**Figure 13.3**).
   If you do not check the Animate in the Background checkbox, the projector pauses when a user switches to another program and resumes playing the movie when the user reactivates the projector window.

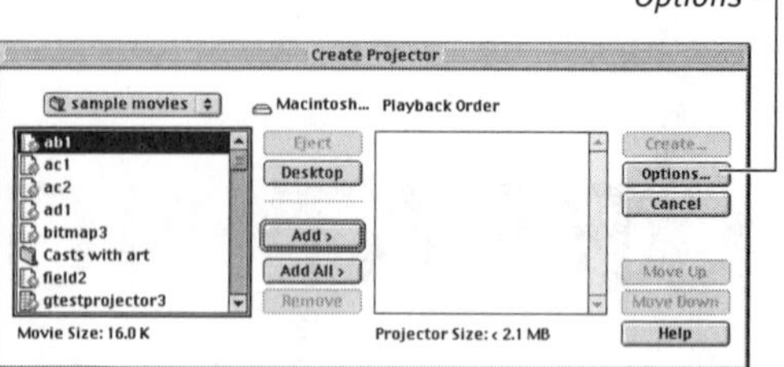

Figure 13.2 Setting the projector's playback options is the first step in creating a projector. You click Options in the Create Projector dialog box.

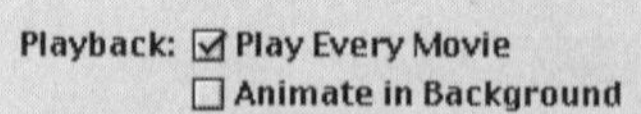

Figure 13.3 If you compile multiple movies in a projector and want them to play in the order listed, check Play Every Movie. If you want the movie to keep playing when users switch to other tasks, check Animate in Background.

Figure 13.4 With the Full Screen option selected, this movie fills the screen; no desktop or menu bar appears.

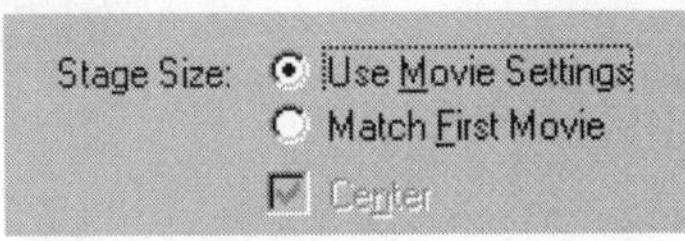

Figure 13.5 If you have multiple movies in a projector, choose a Stage Size setting.

Use Movie Settings *Match First Movie*

Figure 13.6 If you choose Use Movie Settings for the Stage Size, the stage changes if the movies in a projector have different stage sizes. Choose Match First Movie to keep the stage size uniform.

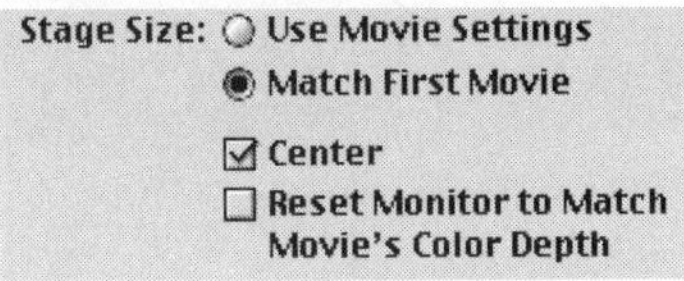

Figure 13.7 Check Center to place the stage at the center of the user's screen.

6. Select the Full Screen option if you want the movie to occupy the full screen when playing (**Figures 13.4**).

   This mode of playing hides the computer's desktop. Any menu bar used in the movie appears at the top of the stage.

7. If you want the stage to resize itself to match each new movie in the projector, choose Use Movie Settings (**Figures 13.5–13.6**).

   or

   If you want to set the stage size to match the first movie in the projector and to remain that size through any other movies included in the projector, choose Match First Movie.

8. If you want, check the Center checkbox (**Figure 13.7**) to center the stage on the screen.

   This option comes in handy when the stage is smaller than the full screen dimensions. If you do not choose Center, the projector positions the stage according to the specifications of the included movies.

continues on next page

9. Check the Compress (Shockwave Format) checkbox (**Figure 13.8**) to compress your projector's movie data in the Shockwave format.

   This option reduces the projector's file size but could increase the time needed to load it, because the movie data needs to be decompressed before it plays. Don't confuse this option with creating an actual Shockwave movie

10. Choose a Player option (**Figure 13.9**).

    - **Standard** embeds an uncompressed version of the Director player in your projector. This option creates the largest projector file, but one that starts quickly compared with some other options.
    - **Compressed** includes a compressed version of the player, which reduces projector size but adds a few seconds' delay before playback, because the player must be decompressed.
    - **Shockwave** makes your projector the smallest by not embedding the player and relying on the Shockwave player installed on the user's system. If the player is not installed, the user is prompted to download it. This type of projector is called a Shockwave projector or a slim projector.

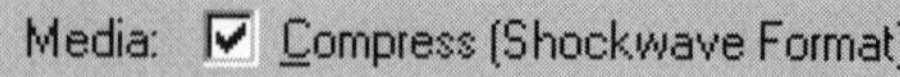

Figure 13.8 Check Compress (Shockwave Format) to condense the projector's movie data in the Shockwave format.

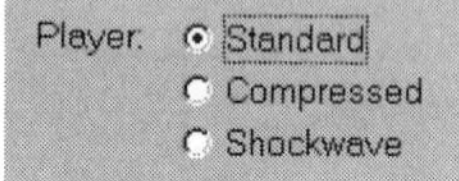

Figure 13.9 Choose a player option for your projector.

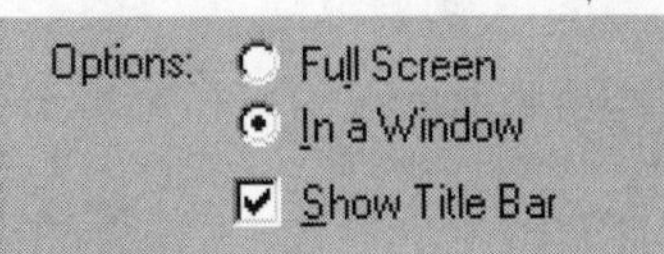

Figure 13.10 In Windows, you can opt to show the movie in a window, with or without a standard Windows title bar at the top.

Figure 13.11 A projector movie in a window, with Show Title Bar selected.

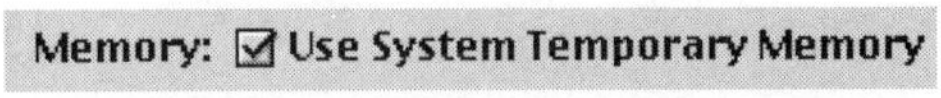

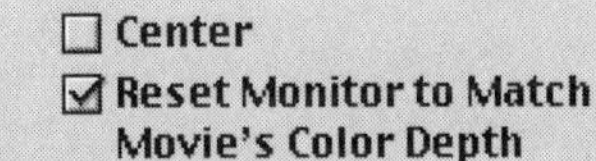

Figure 13.12 On the Macintosh, check Use System Temporary Memory to allow Director to use system memory when its own partition is full.

Center
Reset Monitor to Match Movie's Color Depth

Figure 13.13 On the Macintosh, if you plan to have movies with different color depths incorporated into the same projector, check Reset Monitor to Match Movie's Color Depth to have the monitor automatically change color depth to match each movie as it loads.

A couple of options are specific to Windows.

To set Windows projector options:

1. Choose the In a Window option (**Figure 13.10**) to display the movie in a window as opposed to occupying the full screen.
2. Check the Show Title Bar checkbox to display a title bar for a movie in a window (**Figure 13.11**).

   Users can move a window only when it has a title bar.

There are also Macintosh-specific options.

To set Macintosh projector options:

1. Check the Use System Temporary Memory option (**Figure 13.12**) if you want Director to be able to use system memory when the Director memory partition is full.
2. Check the Reset Monitor to Match Movie's Color Depth checkbox (**Figure 13.13**) so the monitor's color depth changes to match the color depth of each movie in the projector play list.

Making a Projector

A single projector file can embed just about all data necessary to form a complete multimedia production; the exception is any linked media. This data includes multiple Director movies.

Each internal cast is included in the projector file automatically. You can choose to embed external casts within the projector file as well. You also can embed Xtras in the projector file or provide them separately. Any linked media cannot be encapsulated, though, and each such file must be in the same folder as the projector file for distribution.

The projector normally embeds the Director player to make it truly stand-alone. You can exclude the player to make the projector file size smaller. This type of file is called a Shockwave projector or a slim projector. In this case, users view your projector by means of the Shockwave player. If the Shockwave player is not installed on their systems, users are prompted to download the Shockwave player from the Internet so that they can run your projector.

When the files are ready and you have chosen the appropriate projector options, you're ready to create the projector.

To create a projector:

1. Choose File > Create Projector to open the Create Projector dialog box.
2. Set projector options as described in the preceding section.
3. Select the first movie to include in the projector, and click Add (**Figure 13.14**).

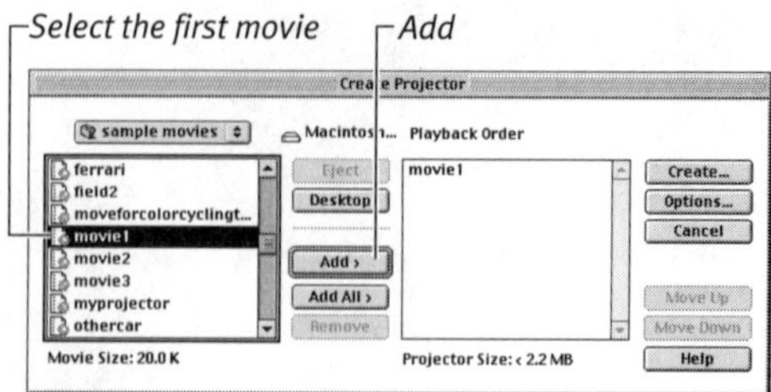

Figure 13.14 In the Create Projector dialog box, select the first movie in your projector and click Add.

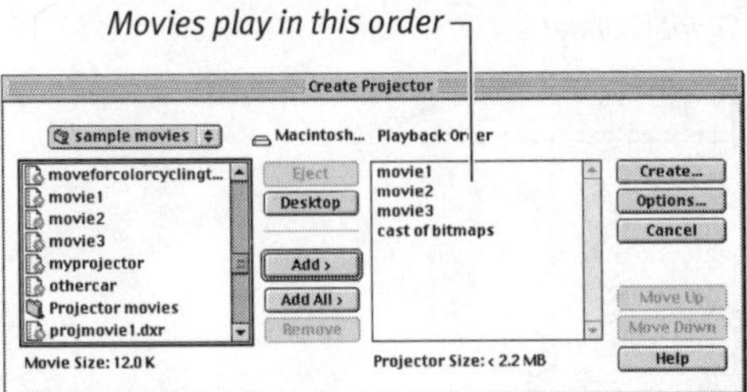

Figure 13.15 Movies in a projector play back in the order of the play list.

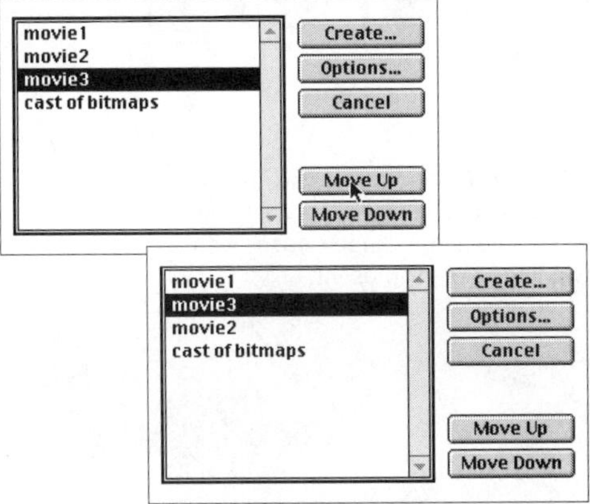

Figure 13.16 You can change the order of movies in the projector by clicking the Move Up and Move Down buttons.

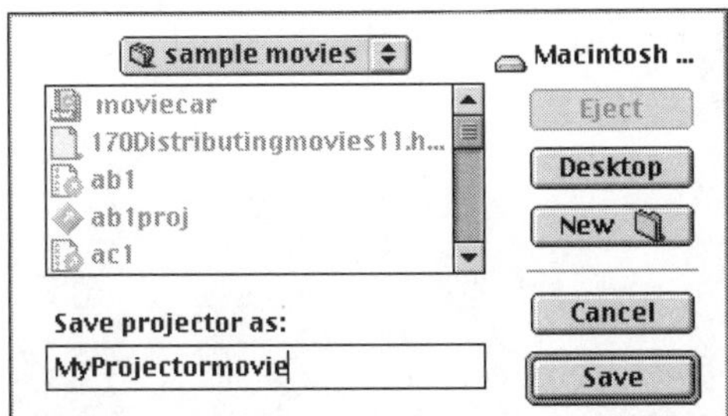

Figure 13.17 After you double-check all the settings, name the projector and click Save.

4. Add any other movies and external casts you need.

   Movies play back in order (assuming that the Play Every Movie option is on), so add movies in the desired sequence (**Figure 13.15**).

   If necessary, change the order of movies in the play list by selecting a movie and clicking Move Up or Move Down (**Figure 13.16**).

   If necessary, remove a movie by selecting it and then clicking Remove.

   If you want a stand-alone projector that doesn't need anything extra in the distribution folder, include all external casts and external movies in this play list. Everything in this play list is encapsulated within the projector.

5. Click Options to double-check the settings.
6. Recheck the order in the movie play list.
7. Click Create.

   The Save dialog box appears.

8. Name the projector, designate its folder, and click Save (**Figure 13.17**).
9. Double-click the projector to test it.

✔ Tips

- After you save a projector, you can't modify it, so check all the settings carefully before you complete the process.
- Make it a habit always to test projectors by playing them as users would.

Projectors that include movies with links to external media files, such as sounds or Flash movies, must be packaged carefully to ensure that they play properly for users.

To prepare a projector with linked files for distribution:

1. Create the projector with all the necessary movies, Xtras, and external casts.
2. Put the projector in the same folder with all linked external media files, such as sounds or Flash movies.

Creating a projector that consists of many movie files has a drawback: If you change a single movie, you must create the entire projector from scratch.

There's a clever way to organize your production that leaves you free to edit any of the movies the projector launches — without having to create the projector file over and over again. This technique doesn't really create a projector that you can modify, but it allows you to change movies easily after you create the projector that plays them. The single short movie you create — actually, nothing more than a Lingo script in a frame of the score—launches all the movie files that form your multimedia production.

To create a projector that's easy to modify:

1. Choose File > New > Movie to begin creating a new Director movie.
2. Open the score.
3. Double-click the first frame in the Script channel to open a Script window (**Figure 13.18**).

   The beginning and ending lines for the exitFrame handler automatically appear in the script window.

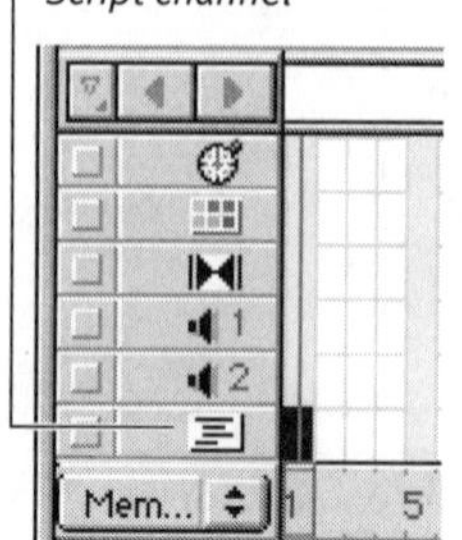

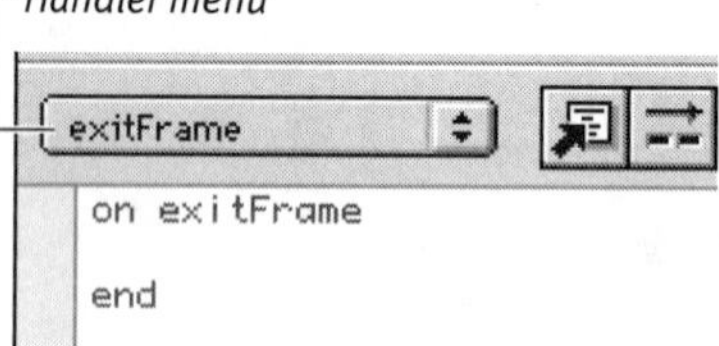

Figure 13.18 Double-click the first frame in the Script channel to open a frame script. The Script window opens with two lines already present.

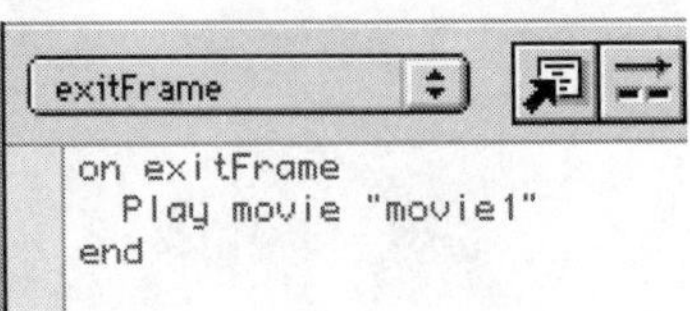

Figure 13.19 Enter the Play Movie command between the two lines provided in the Script window.

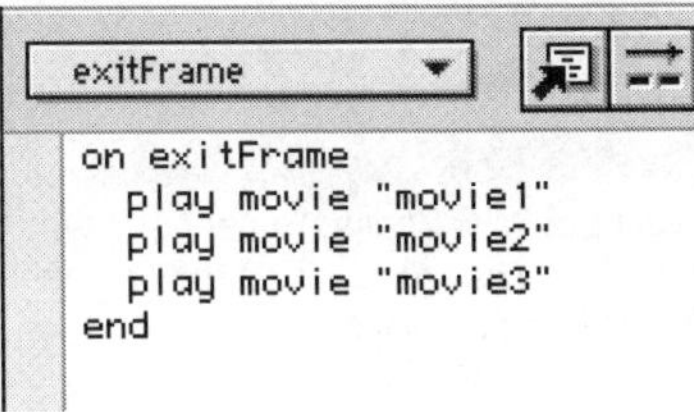

Figure 13.20 Add as many Play Movie commands as you need to launch the movies you want to have played in sequence.

Figure 13.21 This folder contains all necessary files for the script that you put in the projector.

4. In the Script window, enter a Play Movie command between the two lines provided: `Play movie "mymovie"` (**Figure 13.19**).

   Substitute your first movie's name for *mymovie*.

5. Add Play Movie commands for all movies you want the projector to launch, in the sequence in which you want them played (**Figure 13.20**).

   You can include Shockwave movies in the sequence. All movies must be saved in or updated to the Director 8 format.

6. Save the movie.
7. Choose File > Create Projector to open the Create Projector dialog box.
8. Add the movie that you saved in step 7.
9. Click Options to set any projector options you want to use.
10. Create the projector.
11. Put together a distribution folder that contains the projector, all the movies called for in the script, and any external casts and linked media (**Figure 13.21**).

✔ Tip

- You can use the Update Movies command to protect the movies and external cast files included in the folder with a projector to prevent users from tampering with or borrowing from them (see the next section).

Protecting Movie Files

You can protect external movie and cast files from being opened and edited in Director. When you create a projector file that launches other movies or calls on external casts that are not incorporated into the projector file, you may want to protect those accessible files.

Keep in mind that protecting the external files prevents users from tampering with them, but it does not compress the data into a smaller package. If you need to compress the external files as well as protect them, see the instructions for converting multiple movies and casts to Shockwave movies in Chapter 14, Making Movies for the Web.

Most of the time, you probably want to preserve the original movies and cast files as you protect the package that you plan to distribute.

To protect movie and cast files while preserving the originals:

1. Choose Xtras > Update Movies.
   The Update Movies dialog box opens.
2. Choose Protect (**Figure 13.22**).
3. Choose Back Up into Folder to set aside the original movie and cast files in a safe place (**Figure 13.23**).
4. Click Browse and select the folder where you want to put the original files.
5. Click OK.
   The Choose Files dialog box appears.
6. Navigate through folders and then, from the list at the top of the dialog box, select a movie or external cast file that you want to protect (**Figure 13.24**).
   Unprotected Director movies use the .dir extension. External casts use the .cst extension.

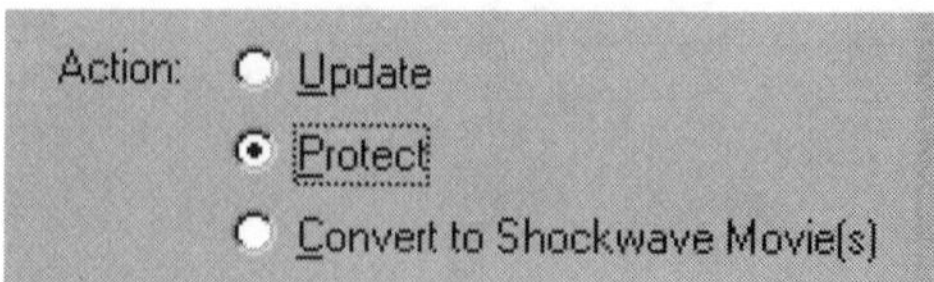

Figure 13.22 Choose the Protect option in the Update Movie dialog box.

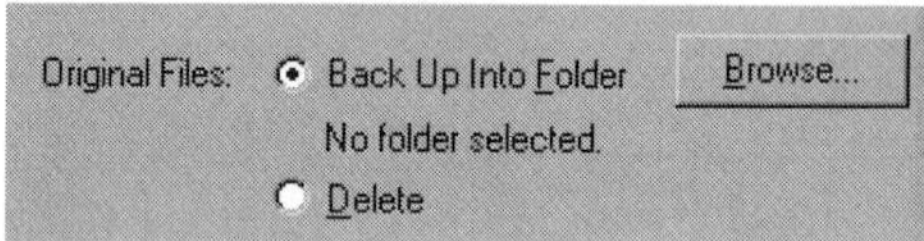

Figure 13.23 Select the Back Up into Folder option in the Update Movie dialog box to set aside the original movie and cast files in a safe place.

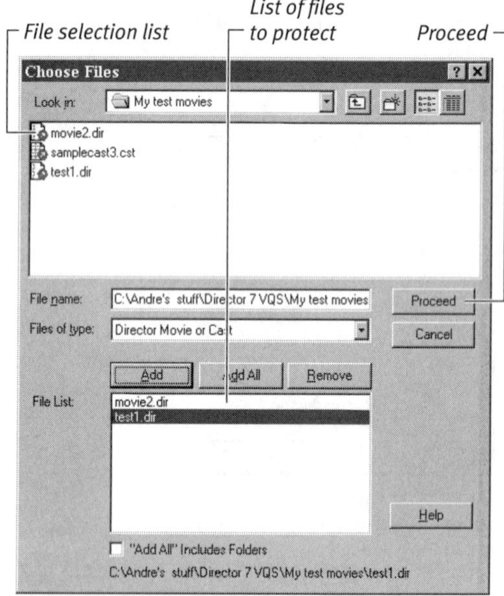

Figure 13.24 In the Choose Files dialog box, select the files you want to protect from the File Selection List at the top of the dialog box.

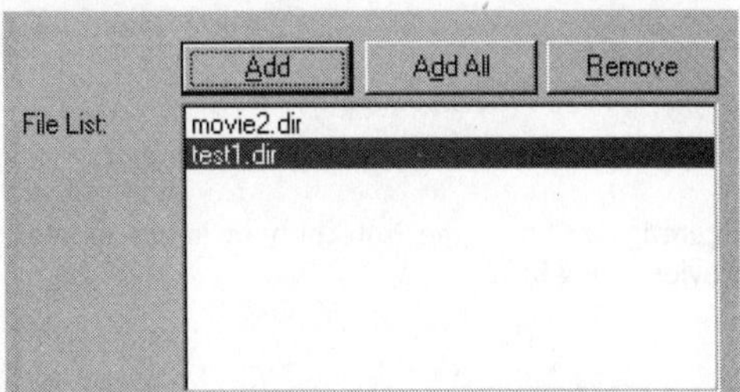

Figure 13.25 Click Add to add the selected file to the list of files to protect.

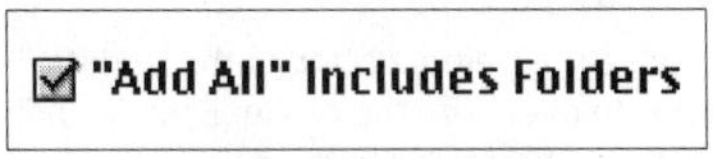

☑ **"Add All" Includes Folders**

Figure 13.26 Check the "Add All" Includes Folders checkbox at the bottom of the Choose Files dialog box to include folders when you click Add All.

7. Click Add (**Figure 13.25**).

   The protected file's name goes into the list in the bottom half of the dialog box.

8. One by one, select the files to protect and then click Add.

   or

   Click Add All to add all the files in the current folder to the list.

9. Click Proceed.

   Director adds the .dxr extension to protected movie files and the .cxt extension to protected casts.

✔ Tip

- If you want to include folders in addition to all files when you click Add All, check the "Add All" Includes Folders checkbox at the bottom of the dialog box (**Figure 13.26**).

In rare instances, you may want to delete original movies and cast files when you protect files before distributing them. You may already have a backup of your originals, for example, and want to remove them from a Zip cartridge before you pass the cartridge along to a tester.

To protect movie and cast files while deleting the originals:

1. Make sure that you have backed up the original files somewhere; you cannot unprotect them.
2. Choose Xtras > Update Movies to open the Update Movies dialog box.
3. Choose Protect (**Figure 13.27**).
4. Choose Delete to overwrite the originals with the new protected files (**Figure 13.28**).
5. Click OK.

   The Choose Files dialog box opens.
6. Select a movie or cast file that you want to protect, and click Add (**Figure 13.29**).

   The protected file's name goes into the list in the bottom half of the dialog box.
7. One by one, select the files to protect and then click Add.

   or

   Click Add All to add all the files in the current folder to the list.
8. Click Proceed.

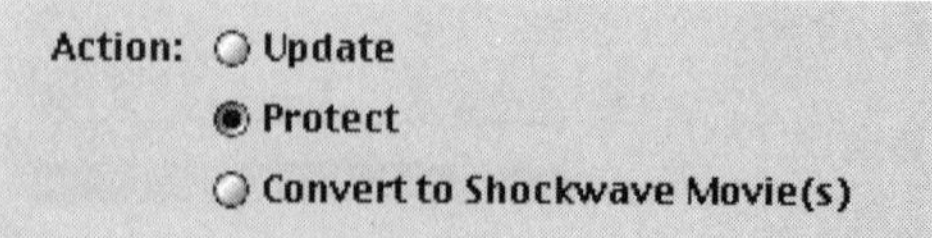

Figure 13.27 Choose the Protect option in the Update Movies dialog box.

Figure 13.28 Choose the Delete option in the Update Movies dialog box to overwrite the original movie and cast files with the new protected versions.

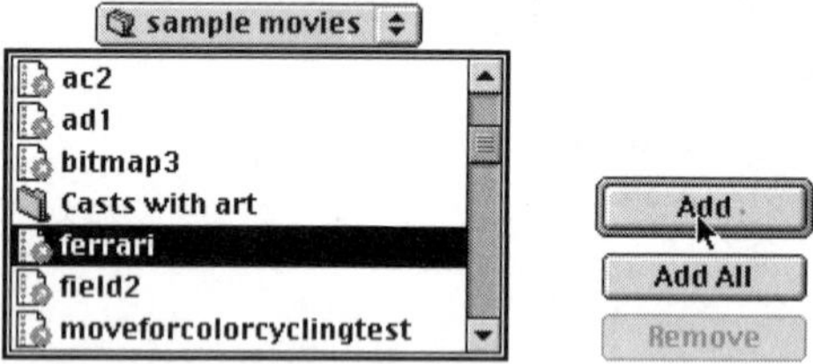

Figure 13.29 In the Choose Files dialog box, select a Director movie or cast file that you want to protect and then click Add.

14 MAKING MOVIES FOR THE WEB

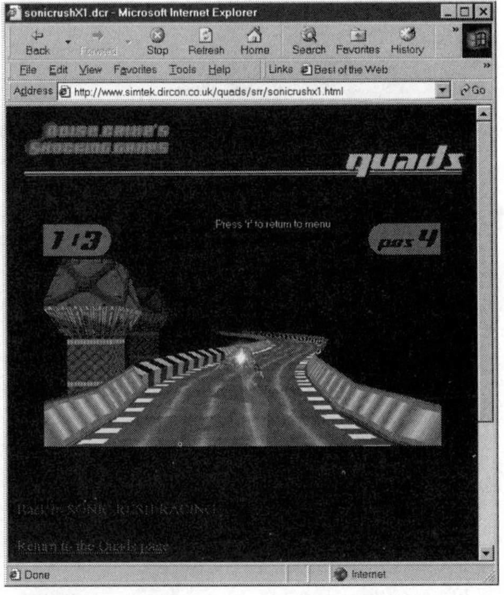

Figure 14.1 A Shockwave movie, shown with other content in a Web browser. (Sonic Rush Racing, created by Noisecrime)

Looking to add some pizzazz to your Web site? Just include a Shockwave movie—a Director movie converted for playback in a Web browser. All that your site's visitors need to do to view it is download and install the free Macromedia Shockwave 8 Player, available at the Macromedia Web site. When they've done so, their Web browsers will play Shockwave movies, which you can integrate with the other content on your Web page (**Figure 14.1**). Unlike projector movies, Shockwave movies don't require your users to exit their browsers and run a separate file.

Statistics have shown that offering Shockwave movies on Web sites increases both traffic and user retention, so it's no surprise that Shockwave is the most popular way of distributing Director movies. And with more than 130 million Shockwave Player downloads, you can be sure that you're reaching a very large audience.

This chapter explains all the basics of publishing a Director movie production in the Shockwave format. You learn how to create and organize all supporting files, how to set the various browser display options, and how to set Shockwave movies to stream as they download. You'll even find tips for smoothing out streaming over challenging Internet connections.

Working with Shockwave

As you've learned, a Shockwave movie is a Director movie converted for playback in a Web browser. Another notable feature: A Shockwave movie file includes all internal casts but can't embed external casts, which must be provided separately in the Shockwave format. (Director's Publish command creates Shocked external casts for you automatically, in addition to the other Shockwave-related files.) Any linked cast members, such as QuickTime movies, must also be provided separately.

After you create a Shockwave movie, you must embed it in an HTML file so that a Web browser can play it. (Web browsers can't open Shockwave movies directly. Director can create the HTML file for you automatically, with all necessary tags (**Figure 14.2**) to display the movie in a browser. You also can use a program such as Dreamweaver to insert a Shockwave movie and to further customize the HTML document for other content on the Web page.

While users watch your Shockwave movie, they can right-click (Control+click, on the Mac) the browser window to display a context menu that contains various playback commands (**Figure 14.3**). The available choices are determined by the playback settings in the Shockwave tab of the Publish Settings dialog box (*see "To change the Shockwave tab settings" later in the chapter*).

A Shockwave movie's data is compressed to help minimize download times. Shockwave movies also are protected, in that they lack the data that would allow users to open and edit them in Director. Shockwave movies can be viewed in a browser when the Shockwave Player has been installed, or they can be played back by a projector or another Shockwave movie. A Shockwave movie can't embed the player, so you can't make a stand-alone Shockwave movie, like a projector file, that runs all by itself.

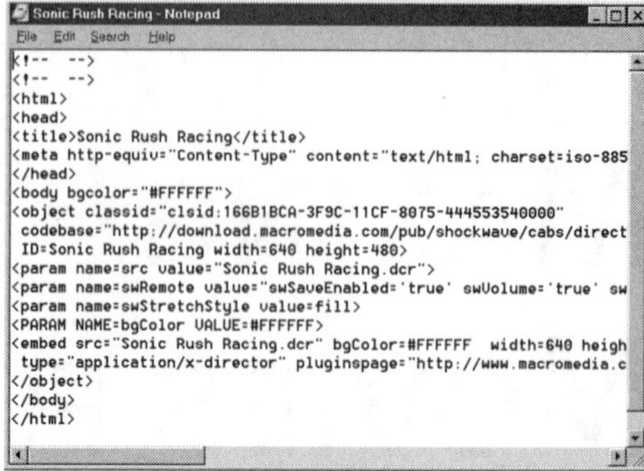

Figure 14.2 After you create a Shockwave movie, you embed it in an HTML file so that a Web browser can play it. Director's Publish command can generate such a file for you automatically.

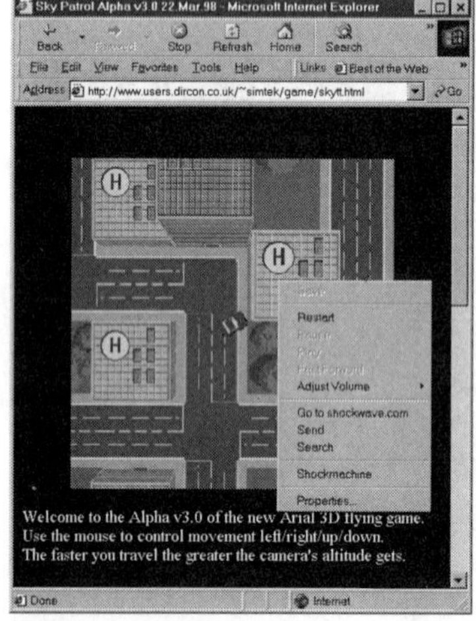

Figure 14.3 Right-click (Control+click, on the Mac) in a browser window while a Shockwave movie is playing to display a context menu with various playback commands. (Noisecrime's GTA, created by Noisecrime)

✔ Tip

- Some people create Shockwave versions of their movies even if they plan to distribute them on disk or other non-Internet means. That's because Shockwave movie offer the convenience of being compressed and protected.

Download if Needed

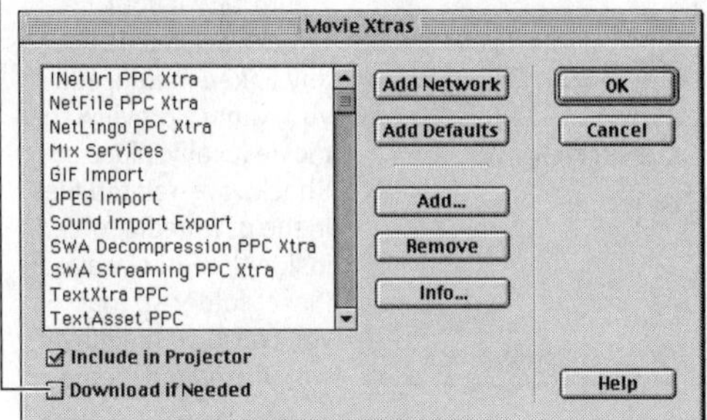

Figure 14.4 Use the Movie Xtras dialog box to specify which Xtras you want your Shockwave movie to attempt to download from the Internet if they are not installed on the user's system.

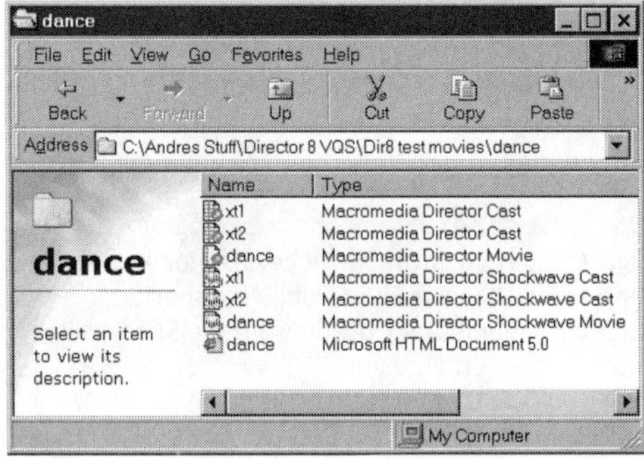

Figure 14.5 All Shockwave-related files—the Shockwave movie, HTML file, and any external casts—are by default placed in the same folder as your Director movie.

Figure 14.6 Director launches your default browser and plays the Shockwave movie.

Creating a Shockwave Movie

Director's Publish command creates all files necessary to view your Shockwave movie. In one step, the Publish command creates the Shockwave file (which has a .DCR extension), the HTML file, and new Shockwave versions of any linked external casts (these files have a .CCT extension).

To create and view a Shockwave movie:

1. Choose File > Save and Compact.

   This command saves your Director movie while removing fragmented and redundant data from the movie and cast files.

2. If your movie uses any nonstandard Xtras, choose Modify > Movie > Xtras to specify which Xtras the movie should prompt users to download, if needed (**Figure 14.4**).

   The most commonly used Xtras are built into the Shockwave Player, so you normally don't need to provide for them. But if your movie uses any Xtras that are not built into the player, you need to set options by using the Modify > Movie > Xtras command (*see Chapter 15, section "Including Xtras in Distributed Movies"*).

3. Choose File > Publish.

   Director creates a Shockwave-file version of your movie, an HTML file (assuming that you selected a template in the Publish Settings dialog box), and Shockwave versions of any external casts used by your movie. By default, all these files are placed in the same directory as your Director movie (**Figure 14.5**). Then Director launches your default browser and plays the Shockwave movie (**Figure 14.6**), assuming that the View in Browser option is enabled in the Formats tab of the Publish Settings dialog box (by default, it should be).

continues on next page

Director uses the settings in the Publish Settings dialog box when it creates your Shockwave movie and other files. If you have not changed these settings, the default settings are used (*see "Default Publish Settings" later in this chapter*). These settings should allow users to view your Shockwave movie right off the bat.

Note: If your movie uses any linked media or external casts, these elements will *not* appear in your Shockwave movie when you preview it in the browser unless the files are contained in the dswmedia folder inside the Shockwave Player folder, along with the .DCR and HTML files. This inconvenience is because of a security restriction that prevents the movie from accessing the local disk. (Your users will not have this problem when they view the movie from your Web site.) To overcome this problem when previewing the movie locally, place the Shockwave movie, HTML file, external casts, and all linked media in the dswmedia folder inside the Shockwave Player folder (**Figure 14.7**).

✔ Tips

- Hold down the Alt key (Option key, on the Mac) while choosing File > Publish to specify an alternative location and/or names for the Shockwave movie and any external casts (.CCT files) (**Figure 14.8**).
- When you create a Shockwave movie or cast, you cannot decompress it and recover the original file, so be sure not to delete the original Director movie and cast files.

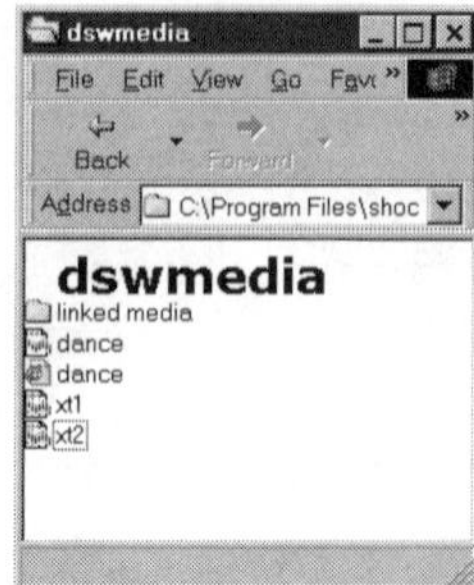

Figure 14.7 If your Shockwave movie uses any linked media, and you want to preview the movie locally, place all Shockwave-related files in the dswmedia folder inside the Shockwave Player folder so that you can view the movie with the linked media.

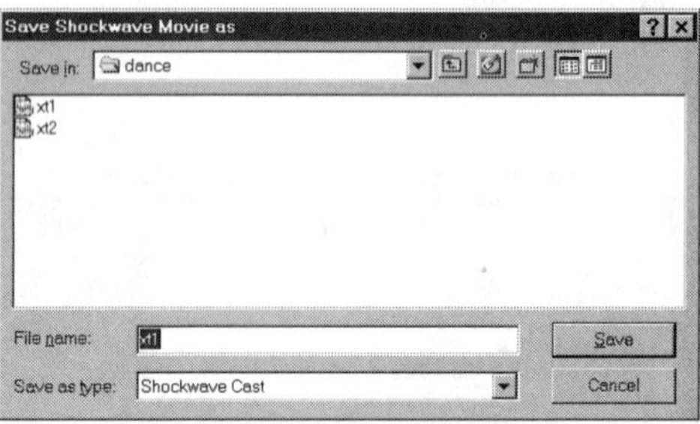

Figure 14.8 Hold down the Alt key (Option key, on the Mac) while choosing File > Publish to specify alternative names and locations for the Shockwave movie and external casts

Figure 14.9 Group a Shockwave movie and its related files and then upload the movie to your Web server with an FTP utility.

To prepare a Shockwave movie for Web distribution:

1. Place your Shockwave movie file, HTML document, any Shocked external casts, and linked media in the same folder (**Figure 14.9**).

   Alternatively, the linked media and external casts can be located at remote URLs, which you can set for each object in the Property Inspector.

2. If the Shockwave movie branches to other movies, place them in the folder as well.

   A Shockwave movie can play other Shockwave movies, as well as Director movies and protected movies.

3. Use an FTP (File Transfer Protocol) utility to transfer this folder to your Internet server.

Extensions Decoder

You can tell apart all the different kinds of Director files by their file extensions. Director movie files end with the extension .DIR. A Shockwave movie ends with .DCR. Protected Director movies end with the extension .DXR, and protected casts end with .CXT. (*See "Protecting Movie Files" in Chapter 13 "Creating a Projector" for details.*)

External casts saved in the Shockwave format end with .CCT.

HTML files end with .HTML on the Mac and .HTM in Windows.

Playing a Shockwave Movie

If you don't already have the latest Shockwave 8 Player installed, go to Macromedia's Web site and download it before proceeding. The Shockwave 8 Player can play Shockwave movies back to version 5. The Shockwave 8 Player is implemented either as a browser plug-in or an ActiveX control, depending on your platform.

The Shockwave Player works with Netscape Navigator 3 and later on both Mac and Windows computers. It works with Internet Explorer 3 and later in Windows and with IE 4.01 and later on the Mac. It also works with browsers that are compatible with Netscape Navigator 3's plug-in architecture, such as America Online.

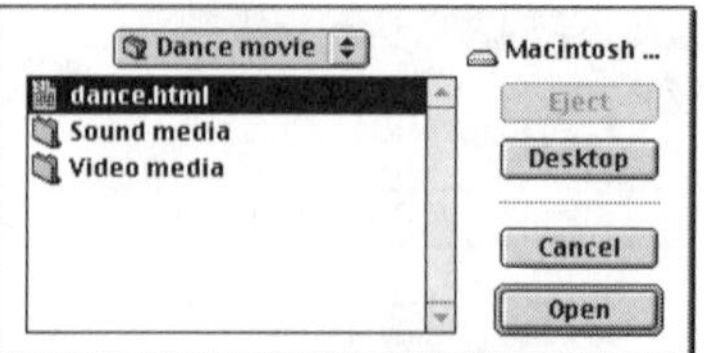

Figure 14.10 From your Web browser, choose File > Open File and select the HTML document for the Shockwave movie.

Figure 14.11 Enter the URL of the HTML document for your Shockwave movie.

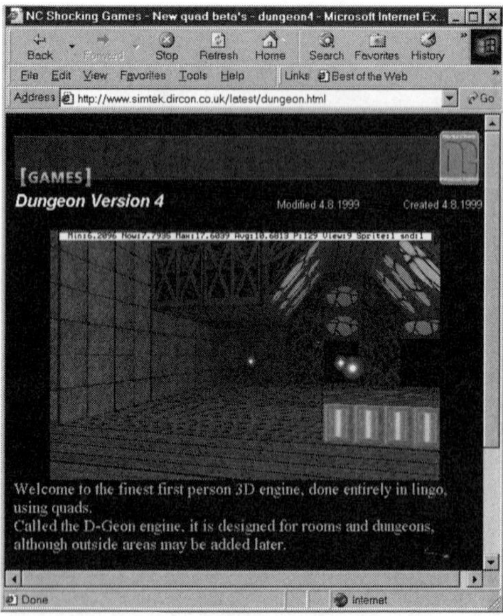

Figure 14.12 The Shockwave movie opens and plays in the browser window. (Dungeon, created by Noisecrime)

To play a Shockwave movie that's local to your system:

1. Launch your Web browser.
2. From the Web browser, choose File > Open File, and select the HTML document that runs the Shockwave movie (**Figure 14.10**).
3. Click Open.

   The Shockwave movie opens and plays in the browser window.

To play a Shockwave movie on the Web:

1. Connect to the Internet and launch your Web browser.
2. In the Web browser, enter the URL of the HTML document that runs the Shockwave movie you want to view (**Figure 14.11**).

   The Shockwave movie opens and plays in the browser (**Figure 14.12**) unless it's been set to pause until the user takes some action.

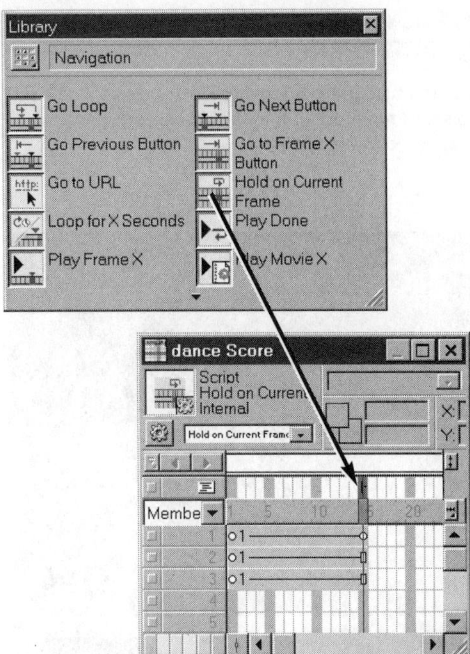

Figure 14.13 Drag the Hold on Current Frame behavior to the last frame of your movie in the script channel.

Shockwave movies are set to loop by default. Before creating your Shockwave movie, use the following procedure to set it to play through only once in the browser.

To set a Shockwave movie to play through once:

1. Open the Director movie.
2. Choose Window > Library Palette to open the Library Palette window.
3. Click the Library List button to display a pop-up menu of behavior categories.
4. Choose Navigation from the pop-up menu.
5. Drag the Hold on Current Frame behavior to the script channel of the last frame of your movie in the score (**Figure 14.13**).

If you are in the design-and-testing stage, you can preview your Shockwave movie by using the Preview in Browser command instead of the Publish command. The difference is that Preview in Browser creates temporary versions of the .DCR and HTML files.

To preview a Shockwave movie in a browser from Director:

1. Open the Director movie that you want to preview in a browser.
2. Choose File > Preview in Browser.

   Director launches the default browser to preview your movie.

   Note: Certain features, such as the context menu and being able to resize a Shockwave movie window, may not work when you preview a Shockwave movie with the Preview in Browser command as opposed to the Publish command.

To specify a browser for previewing a movie:

1. Choose File > Preferences > Network to display the Network Preferences dialog box.
2. Click Browse.
   The Select Browser dialog box appears.
3. Choose the browser program file you want Director to use for previewing your movie (**Figure 14.14**).
4. Click Open.

✔ Tip

- You can download a free application called Shockmachine (**Figure 14.15**) from the Shockwave.com Web site. You can use this application to play Shockwave movies, as well as organize and keep track of them (*see Chapter 18, "Shockmachine"*).

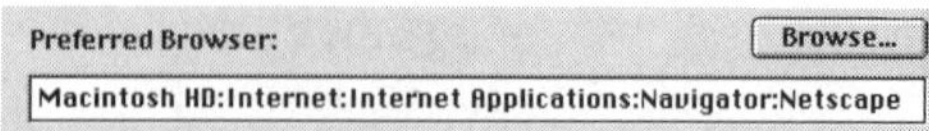

Figure 14.14 Use the Network Preferences dialog box to select the browser that Director uses to preview your Shockwave movie.

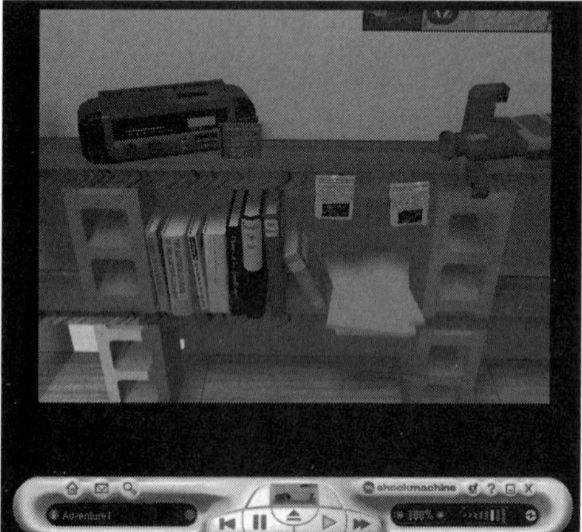

Figure 14.15 You can play back and organize Shockwave movies by using Shockmachine.

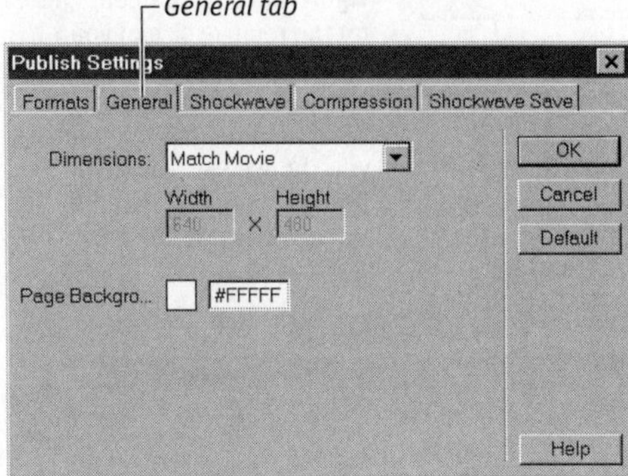

Figure 14.16 Select the General tab.

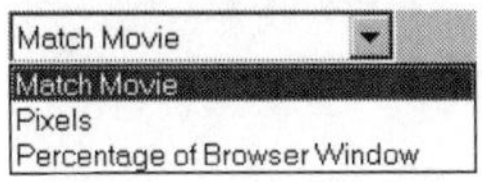

Figure 14.17 Choose sizing options from the Dimensions pop-up menu.

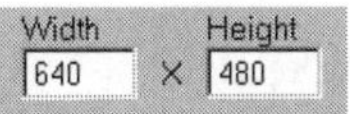

Figure 14.18 Set fixed rectangular dimensions for your movie by using the Width and Height fields when you choose Pixels from the Dimensions pop-up menu.

Making Stretchable Shockwave Movies

In Director 8, you can control how your Shockwave movie behaves when a user resizes a browser window. You can set the Shockwave movie to resize along with the browser window, for example, or to not stretch so that it remains the same size.

To set Shockwave movie resizing options:

1. Choose File > Publish Settings to display the Publish Settings dialog box.
2. Select the General tab (**Figure 14.16**).
3. Make a choice from the Dimensions pop-up menu (**Figure 14.17**):
   - Choose Match Movie to make your Shockwave movie match the exact dimensions of your Director movie. In this case, your Shockwave movie will not resize along with the browser window, regardless of the settings in the Shockwave tab. Your movie will be cropped if it doesn't fit within the resized browser window. Then click OK. You don't need to follow steps 4-8 if you choose this option.
   - Choose Pixels to set fixed rectangular dimensions for your Shockwave movie by using the Width and Height fields below the pop-up menu (**Figure 14.18**). Your movie will not change size if the browser window is resized. The aspect ratio of your movie within the new dimensions is determined in step 5.

continues on next page

Making Stretchable Shockwave Movies

- You must choose Percentage of Browser Window if you want your Shockwave movie to resize along with the browser window. If you choose this option, you also must choose Preserve Proportions, Stretch to Fill, or Expand Stage Size in step 5. Set percentages in the Width and Height fields below the pop-up menu (**Figure 14.19**) to determine the size of your Shockwave movie relative to the browser window. If you set both of these to 50 percent, for example, then your Shockwave movie will always be half the size of the browser window (assuming you select a compatible option in step 5). These default to 100 percent each.

4. Select the Shockwave tab (**Figure 14.20**).
5. Make a choice from the Stretch Style pop-up menu (**Figure 14.21**):
   - Choose No Stretching to make the movie play at the size, specified in the General tab's Dimensions pop-up menu. Resizing the browser crops your movie if it doesn't fit.
   - Choose Preserve Proportions to retain the same aspect ratio of your movie regardless of the size of the browser window (**Figure 14.22**). The movie is aligned with respect to the tags in step 6.

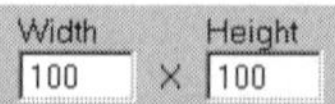

Figure 14.19 Set percentages for the relative size of your movie with respect to the browser window by using the Width and Height fields when you choose Percentage of Browser Window from the Dimensions pop-up menu.

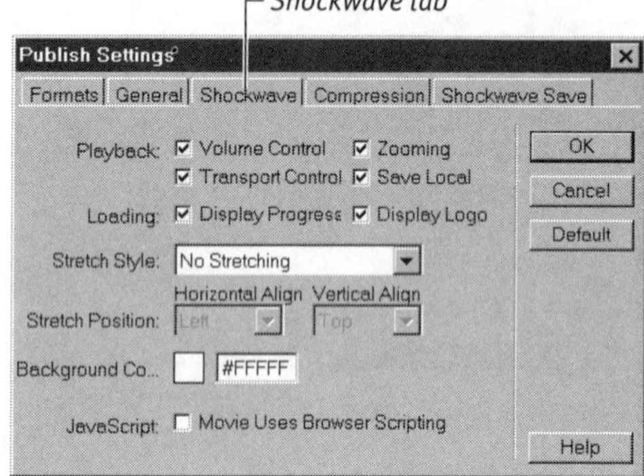

Figure 14.20 Select the Shockwave tab.

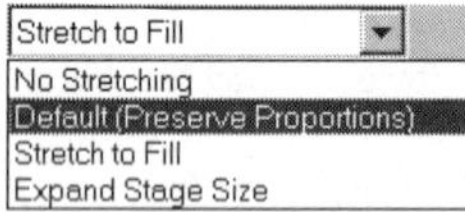

Figure 14.21 Make a selection from the Stretch Style pop-up menu, which determines how your Shockwave movie responds when a user resizes the browser window.

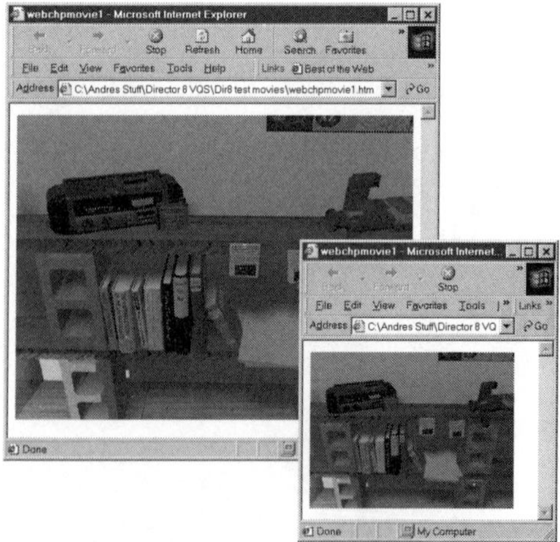

Figure 14.22 How a Shockwave movie resizes using Preserve Proportions.

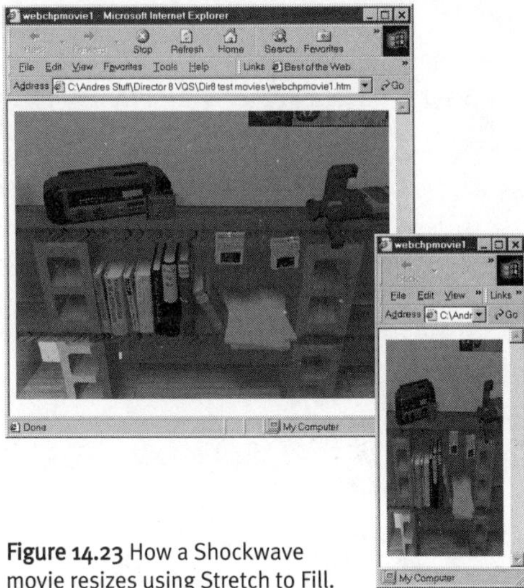

Figure 14.23 How a Shockwave movie resizes using Stretch to Fill.

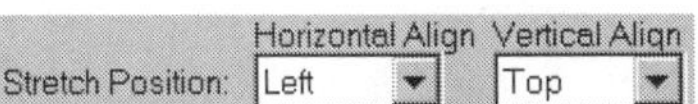

Figure 14.24 Align your movie in the browser window by making choices from the Horizontal Align and Vertical Align pop-up menus.

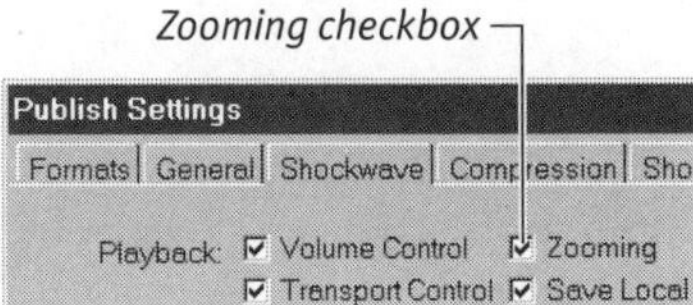

Figure 14.25 Choose the Zooming option if you have set your movie to resize along with the browser window (by using the Dimensions and Stretch Style pop-up menus).

- Choose Stretch to Fill to stretch the movie to fill the browser window. The aspect ratio of your movie may change, which can distort the appearance of sprites (**Figure 14.23**). The alignment tags set in step 6 are ignored for this option.
- Choose Expand Stage Size to expand the stage size to equal the height and width dimensions in the HTML file. Only the stage changes size; sprites remain the same. The movie is aligned with respect to the tags in step 6.

6. Use the Horizontal Align and Vertical Align pop-up menus to specify how your movie lines up in the browser window (**Figure 14.24**).
7. If you have set options for your movie to resize along with the browser window, check the Zooming checkbox (**Figure 14.25**).
8. Click OK.

✔ Tip

- Choose Fill Browser Window as your HTML template to automatically set the Dimensions and Stretch Style options so that your Shockwave movie always stretches to occupy the full size of the browser window without preserving the aspect ratio. Choose this template by opening the Publish Settings dialog box, selecting the Formats tab, and choosing Fill Browser Window from the HTML Template pop-up menu.

Working with Publish Settings

Choose File > Publish Settings to change the settings used by the Publish command when you create your Shockwave movie. These settings are saved when you save your Director movie.

The Publish Settings dialog box contains up to six tabs, depending on which HTML template you select. This section serves as a reference for these settings.

Default Publish Settings

The .DCR and HTML files use the same name as your Director movie (.DIR) file, except for the different file extensions. Likewise, any .CCT files use the same name as the external casts.

The .DCR and HTML files are configured so that if the browser is resized, your Shockwave movie stays the same size.

Your Shockwave movie's width and height are set to match the dimensions of your Director movie.

When your Shockwave movie loads, the same background color is used as the stage color in the movie.

Bitmap images and sounds are compressed via JPEG compression. If certain cast-member images have already been compressed, those settings take precedence over the Publish Settings.

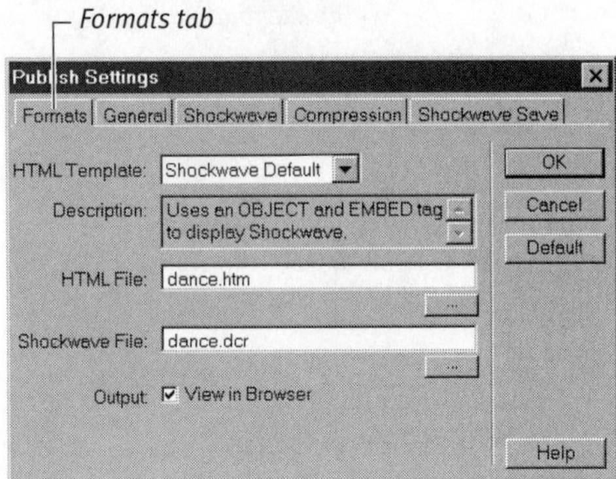

Figure 14.26 Select the Formats tab.

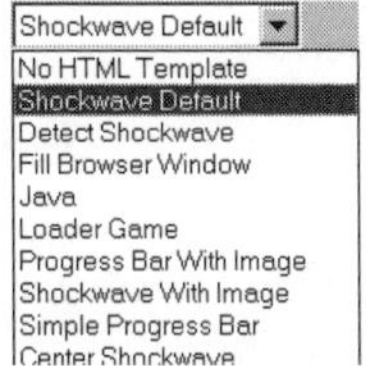

Figure 14.27 Choose a template from the HTML Template pop-up menu.

To change the Formats tab settings:

1. Select the Formats tab in the Publish Settings dialog box (**Figure 14.26**).

2. Choose a template from the HTML Template pop-up menu (**Figure 14.27**) to customize the HTML file:

   - Choose No HTML Template to create only the Shockwave file without the HTML file.

   - Choose Shockwave Default to create an HTML file that runs your Shockwave movie in a browser by including the necessary OBJECT and EMBED tags .

   - Choose Detect Shockwave to use VBScript and JavaScript to detect whether users have the correct version of the Shockwave Player installed. If they don't, they receive a message to update their Players.

   - Choose Fill Browser Window to expand the Shockwave movie to fill the entire browser window.

   - Choose Loader Game to display a game with a progress bar while your Shockwave movie loads.

   - Choose Progress Bar with Image to display a progress bar and an image while your Shockwave movie loads. (The Image tab of the Publish Settings dialog box appears when you choose this option.)

continues on next page

- Choose Shockwave with Image to automatically install the Windows version of the Shockwave Player (an ActiveX control) if the Windows user doesn't already have it installed. In all other cases, the user's computer displays the image that you specify in the Image tab of the Publish Settings dialog box. (This tab becomes available when you choose this option.)
- Choose Simple Progress Bar to display a progress bar while your Shockwave movie loads.
- Choose Center Shockwave to center the movie in the browser window.

3. Set the HTML and Shockwave File fields to indicate the names and locations of the respective files by typing in the fields (**Figure 14.28**) or by clicking the Browse buttons and then selecting the files.
4. Check the View in Browser checkbox (**Figure 14.29**) to launch the browser and view your Shockwave movie when you use the Publish command.

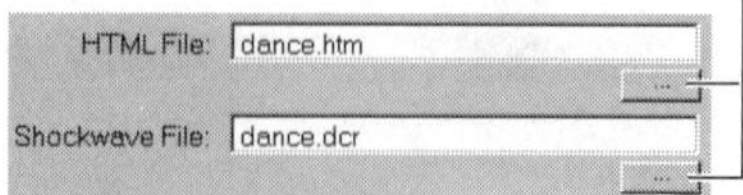

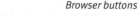

Figure 14.28 Specify the names and locations of the HTML and Shockwave files by using the HTML and Shockwave File fields.

Output: View in Browser

Figure 14.29 Check the View in Browser option if you want Director to automatically launch the default browser and play your Shockwave movie when you use the Publish command to create a Shockwave movie.

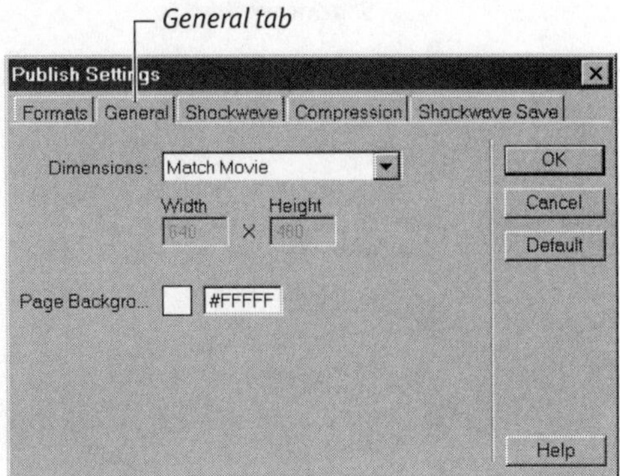

Figure 14.30 Select the General tab.

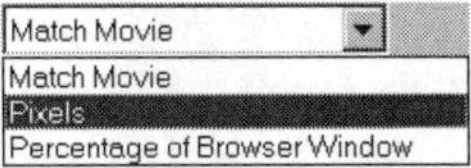

Figure 14.31 Use the Dimensions pop-up menu to set the size of your Shockwave movie.

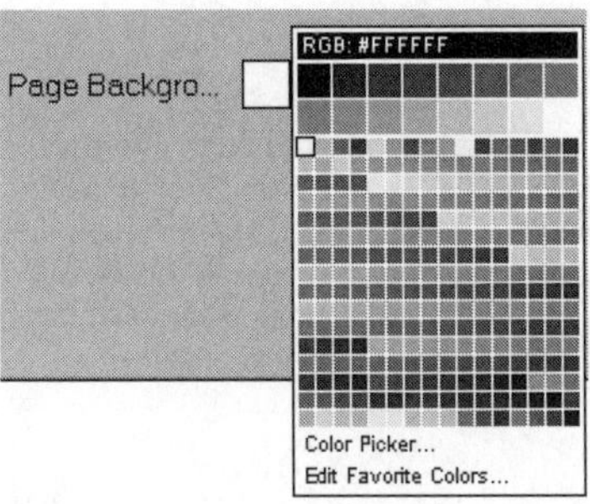

Figure 14.32 Use the Page Background color chip to set a new background color for your HTML document.

To change the General tab settings:

1. Select the General tab in the Publish Settings dialog box (**Figure 14.30**).
2. Set the size of your Shockwave movie by making a choice from the Dimensions pop-up menu (**Figure 14.31**):
   - Choose Match Movie to make your Shockwave movie match the dimensions of your Director movie.
   - Choose Pixels to set rectangular dimensions for your Shockwave movie by using the Width and Height fields below the pop-up menu. Your movie will be resized only if you did not choose the No Stretching option from the Stretch Style pop-up menu in the Shockwave tab.
   - Choose Percentage of Browser Window to set rectangular dimensions for your Shockwave movie based on the size of the browser window by using the Width and Height fields below the pop-up menu. Your movie will be resized only if you did not choose the No Stretching option from the Stretch Style pop-up menu in the Shockwave tab. *(For details on Shockwave options for browser resizing, see "Making Stretchable Shockwave Movies" earlier in this chapter.)*
3. Change the background color of your HTML file by clicking the Page Background color chip, holding down the mouse button, and choosing a color from the Color menu (**Figure 14.32**) or by entering a hexadecimal value in the adjoining field.

To change the Shockwave tab settings:

1. Select the Shockwave tab in the Publish Settings dialog box (**Figure 14.33**).
2. Set Playback options to control which menu choices are available to your users from the context menu during playback (**Figure 14.34**):
   - Check Volume Control to allow your users to adjust the volume of your movie.
   - Check Transport Control to give your users controls for restarting, pausing, playing, and fast-forwarding your movie.
   - Check Zooming to enable stretchable Shockwave.
   - Check Save Local to allow your users to save the movie in Shockmachine (*see Chapter 18, "Shockmachine"*).
   - Check Display Progress and Display Logo to display a progress bar and logo while the movie loads in the browser.
3. Make a choice from the Stretch Style pop-up menu to specify how your movie responds when you resize the browser window (**Figure 14.35**):

   Note: For your movie to resize when you resize the browser, you must choose Percentage of Browser Window from the Dimensions pop-up menu in the General tab and check the Zooming checkbox in this tab.

   - Choose No Stretching to make the movie play at its original size. Resizing the browser crops your movie when it doesn't fit.

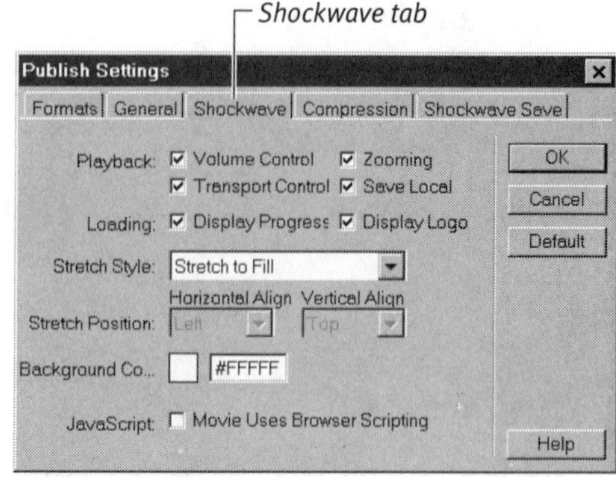

Figure 14.33 Select the Shockwave tab.

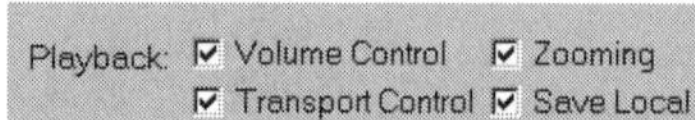

Figure 14.34 The Playback options determine which menu choices are available from a Shockwave movie's context menu during playback.

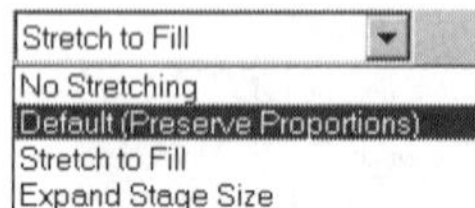

Figure 14.35 Choices from the Stretch Style pop-up menu determine how your Shockwave movie responds to browser resizing.

WORKING WITH PUBLISH SETTINGS

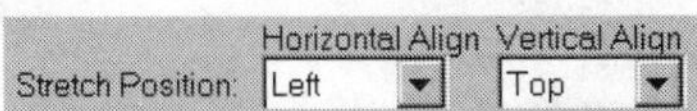

Figure 14.36 Align your movie in the browser window by making choices from the Horizontal Align and Vertical Align pop-up menus.

Figure 14.37 Use the Background color chip to change the background color while your Shockwave movie loads.

Figure 14.38 Enable the Movie Uses Browser Scripting option if your movie includes any Lingo calls to JavaScript.

- Choose Preserve Proportions to maintain the same aspect ratio of your movie regardless of the size of the browser window.
- Choose Stretch to Fill to stretch the movie to fill the browser window. The aspect ratio of your movie may change, which can distort the appearance of sprites.
- Choose Expand Stage Size to expand the stage size to equal the height and width dimensions in the HTML file. Only the stage changes size; sprites remain the same.

4. Make choices from the Horizontal Align and Vertical Align pop-up menus (**Figure 14.36**) to specify how your movie lines up in the browser window.

   These menus are available only if you choose Preserve Proportions or Expand Stage Size from the Stretch Style pop-up menu.

5. To change the background color while your .DCR file is loading, click the Background color chip (**Figure 14.37**), hold down the mouse button, and choose a color from the Color menu, or type a hexadecimal value in the adjoining field.

6. If your movie includes any Lingo calls to JavaScript, check the Movie Uses Browser Scripting checkbox (**Figure 14.38**).

Use the Compression tab to compress all bitmap cast members and sounds used in your movie. You can set individual compression quality for a specific bitmap cast member via the Compression pop-up menu in the Property Inspector (**Figure 14.39**), which overrides the Compression tab settings.

To change the Compression tab settings:

1. Select the Compression tab in the Publish Settings dialog box (**Figure 14.40**).
2. Choose Standard to apply the compression techniques used in Director 4 through 7, which is acceptable when your movie employs graphics with few colors.

   or

   Choose JPEG and then specify the image quality by using the slider (**Figure 14.41**). The lower the percentage, the more your image is compressed.
3. Check the Compression Enabled checkbox (**Figure 14.42**) to compress sounds in your movie; then choose a compression level from the pop-up menu below (*see "Compressing Sounds" in chapter 12*).
4. Check the Convert Stereo to Mono checkbox to convert stereo sounds to monaural.
5. Check the Include Cast Member Comments checkbox (**Figure 14.43**) to include any cast-member comments set in the Property Inspector for the Shockwave file.

   You can use Lingo to access these comments.

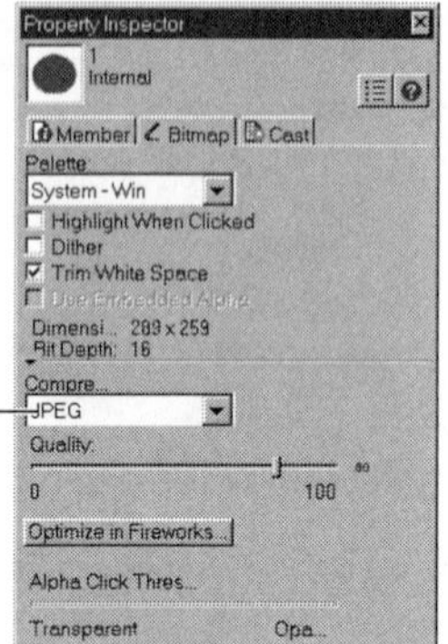

Figure 14.39 Use the Compression pop-up menu in the Property Inspector to set individual compression quality for a selected bitmap cast member. This setting overrides the general settings under the Compression tab in the Publish Settings dialog box.

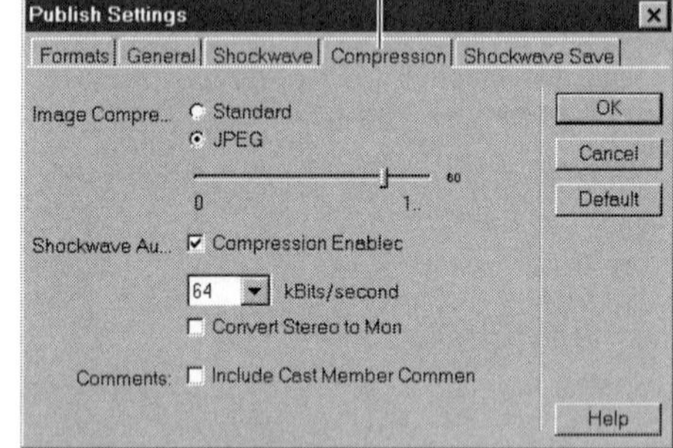

Figure 14.40 Select the Compression tab.

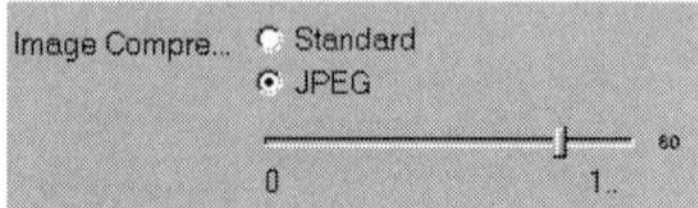

Figure 14.41 Choose JPEG and specify image quality by using the slider.

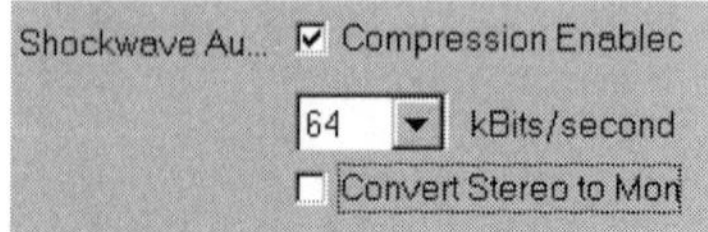

Figure 14.42 Choose Compression Enabled to compress sounds in your movie.

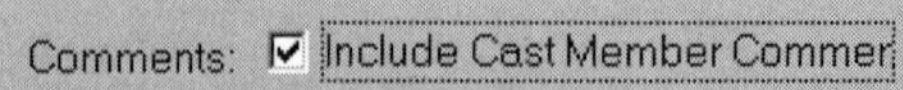

Figure 14.43 Enable the Include Cast Member Comments option to include in the Shockwave file any cast-member comments set in the Property Inspector.

Working with Publish Settings

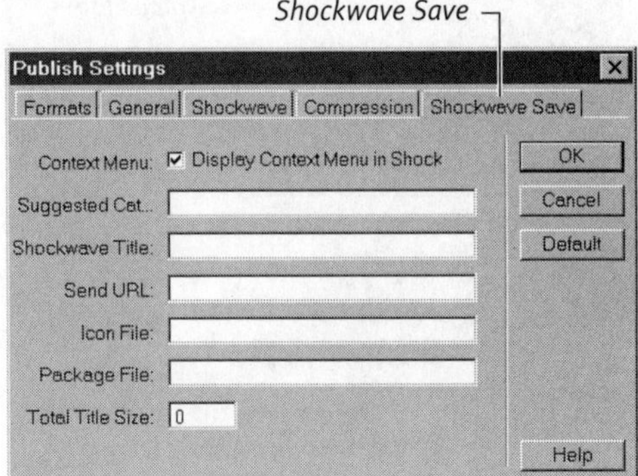

Figure 14.44 Select the Shockwave Save tab.

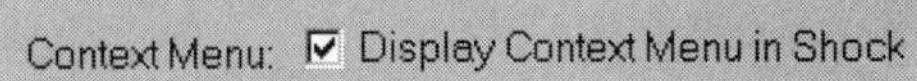

Figure 14.45 Enable Display Context Menu to display a context menu when a user right-clicks (Control+clicks, on the Mac) your Shockwave movie.

Configure your Shockwave file for playback with Macromedia's Shockmachine by filling out the fields in the Shockwave Save tab. (*See Chapter 18, "Shockmachine,"* for details.)

To change the Shockwave Save tab settings:

1. Select the Shockwave Save tab in the Publish Settings dialog box (**Figure 14.44**).
2. Check the Display Context Menu in Shockwave checkbox (**Figure 14.45**) to display the Shockwave context menu when a user right-clicks (Control+clicks, on the Mac) your Shockwave movie playing in a browser.
3. In the Suggested Category field, type a description to suggest a Shockmachine category.
4. In the Shockwave Title field, type a title to appear in the user interface in Shockmachine.
5. If you need to override the URL that Shockmachine detects for the given Shockwave movie, type a new URL in the Send URL field.
6. In the Icon File field, specify a path to a .BMP file to be used as the icon for your Shockwave movie in Shockmachine.
7. In the Package File field, type a relative URL or a fully qualified URL to a package text file. Such a text file in XML contains a list of URLs with the supporting files to download in order to completely save the current project.
8. For content with packages, use the Total Title Size field to indicate the size of all the content that needs to be downloaded for the movie to save successfully.

When you choose Progress Bar with Image or Shockwave with Image from the HTML Template pop-up menu in the Formats tab, the Image tab becomes available. Use this tab to specify an image that should appear if your user doesn't have the Shockwave Player installed.

To change the Image tab settings:

1. Select the Image tab in the Publish Settings dialog box (the label on this tab may not be visible, but it's the one furthest to the right) (**Figure 14.46**).
2. In the Poster Frame field (**Figure 14.47**), type a frame from your movie's score that will be displayed as a JPEG image for users who cannot view your Shockwave movie.
3. Specify a compression level for the image by using the Quality slider (**Figure 14.48**).

   The lower the percentage, the more the image is compressed.
4. Check the Progressive checkbox (**Figure 14.49**) if you want the image to download as a progressive JPEG, which means that the image will initially display at a low resolution but increase in quality as it downloads.

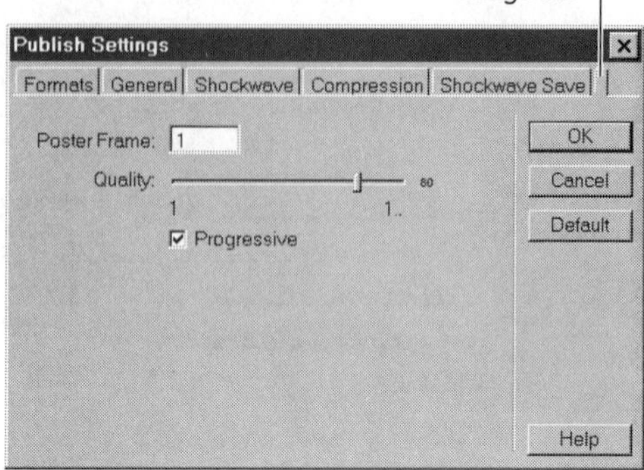

Figure 14.46 Select the Image tab.

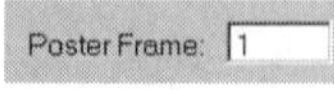

Figure 14.47 Use the Poster Frame field to select a frame from your movie to be displayed as a JPEG image when a user can't view your Shockwave movie.

Figure 14.48 Set a compression level for the JPEG by using the quality slider.

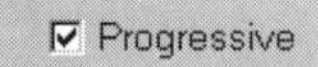

Figure 14.49 Choose Progressive to make the image download as a progressive JPEG.

Working with Publish Settings

Streaming: ☑ Play While Downloading Movie
Download [1] Frames Before Playing
☐ Show Placeholders

Figure 14.50 If you want to set a Shockwave movie to stream, choose the Play While Downloading Movie option in the Movie Playback Properties dialog box before creating the Shockwave movie.

Download [5] Frames Before Playing

Figure 14.51 Type a value for how many frames to download before the movie starts to play.

Making Streaming Shockwave Movies

Streaming is the process that allows users to view a movie or hear a sound while it continues to download. It's a trick that keeps typically impatient Web users contented; they don't have to wait for the entire file to download before something happens. Even though streaming does not decrease the total time needed to download a movie, it can greatly improve the viewing experience by involving the user right from the start.

To create a streaming Shockwave movie:

1. Choose Modify > Movie > Playback to display the Movie Playback Properties dialog box.
2. Choose the Play While Downloading Movie option (**Figure 14.50**).
3. Type a value in the Download Frames Before Playing field to specify the number of complete frames to download before starting to play the movie (**Figure 14.51**).
   If you enter 5, for example, your movie starts playing after all the cast-member media—both internal and linked—used in the first five frames of the score have completely downloaded. By default, this value is set to 1 frame. *(See "Tips for Effective Streaming" later in this chapter for a tip about setting this value.)*
4. Choose the Show Placeholders option if you want rectangular placeholders to appear during playback for media elements that have not yet downloaded.
5. Choose File > Save and Compact.
6. Choose File > Publish to create the Shockwave movie.

Because Internet bandwidth is still limited, Shockwave movies often are too big to stream without hiccups. One useful strategy to make streaming more effective is to loop a sequence of your movie while cast-member media download in the background.

To loop a Shockwave movie scene while loading cast-member media:

1. Open the score.
2. Choose Window > Library Palette to display the Library palette.
3. Click the Library List button to display a pop-up menu of behavior categories
4. Choose Internet > Streaming to display behaviors pertaining to streaming.
5. Drag a Loop Until behavior (**Figure 14.52**) into the script-channel frame where you want to initiate looping until the specified media become available (**Figure 14.53**). A Parameters dialog box appears.
   - Loop Until Next Frame Is Available loops until all media in the next frame have downloaded.
   - Loop Until Member Is Available loops until a cast member you specify has downloaded completely.
   - Loop Until Media in Frame Is Available loops until all media in a specific frame have downloaded.
   - Loop Until Media in Marker Is Available loops until all media between the marker you specify and the next marker are downloaded fully.
6. In the Parameters dialog box, specify the loop type, which frame or marker to loop to, and any other required parameters for the Loop Until behavior (**Figure 14.54**).
7. Click OK.

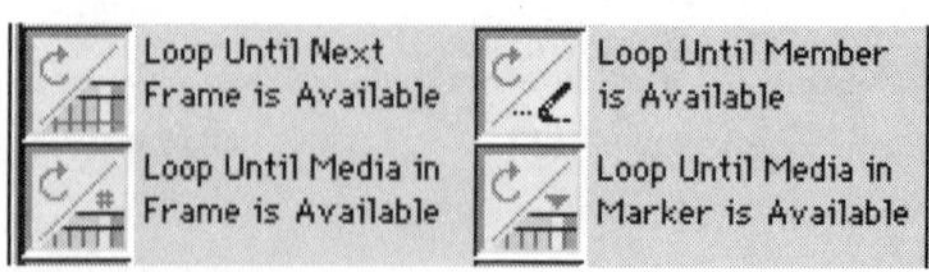

Figure 14.52 Use the Loop Until behaviors in the Library palette to establish the type of looping you need.

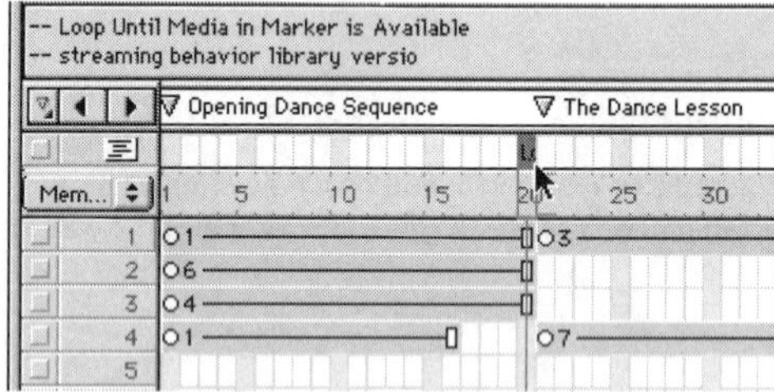

Figure 14.53 Drag a Loop Until behavior into the script channel where you want to initiate looping in your movie.

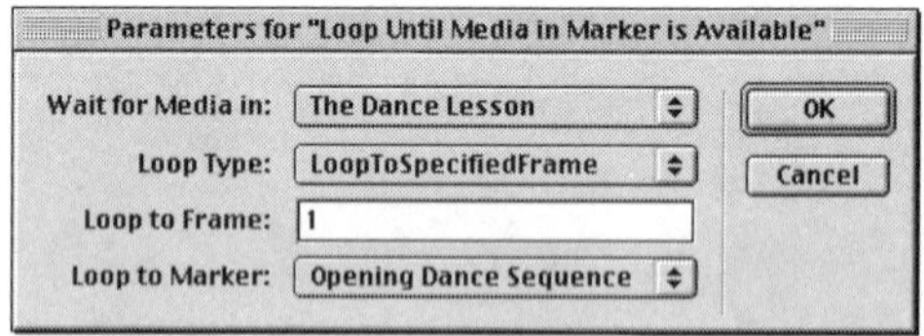

Figure 14.54 Specify the loop type, the start and end of the loop, and other required parameters for the specified Loop Until behavior.

Tips for Effective Streaming

If you're creating a streaming Shockwave movie, careful planning can increase its chances of streaming smoothly.

- Try to prevent users from jumping far ahead in a movie. If you're using scripts or behaviors to jump around in the score—because you are offering navigational controls to the user, for example—restrict the user to short hops. Because Director downloads cast-member data in frame order, a sudden jump over many frames means waiting for *all* intervening cast members to load, even if the users never see those cast members.
- Try to use cast members that require minimal storage space, such as vector shapes. A 32-bit bitmap cast member may occupy more than 100KB of storage, whereas a vector-shape cast member may occupy less than 1KB.
- Large linked sound files or QuickTime movies may seem impressive, but the time required to download these media over most of today's Internet connections could cancel out the effectiveness of streaming.
- Where possible, use tweening as the basis for animated sequences to limit the number of different cast members. Clever tweening of sprite properties can create the illusion of many cast members when only a few are employed.
- If your movie requires large, memory-hungry cast members, such as QuickTime movies or 32-bit bitmaps, start the movie with a simple scene that uses compact cast members; then use one of Director's streaming behaviors to loop the scene until the bigger media have downloaded fully. The looping scene can entertain the user immediately while the movie continues loading in the background.
- Instead of looping, you can try to time animations using the tempo channel to allow the process of downloading media to stay ahead of the end of the animation sequence. Estimating the time required is guesswork, but you can safely assume that most Internet connections today download at an average rate of about 2KB per second. This means that if you have 20KB worth of compressed cast-member media to download for the next scene, you try to make the current animated sequence about 10 seconds long.
- Experiment with the Download Frames Before Playing value in the Movie Playback Properties dialog box to find a reasonable compromise between streaming and letting the user wait for downloading. If the value is too low, too many placeholders boxes clutter the scene. If the value is too high, the user may give up and surf elsewhere.

Converting Multiple Movies

If you have multiple Director movies and casts to save as Shockwave files, you can batch-process them instead of opening and saving each one individually. You have the option of converting the files while preserving the originals or converting the files and throwing away the original files. Note that this process will not create the HTML file for a Shockwave movie, as the Publish command does.

To batch-convert files while preserving the originals:

1. Choose Xtras > Update Movies.

   The Update Movies Options dialog box opens.
2. Choose the Convert to Shockwave Movie(s) option (**Figure 14.55**).
3. Choose Back Up into Folder to set aside the original movie and cast files in a safe place (**Figure 14.56**).
4. Click Browse.
5. Double-click the folder where you want to put the original files and click the Select Folder button.
6. Click OK in the Update Movies dialog box.

   The Choose Files dialog box opens.

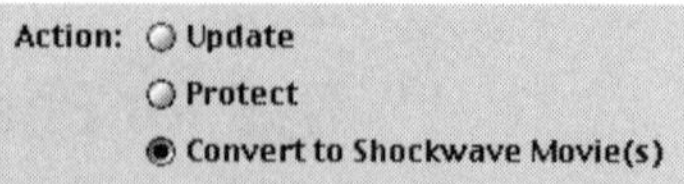

Figure 14.55 Choose the Convert to Shockwave Movies option in the Update Movies dialog box to convert several movies or casts at the same time.

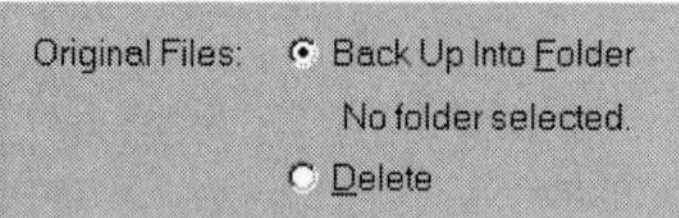

Figure 14.56 Choose Back Up into Folder to set aside the original movie and cast files in a safe place.

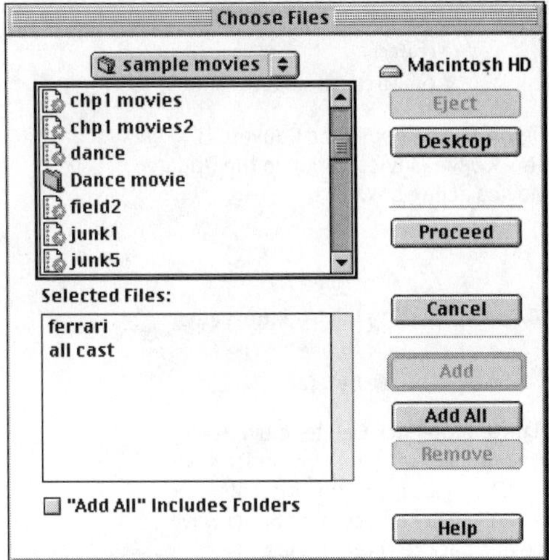

Figure 14.57 Add the Director movies or external casts that you want to convert to Shockwave by clicking Add. Added files appear in the list at the bottom of the dialog box.

"Add All" Includes Folders

Figure 14.58 If you want to select the entire contents of a folder, including any folders it contains, check the "Add All" Includes Folders checkbox and then click Add All.

7. Navigate through folders and select a movie or external cast file to convert (**Figure 14.57**).

   Unlike the Publish command, the Update Movies command does not convert linked external casts automatically. You must manually add each external cast that you want to convert.

8. Click Add.

   The file's name goes into the list in the bottom half of the dialog box.

9. One by one, select the other files to convert to Shockwave and click Add after each selection.

   or

   Click Add All to add all the files in the current folder to the list.

10. Click Proceed.

✔ Tip

- To include folders in addition to files when you click Add All, check the "Add All" Includes Folders checkbox at the bottom of the Choose Files dialog box (**Figure 14.58**).

To batch-convert files while deleting the original files:

1. Make sure that you have backed up the original files somewhere, because you cannot convert Shockwave files back to Director files.
2. Choose Xtras > Update Movies to display the Update Movie dialog box.
3. Choose the Convert to Shockwave Movie(s) option (**Figure 14.59**).
4. Click Delete to overwrite the originals with the new Shockwave files (**Figure 14.60**).
5. Click OK.

   The Choose Files dialog box opens.
6. In the list at the top of the dialog box, select a movie or cast file that you want to convert (**Figure 14.61**).
7. Click Add.

   The file's name goes into the list at the bottom of the dialog box.
8. One by one, select the other files to convert to Shockwave and click Add after each selection.

   or

   Click Add All to add all the files in the current folder to the list.
9. Click Proceed.

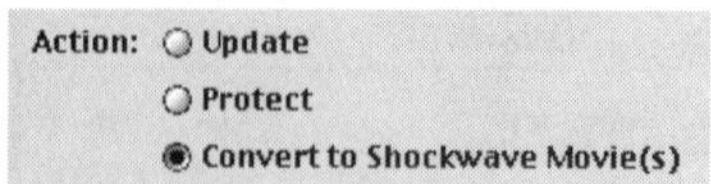

Figure 14.59 Choose the Convert to Shockwave Movies option in the Update Movies dialog box.

Figure 14.60 Click Delete to overwrite the originals with the new Shockwave files. Keep a copy of the originals, because you can't convert Shockwave movies back to Director files.

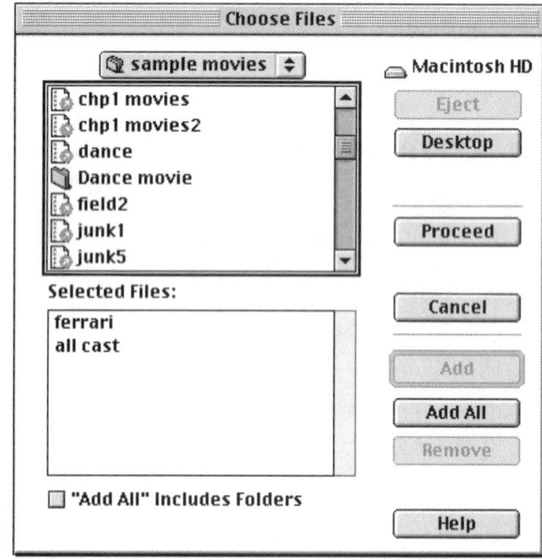

Figure 14.61 From the list at the top of the Choose Files dialog box, select and add the Director movies or external casts that you want to Shock. Added files appear in the list at the bottom of the dialog box.

15

USING XTRAS

Director allows you to add software modules called *Xtras*, which extend what you can do with Director. With Xtras you can add new cast-member types, expand Director's built-in set of transition effects, import Photoshop layered images, and even add authoring tools. Even Macromedia has used Xtras to improve on Director's features.

Director includes several Xtras, and you can buy them from other companies. *Xtravaganza! The Essential Sourcebook for Macromedia Xtras* (Peachpit Press, 1998) serves as a printed reference on Xtras. Or you can find Xtras on the Web; Start with Macromedia's Web site; the Downloads section offers several Macromedia Xtras as well as a long list of third-party Xtras. Also, you can write custom Xtras if you have enough programming experience.

Xtras are not the only way to add functionality in Director. In the Windows version of the program, you can also incorporate ActiveX controls, which are covered in this chapter.

Xtras open a world of possibilities in Director. Read on to discover how to install them and incorporate them into your movie files.

Understanding Xtra Types

Xtras can be classified in five general types:

- **Cast-member Xtras,** which add new media types that could be practically anything from a spreadsheet to a database.
- **Importing Xtras,** which allow Director to bring in certain external media during movie playback, such as animated GIFs or Flash movies. Numerous importing Xtras ship with Director.
- **Transition Xtras,** which add transition effects that are not built into Director (see Chapter 5, "Playing and Refining Movies").
- **Lingo or scripting Xtras,** which add new language elements to Lingo—Director's scripting language. (See Chapter 17, "Scripting Lingo," for information on how to use these Xtras.)
- **Tool Xtras,** which are designed to help you with authoring. An example is the tool Xtra that ships with the Windows version of Director, which allows you to convert WAV audio files to SWA (Shockwave audio) files. Unlike most other Xtra types, you don't distribute tool Xtras with your movies; they serve their purpose during authoring, not during playback.

✔ Tip

- Image filters, which are installed just like Xtras, are technically not considered to be Xtras (See "Applying Image Filters" in the Using Paint Tools chapter).

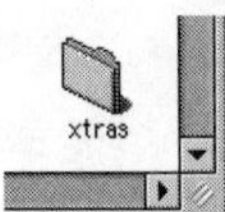

Figure 15.1 Install Xtras in the Xtras folder.

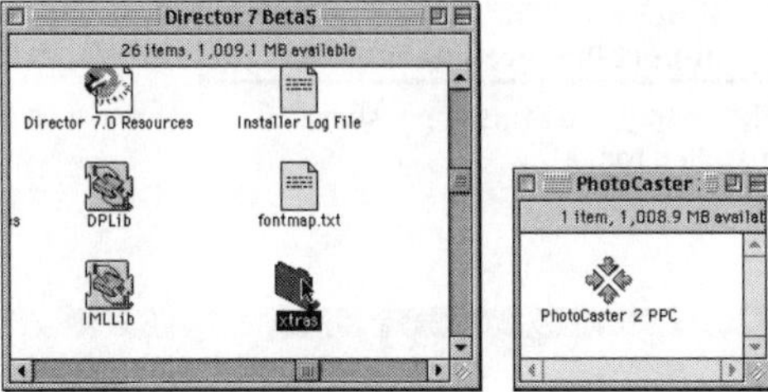

Figure 15.2 Install Xtras by dragging them into the Xtras folder.

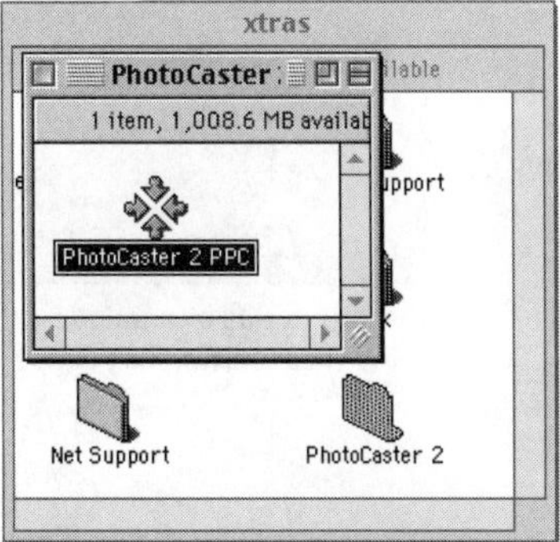

Figure 15.3 This Xtra is nested two layers deep within the Xtras folder. Avoid enclosing Xtras within too many folders.

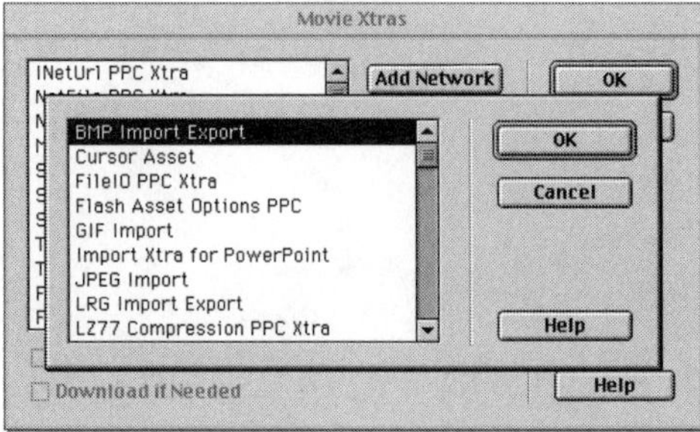

Figure 15.4 Click Add to see the rest of the installed Xtras in a separate list.

Installing Xtras

The first step in using any type of Xtra in Director is installing it. The process is simple.

To install an Xtra:

1. Find the Xtras folder in the Director application folder (**Figure 15.1**).
2. Place the new Xtra in the Xtras folder (**Figure 15.2**).
3. Quit Director.
4. Start Director again.

✔ Tip

■ Put the Xtra file no more than five layers deep within nested folders in the Xtras folder (**Figure 15.3**). If you nest the file within more folders, the program can't find the Xtra.

In addition to simply looking in the Xtras folder, you can see which Xtras are installed from within Director.

To see which Xtras are installed:

1. Choose Modify > Movie > Xtras.

   The Movie Xtras dialog box appears, listing a partial set of the installed Xtras—the ones required for the current movie.
2. Click Add to see the rest of the installed Xtras in a separate list (**Figure 15.4**).
3. Click Cancel to close the dialog box without making any changes.

Note: You may think the Movie Xtras dialog box is a means of installing or uninstalling Xtras. This is not so. Its purpose is to help you keep track of which Xtras are required for a particular movie (see "Preparing the Movie Xtras dialog box list") and to manage the bundling of Xtras for Shockwave and Projector movies.

Using Xtras

Some Xtras come into play transparently, like most importing Xtras; others, you have to explicitly choose from a menu in Director. Because there are so many different types and flavors of Xtras, how you use them depends largely on the Xtra. This section describes some typical ways of employing common types of Xtras. Keep in mind that there are many exceptions, so read your Xtra developer's instructions for specific use.

Installed tool Xtras usually are added to the Xtras menu, from which you can call them.

To use a tool Xtra:

1. Choose Xtras > *Xtra name* (**Figure 15.5**). A custom tool Xtra dialog box appears.
2. Specify any necessary settings in the tool Xtra dialog box (**Figure 15.6**).

Figure 15.5 The Xtras menu shows installed tool Xtras.

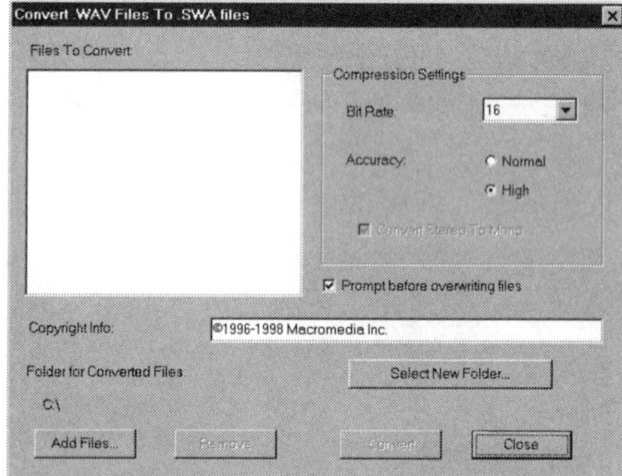

Figure 15.6 Each tool Xtra may have its own unique dialog box. The Convert WAV Files to SWA Files dialog box is shown here.

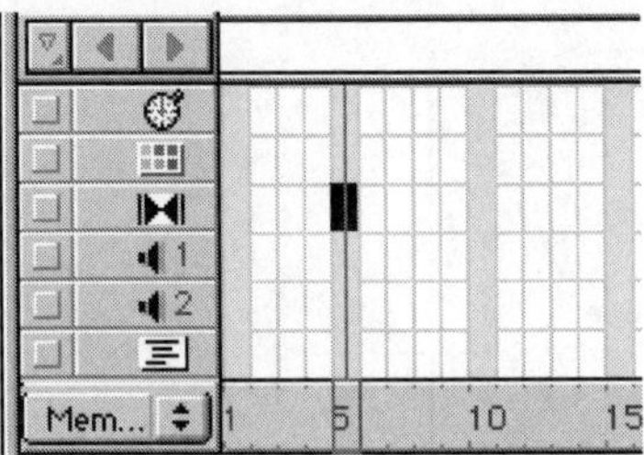

Figure 15.7 Select a cell in the transition channel where you want to use the transition Xtra.

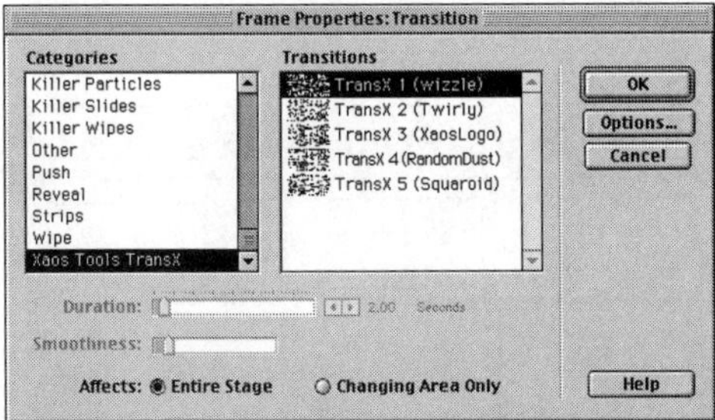

Figure 15.8 Installed transition Xtras should appear in the Categories and Transitions lists in the Frame Properties: Transition dialog box.

To use a transition Xtra:

1. In the score, select a cell in the transition channel where you want to use the transition Xtra (**Figure 15.7**).
2. Choose Modify > Frame > Transition.

   The Frame Properties:Transition dialog box appears. Installed transition Xtras should appear in the Categories and Transitions lists (**Figure 15.8**).
3. Select the Transition Xtra you want to use, and specify any necessary settings in the Transition dialog box.

   See chapter 5, Playing and Refining Movies, section "Using Scene Transitions" for more details).
4. Click OK.

✔ Tip

■ You need to keep track of what Xtras your movie uses, because most Xtras need to be included or bundled when you distribute the movie (see "Including Xtras in Distributed Movies"). If you delete a sprite that requires an Xtra, for example, you may no longer need the Xtra, but Director doesn't delete it automatically—and Xtras consume valuable RAM.

Cast-member Xtras add new media types to a Director movie. Cast-member Xtras allow you to create new cast-member media in Director or to create a cast member that controls a new type of external media, such as a new graphics or sound technology. Third-party cast-member Xtras that you can install include databases, 3-D graphics processors, and even a spreadsheet.

To add cast-member Xtras to a cast:

1. Install the cast-member Xtra by placing it in the Xtras folder and restarting Director.
2. Select an empty position in a cast window where you want to insert the cast-member Xtra.
3. Choose Insert > *cast-member Xtra.*

   If the Xtra has been installed properly, you should see it below the Control command in the Insert menu (**Figure 15.9**).
4. Use the Media Editor window or Properties dialog box that appears to customize the cast-member Xtra for your movie.

   After you add a cast-member Xtra to a cast (**Figure 15.10**), you can place it in a movie as you would any other cast member.

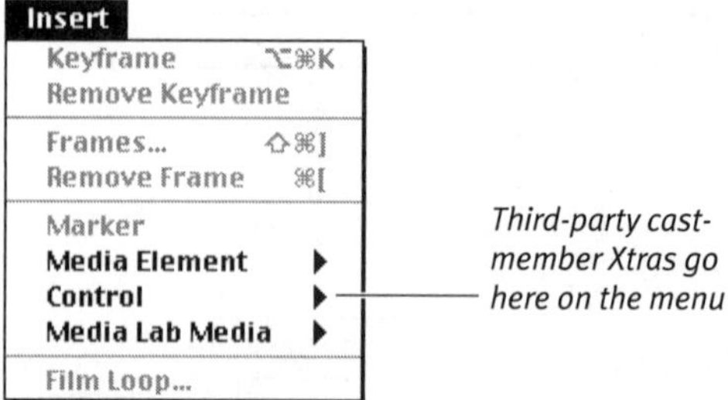

Figure 15.9 Third-party cast-member Xtras usually appear below the Control command in the Insert menu.

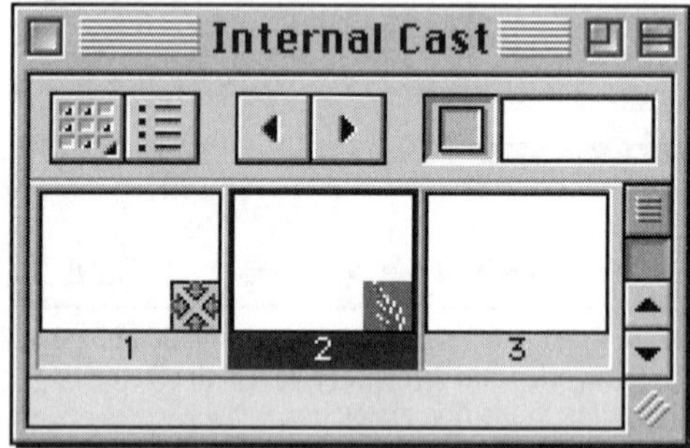

Figure 15.10 You can incorporate cast-member Xtras into your movie just like any other types of cast members.

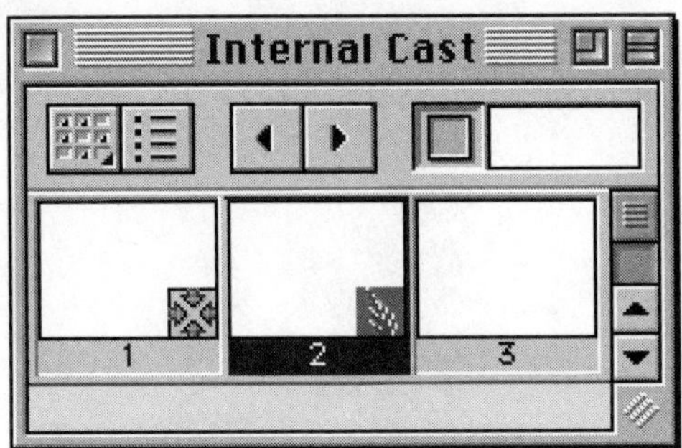

Figure 15.11 Select a cast-member Xtra in a cast window.

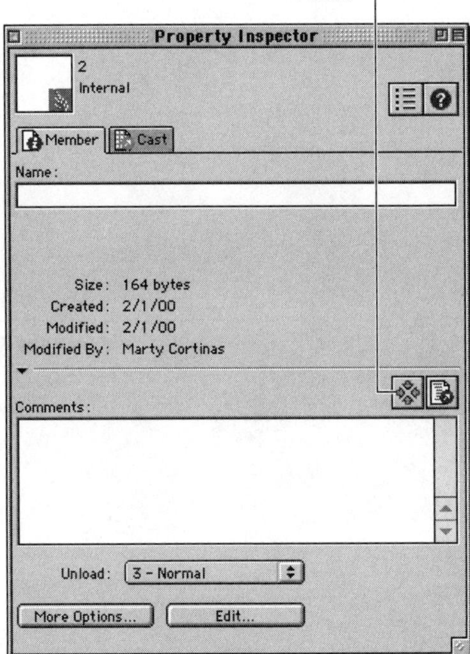

Figure 15.12 Click About in the Property Inspector window.

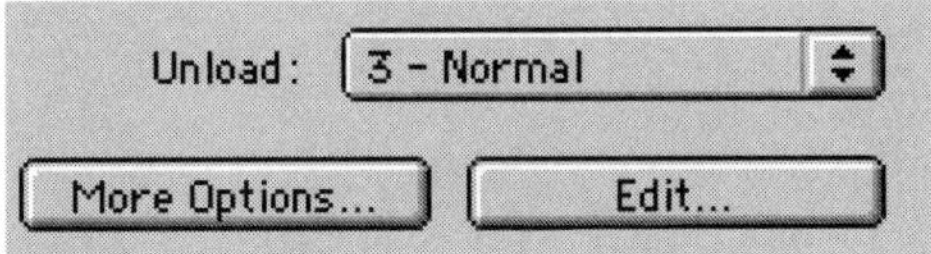

Figure 15.13 Click More Options for additional Xtra settings.

Some types of cast-member Xtras have their own Options dialog boxes and About boxes.

To view and set cast-member Xtra options:

1. In the Cast window, select a cast-member Xtra (**Figure 15.11**).
2. Click the Cast Member Properties button.

   The Property Inspector appears (**Figure 15.12**).
3. Click About to review any About-box information.
4. If you need to change options, click More Options, make selections in the Properties dialog box (**Figure 15.13**), and click OK.

✔ Tip

- An Xtra cast member may have its own media editor, which you can open by double-clicking the Xtra in the Cast window.

Including Xtras in Distributed Movies

When you distribute your movie as a projector or Shockwave file, you must make available all Xtras that the movie uses. Tool Xtras are the single exception, because they are used only during authoring.

If you are deploying your movie as a stand-alone projector, you must include all Xtras with it. You can do this in two ways, as described in the section "Including Xtras with Projectors." On the other hand, if your projector is a Shockwave projector or a slim projector—one that requires the Shockwave player to be installed—most commonly used Xtras are already built into the player, so you have to include only any additional Xtras that the projector requires.

When you create a Shockwave movie, the most common Xtras are already bundled into the Shockwave player, so you need to account only for any additional Xtras, much as you would with a Shockwave projector. The difference with a Shockwave movie is that you don't actually include additional Xtras; that would bloat the file size and time your users would spend downloading the movie. Instead, you set options in the Movie Xtras dialog box to allow the Shockwave movie to download the additional Xtras from the Web automatically when they are needed during playback. (See "Using Xtras for Shockwave Movies" later in this chapter for more details.)

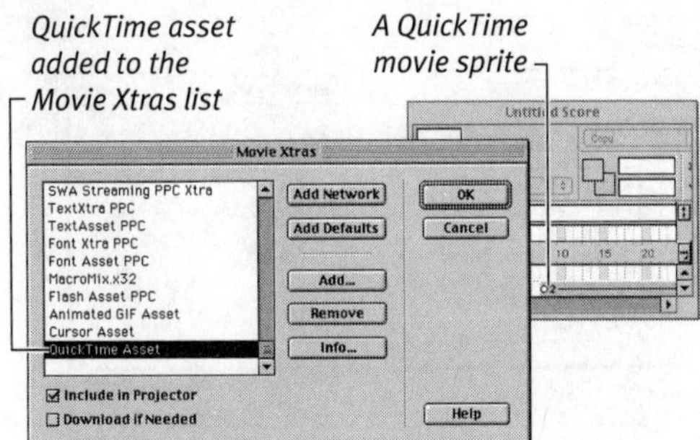

Figure 15.14 When you add a sprite to the score (such as a QuickTime movie sprite, added here), Director adds any necessary corresponding Xtra automatically (the QuickTime Asset Xtra, in this case) to the Movie Xtras dialog box. Director won't remove the Xtra if you remove the sprite; you must do that yourself.

Preparing the Movie Xtras dialog box list

Before you create a projector or Shockwave movie, you need to account for all the Xtras used in it. The Movie Xtras dialog box displays the Xtras required for the current movie. Unfortunately, this list is not always 100 percent accurate, because some Xtras are added to it only at the point where they are used in your movie, and unlisted Lingo Xtras are never added automatically. In these cases, you should add such Xtras to the list manually.

Similarly, you should manually remove all Xtras that you know are not required by your movie, because Director won't do this for you. When you create a sprite that requires an Xtra, for example, Director adds it to the Movie Xtras list (**Figure 15.14**) but won't remove the Xtra if you remove the sprite. Be sure to do this housekeeping chore before you create a projector or Shockwave movie, so that the list truly reflects all required Xtras.

To manually add Xtras to or remove Xtras from the Movie Xtras dialog-box list:

1. Choose Modify > Movie > Xtras to display the Movie Xtras dialog box.
2. Click Add if you want to add Xtras

   In the Add Xtras dialog box which appears, select any Xtra that your movie requires but that is not displayed in the Movie Xtras dialog-box list (**Figure 15.15**), and click OK.

   or

   Select an Xtra in the Movie Xtras list and click Remove to remove it (**Figure 15.16**).

   Be absolutely certain that your movie doesn't require this Xtra. Remember that you must have an importing Xtra for any linked external media files.
3. Repeat step 2 as many times as necessary.
4. If your movie connects to the Internet, you should add the Network Xtras by clicking Add Network.
5. Click OK

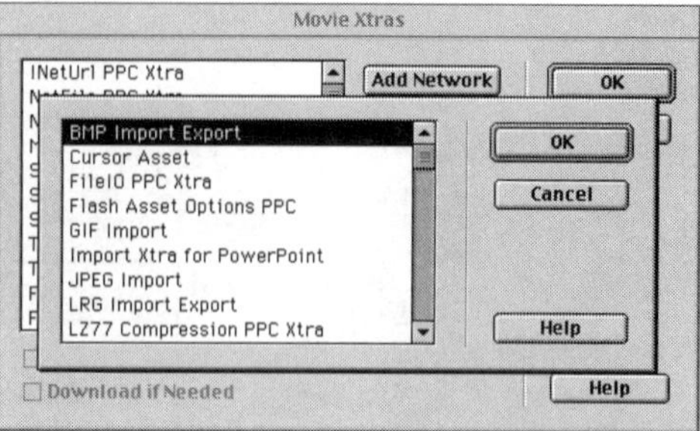

Figure 15.15 Click Add to select and add an Xtra to the Movie Xtras dialog-box list.

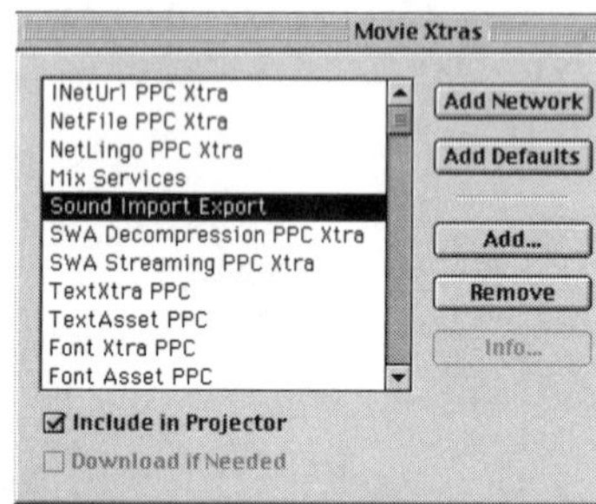

Figure 15.16 Remove an Xtra by selecting it and clicking Remove.

To restore Director's default Xtras to a movie:

1. Choose Modify > Movie > Xtras to open the Movie Xtras dialog box.
2. Click Add Defaults (**Figure 15.17**).

   This step puts back any default Xtras that had been removed. It does not delete Xtras that you have added to a movie.

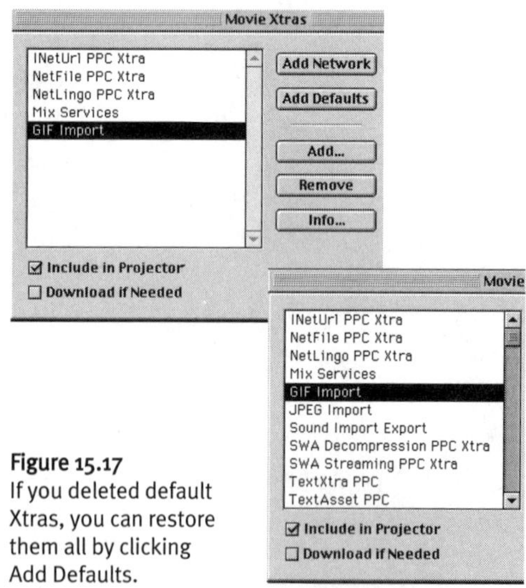

Figure 15.17 If you deleted default Xtras, you can restore them all by clicking Add Defaults.

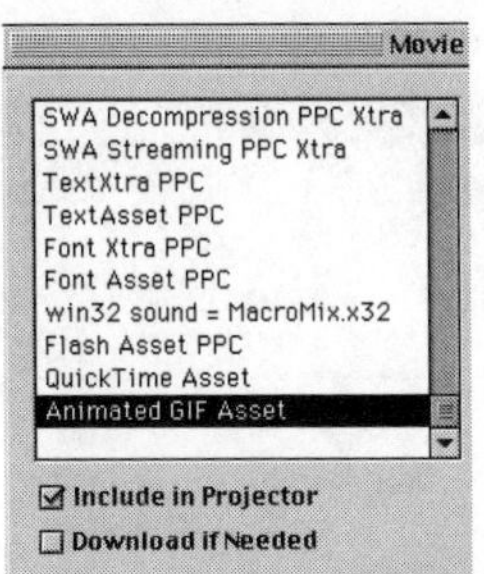

Figure 15.18 Check the Include in Projector checkbox for any Xtra in the Movie Xtras list that you want to embed in the projector.

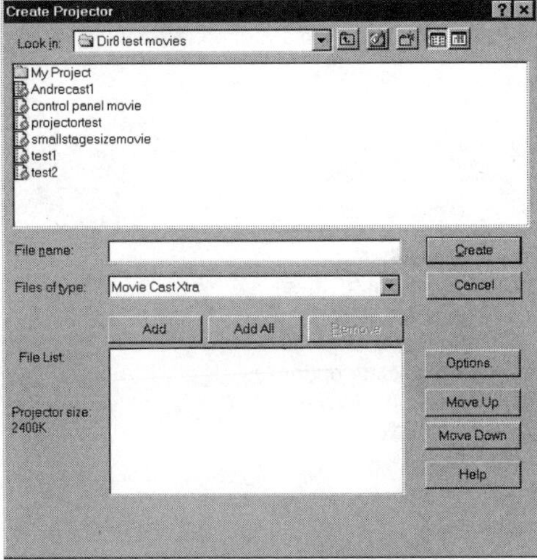

Figure 15.19 The Create Projector dialog box.

Including Xtras with Projectors

There are two approaches to including Xtras with a projector: You can embed the Xtras in the projector to make it one self-sufficient file, or you can include an Xtras folder inside the folder that contains the projector. If you choose the latter approach, anyone can easily see which Xtras the projector uses. Also, if you add movies that require more Xtras, you won't have to re-create the entire projector; you just update the Xtras folder.

To embed Xtras in a stand-alone or slim projector:

1. Choose Modify > Movie > Xtras to open the Movie Xtras dialog box.
2. If you need to add any Xtras that are not included in the Movie Xtras list, click Add, select the Xtra, and click OK.
3. If you want an Xtra in the Movie Xtras list to be embedded in your projector, select that Xtra and make sure that the Include in Projector checkbox is checked (**Figure 15.18**).

   By default, all Xtras in the Movie Xtras dialog box are included in a projector. If you followed the steps in the previous section "Preparing the Movie Xtras dialog box list," this list accurately reflects all the Xtras you need, so you should not have to change anything for a stand-alone projector.

   If you are creating a Shockwave projector or a slim projector, Director's default Xtras are built into the Shockwave player, but you still need to include any third-party Xtras you might be using.
4. Choose File > Create Projector (**Figure 15.19**).

   See the Creating a Projector chapter.

To package Xtras with stand-alone or slim projectors without embedding them:

1. Create a folder called Xtras in the same folder where the projector file resides (**Figure 15.20**).
2. Copy all Xtras that your projector needs from the Director Xtras folder to the Xtras folder inside the projector folder.

   If your projector is stand-alone, you need to copy all the Xtras listed in the Movie Xtras dialog box. If you're using a slim projector, you don't need to copy default Xtras—only any third-party Xtras you're using that aren't built into the Shockwave 8 player.
3. Choose Modify > Movie > Xtras to open the Movie Xtras dialog box.
4. Deselect the Include in Projector option for all Xtras (**Figure 15.21**).

   If you don't do this, the projector may not initialize properly.
5. Click OK.

✔ Tip

- If you projector contains multiple Director movies, you don't need to add the same Xtras in each movie, because they stay in RAM. Just add all of them in the first movie.

Figure 15.20 Create a folder called Xtras, and place it in the folder that contains your projector.

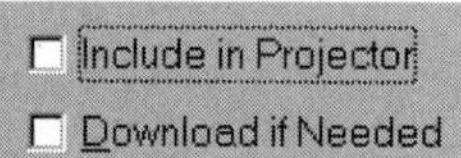

Figure 15.21 When you choose to distribute Xtras separately from your projector file, deselect the Include in Projector option for all Xtras in the Movie Xtras dialog box.

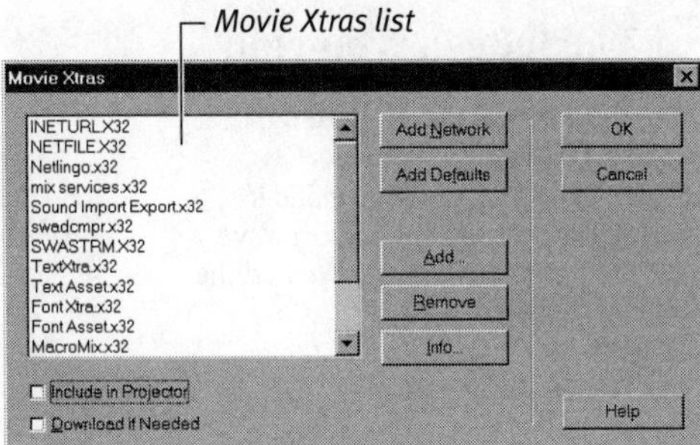

Figure 15.22 Add and remove Xtras in the Movie Xtras dialog box so that the list accurately reflects all required Xtras in your movie.

Using Xtras for Shockwave Movies

You can't embed Xtras in a Shockwave movie, but you can set a Shockwave movie to prompt users to download any required Xtras that are not included in the Shockwave player and not installed on the user's system. (The Shockwave player already includes common Xtras that support Flash movies, text, PICT, BMP, GIF, and JPEG importing, sound management, and Shockwave Audio.)

The Shockwave movie automatically embeds the Web addresses of each Xtra it might need to download, so your users don't have to do anything other than be connected to the Internet.

To set a Shockwave movie to download an Xtra during playback:

1. Make sure that the Xtras you plan to set for downloading are properly installed on your computer.

   If the required Xtras are properly installed on your authoring system, the URL information is automatically stored in the Xtrainfo.txt file inside your Director application folder.

2. Choose Modify > Movie > Xtras to open the Movie Xtras dialog box.

   Make sure that at this point, the Movie Xtras dialog box list (**Figure 15.22**) accurately reflects all the Xtras that your movie needs. (See "Preparing the Movie Xtras dialog box list.")

continues on next page

3. Select an Xtra for downloading.

   Remember that most default Xtras are built into the Shockwave player, so you won't need to include most of the Xtras listed in the Movie Xtras dialog box. Select only nondefault or third-party Xtras that you have added to your movie.

4. Check the Download if Needed checkbox (**Figure 15.23**).

   The movie gets the URL for the selected Xtra from the Xtrainfo.txt file in your Director application folder and embeds it in your Shockwave file when you create it.

   Director verifies the URL, so you must have an active Internet connection during this step.

5. Repeat steps 3 and 4 to include as many Xtras for downloading as necessary.

6. Choose File > Publish to create the Shockwave movie.

   See the Making Movies for the Web chapter.

☐ Include in Projector

☑ Download if Needed

Figure 15.23 Check the Download if Needed checkbox to set a Shockwave movie to prompt users to download the Xtra if necessary.

Developing Xtras

If you have the programming skills, you can write your own Xtras. Most Xtras developers work in the programming language C++, but some use Lingo. If you are interested in creating Xtras, start with the Xtras Developer Kit (XDK) on the Director CD-ROM.

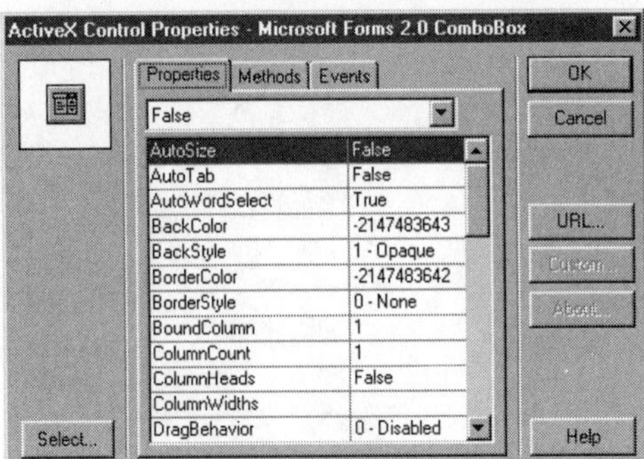

Figure 15.24 Select an ActiveX control to insert into a movie.

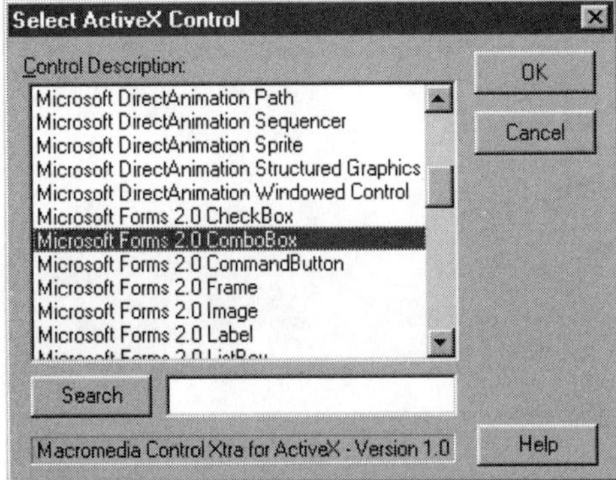

Figure 15.25 View and edit information about the control's properties, methods, and events in the ActiveX Control Properties dialog box.

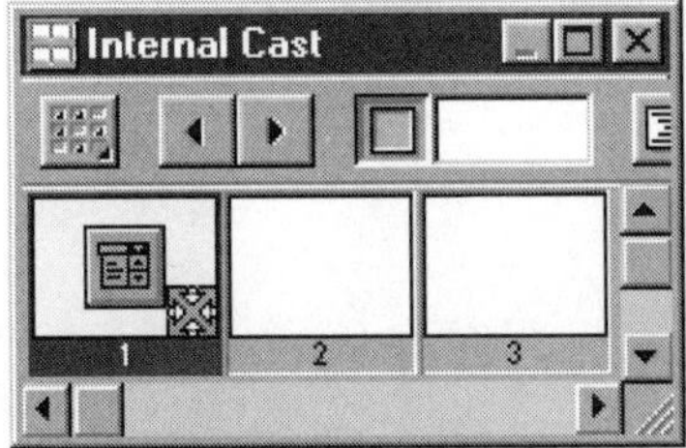

Figure 15.26 The ActiveX control becomes a cast member.

ActiveX Controls (Windows)

Director for Windows allows you to incorporate ActiveX controls into your movies as sprites. ActiveX controls, much like Xtras, can extend the functionality of Director in many ways. You can install the Microsoft Web Browser control (available with Internet Explorer 3.0 or later) to allow your users to browse the Internet from within a movie, for example.

To add an ActiveX control to a movie (Windows):

1. Make sure that any ActiveX controls you want to include in a movie are installed on your system.
2. Choose Insert > Control > ActiveX.

   The Select ActiveX Control dialog box opens.
3. Choose an ActiveX control (**Figure 15.24**).
4. Click OK.
5. Use the Select ActiveX Control dialog box to view and edit information about the control's properties, methods, and events (**Figure 15.25**).
6. Click OK to add the ActiveX control to the active Cast window (**Figure 15.26**).
7. Drag the ActiveX control from the Cast window to the score or to the stage, where it can be resized and positioned like a sprite Xtra.

16

Adding Behaviors

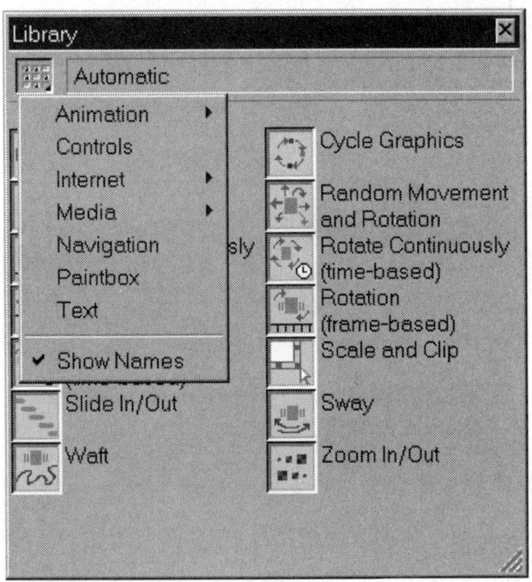

Figure 16.1 The Library Palette contains ready-to-use behaviors grouped by category.

You can add interactive features to movies without having to write or understand Lingo, Director's scripting language. You simply drag a *behavior* (a prefabricated Lingo script) onto a sprite or frame to make it perform certain actions automatically or in response to specific events during your movie. Typical events include a click of a sprite or the entry of the playback head into a specific frame.

Director provides a Library Palette of ready-to-use behaviors grouped by categories, including Animation, Internet, and Navigation (**Figure 16.1**).

In this chapter, you learn to assign Director's drag-and-drop behaviors to sprites and frames, how to modify the supplied behaviors, and even how to create your own behaviors within the Behavior Inspector. A couple of specific examples get you started building behavior interactivity into your movies.

Even if you plan to acquire Lingo scripting skills, it's a good idea to experiment first with behaviors to develop a feel for what Lingo can do.

Assigning Behaviors

You incorporate a behavior into your movie by assigning it to a sprite in a sprite channel (**Figure 16.2**) or a frame in the script channel (**Figure 16.3**). You can assign multiple behaviors to a single sprite, but only one to a frame.

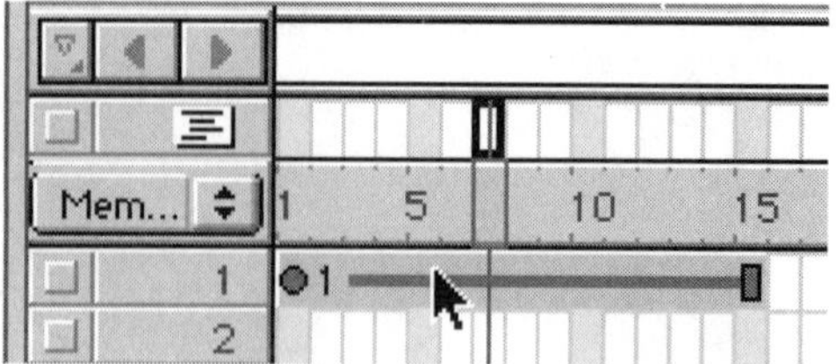

Figure 16.2 A behavior dragged to a sprite channel.

If the behavior is interactive, you specify what event, usually in the form of user input, triggers the behavior assigned to a sprite. A mouse click, for example, can trigger the action. A behavior assigned to a frame is triggered only when the specified event occurs while the playback head is in that frame.

Figure 16.3 A behavior dragged to a frame in the script channel.

Certain behaviors make sense only when applied to sprites, such as the Animation > Automatic behaviors such as Fade In/Out or Sway. Certain other behaviors belong only to frames, such as the Streaming behavior called Jump When Media in Frame Is Available.

Behavior description

Library

Automatic

Color Cycling | Cycle Graphics | Fade In/Out | Random Movement and Rotate to Follow Path | Rotate Continuously (frame-based) | Rotate Continuously (time-based) | Scale and Clip | Slide In/Out | Sway | Wait | Zoom In/Out

Zoom In/Out

Zooms sprite in and out. Use with graphic and text sprites. A sprite can zoom in once, multiple times, or continuously.

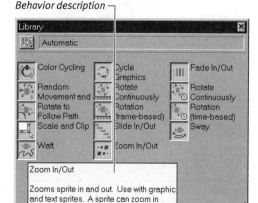

Figure 16.4 Hold the mouse pointer over a behavior icon in the Library Palette to display a description of the behavior.

The Library Palette comes with a built-in cheat sheet: If you hold the mouse pointer over a behavior icon in the Library Palette, a description of the behavior pops open, including a brief tip on how to use it (**Figure 16.4**).

After you assign a built-in behavior to a sprite or frame, that behavior goes into the Cast window (**Figure 16.5**), where you are free to modify it. Then you can assign that single behavior from the cast window to multiple sprites and frames. You cannot modify the original behaviors stored in the Library Palette. Any new behaviors you create are also stored in the Cast window.

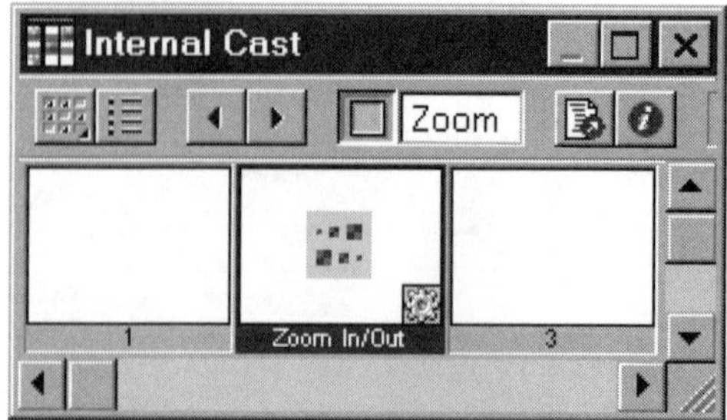

Figure 16.5 A behavior cast member.

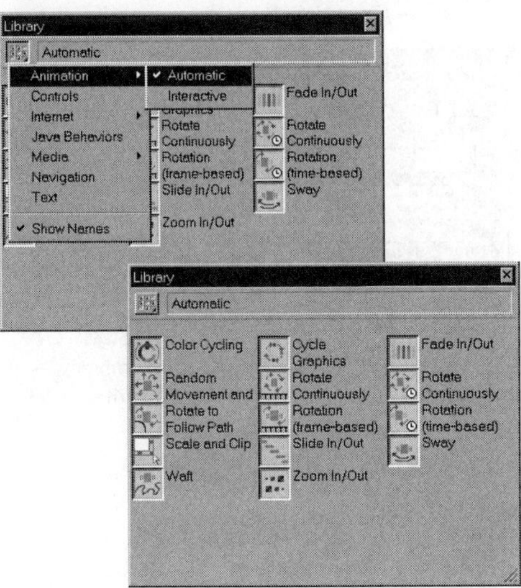

Figure 16.6 Choose a category of behaviors from the Library List pop-up menu.

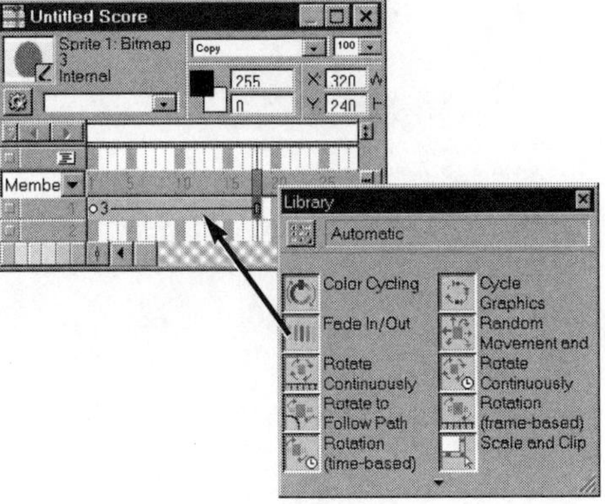

Figure 16.7 Drag a behavior from the Library Palette to a sprite in the score.

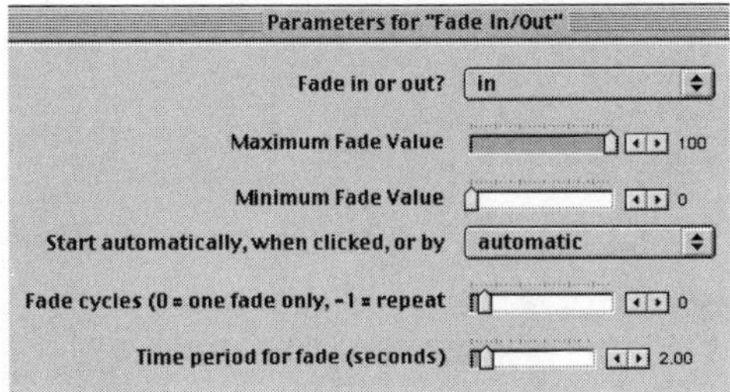

Figure 16.8 Choose settings for the behavior—in this case, parameters for the Fade In/Out behavior.

To assign a built-in behavior to a sprite or frame:

1. Choose Window > Score.
2. Choose Window > Library Palette.
3. In the Library Palette window, choose a category of behaviors from the Library List pop-up menu (**Figure 16.6**).
4. Drag a behavior from the Library Palette to a sprite in the score (**Figure 16.7**) or on the stage, or to a frame in the script channel (**Figure 16.3**).

   Director copies the behavior to the active cast. Dragging the same behavior from the Library Palette multiple times to different sprites or frames creates a new behavior cast member for each instance. Alternatively, one behavior can be assigned to multiple sprites.

   As already discussed,whether you drag the behavior to a sprite or the script channel depends on the type of behavior and what you're trying to accomplish with it.
5. If a Parameters window appears, provide the additional information requested to tailor how the behavior works; then click OK.

   If you assign the Fade In/Out behavior, for example, enter the parameters shown in **Figure 16.8**.

After you assign a built-in behavior to a sprite or frame, a behavior cast member is created, and you can reuse it over and over. Remember that each time you drag a behavior from the Library Palette to a sprite or frame, a new behavior cast member is created even if the same one is already in a cast.

To assign a behavior cast member to a sprite or frame:

1. Open the cast window that contains the required behavior.
2. Open the Score window.
3. Drag the behavior from the cast to a sprite or a frame in the script channel.

If the cast-member behavior uses parameters, you are prompted to set them for each instance to which the behavior is assigned. The original cast-member behavior is not altered. (See the section titled "To re-enter parameters for an assigned behavior" to learn how to change behavior parameters for a specific instance.)

To delete all behaviors assigned to a sprite or frame:

1. In the score, select the sprite or frame in the script channel.
2. Choose Clear All Behaviors from the Script pop-up menu in the Score's Sprite toolbar (**Figure 16.9**).

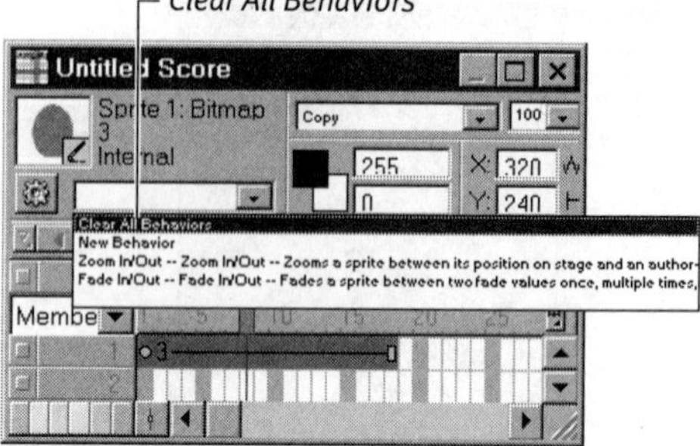

Figure 16.9 Choose Clear All Behaviors from the Script pop-up menu in the Score's Sprite toolbar.

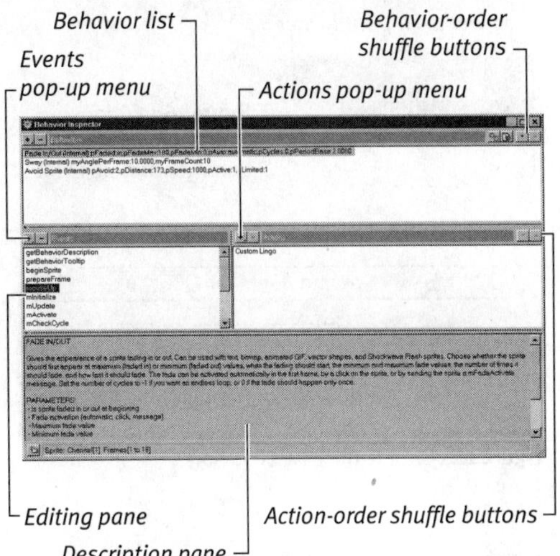

Figure 16.10 You control behaviors in the Behavior Inspector. This one is for the Library behaviors.

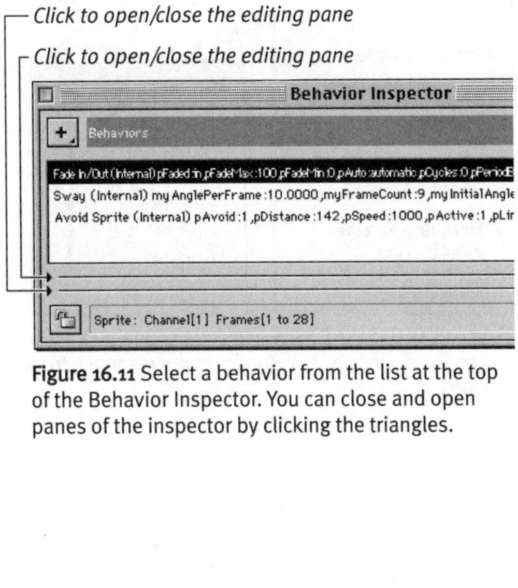

Click to open/close the editing pane

Click to open/close the editing pane

Figure 16.11 Select a behavior from the list at the top of the Behavior Inspector. You can close and open panes of the inspector by clicking the triangles.

Using the Behavior Inspector

Use the Behavior Inspector when you want to create a new behavior, modify an existing one, or change the order in which behaviors are executed for a given sprite.

To open and use the Behavior Inspector:

1. Select a sprite or a frame in the script channel.

   If you are creating a new behavior, you don't need to select a sprite or frame first. But if you want to view or modify a sprite or frame's behavior, select the object first.

2. Choose Window > Inspectors > Behavior.

   The Behavior Inspector opens (**Figure 16.10**). The top of the inspector lists all behaviors that have been assigned to the sprite or frame.

3. Select a behavior from the behavior list at the top of the Behavior Inspector (**Figure 16.11**).

4. If you want to modify the behavior, open the editing pane, if necessary, by clicking its small triangle.

5. If you need information about the behavior, open the description pane by clicking its triangular button (**Figure 16.10**).

   All built-in behaviors have a description.

✔ Tip

- To adjust the size of the editing and description panes, drag the dark line at the bottom of each section.

Creating Behaviors

Although Director's built-in behaviors provide a wealth of interactive possibilities, you may need to go further and create your own custom behaviors. This section shows you how to do so and provides two simple examples. One example behavior triggers a beep when a user clicks a sprite. The other example is a navigation behavior that makes the movie reset to a specific frame when the user removes the mouse pointer from a sprite.

To create a behavior:

1. Open the Behavior Inspector.
2. Choose New Behavior from the Behavior pop-up menu (**Figure 16.12**).

   The Name Behavior dialog box opens.
3. Type a name for the behavior and click OK (**Figure 16.13**).

   The behavior is added to the cast window as a behavior cast member. So far, the cast member is an empty shell.

   Next, you need to define the behavior by specifying which actions should occur in response to specific events.
4. If necessary, click the triangular open-pane buttons in the Behavior Inspector to display the editing and description panes.
5. Choose from the Events pop-up menu an event that should trigger your behavior's action (**Figure 16.14**).
6. From the Actions pop-up menu, choose a category of action and then a specific action that the event should trigger.
7. Set parameters, if necessary, for the given action.

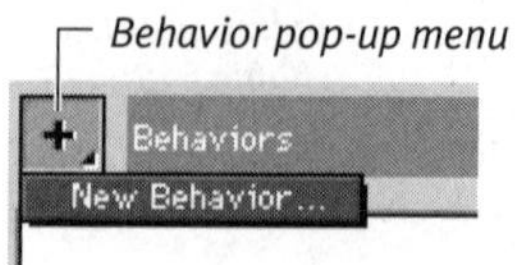

Figure 16.12 Choose New Behavior from the Behavior pop-up menu.

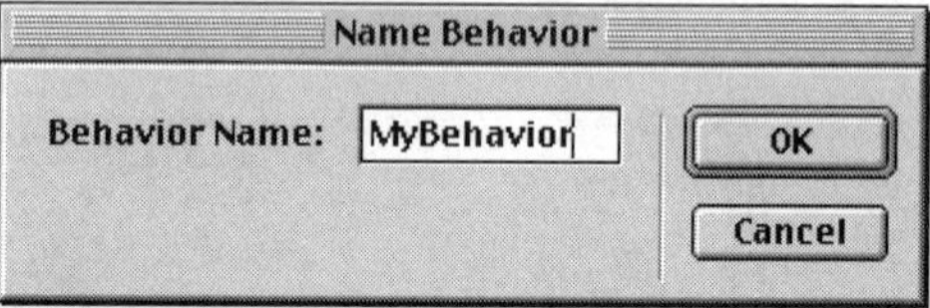

Figure 16.13 Name the new behavior.

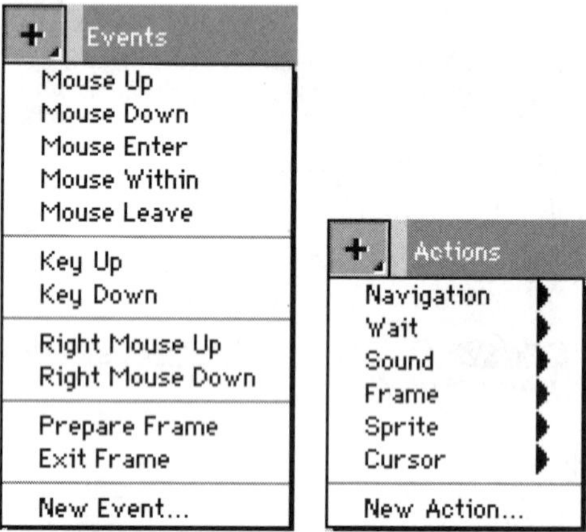

Figure 16.14 Use the Events and Actions pop-up menus to specify which actions occur in response to which events.

Figure 16.15 Open the Behavior Inspector.

Figure 16.16 Choose Mouse Down to have the sprite make a sound when a user clicks.

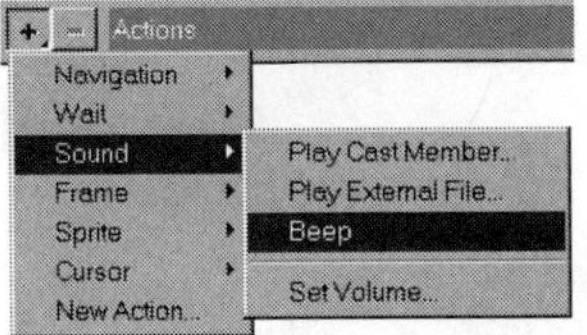

Figure 16.17 Choose Sound > Beep from the Actions pop-up menu.

8. Repeat steps 5–7 to add as many events and actions as necessary.

   Remember that a behavior can have multiple events, and each event can trigger multiple actions. Actions for any event are executed in the order listed in the Actions list.

9. Close the Behavior Inspector.

10. Drag the behavior from the cast window to a sprite in the movie or a frame in the score.

✔ Tip

- Always play back the movie to check the new behavior and then adjust the behavior settings, if necessary.

The following behavior makes a sprite produce a beep when clicked.

To create a sound behavior:

1. Open the Behavior Inspector (**Figure 16.15**).

2. Choose New Behavior from the Behavior pop-up menu to display the Name Behavior dialog box.

3. Name the behavior and click OK.

   The behavior is added to the cast window.

4. Open the editing pane, if necessary.

5. Choose Mouse Down from the Events pop-up menu (**Figure 16.16**).

6. Choose Sound > Beep from the Actions pop-up menu (**Figure 16.17**).

7. Close the Behavior Inspector.

8. Drag the new behavior from the cast window to a sprite in your movie.

9. Play back the movie and click the sprite to test the sound.

Sometimes, you want to be able to reset the frame when a user finishes an activity. The following example is a simple way to enhance a sprite with a behavior. When the mouse pointer leaves the bounding box of the sprite, the playback head jumps to a frame that you specify.

To create a frame-reset behavior:

1. Open the Behavior Inspector.
2. Choose New Behavior from the Behavior pop-up menu to display the Name Behavior dialog box.
3. Name the behavior and click OK.
   The behavior is added to the cast window.
4. Open the editing pane in the Behavior Inspector by clicking the top small triangle (**Figure 16.18**).
5. Choose Mouse Leave from the Events pop-up menu (**Figure 16.19**).
6. Choose Navigation > Go to Frame from the Actions pop-up menu (**Figure 16.20**).
   The Specify Frame dialog box opens.
7. Type a frame number and click OK (**Figure 16.21**).
8. Close the Behavior Inspector.
9. Drag the new behavior from the cast window to a sprite in your movie.

Figure 16.18 Open the editing pane by clicking the small triangle, if the pane is not already open.

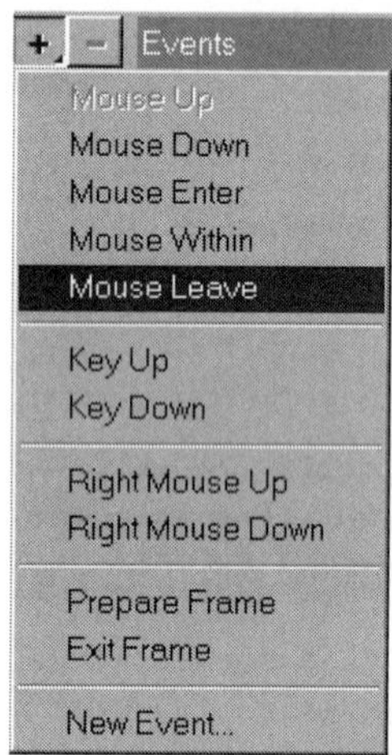

Figure 16.19 Choose Mouse Leave from the Events pop-up menu.

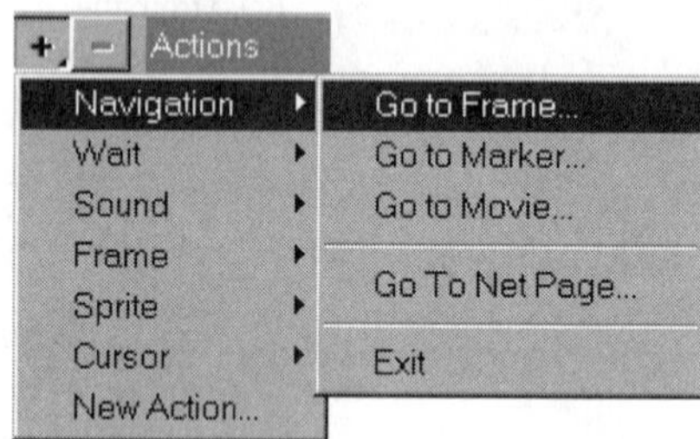

Figure 16.20 Choose Navigation > Go to Frame from the Actions pop-up menu.

Figure 16.21 Enter a frame number and click OK.

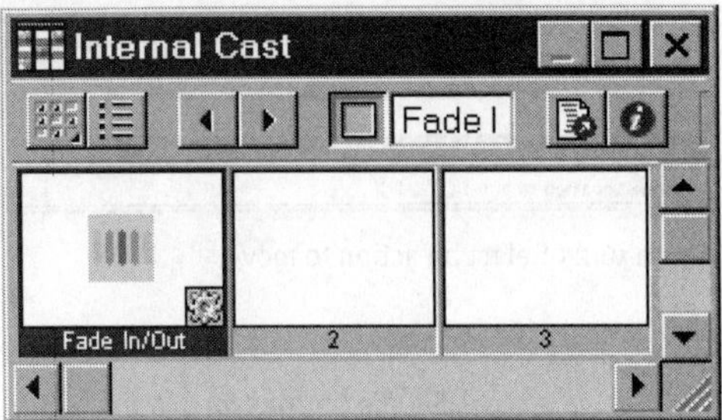

Figure 16.22 Drag a behavior to a cast window.

Figure 16.23 If the editing pane is hidden, click the small triangle to open it.

Figure 16.24 Modify the behavior actions and events with the pop-up menus in the editing pane.

Modifying Behaviors

Some behaviors come ready to use without modification, but most need a little tweaking to fit your needs. Modifying a behavior is simple, especially if you adjust the behavior before you assign it to any cast members, sprites, or frames.

To modify a built-in behavior:

1. Choose Window > Library Palette to display the Library Palette.
2. Drag a behavior to a cast window (**Figure 16.22**).
3. In the cast window, double-click the behavior.

   The Behavior Inspector opens, containing the selected behavior.
4. If necessary, click the small triangle to open the editing pane (**Figure 16.23**).
5. In the editing pane, use the Events and Actions pop-up menus to change which events trigger which actions and/or to add new events and actions (**Figure 16.24**).
6. Close the Behavior Inspector.
7. Drag the modified behavior cast member to a sprite or frame to test it.

✔ Tip

- You can make more detailed changes in a behavior by editing its Lingo script directly. To do so, select the behavior in the cast window and click the Script button to open the Script window.

Sometimes, after testing, you realize that a behavior would work better if you could rearrange its sequence of actions. Remember that if you change the behavior cast member, you change the behavior of any sprites to which it is assigned.

To reorder actions in a behavior:

1. Double-click a behavior in the cast window to open it in the Behavior Inspector.
2. If necessary, open the editing pane by clicking the small triangle.
3. In the Events list, select the event for which you want to reorder actions.
4. Select an action to move within the sequence of actions (**Figure 16.25**).
5. In the Behavior Inspector, click the Shuffle Up or Shuffle Down button to move the selected action up or down in the list (**Figure 16.26**).
6. Close the Behavior Inspector and test the modified behavior.

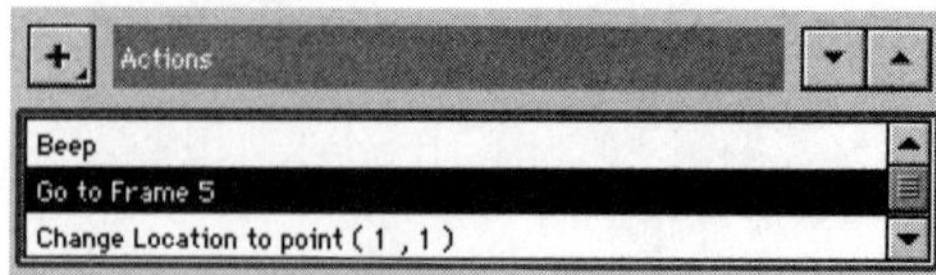

Figure 16.25 Select an action to move.

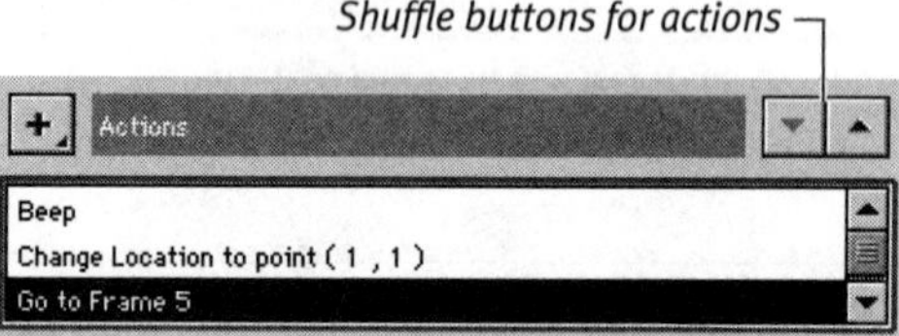

Figure 16.26 Click the Shuffle Up or Shuffle Down button to move the selected action to a new place in the sequence.

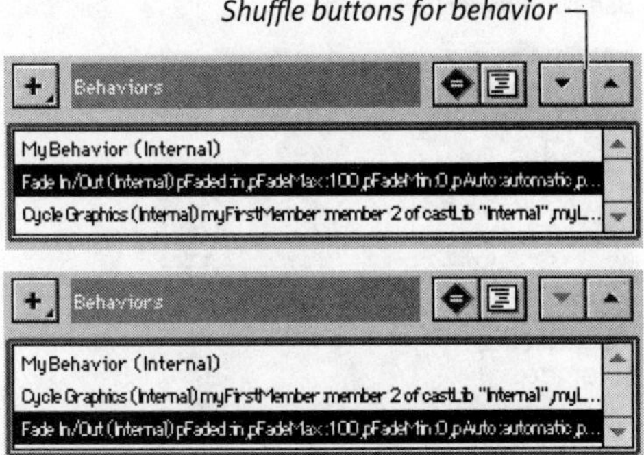

Figure 16.27 Click the Shuffle Up or Shuffle Down button to reorder the selected behavior. Here, the selected behavior moves down in the list.

To remove an action or event from a behavior:

1. Double-click a behavior in the cast window to open it in the Behavior Inspector.
2. Open the editing pane by clicking the small triangle.
3. Select the action or event in the Actions or Events box.
4. Press Delete.

To change the order of behaviors assigned to a sprite:

1. Select a sprite with behaviors that require reordering.
2. Open the Behavior Inspector.
3. Select a behavior from the list.
4. Use the Shuffle Up and Shuffle Down buttons at the top of the window to change the order of the selected behavior (**Figure 16.27**).
5. Select any other behaviors that you want to move, and shuffle them in the list.
6. When you finish moving behaviors around, close the Behavior Inspector and test the sprite's behaviors.

You can change the parameters for a behavior already assigned to a sprite or frame without altering the cast-member behavior or reassigning the behavior. You may want to change the number of degrees through which a sprite rotates for the Animation > Automatic > Rotation (frame-based) behavior, for example.

To re-enter parameters for an assigned behavior:

1. In the score, select a sprite or frame with an assigned behavior.
2. In the Sprite toolbar, click the Behavior Inspector button (**Figure 16.28**) to display the Behavior Inspector.
3. Select the behavior for which you want to modify parameters.
4. Click the Parameters button (**Figure 16.29**).
5. Change the parameters and click OK.

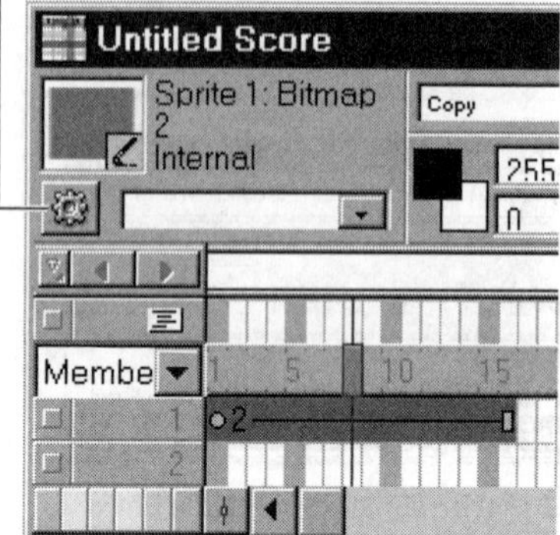

Figure 16.28 Click the Behavior Inspector button in the Sprite toolbar.

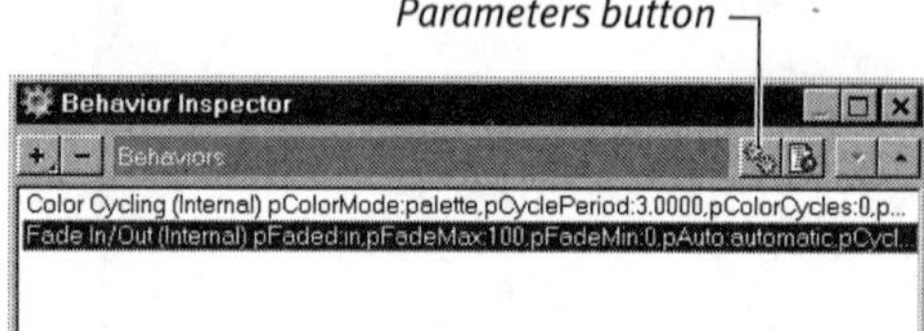

Figure 16.29 Click the Parameters button in the Behavior Inspector.

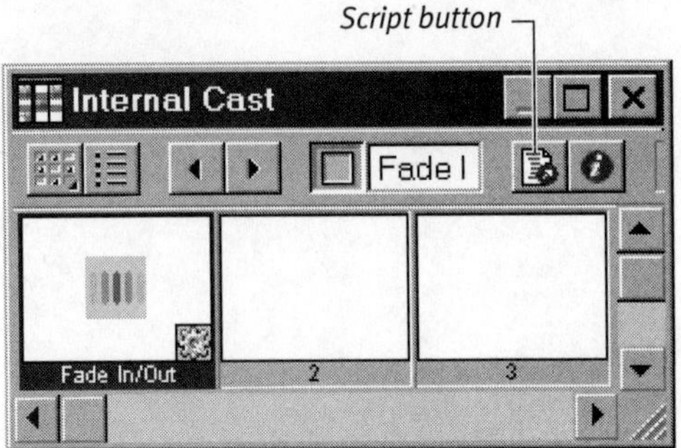

Figure 16.30 Open a behavior's script by clicking the Script button in a cast window.

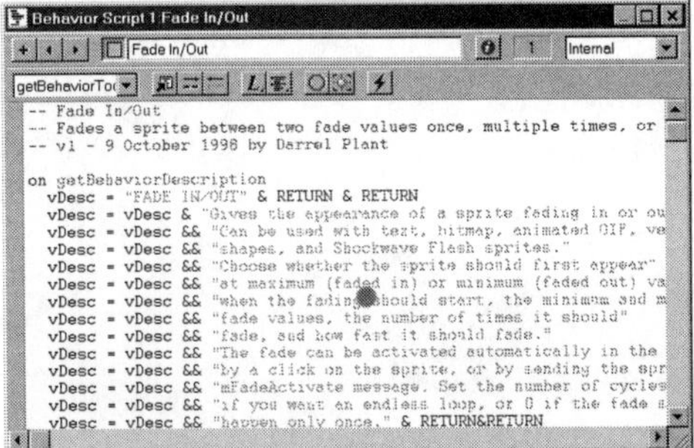

Figure 16.31 In the Script window, make any desired changes in the script and then close the window.

Because a behavior is technically a script cast member, if you know how to do scripting, you can edit its Lingo code in a Script window. Doing so affects all sprites and frames to which the behavior is assigned.

To edit a behavior in a Script window:

1. Select a behavior in a cast window.
2. Click the script button to open the Script window (**Figure 16.30**).
3. Modify the script (**Figure 16.31**).
4. Close the Script window and test the modified behavior.

17 Scripting Lingo

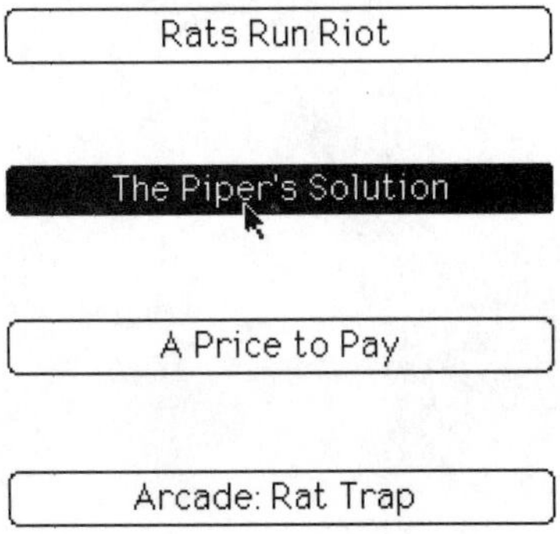

Rats Run Riot

The Piper's Solution

A Price to Pay

Arcade: Rat Trap

Figure 17.1 One application of Lingo is adding navigational controls to your movie. Your users need not view scenes in the order set in the score; they can choose where to begin—or resume.

Lingo, Director's scripting language, adds an intelligent, interactive dimension to your multimedia productions. Through Lingo, you enable users to communicate with your movie; they can type text and click on sprites, and your movie can respond to these inputs in limitless ways.

Lingo allows your movie to go beyond what is normally possible when you are authoring only through the score. You can use Lingo to offer your users navigational control of the order in which the scenes of your movie are played (**Figure 17.1**), or you can script sprites or cast members to change in response to user input. You can write a script that causes a sprite's color to change when a user clicks it, for example. In fact, you can write scripts that allow user input to affect virtually every aspect of your movie — sound, positions of sprites, text input/output, and many other attributes for limitless interactive possibilities.

Suppose that you want something to happen when a user clicks a particular sprite in your movie. What do you do to set it up? To put a response in place, you need to write a script (**Figure 17.2**) or use the prefabricated scripts known as *behaviors*, covered in Chapter 16, "Adding Behaviors." Writing a script gives you more control over how your movie responds than using behaviors from the Library palette.

This chapter introduces the basics of Lingo scripts, with a few examples that will help you put Lingo to work. The chapter covers types of scripts and how they differ, the basics of writing a script, ways to assign a script to a movie or one of its elements, and specific instructions for navigation and simple sprite and cast-member interactivity.

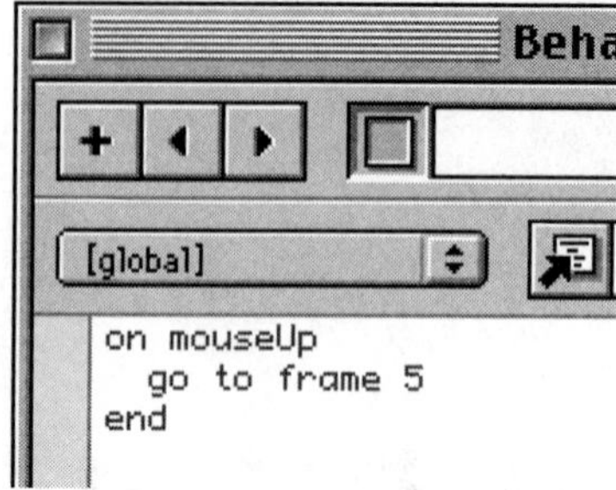

Figure 17.2 A Lingo script tells Director how your movie should respond when specific events occur during play. You write and edit scripts in the Script window.

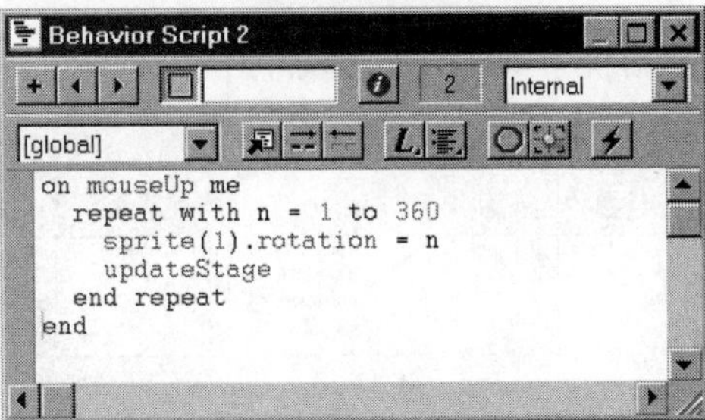

Figure 17.3 A sample Lingo script.

Understanding Scripts

A Lingo *script* is a set of instructions that you write in a script window to tell Director how your movie should respond when specific events occur during play. Examples of events include user input through the mouse and keyboard. Other events are non-input-oriented, such as the playback head entering a new frame. (Events are discussed in detail in "Understanding Handlers, Messages, and Events" later in this chapter

The instructions in a Lingo script are organized into *handlers*. Each handler starts with the word `on` and ends with the word `end`. The word after `on` is the specific event the handler should respond to (such as `on mouseDown`). Handlers are discussed in "Understanding Handlers, Messages, and Events" later in this chapter

Lingo instructions must always be valid combinations of Lingo elements, some of which are introduced throughout this chapter in sample scripts (**Figure 17.3**). All Lingo elements are defined in Director's Lingo Dictionary, which you can open by choosing Help > Lingo Dictionary.

You attach a script to one of the following objects or elements in your Director movie: a sprite, a frame in the script channel, a cast member, or the movie itself. The object or element to which you attach a script determines when and where its instructions are available for execution. This is very important. Because many scripts in a movie can respond to the same kind of event (such as releasing the mouse button), Director uses a precise hierarchy in determining which scripts get the first chance to respond *(see "Understanding Handlers, Messages, and Events" later in this chapter).* The type of object or element to which you attach the script also determines the *script type*—either *behavior, cast member, or movie* . (Behavior scripts include scripts

UNDERSTANDING SCRIPTS

attached to frames or sprites, also known as *score scripts.*) Director includes an advanced script type called *parent scripts*, a topic that is beyond the scope of this book.

All script types except cast-member scripts are themselves cast members (**Figure 17.4**). Following is a summary of the characteristics of behavior, cast-member, and movie script types. The next section shows you how to write them.

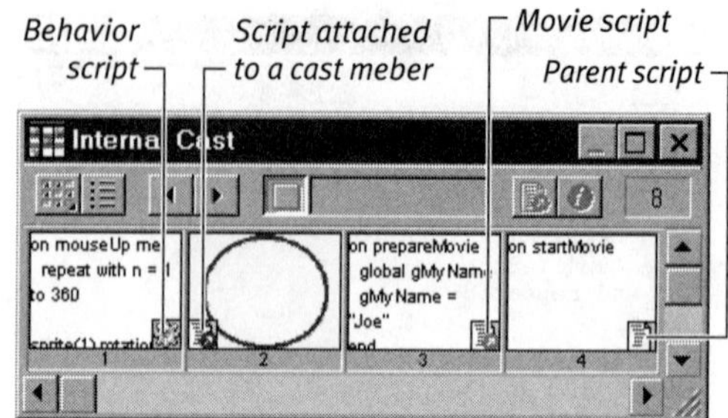

Figure 17.4 The various script cast members. Note that scripts attached to cast members are not themselves cast members.

Behavior scripts

Behaviors (*see Chapter 16, "Adding Behaviors"*) and *behavior scripts* are the same thing. The only difference is how you go about creating them. You can use the Behavior Inspector (**Figure 17.5**)—a menu-driven approach that involves the Events and Actions pop-up menus—or you can get under the hood and create a behavior by writing the script yourself (**Figure 17.6**). In either case, the cast-member types are the same. You use a behavior script by attaching it to a sprite or to a frame in the script channel. You do so by dragging the script from a cast window onto a sprite or frame in the script channel (just like you did in Chapter 16).

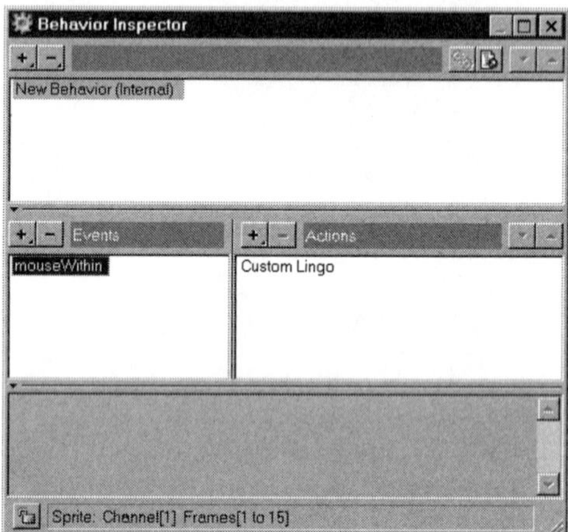

Figure 17.5 The Behavior Inspector offers a menu-driven approach to creating behaviors.

You can attach multiple behavior scripts to one sprite, but you can attach only one script per frame in the script channel. If a sprite has multiple behaviors that respond to the same event, each of them is executed in the order in which you attached them. You can see which behaviors have been attached to a sprite, and their order, by selecting the sprite and opening the Behavior Inspector. Other sprites based on the same cast member do not respond unless the script is attached to them as well.

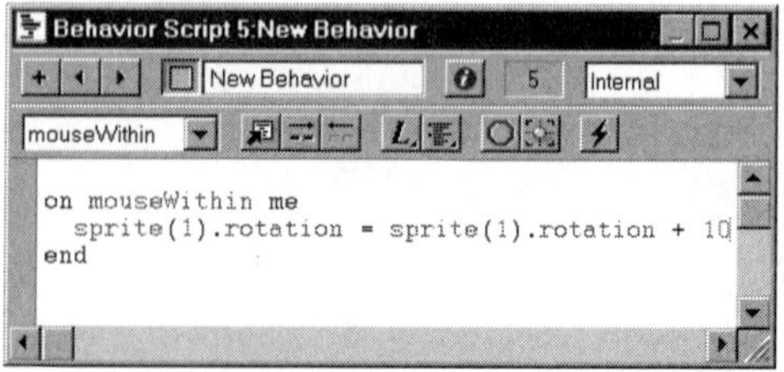

Figure 17.6 Writing behavior scripts gives you much more control than using the Behavior Inspector.

The events that can activate a behavior script attached to a sprite generally are mouse or keyboard input when the pointer is positioned on the sprite, or when the sprite begins or ends in the score (situations that are considered

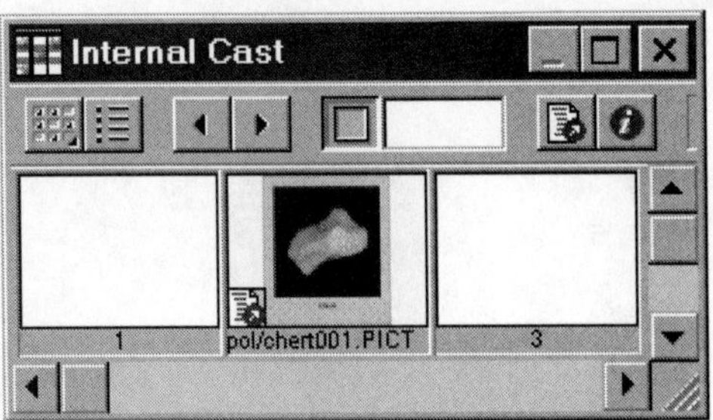

Figure 17.7 A cast member with an attached script.

to be events). When attached to a frame, the instructions in a behavior script are available to be executed only when the playback head is in a frame containing the script and when the specified event for which the script is waiting occurs, such as the `exitFrame` event.

Cast-member scripts

A *cast-member script* is attached to one cast member and can't be shared and reassigned the way a behavior script can. A cast-member script is the only script type that is not itself a cast member. When a cast member has been assigned a cast-member script, its thumbnail displays a special script symbol that is visible in the cast window (**Figure 17.7**). Only one script can be attached to a single cast member.

The type of events that can activate a cast-member script are limited to user input through the mouse or keyboard when the mouse pointer is on the cast member during play.

One advantage of a cast-member script is that its Lingo instructions can run when any sprite based on the cast member is activated—unlike a behavior script, which may or may not be attached to a particular sprite instance. You may want a button cast member to always produce the same response when it's clicked, no matter which sprite instance you click.

If a sprite has both a cast-member script and a behavior script associated with it, the behavior script takes precedence in trapping events. This is important to keep in mind when you decide which type of script to use. If a cast member should always perform the same function throughout your movie, such as causing a jump to a certain movie segment, use a cast-member script. On the other hand, if your cast member should respond differently depending on where it is activated in your movie, attach behavior scripts to the sprite instances.

Movie scripts

Movie scripts are available to the entire movie and are not explicitly attached to any object. Handlers in movie scripts generally are the most accessible, because they are available any time during playback. Consequently, the type of events movie scripts are used to trap usually are not sprite-specific. Movie scripts are a good place to handle events relating to the movie's starting and stopping (which correspond to the `startMovie` and `stopMovie` handlers).

If your movie contains two movie scripts that respond to the same event (they both use the same handler), only the first one that Director finds is executed. The other movie script is ignored.

Figure 17.8 The title bar in a script window indicates its type.

Writing Scripts

Before you learn the technical details about how Director processes scripts, as well as their hierarchy, you need to learn the basics of writing scripts. Lingo scripts are written in script windows, which you can open in Director in several ways. How you open a script window is important, because it determines the type of script the window will contain. A script window's type is indicated in its title bar (**Figure 17.8**).

The examples in this section show you how to create behavior, cast-member, and movie scripts. The following section elaborates on handlers, messages, and events, and how they affect the type of script you choose to create. An explanation of the various language elements of Lingo is provided in the section "Understanding Lingo Elements."

As you write in a script window, you'll notice that Director automatically indents and color-codes the various elements of your Lingo statements.

The following example shows you how to create a behavior script attached to a frame. (Remember that scripts attached to frames or sprites are collectively called behavior scripts.) This script causes the playback head to jump to frame 1 each time it reaches frame 5 as your movie is playing.

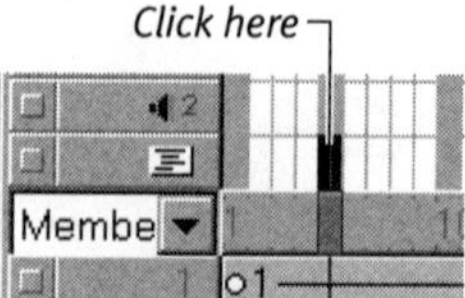

Figure 17.9 Select the fifth frame in the script channel.

To write a behavior script attached to a frame:

1. Open the score window.
2. Click to select the fifth frame in the script channel (**Figure 17.9**).
3. Choose New Behavior from the Behaviors pop-up menu in the score window (**Figure 17.10**) to open a script window.

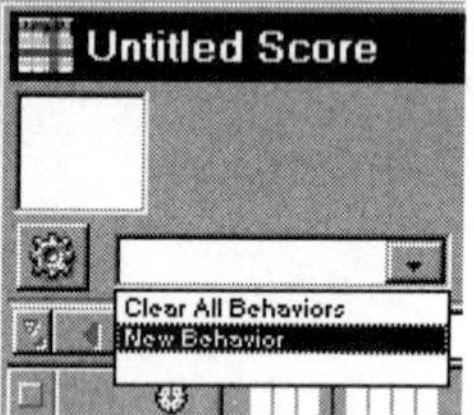

Figure 17.10 Choose New Behavior from the Behaviors pop-up menu.

4. In the script window that opens, type `go to frame 1` in the middle line (**Figure 17.11**).

   The first and last lines are provided automatically.

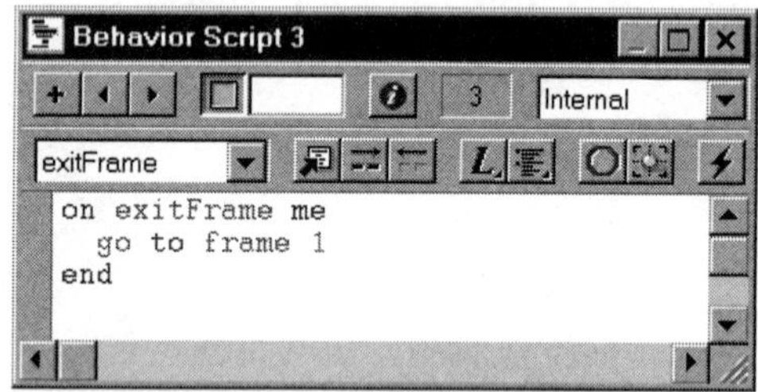

Figure 17.11 This script causes the playback head to loop back to frame 1.

5. Close the script window.

   The script becomes a behavior-script cast member that you can attach to other frames by dragging it from the cast window to another frame in the script channel.
6. Rewind and play your movie with the score still open.

   You should be able to see the playback head looping between frames 1 and 5 in the score.

✔ Tip

- As a shortcut, you can double-click a frame in the script channel to open the behavior script window.

Figure 17.12 Select the sprite.

Figure 17.13 This script makes the sprite move to the right each time it's clicked.

The following example shows you how to create a behavior script attached to a sprite. This particular script makes the sprite move to the right each time it's clicked on the stage.

To write a behavior script attached to a sprite:

1. Choose File > New > Movie.
2. Create a simple bitmap cast member in the paint window.
3. Place the cast member in the score to create a sprite.
4. Select the sprite in the score (**Figure 17.12**).
5. Choose New Behavior from the Behaviors pop-up menu in the score window to open a script window.
6. In the script window that opens, type `sprite(1).locH = sprite(1).locH + 10` on the middle line (**Figure 17.13**).

   The first and last lines are provided automatically.
7. Close the script window.

   The script becomes a behavior script cast member.
8. Choose Control > Loop Playback to set your movie to repeat.
9. Rewind and play your movie.
10. Click the sprite on the stage.

    The sprite should move to the right.

To write a behavior script that you can later attach to a sprite or frame:

1. Open a cast window and select an empty position.
2. Choose Window > Inspectors > Behavior to display the Behavior Inspector.
3. Click the Behavior button and choose New Behavior from the pop-up menu (**Figure 17.14**).
4. In the dialog box that opens, enter a name for the new behavior and click OK.
5. Click the Script Window button in the Behavior Inspector (**Figure 17.15**).
   An empty script window opens.
6. Type a script.
   For this example, enter the following script (**Figure 17.16**):
   ```
   on mouseUp
   alert "hello world"
   end
   ```
7. Close the script window.
8. Close the Behavior Inspector.
   Now you can attach this behavior script cast member to any sprite or frame in the score.

Figure 17.14 Click the Behavior pop-up button and choose New Behavior.

Figure 17.15 Click the Script Window button to open a Behavior Script window.

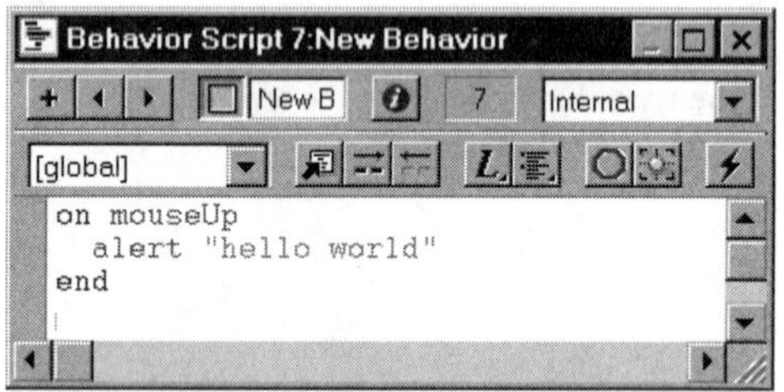

Figure 17.16 Attaching this script to a sprite, and clicking the sprite during playback, causes it to display the words "hello world" in a dialog box.

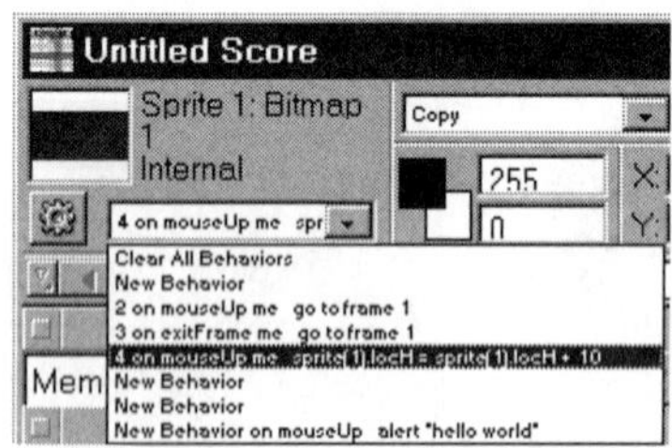

Figure 17.17 You can attach a behavior to a sprite by selecting the sprite and then choosing the behavior from the Behaviors pop-up menu in the score.

✔ Tips

- You can also attach a behavior to a sprite by selecting the sprite in the score and choosing the desired behavior from the Behaviors pop-up menu in the score (**Figure 17.17**). You can repeat this procedure as often as necessary to attach multiple behaviors.
- When you select a sprite in the score, the Behaviors pop-up menu displays which behavior has been attached to the sprite. If multiple behaviors have been attached, the pop-up menu displays <Multiple>.
- You can remove all behaviors attached to a sprite by selecting the sprite in the score and then choosing Clear All Behaviors from the Behaviors pop-up menu in the score.

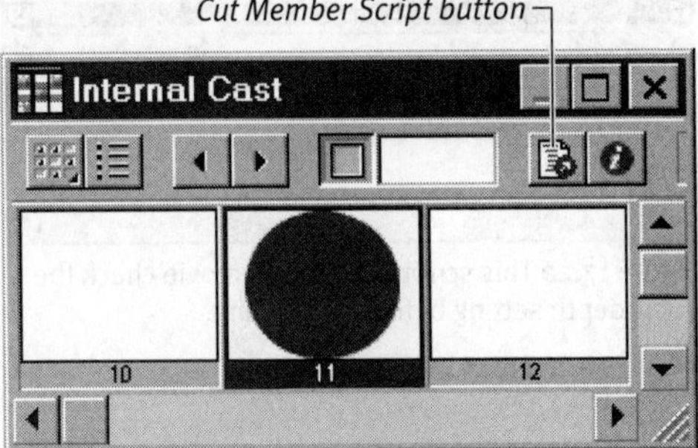

Figure 17.18 Select the cast member.

```
on mouseUp
  beep
end
```

Figure 17.19 This script makes a cast member beep when clicked during playback.

The following example shows you how to create a cast-member script. This script causes a cast member to beep when any sprite based on it is clicked on the stage.

To write a cast-member script:

1. Choose File > New > Movie.
2. Create a simple bitmap cast member in the paint window.
3. Place the cast member in the score to create a sprite.
4. Select this cast member in the cast window (**Figure 17.18**).
5. In the cast window, click the Cast Member Script button.
6. In the script window that opens, type **beep** on the middle line (**Figure 17.19**).

   The first and last lines are provided automatically.
7. Close the script window.

   The script is attached to the cast member but does *not* become a cast member itself. (Remember that cast-member scripts are the only type that are not cast members themselves.)
8. Choose Control > Loop Playback to set your movie to repeat.
9. Rewind and play your movie.
10. Click the sprite on the stage.

    You should hear a beep.

The following example shows you how to create a movie script. This script checks to see whether your computer's color depth is set to 16 bits or greater. If not, the script generates an alert message in a dialog box and then exits the movie.

To write a movie script:

1. Open the cast window and select an empty position.
2. Choose Window > Script.
   The Movie Script window opens and is empty.
3. Type a script.
   For this example, type the following (**Figure 17.20**):

```
on startMovie
   if the colorDepth < 16 then
      alert "This movie requires 16
      → bit or greater color depth
      → to run"
      halt
   end if
end
```

4. Close the script window.
   The script becomes a movie script cast member.
5. Rewind and play your movie.
   If your computer's color depth is set to at least 16 bits, nothing should happen. Try changing the setting to less than 16 bits and running the movie again to see the alert message.

✔ Tip

- Lingo is not case-sensitive. For the sake of readability, however, use capital letters consistently in your scripts. Follow the conventions used in the Lingo Dictionary, as well as those provided in the example scripts throughout this chapter.

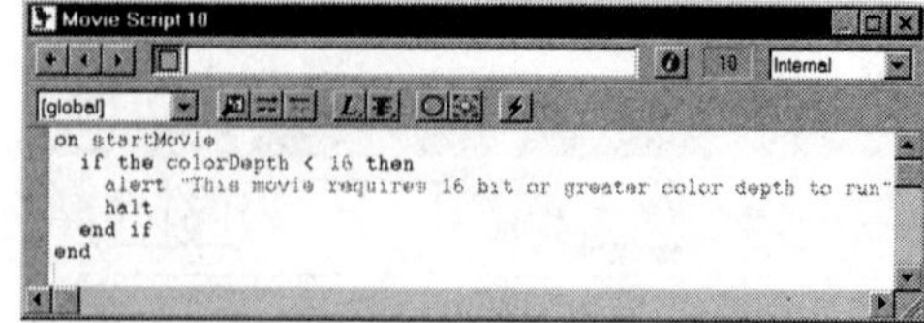

Figure 17.20 This script makes your movie check the color-depth setting before proceeding.

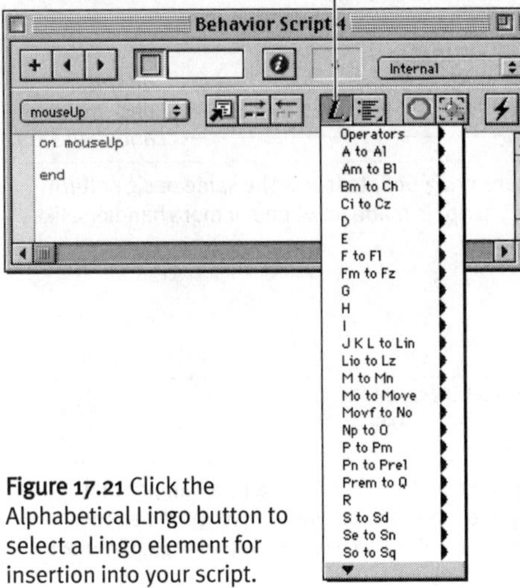

Figure 17.21 Click the Alphabetical Lingo button to select a Lingo element for insertion into your script.

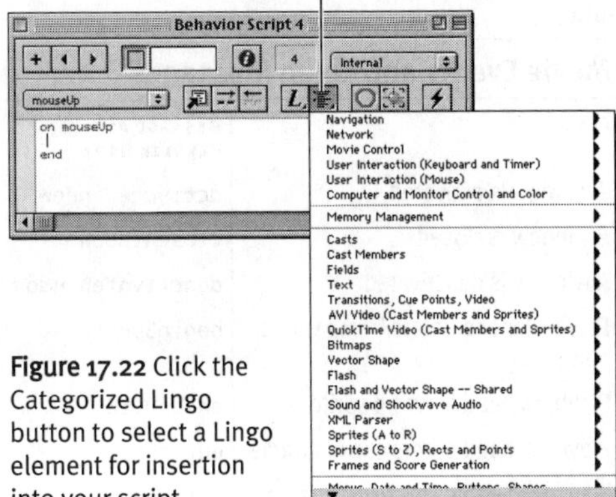

Figure 17.22 Click the Categorized Lingo button to select a Lingo element for insertion into your script.

To edit an existing script:

1. Open the cast window that contains the script you want to edit.
2. Select the script cast member.

   or

   If the script you want to edit is a cast-member script type, select the cast member to which it is attached.
3. Click the Cast Member Script button in the cast window.

   A script window opens.
4. Edit the script.
5. Close the window.

✔ Tips

- Double-clicking a movie or parent script cast member opens the script in a script window, as you would expect. But double-clicking a behavior script opens it in the Behavior Inspector. From there, you can access the script by clicking the Script Window button.
- Editing a behavior script affects the behavior of all sprites and frames to which it is attached.

To insert Lingo elements into a Script window automatically:

1. Open a Script window.
2. Click the script to place the insertion point where you want to insert the Lingo element.
3. Click either the Alphabetical Lingo (**Figure 17.21**) or Categorized Lingo button (**Figure 17.22**).
4. From the pop-up menu, choose the Lingo element that you want to insert into your script.

Understanding Handlers, Messages, and Events

The basic building block of Lingo scripts is the *handler*, which is triggered to run by a specific event during the playback of your movie (**Figure 17.23**) (technically, a handler is triggered by a message generated by the specific event, see "Events and Messages" below). A Lingo script is composed of one or more handlers.

A handler always starts with the word on, followed by the name of the message to which the handler should respond. Handlers go by the name of the message that triggers them. The example in **Figure 17.23** is called a mouseUp handler; it responds to a mouse message sent when a user releases the mouse button in a particular place in the movie.

The body of the handler script, which is the indented part, contains the commands, which are executed one after another when the handler is triggered. Handlers always end with the word end.

Events and messages

Events are the actions that occur in a movie to generate messages. The handlers wait for a corresponding message and then spring into action. Events include typing, clicking the mouse button, activating a window, and closing a window. Some events occur without the direct intervention of the user, such as the playback head entering a new frame as the movie plays (**Figure 17.24**).

Table 17.1 shows a partial list of common events that can occur while a movie is playing and the messages that they send. You can write handlers that respond to any of these built-in messages. You can also create custom handlers that respond to messages that you define, much like function calls, but that topic is beyond the scope of this book.

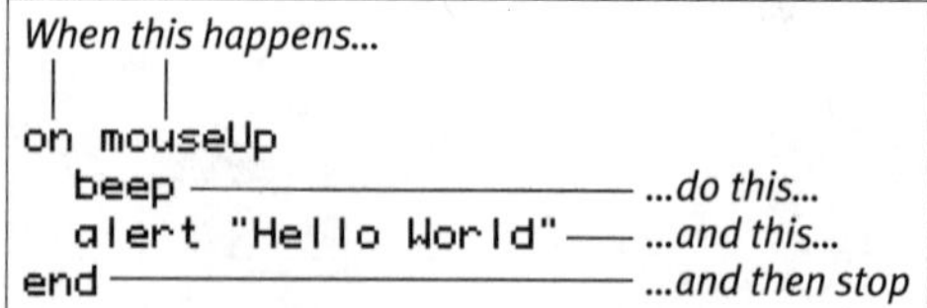

Figure 17.23 Scripts follow the same basic pattern. Each script is made up of one or more handlers, like this one.

```
on exitFrame
  go to frame 1
end
```

Figure 17.24 This script contains a handler that responds to the exitFrame message. When the handler receives an exitFrame message, the movie jumps to frame 1.

Table 17.1

Movie Events and Lingo Messages

Event	Message and Handler Name
A window is activated	activateWindow
A window is closed	closeWindow
A window is deactivated	deactivateWindow
Playback head enters frame with a new sprite	beginSprite
Playback head leaves a sprite	endSprite
Playback head enters current frame	enterFrame
Playback head exits current frame	exitFrame
No event occurred	idle
A key is pressed	keyDown
A key is released	keyUp
Mouse button pressed	mouseDown
Mouse button released	mouseUp
Pointer enters sprite's region	mouseEnter
Pointer leaves sprite's region	mouseLeave
Pointer stays within sprite's region	mouseWithin
Playback head enters a frame but has not drawn it yet	prepareFrame
Movie starts playing	startMovie
Movie stops playing	stopMovie

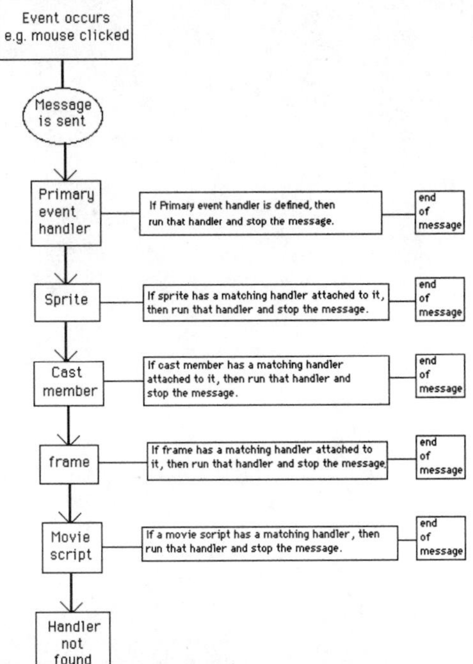

Figure 17.25 When the mouse pointer is positioned over a sprite, Director sends mouseUp, mouseDown, keyUp, and keyDown messages along in the order shown until it finds a handler. If no handler is found, nothing happens.

Handler hierarchy

Imagine that as Director is playing a movie, it is listening for any messages generated by all these events. Director checks to find out whether any handlers are present that are waiting for those messages. But because your movie can have multiple handlers responding to the same message (such as a mouseUp handler), there's a priority established for which handlers are given the chance to respond first.

Director uses a specific order for the type of scripts it looks in to find matching handlers. The order varies depending on the message and, in some cases, depending on which object in your movie is activated with the mouse pointer (as the following examples will make clear). Understanding this order is necessary to know where to put your scripts (which objects or elements to attach them to in Director).

Following is the order that Director uses to check for matching handlers for some common events/messages:

- For keyUp, keyDown, mouseUp, and mouseDown messages, the first thing Director looks for is a *primary event handler*, a handler that you define as the top-priority handler for a small subset of events (*see "Setting Up Primary Event Handlers" later in the chapter*). If no primary event handler is found, Director continues checking for a handler in one of two possible orders. If the mouse pointer is positioned over a sprite when any of these messages is generated, Director checks the following places for scripts with matching handlers (**Figure 17.25**): the activated sprite, the activated sprite's cast member, the current frame, and the movie (which can have many movie scripts, all of which are checked for a matching handler). If the mouse pointer is not positioned over a sprite, the order for `mouseUp`, `mouseDown`, `keyUp`, and `keyDown` messages is primary event handler, current frame, and movie scripts.

- For both the `enterFrame` and `exitFrame` messages, Director first checks the current frame for a matching handler (technically, in the script channel of the current frame) and then checks movie scripts.
- Director looks for matching handlers for the `idle`, `activateWindow`, `closeWindow`, `deactivateWindow`, `startMovie`, `stopMovie`, and `zoomWindow` messages in movie scripts.

  The Lingo Dictionary includes the order for other built-in messages.

Generally, when Director finds a matching handler for a particular message, the handler is executed, and the message does not continue to other objects in the hierarchy. One exception is when a sprite has multiple behavior scripts attached to it with the same handler. In this case, the scripts are executed in the order in which they were attached.

✔ Tip

- You can use the `Pass` and `StopEvent` commands to pass a message or to stop it from going on to the next level in the hierarchy after it has already encountered a matching handler. See the Lingo Dictionary for details.

Understanding Lingo Elements

You've learned that Lingo scripts are composed of handlers. Now you're ready to learn about the content of handlers.

A handler is composed of a combination of Lingo elements, which form the statements that you want to be executed when the handler is triggered. Like any other programming language, Lingo has rules about how you can use Lingo elements to produce valid statements. By working through the scripts in this chapter, you should get a good feel for the language structure (which is fairly simple, as programming languages go).

To get you started, here are the different categories of Lingo elements.

- **Commands** instruct your movie to do something. Following are some examples:

  `beep` – produces a beep

  `go to` – moves the playback head to a specified frame

  `updateStage` – makes Director redraw the stage immediately instead of between frames only

- **Functions** return a value. `time`, for example, returns the current time set in the computer.

- **Keywords** are reserved words in Lingo that have a special meaning. Examples include `the` and `me`.

- **Constants** are elements that never change. `TRUE` and `FALSE` are constants that always have the values 1 and 0, respectively.

- **Operators** are terms that compare, combine, or change one or more values. Examples include +, >, and -.

- **Properties** are the various attributes of an object. `locH`, for example, is a property of a sprite, indicating its horizontal position on the stage. You can use two syntaxes to refer to a property. You can use dot syntax, such as `sprite(1).locH`, or you can use Lingo's `the` keyword in the following manner: `the locH of sprite 1`. The former syntax tends to be more compact.
- **Variables** are storage places that you name and assign values to. Typing `a = 0` in your script, for example, creates a local variable named `a` and assigns the value `0` to it.
- **Expressions** are parts of Lingo statements that generate values, such as `(3 * 5) + 10`.

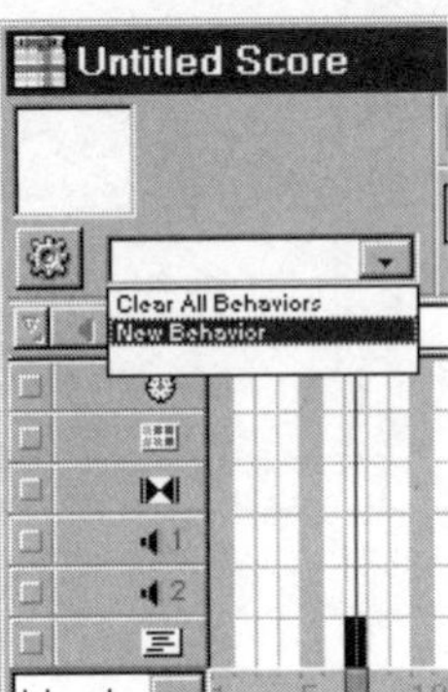

Figure 17.26 Select the last frame of the section you want to loop.

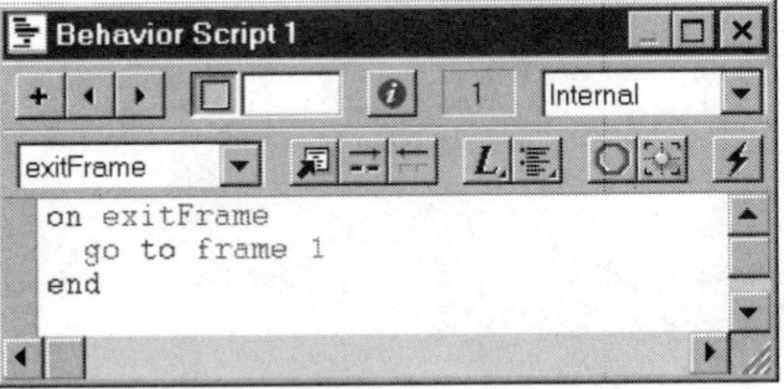

Figure 17.27 This script loops from the designated frame back to the first frame of the movie.

Scripting Navigation

All the techniques in this section script ways to jump around in a movie, from looping to jumping to a marker. You may notice that the example scripts omit the keyword `me`, which Director may include in your scripts automatically. For these examples, it won't make any difference whether you include or omit this keyword.

The following steps create a behavior script that causes the playback head to loop back to a previous frame each time it reaches the designated frame as your movie is playing.

To script a playback loop:

1. In the script channel of the score, select the last frame of the section you want to loop (**Figure 17.26**).
2. Choose New Behavior from the Behaviors pop-up menu in the score to open a Script window.
3. In the Behavior Script window that opens, type `go to frame x` as the middle line (**Figure 17.27**), with x being the frame to which you want to loop back.
4. Close the Script window.
5. Play the movie and make any necessary adjustments.

The following steps create an interactive cast member that, when clicked, causes a movie to jump to a new frame.

To script a jump to a specific frame:

1. Open the Cast window and select a cast member (**Figure 17.28**).
2. Click the Script button at the top of the Cast window.
3. As the middle line of the script, type `go to frame number` (**Figure 17.29**).
4. In the `number` field, enter the actual frame number for the destination of the jump (frame 57 in the example shown in **Figure 17.29**).
5. Close the Script window.
6. Play the movie and make any necessary adjustments.

✔ Tip

- You could just as well attach the script in this example to a sprite instead of a cast member, so that only that specific sprite causes a jump to a new frame when clicked.

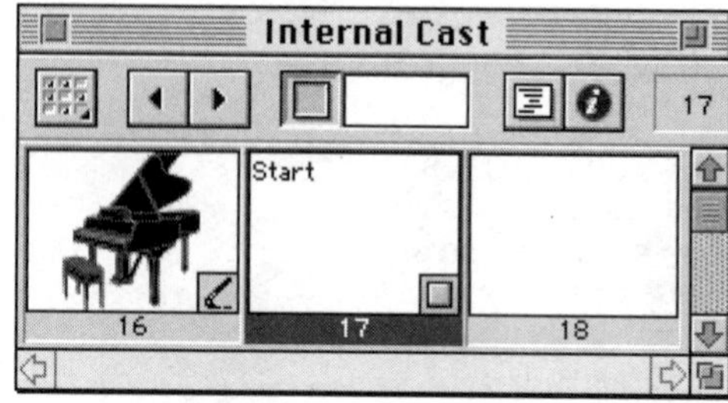

Figure 17.28 Select a cast member that will trigger a jump to a new frame.

```
on mouseUp
  go to frame 57
end
```

Figure 17.29 When attached to a cast member, this script causes the playback head to jump to frame 57 when the cast member is clicked.

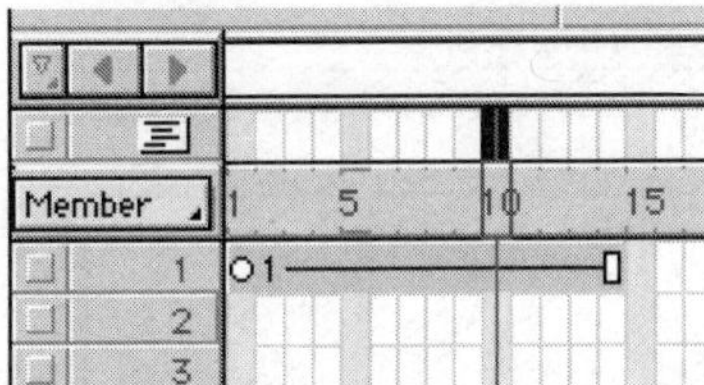

Figure 17.30 Select a frame in the script channel for the pause.

```
on exitFrame
  go to the frame
end
```

Figure 17.31 This script makes your movie pause when attached to a frame in the script channel.

The following steps create a behavior script that causes a movie to pause in a specific frame during playback.

To set a pause at a frame:

1. Open the score and select the frame in the script channel where you want the movie to pause (**Figure 17.30**).
2. Choose New Behaviors from the Behaviors pop-up menu in the score.
3. Type `go to the frame` between the two script lines that appear in the Script window (**Figure 17.31**).
4. Close the Script window.
5. Play the movie.

   The movie pauses at the designated frame, and remains paused until you stop the movie or until another script is activated that moves the playback head to a new frame.

✔ Tip

- As a means of unpausing the movie, you could attach a script to a sprite in this frame that would jump the movie to a new frame when the sprite is clicked.

The following steps create an interactive cast member that functions as a pause button. When the user clicks the cast member, the movie pauses. When the user clicks the cast member again, the movie resumes play.

To script a cast member to function as a pause button:

1. Open the Cast window and select a cast member that appears in your movie (**Figure 17.32**).
2. Click the Cast Member Script button at the top of the Cast window.
3. Delete the two lines that already appear in the Script window.
4. Type this script (**Figure 17.33**):

```
on mouseDown
   if the pauseState = TRUE then
      go to the frame+1
      else
      pause
   end if
end
```

5. Close the Script window.
6. Test the results and make any necessary changes.

✔ Tips

- PauseState is a movie property that is TRUE when the movie is paused and FALSE when it is not.
- The If-Then structure evaluates a statement and then branches, depending on the situation. If the statement is TRUE, the command after then is executed. If the statement is FALSE, the command after else is executed. (Look up the If keyword entry in the Lingo Dictionary for more details on the If-Then structure.)

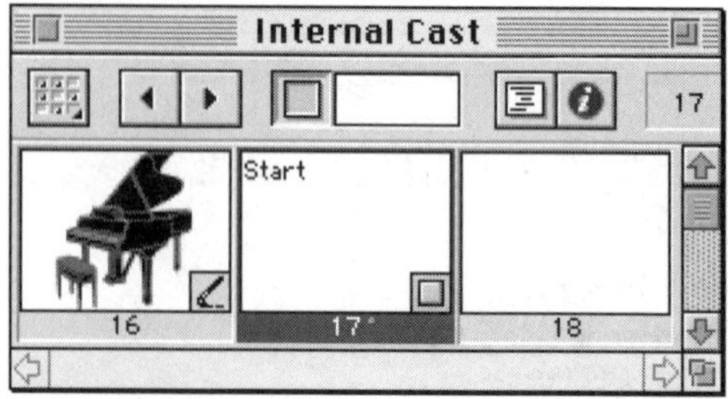

Figure 17.32 Select a cast member to pause your movie when clicked.

```
on mouseDown
  if the pauseState = TRUE then
    go to the frame+1
  else
    pause
  end if
end
```

Figure 17.33 When attached to a cast member, this script makes the cast member pause your movie when clicked and resume playing the movie when clicked again.

```
on mouseUp
  go to the frame -5
end
```

Figure 17.34 This script causes a jump to five frames before the current frame.

The following example uses a behavior script to demonstrate how to jump to a frame relative to the current frame. When the sprite is clicked, the playback head makes the jump.

To jump frames with the go to command:

1. Select a sprite in the score.
2. Choose New Behavior from the Behaviors pop-up in the score.
3. In the Script window that opens, type `go to the frame x` as the middle line of the script (**Figure 17.34**).

   `x` can be a positive or negative number that indicates the number of frames before or after the current frame for the jump.
4. Close the Script window.
5. Test the results and make any necessary changes.

You can use the `go to` command to move the playback head to a specific marker instead of to a frame number. Markers can label different segments of a movie (**Figure 17.35**).

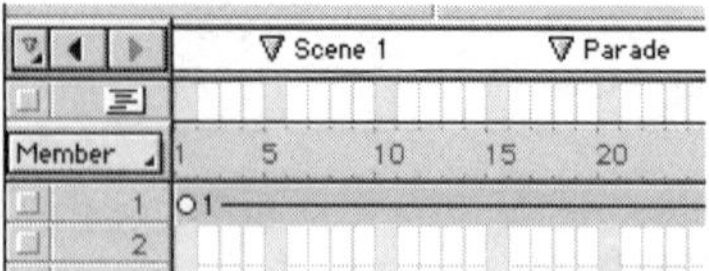

Figure 17.35 Markers label different segments of your movie, here in frames 5 and 18.

Lingo allows you to refer to a marker in relation to how many markers it is ahead of or behind the current frame. To jump to the nth marker ahead of the current frame, include the statement `go to marker(n)` in your script, such as `go to marker(2)` (**Figure 17.36**). This statement tells Director to jump to the second marker after the current frame.

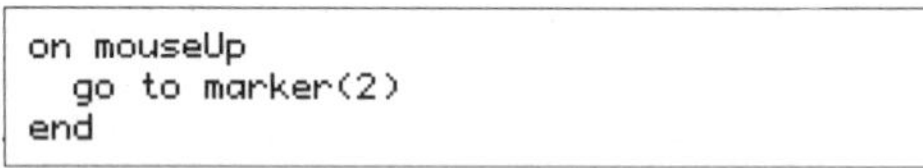

```
on mouseUp
  go to marker(2)
end
```

Figure 17.36 This script makes your movie jump to the second marker ahead of the current frame.

Similarly, to jump to the nth marker before the current frame, include the same statement, but make `n` a negative number. You can also jump to the next marker after the current frame by using the statement `go to next` (**Figure 17.37**). To jump to the marker immediately before the current frame, use `go to previous`. These commands are equivalent to `go to marker(1)` and `go to marker(-1)`.

```
on mouseUp
  go to next
end
```

Figure 17.37 This script makes a movie jump to the next marker after the current frame.

To use go to with a marker label:

In the body of a handler in your script, type the following line:

```
go to "Marker"
```

`Marker` is the name of the marker for the jump (**Figure 17.38**), In the example script, the marker is named Parade.

```
on mouseUp
  go to "Parade"
end
```

Figure 17.38 This script makes a movie jump to the frame of the movie labeled Parade.

```
on mouseUp
  play "scene3"
end
```

Figure 17.39 This script makes a movie branch to the marker labeled scene3.

```
on mouseUp
  play done
end
```

Figure 17.40 The `Play done` command returns the playback head to the frame where the branch occurred.

```
on mouseUp
  play movie "starblast"
end
```

Figure 17.41 This script makes a movie branch to a movie named starblast.

```
on mouseUp
  play frame "scene5" of movie "starblast"
end
```

Figure 17.42 This script branches to a marker label in a different movie.

Branching is the process in which the playback head jumps to a certain movie segment, plays that segment, and returns to the original frame. Suppose that your movie offers a tour of restaurants. This movie starts with a main menu of button sprites, each corresponding to a specific restaurant that you can view. When you click a button, Director jumps to a particular restaurant segment, plays that segment, and returns to the main menu. This branching is best accomplished by using the Lingo branch command `play` in your scripts.

To branch to a marker or frame:

1. Open a Script window for the script in which a branch should take place.
2. Type `play "marker"` and include the name of the destination marker (**Figure 17.39**).

   You can also type `play frame number`, in which `number` is the number of the destination frame.
3. At the end of the movie segment that is branched to in step 2, place the command `play done` in an appropriate script.

   This command returns the playback head to the frame from which the branch occurred (**Figure 17.40**).

✔ Tip

- You can branch to a different movie by using the Lingo statement `play movie "moviename,"` in which `moviename` is the name of the movie file (**Figure 17.41**). To branch to a marker in a different movie, use the statement `play frame "marker" of movie "moviename"` (**Figure 17.42**).

Using the Message Window

Director's Message window allows you to execute and evaluate Lingo commands and expressions immediately, simply by typing them. The Message window is also a very useful tool for debugging scripts.

To execute commands from the Message window:

1. Choose Window > Message to open the Message window.
2. Type a valid Lingo command or expression and then press Enter or Return.

   Type `go to frame 15` to move the playback head to frame 15, for example (**Figure 17.43**).

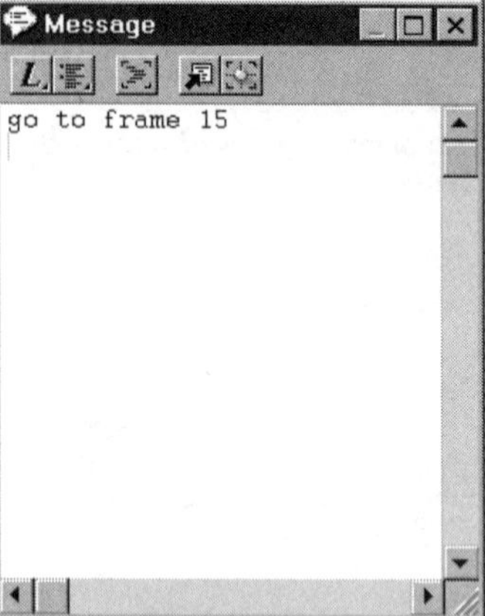

Figure 17.43 You can execute Lingo commands immediately from the Message window.

Use the `put expression` command to output the result of the expression to the Message window. You can type the `put` command in the Message window or use it from your scripts. When placed in a script, the `put` command can work as an effective debugging tool by outputting the current value of a variable, for example. Try typing the following examples in the Message window (**Figure 17.44**):

```
put 5 + 15
```

```
put the time
```

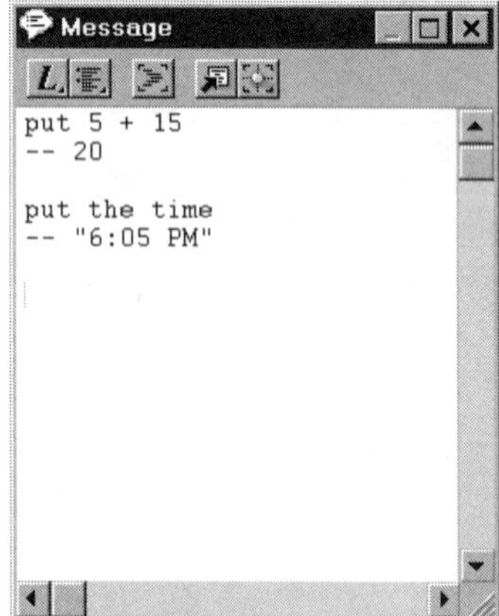

Figure 17.44 Type these commands in the Message window.

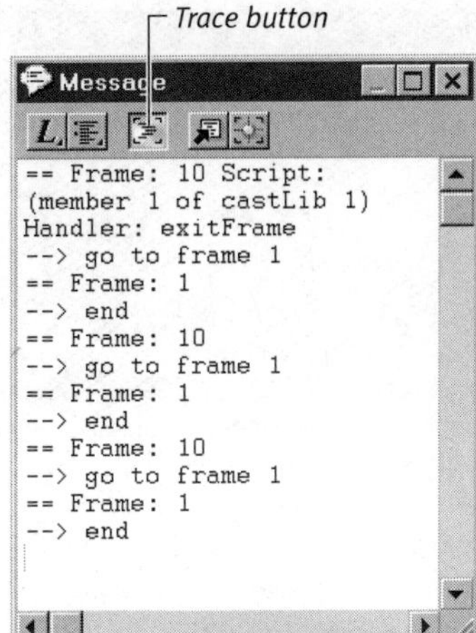

Trace button
Message
== Frame: 10 Script:
(member 1 of castLib 1)
Handler: exitFrame
--> go to frame 1
== Frame: 1
--> end
== Frame: 10
--> go to frame 1
== Frame: 1
--> end
== Frame: 10
--> go to frame 1
== Frame: 1
--> end

Figure 17.45 With Trace mode selected, the Message window displays each handler that Director executes.

The Message window allows you to monitor which handlers Director is currently executing. If your scripts aren't working as expected, this technique can help you uncover the problem.

To trace handlers by using the Message window:

1. Open the Message window.
2. Click the Trace button to select it.
3. Run your movie.

Notice that each handler and the Lingo statements that Director executes are displayed one after another (**Figure 17.45**). They can go by very quickly, so you may need to use the vertical scroll bar in the Message window after you stop the movie to back up.

Using Variables

Like most programming languages, Lingo supports both local and global variable types. Local variables exist only within the confines of a handler and are no longer available as soon as the handler ends. In most cases—in keeping with general programming principles—using local variables is the best approach, because it prevents other handlers from inadvertently modifying the variable value. There is no need to declare local variables. Before using a local variable in a handler, you need to assign a value to it; otherwise, you'll get an error message.

The following example uses a local variable.

To use local variables in a handler:

1. Create and attach the following behavior script to a sprite in your movie (**Figure 17.46**):

```
on mouseDown
   n = 0
   put n
   n = n +10
      put n
   end
```

2. Choose Window > Message to open the Message window.

3. Play your movie and click the sprite with the attached behavior.

   Each time you click the sprite, you should see a 0 followed by a 10 in the Message window (**Figure 17.47**).

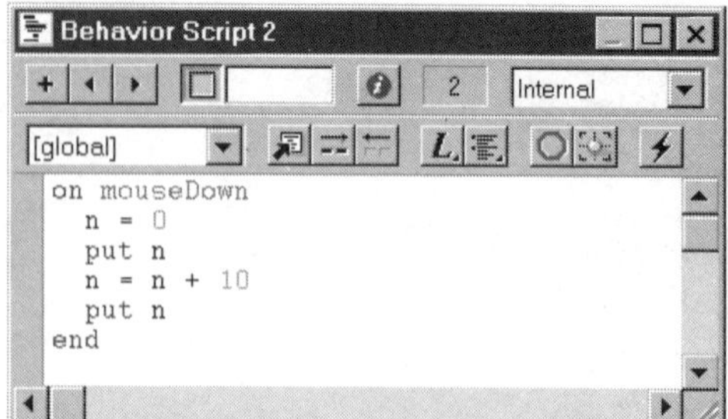

Figure 17.46 This script creates a local variable, modifies it, and outputs its value twice to the Message window.

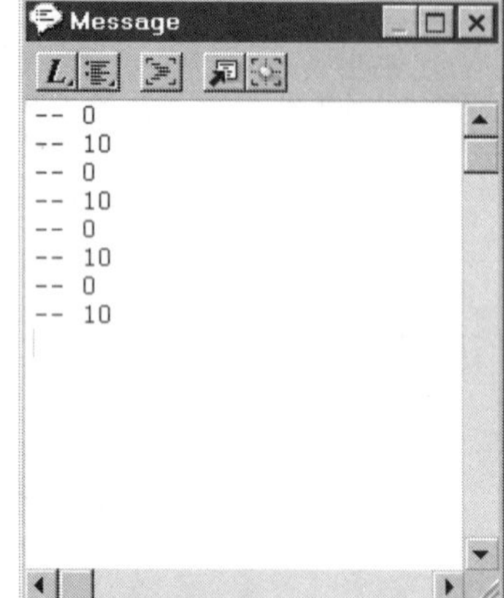

Figure 17.47 The output shown in the Message window.

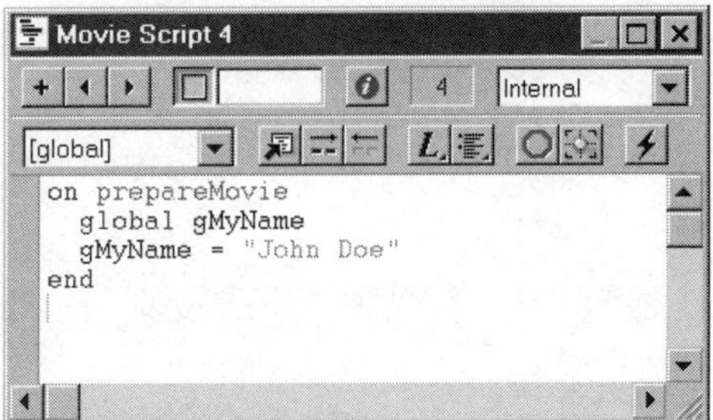

Figure 17.48 This script declares and initializes a global variable.

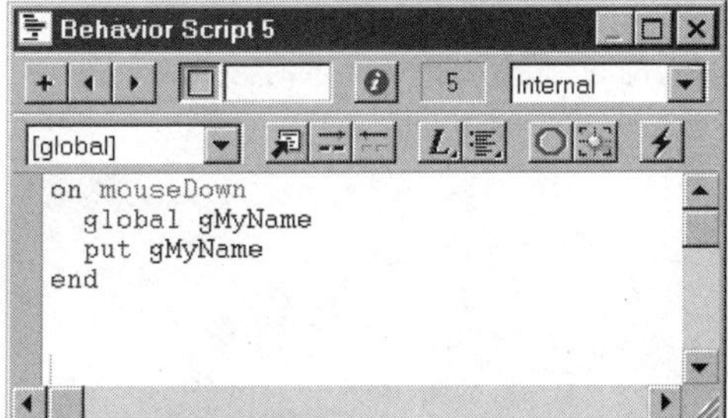

Figure 17.49 This script outputs the value of a global variable to the Message window.

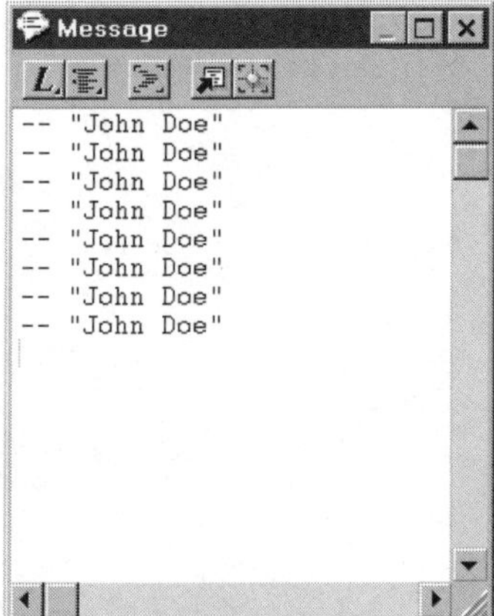

Figure 17.50 The output shown in the Message window.

Unlike the value of a local variable, a global variable's value can be accessed and set by all handlers in a movie and, in some cases, even by handlers in other movies.

Use the `global` keyword to declare a variable to be global. You can do so from any handler. Every subsequent or previous handler must also declare the variable as global before using it; otherwise, you will be working with a local variable with the same name.

The following example creates and modifies a global variable named `gMyName`. This variable is initialized in the `prepareMovie` handler—a good place to initialize all global variables, because this handler automatically runs before the start of any movie.

To use global variables:

1. Create the following movie script (**Figure 17.48**):

```
on prepareMovie
   global gMyName
   gMyName = "John Doe"
end
```

2. Create the following behavior script and attach it to a sprite in your movie (**Figure 17.49**):

```
on mouseDown
   global gMyName
   put gMyName
end
```

3. Choose Window > Message to open the Message window.
4. Play the movie and click the sprite to which you attached the script.

   Each time you click, "John Doe" should appear in the Message window (**Figure 17.50**).

✔ Tip

- When you define variables in the Message window, they are automatically set to be global.

Making Sprites Interactive

This section offers several practical examples to get you going in scripting sprite interactivity. In the process, you'll learn some additional and very useful properties and language elements of Lingo.

In many situations in a movie, you may want a sprite's image to change when the user moves the mouse pointer over it (without clicking). You may want to create a menu in which the choices become highlighted, or pop out, as soon as the user moves the pointer over one (**Figure 17.51**). The following example shows you how to do so.

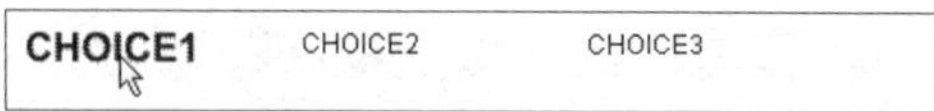

Figure 17.51 A menu choice is highlighted when the mouse pointer moves over it.

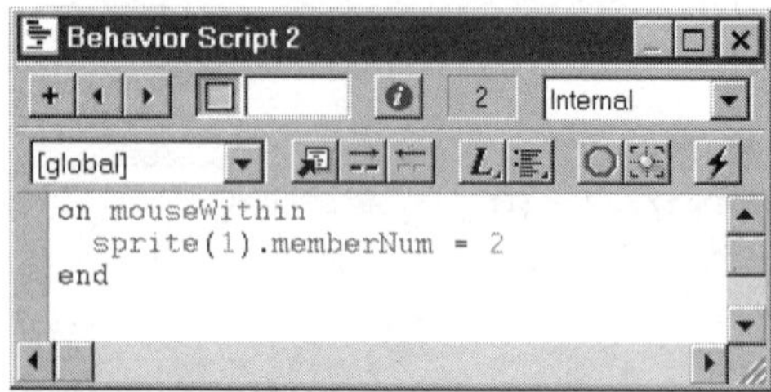

Figure 17.52 The script switches the cast member associated with a sprite when the mouse pointer movies within the sprite.

To make a sprite's image change when the mouse pointer moves within or leaves it:

1. Using the paint window, create two different graphical cast members and place them in positions 1 and 2 in the internal cast.
2. Place the first cast member in sprite channel 1 in the score.
3. Create a behavior script with the following Lingo statements (**Figure 17.52**):

   ```
   on mouseWithin
      sprite(1).memberNum = 2
   end
   ```

   The event handler `mouseWithin` is activated whenever the mouse pointer is over the sprite with the attached handler.

   The sprite property `memberNum` identifies which cast member is associated with the given sprite. Above, the cast member associated with sprite 1 is switched to cast member 2.

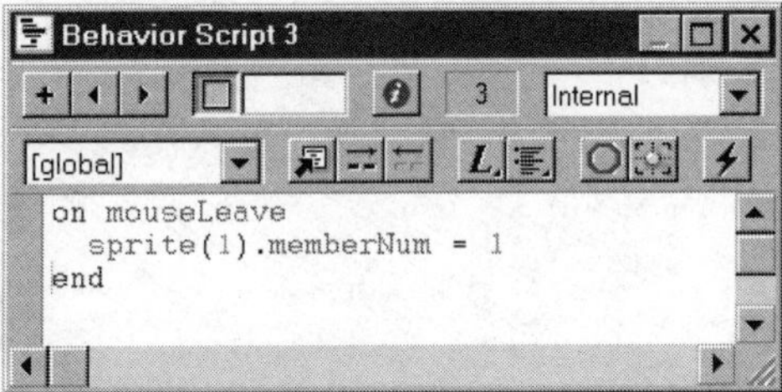

Figure 17.53 The script switches the cast member associated with a sprite when the mouse pointer leaves the sprite.

4. Attach this script to the sprite in the score.
5. Create a second behavior script (**Figure 17.53**):

```
on mouseLeave
   sprite(1).memberNum = 1
end
```

   The event handler `mouseLeave` is activated whenever the mouse pointer leaves the sprite.
6. Attach this script to the sprite in the score.
7. Play the movie.

   Notice that the sprite's image changes whenever the mouse pointer moves into or out of the sprite.

The following behavior script uses Lingo's `repeat with` statement to repeat an action a specified number of times. In this example, the script makes a sprite rotate 360 degrees when you click it, as long as you keep the mouse pointer within its region. If the pointer leaves the sprite while it's rotating, the sprite stops rotating.

To repeat an action a specified number of times:

1. Place a graphical cast member in the score to create a sprite.
2. Create and attach the following behavior script to this sprite (**Figure 17.54**):

```
on mouseDown
   repeat with n = 1 to 360
      sprite(1).rotation = n
      updateStage
      If rollover(1) = FALSE then
      → exit repeat
   end repeat
end
```

3. Play the movie and click the sprite.

   The body of the `repeat` statement above repeats 360 times, with the local variable `n` used as the index. The `rotation` property of the sprite is set to these values. When the repeat loop initiates, the playback head becomes stuck in the same frame until the loop completes. This is why it is necessary to use the `updateStage` command to redraw the stage, because the stage normally gets redrawn only between frames. The `rollover` function is used to exit the repeat loop early if the pointer leaves the sprite region (the `rollover` function returns TRUE when the pointer is over the specified sprite).

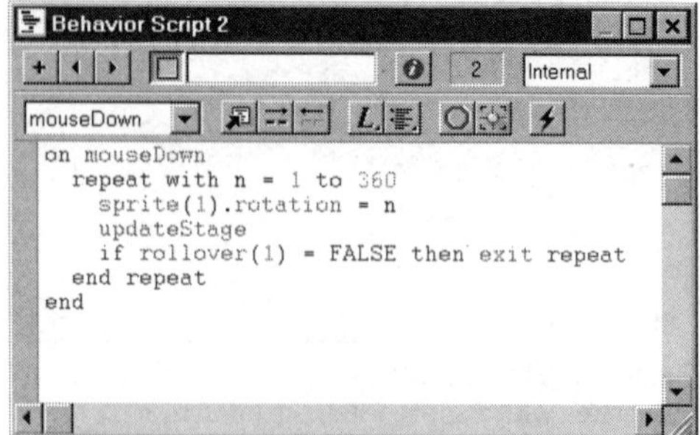

Figure 17.54 When attached to a sprite, this script causes the sprite to rotate 360 degrees when clicked, so long as the mouse pointer remains within the region of the sprite.

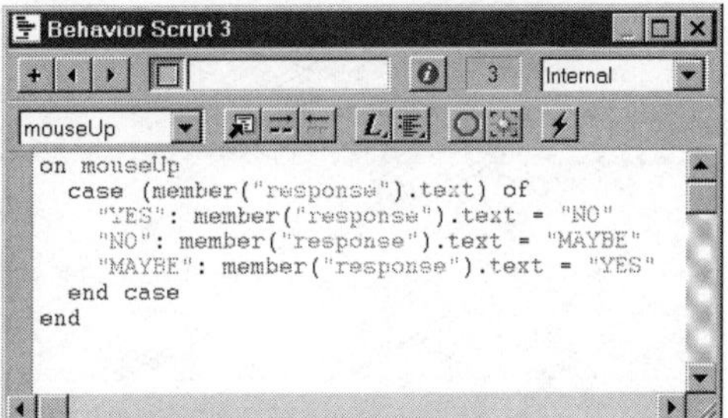

Figure 17.55 This script causes a text cast member's text to change each time it's clicked on the stage.

The following behavior script causes the text in a text cast member to change whenever you click it on the stage. The script causes the text to cycle among the words "YES", "NO", and "MAYBE" as the cast member is clicked.

To make a text cast member's text change when clicked:

1. Choose Window > Text to open the text window.
2. Type "YES".
3. Close the window.
4. In the cast window, name this text cast member "response".
5. Place the text cast member in the score.
6. Create and attach the following behavior script to the text sprite in the score (**Figure 17.55**):

```
on mouseUp
  case (member("response").text) of
    "YES": member("response").text =
    → "NO"
    "NO": member("response").text =
    → "MAYBE"
    "MAYBE": member("response").text =
    → "YES"
  end case
end
```

7. Play the movie and click the text sprite on the stage to see the text alternate.

   The `case` statement is used to replace a chain of `if then` statements. Lingo compares the `case expression` with the expressions in the lines below it, before the colons. If Lingo finds a match, it executes the corresponding line of code and then exits the `case` structure. (*See the Lingo Dictionary for more details on the* `case` *statement.*) `Member("response").text` refers to the text property of the text cast member named "response".

Using Lingo for Animated Cursors

You use Lingo to animate cursor cast members (which are covered in Chapter 4, "Animating Sprites").

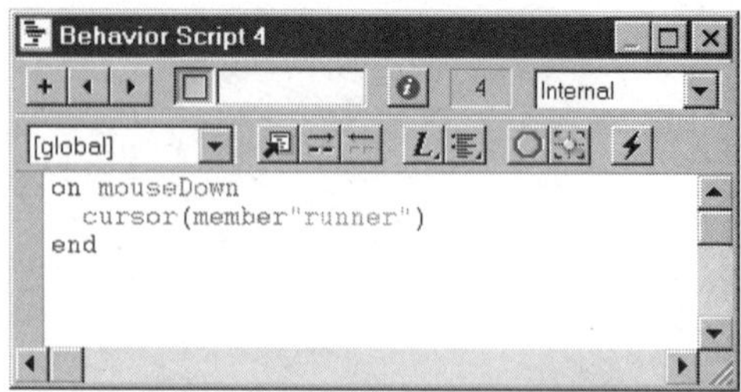

Figure 17.56 A script to activate an animated cursor.

To write a script that activates an animated cursor:

1. Create an animated cursor.

   (*For details, see Chapter 4, "Animating Sprites."*)

2. In the part of a script where you want to activate the animated cursor, add the following statement:

   ```
   cursor (member "MyAnimatedCursor")
   ```

   Substitute your cursor's cast member number or name for `MyAnimatedCursor`.

   You could attach the following behavior script to a sprite to activate the cursor when the sprite is clicked (**Figure 17.56**):

   ```
   on mouseDown
      cursor (member "runner")
   end
   ```

3. Turn off the animated cursor by including the following Lingo statement in a script:

   ```
   cursor -1
   ```

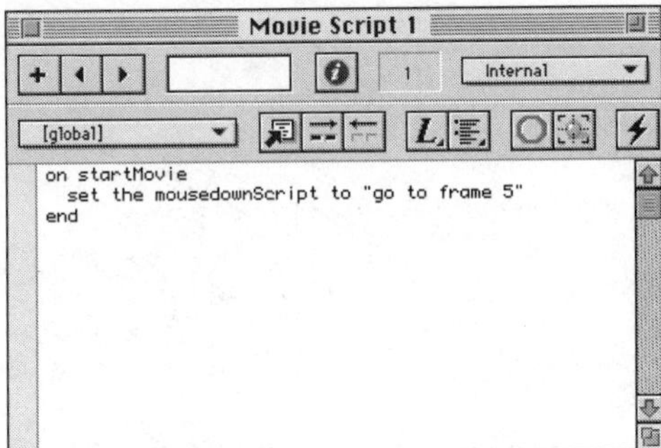

Figure 17.57 This script defines a primary event handler to trap a `mouseDown` message.

Table 17.2

Primary Event-Handler System Properties

PROPERTY	MESSAGE
keyupScript	keyUp
keydownScript	keyDown
mouseupScript	mouseUp
mousedownScript	mouseDown

Setting Up Primary Event Handlers

Primary event handlers provide the first opportunity for your movie to respond to messages. They are first in the hierarchy of objects that messages are sent to. **Table 17.2** contains some of the Lingo properties you use in defining a primary event handler, as well as their corresponding messages. Only a subset of Director's built-in messages can work with a primary event handler. The Lingo Dictionary includes the complete list of the messages.

To set up a primary event handler:

1. Open a movie script.
2. Create a `startMovie` handler.

   This handler generally is the best place to define a primary event handler.
3. In the middle of the handler, type `set the "property" to "your script"`.

   Replace `property` with the primary event-handler property corresponding to the message you want to trap, and replace `your script` with the actual script statement in quotes that you want to execute. (You could also place a custom handler name here.)

   In the example (**Figure 17.57**), the `mouseDownScript` has been set to move the playback head to frame 5. So every time someone clicks the mouse button in the movie, the movie loops back to frame 5, and the `mouseDown` message does not continue on to other scripts (unless you include the `Pass` command in the primary event handler's script response).
4. Close the Script window and run the movie to test the script.

To turn off a primary event handler:

1. Open the script window for the primary event handler that you want to turn off.
2. Include the following statement:

   `Set the "property" to EMPTY`, in which `property` is the primary event-handler property you want to turn off.
3. Close the Script window and test the results.

18

SHOCKMACHINE

Shockmachine is a separate application from Director that lets you play, collect, and manage your favorite Shockwave movie titles—referred to as *cartridges* in Shockmachine. This book covers it here because many of your users will likely be using it to view your Shockwave movies. This chapter also covers several settings in Director specifically geared toward customizing certain playback features of your Shockwave movies in Shockmachine.

You can download Shockmachine for free from the Shockwave.com Web site. The Shockwave.com site also includes lots of titles in many categories to get your collection started.

Understanding Shockmachine Basics

Take a moment to learn the basics of storing, playing, and organizing Shockwave titles in Shockmachine (**Figure 18.1**).

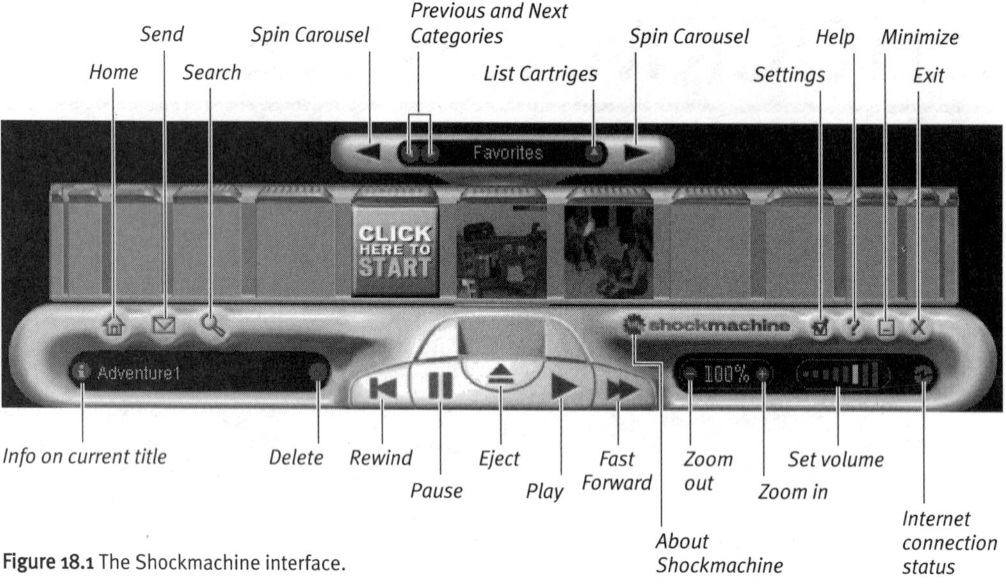

Figure 18.1 The Shockmachine interface.

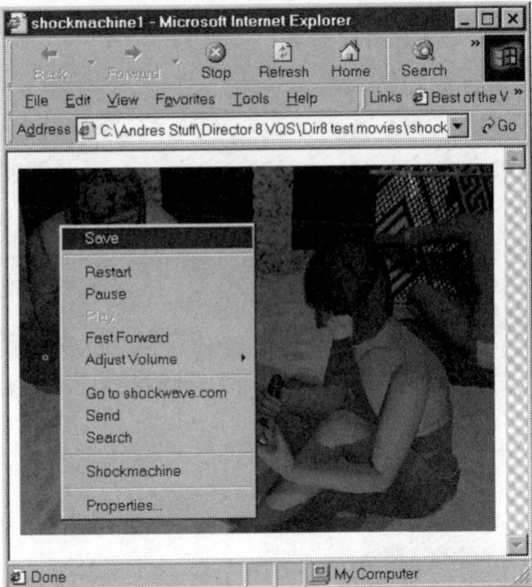

Figure 18.2 Right-click (Control+click, on the Mac) a Shockwave movie in a browser to display a context menu that allows you to save the movie to Shockmachine.

Figure 18.3 Save a Shockwave movie title from the Shockwave.com Web site by selecting the title and then clicking the Save button at the bottom of the Web page.

Figure 18.4 Click OK to save the Shockwave movie to Shockmachine.

To save a Shockwave movie to Shockmachine:

1. While playing a Shockwave movie in a browser window, right-click it (Control+click, on the Mac) and then choose Save from the pop-up menu (**Figure 18.2**).

   Note: Save is available only if the author of the movie chose to allow users to save it *(see "To set a Shockwave movie to be savable to Shockmachine" later in this chapter).*

   or

   If you want to save content from the Shockwave.com Web site, select a title to play and then click the Save button at the bottom of the Web page (**Figure 18.3**).

2. In the Save to Shockmachine dialog box that appears, click OK to save the Shockwave movie under the name and category already provided (**Figure 18.4**), or first change the name and select a new category

To select and play a Shockwave cartridge:

1. Launch Shockmachine.
2. Click the Previous or Next Category button to select the category that contains the cartridge you want to play.
3. Click the Spin Carousel buttons to cycle through the cartridges in the current carousel.
4. In the carousel, click the cartridge that you want to play.

   Shockmachine loads and plays the cartridge (**Figure 18.5**).
5. Use the controls at the bottom of Shockmachine to rewind, pause, eject, and fast-forward the Shockwave movie.

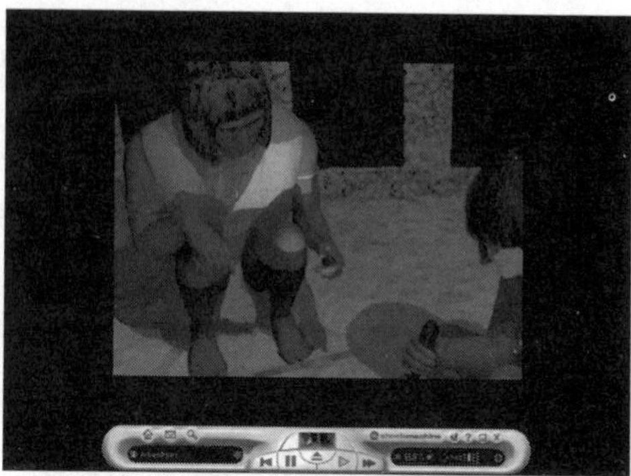

Figure 18.5 A Shockwave movie cartridge playing in Shockmachine.

✔ Tip

- When selecting a cartridge for playback, click the List Cartridges button to display a list of all the cartridges in the current category. Above this list, click the Show All button to display a list of all cartridges in all categories.

To manage and organize Shockwave cartridges:

1. Right-click (Control-click, on the Mac) any visible cartridge in the carousel to display a pop-up menu (**Figure 18.6**).
2. From this pop-up menu, choose Play, Delete, Rename, Change Category, Info, or Visit Web Site.
3. If you are renaming a cartridge, enter a new name in the name field at the bottom-left corner of the Shockmachine interface (**Figure 18.7**).
4. Reposition a cartridge by dragging it to a different slot in the carousel.

   The other cartridges are rearranged automatically.

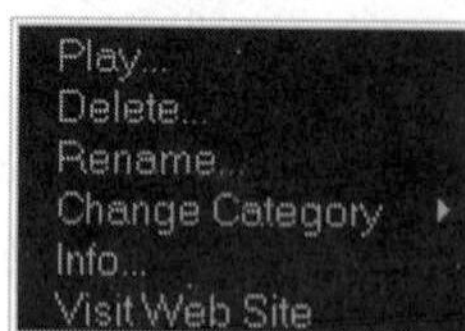

Figure 18.6 Right-click (Control+click, on the Mac) a cartridge in the carousel to display a pop-up menu.

Figure 18.7 Type a new name for a Shockwave cartridge in the Name field in the bottom-left corner of Shockmachine.

Understanding Shockmachine Basics

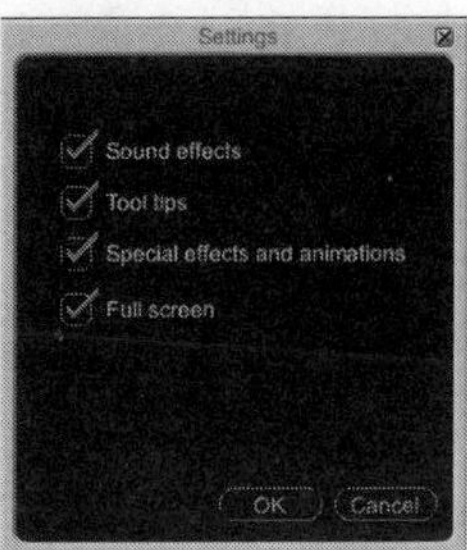

Figure 18.8 Click to select or deselect Shockwave options.

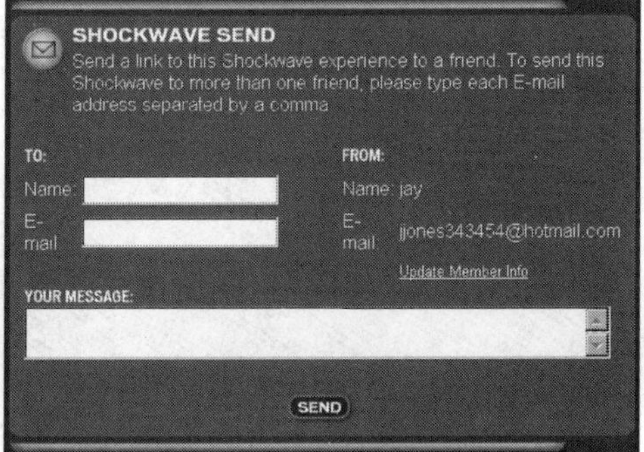

Figure 18.9 Type a friend's e-mail address and click Send to send the URL to the Shockwave cartridge.

To modify Shockmachine settings:

1. Click the Settings button.
2. Click to select or deselect the Sound Effects, Tool Tips, Special Effects and Animations, and Full Screen options (**Figure 18.8**).

To zoom the Shockmachine window:

- Click the Zoom In or Zoom Out button.

  For a Shockwave movie to zoom, the author must have set the Zooming option in the Shockwave tab of the Publish Settings dialog box *(see "To set a Shockwave movie to be zoomable in Shockmachine" later in this chapter).*

To share a Shockmachine title with a friend:

1. Connect to the Internet, if you're not already online.
2. Click the Send button while a Shockwave cartridge is playing.

   A browser window opens and takes you to Shockwave.com.
3. Type your friend's e-mail address and click Send (**Figure 18.9**).

   Shockwave.com sends the URL (not the actual file) of the Shockwave cartridge to the specified e-mail address. You can change this URL, if you want *(see "To set Shockwave Save tab settings" later in this chapter).*

Preparing Shockwave Movies for Playback in Shockmachine

Before you create a Shockwave movie from your Director movie, you can set several Shockmachine-related options to customize how the movie is saved to Shockmachine, as well as to determine the availability of certain controls during playback in Shockmachine.

To set a Shockwave movie to be savable to Shockmachine:

1. Choose File > Publish Settings to display the Publish Settings dialog box.
2. Select the Shockwave tab.
3. Check the Save Local checkbox (**Figure 18.10**).
4. Choose File > Publish when you're ready to create your Shockwave movie.

   When a user right-clicks (Control+clicks, on the Mac) your Shockwave movie in a Web browser, the Save command is available.

To set a Shockwave movie to be zoomable in Shockmachine:

1. Choose File > Publish Settings to display the Publish Settings dialog box.
2. Select the Shockwave tab.
3. Check the Zooming checkbox (**Figure 18.10**).
4. Choose File > Publish when you're ready to create your Shockwave movie.

   When a user clicks the Zoom In or Zoom Out button in Shockmachine, the size of your movie increases or decreases (**Figure 18.11**).

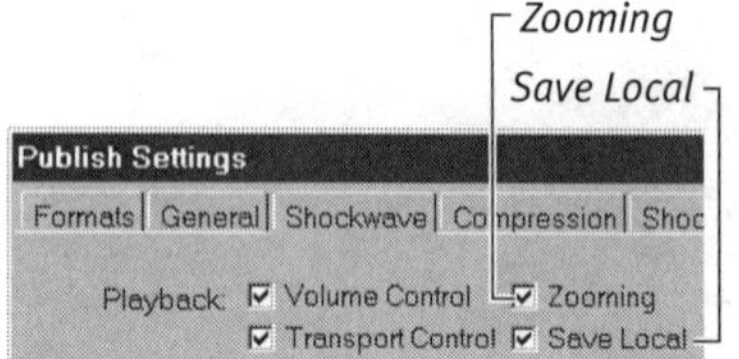

Figure 18.10 Enable the Save Local and Zooming options to allow your users to save and zoom your Shockwave movie in Shockmachine.

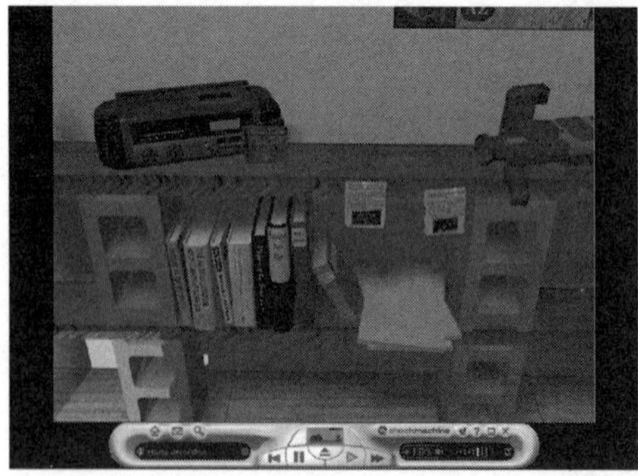

Figure 18.11 Click Zoom In or Zoom Out in Shockmachine to increase or decrease the size of the movie.

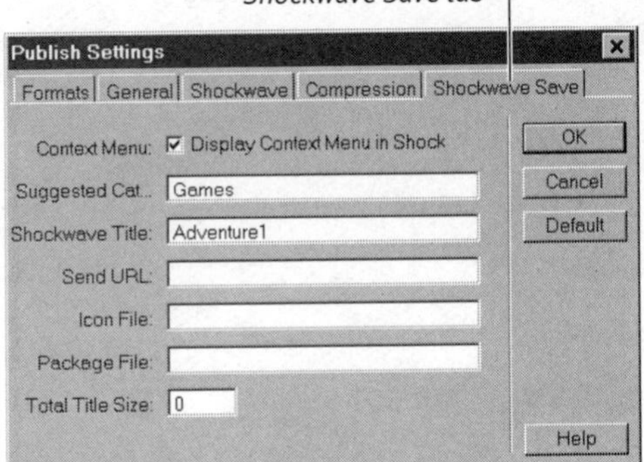

Figure 18.12 Select the Shockwave Save tab.

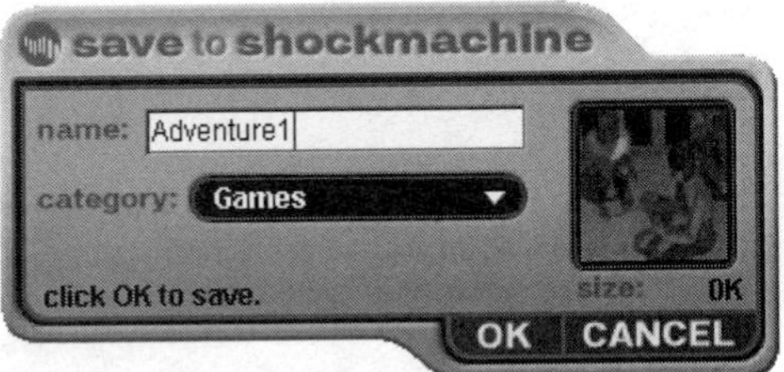

Figure 18.13 Text entered in the Suggested Category and Shockwave Title fields appears in the Save to Shockmachine dialog box.

To set Shockwave Save tab settings:

1. Choose File > Publish Settings to display the Publish Settings dialog box.
2. Select the Shockwave Save tab (**Figure 18.12**).
3. Check the Display Context Menu in Shockwave checkbox to display the Shockwave context menu when a user right-clicks (Control-clicks, on the Mac) your Shockwave movie playing in a browser.
4. Type an existing category name in the Suggested Category field to suggest a Shockmachine category.

   This category will appear in the Category field of the Save to Shockmachine dialog box when a user saves your Shockwave movie to Shockmachine (**Figure 18.13**).
5. In the Shockwave Title field, type a title to appear in the Name field of the Save to Shockmachine dialog box when a user saves your Shockwave movie to Shockmachine.
6. If you need to override the URL that Shockmachine detects for the given Shockwave movie, type a new URL in the Send URL field.

   This new URL is used when a user clicks the Send button in Shockmachine to send the title to a friend.
7. In the Icon File field, type a path to a .BMP file to be used as the icon for your Shockwave movie in Shockmachine.

GLOSSARY

Anti-aliasing

Removes or reduces the rough and jagged edges around an image.

Bit depth

The number of bits used to display each pixel. In Director, bit depth can be set to 1, 2, 4, 8, 16, 24, and 32-bit color.

Cast window

A Cast window is the storage area in Director that contains your multimedia elements, such as graphics, sounds, color palettes, film loops, buttons, QuickTime movies, and scripts.

Control Panel

Provides VCR-type control over the playback of your movie, including Rewind, Play, and Step Forward buttons.

Cast member

An individual multimedia element that can be incorporated into your movie, such as a graphic, sound, film loop, color palette, or QuickTime movie.

Cell

The individual storage units that make up the Score. Each cell contains information about one cast member.

Channel

A row of cells in the score. Each channel holds a specific cast member type. There are animations channels, five effects channels (Tempo, Palette, Transition, Sound 1 & 2) and a script channel.

Color cycling

A color effect, which rotates colors through a specified range in a color palette. Cast members that appear in these colors appear to pulsate and change color.

Color depth

The bit depth of a cast member, indicating how many colors it can display.

Common palette

A specially constructed palette that incorporates many of the colors shared by your entire cast. Its purpose is to replace the many cast member palettes your movie may be using with a single palette that can display your entire cast in approximately accurate colors.

Current frame

The frame that is currently displayed on the stage. You can change the current frame by using the frame counter in the Control Panel, or the Playback head in the score.

Current palette

The color palette used to display the colors of the cast members in the current frame on the stage. You can change the current palette in the Palette channel of the score.

Foreground

Sprites that appear to be in front of other sprites on the stage are in the foreground. A sprite's foreground priority is determined by its placement in the animation channels. A sprite closer to the bottom animation channel is closer to the foreground.

Foreground color

The main color used to paint artwork in the Paint window, and to paint QuickDraw shapes and text in the Tool Palette. It is selected using the Foreground color chip.

Frame

A column of cells in the score that represents a segment of time in your movie. Each frame contains information about what your cast members are doing in that time segment.

Film loop

A cast member that is composed of a sequence of graphical cast members to form a looping animation.

In-Between

A command in Director that helps create an animation sequence by filling in the frames between two key frames that you specify.

Ink Effects

Ink effects determine how your sprites appear when they overlap each other and background artwork on the stage. Ink effects are applied to sprites using the score's ink pop-up menu. Ink effects can also be applied to cast members to permanently affect their colors, by using the Paint window's Ink pop-up menu.

Mask

An image that allows you to control which parts of an artwork selection are transparent (you can see background artwork through these parts) and which parts are opaque. A mask could be used to make the windows in a house transparent and the rest of the house opaque, for example.

Movie

The term used to describe any multimedia animation created in Director.

Palette
A subset of colors used to display your cast members if you are working with index-palette mode, for limited bit-depth monitors. Only one color palette can be active at a time.

Playback head
The position of the Playback head in the score indicates which frame is currently displayed on the stage. You can drag the Playback head to display different frames on the stage.

Projector
A play-only version of a Director movie. Projectors cannot be opened or edited in Director and are the best way to distribute your movies to the public. It is not necessary to own a copy of Director to run a projector movie.

Real-time recording
A feature in Director that allows you to record the path of mouse movements, and then substitute any graphical cast member to follow this path to form an animation.

Registration point
A reference point used to align the positions of cast members in an animation sequence.

Score
A frame-by-frame record of your movie, used to direct all your cast members. The score is organized into animation channels, five effects channels (Tempo, Palette, Transitions, Sound 1 & 2), and one script channel.

Stage
The background upon which your movie animations are played and viewed.

Step Recording
The most basic animation technique in Director, where you arrange and record each frame on an individual basis to create an animation sequence.

Tempo
The rate at which the frames of your movie are played. Tempo is measured in frames per second.

INDEX

A

activating frames, 65
ActiveX controls (Windows), 355
Air Brush tool
  adjusting spray pattern for, 157
  assigning shape to brush, 158
  choosing shape for, 158
  painting with, 153
aligning
  registration points, 114
  Shockwave movie in browser, 325, 331
  sprites, 88
  text margins, 270–271
animated GIFs, 262
animated sequences, 113–117
animating sprites, 99–127
anti-aliasing
  for text, 276
  for vector shapes, 200
asset-management fields, 60
Automask option, 122
AVI movies, 250–251, 253

B

background color
  changing stage, 203
Background color chip, 219
Background Color tool, 144
batch-converting Shockwave files, 338–340
Behavior Inspector
  Behavior pop-up menu, 362
  editing pane for, 361
  Shuffle buttons for, 361, 366, 367
  See also behaviors
behaviors, 357–369
  assigning, 358–360
  changing order of sprite's, 367
  creating, 362–364
  deleting all assigned, 360
  editing, 79, 369
  Hold on Current Frame, 321
  Library Palette of, 357
  modifying built-in, 365
  re-entering parameters for assigned, 368
  removing action or event from, 367
  reordering actions in, 366, 367
  scripting, 372, 374–375
  using Behavior Inspector, 361
  writing scripts for cast member, 381
Bézier curves, 188
bit depth
  recommendations for sound, 288
  specifying movie, 214
  See also color depth
bitmap images
  setting image options for cast members, 43–44
  vector shapes vs., 185
bitmapped text
  adding, 173–174
  advantages of, 264
  converting regular or field text to, 277
blending colors, 229
bounding box
  removing, 259
  resizing, 258
branching, 395
browsers
  aligning Shockwave movie in, 325
  compatibility of Shockwave Player with, 320
  displaying Shockwave playback commands (Macintosh), 316
  enabling browser scripting, 331
  opening Shockwave movies from, 316

browsers *(continued)*
playing Shockwave movies locally and on Web with, 320–321
previewing Shockwave movie in, 321
specifying for movie preview, 322
Brush Settings dialog box, 154, 155
Brush tool, 144
See also Paint Brush tool
buttons
on Control Panel, 11, 21, 130, 131
creating on stage, 211
on toolbar, 4

C

cast members
adding from Paint window, 145
aligning registration points for, 114
building optimal color palette for, 241
changing
color depth for, 218
color of text, 270
text fonts for, 269
checking palette for, 235
choosing for animated cursor, 121
copying, moving, or deleting selection of, 52
creating
internally, 15–16
sprite by dragging to stage, 69
tile from, 166–167
vector-shape, 189
deleting unused, 46–47
displaying original colors in imported, 240
editing
properties of, 79
text cast members during playback, 284
exchanging within sprite, 113
film loop, 119
filtering bitmapped, 184
icons used for, 32
importing, 39–47
internal sound, 288
linked, 37
loading while looping Shockwave movie scenes, 336
managing properties for, 57–61
mapping colors to specific color positions on palette, 234
moving
with Place button, 55
shape within multiple-shape vector, 198
naming in Thumbnail view, 53
onion skinning and creating, 182, 183
placing
in frame as one sprite, 114
in score, 17–18
remapping 8-bit members to Web216 palette, 239
renaming in List view mode, 50
repositioning, copying, or moving in Cast window, 54–55
scripts for, 375
selecting
in List view mode, 51
multiple nonadjacent, 53
setting
media options for Flash, 124
options for imported Flash, 123
playback options for Flash, 125–127
priority in memory, 59
properties for digital video, 256–258
sorting, 49
streaming and optimal size of, 337
text, 268
tweening size of, 102
writing scripts for behaviors, 381
See also casts
Cast to Time command, 114
Cast window, 31
changing preferences in, 56
choosing casts in, 36
opening, 36
repositioning, copying, or moving cast members in, 54–55
resizing columns in, 50
setting column attributes for, 48
toggling view style for, 48
cast-member Xtras, 342, 346–347
casts, 31–61
adding cast-member Xtras to, 346
Cast windows, 31
choosing, 36
creating, 35
cast members internally, 15–16
members on stage, 16
deleting unused cast members, 46–47
icons for types of, 32
importing cast members, 14–15
internal and external, 33–34
managing properties for members and, 57–61
opening
Cast window, 36
external, 10–11, 46–47
placing cast members in score, 17–18
saving changes in external, 38
unlinking external, 38
updating, 29
See also cast members; external casts; internal casts

.CCT files, 317, 319, 326
cell
  indicating for field cast member, 282
  selecting
    for new tempo, 135
    in transition channel, 140
    for transition in palette channel, 237
channels
  function of, 66
  Tempo, 134
  Transitions, 140
  turning on/off, 96
color, 213–247
  adding to optimal color palette, 243–244
  blending colors within palette, 229
  changing
    or setting current color palette, 222
    sprite's, 84
    text cast member's, 270
  checking current mode for, 219
  choosing, 221
  color depth, 214–218
  color modes, 220
  copying and pasting within palette, 228
  cycling in color palette, 245–247
  displaying original colors in imported cast member, 240
  fill foreground and background, 210
  foreground, 161, 209
  foreground, background, and gradient destination, 161
  mapping to positions on color palette, 234
  matching in sprites, 230
  opening color menu, 219
  organizing on color palette, 242
  reversing order of palette's, 231
  RGB and palette-index color modes, 220
  setting gradient color range, 172
  sorting on palette, 232
  stroke, 191
  See also color menu; color palette; limited color displays
color cycling, 245–247, 416
Color Cycling option (Frame Properties dialog box), 246
color depth, 214–218
  changing
    cast member's, 218
    Macintosh, 215
    Windows, 216
  checking movie, 216
  resetting monitor to match movie's (Macintosh), 307
  viewing for cast member, 217
  See also limited color displays
color menu
  choosing colors from, 221
  editing favorite colors for, 223
  opening, 219
  setting current color palette for, 222
color modes, 219–220
  checking current, 219
  RGB and palette-index, 220
  setting, 220
color palette, 224–232
  assigning to certain frames, 236
  blending colors within palette, 229
  changing or setting current palette, 222
  checking cast member's, 235
  copying and pasting colors within palette, 228
  cycling colors in, 245–247
  default, 235
  duplicating, 226
  editing colors in, 227
  importing, 224, 225
  mapping cast member colors to, 234
  matching colors in sprites, 230
  remapping cast member to different, 239
  reversing order of palette's colors, 231
  selecting options for imported cast members, 43
  setting transition, 237–238
  sorting colors on, 232
  See also current color palette; optimal color palette; palette channel
columns
  resizing, 50
  setting attributes for, 48
  sorting, 49
commands
  executing Lingo from Message window, 396
  keyboard shortcuts next to, 26
  Lingo, 387
  See also specific commands
common palette, 416
compression
  options for files, 34
  for Shockwave movies, 332
  sound, 297–299
  stretching/compressing selections, 152
constraining
  control handles, 195
  shapes, 144, 186
context menus, 26
Control Panel, 130–133
  adjusting movie volume, 131, 289
  buttons on, 11, 21, 130, 131

INDEX

Control Panel *(continued)*
  display for target and actual tempo, 136
  jumping to specific frame, 133
  opening, 130
  rewinding movie to frame 1, 130
  starting playback, 131, 132
  stepping
    backward, 132
    through movie, 131
  stopping playback, 130, 132
  tempo display in, 112
  See also playback
copying
  keyframes, 100
  selection with Marquee tool, 152
copying and pasting
  colors within Color Palette, 228
  digital video frames, 260–261
corner point
  adding, 198
  converting, 196
  selecting, 196
  See also points
creating
  behaviors, 362–364
  movies, 13–24
    adding interactive controls, 20
    assembling cast, 14–16
    customizing and animating sprites, 18–19
    customizing authoring environment and movie properties, 13–14
    incorporating cast members into movie, 17–18
    publishing movies, 23
    testing and refining movies, 21–22
    updating movies, 29
  projectors, 308–309
cross-platform issues, xii
current color palette
  changing or setting, 222
  numbering of colors in, 220
  remapping sprites on stage to, 240
  switching for each frame, 233
  See also color palette
current frame
  copying contents of to next frame, 131
  holding on, 321
current palette
  changing or setting colors of, 222
  remapping sprites on stage to, 240
cursors
  animating, 121–122, 404
  positioning hotspot for, 122
curve point
  adding, 198
  adjusting, 195
  converting
    to corner point, 196
    corner point to, 196
  displaying handles for, 195
  See also points
custom line width, 147
custom Xtras, 354
customized Lingo behaviors, 372
.CXT files, 319

D

.DCR files, 317, 319, 326
deleting
  all behaviors assigned to sprite or frame, 360
  files, 29
  frame from score, 76
  markers, 97
  points, 195
  sprite selection, 72
  unused cast members, 46–47
digital video, 249–262
  editing, 260
  extending video sprite to cover enough frames, 255
  importing, 250–251
  importing animated GIFs, 262
  overview, 249
  placing in movie, 254
  previewing, 252–253
  setting properties for cast members, 256–258
  setting properties for sprites, 259
digitizing sounds (Macintosh), 302
.DIR files, 319
Director, 1–29
  cast, score, and stage interaction in, 5
  context menus, 26
  creating movies, 13–24
  filename extensions used by, 319
  formatting imported HTML documents, 279
  Help for, 24–25
  hiding interface for, 21
  inspectors, 8–9
  keyboard shortcuts for, 26
  sprites and cast members, 4
  stage and toolbar, 4
  types of projects created with, 2–3
  updating movies, 29
  windows in, 7
dissolve, adding, 22
distorting artwork, 177

INDEX

distributing
projector files, 303, 310
Shockwave movies, 23, 319
distribution folder, 311
dither-type gradients, 170–171
downloading
options for streaming movies, 335, 337
Shockmachine, 407
times and streaming performance, 337
Xtras for Shockwave movies during playback, 353–354
dragging
cast members to stage, 69
sprites on stage, 19
drawing
buttons and checkboxes, 211
filled and hollow shapes on stage, 209
line on stage, 208
See also painting
Dreamweaver, 2
drop shadows, 283
Drumbeat 2000, 2
duplicating
cast-member selection, 52
color palette, 226
.DXR files, 319

E

editing
behavior in Script window, 369
color swatches, 227
colors in color palette, 227
existing Lingo scripts, 383
patterns, 163, 164
preset patterns, 166
sound, 287
sound to fit frames required, 291
sprite frames, 76
vector shapes, 194–200
editing pane (Behavior Inspector), 361
effects
applying various, 178
creating sequence of in-between images, 179
distorting artwork, 177
flipping artwork, 177
rotating artwork
in 1-degree increments, 176
90 degrees, 176
See also ink effects
Effects toolbar, 162, 175
8-bit color. *See* limited color displays; palette-index mode
elements, Lingo, 387–388
Ellipse tool, 144
embedded fonts
best size for, 281
in movie, 280
embedding Xtras in stand-alone projectors, 351
end points, 197
Eraser tool, 144, 153
erasing
images, 153
selections, 152
events
removing from behavior, 367
exchanging cast member within sprite, 113
extending sprites, 21, 74
external casts
alternate names and locations for Shockwave (Macintosh), 318
checking Use in Current Movie option, 35
choosing internal vs., 34
distinguishing between linked cast members and linked, 37
linking to current movie, 37
opening, 10–11, 46–47
as projectors, 33
saving changes in, 38
unlinking, 38
external Shockwave Audio files, 299
Eyedropper tool, 144
matching colors in sprites, 230
replacing colors with, 162

F

fading sprites in/out, 102
field text
adding drop shadows and borders to, 283
advantages of, 264
converting to bitmapped text, 277
creating, 282–283
editing cast members during playback, 284
field text window, 7
Field tool, 282
Field window, 283
files
applying options to imported images, 43
batch-converting Shockwave files, 338–340
choosing Bitmap Image option for, 14
created with Publish command, 317
deleting, 29
original while protecting movie and cast, 314
filename extensions for Director, 319

files *(continued)*
formats
for imported sound, 288
for importing text, 278
supported for import, 39
importing
cast members from external, 42
digital video, 250–251
Scrapbook or PICS files (Macintosh), 45–46
Shockwave Flash, 123
minimizing size of font cast member, 280–281
naming linked Flash movies, 124
preserving original movie and cast files when decompressing Shockwave movies, 318
protecting original while protecting movie and cast, 312–313
selecting and choosing, 312
setting compression for, 34
specifying, HTML and Shockwave, 328
updating movies, 29
See also projectors
fill
selecting foreground and background colors for, 210
stage, 202
Filled Ellipse tool, 144
Filled Polygon tool, 144
Filled Rectangle tool, 15, 144
filled shape tools, 209
film loops, 118–120
creating, 119
ink effects for, 119
looping Flash sprites, 127
overview, 118
real-time recording with, 120
Fireworks, 2
Flash movies, 123–127
controlling playback of, 127
importing, 123
ink effects for Flash sprites, 127
setting media options for cast members, 124
setting playback options for cast member, 125–127
Flash Player, 2
flipping
artwork, 177
sprites, 82
folders
distributing Xtras for projectors in, 352
distribution, 311
installing Xtras in Xtras, 343
moving Shockwave-related files to Shockwave Player, 318
Xtras, 141, 184
fonts
changing for text cast members, 269
embedded, 264, 280, 281
foreground color
for cast member's and sprite's text, 270
for filled shape, 209
Foreground color chip
opening color menu with, 219
selecting color from Color menu, 153
Foreground Color tool, 144
fps (frames per second), 134, 137
frame number display, 11
frame-reset behavior, 364
frames
assigning
behavior cast member to, 360
behaviors to, 359
color palette to certain, 236
branching to, 395
converting sprites to animated sequences, 115–116
copying contents of to next frame, 131
creating
animated cursors with variable frame rates, 122
keyframes, 100
determining required number for sound, 291
editing, inserting, and removing, 76
extending
sound sprites to fit, 291
video sprite to cover enough, 255
jumping to specific, 133, 390
making text editable during ranges of, 285
pausing movie at specific, 391
placing series of cast members in as one sprite, 114
playing only marked, 133
repositioning selected sprite, 73
selecting, 65, 71
setting color-palette transitions, 237, 238
specifying quantity to download before playing movies, 335, 337
step recording, 109–110
switching current color palettes for each, 233
writing scripts
attached to, 378
for later attachment to, 380
See also keyframes
frames per second (fps), 134, 137
FreeHand, 2
FTP (File Transfer Protocol) utility, 319
Full Screen mode, 203

G

Generator, 2
global variables, 399
go to command (Lingo), 393
gradient color chip, 168
Gradient Colors tool, 144
gradient destination color, 161
gradients, 168–172
  color range, 172
  color-blending method, 170–171
  creating, 168
  direction of, 169
  repeat settings, 170
  setting spread, 172
  using Gradient Settings dialog box, 169
graphical cast members, 69
grids
  displaying and configuring stage, 206
  turning on/off, 13
guides
  adding to stage, 207
  turning on/off, 13

H

Hand tool, 144, 152, 204, 205
handlers
  elements in, 387–388
  hierarchy of, 385–386
  setting up primary event, 405
  tracing from Message window, 397
  turning off primary event, 406
  using local variables in, 398–399
handles
  displaying for curve point, 195
  sprite's resize, 80
height
  adjusting tile, 167
  setting for Shockwave movies, 323
Help, 24–25
hiding
  Director interface, 21
  effects of channels, 92
  keyframes in score, 93
  paint tool palette, 146
  rulers, 146
  Sprite toolbar, 79
hollow shape tools, 209
horizontal guide lines, 207
HTML documents
  importing, 278, 279
  setting background colors for, 329
HTML files
  embedding Shockwave movies in, 316
  options for publishing for Shockwave movies, 327
  specifying and selecting, 328
hyperlink text, 286

I

icons
  for cast member types, 32
  lock, 91
  movie, 10
  program, 10
If-Then structure, 392
image filters, 184, 342
images
  erasing, 153
  file formats supported for still, 39
  in-between, 179, 416
  selecting and moving, 148–152
importing
  animated GIFs, 262
  cast members, 39–47
    changing size of bitmap cast members, 44
    choosing Standard Import or Link to External File option, 42
    deleting unused cast members, 46–47
    setting image options for bitmap cast members, 43–44
  color palette, 224, 225
  digital video files, 250–251
  HTML documents from Web, 279
  PowerPoint presentation, 47
  Scrapbook or PICS files (Macintosh), 45–46
  sound, 288–289
  text, 278–279
  Xtras, 342
in-between images, 179, 416
ink effects
  choosing, 159
  description of, 160
  for film loops, 119
  for Flash sprites, 127
  options for, 86, 87
  setting for sprite, 86
ink masks, 180–181
Ink pop-up menu, 86, 159
inserting frames in score, 76
inspectors, 8–9
installing Xtras, 343
interactive controls, 20
interactive sprites, 400–403
  changing image when pointer moves in or out, 400–401

interactive sprites *(continued)*
changing text cast member's text when clicked, 403
specifying repeated actions, 402
Internal Cast window, 5
internal casts
choosing external vs., 34
creating, 15–16
as projectors, 33
internal sound cast members, 288

J

joining sprites, 75
JPEG file compression, 334
jumping
frames with go to command, 393
restricting users to short hops, 337
to specific frame, 133, 390

K

kerning, 272–273
keyboard shortcuts
for Cast to Time command, 114
for Director, 26
modifier keys for, xii
sparing use of, xi
for toggling looping, 132
See also listings on reference card
keyframes
creating, 100
and changing sprite property simultaneously, 104
hiding or displaying, 93
refining tweening between, 103
repositioning in score, 101
of sprite, 67
using to synchronize sound, 293
See also frames
keywords for Help, 25

L

Lasso tool
choosing options with, 151
erasing selections, 152
Marquee tool vs., 148
repositioning selection with, 151
selecting images with, 150
using special effects with, 178
See also Marquee tool
Library Palette, 7, 20, 321, 357
limited color displays, 233–247
adding colors to optimal palette, 243–244
assigning color palette to certain frames, 236
building optimal color palette for cast members, 241
checking cast member's palette, 235
current color palette, 233
cycling colors in palette, 245–247
displaying original colors in imported cast member, 240
mapping cast member colors to specific color positions, 234
organizing used and unused colors, 242
remapping, 239–240
setting color-palette transition, 237–238
setting default color palette, 235
line spacing, 274
Line tool
constraining lines with, 144
drawing line on stage with, 208
line width, 147
linear gradients, 193
Line-width selector tool, 144
Lingo, 371–406
animated cursors for, 404
elements of, 387–388
enabling browser scripting for, 331
handlers, messages, and events for, 384–387
hierarchy of handlers, 385–386
making sprites interactive, 400–403
scripting navigation, 389–395
scripts, 373–376
setting up primary event handlers for, 405–406
synchronizing sound with, 295, 296
tracing handlers from Message window, 397
using the Message window, 396–397
variables, 398–399
writing scripts, 377–383
Lingo Xtras, 342
linked cast members
distinguishing between linked external casts and, 37
setting option for Flash cast members, 124
linked external casts, 37
linked files
preparing projectors for distribution with, 310
for sound, 288, 300–301
List view mode, 48–52
local variables, 398
locking
playback speed, 138
sprites, 91
looping
creating film loops, 118–120
enhancing streaming performance with, 337

Flash sprites, 127
scripting playback loops, 389
setting Shockwave movie to play only once, 321
Shockwave movie scenes while loading cast-member media, 336
sound, 291, 292
stopping/starting loop playback, 132
See also film loops

M

Macintosh platform
changing movie color depth, 215
creating external Shockwave Audio files, 299
displaying Shockwave playback commands in browser, 316
Help window for, 25
importing Scrapbook or PICS files to, 45–46
keyboard shortcut symbols for, 26
modifier keys for, xii
previewing QuickTime files, 252
projector settings for, 307
recording sounds in Director, 302
reinstalling stored patterns, 165
resetting monitor to movie's color depth, 27
reversing sort order in Cast window, 49
selecting
cast members in List view mode, 51
single frame in sprite, 104
specifying alternate names and location for Shockwave movies, 318
storing
custom brushes on, 156
custom patterns for, 164
Macromedia Director. *See* Director
Macromedia software applications, 2
Magnifying Glass tool, 144, 204
margins
aligning text, 270–271
changing, 271
Marker channel, 97
markers, 97–98
annotating in Markers window, 98
branching to, 395
creating, 97
navigating score by, 97
positioning in Marker channel, 97
using go to command with marker label, 394
Markers window, 98
Marquee tool, 144
choosing options for, 149
copying selection with, 152
erasing selections, 152
Lasso tool vs., 148
selecting images with, 148
stretching/compressing selections, 152
using Effects toolbar with, 175
See also Lasso tool
masks
ink, 180–181
Memory Inspector, 9
menus
checks, diamonds, or bullets on, 7
conventions for referring to commands, xi
keyboard shortcuts on, 26
using context, 26
Message window
executing Lingo from, 396
tracing handlers from, 397
modifying
built-in behaviors, 365
settings for Shockmachine, 411
monitor
resetting to match movie's color depth (Macintosh), 307
See also limited color displays
mouse
changing
interactive sprites when pointer moves in or out, 400–401
text cast member's text when clicked, 403
clicking and dragging with, xi
moving points in vector shapes, 194
pausing and restarting movie with, 392
selecting continuous range of sprites with, 71
movie scripts, 376
movies, 13–24, 129–141, 315–340
adding interactivity to, 20
adjusting
Publish settings for Shockwave movies, 326–334
tempo of, 14, 22
changing
actual-tempo and target-tempo value, 137
sprite properties, 18–19
stage size and location for, 202
color depth of, 214
comparing target tempo with actual tempo, 136
compression options for Shockwave movies, 332
creating
cast members internally, 15–16
cast members on stage, 16
and viewing Shockwave, 317–318
default color palette for, 235
default setting for looping, 132

movies *(continued)*
embedding text fonts in, 280
fine-tuning, 21–22
function of score for, 63
importing cast members, 14–15
including Xtras in distributed, 348–350
jumping to specific frame, 133
linking external cast to current, 37
locking playback speed, 138
looping Shockwave scenes while loading cast-member media, 336
making streaming Shockwave, 335–336, 337
opening
existing, 10–11
new, 11
options for stretchable Shockwave, 323–325, 330–331
pausing, 139, 391, 392
placing
cast members in score, 17–18
digital video in, 254
playing, 11
only marked frames, 133
Shockwave, 320–322
Shockwave movie only once, 321
previewing Shockwave movie in browser, 321
protecting movie and cast files while deleting projector files, 314
publishing, 23
remapping 8-bit cast members to Web216 palette, 239
reverting to last saved version, 12
rewinding to frame 1, 130
saving, 12, 38, 46
scene transitions, 140–141
setting
pauses in, 139
properties for, 13–14, 28
sprites to be moveable during playback, 85
tempo of, 134–135
specifying alternate names and location for Shockwave (Macintosh), 318
speeding text display in, 277
starting
frame of, 64
playback, 131
stepping
backward in, 132
through, 131
stopping playback, 130
updating, 29
writing Lingo scripts for, 382
See also Flash movies; limited color displays; Shockwave movies
moving
points in vector shape, 194
selections with Hand tool, 152
shape within multiple-shape vector cast member, 198
MPEG3 sound files
settings for streaming, 300
streaming, 301
multiple image file formats supported, 39
Multiuser Server 2, 3

N

naming
cast member in Thumbnail view, 53
custom color palette, 226
navigation, 389–395
branching to marker or frame, 395
creating in Lingo controls for, 371
designating cast member to function as pause button, 392
jumping
frames with go to command, 393
to specific frame, 390
pausing movie at specific frame, 391
playback loops, 389
through score by markers, 97
using go to command with marker label, 394

O

Onion Skin toolbar, 182
onion skinning, 182–183
opening
Brush Settings dialog box, 156
color menu, 219
Control Panel, 130
external casts, 10–11, 46–47
inspectors, 5, 9
linked and unlinked external casts, 36–37
media editor for Xtra cast member, 347
new movies, 11
Paint window, 145
Property Inspector for sprites, 78
reference cast member, 182
score, 65
Shockwave movies on Web, 320–321
stage, 66
Text Inspector, 269
options for ink effects, 86, 87
order indicator for sort order, 49
outline, 186
overlapping sprites, 77

P

Page Background color chip, 329
Paint Brush tool
  assigning color to brush, 155
  changing brush shape of, 154
  choosing shape of, 154
  editing brush shape, 155
  painting with, 153
  retrieving custom brush shapes, 156
  storing custom brush shapes, 156
  See also Brush tool
Paint Bucket tool, 144
Paint toolbar
  hiding and displaying, 146
Paint window
  adding cast member from, 145
  checking movie color depth in, 216
  erasing contents of, 153
  ink effects in, 86
  opening, 145
  placing graphic on stage from, 145
  scrolling, 152
painting, 143–184
  adding
    cast member from Paint window, 145
    text, 173–174
  adjusting Air Brush spray pattern, 157
  applying
    effects, 175–179
    image filters, 184
  assigning color to brush, 155
  changing brush shape of Paint Brush tool, 154
  choosing
    and assigning shape to Air Brush tool, 158
    colors, 161
    Paint Brush shape, 154
    patterns, 163
  customizing line width, 147
  editing
    brush shape, 155
    or creating patterns, 163
    preset patterns, 166
  erasing images, 153
  foreground, background, and gradient destination colors, 161
  with gradients, 168–172
  hiding and displaying
    paint tool palette, 146
    rulers, 146
  ink effects, 159–160
  ink masks, 180–181
  onion skinning, 182–183
  opening Paint window, 145
  overview, 143–144
  placing graphic on stage from Paint window, 145
  reinstalling stored patterns, 165
  retrieving custom brush shapes, 156
  selecting and moving images, 148–152
  setting width of line or shape's outline, 147
  storing
    custom brush shapes, 156
    custom pattern sets, 164
  switching colors in cast members, 162
  See also specific tools by name
palette channel
  function of, 66
  setting color-palette transition
    over series of frames, 238
    over single frame, 237
palette-index mode
  RGB mode and, 220
palettes, defined, 417
Parameters window, 359
parent scripts, 374
Pass command, 386
Paste Relative command, 116
pasting
  colors within Color Palette, 228
  digital video frames, 260–261
  sprites in score and selection, 72
paths
  accelerating or decelerating sprites along, 108
  closing, 188
  curving sprite's tweened, 106
  real-time-recorded, 111
  See also points
pattern chip, 163
Pattern tool, 144
patterns
  adjusting spray, 157
  choosing, 163
  creating, 163
    tiles from cast member, 166–167
  editing, 163, 164
    preset, 166
  reinstalling stored, 165
  storing custom, 164
pausing movies
  and restarting with mouse, 392
  setting pause, 139
  at specific frame, 391
Pen tool
  creating points for vector shape with, 187
  ending distinct vector shapes with, 189
Pencil tool, 144, 153
Perspective tool, 177

PICS files (Macintosh), 45–46
play list for projector, 309
Play Movie command, 311
playback, 129–141
  adding user controls for QuickTime, 258
  changing actual-tempo and target-tempo value, 137
  controlling for Flash movies, 127
  downloading Xtras during Shockwave movie, 353–354
  editing text cast members during, 284
  jumping to specific frame, 133
  locking playback speed, 138
  options
    for Flash cast members, 125–127
    for projector, 304–307
    for Shockwave movies, 330
  playing
    movies, 11
    Shockwave movies, 320–322
  preparing Shockwave movies for, 412–413
  resizing bounding box for, 258
  scene transitions, 140–141
  scripting loops, 389
  of selected frames, 133
  setting
    movie tempo, 134–135
    pauses in movies, 139
  starting, 131
  stepping
    backward, 132
    through movie, 131
  stopping/starting loop, 132
  testing behaviors, 363
  using Control Panel, 130–133
  See also Control Panel
playback head
  dragging to frame, 65
players
  embedding in projector, 308
  Shockwave, 2, 308, 316
points
  adding to vector shapes, 197
  adjusting curve, 195
  deleting, 195
  moving, 194
  selected, 190
  See also corner point; curve point
Polygon tool, 144
polygons, 150
PowerPoint presentation, importing, 47
preparing files for distribution
  projectors with linked files, 310
  Shockwave movies, 23, 319
previewing
  Air Brush spray pattern, 157
  AVI movies, 253
  digital video, 252–253
  Shockwave movie in browser, 321
  sounds, 290
primary event handlers, 405–406
projectors, 303–314
  creating, 308–309
  distributing Xtras with, 351–352
  internal and external casts as, 33
  protecting movie files, 312–313
  setting playback options for, 304–307
projects created with Director, 2–3
properties
  aligning sprites, 88
  changing
    color of sprites, 84
    for locked and unlocked sprites, 91
    sprite, 18–19, 78–91
  creating keyframe and changing, 104
  editing
    behavior, 79
    cast members, 79
  flipping sprites, 82
  managing for casts and cast members, 57–61
  for primary event handlers, 406
  resetting sprites to original, 83
  resizing sprites, 80
  rotating sprites, 81
  setting
    blend percentage of sprites, 85
    for digital video cast members, 256–258
    for digital video sprites, 259
    movie, 13–14, 28
    sprite properties in keyframe, 101
    sprites to be moveable during movie playback, 85
  skewing sprites, 83
  for sprite tweening, 102
  tweaking sprites, 89
  viewing sprite properties on stage, 79
Property Inspector
  choosing stage size in, 13
  color chips and pop-up color palette in, 84
  List view mode in, 8
  setting cast member priorities, 59
  setting movie properties in, 28
  in table view, 58
  viewing cast member's color depth in, 217
protecting movie files, 311, 312–314
publishing
  movies, 23
  Shockwave movies, 327
Push Button tool, 16

Q

QuickDraw graphics, 210
QuickTime
  copying and pasting digital video frames in, 260–261
  importing files, 250–251
  previewing files, 252

R

radial gradients, 193
radio buttons, 211
real-time recording
  with film loop, 120
  setting up, 111–112
Rectangle tool, 144
reference cast members, 182, 183
registration point
  aligning, 114
  resetting to center of vector shape, 199
Registration Point tool, 144, 199
regular text
  advantages of, 264
  converting to bitmapped text, 277
  creating and editing, 266–267
  kerning for, 272
reinstalling stored patterns, 165
remapping sprites on stage to current palette, 240
removing
  action or event from behavior, 367
  sprite frames, 76
renaming cast members, 50
reordering
  actions in behavior, 366, 367
  cast members, 52
repeating
  sounds, 292
  specified actions for interactive sprites, 402
repositioning
  keyframes in score, 101
  markers, 97
  selections, 151
  sprite on stage, 73
resetting
  mode for actual-tempo display, 137
  sprites to original shape and orientation, 83
resize handles for sprites, 80
resizing
  bitmap cast members, 44
  columns in Cast window, 50
  options for Shockwave movies, 323–325, 330–331
  playback area, 258
  sprites, 80
  vector shapes, 197
restoring
  defaults for Xtras, 350
  registration point to default position, 90
reversing
  animated sequences, 117
  order of Color Palette's colors, 231
reverting to last saved version of movie, 12
Rich Text Format (RTF) format, 278
rotating
  artwork
    in 1-degree increments, 176
    90 degrees, 176
  handles of point, 195
  images to create in-between images, 179
  sprites, 81, 99, 102
Rotation and Skew tool, 81, 83
Rotation tools, 176
RTF (Rich Text Format) format, 278
rulers, 146
  adjusting tabs on, 272
  setting text margins with, 271

S

saturation controls (Color Palette), 227
saving
  changes in external casts, 38
  and compacting movies, 46
  movies, 12
  projector, 309
  Shockwave movie to Shockmachine, 409, 412, 413
  Shockwave movies, 333
scene transitions, 22, 140–141
score, 63–98
  centering playback head in window, 92
  changing
    default sprite-span duration, 70
    display option for sprite labels, 95
    order of overlapping sprites, 77
    view of, 92–96
  creating, ink masks in, 181
  displaying in Director 5 style, 96
  editing, inserting, and removing frames in, 76
  function of channels in, 66
  hiding or displaying
    effects of channels, 92
    keyframes in, 93
  opening, 65
  placing cast members in, 17–18, 254
  real-time recording in, 111
  repositioning keyframes in, 101
  selecting frame in, 65

score (continued)
setting markers in, 97–98
sound channels for, 287
sprites
changing sprite properties, 18–19, 78–91
creating by dragging cast members to stage, 69
creating in, 68
cutting and pasting in, 72
joining and splitting, 75
locking and unlocking, 91
moving in, 72
selecting frames in, 71
working with, 67
turning channel on or off, 96
using frames and channels, 64–66
viewing
in multiple windows, 93
sprite labels in, 94
zooming in and out in, 92
See also sprites
score scripts, 374
script channel
dragging Loop Until behaviors to, 336
function of, 66
Script window, 7, 296, 369, 383
scripting
animated cursors, 404
enabling browser, 331
Lingo, 373–376
navigation, 389–395
writing scripts, 377–383
Xtras, 342
selecting
area for transition, 141
cast members, 51, 53
copying selections with Marquee tool, 152
erasing selections, 152
first frame in first sprite channel, 16
frames, 65, 71
images
with Lasso tool, 150
with Marquee tool, 148
moving selections with Hand tool, 152
options for imported cast members, 43
and playing Shockwave cartridges, 410
range of digital video frames for copying and pasting, 260
repositioning selections, 151
sprites, 70–71
stretching/compressing selections, 152
text sprites, 267
Selection tool, 194
Shape tools, 186
shapes
filled and hollow shape tools, 209
setting width of outline, 147
See also vector shapes
Shockmachine, 407–413
managing and organizing Shockwave cartridges, 410
modifying settings for, 411
preparing Shockwave movies for playback, 412–413
saving Shockwave movie to, 409, 412, 413
selecting and playing Shockwave cartridge, 410
zooming window for, 411
Shockwave Audio sound files, 300, 301
Shockwave Audio (SWA) compression, 297
Shockwave movies, 315–340
adjusting Publish settings, 326–334
converting multiple movies to, 338–340
creating and viewing, 317–318
internal and external casts as, 33
looping movie scenes while loading cast-member media, 336
making streaming, 335–336
overview, 315–316
playing, 320–322
preparing, 23, 319
preparing for playback in Shockmachine, 412–413
saving to Shockmachine, 409, 412, 413
setting resizing options for stretchable, 323–325, 330–331
tips for effective streaming, 337
Shockwave Player, 2, 308, 316, 320
shortening sprites, 17, 74
shrinking sprites, 19
Skew tool, 177
skewing sprites, 83
sorting
colors on color palette, 232
columns in Cast window, 49
sound, 287–302
compressing, 297–299
file formats supported, 39, 288
importing, 288–289
looping, 292
placing in score, 290–292
recording in Director (Macintosh), 302
repeating, 292
streaming linked Shockwave audio or MPEG3 sound files, 300–301
synchronizing, 293–296
volume, 289
sound behaviors, 363

Sound Channel pop-up menu, 300
sound channels
availability of, 287
dragging sound into, 290
function of, 66
placing imported sound in, 288
splitting sprites, 75
sprite channels, 64, 66
sprite labels, 6, 94, 95
sprite overlay, 79
sprite span
changing duration of, 70
Sprite toolbar
hiding and showing, 79
Sprite Tweening dialog box, 19, 102
sprites, 67–77, 99–127
accelerating or decelerating along path, 108
adjusting
motion for animated, 105–108
number of frames assigned to sound, 290
aligning, 88
assigning
behavior cast member to, 360
behaviors to, 359
changing
color of, 84
text color, 270
converting to animated sequences, 115–116
creating
by dragging cast members to stage, 69
circular path for, 107
keyframes within, 100
in score, 68
cutting and pasting in score, 72
editing
individual frames, 76
length of span, 73
order of overlapping, 77
orders of behaviors, 367
properties of, 18–19, 78–91
exchanging cast member within, 113
extending, 21, 74
sound sprites to fit frames, 291
video sprite to fit frames, 255
fading in and out, 102
flipping, 82
interactive, 400–403
joining and splitting, 75
keyframe of, 67
locking, 91
looping Flash, 127
matching colors in, 230
moving to new location in score, 72
opening Property Inspector for, 78
placing series of cast members in frames as single, 114
refining tweening, 103
remapping to current palette, 240
repositioning on stage, 73
resetting to original shape and orientation, 83
resizing, 80
rotating, 81, 99, 102
selecting, 70–71
first frame in first sprite channel, 16
text, 267
setting
to be moveable during movie playback, 85
blend percentage of, 85
ink effect for, 86–87
properties for, 259
text in transparent ink, 270
Trails property for, 85
shortening, 17, 74
shrinking, 19
skewing, 83
smoothing speed changes of moving, 108
toggling display of Sprite toolbar, 79
tweaking, 89
tweening, 101–102
viewing
properties on stage, 79
and setting cast member's registration point, 90
writing scripts
attached to, 379
for later attachment to, 380
See also interactive sprites
stage, 201–212
adding guides to stage, 207
changing
background color of, 203
size and location for movie, 202
choosing size for, 13
creating
buttons on, 211
cast members on, 16
sprite by dragging cast members to, 69
text on, 212
displaying and configuring stage grid, 206
drawing
filled shape on, 209
hollow shape on, 209
line on, 208
editing text on, 211, 267
field text box on, 282
opening, 66
overview, 201
positioning cast members on, 5

stage *(continued)*
- repositioning sprite on, 73
- scrolling, 204
- selecting area for transition, 141
- setting
  - color and pattern of QuickDraw graphics on, 210
  - preferences for, 27
  - title of, 203
- viewing
  - and adjusting sprite path on, 105
  - in Full Screen mode, 203
  - sprite properties on, 79
- zooming, 204

step recording, 109–110, 417
still image file formats supported, 39
StopEvent command, 386
stopping playback, 130
storing custom pattern sets, 164
streaming
- linked Shockwave audio or MPEG3 sound files, 300–301
- Shockwave movies, 335–336, 337

stretchable Shockwave movies, 323–325, 330–331
stretching/compressing selections, 152
stroke color, 191
Stroke Width pop-up menu, 186, 187
SWA (Shockwave Audio) compression, 297
synchronizing sound, 293–296
- to animation with cue points, 294–295
- with Lingo, 295, 296

T

Table view, 58
tabs, types of text, 272
tempo
- adjusting for real-time recording, 112
- adjusting movie, 14, 22
- adjusting sound play with playback, 291
- changing actual-tempo and target-tempo value, 137
- comparing target with actual, 136
- setting movie, 134–135

Tempo channel
- selecting frame where playback head waits for cue point, 294

testing
- behaviors, 363
- playback tempo, 135
- projectors, 309
- and refining movies, 21–22

text, 263–286
- adding
  - bitmapped, 173–174
  - drop shadows and borders to field, 283
- adjusting line spacing, 274
- changing
  - color of cast member's and sprite's, 270
  - fonts of cast member, 269
  - margins, 271
- choosing type of, 264
- comparison of types, 265
- converting regular or field text to bitmapped, 277
- creating
  - field, 282–283
  - regular text, 266–267
  - on stage, 212
  - in Text window, 268
- editing
  - cast members during playback, 284
  - on stage, 211, 267
  - in Text window, 269
- embedding fonts
  - in movie, 280
  - that look best at small sizes, 281
- hyperlink, 286
- imported file formats supported, 39
- importing, 278–279
- kerning, 272–273
- making editable during ranges of frames, 285
- minimizing file size of font cast member, 280–281
- reformatting with Text Inspector, 275
- resetting anti-aliasing, 276
- speeding display in movie, 277
- tab settings for, 272
- in transparent ink, 270
- types of, 263
- *See also* bitmapped text

text cast member, 403
Text Inspector
- opening, 269
- reformatting text with, 275

Text tool, 15, 144, 173, 266
Text window
- alignment buttons in, 271
- creating text in, 268
- editing text in, 269

Thumbnail view mode, 53–56
- changing Cast-window preferences in, 56
- moving cast members with Place button, 55
- naming cast member in, 53
- reordering cast members in, 52

repositioning, copying, or moving cast members in Cast window, 54–55
selecting cast members in, 53
toggling between List view and, 48
thumbnails for cast members, 61
titling stage, 203
Tool palette
choosing button on, 211
Rotation and Skew tool on, 81, 83
tool Xtras, 342, 344
toolbar
buttons on, 4
Effects, 175
Onion Skin, 182
Paint, 15, 144
Rewind, Stop, and Play buttons on, 11
Sprite, 78, 79
tools
hollow and filled shape, 209
See also specific tools
tracing handlers from Message window, 397
Trails option
for handwriting effect, 112
setting for sprites, 85
transition channel, 22, 64, 66
transition Xtras, 342, 345
transitions
adding scene, 22
types of, 129, 140
Transitions channel, 140
troubleshooting sound synchronization, 293
Tweak window, 89
tweaking sprites, 89
tweening, 100–104
creating
keyframe, 100
keyframe while changing sprite property, 104
curving sprite's tweened path, 106
film loops, 118
refining, 103
repositioning keyframes in score, 101
sprites, 101–102
streaming performance and, 337

U

Undo command, 12, 44
unlinking external casts, 38
unlocking sprites, 91
Update Movies command, 311
updating movies, 29
uploading Shockwave movies to Web server, 319

V

variables, 398–399
Vector Shape window, 7, 186
vector shapes, 185–200
adding
new end point to open, 197
new point to open vector shape, 198
point to, 197
adjusting
curve point, 195
registration point for, 199
bitmaps vs. vector shapes, 185
converting, 196
deleting points, 195
filling with solid color, 192
joining two curves or, 191
moving
points, 194
shape within multiple-shape vector cast member, 198
resizing, 197
setting
background color for, 192
gradient fill, 193
splitting, 190
undoing fill, 192
vertical guide lines, 207
viewing
asset-management fields, 60
cast-member Xtra options, 347
color depth for cast members, 217
registration point for cast members, 90
score, 92–96
Shockwave movies, 317–318
sprite labels in score, 94
sprite path on stage, 105
sprite properties on stage, 79
stage in Full Screen mode, 203
toggling view style for Cast window, 48
Xtras installed, 343
See also List view mode; Thumbnail view mode
volume, adjusting movie, 131, 289

W

Warp tool, 177
Web216 palette, 239
Web browser. *See* browsers
Web sites
importing HTML documents from, 279
opening Shockwave movies on, 320–321
playing Shockwave movies on, 320–321
uploading Shockwave movies to Web server, 319

width
adjusting tile, 167
changing with Stroke Width pop-up menu, 187
setting line or shape outline, 147
of Shockwave movies, 323
windows
centering playback head in, 92
types of, 7
See also specific windows
Windows platform
changing color depth, 216
creating external Shockwave Audio files, 299
Help window for, 25
modifier keys for, xii
previewing AVI movies, 253
projector settings for, 307
reinstalling stored patterns, 165
selecting cast members in List view mode, 51
storing
custom brushes on, 156
custom patterns for, 164
using ActiveX controls, 355

X

Xtra transitions file, 141
Xtras, 341–355
ActiveX controls (Windows), 355
developing custom, 354
distributing with projectors, 351–352
downloading for Shockwave movies during playback, 353–354
including in distributed movies, 348–350
installing, 343
specifying for Shockwave movies, 317
types of, 342, 344–347
Xtras folder
copying Xtra transitions file, 141
placing image filters in, 184

Z

zooming
in and out in score, 92
Shockwave movie in Shockmachine, 412
stage window, 204

Director 8 Keyboard Shortcuts

File Menu	Windows	Mac
New Movie	Ctrl N	⌘ N
New Cast	Ctrl Option N	⌘ Option N
Open	Ctrl O	⌘ O
Close	Ctrl F4	⌘ F4
Save	Ctrl S	⌘ S
Import	Ctrl R	⌘ R
Export	Ctrl Shift R	⌘ Shift R
Page Setup	Ctrl Shift P	⌘ Shift P
Print	Ctrl P	⌘ P
Preferences	Ctrl U	⌘ U
Exit/Quit	Alt F4	⌘ Q

Edit Menu	Windows	Mac
Undo	Ctrl Z	⌘ Z
Repeat	Ctrl Y	⌘ Y
Cut	Ctrl X	⌘ X
Copy	Ctrl C	⌘ C
Paste	Ctrl V	⌘ V
Clear	Del	Del
Duplicate	Ctrl D	⌘ D
Select All	Ctrl A	⌘ A
Find Text	Ctrl F	⌘ F

Edit Menu (cont.)	Windows	Mac
Find Handler	Ctrl Shift ;	⌘ Shift ;
Find Cast Member	Ctrl ;	⌘ ;
Find Selection	Ctrl H	⌘ H
Find Again	Ctrl Alt F	⌘ Option F
Replace Again	Ctrl Alt E	⌘ Option E
Edit Sprite Frames	Ctrl Alt]	⌘ Option]
Edit Entire Sprite	Ctrl Alt [	⌘ Option [
Exchange Cast Members	Ctrl E	⌘ E
Launch External Editor	Ctrl ,	⌘ ,

View Menu	Windows	Mac
Next Marker	Ctrl right arrow	⌘ right arrow
Previous Marker	Ctrl left arrow	⌘ left arrow
Zoom in	Ctrl +	⌘ +
Zoom out	Ctrl - (minus)	⌘ - (minus)
Show Grid	Ctrl Shift Alt G	⌘ Shift Option G
Snap to Grid	Ctrl Alt G	⌘ Option G
Show Info	Ctrl Shift Alt O	⌘ Shift Option O
Show Paths	Ctrl Shift Alt H	⌘ Shift Option H
Sprite Toolbar	Ctrl Shift H	⌘ Shift H
Keyframes	Ctrl Shift Alt K	⌘ Shift Option K
Full Screen	Ctrl Alt 1	⌘ Option 1

Insert Menu	Windows	Mac
Keyframe	Ctrl Alt K	⌘ Option K
Insert Frame	Ctrl Shift]	⌘ Shift]
Remove Frame	Ctrl [	⌘ [